Elementary Algebra

THIRD EDITION

Terentie Bortis

Printed in the United States of America

ISBN 13: 978-1-50669-547-1

Acknowledgments:

Cover Image: © Can Stock Photo Inc./nalinratphi

530 Great Road
Acton, MA 01720
800-562-2147
www.xanedu.com

Acknowledgements

I sincerely appreciate the time and effort of Dr. Lilian Metlitzky, California Polytechnic University, Pomona who reviewed the manuscript and made invaluable comments and suggestions. Her dedication and patience for the tremendously detailed and accurate checking of any definition or statement to make sure they are mathematically precise was far beyond any reviewer's task. I would also like to thank Mrs. Tesla Kavena Thurman and Mrs. Tracy Jayasinghe who proofread part of the manuscript. I am grateful to Professor Ratana Ngo, Long Beach City College, who enthusiastically accepted the class-testing of the first edition. I would also like to thank Professor Dimos Arsenidis, CSU Long Beach, for his thoughtful comments and suggestions.

I would like to express my gratitude to the professional staff at XanEdu especially to Krishna Gil for her enthusiasm, excellent cooperation and assistance throughout this project. Without their support this project would not have been possible.

Special thanks to my family for their patience and encouragement during this project.

To my wife Dorina, and
our sons Gerald, Daniel, and Michael

Preface

My primary goal in writing this textbook was to provide students and instructors with an introductory algebra textbook that is straightforward and provide the simplest and shortest explanation for every mathematical concept included in the book. To help make this book usable in a class lecture format, first I have defined the topic in a plain and concise language, and then I built on it using numerous examples that increase in difficulty from simple to more challenging. I ended each section with more than enough exercises for a fifty minutes lecture, and homework assignment.

As a math teacher for over thirty years, one of the things my students have told me over and over again at the beginning of a course is how scared they are of taking math classes. I have listened to their feedback, and I decided to write a textbook that makes the subject approachable for all students, in a simple language that they understand, to help dispel their fears. This textbook provides basic concepts of algebra in a simple, straightforward manner. The content and level of detail is appropriate for an introductory college algebra course, and by the time students complete each of the nine chapters, they should have the knowledge to continue with confidence on to an intermediate algebra course.

Each section in this book begins with an introduction of the most basic elements of the algebraic concept discussed in the section. I have taken great care to ensure that the definitions and description of the mathematical concepts described within are as accurate as possible. Also, the logic in which the material in each section is introduced, and the connection between the sections in each chapter makes this textbook easy to read and understand. For example, in chapter one, I provide at an appropriate level a detailed introduction to the real number system, I then define the operations that can be performed on real numbers, beginning with integers and then expanding to rational numbers (fractions). This provides a logical sequence, that help students grasp the operations without requiring prior knowledge. I also avoid introducing concepts prematurely before laying the foundation, since this can be a source of confusion for many students.

I then expand the basic concepts into more complicated ones, creating logical connections between them along the way to make it easy for students to follow and connect to dots to complete the big picture. For example, in chapter two, I begin by defining a basic first degree equation in general. I then define linear equations, and finally expand the concept to any first degree equation that can be reducible to a linear equation (fractional, decimal, etc.). Each section in the chapter also includes a set of exercises in logical and progressive order, ending with word problems. I include only the most common and appropriate examples for each section to reinforce the concepts, paying special attention to the degree of difficulty at each step to avoid frustrating students.

Finally, I ended each chapter with applications that can be solved using the techniques learned in the chapter. The applications are designed to help students see the entire picture, and tie together all of the sections within the chapter. Each chapter also includes a chapter review exercises with the most important problems from each section. These are useful for the students to asses their understanding and prepare for tests and for instructors to choose the appropriate problems for the chapter test.

The content of this textbook was conceived and tested over many years of lectures, and I hope that the students and instructors will find it useful.

Contents

1 FUNDAMENTAL CONCEPTS

1.1 THE REAL NUMBER SYSTEM

□ Sets □ The Real Number System □ The Real Number Line
□ Ordering Numbers □ Opposite Numbers □ Absolute Value

□ SETS

> **Definition**
>
> *A **set** is a collection (group) of objects.*

The objects of a set are called the elements of the set. If a set has no elements, it is called the **empty set** or **null set** and is denoted by the Greek letter phi, φ or { }. The set of students in an empty classroom is an example of an empty set.

Examples of sets:

- The set of all the students in a classroom.
- The set of all the cars in a parking lot.
- The set of all the books in a library.
- The set of all the letters of the alphabet.

Notation

A pair of braces { } is the symbol used to indicate a set.

Capital letters A, B, X . . . are commonly used to label a set, and lowercase letters a, b, c, etc. are used to denote the elements of a set.

The simplest way to represent a set is by listing all the elements within a pair of braces. This method of describing a set is called **roster notation.**

Example 1

A = {1, 2, 3, a} which is read "A is the set with the elements 1, 2, 3, and a."

Another way of describing a set is by listing some properties common to all the elements, within a pair of braces. This method of describing a set is called **set builder notation.**

Example 2

A = {x | x is an even number, greater than 4} which is read "A is the set of all the elements x such that x is an even number greater than four."

This set was described by listing two properties common to all the elements: "even numbers" and "greater than four." The set A can be written in roster notation as follows:

A = {6, 8, 10, . . .}

Example 3

B = {x | x is an odd number, 3 ≤ x ≤ 11} which is read "B is the set of all the elements x such that x is an odd number greater than or equal to three and less than or equal to eleven." In roster notation, this set can be written as follows:

B = {3, 5, 7, 9, 11}

☐ THE REAL NUMBER SYSTEM

*If all the elements of a set are numbers, the set is called a **set of numbers**.*

The following sets are the most common sets of numbers used in algebra.

Natural Numbers: (N)

N = {1, 2, 3, 4, . . .}

Since natural numbers are used to count objects, they are also called **counting numbers**.

Whole Numbers: (W)

W = {0, 1, 2, 3, . . .}

Integers: (Z)

Z = {. . . –3, –2, –1, 0, 1, 2, 3, . . .}

Integers are often called **signed numbers**. The set of integers consists of:

a. *Negative numbers*: . . . –3, –2, –1 (integers listed to the left of zero)

b. *Positive numbers*: 1, 2, 3, 4, . . . (integers listed to the right of zero)

c. *Zero*: 0, which is neither a positive nor a negative number (neutral)

Rational Numbers: (Q)

> A **rational number** is a number that can be written in the form $\dfrac{a}{b}$, where a and b are integers and $b \neq 0$

Rational numbers consist of:

a. *Fractions*: $\dfrac{2}{3}, -\dfrac{4}{5}, \dfrac{15}{7}, \dfrac{5}{5}, \ldots$

b. *Mixed numbers*: $2\dfrac{2}{3} = \dfrac{8}{3}, 5\dfrac{1}{7} = \dfrac{36}{7}, -3\dfrac{2}{5} = -\dfrac{17}{5}, \ldots$

c. *Repeating decimals*: $0.\overline{3} = 0.3333\ldots = \dfrac{3}{9}$, $0.\overline{27} = 0.272727\ldots = \dfrac{27}{99}$

$0.\overline{325} = 0.325325\ldots = \dfrac{325}{999}$, $1.\overline{4} = 1.444\ldots = 1 + 0.444\ldots = 1 + \dfrac{4}{9} = 1\dfrac{4}{9} = \dfrac{13}{9}$

d. *Terminating decimals*: $1.2 = \dfrac{12}{10}, 2.35 = \dfrac{235}{100}, 5.274 = \dfrac{5274}{1000}, 0.72 = \dfrac{72}{100}$

Irrational Numbers: (I)

> An **irrational number** is a number that is **not** rational.

Numbers like $\sqrt{2} = 1.41\ldots$, $\sqrt{3} = 1.7\ldots$ etc. are *not* rational numbers because they cannot be expressed as a quotient of two integers in the form $\dfrac{a}{b}$ as described above. Their decimal form has no repeating decimals and never terminates. In fact, the decimal form has an infinite number of non-repeating decimals. Such numbers are called irrational numbers.

Example 4

Irrational numbers: $\pi = 3.14\ldots$, $\sqrt{12} = 3.46\ldots$, $e = 2.7\ldots$, etc.

Real Numbers: (R)

> The set of **real numbers** consists of natural numbers together with whole numbers, integers, rational and irrational numbers.

Since every natural number, whole number and integer is a rational number ($1 = \dfrac{1}{1}$, $0 = \dfrac{0}{1}$, $-2 = \dfrac{-2}{1}$, etc ...), the set of real numbers consists of rational numbers together with irrational numbers. Hence, every real number is either a rational or irrational number.

Example 5

Determine whether each statement is true or false.

a. Every whole number is an integer.

b. Every rational number is a natural number.

c. Some integers are whole numbers.

d. Every natural number is a whole number.

e. Every irrational number is a real number.

Solution

a. True, because the set of integers consists of the negative numbers and *whole numbers*.

b. False, because 2.3 is a rational number that is not a natural number.

c. True, because 0, 1, and 2 for example, are integers and whole numbers.

d. True, because the set of whole numbers consists of 0 and *natural numbers*.

e. True, because the set of real numbers consists of rational numbers and *irrational numbers*.

Below is an illustration of the real number (**R**) system.

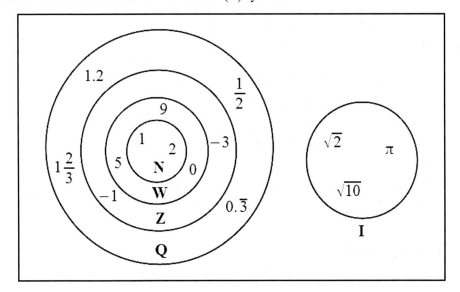

R

Example 6

Consider the set $\left\{2.5, -4, 1\frac{3}{4}, 0, 12, \sqrt{7}, \frac{5}{8}, -18, -\sqrt{3}, 4.576, 1, 0.\overline{23}, 18\right\}$

List the elements of the set that are natural numbers, whole numbers, integers, rational numbers, irrational numbers and real numbers.

Solution

    a. Natural numbers: 1, 12, 18

    b. Whole numbers: 0, 1, 12, 18

    c. Integers: −4, −18, 0, 1, 12, 18

    d. Rational numbers: $2.5, -4, 1\frac{3}{4}, 0, 12, \frac{5}{8}, -18, 4.567, 1, 0.\overline{23}, 18$

    e. Irrational numbers: $\sqrt{7}, -\sqrt{3}$

    f. Real numbers: $2.5, -4, 1\frac{3}{4}, 0, 12, \sqrt{7}, \frac{5}{8}, -18, -\sqrt{3}, 4.576, 1, 0.\overline{23}, 18$ (all)

☐ THE REAL NUMBER LINE

*The **real number line** is usually a horizontal line containing an arbitrary point chosen to represent the number zero and is called the origin and equally spaced points to the left and right of zero along the line.*

The points to the left of zero on the number line correspond to negative numbers, and the points to the right of zero correspond to positive numbers. The arrowhead at the right end of the line shows the direction of increasing numbers.

$$\cdots \quad -4 \ -3 \ -2 \ -1 \quad 0 \quad 1 \quad 2 \quad 3 \quad 4 \quad \cdots$$

Any **real number** can be plotted on the **real number line**. To plot or graph a real number on the real number line, place a dot on the number line above the number.

Note: Sometimes, we will refer to the real number line as simply "the number line."

Example 7

Plot −4, 0, and 2 on the number line.

Solution

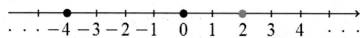

Example 8

Graph on the number line.

a. $2\dfrac{3}{4}$,   b. 1.2   c. $0.\overline{6}$

Solution

a. $2\dfrac{3}{4}$ is located between 2 and 3. First, divide the interval between 2 and 3 into 4 equal
    subintervals and then place the dot on the third dividing segment.

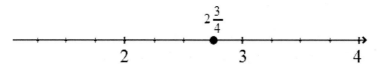

b. 1.2 is located between 1 and 2. Divide the interval between 1 and 2 into 10 equal subin-
    tervals and then place the dot on the second dividing segment.

c. $0.\overline{6} = \dfrac{6}{9} = \dfrac{2}{3}$ is located between 0 and 1. Divide the interval between 0 and 1 into 3 equal
    subintervals and place the dot on the second dividing segment.

□ ORDERING REAL NUMBERS

If a *real number n* is located to the left of a *real number m* on the **real number line**, then *n* is
smaller than *m* which is written n < m.

If a *real number n* is located to the right of a *real number m* on the real number line, then *n* is
greater than *m* which is written n > m.

The following symbols, called **inequality symbols**, are used to compare real numbers.

a. < "is less than"   Ex.: 3 < 5, −12 < −1

b. ≤ "is less than or equal to"   Ex.: 2 ≤ 3 because 2 < 3

                                          5 ≤ 5 because 5 = 5)

c. > "is greater than"   Ex.: 0 > −7, 10 > 6

d. ≥ "is greater than or equal to"   Ex.: 10 ≥ −10 because 10 > −10,

                                          8 ≥ 8 because 8 = 8)

The symbol $<$ may be used when a number n is strictly less than a number m ($n < m$) and the symbol $\leq$ may be used when $n < m$ or $n = m$.

Note: There is a difference between "5 less than a number" which is translated n -5, and "5 is less than a number" which is translated $5 < n$.

Example 9

Place the correct inequality symbol ($<$ or $>$) between each pair of numbers.

   a. -4 ___ 2 b. -7 ___ -4 c. 3 ___ -3 d. 1 ___ -8

Solution

   a. $-4 < 2$ because -4 lies to the left of 2 on the number line.

   b. $-7 < -4$ because -7 lies to the left of -4 on the number line.

   c. $3 > -3$ because 3 lies to the right of -3 on the number line.

   d. $1 > -8$ because 1 lies to the right of -8 on the number line.

□ OPPOSITE NUMBERS

> **Definition**
>
> *Two numbers that have the same distance from zero in opposite directions on the number line are called **opposite numbers**.*

The opposite of a number is also called the **additive inverse** of the number.

Example 10

Find the opposite of each number:

   a. 10   b. -3 c. 0

Solution

   a. The opposite of 10 is -10 (because 10 and -10 have the same distance from zero in opposite directions on the number line).

   b. The opposite of -3 is 3.

   c. The opposite of 0 is $-0 = 0$.

Note: The opposite or additive inverse of areal number n is $-$n.

Thus, one easy way to indicate the opposite of a number is to place a negative sign in front of the number. Since the opposite of -2 is 2, we conclude that $-(-2) = 2$.

This can be summarized in the following property:

***Double Negative Property*:** If n is a real number, then $-(-$n$) =$ n (the opposite of $-$n is n).

Example 11
_____

Find the opposite of each number.

   a. 50   b. −8   c. −53

Solution

   a. The opposite of 50 is −50.

   b. The opposite of −8 is −(−8) = 8.

   c. The opposite of −53 is −(−53) = 53.

□ ABSOLUTE VALUE

Definition

*The **absolute value** of a real number n is the distance from zero to the number n on the real number line and is denoted by |n|.*

Example 12
_____

$|3| = 3$ because the distance from 0 to 3 is 3 units.

$|{-5}| = 5$ because the distance from −5 to zero is 5 units.

$\left|\dfrac{2}{3}\right| = \dfrac{2}{3}$ because the distance from $\dfrac{2}{3}$ to zero is $\dfrac{2}{3}$ units.

$|0| = 0$ because the distance from 0 to 0 is 0 units.

Since the distance cannot be a negative number, the absolute value of a nonzero real number is always positive and the absolute value of zero is zero.

This conclusion is not contradicted by the following examples:

$-|6| = -6$ because $-|6|$ is the opposite of $|6| = 6$.

$-|{-23}| = -23$ because $-|{-23}|$ is the opposite of $|{-23}| = 23$.

1.1 EXERCISES

Use roster notation to write the following sets:

   1. The set of integers between −3 and 4.

   2. The set of natural numbers less than or equal to 5.

   3. The set of positive integers less than 6.

   4. The set of negative integers greater than −5.

5. The set of whole numbers between 2 and 3.

6. The set of counting numbers greater than –7.

7. The set of whole numbers less than $\dfrac{9}{2}$.

Determine whether the statement is true or false. Explain your answer.

8. Every irrational number is a real number.

9. Every natural number is a rational number.

10. Every counting number is a whole number.

11. Zero is a natural number.

12. Every whole number is a natural number.

13. Some rational numbers are integers.

14. Some real numbers are irrational numbers.

15. Some irrational numbers are rational numbers.

16. Consider the set: $\left\{-8, 0, 5.3, \dfrac{4}{5}, \sqrt{8}, 12, -3, 2\dfrac{1}{4}, \sqrt{16}, 4.28, 10, \sqrt{6}, 0.\overline{58}, 7.935...\right\}$
    List the elements that are:

    a. natural numbers

    b. whole numbers

    c. integers

    d. rational numbers

    e. irrational numbers

17. Consider the set: $\left\{1, -10, 2.53, 17, 0, \dfrac{5}{7}, -3, 4\dfrac{2}{5}, \sqrt{2}, 0.\overline{23}, \pi, -\dfrac{3}{2}, 80\right\}$
    List the elements that are:

    a. natural numbers

    b. whole numbers

    c. integers

    d. rational numbers

    e. irrational numbers

    f. real numbers

Graph the numbers on the real number line:

18. $-3, 1\dfrac{2}{3}, \dfrac{1}{4}, 2, 3.4$

19. $-2.3, 2\dfrac{3}{5}, 4, \dfrac{3}{2}$

Find the opposite of each number:

20. -12

21. 16

22. $\dfrac{5}{7}$

23. -5

24. 3.5

25. $1\dfrac{1}{8}$

Evaluate:

26. $|-9|$

27. $|-12|$

28. $|5\frac{7}{9}|$

29. $|\frac{11}{2}|$

30. $-|-15|$

31. $-|-1.23|$

32. $-(-5)$

33. $-(-35)$

34. $-|5|$

35. $-|17|$

36. $|0|$

37. $-|-0.6|$

Place the correct symbol (<, > or =) between each pair of numbers.

38. $-16 \ldots \ldots 12$

39. $-8 \ldots \ldots -5$

40. $0 \ldots \ldots -\frac{2}{5}$

41. $-14 \ldots \ldots \frac{3}{8}$

42. $|9| \ldots \ldots |-9|$

43. $|\frac{2}{3}| \ldots \ldots |-\frac{2}{3}|$

44. $-|-5| \ldots \ldots |-3|$

45. $-|-2| \ldots \ldots |-2|$

46. $1.531 \ldots \ldots 1.534$

47. $3.8 \ldots \ldots 3.79$

48. $\frac{2}{3} \ldots \ldots \frac{4}{5}$

49. $\frac{1}{2} \ldots \ldots \frac{3}{4}$

Write the following numbers in order from smallest to largest.

50. $8, -3, 2\frac{4}{5}, |-7|, -4.3, 6$

51. $0.3, 4, -3.21, -3.22, |-11|, \frac{7}{3}$

For what values x are the following statements true?

52. $|x| = x$.

53. $|x| = -x$

Write each set in roster and builder notation.

54. The set of whole numbers less than 5.

55. The set of natural numbers less than or equal to 7.

56. The set of negative integers greater than –4.

57. The of integers between –3 and 3.

58. The set of positive integers less than or equal to 8.

1.2 ADDITION AND SUBTRACTION OF INTEGERS

□ Adding Integers with the Same Sign □ Adding Integers with Different Signs □ Subtraction of Integers

□ ADDING INTEGERS WITH THE SAME SIGN

In this section we will use the concept of absolute value to define the addition of integers. The integers being added are called **terms** or **addends** and the result is called **sum**.

> **Rule 1**
>
> To add two or more integers with the same sign, add their absolute values, and give the sum their common sign.

Example 1

Use the rule of addition to add.

a. $(+2) + (+5)$

b. $(-3) + (-2)$

Solution

a. In the first example, $|+2| = 2$ and $|+5| = 5$. If we add their absolute values, the sum is $2 + 5 = 7$. Then, give the sum their common sign $(+)$, to obtain $(+2) + (+5) = (+7)$.

b. Similarly, $|-3| = 3$ and $|-2| = 2$. If we add their absolute values, the sum is $3 + 2 = 5$. Then, give the sum their common sign $(-)$, to obtain $(-3) + (-2) = (-5)$.

We can use the number line to illustrate the addition of integers. If we represent a positive integer by an arrow pointing to the right and a negative integer by an arrow pointing to the left then we can illustrate the addition of the integers from the above examples on the number line as follows:

$(+2) + (+5) = (+7)$

Start at zero and draw an arrow 2 units to the right, then from the tip, draw another arrow 5 units to the right. Since we end up at $(+7)$, we conclude that $(+2) + (+5) = (+7)$.

$(-3) + (-2) = (-5)$

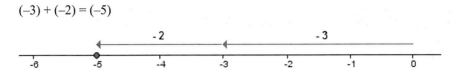

Start at zero and draw an arrow 3 units to the left, then from the tip, draw another arrow 2 units to the left. We end up at (–5). Thus, $(-3) + (-2) = (-5)$.

Example 2
___

Use the rule of addition to find the sum. a) $(+ 10) + (+ 20)$ b) $(-6) + (-4)$

Solution

a. First, find the absolute value of the integers being added. $|+10| = 10$, $|+20| = 20$. Since both integers have the same sign (+), we add their absolute values. $10 + 20 = 30$. Then give the sum their common sign (+). Thus, $(+10) + (+20) = (+30) = 30$

b. Find the absolute values of the integers to be added. $|-6| = 6$, $|-4| = 4$. Since both integers have the same sign (–), we add their absolute values. $6 + 4 = 10$. Then give the sum their common sign. Thus, $(-6) + (-4) = -10$.

☐ ADDING INTEGERS WITH DIFFERENT SIGNS

Rule 2

To add two integers with different signs, subtract the smaller absolute value from the larger absolute value and give the sum the sign of the number larger in absolute value.

Example 3
___

Use the rule of addition to add.

a. $(-41) + (+1)$

b. $(+25) + (-20)$

Solution

Let's follow the rule of addition for the above examples.

a. The absolute values of the addends in the first example are $|-41| = 41$ and $|+ 1| = 1$. Since the integers have different signs, we subtract the smaller absolute value from the larger absolute value $41 - 1 = 40$. Then, give the result the sign of the integer larger in absolute value (–), to obtain $(-41) + (+ 1) = -40$.

b. The absolute value of the integers being added in the second example are $|+ 25| = 25$ and $|-20| = 20$. Again, the integers have different signs and therefore we subtract the smaller absolute value from the larger one, $25 - 20 = 5$. If we give the result the sign of the integer larger in absolute value (+), we obtain $(+ 25) + (-20) = 5$.

Example 4

Use the rule of addition to add.

a. $(-12) + (+15)$

b. $(+8) + (-8)$

Solution

a. Find the absolute values of the integers being added. $|-12| = 12$, and $|+15| = 15$. Since the integers have different signs, subtract the smaller absolute value from the larger absolute value. $15 - 12 = 3$. Then give the result the sign of the integer larger in absolute value $(+)$. Thus, $(-12) + (+15) = 3$.

b. The absolute values of the integers to be added are $|+8| = 8$ and $|-8| = 8$. Since the integers have different signs, we subtract their absolute values $8 - 8 = 0$. Thus, $(+8) + (-8) = 0$. Since $+0 = -0 = 0$, this example does not contradict Rule 2.

Note: The sum of two opposite integers is always zero.

The addition of two integers with different signs can also be illustrated on the number line.

Example 5

Use the real number line to add or subtract.

a. $(-4) + (+2)$

Start at zero and draw an arrow 4 units to the left, then from the tip draw another arrow 2 units to the right. We end up at (-2). Thus, $(-4) + (+2) = -2$

b. $(+6) + (-4)$

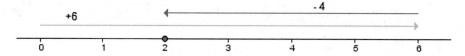

Start at zero and draw an arrow 6 units to the right, then from the tip draw another arrow 4 units to the left. We end up at $(+2)$. Hence, $(+6) + (-4) = 2$.

The following note summarizes the most important part from the above rules that one should remember.

Note: When adding two integers:

a. If the integers have the same signs, add their absolute values.

b. If the integers have different signs, subtract their absolute values.

Example 6

Find the sum.

a. $3 + (-5) + (-4) + 7 + 0$

b. $-6 + 10 + (-2) + 12$

Solution

a. $3 + (-5) + (-4) + 7 + 0 =$

$(-2) + (-4) + 7 + 0 =$

$(-6) + 7 + 0 =$

$1 + 0 = 1$

b. $-6 + 10 + (-2) + 12 =$

$4 + (-2) + 12 =$

$2 + 12 = 14$

□ SUBTRACTION OF INTEGERS

Definition

If a and b are two integers, then a − b = a + (−b). In other words, to subtract two integers, add the first integer to the opposite of the second integer.

Thus, the subtraction of two integers is equivalent to an addition in which the first integer is added to the opposite (additive inverse) of the second integer.

Example 7

a. $(+ 8) - (+ 2) = (+ 8) + (-2) = 6$

b. $(-10) - (+ 5) = (-10) + (-5) = -15$

c. $(+ 12) - (-8) = (+ 12) + (+ 8) = 20$

d. $(-18) - (-16) = (-18) + (+ 16) = -2$

Example 8

Subtract

a. $-11 - 4$

b. $7 - 3$

c. $5 - (-9)$

d. $-25 - (-15)$

Solution

First, rewrite each subtraction as an addition.

a. $-11 - 4 = -11 + (-4) = -15$

b. $7 - 3 = 7 + (-3) = 4$

c. $5 - (-9) = 5 + (+9) = 14$

d. $-25 - (-15) = -25 + (+15) = -10$

1.2 EXERCISES

In exercises 1–6, find the sum by using the number line:

1. $2 + 3$

2. $1 + 4$

3. $-3 + (-1)$

4. $-4 + (-2)$

5. $-5 + 3$

6. $4 + (-3)$

Find the sum:

7. $2 + 7$

8. $4 + 11$

9. $-3 + 8$

10. $35 + (-10)$

11. $-6 + (-7)$

12. $-14 + 20$

13. $-24 + 12$

14. $-15 + (-45)$

15. $-18 + (-32)$

16. $75 + (-25)$

17. $-53 + 9$

18. $-24 + 16$

19. $49 + 11$

20. $73 + 25$

21. $-21 + 21$

22. $87 + (-87)$

23. $-8 + (-12)$

24. $-45 + (-13)$

25. $-10 + 3$

26. $-33 + 9$

27. $23 + (-10)$

28. $-4 + (-6) + 8$

29. $(-14) + (-6) + 15$

30. $16 + (-9) + (-3)$

31. $28 + (-10) + (-7)$

32. $-20 + 27 + (-9)$

33. $-80 + 15 + (-26)$

34. $120 + 60 + (-40)$

35. $75 + 35 + (-100)$

36. $77 + (-40) + 0$

37. $[-6 + 2] + [-5 + (-3)]$

38. $[9 + (-5)] + [-14 + 26]$

39. $[20 + (-3)] + [-7 + 15]$

40. $[-31 + 16] + [-12 + (-13)]$

41. $[-85 + (-15)] + [-32 + 142]$

42. $[18 + (-9)] + [-1 + 6]$

43. $[-7 + (-4)] + [9 + (-3)] + 5$

44. $[12 + (-11)] + [-63 + 3] + 9$

45. $[-6 + 8] + [7 + (-5)] + [-4 + (-9)]$

46. $[-2 + (-5)] + [18 + (-11)] + [-8 + 1]$

Find the difference:

47. $15 - 6$

48. $18 - 30$

49. $24 - (-3)$

50. $35 - (-12)$

51. $-26 - (-14)$

52. $-10 - (-18)$

53. $-8 - 16$

54. $-32 - 11$

55. $49 - 10$

56. $5 - 13$

57. $9 - (-8)$

58. $14 - (-30)$

59. $2 - 48$

60. $-4 - (-4)$

61. $-52 - (-52)$

62. $-28 - 6$

63. $-104 - 60$

64. $-4 - 9$

65. $6 - (-34)$

66. $8 - (-12)$

67. $-3 - 10$

Add or subtract:

68. $9 - 4 - (-8)$

69. $-6 - (-7) - 16$

70. $-18 - 5 - 3$

71. $-21 - 12 - (-3)$

72. $-26 - 24 - (-9)$

73. $7 - (-33) - 10$

74. $14 - 10 - (-28)$

75. $64 - 23 - (-2)$

76. $-85 - 105 - 8$

77. $[-7 - (-1)] + [15 - (-4)]$

78. $[-5 - (-8)] + [23 - (-10)]$

79. $[22 - (-50)] - [-18 - 3]$

80. $[71 - (-49)] - [-25 - 7]$

81. $[-16 - (-30)] - [15 + (-3)] - 8$

82. $[-80 - (-16)] + [-9 + 11] + (-12)$

83. $[5 - (-2)] - [-6 - (-8)] + [-10 - 3]$

84. $[-11 - (-5)] + [-27 - 3] - [-16 + 10]$

85. Subtract 12 from 30

86. Subtract 15 from -28

87. Subtract -35 from 43

88. Subtract -11 from -63

89. Subtract 5 from the sum of 18 and -3

90. Subtract -9 from the difference of -4 and 25

91. Increase -5 by -8

92. Increase 12 by -3

93. Decrease -15 by 7

94. Decrease -20 by -11

95. Subtract the sum of -2 and 4 from 15

96. Subtract the sum of 9 and -6 from -19

Application problems:

97. In 2000 the population of California was 33,871,000 and in 2012 the population was 38,041,000. Find the increase in population between 2000 and 2012.

98. At the beginning of a week, John had $1500 in his account. During the week he withdrew $625 and $350. Before the week was over he deposited $800. What was his balance at the end of the week?

99. Jane had $2000 in her account. She wrote two checks, one for $83 and the other for $60. Two days later she deposited $240 in her account. What is her account balance after those three transactions?

100. The temperature in the morning is 8° below zero Celsius. At noon the temperature has risen 10°C. At 4 o'clock, the temperature dropped 3°C. Write an expression to describe the change in temperature and then simplify it.

101. The high temperature for a day in Denver was 12°F, and the low temperature was −5°F. Find the difference between the high and low temperature for the day.

102. At the beginning of the year, John weighed 160 pounds. In January he lost 4 pounds, in February he lost another 3 pounds and he gained 2 pounds in March. What does John weigh at the end of March?

1.3 MULTIPLICATION AND DIVISION OF INTEGERS

□ **Multiplying Integers** □ **Exponential Expressions** □ **Dividing Integers**

□ MULTIPLYING INTEGERS

*When multiplying integers, the result is referred to as the **product** and the integers being multiplied are called **factors**.*

For example, when multiplying $2 \cdot 4 = 8$, the integers 2 and 4 are factors and 8 is the product of those two integers.

Notation used for multiplication: 2×4, $2 \cdot 4$, or $(2)(4)$

Example 1

Find each product:

   a. $3 \cdot 4$ c. $(-3)(5)$

   b. $(4)(-6)$ d. $(-4)(-2)$

Solution

The product of two integers can be obtained indirectly by interpreting the multiplication as a short form representation of a repeated addition of the same number.

   a. $3 \cdot 4 = 4 + 4 + 4 = 12$ (4 is repeated 3 times)

   b. $(4)(-6) = (-6) + (-6) + (-6) + (-6) = -24$ (−6 is repeated 4 times)

   c. $(-3)(5) = ?$

To find the product of a negative integer and a positive integer, we consider the following pattern:

$(3)(5) = 15$

$(2)(5) = 10$

$(1)(5) = 5$

$(0)(5) = 0$

The product on the right side is decreasing by 5 as the first factor on the left side is decreasing by one. If we continue this pattern we have:

$(-1)(5) = -5$

$(-2)(5) = -10$

$(-3)(5) = -15$

Thus, $(-3)(5) = -15$

  d. $(-4)(-2) = ?$

Again, to find the product of two negative integers, we consider the following pattern:

$(4)(-2) = (-2) + (-2) + (-2) + (-2) = -8$ (–2 repeated 4 times)

$(3)(-2) = (-2) + (-2) + (-2) = -6$

$(2)(-2) = (-2) + (-2) = -4$

$(1)(-2) = -2$

$(0)(-2) = 0$

Thus, $(4)(-2) = -8$

$(3)(-2) = -6$

$(2)(-2) = -4$

$(1)(-2) = -2$

$(0)(-2) = 0$

The product on the right side is increasing by 2 as the first factor on the left side is decreasing by one. If we continue this pattern we have:

$(-1)(-2) = 2$

$(-2)(-2) = 4$

$(-3)(-2) = 6$

$(-4)(-2) = 8$

Thus, $(-4)(-2) = 8$

We are using these examples to justify the rules for multiplication of any two integers. Regarding the sign of the product, examples a) and d) lead us to the conclusion that the product of two integers with the same sign (both positive or both negative) is always positive. From examples b) and c) we conclude that the product of two integers with different signs (one positive and one negative) is always negative.

Rule 1

To multiply two integers with the same sign, multiply their absolute values and the product is always a positive integer.

  $(+) \cdot (+) = +$

  $(-) \cdot (-) = +$

Rule 2

To multiply two integers with different signs, multiply their absolute values and the product is always a negative integer.

$$(+) \cdot (-) = -$$

$$(-) \cdot (+) = -$$

Each product of two integers in example one can be obtained directly by multiplying their absolute values and using the appropriate rule to determine the sign of the product.

   a. Since $|3| \cdot |4| = 3 \cdot 4 = 12$ by the Rule 1 $3 \cdot 4 = 12$

   b. Since $|4| \cdot |-6| = 4 \cdot 6 = 24$ by the Rule 2 $(4)(-6) = -24$

   c. Since $|-3| \cdot |5| = 3 \cdot 5 = 15$ by the Rule 2 $(-3)(5) = -15$

   d. Since $|-4| \cdot |-2| = 4 \cdot 2 = 8$ by the Rule 1 $(-4)(-2) = 8$

Example 2

Find each product:

   a. $4 \cdot 5$

   b. $(-11)(-3)$

   c. $(-6)(2)$

   d. $(8)(-5)$

Solution

   a. First, find the product of the absolute values:

       $|4| \cdot |5| = 4 \cdot 5 = 20$

       Since 4 and 5 have the same sign (+), the product is positive.

       $4 \cdot 5 = 20$

   b. The product of the absolute values is:

       $|-11| \cdot |-3| = 11 \cdot 3 = 33$

       Because -11 and -3 have the same sign (−), the product is positive.

       $(-11)(-3) = 33$

   c. The product of the absolute values is:

       $|-6| \cdot |2| = 6 \cdot 2 = 12$

       Because -6 and 2 have different signs, the product is negative.

       $(-6)(2) = -12$

   d. The product of the absolute values is:

       $|8| \cdot |-5| = 8 \cdot 5 = 40$

Because 8 and –5 have different signs, the product is negative.

$(8)(-5) = -40$

Example 3

Evaluate the products.

a. $5 \cdot 0$ b. $0(-3)$

Solution

a. $5 \cdot 0 = 0$ b. $0(-3) = 0$

Note: Any integer multiplied by zero is zero. $n \cdot 0 = 0 \cdot n = 0$

Example 4

Evaluate the product.

$(-2)(-3)(-4)$

Solution

Multiply the first two integers and the product with the next integer to get
$(-2)(-3)(-4) = (6)(-4) = -24$.

Note: The product of an odd number of negative integers is negative.

Example 5

Evaluate the product.

$(-5)(-1)(-2)(-3)$

Solution

$(-5)(-1)(-2)(-3) = (5)(-2)(-3) = (-10)(-3) = 30$

Note: The product of an even number of negative integers is positive.

Example 6

Evaluate the product.

$(-10)(-2)(-1)(3)$

Solution

Since there are an odd number of negative integers, the product is negative.

$(-10)(-2)(-1)(3) = (20)(-1)(3) = (-20)(3) = -60$

Example 7

Evaluate.

   a. $(-4)(-6)+(-3)(12)$

   b. $(-8)(3)-0(-15)$

   c. $(7)(-1)-(-9)$

Solution

   a. $(-4)(-6)+(-3)(12)=(24)+(-36)=-12$

   b. $(-8)(3)-0(-15)=(-24)+0=-24$

   c. $(7)(-1)-(-9)=(-7)+9=2$

☐ EXPONENTIAL EXPRESSIONS

> *When performing a multiplication by repeating the same factor, the multiplication can be represented in a compact (shorthand) form called **exponential form**.*

Example 8

$$3 \cdot 3 \cdot 3 \cdot 3 = 3^4$$

The factor 3 that is repeated is called the **base** and the number 4 that indicates how many times the base is repeated is called the **exponent** or **power**. The expression 3^4 is read "three to the fourth power" or "the fourth power of three" and is called an **exponential expression**.

Note: If the exponent is 1, the exponent can be omitted. $3^1 = 3$

Example 9

Write each product in exponential form.

   a. $5 \cdot 5 \cdot 5 \cdot 5 \cdot 5 \cdot 5 = 5^6$

   b. $(-4)(-4)(-4) = (-4)^3$

   c. $a \cdot a \cdot a \cdot \ldots \cdot a = a^n$ (a is repeated n-times)

      Warning: $a+a+a+a=4a$ and $a \cdot a \cdot a \cdot a = a^4$

Example 10

Evaluate.

   a. 2^5 b. $(-3)^2$ c. -3^2 d. $(-2)^3$ e. -2^5

Solution

    a. $2^5 = 2 \cdot 2 \cdot 2 \cdot 2 \cdot 2 = 32$

    b. $(-3)^2 = (-3)(-3) = 9$ (the base is –3)

    c. $-3^2 = -3 \cdot 3 = -9$ (the base is 3 only)

    d. $(-2)^3 = (-2)(-2)(-2) = -8$ (the base is –2)

    e. $-2^5 = -2 \cdot 2 \cdot 2 \cdot 2 \cdot 2 = -32$ (the base is 2 only)

Note:3^2 is read " three squared" or "the second power of 3"

        2^3 is read "two cubed" or "the third power of 2"

□ DIVIDING INTEGERS

*The division of two integers **a** and **b**, $(b \neq 0)$ can be written as $a \div b = q$,where **a** is called the **dividend**, **b** is called the **divisor** and the result **q** is referred to as the **quotient**.*

Notation used for division: $6 \div 2$, $\dfrac{6}{2}$, 6/2.

Rule 3

To divide two non-zero integers with the same sign, divide their absolute values and the quotient is always a positive integer.

$$\frac{+}{+} = + \qquad \frac{-}{-} = +$$

Rule 4

To divide two non-zero integers with different signs, divide their absolute values and the quotient is always a negative integer.

$$\frac{+}{-} = - \qquad \frac{-}{+} = -$$

Example 11

Divide.

   a. $24 \div 2$ b. $(-9) \div (-3)$ c. $(12) \div (-4)$ d. $(-15) \div (3)$

The rules for dividing integers are similar to the rules of multiplication. The number involved in the quotient of the two integers can be obtained by dividing the absolute value of the dividend by the absolute value of the divisor.

   a. $|24| \div |2| = 24 \div 2 = 12$ c. $|12| \div |-4| = 12 \div 4 = 3$

   b. $|-9| \div |-3| = 9 \div 3 = 3$ d. $|-15| \div |3| = 15 \div 3 = 5$

The sign of the quotient is given by the above rules.

Since the dividend and the divisor in examples a) and b) have the same signs, the quotients are positive.

   a. $24 \div 2 = 12$ b. $(-9) \div (-3) = 3$

The quotients in examples c) and d) are negative because the integers being divided have different signs.

   c. $(12) \div (-4) = -3$ d. $(-15) \div (3) = -5$

Note: To divide any two integers, first find the quotient of their absolute values and then apply the above rules to determine the sign of the quotient.

Example 12

Divide.

   a. $10 \div 2$ b. $(-20) \div (-5)$ c. $(16) \div (-8)$ d. $(30) \div (-3)$

Solution

   a. First find the quotient of the absolute values of the two integers.

$$\frac{|10|}{|2|} = \frac{10}{2} = 5$$

Since both integers have the same sign (+), the quotient is positive.

$$10 \div 2 = 5$$

   b. The quotient of the absolute values of the integers is:

$$\frac{|-20|}{|-5|} = \frac{20}{5} = 4$$

Because –20 and –5 have the same sign (–), the quotient is positive.

$$(-20) \div (-5) = 4$$

c. The quotient of the absolute values of the integers is:

$$\frac{|16|}{|-8|} = \frac{16}{8} = 2$$

Since the integers being divided have different signs, the quotient is negative.

$$(16) \div (-8) = -2$$

d. The quotient of the absolute values of the integers is:

$$\frac{|30|}{|-3|} = \frac{30}{3} = 10 \quad \text{Because 30 and } -3 \text{ have different signs, the quotient is negative.}$$

$$(30) \div (-3) = -10$$

Example 13

Divide.

a. $\dfrac{0}{3}$ b. $\dfrac{5}{0}$ c. $\dfrac{0}{0}$

Solution

We know that $\dfrac{6}{2} = 3$ because $2 \cdot 3 = 6$. Using this relation between division and multiplication, we try to determine the quotient in each case.

a. $\dfrac{0}{3} = 0$ because $0 = 3 \cdot 0$

b. If $\dfrac{5}{0} = a$, then $5 = 0 \cdot a$ There is no such integer **a**, because zero multiplied by any integer is zero. Therefore, $\dfrac{5}{0}$ cannot be defined.

c. If $\dfrac{0}{0} = a$ then $0 = 0 \cdot a$ Since zero multiplied by any integer is equal to zero, **a** can be any integer. In other words **a** cannot be determined. Therefore $\dfrac{0}{0}$ is indeterminate.

Note: When zero is divided by any non-zero integer, the quotient is **zero** ($\dfrac{0}{a} = 0$). When a non-zero integer is divided by zero the quotient is **undefined** ($\dfrac{a}{0}$ is undefined). When zero is divided by zero, the quotient is **indeterminate** ($\dfrac{0}{0}$ is indeterminate).

1.3 EXERCISES

Multiply.

1. $5 \cdot 4$

2. $3 \cdot 12$

3. $6(-5)$

4. $8(-3)$

5. $(-9)10$

6. $(-14)2$

7. $(-6)(-20)$

8. $(-7)(-5)$

9. $25(-4)$

10. $3(-50)$

11. $(-200)8$

12. $(-5)21$

13. $(-4)(-4)$

14. $325(-1)$

15. $(-816)0$

16. $32 \ 0$

17. $(-81)(-1)$

18. $27 \cdot 1$

19. $5(-8)$

20. $(-9)7$

21. $(-6)4$

22. $(-8)(-4)2$

23. $(-10)(-5)3$

24. $6(-3)20$

25. $16(-2)4$

26. $(-2)(-3)(-4)$

27. $(-12)(-10)(-1)$

28. $(-6)(-7)5(-2)$

29. $(-25)(-4)(-1)8$

30. $(-5)(-2)(-4)(-3)$

Determine the sign of each product.

31. $(-15)(-32)(-87)$

32. $(-24)(-8)(-13)$

33. $(-12)(-4)(-5)6$

34. $(-16)(-7)(-18)(-9)$

35. $(-200)(-30)5 \cdot 40$

36. $(-2)(-2)(-2)(-2)$

37. $(-4)(-5)(-6)(-7)(-8)$

38. $(-59)12 \cdot 15 \cdot 38$

39. $(-8)(-9)43 \cdot 7 \cdot 9$

Divide.

40. $15 \div 3$

41. $(-21) \div (-7)$

42. $18 \div (-6)$

43. $32 \div (-8)$

44. $(-45) \div 9$

45. $(-33) \div 11$

46. $(-14) \div (-2)$

47. $(-48) \div (-12)$

48. $80 \div (-20)$

49. $\dfrac{100}{-5}$

50. $\dfrac{-36}{9}$

51. $\dfrac{-42}{-7}$

52. $\dfrac{-90}{-30}$

53. $\dfrac{28}{-4}$

54. $\dfrac{35}{-5}$

55. $\dfrac{-27}{3}$

56. $\dfrac{0}{18}$

57. $\dfrac{0}{-38}$

58. $\dfrac{5}{0}$

59. $\dfrac{-10}{0}$

60. $\dfrac{98}{-1}$

61. $(-56) / 7$

62. $60 / (-3)$

63. $(-41) / (-41)$

Evaluate.

64. 10^2

65. $(-4)^2$

66. -4^2

67. -3^4

68. $(-3)^4$

69. 5^3

70. $(-1)^{10}$

71. $(-1)^{11}$

72. $(-11)^2$

73. 3^3

74. -9^2

75. $(-9)^2$

Problem Solving

76. John used his credit card to buy a $750 television set. After he makes 8 payments of $50 each, how much will he still owe?

77. A student saved $250 per month to attend graduate school. How much did he save in two years?

78. The cost of an admission ticket at a basketball game was $15 per person. If the attendance at the game was 12,000 people, what was the total gate receipts for the game?

79. A computer printer can print 25 pages per minute. How many pages can be printed in 2 hours?

80. At the end of the year, Jane received a bonus from her employer and decided to buy a car. She agrees to pay $10,000 down and $300 a month for 36 month. What is the total cost of the car?

81. A student received a gift card of $50 and she purchased 3 DVD's at $12.50 each. How much was left on her gift card?

1.4 SIMPLIFYING FRACTIONS

□ Factors □ Prime Numbers □ Fractions □ Simplifying Fractions

□ FACTORS

From the previous section we know that in the multiplication $3 \cdot 4 = 12$ *the integers 3 and 4 are called* **factors** *and 12 is called the* **product***. Note that 12 has more than two factors.*

$$2 \cdot 6 = 12$$

$$4 \cdot 3 = 12$$

$$1 \cdot 12 = 12$$

Since $2 \cdot 6 = 12$, the factors 2 and 6 divide 12 exactly (without remainder): $12 \div 2 = 6$, and $12 \div 6 = 2$. Also, 3 is a factor of 12 and therefore 3 divides 12 exactly: $12 \div 3 = 4$.

Thus, an easy way to find all the factors of 12 is to divide 12 by 1, 2, 3 . . . 12, and choose as factors of 12 only those integers from the set $\{1, 2, 3 \ldots 12\}$ that divide 12 exactly.

$12 \div 1 = 12$ 1 is a factor	$12 \div 7 = ?$ 7 is not a factor
$12 \div 2 = 6$ 2 is a factor	$12 \div 8 = ?$ 8 is not a factor
$12 \div 3 = 4$ 3 is a factor	$12 \div 9 = ?$ 9 is not a factor
$12 \div 4 = 3$ 4 is a factor	$12 \div 10 = ?$ 10 is not a factor
$12 \div 5 = ?$ 5 is not a factor	$12 \div 11 = ?$ 11 is not a factor
$12 \div 6 = 2$ 6 is a factor	$12 \div 12 = 1$ 12 is a factor (improper factor)

Hence, the factors of 12 are: 1, 2, 3, 4, 6, and 12.

Similarly, the factors of 18 are: 1, 2, 3, 6, 9, and 18.

The numbers 18 and 12 have some common factors: 1, 2, 3 and 6. The common factor 6 is the largest common factor that divides both 18 and 12 exactly.

The factor 6 is called **the greatest common factor** (GCF) of 18 and 12.

For large numbers it is an inconvenience to list all the factors in order to find the GCF. Therefore, we will introduce another method to find the GCF using the concept of prime numbers. This method will be easy to use regardless how large the numbers are.

□ PRIME NUMBERS

> **Definition**
>
> *A natural number greater than one whose only factors are 1 and itself is called a **prime number**.*

Example 1

2, 3, 5, 7, 11, 13, 17, 19, 23 . . . are prime numbers because each number has only two factors, one and itself $2 = 1 \cdot 2$, $3 = 1 \cdot 3$, $5 = 1 \cdot 5$, $7 = 1 \cdot 7$, etc.

> **Definition**
>
> *A natural number greater than 1 that is not a prime number is called a **composite number**.*

Example 2

4, 6, 8, 9, 10, 12, 14, 15 are composite numbers because each number has at least one factor other than one and itself.

Note: From the above definitions we conclude that 1 is *neither* prime nor composite.

> **Definition**
>
> *The process of writing a number as a product of its factors is called **factorization**.*

Example 3

$24 = 3 \cdot 8$, $24 = 2 \cdot 3 \cdot 4$, $24 = 1 \cdot 24$, $24 = 1 \cdot 6 \cdot 4$ are factorizations of 12.

Note: A composite number has more than one factorization.

> **Definition**
>
> *The process of writing a number as a product of its prime factors is called **prime factorization**.*

Example 4

$12 = 2 \cdot 2 \cdot 3$ is the prime factorization of 12.

Note: The prime factorization of a composite number involves unique factors that can be written in any order. For example: $12 = 2 \cdot 2 \cdot 3$, $12 = 3 \cdot 2 \cdot 2$, $12 = 2 \cdot 3 \cdot 2$.

Next, we will introduce two methods to find the prime factorization of a composite number: Tree Diagram and Bar Chart.

Example 5

Use the Tree Diagram to find the prime factorization.

   a.   24

   b.   15

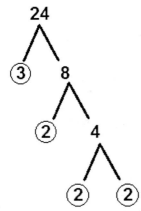

   a.

   Step 1   Find any two numbers whose product is 24, for example: $3 \cdot 8 = 24$.

   Step 2   Circle the prime number (3), and repeat Step 1 for the composite number (8).

   Step 3   Circle the prime number (2), and repeat Step 1 for the composite number (4).

   Step 4   Circle both prime numbers (2) and the diagram is completed.

   Step 5   Write 24 as a product of its prime factors (inside the circles) from smallest to largest: $24 = 2 \cdot 2 \cdot 2 \cdot 3$.

   b.

   Step 1   Find any two numbers whose product is 15 ($3 \cdot 5 = 15$).

   Step 2   Since 3 and 5 are prime numbers, circle both numbers and the diagram is completed.

   Step 3   Write 15 as a product of its prime factors from smallest to largest: $15 = 3 \cdot 5$.

Example 6

Use the Bar Chart to find the prime factorization.

   a.   42   b.   18   c.   35

Solution

a. We begin the process by finding the smallest prime number that is a factor of 42.

$$\begin{array}{r|l} 42 & 2 \\ 21 & 3 \\ 7 & 7 \\ 1 & \end{array} \qquad \begin{array}{l} 42 \div 2 = 21 \\ 21 \div 3 = 7 \\ 7 \div 7 = 1 \end{array}$$

We can divide 42 exactly by the smallest prime number, which is 2.

$$42 \div 2 = 21$$

Next, divide 21 exactly by the smallest prime number. Since 21 cannot be divided by 2, we try the next prime number 3.

$$21 \div 3 = 7$$

Since 7 is the only prime factor of 7, divide 7 by 7.

$$7 \div 7 = 1$$

Thus, the chart is completed. Use the right column to write 42 as a product of its prime factors, usually from smallest to largest.

$$42 = 2 \cdot 3 \cdot 7$$

$$\begin{array}{r|l} 18 & 2 \\ 9 & 3 \\ 3 & 3 \\ 1 & \end{array} \qquad\qquad\qquad\qquad\qquad \begin{array}{r|l} 35 & 5 \\ 7 & 7 \\ 1 & \end{array}$$

b. $18 = 2 \cdot 3 \cdot 3$ c. $35 = 5 \cdot 7$

Now, we can use the prime factorization to find the GCF.

Rule

To find the GCF of two or more numbers:

Step 1 Write each number as a product of its prime factors (prime factorization). Repeated factors should be written in exponential form.

Step 2 Choose only factors common to each number with the lowest exponent.

Step 3 Multiply the factors from Step 2 to find the GCF.

Example 7

a. Find the GCF of 18 and 42.   b. Find the GCF of 30 and 70.

$$\begin{aligned} 18 &= 2 \cdot 3^2 \\ 42 &= 2 \cdot 3 \cdot 7 \end{aligned}$$
$$\begin{aligned} 30 &= 2 \cdot 3 \cdot 5 \\ 70 &= 2 \cdot 5 \cdot 7 \end{aligned}$$

$$GCF = 2 \cdot 3 = 6$$ $$GCF = 2 \cdot 5 = 10$$

Example 8

Find the GCF of 120, 90, and 84.

120	2		84	2		90	2
60	2		42	2		45	3
30	2		21	3		15	3
15	3		7	7		5	5
5	5		1			1	
1							

$$120 = 2^3 \cdot 3 \cdot 5$$
$$84 = 2^2 \cdot 3 \quad \cdot 7$$
$$90 = 2 \cdot 3^2 \cdot 5$$
$$\overline{GCF = 2 \cdot 3 = 6}$$

☐ FRACTIONS

Examples of fractions. $\dfrac{2}{3}, \dfrac{7}{-2}, \dfrac{-4}{5}, \dfrac{1}{9}$

Definition

*A **fraction** is a number of the form $\dfrac{a}{b}$ where $b \neq 0$.*

The top number **a** is called the **numerator**, and the bottom number **b** is called the **denominator** and they are separated by the **fraction bar**.

Fractions can be classified as **proper fractions** and **improper fractions**.

Examples of proper fractions: $\dfrac{1}{7}, \dfrac{2}{5}, \dfrac{23}{27}$

Definition

*A fraction is called a **proper fraction** if the numerator is less than the denominator.*

Examples of improper fractions: $\dfrac{8}{3}, \dfrac{24}{15}, \dfrac{12}{12}$

Definition

*A fraction is called an **improper fraction** if the numerator is greater than or equal to the denominator.*

Note: An improper fraction can be expressed as a mixed number in simplest form.

Example 9

a. $\dfrac{8}{3} = \dfrac{6}{3} + \dfrac{2}{3} = 2 + \dfrac{2}{3} = 2\dfrac{2}{3}$

b. $\dfrac{24}{15} = \dfrac{15}{15} + \dfrac{9}{15} = 1 + \dfrac{9}{15} = 1\dfrac{9}{15} = 1\dfrac{3}{5}$

☐ SIMPLIFYING FRACTIONS

> **Definition**
>
> *A fraction is in **simplest form** (lowest terms) when the numerator and denominator have no common factors other than 1.*

Fundamental Property of Fraction

If $\dfrac{a}{b}$ is a fraction and $c \neq 0$, then $\dfrac{a \cdot c}{b \cdot c} = \dfrac{a}{b}$

> **Rule**
>
> To simplify a fraction:
>
> **Step 1** Find the GCF of the numerator and denominator.
>
> **Step 2** Divide both the numerator and denominator by their GCF.

Example 10

Write each fraction in simplest form.

a. $\dfrac{24}{60}$ b. $\dfrac{15}{35}$ c. $\dfrac{64}{56}$ d. $\dfrac{13}{26}$ e. $\dfrac{11}{15}$

Solution

a. The greatest common factor of 24 and 60 is 12. To simplify the fraction, divide both the numerator and denominator by 12.

$$\frac{24}{60} = \frac{24 \div 12}{60 \div 12} = \frac{2}{5}$$

$\dfrac{2}{5}$ is the simplest form because 2 and 5 have no common factors other than 1.

b. The GCF of 15 and 35 is 5. Divide both the numerator and denominator by 5.

$$\frac{15}{35} = \frac{15 \div 5}{35 \div 5} = \frac{3}{7}$$

c. The GCF of 64 and 56 is 8. Divide both the numerator and denominator by 8.

$$\frac{64}{56} = \frac{64 \div 8}{56 \div 8} = \frac{8}{7}$$

d. The GCF of 13 and 26 is 13. Divide both the numerator and denominator by 13.

$$\frac{13}{26} = \frac{13 \div 13}{26 \div 13} = \frac{1}{2}$$

e. $\frac{11}{15}$ Since the numerator and denominator have no common factors other than 1, the fraction is in lowest terms.

Note: If you cannot see the GCF by observation, use the rule discussed in this section to find the GCF.

If the fraction involves large numbers and you try to avoid the process of finding the GCF it is still possible to simplify the fraction in more than one step.

First, recognize by observation any common factor for the numerator and denominator. Then, divide both the numerator and denominator by that common factor. Repeat this process until the fraction is in simplest form.

Example 11

Simplify.

$$\frac{24}{60}$$

Step 1 $\dfrac{24 \div 2}{60 \div 2} = \dfrac{12}{30}$ 2 is a common factor for 24 and 60, divide by 2.

Step 2 $\dfrac{12 \div 2}{30 \div 2} = \dfrac{6}{15}$ 2 is a common factor for 12 and 30, divide by 2.

Step 3 $\dfrac{6 \div 3}{15 \div 3} = \dfrac{2}{5}$ 3 is a common factor for 6 and 15, divide by 2.

Thus, $\dfrac{24}{60} = \dfrac{2}{5}$. The fraction $\dfrac{2}{5}$ is in lowest terms or simplest form. For this fraction (see example a) we obtained the same answer in one step by dividing 24 and 60 by the GCF = 12.

The fractions $\dfrac{24}{60}$ and $\dfrac{2}{5}$ are called equivalent fractions $\left(\dfrac{24}{60} = \dfrac{2}{5} \right)$.

Definition

*Two fractions are called **equivalent fractions** if one fraction can be obtained from the other fraction by multiplying or dividing both the numerator and denominator by the same non-zero number.*

Example 12

$$\frac{12}{18} = \frac{12 \div 3}{18 \div 3} = \frac{4}{6} \qquad \frac{12}{18} \text{ and } \frac{4}{6} \text{ are equivalent fractions}$$

$$\frac{2}{5} = \frac{2 \cdot 4}{5 \cdot 4} = \frac{8}{20} \qquad \frac{2}{5} \text{ and } \frac{8}{20} \text{ are equivalent fractions}$$

Note: Equivalent fractions: $-\dfrac{a}{b} = \dfrac{-a}{b} = \dfrac{a}{-b} = -\dfrac{-a}{-b}$

Example 13

Write equivalent fractions with the given denominator.

a. $\dfrac{3}{7} = \dfrac{}{21}$ 　　　b. $\dfrac{15}{36} = \dfrac{}{12}$ 　　　c. $\dfrac{4}{5} = \dfrac{}{30}$ 　　　d. $\dfrac{16}{40} = \dfrac{}{10}$

Solution

a. $\dfrac{3}{7} = \dfrac{3 \cdot 3}{7 \cdot 3} = \dfrac{9}{21}$ 　　　$\dfrac{3}{7}$ and $\dfrac{9}{21}$ are equivalent fractions

b. $\dfrac{15}{36} = \dfrac{15 \div 3}{36 \div 3} = \dfrac{5}{12}$ 　　　$\dfrac{15}{36}$ and $\dfrac{5}{12}$ are equivalent fractions

c. $\dfrac{4}{5} = \dfrac{4 \cdot 6}{5 \cdot 6} = \dfrac{24}{30}$ 　　　$\dfrac{4}{5}$ and $\dfrac{24}{30}$ are equivalent fractions

d. $\dfrac{16}{40} = \dfrac{16 \div 4}{40 \div 4} = \dfrac{4}{10}$ 　　　$\dfrac{16}{40}$ and $\dfrac{4}{10}$ are equivalent fractions

1.4 EXERCISES

Find all factors of each number.

1. a. 36 　　　b. 15 　　　c. 40

2. a. 28 　　　b. 64 　　　c. 19

3. a. 45 　　　b. 12 　　　c. 50

Identify each number as prime, composite or neither.

4. a. 212 　　　b. 35 　　　c. 23

5. a. 81 　　　b. 1 　　　c. 17

6. a. 37 　　　b. 56 　　　c. 31

Find the prime factorization of each number.

7. a. 100   b. 210   c. 90

8. a. 35   b. 40   c. 84

9. a. 88   b. 154   c. 17

Find the greatest common factor

10. a. 20, 42   b. 64, 84   c. 15, 27

11. a. 36, 90   b. 48, 54   c. 12, 66

12. a. 240, 180, 72   b. 66, 88, 154   c. 28, 60, 40

Simplify each fraction.

13. a. $\dfrac{18}{60}$ b. $\dfrac{56}{72}$ c. $\dfrac{15}{35}$

14. a. $\dfrac{45}{90}$ b. $\dfrac{36}{144}$ c. $\dfrac{16}{49}$

15. a. $\dfrac{75}{125}$ b. $\dfrac{44}{76}$ c. $\dfrac{21}{32}$

Write equivalent fractions with the given denominator.

16. a. $\dfrac{6}{9} = \dfrac{}{3}$ b. $\dfrac{12}{64} = \dfrac{}{16}$ c. $\dfrac{5}{17} = \dfrac{}{51}$

17. a. $\dfrac{3}{20} = \dfrac{}{120}$ b. $\dfrac{18}{60} = \dfrac{}{10}$ c. $\dfrac{42}{54} = \dfrac{}{9}$

18. a. $\dfrac{36}{76} = \dfrac{}{19}$ b. $\dfrac{15}{75} = \dfrac{}{5}$ c. $\dfrac{24}{60} = \dfrac{}{15}$

Identify each fraction as proper or improper. Express each improper fraction as a mixed number.

19. a. $\dfrac{15}{18}$ b. $\dfrac{21}{18}$ c. $\dfrac{14}{14}$

20. a. $\dfrac{9}{11}$ b. $\dfrac{43}{43}$ c. $\dfrac{24}{12}$

21. a. $\dfrac{25}{19}$ b. $\dfrac{16}{12}$ c. $\dfrac{102}{501}$

Convert each improper fraction to a mixed number.

22. a. $\dfrac{26}{20}$ b. $\dfrac{12}{9}$ c. $\dfrac{84}{79}$

23. a. $-\dfrac{16}{11}$ b. $\dfrac{14}{3}$ c. $\dfrac{65}{60}$

24. a. $\dfrac{24}{5}$ b. $-\dfrac{100}{3}$ c. $\dfrac{15}{8}$

1.5 MULTIPLICATION AND DIVISION OF RATIONAL NUMBERS

□ **Multiplying Fractions** □ **Multiplying Mixed Numbers** □ **Dividing Fractions** □ **Dividing Mixed Numbers**

□ MULTIPLYING FRACTIONS

Rule

To find the product of two fractions, multiply the numerators and multiply the denominators. Then, write the product in simplest form.

$$\frac{a}{b} \cdot \frac{c}{d} = \frac{a \cdot c}{b \cdot d} \quad (b \neq 0, d \neq 0)$$

Note: To avoid large numbers, if the numerator and denominator have some common factors, cancel those factors before performing the multiplication.

Example 1

Multiply.

Write the product in simplest form.

a. $\dfrac{4}{5} \cdot \dfrac{2}{7} = \dfrac{4 \cdot 2}{5 \cdot 7} = \dfrac{8}{35}$ Multiply the numerators and denominators

b. $(-11)\left(\dfrac{5}{3}\right) = \left(-\dfrac{11}{1}\right)\left(\dfrac{5}{3}\right) = -\dfrac{11 \cdot 5}{1 \cdot 3} = -\dfrac{55}{3}$

c. $\left(-\dfrac{6}{15}\right)\left(-\dfrac{21}{18}\right) =$ Product of two negative numbers is positive

$\dfrac{6}{15} \cdot \dfrac{21}{18} =$ *Use cross cancellation* : Divide 6 and 18 by the GCF (6).

Divide 15 and 21 by the GCF (3)

$\dfrac{1 \cdot 7}{5 \cdot 3} =$ Multiply the numerators and denominators.

$\dfrac{7}{15}$

d. $\dfrac{24}{40} \cdot \dfrac{10}{16} =$ *Use cross cancellation:* Divide 24 and 16 by the GCF (8)

Divide 10 and 40 by the GCF (10)

$\dfrac{3 \cdot 1}{4 \cdot 2} =$ Multiply the numerators and denominators.

$\dfrac{3}{8} =$

Warning: There is no need for common denominator when multiplying fractions.

In Section 1.4 we have seen that an improper fraction can be expressed as a mixed number. Also, mixed numbers can be expressed as improper fractions (multiply the denominator of the fractional part by the whole part, add the result to the numerator, and then divide by the denominator of the fractional part).

Example 2

Rewrite each mixed number as an improper fraction.

a. $2\dfrac{3}{5} = \dfrac{5 \cdot 2 + 3}{5} = \dfrac{10 + 3}{5} = \dfrac{13}{5}$

b. $4\dfrac{7}{12} = \dfrac{12 \cdot 4 + 7}{12} = \dfrac{48 + 7}{12} = \dfrac{55}{12}$

Next, we will expand the multiplication of fractions to multiplication of mixed numbers.

☐ MULTIPLYING MIXED NUMBERS

Warning: Before multiplying mixed numbers, rewrite the mixed numbers as improper fractions. Do not multiply mixed numbers in mixed number form. $\left(2\dfrac{4}{7} \cdot 3\dfrac{2}{5} \neq 6\dfrac{8}{35} \right)$

Example 3

Multiply.

Write the answer in simplest form.

a. $4\dfrac{1}{6} \cdot 2\dfrac{3}{5}$ b. $\left(-3\dfrac{6}{5} \right)\left(-6\dfrac{8}{7} \right)$ c. $1\dfrac{5}{7} \cdot 6\dfrac{2}{3}$ d. $\left(-\dfrac{2}{5} \right) \cdot 5\dfrac{5}{4}$

Solution

a. $4\dfrac{1}{6} \cdot 2\dfrac{3}{5} = \dfrac{25}{6} \cdot \dfrac{13}{5} = \dfrac{5}{6} \cdot \dfrac{13}{1} = \dfrac{65}{6}$

b. $\left(-3\dfrac{6}{5} \right)\left(-6\dfrac{8}{7} \right) = \dfrac{21}{5} \cdot \dfrac{50}{7} = \dfrac{3}{1} \cdot \dfrac{10}{1} = \dfrac{30}{1} = 30$

c. $1\dfrac{5}{7} \cdot 6\dfrac{2}{3} = \dfrac{12}{7} \cdot \dfrac{20}{3} = \dfrac{4}{7} \cdot \dfrac{20}{1} = \dfrac{4 \cdot 20}{7 \cdot 1} = \dfrac{80}{7}$

d. $\left(-\dfrac{2}{5}\right) \cdot 5\dfrac{5}{4} = \left(-\dfrac{2}{5}\right) \cdot \dfrac{25}{4} = \left(-\dfrac{1}{1}\right) \cdot \dfrac{5}{2} = -\dfrac{1 \cdot 5}{1 \cdot 2} = -\dfrac{5}{2}$

☐ DIVIDING FRACTIONS

Rule

To divide two fractions, multiply the first fraction by the reciprocal of the second fraction. Then, write the quotient in simplest form.

$$\dfrac{a}{b} \div \dfrac{c}{d} = \dfrac{a}{b} \cdot \dfrac{d}{c} = \dfrac{a \cdot d}{b \cdot c} \quad (b \neq 0, d \neq 0, c \neq 0)$$

Note: The reciprocal of $\dfrac{c}{d}$ is $\dfrac{d}{c}$ $(c \neq 0, d \neq 0)$

Example 4

Divide.

Write the answer in simplest form.

a. $\dfrac{7}{8} \div \left(-\dfrac{21}{24}\right)$ b. $\dfrac{15}{32} \div \dfrac{10}{8}$ c. $\left(-\dfrac{12}{40}\right) \div \left(-\dfrac{18}{8}\right)$ d. $\dfrac{6}{21} \div 30$

Solution

a. $\dfrac{7}{8} \div \left(-\dfrac{21}{24}\right) = \dfrac{7}{8} \cdot \left(-\dfrac{24}{21}\right) = -\dfrac{1}{1} \cdot \dfrac{3}{3} = -\dfrac{1 \cdot 3}{1 \cdot 3} = -\dfrac{3}{3} = -1$

b. $\dfrac{15}{32} \div \dfrac{10}{8} = \dfrac{15}{32} \cdot \dfrac{8}{10} = \dfrac{3}{4} \cdot \dfrac{1}{2} = \dfrac{3 \cdot 1}{4 \cdot 2} = \dfrac{3}{8}$

c. $\left(-\dfrac{12}{40}\right) \div \left(-\dfrac{18}{8}\right) = \left(-\dfrac{12}{40}\right)\left(-\dfrac{8}{18}\right) = \dfrac{2}{5} \cdot \dfrac{1}{3} = \dfrac{2 \cdot 1}{5 \cdot 3} = \dfrac{2}{15}$

d. $\dfrac{6}{21} \div 30 = \dfrac{6}{21} \div \dfrac{30}{1} = \dfrac{6}{21} \cdot \dfrac{1}{30} = \dfrac{1}{21} \cdot \dfrac{1}{5} = \dfrac{1 \cdot 1}{21 \cdot 5} = \dfrac{1}{105}$

Note: If there are negative fractions involved in multiplication, find the sign of the product then simplify.

□ DIVIDING MIXED NUMBERS

Warning: Before dividing mixed numbers, rewrite the mixed numbers as improper fractions.

Example 5

Divide.

Write the answer in simplest form.

a. $2\dfrac{1}{7} \div 1\dfrac{5}{35}$

c. $\left(-4\dfrac{4}{9}\right) \div \left(-1\dfrac{2}{3}\right)$

b. $5\dfrac{1}{3} \div 8\dfrac{2}{6}$

d. $12\dfrac{1}{4} \div 14$

Solution

a. $2\dfrac{1}{7} \div 1\dfrac{5}{35} = \dfrac{15}{7} \div \dfrac{40}{35} = \dfrac{15}{7} \cdot \dfrac{35}{40} = \dfrac{3}{1} \cdot \dfrac{5}{8} = \dfrac{15}{8} = 1\dfrac{7}{8}$

b. $5\dfrac{1}{3} \div 8\dfrac{2}{6} = \dfrac{16}{3} \div \dfrac{50}{6} = \dfrac{16}{3} \cdot \dfrac{6}{50} = \dfrac{8}{1} \cdot \dfrac{2}{25} = \dfrac{16}{25}$

c. $\left(-4\dfrac{4}{9}\right) \div \left(-1\dfrac{2}{3}\right) = \left(-\dfrac{40}{9}\right) \div \left(-\dfrac{5}{3}\right) = \left(-\dfrac{40}{9}\right)\left(-\dfrac{3}{5}\right) = \dfrac{8}{3} \cdot \dfrac{1}{1} = \dfrac{8}{3} = 2\dfrac{2}{3}$

d. $12\dfrac{1}{4} \div 14 = \dfrac{49}{4} \div \dfrac{14}{1} = \dfrac{49}{4} \cdot \dfrac{1}{14} = \dfrac{7}{4} \cdot \dfrac{1}{2} = \dfrac{7}{8}$

1.5 EXERCISES

Convert each mixed number to an improper fraction.

1. a. $3\dfrac{5}{6}$ b. $-8\dfrac{7}{11}$ c. $2\dfrac{3}{9}$

2. a. $-4\dfrac{2}{8}$ b. $5\dfrac{3}{10}$ c. $18\dfrac{1}{2}$

3. a. $24\dfrac{2}{3}$ b. $5\dfrac{8}{9}$ c. $1\dfrac{5}{31}$

Multiply. Write the answer in simplest form.

4. a. $\dfrac{9}{12} \cdot \dfrac{36}{27}$ b. $\left(-\dfrac{3}{8}\right)\left(\dfrac{72}{90}\right)$ c. $\dfrac{11}{5} \cdot \dfrac{30}{18}$

5. a. $\left(-\dfrac{7}{15}\right)\left(-\dfrac{45}{49}\right)$ b. $\dfrac{42}{90}\cdot\dfrac{15}{21}$ c. $\dfrac{16}{28}\cdot\dfrac{49}{64}$

6. a. $\dfrac{24}{33}\cdot\dfrac{22}{60}$ b. $7\cdot\dfrac{8}{56}$ c. $\dfrac{1}{2}\left(-\dfrac{50}{87}\right)$

7. a. $\dfrac{11}{3}\cdot(-21)$ b. $\left(-\dfrac{15}{8}\right)\left(-\dfrac{24}{45}\right)$ c. $\dfrac{5}{35}\left(-\dfrac{20}{6}\right)$

Divide. Write the answer in simplest form.

8. a. $\dfrac{5}{16}\div\dfrac{3}{8}$ b. $\dfrac{14}{15}\div\dfrac{21}{35}$ c. $\left(-\dfrac{19}{24}\right)\div\dfrac{5}{32}$

9. a. $\left(-\dfrac{7}{12}\right)\div\left(-\dfrac{1}{4}\right)$ b. $\dfrac{4}{9}\div\dfrac{2}{3}$ c. $\dfrac{16}{25}\div\dfrac{8}{20}$

10. a. $\dfrac{3}{10}\div\dfrac{12}{50}$ b. $\dfrac{5}{18}\div\left(-\dfrac{4}{63}\right)$ c. $9\div\dfrac{15}{11}$

11. a. $-14\div\dfrac{28}{6}$ b. $\dfrac{22}{15}\div\dfrac{55}{45}$ c. $\dfrac{12}{8}\div(-36)$

Multiply. Write the answer in simplest form

12. a. $3\dfrac{3}{4}\cdot1\dfrac{5}{9}$ b. $\left(-5\dfrac{2}{3}\right)\left(-1\dfrac{4}{17}\right)$ c. $2\dfrac{4}{5}\cdot6\dfrac{3}{7}$

13. a. $\left(-4\dfrac{2}{7}\right)\cdot9\dfrac{4}{5}$ b. $8\dfrac{1}{6}\cdot1\dfrac{4}{14}$ c. $\dfrac{2}{7}\cdot2\dfrac{5}{8}$

14. a. $\dfrac{12}{15}\cdot1\dfrac{7}{18}$ b. $8\dfrac{2}{3}\left(-1\dfrac{5}{13}\right)$ c. $3\dfrac{4}{9}\cdot5\dfrac{2}{5}$

15. a. $2\dfrac{5}{8}\cdot3\dfrac{3}{7}$ b. $\left(-8\dfrac{1}{3}\right)\left(-3\dfrac{3}{5}\right)$ c. $4\dfrac{5}{7}\cdot\left(-\dfrac{21}{22}\right)$

Divide. Write the answer in simplest form.

16. a. $3\dfrac{5}{8}\div4\dfrac{1}{4}$ b. $7\dfrac{3}{5}\div1\dfrac{9}{10}$ c. $\left(-11\dfrac{2}{3}\right)\div\left(-1\dfrac{1}{6}\right)$

17. a. $4\dfrac{2}{9} \div 1\dfrac{1}{18}$ b. $\left(-5\dfrac{3}{4}\right) \div 1\dfrac{2}{24}$ c. $4\dfrac{8}{9} \div 3\dfrac{3}{10}$

18. a. $6\dfrac{2}{3} \div \left(-1\dfrac{7}{18}\right)$ b. $3\dfrac{9}{12} \div 3\dfrac{3}{4}$ c. $5\dfrac{2}{3} \div 4\dfrac{1}{4}$

Problem Solving

19. A recipe for pumpkin pie calls for $2\dfrac{1}{4}$ cups of brown sugar for each pie. How many cups of sugar are needed for 8 pies?

20. A $24\dfrac{1}{2}$ inches rope is to be cut into 7 equal pieces. How long is each piece?

21. There are 42 students in an algebra class. At the end of the semester $\dfrac{1}{6}$ of the students ended up with an A grade and $\dfrac{2}{7}$ of the students a B grade. How many A's and B's were in the algebra class?

22. A batch of 10 cookies calls for $4\dfrac{1}{2}$ cups of flour, $\dfrac{2}{3}$ cup of butter, and $\dfrac{1}{2}$ cup of sugar. How many cups of flour, butter and sugar are needed for 60 cookies?

1.6 ADDITION AND SUBTRACTION OF RATIONAL NUMBERS

□ **Addition and Subtraction of Fractions with the Same Denominator** □ **Addition and Subtraction of Fractions with Different Denominators** □ **Addition and Subtraction of Mixed Numbers**

□ ADDITION AND SUBTRACTION OF FRACTIONS WITH THE SAME DENOMINATOR

Rule

To add or subtract fractions with the same (like) denominator, add or subtract the numerators and keep the same denominator.

$$\frac{a}{c}+\frac{b}{c}=\frac{a+b}{c} \text{ and } \frac{a}{c}-\frac{b}{c}=\frac{a-b}{c} \ (c \neq 0)$$

Example 1

Add or subtract. Write the answer in lowest terms.

a. $\dfrac{2}{15}+\dfrac{8}{15}=\dfrac{2+8}{15}=\dfrac{10}{15}=\dfrac{2}{3}$

b. $\dfrac{5}{12}-\dfrac{2}{12}=\dfrac{5-2}{12}=\dfrac{3}{12}=\dfrac{1}{4}$

c. $-\dfrac{3}{7}+\dfrac{4}{7}=\dfrac{-3+4}{7}=\dfrac{1}{7}$

d. $-\dfrac{8}{11}-\dfrac{3}{11}=\dfrac{-8-3}{11}=\dfrac{-11}{11}=-1$

e. $\dfrac{4}{9}+\dfrac{2}{9}-\dfrac{7}{9}=\dfrac{4+2-7}{9}=\dfrac{6-7}{9}=\dfrac{-1}{9}=-\dfrac{1}{9}$

□ ADDITION AND SUBTRACTIONS OF FRACTIONS WITH DIFFERENT DENOMINATORS

> **Rule**
>
> To add or subtract fractions with different (unlike) denominators:
>
> **Step 1** Find the least common denominator (LCD) of the fractions.
>
> **Step 2** Rewrite each fraction as an equivalent fraction with the LCD as a denominator.
>
> **Step 3** Add or subtract the fractions with the same denominator.

Before we attempt to find the least common denominator, we need to understand the concept of *multiples* of a number. To find the multiples of a number, just multiply the number by 1, 2, 3, ...

Example 2

Find the multiples of 12 and 18. Then, find the LCM.

     12: 12, 24, 36, 48, 60, 72, . . . (12 is an improper multiple)

     18: 18, 36, 54, 72, 90, . . . (18 is an improper multiple)

The numbers 12 and 18 have many common multiples: 36, 72, ... Since 36 is the smallest common multiple, it is called the **least common multiple** (LCM).

In other words, the least common multiple 36 is the smallest number that can be divided exactly by 12 and 18.

For large numbers this is an inconvenient method to find the LCM. Next, we will use prime factorization to introduce another method to find the LCM.

> **Rule**
>
> To find the least common multiple for two or more numbers:
>
> **Step 1** Write each number as a product of its prime factors (prime factorization). Repeated factors should be written in exponential form.
>
> **Step 2** Choose common and uncommon factors with the largest exponents.
>
> **Step 3** Multiply the factors from Step 2 to find the LCM.

Example 3

Find the least common multiple for 12 and 18.

To find the prime factorization of 12 and 18, we can use the tree diagram or the bar chart.

$$12 = 2^2 \cdot 3$$
$$18 = 2 \ \cdot 3^2$$
$$\overline{}$$
$$LCM = 2^2 \cdot 3^2 = 4 \cdot 9 = 36$$

Example 4

Find the least common multiple for 30 and 36.

$$30 = 2 \ \cdot 3 \ \cdot 5$$
$$36 = 2^2 \cdot 3^2$$
$$\overline{}$$
$$LCM = 2^2 \cdot 3^2 \cdot 5 = 4 \cdot 9 \cdot 5 = 180$$

Thus, LCM = 180 is the smallest number that can be divided exactly by 30 and 36.

In the last example, 2 and 3 are common factors. Therefore, we chose 2 and 3 with the largest exponents 2^2 and 3^2. Also, according to the rule we had to take the uncommon factor 5. Since 30 and 36 are two random numbers, 180 is called the least common multiple (LCM) of those two numbers.

If 30 and 36 are the denominators of some fractions like $\dfrac{1}{30}$ and $\dfrac{1}{36}$, then 180 is called the least common denominator (LCD) of those two fractions. Thus, the process of finding the LCM for 30 and 36 is the same as finding the LCD for $\dfrac{1}{30}$ and $\dfrac{1}{36}$. Next, we will apply the concept of least common denominator to add or subtract fractions with different (unlike) denominators.

Example 5

Add.

$$\frac{5}{12} + \frac{7}{18}$$

Solution

Step 1 Find the LCD of $\dfrac{1}{12}$ and $\dfrac{1}{18}$. From Example 3 we know that the LCM of 12 and 18 is LCM = 36.

Step 2 Rewrite each fraction as an equivalent fraction with the denominator 36.

$$\frac{5}{12} = \frac{}{36} \quad \text{Since } 36 \div 12 = 3 \text{, we multiply the fraction by } \frac{3}{3}, \ \frac{5 \cdot 3}{12 \cdot 3} = \frac{15}{36}$$

$$\frac{7}{18} = \frac{}{36} \quad \text{Since } 36 \div 18 = 2 \text{, we multiply the fraction by } \frac{2}{2}, \ \frac{7 \cdot 2}{18 \cdot 2} = \frac{14}{36}$$

Then, $\dfrac{5}{12} + \dfrac{7}{18} = \dfrac{15}{36} + \dfrac{14}{36} = \dfrac{15 + 14}{36} = \dfrac{29}{36}$

Example 6

Subtract

$$\frac{3}{20} - \frac{2}{15}$$

Solution

Step 1 Find LCD

$$15 = \quad 3 \cdot 5$$
$$20 = 2^2 \quad \cdot 5$$
$$\overline{\quad\quad\quad\quad\quad\quad}$$
$$LCD = 2^2 \cdot 3 \cdot 5 = 60$$

Step 2 Rewrite each fraction as an equivalent fraction with denominator 60

$$\frac{3}{20} = \frac{3 \cdot 3}{20 \cdot 3} = \frac{9}{60}, \quad \frac{2}{15} = \frac{2 \cdot 4}{15 \cdot 4} = \frac{8}{60}$$

Hence, $\dfrac{3}{20} - \dfrac{2}{15} = \dfrac{9}{60} - \dfrac{8}{60} = \dfrac{9-8}{60} = \dfrac{1}{60}$

Warning: $\dfrac{1}{2} + \dfrac{1}{3} \neq \dfrac{2}{5}$ **Correct:** $\dfrac{1}{2} + \dfrac{1}{3} = \dfrac{3}{6} + \dfrac{2}{6} = \dfrac{5}{6}$

When the denominators are small numbers, there is a shortcut to find the LCD by inspection.

Hint: Since the LCD is a multiple of the denominators, choose the largest denominator and multiply it by 1, 2, 3 . . . until you find the smallest number (multiple) that can be divided exactly by all denominators. If the denominators have no common factors, multiply the denominators to find the LCD.

Example 7

Add.

$$\frac{5}{24} + \frac{3}{16}$$

Solution

The largest denominator is 24. Multiply 24 by 1, 2, 3 . . . until we find the LCD.

$24 \cdot 1 = 24$ 24 cannot be divided evenly by 16. Thus, 24 is not the LCD.

$24 \cdot 2 = 48$ 48 can be divided by both, 24 and 16. Therefore, 48 is the LCD.

Then, $\dfrac{5}{24} + \dfrac{3}{16} = \dfrac{5 \cdot 2}{24 \cdot 2} + \dfrac{3 \cdot 3}{16 \cdot 3} = \dfrac{10}{48} + \dfrac{9}{48} = \dfrac{10+9}{48} = \dfrac{19}{48}$

Example 8

Subtract.

$$\frac{4}{7} - \frac{5}{9}$$

Solution

Since the denominators 7 and 9 have no common factors, the $LCD = 7 \cdot 9 = 63$

Hence, $\dfrac{4}{7} - \dfrac{5}{9} = \dfrac{4 \cdot 9}{7 \cdot 9} - \dfrac{5 \cdot 7}{9 \cdot 7} = \dfrac{36}{63} - \dfrac{35}{63} = \dfrac{36 - 35}{63} = \dfrac{1}{63}$

Example 9

Add or subtract.

Write the answer in simplest form. $\dfrac{5}{42} + \dfrac{11}{14} - \dfrac{8}{63}$

Solution

The largest denominator is 63. Multiply 63 by 1, 2, 3, . . . until we find the LCD.

$63 \cdot 1 = 63$ 63 cannot be divided evenly by 42 and 14.

Hence, 63 is not the LCD.

$63 \cdot 2 = 126$ 126 can be divided exactly by 42 and 14.

Thus, LCD = 126.

Then,

$\dfrac{5}{42} + \dfrac{11}{14} - \dfrac{8}{63} = \dfrac{5 \cdot 3}{42 \cdot 3} + \dfrac{11 \cdot 9}{14 \cdot 9} - \dfrac{8 \cdot 2}{63 \cdot 2} = \dfrac{15}{126} + \dfrac{99}{126} - \dfrac{16}{126} = \dfrac{15 + 99 - 16}{126} = \dfrac{98}{126} = \dfrac{7}{9}$

☐ ADDITION AND SUBTRACTION OF MIXED NUMBERS

Rule

To add or subtract mixed numbers in mixed number form:

Step 1 Find the least common denominator for the fractional parts.

Step 2 Rewrite the fractional parts as equivalent fractions with the LCD as the denominator.

Step 3 First, add or subtract the whole parts and then the fractional parts with the same denominator.

Example 10

Add

$2\dfrac{3}{4} + 5\dfrac{1}{6}$

Solution

The least common denominator for the fractional parts $\dfrac{3}{4}$ and $\dfrac{1}{6}$ is LCD = 12.
Rewrite each fraction as an equivalent fraction with the denominator LCD = 12.

$$\frac{3}{4} = \frac{3 \cdot 3}{4 \cdot 3} = \frac{9}{12} \text{ and } \frac{1}{6} = \frac{1 \cdot 2}{6 \cdot 2} = \frac{2}{12}$$

Add the whole parts and fractional parts. $2\dfrac{3}{4} + 5\dfrac{1}{6} = 2\dfrac{9}{12} + 5\dfrac{2}{12} = 7\dfrac{9+2}{12} = 7\dfrac{11}{12}$

Example 11

Subtract.

$$5\frac{7}{9} - 3\frac{1}{5}$$

Solution

The least common denominator for the fractional parts $\dfrac{7}{9}$ and $\dfrac{1}{5}$ is $9 \cdot 5 = 45$.
Rewrite each fraction as an equivalent fraction with the denominator LCD = 45

$$\frac{7}{9} = \frac{7 \cdot 5}{9 \cdot 5} = \frac{35}{45} \text{ and } \frac{1}{5} = \frac{1 \cdot 9}{5 \cdot 9} = \frac{9}{45}$$

Subtract the whole parts and fractional parts. $5\dfrac{7}{9} - 3\dfrac{1}{5} = 5\dfrac{35}{45} - 3\dfrac{9}{45} = 2\dfrac{26}{45}$

Example 12

Add or Subtract.

$$4\frac{5}{8} + 6\frac{1}{12} - 2\frac{3}{32}$$

Solution

The least common denominator for the fractional parts $\dfrac{5}{8}$, $\dfrac{1}{12}$, and $\dfrac{3}{32}$ is $LCD = 32 \cdot 3 = 96$
Rewrite each fraction as an equivalent fraction with the denominator LCD = 96.

$$\frac{5}{8} = \frac{5 \cdot 12}{8 \cdot 12} = \frac{60}{96}, \frac{1}{12} = \frac{1 \cdot 8}{12 \cdot 8} = \frac{8}{96}, \text{ and } \frac{3}{32} = \frac{3 \cdot 3}{32 \cdot 3} = \frac{9}{96}$$

Add or subtract the whole parts and fractional parts.

$$4\frac{5}{8} + 6\frac{1}{12} - 2\frac{3}{32} = 4\frac{60}{96} + 6\frac{8}{96} - 2\frac{9}{96} = 10\frac{68}{96} - 2\frac{9}{96} = 8\frac{59}{96}$$

If the mixed numbers do not involve large numbers, then convert the mixed numbers into improper fractions and add or subtract fractions instead of mixed numbers.

Example 13

Add or Subtract.

$$2\frac{1}{3} - 1\frac{3}{5} + 6\frac{3}{4}$$

Solution

Rewrite each mixed number as a fraction.

$$2\frac{1}{3} - 1\frac{3}{5} + 6\frac{3}{4} = \frac{3 \cdot 2 + 1}{3} - \frac{5 \cdot 1 + 3}{5} + \frac{4 \cdot 6 + 3}{4} = \frac{7}{3} - \frac{8}{5} + \frac{27}{4}$$

$LCD = 3 \cdot 5 \cdot 4 = 60$

$$\frac{7}{3} - \frac{8}{5} + \frac{27}{4} = \frac{7 \cdot 20}{3 \cdot 20} - \frac{8 \cdot 12}{5 \cdot 12} + \frac{27 \cdot 15}{4 \cdot 15} = \frac{140}{60} - \frac{96}{60} + \frac{405}{60} = \frac{140 - 96 + 405}{60} = \frac{449}{60}.$$

1.6 EXERCISES

Find the least common multiple for each of the following group of numbers.

1. a. 16 and 14   b. 18 and 48   c. 20 and 35

2. a. 28 and 10   b. 45 and 63   c. 50 and 120

Find the least common denominator for each of the following group of fractions.

3. a. $\dfrac{5}{12}, \dfrac{3}{20}$ b. $\dfrac{2}{15}, \dfrac{7}{40}$ c. $\dfrac{9}{28}, \dfrac{4}{35}$

4. a. $\dfrac{2}{11}, \dfrac{1}{10}$ b. $\dfrac{17}{84}, \dfrac{11}{90}$ c. $\dfrac{5}{6}, \dfrac{8}{45}$

5. a. $\dfrac{1}{48}, \dfrac{15}{64}$ b. $\dfrac{1}{18}, \dfrac{1}{8}$ c. $\dfrac{2}{17}, \dfrac{9}{34}$

6. a. $\dfrac{1}{3}, \dfrac{2}{5}, \dfrac{4}{7}$ b. $\dfrac{10}{27}, \dfrac{1}{45}, \dfrac{6}{63}$ c. $\dfrac{8}{15}, \dfrac{13}{18}, \dfrac{1}{60}$

Rewrite each fraction with the indicated denominator

7. a. $\dfrac{5}{6} = \dfrac{}{18}$ b. $\dfrac{3}{7} = \dfrac{}{21}$ c. $\dfrac{2}{15} = \dfrac{}{45}$

8. a. $\dfrac{9}{11} = \dfrac{}{55}$ b. $\dfrac{4}{9} = \dfrac{}{36}$ c. $\dfrac{3}{14} = \dfrac{}{42}$

9. a. $\dfrac{2}{15} = \dfrac{}{60}$ b. $\dfrac{6}{27} = \dfrac{}{54}$ c. $\dfrac{3}{8} = \dfrac{}{56}$

10. a. $\dfrac{8}{45} = \dfrac{}{90}$ b. $\dfrac{5}{3} = \dfrac{}{27}$ c. $\dfrac{11}{28} = \dfrac{}{84}$

Add or subtract. Write the answer in simplest form.

11. a. $\dfrac{1}{8} + \dfrac{3}{8}$ b. $\dfrac{2}{15} + \dfrac{8}{15}$ c. $\dfrac{5}{24} - \dfrac{3}{24}$

12. a. $\dfrac{11}{40} - \dfrac{3}{40}$ b. $\left(-\dfrac{5}{27}\right) + \left(-\dfrac{4}{27}\right)$ c. $\dfrac{7}{9} + \dfrac{2}{9}$

13. a. $\dfrac{5}{12} + \dfrac{7}{12} - \dfrac{9}{12}$ b. $\dfrac{1}{30} - \dfrac{11}{30} + \dfrac{15}{30}$ c. $-\dfrac{2}{9} + \dfrac{5}{9} + \dfrac{4}{9}$

14. a. $\dfrac{2}{3} + \dfrac{3}{5}$ b. $\dfrac{4}{9} - \left(-\dfrac{5}{8}\right)$ c. $\dfrac{2}{15} - \dfrac{3}{35}$

15. a. $\dfrac{5}{6} - \dfrac{4}{27}$ b. $\dfrac{5}{12} - \left(-\dfrac{3}{8}\right)$ c. $\dfrac{3}{16} + \dfrac{7}{40}$

16. a. $\dfrac{5}{11} + 3$ b. $-2 + \dfrac{4}{18}$ c. $5 - \dfrac{2}{7}$

17. a. $8 - \dfrac{3}{5}$ b. $\dfrac{3}{12} + 1$ c. $-6 + \dfrac{3}{8}$

18. a. $\dfrac{3}{20} - \left(-\dfrac{8}{30}\right) + \dfrac{7}{5}$ b. $\dfrac{4}{7} + \dfrac{2}{3} - \dfrac{1}{6}$ c. $2 - \dfrac{5}{12} + \dfrac{1}{9}$

19. a. $\dfrac{4}{17} + \dfrac{3}{34} - \dfrac{1}{2}$ b. $5 + \dfrac{4}{9} - \dfrac{11}{36}$ c. $\dfrac{6}{7} + \dfrac{5}{9} + \dfrac{8}{21}$

Add or subtract. Write the answer in lowest terms.

20. a. $2\dfrac{3}{5} + 4\dfrac{1}{5}$ b. $5\dfrac{4}{7} - 1\dfrac{2}{7}$ c. $-3\dfrac{7}{12} + 8\dfrac{11}{12}$

21. a. $10\dfrac{9}{16} - 4\dfrac{3}{16}$ b. $-2\dfrac{3}{19} + 6\dfrac{8}{19}$ c. $4\dfrac{3}{8} + 6\dfrac{1}{8}$

22. a. $2\dfrac{5}{12} + 4\dfrac{3}{8}$ b. $7\dfrac{1}{6} + 1\dfrac{5}{9}$ c. $3\dfrac{2}{5} - 1\dfrac{1}{4}$

23. a. $9\dfrac{3}{17} - 5\dfrac{2}{34}$ b. $-1\dfrac{4}{45} + 2\dfrac{5}{6}$ c. $8\dfrac{2}{15} + 3\dfrac{7}{20}$

24. a. $\left(-5\dfrac{4}{18}\right) + \left(-3\dfrac{11}{60}\right)$ b. $-\dfrac{2}{15} + 6\dfrac{5}{21}$ c. $8\dfrac{1}{7} - 3\dfrac{1}{11}$

25. a. $3\dfrac{5}{24} - \left(-2\dfrac{3}{32}\right)$ b. $\dfrac{9}{10} + 1\dfrac{4}{25}$ c. $5\dfrac{3}{2} - 1\dfrac{4}{3}$

26. Jane walks 7 mi each week. She walks $2\dfrac{3}{4}$ mi on Monday, and $2\dfrac{1}{2}$ mi on Wednesday. How many miles are left for Friday?

27. John tutors mathematics 16 hours per week in the math lab. He tutors $4\dfrac{1}{2}$ hours on Monday, $3\dfrac{3}{4}$ hours on Tuesday, and 4 hours on Wednesday. How many more hours can he work on Thursday?

28. The perimeter of a triangle is the sum of the measure of all three sides. If the sides of a triangle are $2\dfrac{3}{4}$ in., $4\dfrac{1}{5}$ in., and $\dfrac{11}{2}$ in., find the perimeter of the triangle.

29. If the perimeter of a triangle is 20 in and the measures of two sides are $5\dfrac{1}{4}$ in. and $6\dfrac{1}{5}$ in., find the measure of the third side.

30. Find the average of $\dfrac{5}{14}$, $\dfrac{7}{18}$, and $\dfrac{4}{9}$.

31. Find the average of $4\dfrac{1}{3}$, $-1\dfrac{17}{24}$, and $5\dfrac{3}{8}$.

1.7 PROPERTIES OF REAL NUMBERS AND ORDER OF OPERATIONS

□ The Commutative Property □ The Associative Property □ The Identity Property □ The Inverse Property □ The Distributive Property □ Order of Operations

□ THE COMMUTATIVE PROPERTY

Addition

Example 1

$2 + 3 = 5$ and $3 + 2 = 5$. Therefore, $2 + 3 = 3 + 2$

In general, we can write this property for any two real numbers a and b as follows:

$a + b = b + a$

This property is called the **commutative property of addition**.

Multiplication

Example 2

$2 \cdot 3 = 6$ and $3 \cdot 2 = 6$. Therefore, $2 \cdot 3 = 3 \cdot 2$

We can write this property for any two real numbers a and b as follows:

$a \cdot b = b \cdot a$

This property is called the **commutative property of multiplication**. We conclude that the order in which two real numbers are added or multiplied does not matter.

□ THE ASSOCIATIVE PROPERTY

Addition

Example 3

$(2 + 3) + 4 = 5 + 4 = 9$ and $2 + (3 + 4) = 2 + 7 = 9$

Therefore, $(2 + 3) + 4 = 2 + (3 + 4)$

In general, this property can be written for any three real numbers a, b, and c as follows:

$(a + b) + c = a + (b + c)$

This property is called the **associative property of addition**.

Multiplication

Example 4

$(2 \cdot 3) \cdot 4 = 6 \cdot 4 = 24$ and $2 \cdot (3 \cdot 4) = 2 \cdot 12 = 24$

Hence, $(2 \cdot 3) \cdot 4 = 2 \cdot (3 \cdot 4)$

We can write this property for any three real numbers a, b, and c as follows:

$(a \cdot b) \cdot c = a \cdot (b \cdot c)$

This property is called the **associative property of multiplication**.

☐ THE IDENTITY PROPERTY

Addition

Example 5

$2 + 0 = 2$ and $0 + 2 = 2$. Therefore, $2 + 0 = 0 + 2 = 2$

We can write this property for any real number a, as follows:

$a + 0 = 0 + a = a$

This property is called the **identity property of addition**.

Zero is called the identity element of addition.

Multiplication

Example 6

$2 \cdot 1 = 2$ and $1 \cdot 2 = 2$. Therefore, $2 \cdot 1 = 1 \cdot 2 = 2$

We can write this property for any real number a as follows:

$a \cdot 1 = 1 \cdot a = a$

This property is called the **identity property of multiplication**. One is called the identity element of multiplication.

☐ THE INVERSE PROPERTY

Addition

Example 7

$2 + (-2) = 0$ and $(-2) + 2 = 0$.

Therefore, $2 + (-2) = (-2) + 2 = 0$

In general, we can write this property for any real number a as follows:

$a + (-a) = 0$ and $(-a) + a = 0$

This property is called the **inverse property of addition**.

Recall that $-a = -(a)$ is the opposite or additive inverse of a.

Multiplication

Example 8

$2 \cdot \left(\dfrac{1}{2}\right) = 1$ and $\left(\dfrac{1}{2}\right) \cdot 2 = 1$. Therefore, $2 \cdot \left(\dfrac{1}{2}\right) = \left(\dfrac{1}{2}\right) \cdot 2 = 1$

In general, this property can be written for any real number $a \neq 0$ as follows:

$$a \cdot \frac{1}{a} = 1 \text{ and } \frac{1}{a} \cdot a = 1 \text{ for } a \neq 0$$

This property is called the **inverse property of multiplication**.

The number $\dfrac{1}{a}$ where $a \neq 0$ is called the **reciprocal or multiplicative inverse** of a.

Note: None of the above properties hold for subtraction and division.

Example 9

$2 - 3 \neq 3 - 2$, $6 \div 2 \neq 2 \div 6$, $2 - 0 \neq 0 - 2$, $2 \div 1 \neq 1 \div 2$ etc.

□ The Distributive Property

Example 10

$2(3 + 4) = 2 \cdot 7 = 14$ and $2 \cdot 3 + 2 \cdot 4 = 6 + 8 = 14$.

Therefore, $2(3 + 4) = 2 \cdot 3 + 2 \cdot 4$.

In general, this property can be written for any real numbers a, b, and c as follows:

$$a(b + c) = a \cdot b + a \cdot c.$$

This property is called the **distributive property**.

Example 11

Identify each property.

a. $(-3) + 0 = -3$

b. $4 + (-5) = (-5) + 4$

c. $6 \cdot \dfrac{1}{6} = 1$

d. $(x + 2) + 5 = x + (2 + 5)$

e. $7(z + 3) = 7z + 21$

f. $9 + (-9) = 0$

g. $m \cdot n = n \cdot m$

h. $3 + (x + 8) = (x + 8) + 3$

i. $\dfrac{3}{5} \cdot \dfrac{5}{3} = 1$

Solution

a. Identity property of addition

b. Commutative property of addition

c. Inverse property of multiplication

d. Associative property of addition

e. Distributive property

f. Inverse property of addition

g. Commutative property of multiplication

h. Commutative property of addition

i. Inverse property of multiplication

We can summarize the properties of real numbers in the following chart:

Property	Addition	Multiplication
1. Commutative Property	$a+b=b+a$	$a \cdot b = b \cdot a$
2. Associative Property	$(a+b)+c = a+(b+c)$	$(a \cdot b) \cdot c = a \cdot (b \cdot c)$
3. Identity Property	$a+0 = 0+a = a$	$a \cdot 1 = 1 \cdot a = a$
4. Inverse Property	$a+(-a) = (-a)+a = 0$	$a \cdot \dfrac{1}{a} = \dfrac{1}{a} \cdot a = 1\ (a \neq 0)$
5. Distributive Property	$a(b+c) = a \cdot b + a \cdot c$	

☐ ORDER OF OPERATIONS

When evaluating a mathematical expression we must obey the following order of operations:

1. Perform operations inside grouping symbols $\{[(\ldots\ldots\ldots)]\}$. First parentheses followed by brackets and then braces.

2. Simplify exponential expressions.

3. Perform multiplication OR division as they occur from left to right. (Whichever comes first).

4. Perform addition OR subtraction as they occur from left to right. (Whichever comes first).

Example 12

Evaluate.

$$5 + 24 \div 3 \cdot 2 - 5^2$$

Solution

$5 + 24 \div 3 \cdot 2 - 5^2 =$ exponential

$5 + 24 \div 3 \cdot 2 - 25 =$ division

$5 + 8 \cdot 2 - 25 =$ multiplication

$5 + 16 - 25 =$ addition

$21 - 25 =$ subtraction

-4

Example 13

Evaluate.

$$\frac{10 + 6(5-2)^2}{4 + 20 \div 10 \cdot 2}$$

Solution

$\dfrac{10 + 6(5-2)^2}{4 + 20 \div 10 \cdot 2} =$ parenthesis (numerator) & division (denominator)

$\dfrac{10 + 6(3)^2}{4 + 2 \cdot 2} =$ exponential (numerator) & multiplication (denominator)

$\dfrac{10 + 6 \cdot 9}{4 + 4} =$ multiplication (numerator) & addition (denominator)

$\dfrac{10 + 54}{8} =$ addition (numerator)

$\dfrac{64}{8} =$ division

8

Example 14

Evaluate.

$$\frac{(8-3)(2-6) - 4^2}{9 + 3(-2) + 12 \div 4}$$

Solution

$$\frac{(8-3)(2-6)-4^2}{9+3(-2)+12\div4} =$$

$$\frac{5(-4)-16}{9-6+3} =$$

$$\frac{-20-16}{3+3} = \frac{-36}{6} = -6$$

Example 15

Evaluate.

$$3+2[4(10-2^2)\div3+5]$$

Solution

$3+2[4(10-2^2)\div3+5] =$ exponential

$3+2[4(10-4)\div3+5] =$ parenthesis

$3+2[4(6)\div3+5] =$ multiplication

$3+2[24\div3+5] =$ division

$3+2[8+5] =$ brackets

$3+2[13] =$ multiplication

$3+26 =$ addition

29

Example 16

Evaluate.

$$7+2[(-2)(-3)+5(9-1)+(-3)^2]\div11$$

Solution

$7+2[(-2)(-3)+5(9-1)+(-3)^2]\div11 =$ exponential

$7+2[(-2)(-3)+5(9-1)+9]\div11 =$ parenthesis

$7+2[(-2)(-3)+5(8)+9]\div11 =$ multiplication

$7+2[6+40+9]\div11 =$ addition

$7+2[46+9]\div11 =$ addition

$7+2[55]\div11 =$ multiplication

$7+110\div11 =$ division

$7+10 =$ addition

17

1.7 EXERCISES

Identify the property of real numbers.

1. a. $x + 8 = 8 + x$ b. $5 + 0 = 5$ c. $2 \cdot (4 \cdot 6) = (2 \cdot 4) \cdot 6$

2. a. $-7(x + 4) = -7x - 28$ b. $25 \cdot 1 = 25$ c. $\dfrac{2}{3} \cdot \dfrac{3}{2} = 1$

3. a. $(5 + 8) + 9 = 5 + (8 + 9)$ b. $4(m + n) = 4m + 4n$ c. $(a + 1) + 4 = 4 + (a + 1)$

4. a. $6a + (-6a) = 0$ b. $4(5x) = (4 \cdot 5)x$ c. $9 \cdot 7 = 7 \cdot 9$

5. a. $16 + (-16) = 0$ b. $12 \cdot \dfrac{1}{12} = 1$ c. $5(x + y) = 5x + 5y$

Complete the statement using the specified property of real numbers.

6. Associative property: $(x + 2) + 4 =$

7. Commutative property: $(x + 2) + 4 =$

8. Inverse property: $m + (-m) =$

9. Distributive property: $12(p + q) =$

10. Commutative property: $x \cdot y =$

11. Identity property: $4x + 0 =$

12. Inverse property: $\dfrac{c}{d} \cdot \dfrac{d}{c} =$

13. Associative property: $(m \cdot n) \cdot p =$

14. Identity property: $(2x) \cdot 1 =$

15. Distributive property: $11(x + 3) =$

Evaluate.

16. $12 - 5 \cdot 2 + 20$

17. $-19 + 3(-4) + 30$

18. $-16 + (-4)(-6) + 9$

19. $20 - 64 \div 4 - (-18)$

20. $8 - 5(3 - 9) + 24 \div 3 \cdot 2$

21. $6 + 2(7 - 3)^2 \div 4$

22. $(8 - 2)(5 + 3) - 18 \div 3 + 4$

23. $2 + 3(12 \div 4 + 5 \cdot 2 - 5^2)$

24. $[(45 \div 3 \cdot 5 - 35 \cdot 2)^2 - 20]^2$

25. $17 - 48 \div 16 \cdot 2^2 + 5(1 - 23)$

26. $-4 + 2[(-3)(-4) + 18 \div 2 \cdot 3 - 7]$

27. $(15 - 3) \div 4(5 + 7) + (-2)^4$

28. $6(-2)^2 - 6(10 - 7) - (-14)$

29. $11 + [54 - 8(7 - 4)] \div 15 + 1$

30. $1 + 3[21 + (11 - 5)^2 \div 4] \div 15 - 5$

31. $\{86 - 5(15 - 11)^2\}^2 \div 4$

32. $4\{30 - [(4 - 5)^2 + 2]^3\} - 12$

33. $1 - \{4 - [14 - 2^3 \div 4]\}^2$

34. $(-5)^2 + [72 \div 9 \cdot 2 - 20]^2$

35. $2\{-18 + 3[-12 + 5(-7 + 10)]\}$

36. $\dfrac{(-4)(-7) - 55 \div 5}{-2(8-3) - 7}$

37. $\dfrac{19 - 4^2 + (-7)(-1)}{8(6-9) - 11(-2)}$

38. $\dfrac{(-3)^2(-2-4) + 80 \div 2}{-7 + 5(6-2) - 2 \cdot 10}$

39. $\dfrac{43 - [9 - (5-3)^2]}{3[4 - 18 \div 3] + 25}$

40. $\dfrac{54 \div 6 - 4^2 + 7(24-19)}{7^2 - 2^3 \cdot 3 + 27 \div 9}$

41. $\dfrac{-10 + 4[5 - 6(16-21)]}{-\{16 - [-1 + (5-7)^2]\}}$

CHAPTER 1 REVIEW EXERCISES

Graph the numbers on the number line.

1. $-2, 2\frac{1}{3}, -\frac{1}{5}, 4, 5.3$

2. $-1.4, 2\frac{1}{5}, -3, \frac{5}{3}, 0.3$

3. Consider the set. $\{-2, \frac{2}{3}, -0.3, \frac{1}{8}, 7, -1, 0, 2\frac{1}{4}, 0.\bar{5}, \sqrt{8}, 3, \pi\}$.

   List the elements that are:
   a. natural numbers.
   b. whole numbers.
   c. integers.
   d. rational numbers.
   e. irrational numbers.

Find the opposite of each number.

4. -8

5. 4

6. $\frac{2}{5}$

7. -3

8. 2.8

9. $-2\frac{3}{4}$

Evaluate.

10. $|-6 + 1|$

11. $|-18|$

12. $|1\frac{6}{9}|$

13. $|-\frac{1}{5}|$

14. $-|-5.75|$

15. $-(-3)$

16. $-(-15)$

17. $-|-20|$

18. $-|17|$

19. $-(-0.3)$

Place the correct symbol (<, > or =) between each pair of numbers.

20. $-18 \ldots\ldots 18$

21. $-11 \ldots\ldots -3$

22. $0 \ldots\ldots -\frac{4}{9}$

23. $-14 \ldots\ldots \frac{3}{8}$

24. $|-6| \ldots\ldots |6|$

25. $-|-4| \ldots\ldots |-2|$

26. $2.351 \ldots\ldots 2.354$

27. $\frac{3}{4} \ldots\ldots \frac{4}{5}$

Write the following numbers in order from smallest to largest.

28. $5, -2, 3\frac{4}{7}, |-10|, -5.6, 7, 0.2, -(-4)$

Find the sum.

29. $[(-5) + 3] + [12 + (-2)] + [(-8) + (-11)]$

30. $[(-6) + (-3)] + [12 + (-21)] + [(-4) + 7]$

Find the difference.

31. $12 - 8$	34. $33 - (-13)$	37. $(-3) - 18$
32. $28 - 37$	35. $(-48) - (-12)$	38. $(-35) - 14$
33. $16 - (-5)$	36. $(-21) - (-15)$	39. $11 - (-29)$

Multiply.

40. $6 \cdot 8$	43. $4(-10)$	46. $(-3)(-33)$
41. $5 \cdot 11$	44. $(-5)(12)$	47. $(-9)(-2)$
42. $7(-3)$	45. $(-18)(2)$	48. $(12)(-4)$

Divide.

49. $18 \div (-6)$	53. $(-46) \div (-23)$	56. $\dfrac{-35}{7}$
50. $(-35) \div 7$	54. $42 \div (-7)$	
51. $(-55) \div 11$	55. $\dfrac{55}{-5}$	57. $\dfrac{-48}{-16}$
52. $(-28) \div (-4)$		

Find all factors of each number.

58. 48	60. 32	62. 128
59. 65	61. 22	63. 23

Find the prime factorization of each number.

64. 99	66. 180	68. 80
65. 42	67. 45	69. 120

Simplify each fraction.

70. $\dfrac{24}{42}$	72. $\dfrac{121}{55}$	74. $\dfrac{64}{80}$
71. $\dfrac{63}{72}$	73. $\dfrac{30}{45}$	75. $\dfrac{66}{18}$

Multiply. Write the answer in simplest form.

76. $\dfrac{14}{18} \cdot \dfrac{36}{21}$

77. $\left(-\dfrac{6}{10}\right)\left(\dfrac{50}{48}\right)$

78. $\dfrac{24}{56} \cdot \dfrac{35}{36}$

79. $\left(-\dfrac{9}{38}\right)\left(-\dfrac{19}{99}\right)$

80. $\dfrac{16}{55} \cdot \dfrac{15}{72}$

81. $\dfrac{49}{23} \cdot \dfrac{46}{14}$

Divide. Write the answer in simplest form.

82. $\dfrac{7}{36} \div \dfrac{21}{12}$

83. $\dfrac{14}{15} \div \dfrac{21}{35}$

84. $\left(-\dfrac{36}{24}\right) \div \dfrac{18}{66}$

85. $\left(-\dfrac{27}{44}\right) \div \left(-\dfrac{9}{4}\right)$

86. $\dfrac{15}{19} \div \dfrac{65}{38}$

87. $\dfrac{64}{75} \div \dfrac{80}{25}$

Add or subtract. Write the answer in simplest form.

88. $\dfrac{3}{5} + \dfrac{1}{5}$

89. $\left(-\dfrac{5}{18}\right) + \left(-\dfrac{4}{18}\right)$

90. $\dfrac{5}{15} + \dfrac{11}{15} - \dfrac{9}{15}$

91. $\dfrac{2}{5} + \dfrac{3}{7}$

92. $\dfrac{3}{7} - \left(-\dfrac{5}{21}\right)$

93. $\dfrac{7}{18} - \left(-\dfrac{1}{24}\right)$

94. $1\dfrac{2}{3} + 3\dfrac{1}{5}$

95. $3\dfrac{2}{7} - 1\dfrac{1}{28}$

96. $-2\dfrac{5}{12} + 3\dfrac{11}{18}$

Evaluate.

97. $-5 + 2[9 + (12-8)^2 \div 8] \div 11 - 3$

98. $8\{12 - [(3-8)^2 - 23]^3\} \div 2 - 12$

99. $\dfrac{(-4)^2(-3+7) + 44 \div 4}{-9 + 3(8-1) + 3 \cdot 11}$

100. $\dfrac{35 - [18 - (1-4)^2]}{2[8 - 21 \div 7] + 3}$

2 EQUATIONS AND INEQUALITIES IN ONE VARIABLE

2.1 ALGEBRAIC EXPRESSIONS

□ **Variable** □ **Algebraic Expression** □ **Term** □ **Like Terms**

□ VARIABLE

> *A letter of the alphabet used to represent an unknown number (quantity) is referred to as a **variable.***

Example of variables: $x, y, z, \ldots$

□ ALGEBRAIC EXPRESSION

> *A combination of numbers, variables, and grouping symbols, connected by operation symbols is called an **algebraic expression** or simply expression.*

Examples of algebraic expressions: $2(x+y)-5x+4$, x^2+2x+3, $5(12-3)+8\div4-2^2$

Algebraic expressions can be classified as follows:

Variable expressions: $x^2+9(x+3)-11y+2$

Numerical expressions: $-8+6(1-5)\div4+16$

A variable expression is an expression that contains one or more variables.

A numerical expression is an expression that contains no variables (numbers only).

□ TERM

> *The variable expression x^2+3x+4 contains three terms: x^2, 3x, and 4.*
>
> *A **term** is a number or a variable or a product or quotient of numbers and variables.*

Examples of terms: 3, z, 2xy, $\dfrac{3}{5}x^2$, $\dfrac{7}{x}$, etc.

The terms of a variable expression can be classified as follows:

a. Variable terms: x^2, $3y$, $-z$, $5mn$

b. Constant terms: 4, -5, $\sqrt{8}$

A variable term is a term that contains one or more variables.

A constant term (usually a number) represents a fixed value.

Note: If a term "c" represents a fixed value then c is considered a constant term.

Any variable term has two parts, a numerical part called **coefficient** and a variable part called simply **variable**.

Example 1

Term	Coefficient	Variable
$-5x$	-5	x
$\frac{1}{4}y$	$\frac{1}{4}$	y
$-t$	-1	t
n	1	n
$2a^2$	2	a

□ LIKE TERMS

*Terms that have the same variable(s) with the same exponents are referred to as **like terms**. In other words, terms that have the same variable part are called like terms.*

Examples of like terms:

$2x^2y^3$, $-x^2y^3$, $7x^2y^3$

$6ab$, $11ab$, ab, $3ab$

$-t$, $5t$, $20t$, $14t$

$9m^2$, $12m^2$, $-m^2$, $\frac{1}{2}m^2$

Note: Numbers are considered like terms. For example, numbers such as 1, -4, 21, 3, 54 are like terms.

If at least one of the two conditions (same variables, same exponents) fails, the terms are referred to as **unlike terms**. The following are some examples of unlike terms.

$5xy$, $3x^2y$, $19xy^2$ (same variables, different exponents)

$2x$, $3y$, $4n$, t (different variables)

$7x^2$, $14x$, $9c$ (different variables and different exponents)

In this section, our goal is to **simplify** and **evaluate** variable expressions.

To **simplify a variable expression** or write the expression in simplest form, use the properties of real numbers to remove the grouping symbols and **combine like terms**.

To combine like terms, add the coefficients and keep the variable part unchanged.

Note: $2x + 3x = 5x$ and $(2x)(3x) = 6x^2$.

Example 2

Simplify.

   a. $3(x + 4) - 5x + 2(y - 1) + 9y + 7$

   b. $19 - 8(2m - 1) + 5(m - 4) + m - 2$

Solution

   a. $3(x + 4) - 5x + 2(y - 1) + 9y + 7 =$ distributive property

        $\mathbf{3x} + 12 - \mathbf{5x} + \mathit{2y} - 2 + \mathit{9y} + 7 =$ combine like terms

        $-2x + 11y + 17$

   b. $19 - 8(2m - 1) + 5(m - 4) + m - 2 =$ distributive property

        $19 - \mathbf{16m} + 8 + \mathbf{5m} - 20 + \mathbf{m} - 2 =$ combine like terms

        $25 - 10m$

To **evaluate a variable expression** for some given values of the variables, substitute the given value for each variable, and use the order of operations to find its numerical value.

Example 3

Evaluate.

$$4a^2 - b^2 + 3ab - 5 \text{ when a} = -1 \text{ and b} = 2.$$

Solution

$$4a^2 - b^2 + 3ab - 5 =$$

$$4(-1)^2 - 2^2 + 3(-1)(2) - 5 = \quad \text{Substitute } -1 \text{ for } a \text{ and } 2 \text{ for } b$$

$$4 \cdot 1 - 4 - 6 - 5 = \quad \text{Evaluate exponential expressions}$$

$$4 - 4 - 6 - 5 = \quad \text{Use the order of operations to simplify}$$

$$0 - 6 - 5 =$$

$$-6 - 5 = \quad -11$$

Example 4

Evaluate

$$\frac{x^2 + 5xy - y^2}{x - y} \text{ when } x = 4 \text{ and } y = -2$$

Solution

$$\frac{x^2 + 5xy - y^2}{x - y} =$$ Substitute 4 for x and -2 for y.

$$\frac{4^2 + 5 \cdot 4(-2) - (-2)^2}{4 - (-2)} =$$ Evaluate exponential expressions.

$$\frac{16 - 40 - 4}{4 + 2} =$$ Use the order of operations to simplify.

$$\frac{-24 - 4}{6} =$$

$$\frac{-28}{6} = -\frac{14}{3} = \quad \frac{-28}{6} = -\frac{14}{3}$$

Example 5
_____

Let x be a number. Translate each phrase to an algebraic expression and simplify, if possible.

Five subtracted from a number	x − 5
Ten more than a number	x + 10
Eleven more than the sum of 2 and a number	11 + (x + 2) = x + 13
Four less than the sum of 9 and a number	(x + 9) − 4 = x + 5
The quotient of 9 and a number	$\dfrac{9}{x}$
Eight less than a number	x − 8
Eleven added to a number	x + 1
The sum of nine and six times a number	9 + 6x
The product of 2 and a number subtracted from 10	10 − 2x

2.1 EXERCISES

Identify the terms of each variable expression and the coefficient of each term.

1. $4x^2 + 5x - y + 3$

2. $9a^2 + 11ab + b - 18$

3. $12mn + m - n + 6$

4. $x^3 + 3x^2 + x - 1$

Determine whether the given terms are like or unlike terms.

5. 2xy, xy, 15xy, −xy

6. $a^2, 6a^2, 4a^2, 2a^2$

7. $x^2 y, 20x^2 y, 5xy^2$

8. 7x, −x, 8y, 12x

Simplify each expression.

9. $14x - 18x + 7$

10. $32x - 20x + 2$

11. $-6x + 15x + 30$

12. $-18x + 40x - 5$

13. $10x - 16 + x + 5$

14. $22y + 4 - 20y - 11$

15. $4(x + 3) - 2x + 1$

16. $-3(a + 4) + 15a + 9$

17. $11 - 5(x - 2) + 3x$

18. $-15 - 7(3 - x) + 9x$

19. $2(x + 3) - 5x + 9x - 4$

20. $-14x + 4(2x - 1) + 3x + 10$

21. $8(a + b) - 12(a - 1) + 3b - 14$

22. $-10(x + y) - (1 - 8x) + 11y + 2$

23. $6x^2y + 7(x^2y - xy^2) + 9xy^2 - 3xy$

24. $24ab - 5(a^2b + 3ab^2) + a^2b - 18ab$

25. $15 - 11(3m - 2) + 4(8m - 9) - 10$

26. $-(3m - 20n - 15) + 8(m - n) - 21$

27. $-2(x - 2y - 3z) + 4(x + z) + 6x$

28. $x^2 + 2y^2 - 3(2x^2 + y^2) - x + y$

29. $3x - 5[x + 2(x - 3)] + 10x - 12$

30. $-16a + 6[4a - 5(a - 1)] + 30 - 25$

31. $-8 + 3[2m - 4(1 - m) + 5] - 20m$

32. $15 - 5[3x - (3 - x) + 4] - 12x + 6$

33. $\dfrac{3}{5}x + \dfrac{2}{3} + \dfrac{1}{5}x - \dfrac{1}{2}$

34. $\dfrac{4}{7}a + \dfrac{3}{5} + \dfrac{2}{3}a - 2$

Evaluate each expression when x = 2, y = –3, and z = –1.

35. $x - 2y + 3z + 4$

36. $-x + xy - 5z + 8$

37. $x^2 + y^2 + xz - 5$

38. $-x^2 - 2y^2 + 3yz - 12$

39. $\dfrac{xy + xz - yz + 21}{y^2 + z^2}$

40. $\dfrac{2xz - 3xz + yz + 13}{x^2 - z^2}$

Evaluate each expression when a = 4 and b = –5.

41. $5a + 3ab - 4b + 1$

42. $-8a + 7b - ab + 5$

43. $3a^2 - 4ab + b^2 - 10$

44. $a^2 + ab - 2b^2 + 22$

45. $\dfrac{a + 2b + ab + 6}{a + b}$

46. $\dfrac{3a - 5b - ab - 7}{2(a + b)}$

Evaluate each expression when $x = \dfrac{1}{3}$ and $y = -\dfrac{1}{2}$.

47. $6x + 10y + 5$

48. $24x + 50y + 20$

49. $2x + 3y - 4$

50. $4x - 7y + 5$

Translate each phrase to an algebraic expression and simplify it, if possible.

51. The sum of 16 and five times a number.

52. Ten more than eight times a number.

53. Eleven less than the sum of seven and twice a number.

54. The difference of a number and six.

55. The quotient of four more than a number and five.

56. The sum of a number and two, increased by twenty.

57. The difference of three and a number decreased by eight.

58. The product of 15 and a number subtracted from 32.

59. The sum of 18 and a number, divided by the difference of 9 and a number.

60. Eight less than the product of 5 and a number.

61. Six added to the quotient of a number and 2.

62. Twenty more than twice a number.

63. Three times the difference of a number and ten.

64. Fourteen less than the square of a number.

2.2 LINEAR EQUATIONS IN ONE VARIABLE

□ Equations □ Linear Equations in One Variable

□ EQUATIONS

Examples of Equations:

a. $2x + 5 = 7$ b. $3(x + 5) - 1 = 2x + 8$ c. $x^2 - 8x + 6 = -7x - 6$

In example a. the left-hand side $2x + 5$ is a variable expression and the right-hand side 7 is a numerical expression.

In example b. the left-hand side $3(x + 5) - 1$ and the right-hand side $2x + 8$ are both variable expressions. Also, both sides in example c. are variable expressions.

We can use the above examples to justify the definition of an algebraic equation.

Definition

*Equality of two algebraic expressions where at least one expression is a variable expression is called an **algebraic equation.***

Note: The following examples are either true or false numerical statements: $2 + 3 = 5$ (true), $11 - 8 = 3$ (true), $4 + 6 = 11$ (false), $3^2 = 6$ (false).

In this chapter, our goal is to find the solution of an equation (solve). Solving an equation is the process of finding the solution(s) of the equation.

Definition

*A number that makes an equation a true numerical statement when substituted for the variable is called a **solution**.*

Example 1

Determine whether x = –1 is a solution of 4x + 3 = 2.

Check: Substitute –1 for x and simplify.

$$4(-1) + 3 = 2$$

$$-4 + 3 = 2$$

$$-1 = 2 \text{ False}$$

Since x = –1 makes the equation a false numerical statement, we conclude that x = –1 is not a solution.

Example 2

Determine whether $x = 3$ is a solution of $2x - 1 = 5$.

Check: Substitute 3 for x and simplify.

$2(3) - 1 = 5$

$6 - 1 = 5$

$5 = 5$ True

Since $x = 3$ makes the equation a true statement, we conclude that $x = 3$ is a solution.

Definition

*Two equations that have the same solution(s) are called **equivalent equations**.*

Example 3

Determine whether $x = 3$ is a solution of $3x + 2 = 11$.

Check: Substitute 3 for x and simplify.

$3(3) + 2 = 11$

$9 + 2 = 11$

$11 = 11$ True

Since $x = 3$ makes the equation a true statement, we conclude that $x = 3$ is a solution.

Also $x = 3$ was a solution of $2x - 1 = 5$. Since both $2x - 1 = 5$ and $3x + 2 = 11$ have the same solution $x = 3$ they are equivalent equations.

☐ LINEAR EQUATIONS IN ONE VARIABLE

Examples of linear equations in one variable: $3x + 6 = 0$, $5x + 4 = 9$, and $11x + 15 = 37$

Definition

*An equation that can be written in the form ax + b = 0, where a and b are real numbers and a ≠ 0 is called a **linear equation in one variable** x or a first degree equation in one variable.*

Note: The form $ax + b = 0$, $(a \neq 0)$ is referred to as the standard form of a linear equation in one variable.

When solving linear equations, our goal is to rewrite each equation as an equivalent equation of the form *variable = constant*. This can be accomplished by using the addition and multiplication properties of equality.

Addition Property of Equality

If A = B, then A + C = B + C for any real numbers A, B, and C.

Since any equation is an equality, according to the addition property of equality, the same number may be added to both sides of an equation without changing the solution. Thus, if A = B is an algebraic equation then A = B and A + C = B + C are equivalent equations.

Example 4

Solve.

$$x - 5 = 3$$

Solution

$$x - 5 = 3$$

$$x - 5 + 5 = 3 + 5 \qquad \text{Addition property: add C = 5 to both sides}$$

$$x = 8$$

Note: Since a − b = a + (−b), we can add (instead of subtract) a negative constant C to both sides of an equation. Hence, there is no need for subtraction property because the addition property covers both the addition and subtraction.

Example 5

Solve.

$$x + 1 = 3$$

Solution

$$x + 1 = 3$$

$$x + 1 + (-1) = 3 + (-1) \qquad \text{Addition property: add C = −1 to both sides}$$

$$x = 2$$

Multiplication Property of Equality

If A = B, then A · C = B · C for any real numbers A, B, and C (C ≠ 0).

Thus, if A = B is an algebraic equation, according to the multiplication property of equality, both sides of the equation may be multiplied by the same nonzero number without changing the solution.

Again, the algebraic equations A = B and $A \cdot C = B \cdot C$, (C ≠ 0) are equivalent equations.

Example 6

Solve.

$$\frac{1}{5}x = 4$$

Solution

$$\frac{1}{5}x = 4$$

$$5 \cdot \frac{1}{5}x = 4 \cdot 5 \quad \begin{array}{l}\text{Multiplication property: multiply} \\ \text{both sides by 5}\end{array}$$

$$x = 20$$

Example 7
___

Solve.

$$\frac{1}{2}x - 1 = 4$$

Solution

$$\frac{1}{2}x - 1 = 4$$

$$\frac{1}{2}x - 1 + 1 = 4 + 1 \quad \begin{array}{l}\text{Addition property:} \\ \text{add 1 to both sides}\end{array}$$

$$\frac{1}{2}x = 5 \quad \text{Simplify}$$

$$2 \cdot \frac{1}{2}x = 2 \cdot 5 \quad \begin{array}{l}\text{Multiplication property: multiply} \\ \text{both sides by 2}\end{array}$$

$$x = 10$$

Example 8
___

Solve.
$$2x + 9 = 15$$

Solution

$$2x + 9 = 15$$

$$2x + 9 - 9 = 15 - 9 \quad \begin{array}{l}\text{Addition property:} \\ \text{add} -9 \text{ to both sides}\end{array}$$

$$2x = 6 \quad \text{Simplify}$$

$$\frac{1}{2} \cdot 2x = 6 \cdot \frac{1}{2} \quad \begin{array}{l}\text{Multiplication property: multiply} \\ \text{both sides by } \frac{1}{2}\end{array}$$

$$x = 3$$

Note: When 2 is multiplied by $\frac{1}{2}$, or 2 is divided by 2 the result is the same: $2 \cdot \frac{1}{2} = \frac{2}{2} = 1$

Hence, to eliminate the coefficient 2 of x, we can either divide both sides of the equation by 2 or multiply both sides of the equation by the reciprocal of 2, which is $\frac{1}{2}$. So, there is no need for the division property because the multiplication property covers both the multiplication and division.

Note: Using the addition property in combination with identity and the inverse property of addition we can remove any term from one side of the equation to the other side by changing the sign.

Example 9

Solve.

$$\frac{2}{3}x - 3 = 11$$

Solution

$\frac{2}{3}x - 3 = 11$ Addition property: remove −3 from the left-hand side to the right-hand side as +3.

$\frac{2}{3}x = 11 + 3$

$\frac{2}{3}x = 14$ Simplify

$\frac{3}{2} \cdot \frac{2}{3}x = 14 \cdot \frac{3}{2}$ Multiplication property: multiply both sides by $\frac{3}{2}$

$x = 7 \cdot 3$ Simplify

$x = 21$

Check: $\frac{2}{3} \cdot 21 - 3 = 11$, $2 \cdot 7 - 3 = 11$, $14 - 3 = 11$, $11 = 11$ True

Thus x = 21 is a solution.

Example 10

Solve.

$6 - 7x = -15$

Solution

$$6 - 7x = -15$$ Addition property: remove 6 from the left-hand side to the right-hand side as –6.

$$-7x = -15 - 6$$ Simplify

$$-7x = -21$$

$$\frac{-7x}{-7} = \frac{-21}{-7}$$ Multiplication property: Divide both sides by –7

$$x = 3$$

Example 11

Solve.

$$\frac{5}{6}x - \frac{4}{6} = \frac{8}{3}$$

Solution

$$\frac{5}{6}x - \frac{4}{6} = \frac{8}{3}$$ Addition property: remove $-\frac{4}{6}$ from the left-hand side to the right-hand side as $\frac{4}{6}$

$$\frac{5}{6}x = \frac{8}{3} + \frac{4}{6}$$

$$\frac{5}{6}x = \frac{16}{6} + \frac{4}{6}$$ Find the LCD = 6. Rewrite each fraction with LCD = 6

$$\frac{5}{6}x = \frac{20}{6}$$ Simplify

$$\frac{6}{5} \cdot \frac{5}{6}x = \frac{20}{6} \cdot \frac{6}{5}$$ Multiplication property: multiply both sides by $\frac{6}{5}$

$$x = 4$$

2.2 EXERCISES

Identify each as an equation or an expression.

1. $2x + 3y - 7$

2. $4(x + 5) - 1 = 6$

3. $7x - 3 = x + 4$

4. $x^2 + 3x + 12$

5. $2a + b + c - 20$

6. $3x - 5 = x$

Determine whether the given value is a solution to the equation.

7. $x + 8 = 3$, $x = -5$

8. $6x - 3 = 9$, $x = 2$

9. $-5x + 1 = 0$, $x = \dfrac{1}{5}$

10. $7 = 3 - 4x$, $x = 3$

11. $12 = -\dfrac{2}{3}x$, $x = 9$

12. $10x + 9 = 12$, $x = \dfrac{1}{2}$

Use the addition property to solve each equation.

13. $x - 9 = 1$

14. $x + 6 = -3$

15. $y + 11 = -6$

16. $-4 = x - 10$

17. $-14 = x - 20$

18. $y - 6 = 18$

19. $z - 1 = -8$

20. $15 = 4 + z$

21. $24 = 12 + x$

22. $x - 19 = -20$

23. $y - 5 = -16$

24. $-15 = -25 + z$

25. $6 = -3 + y$

26. $-10 = x - 19$

27. $y - 5 = -3$

28. $a - 4 = -6$

29. $a + 7 = -9$

30. $n + 15 = 2$

31. $11 + y = 2$

32. $9 + x = -4$

33. $b - 6 = -3$

34. $17 = 5 + x$

35. $-8 = 2 + y$

36. $-20 = z - 5$

37. $-3 + a = -9$

38. $-1 + x = -7$

39. $5 + m = 6$

40. $x + \dfrac{3}{5} = \dfrac{4}{5}$

41. $y + \dfrac{2}{7} = \dfrac{5}{7}$

42. $x - \dfrac{3}{4} = \dfrac{1}{2}$

43. $x - \dfrac{2}{3} = \dfrac{5}{6}$

44. $-\dfrac{3}{6} = y - \dfrac{4}{5}$

45. $-\dfrac{5}{8} = \dfrac{3}{4} + y$

46. $\dfrac{2}{5}x + 4 = \dfrac{7}{5}x$

47. $\dfrac{3}{8}y - 7 = -\dfrac{5}{8}y$

48. $12 - \dfrac{5}{6}z = \dfrac{1}{6}z$

49. $3 + x = 3$

50. $x - 5 = -5$

51. $-15 + x = 15$

52. $x + 2.5 = 7.5$

53. $2.8 + y = -8.2$

54. $m - 2.84 = 0.16$

55. $a - 4.8 = 6.9$

56. $18.3 + x = 20$

57. $8.2 = y - 3.6$

Use the multiplication property to solve each equation.

58. $3x = 12$

59. $8y = 24$

60. $5y = -30$

61. $7x = -56$

62. $-4y = 32$

63. $-6x = -48$

64. $-11y = -33$

65. $15 = 3m$

66. 66. $28 = 7m$

67. $-8x = 24$

68. $-6x = 48$

69. $16 = -4x$

70. $56 = -8x$

71. $-72 = 9z$

72. $-64y = 16$

73. $11z = 121$

74. $13x = 169$

75. $-x = 4$

76. $-x = -14$

77. $-8x = 20$

78. $10z = -22$

79. $\dfrac{1}{2}x = 5$

80. $\dfrac{1}{4}y = 3$

81. $-\dfrac{1}{5}a = 6$

82. $-\dfrac{1}{11}y = 2$

83. $-4 = \dfrac{1}{8}x$

84. $-11 = \dfrac{1}{10}x$

85. $\dfrac{2}{3}x = 8$

86. $\dfrac{3}{4}y = 9$

87. $-\dfrac{4}{5}y = -16$

88. $-\dfrac{5}{8}z = -25$

89. $\dfrac{4}{7}x = \dfrac{12}{21}$

90. $\dfrac{5}{6}m = \dfrac{25}{48}$

91. $\dfrac{1}{3}x = 3.5$

92. $2.1y = 6.3$

93. $2.5m = 10$

94. $0.2a = 5.8$

95. $\dfrac{2}{3}x = -11.2$

96. $-\dfrac{3}{5}y = -2.4$

Use the properties of equations to solve each equation.

97. $2x + 3 = 9$

98. $3y + 5 = 14$

99. $5z - 1 = 9$

100. $8z - 2 = 22$

101. $4x - 9 = -13$

102. $6x - 5 = -17$

103. $9x + 1 = -17$

104. $11a + 8 = -14$

105. $-5m + 2 = -8$

106. $-4m + 3 = -21$

107. $-6x - 54 = 0$

108. $-7x - 56 = 0$

109. $5 - 10y = 35$

110. $4 - 3a = 31$

111. $15 = 12a - 9$

112. $13 = 9x - 14$

113. $-6 = 15 - 7x$

114. $-23 = 11 - 17x$

115. $\dfrac{1}{5}a + 4 = 1$

116. $\dfrac{1}{9}y + 6 = 9$

117. $\dfrac{1}{4}m + 1 = 8$

118. $\dfrac{1}{11}m - 2 = 9$

119. $\dfrac{2}{3}x - 3 = 5$

120. $\dfrac{3}{7}a + 19 = 28$

121. $-4 + \dfrac{3}{5}x = -1$

122. $8 = \dfrac{7}{2}y - 13$

123. $5 = -\dfrac{3}{4}x - 1$

124. $2.6x - 1.7 = 11.3$

125. $5.9y + 2.8 = 20.5$

126. $3.2 + 4.8x = 36.8$

127. $-6.4 + 2.5x = 8.6$

128. $3.7 = -1.8z - 3.5$

129. $11.8 - 7.3x = -10.1$

2.3 MORE ON SOLVING LINEAR EQUATIONS

□ **General Equations Without Grouping Symbols** □ **General Equations Involving Grouping Symbols** □

In this section we will solve more complicated equations that can be simplified to a linear equation $ax + b = 0$, $a \neq 0$

□ GENERAL EQUATIONS WITHOUT GROUPING SYMBOLS

Example 1

Solve.

$$5x + 3 = 2x + 15$$

Solution

Our goal is to rewrite the equation as an equivalent equation of the form: *variable = constant* (isolate the variable). This can be accomplished by removing terms from one side of the equation to the other side (addition property) and making sure to change the sign of each term that has been removed from one side to the other.

Addition property:

$5x + 3 = 2x + 15$ move $2x$ to the left hand-side as $-2x$ and $+3$ to the right-hand side as -3

$5x - 2x = 15 - 3$ Simplify

$3x = 12$

$\dfrac{3x}{3} = \dfrac{12}{3}$ Multiplication property: multiply both sides of the equation by $\dfrac{1}{3}$ (or simply divide by 3)

$x = 4$

Example 2

Solve.

$$10y - 7 = 3y + 14$$

Solution

$10y - 7 = 3y + 14$	Addition property:
$10y - 3y = 14 + 7$	move -7 to the right-hand side as $+7$ and 14 to the left hand side as -14.
$10y - 3y = 14 + 7$	Simplify (combine like terms).
$7y = 21$	
$\dfrac{7y}{7} = \dfrac{21}{7}$	Multiplication property: Divide both sides by 7.
$y = 3$	

□ GENERAL EQUATIONS INVOLVING GROUPING SYMBOLS

Example 3

Solve.

$$3(2x + 4) - 5(x - 7) = 41 - x$$

Solution

$3(2x + 4) - 5(x - 7) = 41 - x$	Distributive property
$6x + 12 - 5x + 35 = 41 - x$	Simplify: combine like terms
$x + 47 = 41 - x$	Addition property: move x to the left-hand side and 47 to the right-hand side.
$x + x = 41 - 47$	
$2x = -6$	Simplify
$\dfrac{2x}{2} = \dfrac{-6}{2}$	Multiplication property: Divide both sides by 2
$x = -3$	

Example 4

Solve.

$$40x + 3[10(x - 5) - 8(3x - 6)] = -4(x + 6)$$

Solution

$$40x + 3[10(x - 5) - 8(3x - 6)] = -4(x + 6)$$

$$40x + 3[10x - 50 - 24x + 48] = -4x - 24$$

$$40x + 3[-14x - 2] = -4x - 24$$

$$40x - 42x - 6 = -4x - 24$$

$$-2x - 6 = -4x - 24$$

$$-2x + 4x = -24 + 6$$

$$2x = -18$$

$$\frac{2x}{2} = \frac{-18}{2}$$

$$x = -9$$

Example 5

Solve.

$$3(x + 5) - 2(x + 3) = x + 9$$

Solution

$$3(x + 5) - 2(x + 3) = x + 9$$

$$3x + 15 - 2x - 6 = x + 9$$

$$x + 9 = x + 9$$

$$x - x = 9 - 9$$

$$0x = 0$$

Solution: *All real numbers.*

Since every real number multiplied by zero is equal to zero, we conclude that every real number is a solution of the original equation. Such equation that is true for any value of the variable is called **identity.**

Example 6

Solve.

$$5(2x - 1) + 4(x - 3) = 7(2x - 3)$$

Solution

$$5(2x - 1) + 4(x - 3) = 7(2x - 3)$$

$$10x - 5 + 4x - 12 = 14x - 21$$

$$14x - 17 = 14x - 21$$

$$14x - 14x = -21 + 17$$

$$0x = -4 \text{ or } 0 = -4$$

Solution: *No solution.*

Since there is no real number that multiplied by zero equals −4, this equation has no solution and it is called a **contradiction.**

☐ FRACTIONAL EQUATIONS

Definition

An equation containing one or more fractions with constant denominators is called a fractional equation.

To solve a fractional equation, first find the Least Common Denominator (LCD), and then multiply both sides of the equation by the LCD to eliminate the denominators. Recall, the Least Common Denominator of two or more fractions is the smallest number that can be divided evenly by each denominator.

Example 7

Solve.

$$\frac{1}{3}x - \frac{6}{4} = \frac{1}{2}x + \frac{5}{6}$$

Solution

$$\frac{1}{3}x - \frac{6}{4} = \frac{1}{2}x + \frac{5}{6}$$

Step 1 Find the LCD. Multiply the largest denominator (6) by 1, 2, 3, . . . until you find the LCD. In our case the LCD = 6 · 2 = 12

Step 2 Eliminate the denominators (Multiply both sides by the LCD = 12).

$$12 \cdot \frac{1}{3}x - 12 \cdot \frac{6}{4} = 12 \cdot \frac{1}{2}x + 12 \cdot \frac{5}{6}$$

$$4x - 18 = 6x + 10$$

$$4x - 6x = 10 + 18$$

$$-2x = 28$$

$$\frac{-2x}{-2} = \frac{28}{-2}$$

$$x = -14$$

Example 8

Solve.

$$\frac{2}{5}(x+3) - \frac{3}{4}(2x-1) = \frac{7}{10}(x-1) - \frac{19}{20}$$

Solution

$$\frac{2}{5}(x+3)-\frac{3}{4}(2x-1)=\frac{7}{10}(x-1)-\frac{19}{20}$$

Step 1 Find the LCD. Multiply the largest denominator (20) by 1, 2, . . . until you find the LCD = 20(1) = 20

Step 2 Eliminate the denominators (Multiply both sides by the LCD = 20).

$$20\cdot\frac{2}{5}(x+3)-20\cdot\frac{3}{4}(2x-1)=20\cdot\frac{7}{10}(x-1)-20\frac{19}{20}$$

8(x + 3) – 15(2x – 1) = 14(x – 1) – 19

8x + 24 – 30x + 15 = 14x – 14 – 19

–22x + 39 = 14x – 33

–22x – 14x = –33 – 39

–36x = –72

$$\frac{-36x}{-36}=\frac{-72}{-36}$$

x = 2

Example 9

Solve.

$$\frac{3}{4}(4x+3)+2=\frac{2}{3}(3x-1)+x$$

Solution

$$\frac{3}{4}(4x+3)+2=\frac{2}{3}(3x-1)+x$$

Step 1 Find the LCD = 12

Step 2 Eliminate the denominators (multiply both sides by the LCD = 12)

$$12\cdot\frac{3}{4}(4x-3)+12(2)=12\cdot\frac{2}{3}(3x-1)+12x$$

9(4x – 3) + 24 = 8(3x – 1) + 12x

36x – 27 + 24 = 24x – 8 + 12x

36x – 3 = 36x – 8

36x – 36x = –8 +3

0x = –5   No solution

☐ DECIMAL EQUATIONS

Definition

*An equation containing one or more decimal numbers is called a **decimal equation**.*

Note: To clear the decimals, multiply both sides of the equation by 10, 100, 1000, etc. (the number of zeros equals the largest number of decimal places).

Example 10

Solve.

$$0.2(3x + 2) - 0.5(2x - 1) = 2.1$$

Solution

$$0.2(3x + 2) - 0.5(2x - 1) = 2.1$$

Step 1 Clear the decimals. Since every decimal number involved in this equation (0.2, 0.5, and 2.1) has one decimal place, we multiply both sides of the equation by 10 to convert all decimal numbers to integers.

Step 2 Solve the resulting equation.

$$2(3x + 2) - 5(2x - 1) = 21 \quad \text{Distributive property}$$
$$6x + 4 - 10x + 5 = 21 \quad \text{Combine like terms}$$
$$-4x + 9 = 21 \quad \text{Addition property}$$
$$t - 4x = 21 - 9 \quad \text{Remove 9 to the right-hand side as } -9$$
$$-4x = 12$$
$$\frac{-4x}{-4} = \frac{12}{-4} \quad \text{Multiplication property. Divide both sides of the equation by } -4$$
$$x = -3$$

Example 11

Solve.

$$0.16(y + 3) + 0.03(4 - 3y) = 0.88$$

Solution

$$0.16(y + 3) + 0.03(4 - 3y) = 0.88$$

Step 1 Clear the decimals. Since every decimal number involved in this equation (0.16, 0.03, and 0.88) has two decimal places, multiply both sides of the equation by 100 to convert all decimals to integers.

Step 2 Solve the resulting equation.

$$16(y + 3) + 3(4 - 3y) = 88$$
$$16y + 48 + 12 - 9y = 88$$
$$7y + 60 = 88$$
$$7y = 88 - 60$$
$$7y = 28$$
$$\frac{7y}{7} = \frac{28}{7}$$
$$y = 4$$

Example 12

Solve.

$$0.625(z - 1) + 1.5 = 0.25(3z - 1)$$

Solution

$$0.625(z - 1) + 1.5 = 0.25(3z - 1)$$

Step 1 Clear the decimals. Since the largest number of decimal places of the decimal numbers involved in this equation is three, we multiply both sides of the equation by 1000.

Step 2 Solve the resulting equation.

$$625(z - 1) + 1500 = 250(3z - 1)$$
$$625z - 625 + 1500 = 750z - 250$$
$$625z + 875 = 750z - 250$$
$$625z - 750z = -250 - 875$$
$$-125z = -1125$$
$$\frac{-125z}{-125} = \frac{-1125}{-125}$$
$$z = 9$$

2.3 EXERCISES

Solve.

1. $2x + 8 + 7x - 4 = 22$

2. $9x - 3 - 5x + 12 = -7$

3. $x + 2 - 6x - 9 = 18$

4. $15x - 8 - 24x + 19 = 29$

5. $4 + 2x - 8x + 10 + 11x = -1$

6. $10y - 4 - 6y + 2y - 3 = 11$

7. $16 = 8 - 3x - x + 1 + 5x$

8. $-21 = 7x - 4 + 4x - 3 + 3x$

9. $4x + 12 = 5x + 9 - x + 3$

10. $7y + 3 = 7y - 7 + 10$

11. $15a - 1 = 27a + 23$

12. $11x - 4 = 4x + 10$

13. $8x + 6 = 2x - 18$

14. $9z + 2 = 14z - 8$

15. $3(z + 5) = 3z + 25$

16. $3x - 7 = 5x + 5$

17. $10x - 8 = 4x + 28$

18. $4m + 19 = 13m - 8$

19. $5m + 3 = 5(m + 1) - 2$

20. $6x + 2 = 8x - 2(x + 1)$

21. $9x - 11 = 4x + 7 - x$

22. $12z - 7 = 5z + 21 + 3z$

23. $4(x - 3) + 2 = 4x - 11$

24. $-2(x + 4) + 22 = 14 - 2x$

25. $-6x + 4 = -5(x + 2) + 8$

26. $-4x - 12 = 7(x - 1) - 2$

27. $3(x+5) = 5(x + 3) - x$

28. $9(2y - 1) + 6 = 4(3y+2) - 19$

29. $2(x - 8) + 12 = 6(3 - x) + 2$

30. $11(m - 4) + 50 = 7(5 - m) + 25$

31. $4(x - 7) - 2(2 - x) = 5(x - 6) + 11$

32. $5(x + 3) - 8(x + 2) = -3(x - 5) - 6$

33. $3x - 2[9x - 4(2x + 1)] = 20 - 5x$

34. $5 - 3[12x - (8x - 3) + 4] = -7x - 21$

35. $\dfrac{1}{2}x + \dfrac{2}{3}x = \dfrac{7}{6}$

36. $\dfrac{3}{5}x - \dfrac{5}{6}x = -\dfrac{7}{15}$

37. $\dfrac{3}{4}x - 5 = \dfrac{1}{2}x - 4$

38. $\dfrac{5}{8}x - 2 = \dfrac{3}{16}x + 12$

39. $\dfrac{1}{2}x + \dfrac{2}{3}x - \dfrac{5}{6} = \dfrac{3}{2}$

40. $\dfrac{4}{9}x + \dfrac{7}{18}x - \dfrac{2}{3} = \dfrac{11}{6}$

41. $\dfrac{x}{4} - 3x = \dfrac{x}{8} - 23$

42. $\dfrac{2}{7}x - 4x = \dfrac{x}{14} - \dfrac{53}{2}$

43. $\dfrac{5}{6}x + \dfrac{1}{3} = \dfrac{1}{12}(x + 4) + \dfrac{3}{2}$

44. $\dfrac{1}{4}y + \dfrac{2}{3}(y - 5) = \dfrac{5}{6}y - \dfrac{79}{24}$

45. $\dfrac{3}{2}(4x + 1) - \dfrac{6}{5}(2x - 3) = \dfrac{87}{10}x$

46. $\dfrac{5}{9}(2z + 1) - \dfrac{3}{2}(z + 2) = \dfrac{2}{9}z$

47. $\dfrac{1}{5}(2x + 1) - \dfrac{1}{2}(x + 3) = \dfrac{1}{10}x - \dfrac{21}{10}$

48. $\dfrac{1}{2}(x - 2) - \dfrac{1}{6}(x + 5) = \dfrac{1}{3}(3 - 2x) + \dfrac{13}{6}$

49. $\dfrac{3}{4}y - 3 + \dfrac{5}{11}(y - 1) = \dfrac{1}{2}y + 5$

50. $\dfrac{2}{7}(x + 3) - 2 + \dfrac{1}{2}x = 2x - 6$

51. $\dfrac{x + 6}{9} + \dfrac{x - 1}{2} - 4 = \dfrac{x - 7}{2}$

52. $\dfrac{x - 4}{3} - \dfrac{x}{4} + 5 = \dfrac{x + 44}{12}$

53. $0.5x - 0.4(3x + 8) = 0.3$

54. $0.8(4x - 3) + 0.3(7 - 10x) = -0.2$

55. $1.3(2x - 5) - 3.5 = 2.1(2x - 4)$

56. $1.1(5x - 7) + 3.6 = 0.2(9 - 2x)$

57. $0.12x + 0.06(3 - x) = 0.09(x - 1)$

58. $0.02(3x - 4) + 0.15x = 0.05(4 - x)$

59. $0.07(4x - 1) - 0.14(x + 2) = 0.21$

60. $0.18(2x - 3) - 0.10(3x + 4) = 0.04$

61. $0.1(5x - 9) - 0.04(10x - 11) = 0.14$

62. $0.09(7x - 3) - 0.2(3x + 1) = 0.025x$

63. $2.03(x - 1) - 3.01x + 2 = 1.21 - x$

64. $4.5(2x + 1) - 10x + 5 = 9.5 - x$

65. $1.012x + 3.25(x + 1) - 3 = 4.261x$

66. $3.216(x - 2) - 2.83(x + 4) = 0.386x$

2.4 APPLICATIONS: INTEGERS AND GEOMETRY PROBLEMS

□ **Integer Problems** □ **Geometry Problems** □ **Supplementary Angles** □ **Vertical Angles** □ **Triangles**

□ INTEGER PROBLEMS

In section 1.1 we have introduced the set of integers: $Z = \{\ldots -3, -2, -1, 0, 1, 2, 3, \ldots\}$

Integers can be classified as:

even integers: $\ldots -4, -2, 0, 2, 4, 6 \ldots$

odd integers: $\ldots -3, -1, 1, 3, 5, 7 \ldots$

In this section, our goal is to solve problems involving integers, consecutive integers, consecutive even integers, consecutive odd integers and some geometry problems.

Definition

*Integers that follow one after the other, in order, are called **consecutive integers**.*

Consecutive Integers

    a. 1, 2, 3, 4   b. 11, 12, 13, 14   c. $-7, -6, -5, -4$

Every integer in these examples can be obtained from the previous integer by adding one.

For example: $3 = 2 + 1$, $12 = 11 + 1$, $-4 = -5 + 1$.

If x represents the first integer, using this observation we can set up three consecutive integers as follows:

    1st   x

    2nd   x + 1

    3rd   x + 2

Consecutive Even Integers

    a. 2, 4, 6, 8   b. 16, 18, 20, 22   c. $-4, -2, 0, 2$

Every integer in the above examples can be obtained from the previous integer by adding two. For example: $8 = 6 + 2$, $18 = 16 + 2$, $0 = -2 + 2$, etc.

If x is the first even integer, we can set up three consecutive even integers as follows:

1st   x

2nd   x + 2

3rd   x + 4

Consecutive Odd Integers

   a.   1, 3, 5, 7   b.   43, 45, 47, 49   c.   −7, −5, −3

Every integer in the above examples can be obtained from the previous integer by adding two. For example: $7 = 5 + 2$, $47 = 45 + 2$, $-3 = -5 + 2$, etc.

Again, if x represents the first integer, we can set up three consecutive odd integers as follows:

1st   x

2nd   x + 2

3rd   x + 4

Note: The setup for even and odd consecutive integers is the same. It depends on the first integer x. If x is even, all three integers will be even and if x is odd all three integers will be odd.

Example 1

The sum of three consecutive even integers is 84. Find the integers.

Solution

Step 1   *Read the problem carefully until you can identify what is given and what the problem is asking for.*

Step 2   *Assign a variable to the unknown quantity.* Let x be the first integer.

Step 3   *Express the other unknown quantities in terms of the variable.* In our case set up three consecutive even integers knowing that x is the first integer.

1st   x

2nd   x + 2

3rd   x + 4

Step 4   *Translate the information into an equation using the variable.*

$$x + (x + 2) + (x + 4) = 84$$

Step 5   *Solve the equation.* $x + x + 2 + x + 4 = 84$

$$3x + 6 = 84$$

$$3x = 84 - 6$$

$$3x = 78$$

$$\frac{3x}{3} = \frac{78}{3}$$

$$x = 26$$

Step 6   *State and check the answer.* Substitute 26 for x to find the integers.

  1st   26

  2nd $26 + 2 = 28$

  3rd $26 + 4 = 30$

Check: $26 + 28 + 30 = 84$

Example 2

Find three consecutive integers such that the sum of the first two integers is four more than the largest integer.

Solution

Step 1 *Read the problem carefully until you can identify what is given and what the problem is asking for.*

Step 2 *Assign a variable to the unknown quantity.* Let x be the first integer.

Step 3 *Express the other unknown quantities in terms of the variable.* In our case set up three consecutive integers such that x is the first integer.

  1st   x

  2nd $x + 1$

  3rd $x + 2$

Step 4 *Translate the information into an equation using the variable.*

  $x + (x + 1) = 4 + (x + 2)$

Step 5 *Solve the equation.* $x + x + 1 = 4 + x + 2$

  $2x + 1 = x + 6$

  $2x - x = 6 - 1$

  $x = 5$

Step 6 *State and check the answer.* Substitute 5 for x to find the integers.

  1st   5

  2nd $5 + 1 = 6$

  3rd $5 + 2 = 7$

Check: $5 + 6 = 4 + 7, 11 = 11$ True.

Example 3

Find two consecutive odd integers such that their sum is five less than three times the smallest.

Solution

Step 1 *Read the problem carefully until you can identify what is given and what the problem is asking for.*

Step 2 *Assign a variable to the unknown quantity.* Let x be the first odd integer.

Step 3 *Express the other unknown quantities in terms of the variable.* In our case set up two consecutive odd integers such that x is the first odd integer.

1st   x

2nd   x + 2

Step 4 *Translate the information into an equation using the variable.*

$$x + (x + 2) = 3x - 5$$

Step 5 *Solve the equation.* $x + x + 2 = 3x - 5$

$$2x + 2 = 3x - 5$$

$$2x - 3x = -5 - 2$$

$$-x = -7$$

$$x = 7$$

Step 6 *State and check the answer.* Substitute 7 for x to find the integers.

1st   7

2nd   7 + 2 = 9

Check: $7 + 9 = (3)(7) - 5$, $16 = 21 - 5$, $16 = 16$ True.

Example 4

The sum of two integers is 13. If the second integer is one more than three times the first integer, find the integers.

Solution

Step 1 *Read the problem carefully until you can identify what is given and what the problem is asking for.*

Step 2 *Assign a variable to the unknown quantity.* Let x be the first integer.

Step 3 *Express the other unknown quantities in terms of the variable.* In our case the second integer is one more then three times the first integer: 2nd integer $= 3x + 1$. Thus,

1st integer $= x$

2nd integer $= 3x + 1$

Step 4 *Translate the information into an equation using the variable.* Since the sum of the two integers is 13, we can write the equation:

$$x + (3x + 1) = 13$$

Step 5 *Solve the equation.* x + 3x + 1 = 13

   4x = 13 − 1

   4x = 12

   x = 3

Step 6 *State and check the answer.* Substitute 5 for *x* to find the integers. Substitute 3 for x to find the integers

   1st 3

   2nd 3(3) + 1 = 9 + 1 = 10

Check: 3 + 10 = 13

☐ GEOMETRY PROBLEMS

Complementary Angles

Definition

*Two angles are called **complementary angles** if the sum of their measures is 90°.*

FIGURE 1

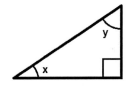 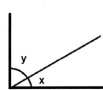

Measure of the angle: x°

Measure of the complement:
y = (90 − x)°

$m\angle x + m\angle y = 90°$

Note: Angle *y* is called the complement of *x* and angle *x* is the complement of *y*.

Example 5

If the measure of an angle *x* is 40°, find the measure of its complement *y*.

Solution

The measure of its complement *y* is 90° − 40° = 50°.

Example 6

The measure of the complement of an angle is 35° more than four times the measure of the angle. Find the measure of the angle.

Solution

Step 1 *Read the problem carefully until you can identify what is given and what the problem is asking for.*

Step 2 *Assign a variable to the unknown quantity.* Let x be the measure of the angle.

Step 3 *Express the other unknown quantities in terms of the variable.* The measure of the complement is $(90 - x)°$.

Step 4 *Translate the information into an equation using the variable.* Since the complement $(90 - x)°$ is 35° more than four times the measure of the angle, we can write the equation:

$$90 - x = 35 + 4x$$

Step 5 *Solve the equation.*

$$90 - 35 = 4x + x$$

$$55 = 5x$$

$$\frac{5x}{5} = \frac{55}{5}$$

$$x = 11$$

Step 6 *State and check the answer.* The measure of the angle is 11°.

Check: $90 - 11 = 35 + (4)(11)$, $79 = 35 + 44$, $79 = 79$ True

☐ SUPPLEMENTARY ANGLES

Definition

*Two angles are called **supplementary angles** if the sum of their measures is 180°.*

FIGURE 2

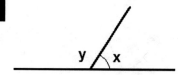

Measure of the angle: $x°$

Measure of the supplement:
$y = (180 - x)°$

$m\angle x + m\angle y = 180°$

Note: Angle x is called the supplement of y and angle y is called the supplement of x.

Example 7

If the measure of an angle x is $110°$, find the measure of its supplement y.

Solution

The measure of its supplement is $y = 180° - 110° = 70°$

Example 8

The measure of the supplement of an angle is $15°$ less than twice the measure of the angle. Find the measure of the angle.

Solution

Step 1 *Read the problem carefully until you understand what is given and what the problem is asking for.*

Step 2 *Assign a variable to the unknown quantity.* Let x be the measure of the angle.

Step 3 *Express the other unknown quantities in terms of the variable.* The measure of the supplement is $(180 - x)°$.

Step 4 *Translate the information into an equation using the variable.* Since the supplement is $15°$ less than twice the measure of the angle we can write the following equation:

$180 - x = 2x - 15$

Step 5 *Solve the equation.*

$-x - 2x = -15 - 180$

$-3x = -195$

$\dfrac{-3x}{-3} = \dfrac{-195}{-3}$

$x = 65$

Step 6 *State and check the answer.* The measure of the angle is $65°$.

Check: $180 - 65 = (2)(65) - 15$, $115 = 130 - 15$, $115 = 115$ True.

Example 9

Three times the measure of the complement of an angle is 26° less than the measure of its supplement. Find the measure of the angle.

Solution

Step 1 *Read the problem carefully until you understand what is given and what the problem is asking for.*

Step 2 *Assign a variable for the unknown quantity.* Let x be the measure of the angle.

Step 3 *Express the other unknown quantities in terms of the variable.* The measure of the complement is $(90 - x)°$ and the measure of the supplement is $(180 - x)°$.

Thus, Measure of the angle = $x°$

Measure of the complement = $(90 - x)°$

Measure of the supplement = $(180 - x)°$

Step 4 *Translate the information into an equation using the variable.* Since 3 times the measure of the complement is 26° less than the measure of the supplement, we can write the following equation:

$$3(90 - x) = (180 - x) - 26$$

Step 5 *Solve the equation.*

$$270 - 3x = 180 - x - 26$$

$$-3x + x = 180 - 26 - 270$$

$$-2x = -116$$

$$\frac{-2x}{-2} = \frac{-116}{-2}$$

$$x = 58$$

Step 6 *State and check the answer.* The measure of the angle is 58°

Check: $3(90 - 58) = 180 - 58 - 26$, $3(32) = 96$, $96 = 96$ True.

□ VERTICAL ANGLES

Definition

*Two angles with a common vertex that lie on opposite sides of the intersection of two lines are called **vertical angles**.*

Note: Vertical angles have the same measure.

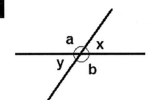

FIGURE 3

a and *b* are vertical angles

x and *y* are vertical angles

Thus, $m\angle a = m\angle b$ (measure of angle a = measure of angle b) and $m\angle x = m\angle y$ (measure of angle x = measure of angle y).

Example 10

Find the measures of *a*, *b* and *y* when the measure of x is 60° (Figure 3).

Solution

Since angles *x* and *y* are vertical angles, they have the same measure:

$m\angle y = m\angle x = 60°$.

Angles *a* and *x* are supplementary angles. Hence, $m\angle a = 180° - 60° = 120°$.

Since *a* and *b* are vertical angles, they have the same measure: $m\angle b = m\angle a = 120°$.

Example 11

Find the measure of each indicated angle.

FIGURE 4

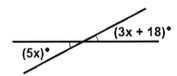

Solution

Step 1 *Read the problem carefully until you understand what is given and what the problem is asking for.*

Step 2 *Translate the information into an equation using the variable.* Since vertical angles have the same measure, we can write the following equation: $5x = 3x + 18$

Step 3 *Solve the equation.* $5x - 3x = 18$

$2x = 18$

$x = 9$

Step 4 *State and check the answer.* Each angle is $(5)(9) = 45°$

☐ TRIANGLES

Note: The sum of the measures of the angles of a triangle is 180°.

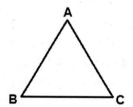

FIGURE 5

$$m \angle A + m \angle B + m \angle C = 180°$$

Example 12

If $m \angle A = (x + 40)°$, $m \angle B = (2x - 30)°$, $m \angle C = (x + 50)°$, find the measure of each angle.

Solution

Step 1 *Read the problem carefully until you understand what is given and what the problem is asking for.*

Step 2 *Translate the information into an equation using the variable.* Since the sum of the measure of the angles of a triangle is 180°, $m \angle A + m \angle B + m \angle C = 180°$, we can write the following equation:

$$(x + 40) + (2x - 30) + (x + 50) = 180$$

Step 3 *Solve the equation.*

$$x + 40 + 2x - 30 + x + 50 = 180$$

$$4x + 60 = 180$$

$$4x = 180 - 60$$

$$4x = 120$$

$$\frac{4x}{4} = \frac{120}{4}$$

$$x = 30$$

Step 4 *State and check the answer.* The measure of each angle is:

$m \angle A = x + 40 = 30 + 40 = 70$	$m \angle A = 70°$
$m \angle B = 2x - 30 = 2(30) - 30 = 60 - 30 = 30$	$m \angle B = 30°$
$m \angle C = x + 50 = 30 + 50 = 80$	$m \angle C = 80°$

Check: $70° + 30° + 80° = 180°$

Example 13

In a triangle, the largest angle is 80° more than the measure of the smallest angle. The medium angle is 20° more than twice the measure of the smallest angle. Find the measure of each angle.

Solution

Step 1 *Read the problem carefully until you understand what is given and what the problem is asking for.*

Step 2 *Assign a variable for the unknown quantity.* Since all the angles are related to the smallest angle, let x be the measure of the smallest angle.

Step 3 *Express the other unknown quantities in terms of the variable.* The measure of the largest angle is $(x + 80)°$, and the measure of the medium angle is $(2x + 20)°$.

Step 4 *Translate the information into an equation using the variable.*

Since the sum of the measures of the angles of a triangle is $180°$, we can write the following equation:

$$x + (x + 80) + (20 + 2x) = 180$$

Step 5 *Solve the equation.*

$$x + x + 80 + 20 + 2x = 180$$

$$4x + 100 = 180$$

$$4x = 180 - 100$$

$$4x = 80$$

$$\frac{4x}{4} = \frac{80}{4}$$

$$x = 20$$

Step 6 *State and check the answer.* The measure of each angle is:

Smallest : $20°$

Medium : $(x + 80)° = (20 + 80)° = 100°$

Largest : $(20 + 2x)° = (20 + 40)° = 60°$

Check: $20 + (20 + 80) + (20 + 40) = 180$

$20 + 100 + 60 = 180,$

$180 = 180$ True.

2.4 EXERCISES

1. The sum of two consecutive odd integers is 56. Find the integers.

2. The sum of three consecutive integers is 75. Find the integers.

3. Find three consecutive integers such that three times the smaller integer is eight more than the sum of the other two integers.

4. Find three consecutive even integers such that five times the middle integer is equal to the sum of the smaller and larger integer.

5. Find three consecutive odd integers such that the sum of the first two smaller integers is five more than the larger integer.

6. Find two consecutive integers such that three times the smaller is 20 more than twice the larger integer.

7. Find three consecutive integers such that three times the middle integer is equal to the sum of the other two.

8. Find two consecutive even integers such that four times the smaller integer is two less than three times the larger integer.

9. Find two consecutive even integers such that six times the smaller integer equals five times the larger integer.

10. The sum of three consecutive even integers is –66. Find the integers.

11. The sum of three consecutive odd integers is –51. Find the integers.

12. The sum of three consecutive odd integers is equal to one more than ten times the larger integer. Find the integers.

13. Find two consecutive integers such that the smaller integer is six more than twice the larger integer.

14. The sum of two positive integers is 53. If the smaller integer is x and the larger integer is 11 more than twice the smaller integer, find the integers.

15. The sum of two positive integers is 29. If the smaller integer is x and the larger integer is one less than four times the smaller integer, find the integers.

16. The difference of two integers is 29. If the larger integer is seven less than four times the smaller integer, find the integers.

17. The difference of two integers is 30. If the larger integer is two more than five times the smaller integer, find the integers.

18. Five less than three times an integer is the same as eleven more than the integer. Find the integer.

19. Sixteen more than five times an integer is the same as eight less than the integer. Find the integer.

20. Eight less than a positive integer is the same as two more than half the integer. Find the integer.

21. The measure of the complement of an angle is 10° more than three times the measure of the angle. Find the measure of the angle, and its complement.

22. The measure of the complement of an angle is 6° more than six times the measure of the angle. Find the measure of the angle, and its complement.

23. The measure of the supplement of an angle is 30° more than twice the measure of the angle. Find the measure of the angle, and its supplement.

24. The measure of the supplement of an angle is 20° less than four times the measure of the angle. Find the measure of the angle and its supplement.

25. Five times the measure of the complement of an angle is 15° less than twice the measure of the supplement of the angle. Find the measure of the angle, its complement, and its supplement.

26. The measure of the supplement of an angle is 15° less than twice the sum of the measure of the angle and its complement. Find the measure of the angle, its complement, and its supplement.

27. The measure of one angle of a triangle is four times the measure of the smallest angle. The measure of the third angle is seven times the measure of the smallest angle. Find the measure of each angle of the triangle.

28. The measure of the medium angle of a triangle is 14° more than the measure of the smallest angle. The measure of the largest angle is 26° more than twice the measure of the smallest angle. Find the measure of each angle of the triangle.

29. The measure of the medium angle of a triangle is 55° less than three times the measure of the smallest angle. The measure of the largest angle is 45° more than the measure of the smallest angle. Find the measure of each angle of the triangle.

30. The smallest angle of a triangle is $\frac{1}{6}$ as large as the largest angle. The medium angle is $\frac{1}{3}$ as large as the largest angle. Find the measure of each angle.

31. Find the measure of each indicated angle.

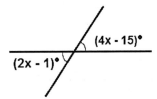

32. Find the measure of each indicated angle.

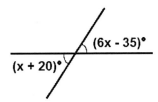

33. Find the measure of each indicated angle

34. Find the measure of each indicated angle.

35. Find the measure of each indicated angle.

36. Find the measure of each indicated angle.

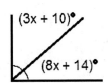

2.5 FORMULAS AND APPLICATIONS: MOTION PROBLEMS

☐ **Formulas** ☐ **Applications: Perimeter Problems**
☐ **Applications: Motion Problems**

☐ FORMULAS

Examples of Formulas:

$$P = 2L + 2W \qquad A = \frac{1}{2}bh \qquad C = \frac{5}{9}(F - 32)$$

$$A = L \cdot W \qquad V = L \cdot W \cdot H \qquad I = P \cdot r \cdot t$$

We can use the above examples of formulas to justify the following definition.

Definition

*A **formula** is an equation involving two or more variables and represents a mathematical or scientific rule.*

In this section our goal is to **evaluate** formulas for some given values and **solve** formulas for a specific variable.

Example 1

Evaluate each formula for the given values.

a. $P = 2L + 2W$ when $L = \frac{1}{2}$ and $W = 5$

b. $P = a + b + c$ when $a = 24$, $b = 6$, and $c = 20$

c. $m = \frac{y_2 - y_1}{x_2 - x_1}$ when $x_1 = 3$, $x_2 = 5$, $y_1 = 10$, and $y_2 = 4$

Solution

a. $P = 2 \cdot \frac{1}{2} + 2 \cdot 5 = 1 + 10 = 11$

b. $P = 24 + 6 + 20 = 50$

c. $m = \frac{4 - 10}{5 - 3} = \frac{-6}{2} = -3$

Example 2

Solve each formula for the indicated variable.

a. $P = 2L + 2W$ for W

b. $A = \dfrac{1}{2}bh$ for b

c. $A = \dfrac{h}{2}(b_1 + b_2)$ for b_1

d. $2x + 3y = 6$ for y

Solution

a. $P = 2L + 2W$ for W

$\quad P - 2L = 2W$ To isolate 2W, subtract 2L from both sides (addition property).

$\quad \dfrac{P - 2L}{2} = \dfrac{2W}{2}$ Divide both sides by 2 (multiplication property).

$\quad W = \dfrac{P - 2L}{2}$

b. $A = \dfrac{1}{2}bh$ for b

$\quad 2 \cdot A = 2 \cdot \dfrac{1}{2}bh$ To eliminate the denominator, multiply both sides by 2.

$\quad 2A = bh$ Simplify.

$\quad \dfrac{2A}{h} = \dfrac{bh}{h}$ Divide both sides by h.

$\quad b = \dfrac{2A}{h}$

c. $A = \dfrac{h}{2}(b_1 + b_2)$ for b_1

$\quad 2 \cdot A = 2 \cdot \dfrac{h}{2}(b_1 + b_2)$ To eliminate the denominator, multiply both sides by 2.

$\quad 2A = h(b_1 + b_2)$ Simplify.

$\quad \dfrac{2A}{h} = \dfrac{h(b_1 + b_2)}{h}$ Divide both sides by h.

$\quad \dfrac{2A}{h} = b_1 + b_2$ Subtract b_2 from both sides.

$\quad \dfrac{2A}{h} - b_2 = b_1$

d. $2x + 3y = 6$ for y

$\quad 3y = -2x + 6$ Subtract 2x from both sides.

$\quad \dfrac{3y}{3} = -\dfrac{2x}{3} + \dfrac{6}{3}$ Divide both sides by 3.

$\quad y = -\dfrac{2}{3}x + 2$ Simplify.

☐ APPLICATIONS: PERIMETER PROBLEMS

a. Triangle

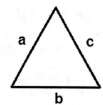

$$P = a + b + c$$

b. Square

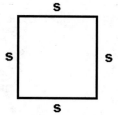

$$P = 4s$$

c. Rectangle

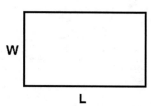

$$P = 2L + 2W$$

d. Circle (circumference)

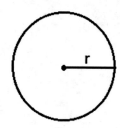

$$c = 2\pi r$$

Example 3

The perimeter of a triangle is 17 cm. The medium side is 2 cm more than the smaller side. The longer side is 1 cm less than twice the smaller side. Find the length of each side.

Solution

Step 1 *Read the problem carefully.*

Step 2 *Assign a variable to the unknown quantity.*

Since two of the three sides of the triangle are related to the smaller side, we let the smaller side of the triangle be *x*.

Step 3 *Express the other unknown quantities in terms of the variable.* Now, we can set up the medium and the longer side of the triangle as follows:

Smaller side: x

Medium side: x + 2

Larger side: 2x − 1

Step 4 *Translate the information into an equation using the variable.* Using the formula for the perimeter of the triangle P = a + b + c, we can write the equation as follows:

x + (x + 2) + (2x − 1) = 17

Step 5 *Solve the equation.*

x + x + 2 + 2x − 1 = 17

4x + 1 = 17

4x = 17 − 1

4x = 16

$$\frac{4x}{4} = \frac{16}{4}$$

x = 4

Step 6 *State and check the answer.* The length of each side is:

Smaller side: x = 4cm

Medium side: x + 2 = 4 + 2 = 6cm

Larger side: 2x − 1 = 2(4) − 1 = 8 − 1 = 7cm

Check: 4 + 6 + 7 = 17 True.

Example 4

The perimeter of a rectangle is 86 in. The length of the rectangle is 3 in more than four times the width. Find the length and width of the rectangle.

Solution

Step 1 *Read the problem carefully.*

Step 2 *Assign a variable for the unknown quantity.* Since the length of the rectangle is expressed in terms of the width we let the width be x.

Step 3 *Express the other unknown quantities in terms of the variable.* The length of the rectangle is 3 in more than four times the width. Hence, the length is L = 4x +3.

Step 4 *Translate the information into an equation using the variable.* Using the formula for the perimeter of the rectangle P = 2L + 2W, we can write the following equation:

$$2(4x + 3) + 2x = 86$$

Step 5 *Solve the equation.*

$$8x + 6 + 2x = 86$$

$$10x + 6 = 86$$

$$10x = 86 - 6$$

$$10x = 80$$

$$\frac{10x}{10} = \frac{80}{10}$$

$$x = 8$$

Step 6 *State and check the answer.* The width of the rectangle is $w = x = 8$ and the length is L = 4x + 3 = 4(8) + 3 = 32 + 3 = 35 in

Check: 2(8) + 2(35) = 86, 16 + 70 = 86, 86 = 86   True

Example 5

The perimeter of a square is 64 ft. Find the length of each side of the square.

Solution

Step 1 *Read the problem carefully.*

Step 2 *Assign a variable for the unknown quantity.* Since the problem is asking for the side of the square we let the length of each side of the square be *s*.

Step 3 *Translate the information into an equation using the variable.* Using the formula for the perimeter of the square P = 4s, we have the following equation:

$$4s = 64$$

Step 4 *Solve the equation.*

$$\frac{4s}{4} = \frac{64}{4}$$

$$s = 16$$

Step 5 *State and check the answer.* The length of each side of the square is

$s = 16.$

Check: $4(16) = 64$

☐ APPLICATIONS: MOTION PROBLEMS

> Motion problems refer to applications involving movement at a constant rate. The formula used to solve motion problems is called distance formula $D = R \times T$ which stands for
>
> **Distance = Rate x Time**

Note: All the units involved in a motion problem must be consistent. For instance if the rate is 50 mph and the time is 30 min, we must convert 30 minutes into hours.

30 min = 0.5 hrs

Example 6

Two cars leave Las Vegas, one car driving east and the other driving west. The eastbound car travels 10 mph faster than the westbound car. After two hours the cars are 220 mi apart. Find the speed of each car.

Solution

Step 1 *Read the problem carefully.*

Step 2 *Assign a variable for the unknown quantity.* Since the rate of the eastbound car is expressed in terms of the rate of the westbound car, we let the rate of the westbound car be $R = x$.

Step 3 *Express the other unknown quantities in terms of the variable.* The rate of the eastbound car is 10 mph faster than the westbound car. Thus, $R = x + 10$.

$$220 \text{ mi}$$

W ---------------------- ←|→ ------------------------- E

$R = x$	$R = x + 10$
$T = 2$ hr	$T = 2$ hr
$D = 2x$	$D = 2(x + 10)$

Step 4 *Translate the information into an equation using the variable.* From the diagram we can see that the distance traveled by the westbound car plus the distance traveled by the eastbound car equals the total distance 220 mi. This can be translated into an algebraic equation.

$2x + 2(x + 10) = 220$

Step 5 *Solve the equation.*

$$2x + 2x + 20 = 220$$

$$4x + 20 = 220$$

$$4x = 220 - 20$$

$$4x = 200$$

$$\frac{4x}{4} = \frac{200}{4}$$

$$x = 50$$

Step 6 *State and check the answer.* The rate of the westbound car is R = 50 mph and the rate of the eastbound car is R = x + 10 = 50 + 10 = 60 mph.

Also, we can use the following chart to organize the information of the problems.

	R	×	T	=	D
Westbound	x		2		2x
Eastbound	x + 10		2		2(x + 10)
					220 mi.

The equation is the same: 2x + 2(x + 10) = 220

Example 7

At 8:00 a.m., a car and a truck leave cities 375 mi apart and travel toward each other. The truck is 15 mph slower than the car. Find the speed of the car and the speed of the truck if they pass each other at 11:00 a.m.

Solution

Step 1 *Read the problem carefully.*

Step 2 *Assign a variable for the unknown quantity.* Since the rate of the eastbound car is expressed in terms of the rate of the westbound car, we let the rate of the westbound car be R = x.

Step 3 *Express the other unknown quantities in terms of the variable.* The truck is 15 mph slower than the car. Thus, the speed of the truck is

R = x − 15.

Step 4 *Translate the information into an equation using the variable.*

375 mi

|→ ------------------|----------------------------------- ←|

Truck   Car

R = x − 15   R = x

T = 3 hrs   T = 3 hrs

D = 3(x − 15)   D = 3x

From the diagram, we can see that the distance traveled by the truck plus the distance traveled by the car equals the total distance 345 mi.

The corresponding equation is:

$3(x - 15) + 3x = 375$

Step 5 *Solve the equation.*

$3x - 45 + 3x = 375$

$6x - 45 = 375$

$6x = 375 + 45$

$6x = 420$

$$\frac{6x}{6} = \frac{420}{6}$$

$x = 70$

Step 6 *State and check the answer.* The rate of the car is R = 70 mph, and the rate of the truck is R = x − 15 = 70 − 15 = 55 mph.

The information given in this problem can be organized in the following chart.

	R	×	T	=	D
Car	x		3		3x
Truck	x − 15		3		3(x − 15)
					375 mi.

The equation is the same: $3x + 3(x - 15) = 375$

Example 8

Two cars heading in the same direction leave a city at the same time. The average speed of the first car is 60 mph and the average speed of the second car is 65 mph. How long does it take for the second car to be 20 mi ahead of the first car?

Solution

Step 1 *Read the problem carefully.*

Step 2 *Assign a variable for the unknown quantity.* Let the time it takes the second car to be 20 mi ahead of the first car be T = x.

We can use the following chart to organize the information of the problem.

	R	×	T	=	D
1st car	60		x		60x
2nd car	65		x		65x

Step 3 *Translate the information into an equation using the variable.* The difference between the distance travelled by the second car and the first car is 20 mi. This can be translated into the following equation:

$65x - 60x = 20$

Step 4 *Solve the equation.*

$5x = 20$

$x = 4$ hours

Step 5 *State and check the answer.* It takes 4 hours for the second car to be 20 mi ahead of the first car

Example 9

On the first part of a 108 mile trip, a car averaged 60 mph. Due to traffic conditions, on the second part of the trip the car averaged 52 mph. If the entire trip took 2 hours, find the travel time for each part of the trip.

Solution

Step 1 *Read the problem carefully.*

Step 2 *Assign a variable for the unknown quantity.* Let the travel time for the first part of the trip be $T = x$.

Step 3 *Express the other unknown quantities in terms of the variable.* Since the entire trip took 2 hours, the travel time for the second part of the trip was $T = 2 - x$.

The information given in the problem can be organized in the following chart.

	R	×	T	=	D
1st part	x		x		60x
2nd part	2 − x		2 − x		52(2 − x)
					108 mi.

Step 4 *Translate the information into an equation using the variable.* Since the entire trip was 108 mi, the corresponding equation is:

$60x + 52(2 - x) = 108$

Step 5 *Solve the equation.*

$60x + 104 - 52x = 108$

$8x + 104 = 108$

$8x = 108 - 104$

$8x = 4$

$x = 0.5$

Step 6 *State and check the answer.* The travel time for the first part of the trip was $T = 0.5$ hours and for the second part of the trip it was $T = 2 - x = 2 - 0.5 = 1.5$ hours.

Example 10

A freight train leaves a station traveling at 48 mph. A passenger train leaves the same station 30 minutes later traveling in the same direction on different tracks at 56 mph. In how many hours after the freight train leaves the station will the passenger train pass the freight train?

Solution

Step 1 *Read the problem carefully.*

Step 2 *Assign a variable for the unknown quantity.* Let the travel time for the freight train be T = x. Since the freight train has 30 minutes head start, the travel time of the passenger train is 30 minutes shorter than the travel time of the freight train, T = x − 0.5.

The information given in the problem can be organized in the following chart.

	R	×	T	=	D
Freight train	48		x		48x
Passenger train	56		x − 0.5		56(x − 0.5)

Step 3 *Translate the information into an equation using the variable.* Since the distance traveled by the freight and passenger trains is the same, the equation is

$$48x = 56(x - 0.5)$$

Step 4 *Solve the equation.*

$$48x = 56x - 24$$

$$24 = 56x - 48x$$

$$24 = 8x$$

$$x = 3$$

Step 5 *State and check the answer.* Thus, the passenger train passes the freight train after 3 hours.

2.5 EXERCISES

Evaluate each formula for the given values.

1. $P = 2L + 2W$ if $L = 12$ *in* and $W = 7$ *in*

2. $A = \dfrac{1}{2}bh$ if $b = 18m$ and $h = 5m$

3. $P = a + b + c$ if $P = 21$ ft, a = 2 ft and b = 10 ft

4. $I = Prt$ if I = $6 , P = $100, and t = 2 years

5. $D = RxT$ if D = 200 mi, and T = 4 hours

6. $C = 2\pi R$ if R = 5 in

7. $m = \dfrac{y_2 - y_1}{x_2 - x_1}$ if $y_2 = 12$, $y_1 = 3$, $x_2 = 4$, and $x_1 = 1$

8. $x = \dfrac{-b + \sqrt{b^2 - 4ac}}{2a}$ if a = 1, b = −6, and c = 8

9. $A = \dfrac{1}{2}h(B+b)$ if A = 15 cm, h = 3 cm, and b = 4 cm

10. $C = \pi R^2$ if R = 2 in

Solve each formula for the indicated variable.

11. $P = 2L + 2W$ for W

12. $D = R \cdot T$ for T

13. $I = P \cdot r \cdot t$ for P

14. $A = \dfrac{1}{2}bh$ for h

15. $C = 2\pi R$ for R

16. $A = \dfrac{1}{2}h(B+b)$ for b

17. $C = \dfrac{5}{9}(F - 32)$ for F

18. $V = l \cdot w \cdot h$ for w

19. $P = a + b + c$ for c

20. $V = \dfrac{1}{3}\pi R^2 h$ for h

21. $y = mx + b$ for m

22. $y - y_1 = m(x - x_1)$ for x

23. $X = \dfrac{m+n+p}{3}$ for p

24. $IR + Ir = E$ for r

Use a known formula to solve each perimeter problem

25. If the width of a rectangle is 3 in less than the length, and the perimeter of the rectangle is 14 in, find the length and the width of the rectangle.

26. The perimeter of a triangle is 35 in. The longest side is 6 in longer than the shortest side and the medium side 3 in less than twice the shortest side. Find the lengths of the three sides.

27. The perimeter of a triangle is 142 cm. The medium side is 8 cm longer than the shortest side and the longest side is 2 cm longer than twice the shortest side. Find the lengths of each side.

28. The perimeter of a square is 48 cm more than the side of the square. Find the side of the square.

29. The perimeter of a square is 96 cm. Find the side of the square.

30. The circumference of a circle is 24π in. Find the radius of the circle.

31. The radius of a circle is 5 in. Find the circumference of the circle.

Use the distance formula to solve each motion problem.

32. A car and a bus start from Los Angeles bus station and travel in opposite directions. The car travels 15 mph faster than the bus. In 2 hours the car and the bus are 230 mi apart. Find the average rate of the car and the average rate of the bus.

33. A passenger train and a freight train leave a station at the same time and travel in opposite directions. The passenger train travels 25 mph faster than the freight train. In 3 hours the trains are 315 miles apart. Find the average speed of the passenger train and the average speed of the freight train.

34. A car and a truck leave cities 360 mi apart at the same time and travel toward each other. If the car travels 10 mph faster than the truck and they pass each other in 3 hours, find the average speed of the car and the average speed of the truck.

35. Two cars start at 8:00 a.m. from cities 330 mi apart and travel toward each other. If one car travels at an average speed of 50 mph and the other at an average speed of 60 mph, at what time do they pass one another?

36. A runner and a jogger start at 7:00 a.m. from the same point, headed in the same direction. The average speed of the jogger is 4 mph and the average speed of the runner is 6 mph. How long does it take for the runner to be 1 mile ahead of the jogger?

37. A car and a bus start at 8:00 a.m. from the same point and travel in the same direction. The average speed of the car is 60 mph. In 2 hours the car is 30 miles ahead of the bus. Find the average speed of the bus.

38. The distance between Los Angeles and San Diego is about 120 mi. A car leaves LA at 8:00AM and travels toward San Diego. Due to traffic conditions in the Los Angeles area, the average speed of the car was 35 mph for the first part of the trip and 60 mph for the last part of the trip. If the car arrived in San Diego at 11:00 a.m., find the travel time for each part of the trip.

39. On the first part of a 390 mi trip an automobile averaged 45 mph and for the remainder of the trip the automobile averaged 60 mph. If the entire trip took 7 hours, find the travel time for each part of the trip.

40. A student leaves home at 7:00 AM headed to a mountain ski resort with an average speed of 65 mph on the highway. On the mountain road, close to the ski resort the average speed was 30 mph. If the distance from home to the ski resort is 110 mi, and the student arrived at the ski resort at 9:30 a.m., find the travel time for each part of the trip.

41. A freight train leaves a station and travels east at an average speed of 48 mph. Later, a passenger train leaves the same station on parallel tracks and follows the freight train at an average speed of 60 mph. If the passenger train overtakes the freight in 2 hours, how much of a head start did the freight train have?

42. A jet plane leaves an airport 1 hour after a small plane leaves the same airport. If the jet plane travels 160 mph faster than the small plane, find the speed of each plane if the jet plane overtakes the small plane in 1.5 hours.

43. Two cars start at the same time from Phoenix and travel toward Los Angeles. One car travels at an average speed of 55 mph and the other car at 65 mph. When the faster car arrives in LA the slower car is 58 miles away. How far is Phoenix from Los Angeles?

2.6 APPLICATIONS: INVESTMENT AND MIXTURE PROBLEMS

□ **Investment Problems** □ **Value Mixture Problems** □ **Percent Mixture Problems**

□ INVESTMENT PROBLEMS

When someone invests a certain amount of money for a period of time in an account with a financial institution, at the end of that period the investor expects to make some money or earn some interest from that investment.

> The *interest earned* from an investment is a percentage of the **amount invested**. The percentage is set by the financial institution and it is called the **interest rate**.
>
> If the interest earned from an account remains unchanged every period, the interest rate is called **simple interest rate**.

The basic formula used to calculate the simple interest earned from an investment is called the simple interest formula: $I = P \cdot r \cdot t$ where,

I = interest earned

P = principal or initial amount invested

r = annual simple interest rate

t = time (years)

If the money is invested for one year (t = 1), the simple interest formula becomes

$$I = P \cdot r$$

Note: When solving investment problems the interest rate r should always be expressed in decimal form.

Example 1

Tim invested $10,000 into two savings accounts. Part of that amount was invested at 3.5% simple interest and the rest at 5% simple interest. If the interest earned in one year from those two accounts was $410, how much did he invest in each account?

Solution

Step 1 *Read the problem carefully.*

Step 2 *Assign a variable to the unknown quantity.* Let *x* be the amount invested at 3.5%.

Step 3 *Express the other unknown quantities in terms of the variable.* Then, the amount invested at 5% is the rest of the money $10,000 - x$. Since $t = 1$, we can use the formula $I = P \cdot r$.

The information of the problem can be summarized in the following chart:

	P	×	r	=	I
1st account	x		0.035		0.035x
2nd account	10,000 – x		0.05		0.05(10,000 – x)
					$410

Step 4 *Translate the information into an equation using the variable.* The interest earned from the first account 0.035x together with the interest earned from the second account 0.05(10,000 – x) equals the total interest earned in one year $410. This can be translated into the following equation:

$$0.035x + 0.05(10,000 - x) = 410$$

Step 5 *Solve the equation.* Multiply both sides of the equation by 1000 to eliminate the decimals.

$$35x + 50(10,000 - x) = 410,000$$

$$35x + 500,000 - 50x = 410,000$$

$$-15x + 500,000 = 410,000$$

$$-15x = 410,000 - 500,000$$

$$-15x = -90,000$$

$$x = 6,000$$

Step 6 *State and check the answer.*

Tim invested $6,000 at 3.5% and $10,000 – $6,000 = $4,000 at 5%.

Example 2

Lisa invested some money in a savings account that paid 4% annual simple interest and $3,000 more than that in a certificate of deposit that pays 5% simple interest per year. How much was invested at each rate if the interest earned from those two investments after one year was $870?

Solution

Step 1 *Read the problem carefully.*

Step 2 *Assign a variable to the unknown quantity.* Let x be the amount invested at 4%.

Step 3 *Express the other unknown quantities in terms of the variable.* The amount invested at 5% is $3,000 more: $x + 3,000$

I = $870 and t = 1

The following chart summarizes the information of the problem,

	P	×	r	=	I
Savings Account	x		0.04		0.04x
CD	x + 3,000		0.05		0.05(x + 3,000)
					$870

Step 4 *Translate the information into an equation using the variable.* The interest earned from the savings account 0.04x plus the interest earned from the certificate of deposit x + 3,000 was $870. This can be expressed in the following equation:

0.04x + 0.05(x + 3,000) = 870

Step 5 *Solve the equation.* Multiply both sides of the equation by 100 to eliminate the decimals.

$$4x + 5(x + 3,000) = 87,000$$

$$4x + 5x + 15,000 = 87,000$$

$$9x + 15,000 = 87,000$$

$$9x = 870,000 - 15,000$$

$$9x = 72,000$$

Step 6 *State and check the answer.* Lisa invested $8,000 in a savings account and x + 3,000 = $8,000 + $3,000 = $11,00 in a certificate of deposit.

Example 3

A student invested some money in an account that paid 4.5% annual simple interest rate and twice as much in an account that paid 6% annual simple interest rate. If the interest earned from those two investments in one year was $330, how much was invested in each account?

Solution

Step 1 *Read the problem carefully.*

Step 2 *Assign a variable to the unknown quantity.* Let x be the amount invested at 4.5%.

Step 3 *Express the other unknown quantities in terms of the variable.* The amount invested at 6% was twice as much: 2x

I = $330 and t = 1.

We can organize the information of the problem in the following chart:

	P	×	r	=	I
1st account	x		0.045		0.045x
2nd account	2x		0.06		0.06(2x)
					$330

Step 4 *Translate the information into an equation using the variable.* The interest earned from the first account 0.045x together with the interest earned from the second account 0.06(2x) equals the total interest earned in one year $390. This can be translated into the following equation:

$$0.045x + 0.06(2x) = 330$$

Step 5 *Solve the equation.* Multiply both sides by 1000 to eliminate the decimals.

$$45x + 60(2x) = 330,000$$

$$45x + 120x = 330,000$$

$$165x = 330,000$$

$$x = 2,000$$

Step 6 *State and check the answer.* The student invested $2,000 at 4.5% and 2x = 2(2,000) = $4,000 at 6%.

Example 4

A teacher invested $8,000 in two savings accounts. Part of it at 5% simple interest rate and the remainder at 7% simple interest rate. If the interest earned in one year by the 7% investment was $320 more than the interest earned by the 5% investment, find the amount invested at each rate.

Solution

Step 1 *Read the problem carefully.*

Step 2 *Assign a variable to the unknown quantity.* Let x be the amount invested at 5%.

Step 3 *Express the other unknown quantities in terms of the variable.* The remainder $8,000 $- x$ was invested at 7%. The time is t = 1.

Again, we can summarize the given information in the following chart:

	P	×	r	=	I
1st account	x		0.05		0.05x
2nd account	8,000 − x		0.07		0.07(8,000 − x)
	$8,000				

Step 4 *Translate the information into an equation using a variable.* The interest earned at 7% in one year 0.07(8,000 − x) was $320 more than the interest earned at 5% in one year 0.05x. Thus the difference between the interest earned at 7% and the interest earned at 5% was $320. This can be expressed by the following equation:

$$0.07(8,000 - x) - 0.05x = 320$$

Step 5 *Solve the equation.* Multiply both sides by 100 to eliminate the decimals:

$$7(8,000 - x) - 5x = 32,000$$

$$56,000 - 7x - 5x = 32,000$$

$$56,000 - 12x = 32,000$$

$$-12x = 32,000 - 56,000$$

$$-12x = -24,000$$

$$x = 6,000$$

Step 6 *State and check the answer.* The teacher invested $6,000 at 7% and the remainder $8,000 − $6,000 = $2,000 at 5%.

☐ VALUE MIXTURE PROBLEMS

When we mix coffee that costs $5 per pound with coffee that costs $7 per pound, we obtain a single blend of coffee with a possible selling price between $5 and $7.

> ***Value mixture problems*** refer to problems in which two or more ingredients (coffee, candy, almonds, etc…) with different costs are combined into a single blend.

The possible selling price for the blend is somewhere between the costs of the ingredients that make up the mixture. The basic formula used to solve value mixture problem is $A \cdot C = V.$

A = amount of ingredient

C = cost per unit of an ingredient

V = value of an ingredient

Example 5

How many pounds of Coffee A that costs $8 per pound and how many pounds of Coffee B that costs $10 per pound should be mixed to obtain 16 pounds of a blend of coffee that sells for $9.25 per pound?

Solution

Step 1 *Read the problem carefully.*

Step 2 *Assign a variable to the unknown quantity.* Let x be the amount of coffee that costs $8.

Step 3 *Express the other unknown quantities in terms of the variable.* The amount of coffee that costs $10 makes up the difference up to 16 pounds: $16 - x$.

The information of the problem can be organized in the following chart:

	A	×	C	=	V
Coffee A	x		8		3x
Coffee B	16 − x		10		10(16 − x)
Mixture	16		9.25		16(9.25) = 148

Step 4 *Translate the information into an equation using the variable.* The value of coffee A plus the value of coffee B equals the total value of the mixture. This can be expressed into the following equation:

$$8x + 10(16 - x) = 16(9.25)$$

Step 5 *Solve the equation.*

$$8x + 160 - 10x = 148$$

$$-2x + 160 = 148$$

$$-2x = 148 - 160$$

$$-2x = -12$$

$$x = 6$$

Step 6 *State and check the answer.* Thus, 6 pounds of Coffee A should be mixed with 16 − 6 = 10 pounds of Coffee B to obtain 16 pounds of the desired blend of coffee.

Example 6

A merchant wants to mix almonds that cost $6.90 per pound with cashews that cost $8.90 per pound to obtain 20 pounds of a blend that sells for $150. How many pounds of each should be mixed to obtain the desired mixture?

Solution

Step 1 *Read the problem carefully.*

Step 2 *Assign a variable for the unknown quantity.* Let x be the amount of almonds.

Step 3 *Express the other unknown quantities in terms of the variable.* The amount of cashews makes the remainder up to 20 pounds: 20 − x.

Let's use the chart to organize the information of the problem.

	A	×	C	=	V
Almonds	x		6.90		6.90x
Cashews	20 − x		8.90		8.90(20 − x)
Mixture	20				$150

Step 4 *Translate the information into an equation using the variable.* The value of almonds $6.90x$ plus the value of cashews $8.90(20 - x)$ equals the value of the mixture $150. This can be expressed into the following equation:

$$6.90x + 8.90(20 - x) = 150 \text{ or}$$

$$6.9x + 8.9(20 - x) = 150$$

Step 5 *Solve the equation.* Multiply both sides by 10 to clear the decimals.

$$69x + 89(20 - x) = 1,500$$

$$69x + 1,780 - 89x = 1,500$$

$$-20x + 1,780 = 1,500$$

$$-20x = 1,500 - 1,780$$

$$-20x = -280$$

$$x = 14$$

Step 6 *State and check the answer.* Thus, the merchant should mix 14 pounds of almonds and $20 - 14 = 6$ pounds of cashews to obtain the desired mixture.

☐ PERCENT MIXTURE PROBLEMS

When alcohol and water are combined, the mixture is called an alcohol solution. If the solution is labeled "65% alcohol solution" then any amount of this solution contains 65% alcohol and 35% water. The percentage 65% is referred to as the *concentration rate* of this solution and is given by the quantity of alcohol in the solution.

If the solution is too strong, and we want to dilute the solution we add some pure water. Since the concentration of the solution is given by alcohol, and pure water has no alcohol, the concentration rate of pure water is 0%. On the other hand, if we want to strengthen this solution, we add some pure alcohol which has the concentration rate 100% ($100\% = \dfrac{100}{100} = 1$) because the entire amount is alcohol.

Percent mixture problems refer to problems in which two or more solutions (salt solution, acid solution, etc...) with different concentration rates are combined into a single solution.

The basic formula used to solve percent mixture problems is $A \cdot r = Q$ where:

A = amount of a solution

r = concentration rate of a solution

Q = quantity of a substance in the solution (salt, acid, etc.)

Example 7

How many liters of a 36% salt solution should be mixed with a 60% salt solution to get 40 liters of a 45% salt solution?

Solution

Step 1 *Read the problem carefully.*

Step 2 *Assign a variable to the unknown quantity.* Let x be the amount of 36% salt solution.

Step 3 *Express the other unknown quantities in terms of the variable.* The amount of 60% salt solution is the difference up to 40 liters: $40 - x$.

The following chart summarizes the information of the problem.

	A	×	r	=	Q
35% solution	x		0.36		0.36x
60% solution	40 − x		0.60		0.60(40 − x)
Mixture	40				40(0.45) = 18

Step 4 *Translate the information into an equation using the variable.* The sum of the quantities of salt in the 36% solution (0.36x liters) and the quantity of salt in the 60% solution (0.60(40 − x) liters) equals the quantity of salt in the mixture (18 liters). This can be expressed by the following equation:

$$0.36x + 0.60(40 - x) = 18$$

Step 5 *Solve the equation.* Multiply both sides by 100 to clear the decimals.

$$36x + 60(40 - x) = 1,800$$

$$36x + 2,400 - 60x = 1,800$$

$$-24x + 2,400 = 1,800$$

$$-24x = 1,800 - 2,400$$

$$-24x = -600$$

$$x = 25$$

Step 6 *State and check the answer.* Thus, 25 liters of a 36% salt solution should be mixed with $40 - 25 = 15$ liters of a 60% solution to get 40 liters of a 45% salt solution.

Example 8

How many liters of a 15% acid solution should be mixed with 3 liters of a 35% acid solution to make a 20% acid solution?

Solution

Step 1 *Read the problem carefully.*

Step 2 *Assign a variable for the unknown quantity.* Let x be the amount of 15% acid solution.

The following chart summarizes the information of the problem.

	A	×	r	=	Q
15% solution	x		0.15		0.15x
35% solution	3		0.35		3(0.35) = 1.05
Mixture	x + 3		0.20		0.20(x + 3)

Step 3 *Translate the information into an equation using a variable.* The sum of the quantities of acid in the 15% solution (0.15x liters) and in the 35% solution (1.05 liters) equals the quantity of acid in the mixture (0.20(x + 3) liters). This can be expressed by the following equation:

$$0.15x + 1.05 = 0.20(x+3)$$

Step 4 *Solve the equation.* Multiply both sides by 100 to clear the decimals.

$$15x + 105 = 20(x+3)$$

$$15x + 105 = 20x + 60$$

$$105 - 60 = 20x - 15x$$

$$45 = 5x$$

$$x = 9$$

Step 5 *State and check the answer.* Thus, 9 liters of a 15% acid solution should be mixed with 3 liters of a 35% acid solution to get 11 liters of a 20% acid solution.

Example 9

If 5 liters of a 10% alcohol solution are mixed with 10 liters of a 70% alcohol solution, find the concentration rate of the mixture.

Solution

Step 1 *Read the problem carefully.*

Step 2 *Assign a variable for the unknown quantity.* Let x be the concentration rate of the solution.

The following chart summarizes the information of the problem.

	A	×	r	=	Q
10% solution	5		0.10		$5(0.10) = 0.5$
70% solution	10		0.70		$10(0.70) = 7$
Mixture	15		x		15x

Step 3 *Translate the information into an equation using the variable.* The equation is:

$$0.5 + 7 = 15x$$

Step 4 *Solve the equation.*

$$7.5 = 15x$$

$$x = 0.5$$

Step 5 *State and check the answer.* The concentration rate of the mixture is $0.5 \cdot 100\% = 50\%$.

Example 10

How many gallons of pure water should be mixed with 6 gallons of a 70% alcohol solution to dilute it to a 40% alcohol solution?

Solution

Step 1 *Read the problem carefully.*

Step 2 *Assign a variable for the unknown quantity.* Let x be the amount of pure water. The concentration rate of pure water is 0%.

The following chart summarizes the information of the problem.

	A	×	r	=	Q
Pure water	x		0		$0 \cdot x = 0$
70% sol.	6		0.70		$6(0.70) = 4.2$
Mixture	x + 6		0.40		$0.40(x + 6)$

Step 3 *Translate the information into an equation using the variable.* The equation is:

$$0 + 4.2 = 0.4(x + 6)$$

Step 4 *Solve the equation.* Multiply both sides by 10 to clear the denominators.

$$42 = 4(x + 6)$$

$$42 = 4x + 24$$

$$42 - 24 = 4x$$

$$18 = 4x$$

$$x = 4.5$$

Step 5 *State and check the answer.* Thus, 4.5 gallons of pure water will dilute the 70% alcohol solution to 40% alcohol solution.

Example 11

How many liters of pure acid should be mixed with 3 liters of a 10% acid solution to get a 60% acid solution?

Solution

Step 1 *Read the problem carefully.*

Step 2 *Assign a variable for the unknown quantity.* Let x be the amount of pure acid. The concentration rate for pure acid is 100% = 1.

The following chart summarizes the information of the problem.

	A	×	r	=	Q
Pure acid	x		1		x(1) = x
10% sol.	3		0.10		3(0.10) = 0.3
Mixture	x + 3		0.60		0.60(x + 3)

Step 3 *Translate the information into an equation using a variable.* The equation is:

$$x + 0.3 = 0.6(x + 3)$$

Step 4 *Solve the equation.* Multiply both sides by 10 to eliminate the decimals.

Step 5 *State and check the answer.* Thus, 3.75 liters of pure acid will strengthen 3 liters of 10% acid solution to a 60% acid solution.

2.6 EXERCISES

Investment Problems

1. Tom invested part of $12,000 in a 5% simple interest account and the remainder in a 7.5% simple interest account. If the total interest earned from the two investments in one year was $775, how much was invested in each account?

2. Jane invested $25,000 in two savings accounts. Part was invested at 4.5% simple interest and the reminder at 6.5% simple interest for one year. If the total interest earned from those two accounts was $1325, how much was invested in each account?

3. John invested some money in a certificate of deposit that earns 5.5% annual simple interest and $8,000 more in a municipal bond that earns 6% annual simple interest. If the amount of interest earned in one year was $1630, how much was invested in the certificate of deposit?

4. A student invested some money in a 7% simple interest savings account and $3,000 more in preferred stock that earns 10% simple interest. If the total interest earned in one year was $980, how much was invested in the savings account?

5. Linda invested some money for one year in bonds that pay 8% simple interest and three times as much in preferred stock that earns 11% simple interest. If the total interest earned from the two investments was $1640, how much was invested in bonds?

6. Paul invested some money in a 6.5% simple interest savings account and twice as much in a municipal bond that earns 8% simple interest. If the interest earned from both investments in one year was $1,350, how much was invested in the savings account?

7. A machinist invested $15,000, part at 6% simple interest and the remainder at 4% simple interest for one year. How much was invested at each rate if each investment earned the same interest?

8. To provide for retirement supplement income a teacher invested $20,000 in preferred stock that earns 10% simple interest. For a safe investment, how much money should the

teacher invest in a certificate of deposit that earns 4% if the total annual interest earned from the two investments is $2,400?

Value Mixture Problems

9. How many pounds of regular coffee that sells for $4 per pound and how many pounds of premium coffee that sells for $8 per pound should be blended to obtain 24 pounds of a gourmet blend that sells for $6 per pound?

10. How many pounds of almonds that sell for $6.90 per pound and how many pounds of cashews that sell for $8.90 per pound should be mixed to obtain 35 pounds of mixture that sells for $7.50 per pound?

11. How many pounds of chocolate covered raisins that sell for $4.90 per pound should be mixed with chocolate buttons with peanuts that sell for $5.21 per pound to obtain 41 pounds of Trail Mix that sells for $204.

12. A merchant wants to mix tea worth $3.50 per pound with tea worth $4.60 per pound to obtain 60 pounds of gourmet tea that sells for $232. How many pounds of each should be mixed to obtain the desired blend?

13. How many pounds of gumdrops worth $1.90 per pound should be mixed with jelly beans worth $1.40 per pound to make 15 pounds of candy mix that sells for $1.69 per pound?

14. A garden store sells fine Fescue grass seed for $5.80 per pound and perennial Rye grass seed for $2.80 per pound. How many pounds of each type of seed should be mixed to obtain 50 pounds of a sun and shade resistance mixture that sells for $185 ?

15. A garden store sells Bermuda grass seed for $3.65 per pound and Argentine Bahia grass seed for $6.30 per pound. How many pounds of Bermuda grass seed should be mixed with 20 pounds of Bahia grass seed to obtain a low maintenance and drought resistance blend that will sell for $4.90 ?

Percent Mixture Problems

16. A chemist wants to mix some 10% acid solution with 20 liters of a 45% acid solution. How many liters of 10% solution should the chemist use to obtain a 30% acid solution?

17. How many gallons of 20% alcohol solution should be mixed with 5 gallons of a 70% alcohol solution to get a 45% alcohol solution?

18. An auto mechanic wants to mix a 10% antifreeze solution and a 60% antifreeze solution to get 20 quarts of a 40% antifreeze solution. How many quarts of each should the mechanic use to obtain the desired mixture?

19. How many liters of a 30% salt solution should be mixed with a 80% salt solution to obtain 120 liters of a 60% salt solution?

20. How many liters of a 5% acid solution and how many liters of pure acid should be mixed to obtain 15 liters of a 43% acid solution?

21. How many liters of a 20% alcohol solution and how many liters of pure alcohol should be mixed to obtain 8 liters of a 70% alcohol solution?

22. How many liters of a 70% alcohol solution and how many liters of water should be mixed to get 7 liters of a 40% alcohol solution?

23. How many quarts of a 60% antifreeze solution and how many quarts of pure water should be mixed to make 12 quarts of a 45% antifreeze solution?

24. If 300 milliliters of a 3% hydrogen peroxide is mixed with 180 milliliters of a 7% hydrogen peroxide, find the concentration rate of the mixture.

25. If 5 grams of a 75% silver alloy is mixed with 65 grams of a 5%, silver alloy, find the concentration of the resulting alloy.

26. How many kilograms of a 10% copper alloy should be mixed with 200 kilograms of a 80% copper alloy to make a 35% copper alloy?

2.7   RATIOS AND PROPORTIONS

□ Rates □ Ratios □ Proportions □ Similar Triangles

□ RATES

Examples of rates: $\dfrac{60mi}{1hr}$, $\dfrac{\$5}{3oz}$, $\dfrac{\$700}{3days}$, $\dfrac{70mi}{2gal}$ etc.

Definition

*A **rate** is the comparison (by division) of two quantities with different units.*

The rate is used to compare quantities with different units. A real-life application of rate is the concept of "price per unit." When a product (item) is offered in different sizes, to decide which size is the best buy, first find the price per unit for each item and then choose the item with the *lowest price per unit*.

Price per unit = price of the item / number of units

Example 1

A grocery store sells sweet peas in 15 oz cans for 88 cents. Find the price per unit.

Solution

Price per unit = price of the item/number of units = $\dfrac{\$0.88}{15oz}$ = \$0.06 /oz.

Thus, the price per unit is 6 cents per ounce.

Example 2

A supermarket sells tomato sauce in four different sizes. Use the price per unit to decide which size is the best buy.

Tomato Sauce	
Size	Price
14 oz	\$1.99
23.9 oz	\$2.99
45 oz	\$4.99
66 oz	\$7.99

Solution

To find the best buy, first find the price per unit.

14 oz price per unit $= \dfrac{\$1.99}{14oz} = 0.142$ 14.2 cents per ounce

23.9 oz price per unit $= \dfrac{\$2.99}{23.9oz} = 0.125$ 12.5 cents per ounce

45 oz price per unit $= \dfrac{\$4.99}{45oz} = 0.11$ 11 cents per ounce

66 oz price per unit $= \dfrac{\$7.99}{66oz} = 0.121$ 12.1 cents per ounce

Because 45 oz has the lowest price per unit, it is the best buy.

☐ RATIOS

Examples of ratios: $\dfrac{5in}{12in}, \dfrac{3min}{7min}, \dfrac{\$4}{\$15}, \dfrac{8hrs}{25hrs}$, etc.

Definition

*A **ratio** is the comparison (by division) of two quantities with the same unit.*

Notation: The ratio of a quantity a to a quantity b (b $\neq$ 0) can be written as follows:

$a \div b$, or $\dfrac{a}{b}$

The ratio is used to compare quantities with the same unit. Hence, a ratio is a special rate.

Example 3

Write as a ratio in lowest terms.

a. The ratio of 15 m to 3 m: $\dfrac{15m}{35m} = \dfrac{15}{35} = \dfrac{3}{7}$

b. The ratio of 15 in to 45 in: $\dfrac{15in}{45in} = \dfrac{15}{45} = \dfrac{1}{3}$

c. The ratio of 5 hrs to 40 min: $\dfrac{5hrs}{40\,min} = \dfrac{5 \cdot 60\,min}{40\,min} = \dfrac{300\,min}{40\,min} = \dfrac{300}{40} = \dfrac{15}{2}$

d. The ratio of 50 cm to 4 m: $\dfrac{50cm}{4m} = \dfrac{50cm}{4 \cdot 100cm} = \dfrac{50cm}{400cm} = \dfrac{50}{400} = \dfrac{1}{8}$

Note: Since the ratio compares quantities with the same unit, we had to convert the units in examples b. and c.

☐ PROPORTIONS

Examples of Proportions: $\dfrac{2}{3} = \dfrac{8}{12}$, $\dfrac{5}{6} = \dfrac{15}{18}$, $\dfrac{1}{7} = \dfrac{10}{70}$, and $\dfrac{10}{15} = \dfrac{2}{3}$

Definition

*Equality of two rates or ratios is called **proportion**.*

In general, a proportion can be written in the form: $\dfrac{a}{b} = \dfrac{c}{d}$ where $b, d \neq 0$

The quantities **a, b, c,** and **d** are called terms. The terms **a** and **d** are called *extremes* and the terms **b** and **c** are called *means*.

If we multiply both sides of a proportion $\dfrac{a}{b} = \dfrac{c}{d}$ by the LCD = bd, we obtain $a \cdot d = b \cdot c$ which can be summarized in the following property:

Property of Proportions

If $\dfrac{a}{b} = \dfrac{c}{d}$ where $b, d \neq 0$, then $a \cdot d = b \cdot c$

(*In a proportion the cross products are equal*)

We conclude that a proportion is true if the cross products are equal.

Example 4

Decide whether each proportion is true or false.

a. $\dfrac{2}{5} = \dfrac{6}{15}$ b. $\dfrac{15}{45} = \dfrac{2}{3}$

Solution

Use the property of proportions to compare the cross products.

a. $2 \cdot 15 = 30$ and $5 \cdot 6 = 30$ Since the cross products are equal, the proportion is true.

b. $15 \cdot 3 = 45$ and $45 \cdot 2 = 90$ Since the cross products are not equal, the proportion is false.

Also, we can use the property of proportions to solve proportions.

Example 5

Solve each proportion.

a. $\dfrac{x}{3} = \dfrac{6}{18}$ b. $\dfrac{5}{m} = \dfrac{15}{6}$

c. $\dfrac{2}{3} = \dfrac{y+2}{12}$

Solution

a. $\dfrac{x}{3} = \dfrac{6}{18}$, $18x = 3 \cdot 6$, $18x = 18$, $x = 1$

b. $\dfrac{5}{m} = \dfrac{15}{6}$, $15m = 5 \cdot 6$, $15m = 30$, $m = 2$

c. $\dfrac{2}{3} = \dfrac{y+2}{12}$, $3(y+2) = 2 \cdot 12$, $3y + 6 = 24$, $3y = 24 - 6$, $3y = 18$, $y = 6$

Example 6

Solve the proportion.

$$\frac{a+5}{4} = \frac{a-3}{3}$$

Solution

$$4(a-3) = 3(a+5)$$

$$4a - 12 = 3a + 15$$

$$4a - 3a = 15 + 12$$

$$a = 27$$

In geometry, proportions can be used to solve similar triangles.

☐ SIMILAR TRIANGLES

Definition

*Two triangles are called **similar triangles** if they have the same shape (not necessarily the same size).*

Property: If two triangles are similar, the corresponding angles have the same measure and the corresponding sides are proportional.

Notation: $\triangle ABC \approx \triangle DEF$ (triangle ABC is similar to triangle DEF)

If two triangles are similar, then:

a. The corresponding angles have the same measure:

$$m\angle A = m\angle D,\ m\angle B = m\angle E,\ m\angle C = m\angle F$$

b. The corresponding sides are proportional: $\dfrac{AB}{DE} = \dfrac{BC}{EF} = \dfrac{AC}{DF}$

Example 7

If triangle ABC is similar to triangle DEF, use proportions to find the unknown sides.

Solution

Since the triangles are similar, the corresponding sides are proportional.

$$\frac{AB}{DE} = \frac{BC}{EF} = \frac{AC}{DF}$$

$$\frac{12}{x} = \frac{6}{y} = \frac{8}{4}$$

Use the first and last ratios, $\frac{12}{x} = \frac{8}{4}$ and solve the proportion.

$$8x = 12 \cdot 4$$
$$8x = 48$$
$$x = 6 \;\; DE = 6\text{in}$$

Use the second and the last ratios, $\frac{6}{y} = \frac{8}{4}$ and solve the proportion.

$$8y = 6 \cdot 4$$
$$8y = 24$$
$$y = 3 \;\; EF = 3\text{in.}$$

Example 8

If the triangle ABC is similar to the triangle DEF, find the perimeter of the triangle DEF.

Solution

To find the perimeter of the triangle DEF, first we have to find the unknown sides of the triangle DEF. Since the triangles are similar, the corresponding sides are proportional.

$$\frac{AB}{DE} = \frac{BC}{EF} = \frac{AC}{DF}$$

$$\frac{15}{x} = \frac{18}{6} = \frac{9}{y}$$

Use the first and second ratios, $\frac{15}{x} = \frac{18}{6}$ and solve the proportion.

$$18x = 15 \cdot 6$$
$$18x = 90$$
$$x = 5 \;\; DE = 5\text{cm}$$

Use the second and last ratios, $\frac{18}{6} = \frac{9}{y}$ and solve the proportion.

$$18y = 9 \cdot 6$$
$$18y = 54$$
$$y = 3 \;\; DF = 3\text{cm}$$

Now, we can find the perimeter of the triangle DEF.

$$P = DE + EF + DF = 5\text{cm} + 6\text{cm} + 3\text{cm} = 14\text{cm}$$

Example 9

Use proportions to solve. If 5 pairs of jeans cost 225, find the cost of 3 pairs of jeans.

Solution

To solve the problem, we can use the following proportion:

Pairs of jeans / cost = pairs of jeans / cost

$$\frac{5}{225} = \frac{3}{x}$$

$$5x = 675$$

$$x = 135$$

Thus, 3 pairs of jeans cost \$135.

Example 10

If the numerator of $\frac{5}{6}$ is multiplied by a number and the denominator is increased by twice the number, the resulting fraction is $\frac{5}{4}$.

Solution

Step 1 *Read the problem carefully.*

Step 2 *Assign a variable for the unknown quantity.* Let x be the unknown number.

Step 3 *Translate the information into an equation using the variable.* The proportion (equation) is:

$$\frac{5n}{6+2n} = \frac{5}{4}$$

Step 4 *Solve the proportion.* Multiply across

$$20n = 5(6+2n)$$

$$20n = 30 + 10n$$

$$20n - 10n = 30$$

$$10n = 30$$

$$n = 3$$

Step 5 *State and check the answer.* The unknown number is $n = 3$

Example 12

On a map of the United States 1 cm represents 400 Km. If New York and Los Angeles are 9.9 cm apart on the map, what is the actual distance between Los Angeles and New York?

Solution

Step 1 *Read the problem carefully.*

Step 2 *Assign a variable for the unknown quantity.* Let x be the actual distance between the two cities.

Step 3 *Translate the information into an equation using the variable.* The proportion (equation) is:

$$\frac{\text{distance on the map}}{\text{actual distance}} = \frac{\text{distance on the map}}{\text{actual distance}}$$

$$\frac{1}{400} = \frac{9.9}{x}$$

Step 4 *Solve the proportion.* Multiply across

$$(1)\, x = 9.9(400)$$

$$x = 3960$$

Step 5 *State and check the answer.* Thus, the distance between Los Angeles and New York is about 3960 Km.

2.7 EXERCISES

Write as a ratio in lowest terms.

1. 6 meters to 14 meters

2. 15 ft to 45 ft

3. 2 hours to 64 minutes

4. 16 inches to 4 feet

5. 14 hours to 3 days

6. 3 dollars to 80 cents

Determine whether each proportion is true or false.

7. $\dfrac{3}{5} = \dfrac{12}{20}$

8. $\dfrac{4}{7} = \dfrac{9}{10}$

9. $\dfrac{5}{9} = \dfrac{10}{18}$

10. $\dfrac{2}{7} = \dfrac{10}{35}$

11. $\dfrac{24}{16} = \dfrac{3}{2}$

12. $\dfrac{6}{7} = \dfrac{12}{15}$

13. $\dfrac{8}{9} = \dfrac{4}{4.5}$

14. $\dfrac{3}{8} = \dfrac{1\frac{1}{2}}{4}$

A supermarket sells the same product in different sizes. Use the price per unit to determine which size is the best buy.

15.

Baked Beans	
16 oz	$2.29
28 oz	$2.99
55 oz	$4.99

16.

Tuna	
5 oz	$1.99
10 oz	$3.69
12 oz	$3.99

17.

Mayonnaise	
8 oz	$3.49
16.5 oz	$3.99
30 oz	$4.99
48 oz	$7.39

18.

Ketchup	
14 oz	$2.69
20 oz	$2.79
38 oz	$3.99
64 oz	$5.39

19.

Pickles	
10 oz	$1.99
24 oz	$2.99
46 oz	$3.49

Solve each proportion.

20. $\dfrac{x}{3} = \dfrac{36}{27}$

21. $\dfrac{m}{9} = \dfrac{14}{18}$

22. $\dfrac{5}{y} = \dfrac{20}{8}$

23. $\dfrac{7}{a} = \dfrac{49}{21}$

24. $\dfrac{x}{4} = \dfrac{x+8}{5}$

25. $\dfrac{y}{6} = \dfrac{y-4}{2}$

26. $\dfrac{10}{k} = \dfrac{11}{k+7}$

27. $\dfrac{x+12}{2} = \dfrac{4x}{7}$

28. $\dfrac{x+5}{9} = \dfrac{6x+2}{18}$

29. $\dfrac{7y+3}{2} = \dfrac{3y-5}{4}$

30. $\dfrac{10}{4a+2} = \dfrac{5}{a+6}$

Use proportions to solve each problem.

31. If 5 shirts cost $175, find the cost of 8 shirts.

32. If 4 ties cost $144, find the cost of 6 ties.

33. If the numerator of $\dfrac{11}{12}$ increased by a number and the denominator is decreased by that number the resulting fraction is $\dfrac{13}{10}$. Find the number.

34. If the numerator of $\dfrac{2}{3}$ is multiplied by a number and the denominator is increased by three times the number, the resulting fraction is $\dfrac{8}{9}$. Find the number.

35. On a wall map 1 inch represents 250 mi. If Tokyo and Singapore are 13.2 inches apart on the map, what is the actual distance between Tokyo and Singapore?

36. On a wall map 1 inch represents 250 mi. If New York and Mexico City are 8.4 inches apart on the map, what is the actual distance between New York and Mexico City?

37. The tax on a property with an assessed value of $350,000 is $3850. Find the tax on a property with an assessed value of $850,000.

38. The tax on a property with an assessed value of $475,000 is $5225. Find the tax on a property with an assessed value of $280,000.

39. A car uses 15 gallons of gasoline for a trip of 300 mi. How many gallons would be needed for an 800 mi trip?

40. A car uses 16 gallons of gasoline for a 400 mi trip. How many gallons would be needed for a 200 mi trip?

Use a proportion to find the lengths *x* and *y*, given that each pair of triangles is similar.

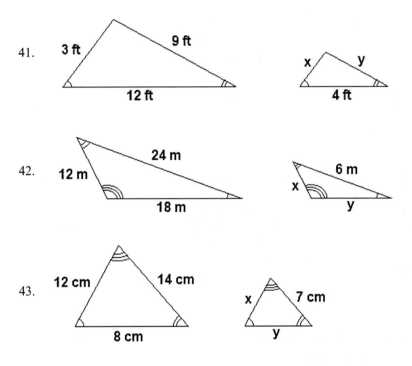

41.

42.

43.

2.8 LINEAR INEQUALITIES IN ONE VARIABLE

□ Solving Linear Inequalities in One Variable □ Addition and Multiplication Properties for Inequalities □ Three-Part Inequalities or Simultaneous Inequalities

□ SOLVING LINEAR INEQUALITIES IN ONE VARIABLE

Examples of linear equations: $2x + 3 = 7$, $4x - 3 = 9$, $\frac{1}{2}x + 1 = 3$, $11x + 5 = 27$

Examples of linear inequalities: $3x + 1 < 7$, $5x - 1 > 9$, $\frac{3}{4}x + 6 \le 1$, $7x - 3 \ge 11$

From the above examples we can see that linear inequalities and linear equations are similar in form. A linear inequality involves one of the following four inequality symbols:

1. $<$ "is less than"
2. $\le$ "is less than or equal to"
3. $>$ "is greater than"
4. $\ge$ "is greater than or equal to"

Definition

*A **linear inequality** or first degree inequality in one variable is an inequality that can be written in the form $ax + b < 0$ where a and b are real numbers and $a \ne 0$.*

Note: The definition is also true if the symbol $<$ is replaced by $\le$, $>$, or $\ge$.

Recall, when we solved linear equations, we used the addition and multiplication properties of equality. Similar properties will be used to solve linear inequalities.

□ ADDITION AND MULTIPLICATION PROPERTIES FOR INEQUALITIES

Addition Property

Before we state the addition property for inequalities, we need to find out what happens to the inequality symbol when the same number is added to both sides of an inequality.

Consider the following true inequality: $10 < 15$ "10 is *less than* 15"

Add 3 to each side, $10 + 3 \ldots 15 + 3$

The inequality symbol remains unchanged. $13 < 18$ "13 is *less than* 18"

Consider another true inequality: $8 < 12$ "8 is *less than* 12"

Add –2 to each side $8 + (-2) \ldots 12 + (-2)$

The inequality symbol remains unchanged $6 < 10$ "6 is *less than* 10"

The above examples lead to the following conclusion: the same positive or negative number may be added to both sides of an inequality without changing the inequality symbol (solution).

This is called the addition property of inequality and it can be expressed in general form as follows:

If $a < b$, then $a + c < b + c$, where a, b, and c are real numbers.

Note: The addition property holds for any inequality symbol ($<, \leq, >, \geq$).

Multiplication Property

Now let's find out what happens to the inequality symbol when both sides of an inequality are multiplied by the same positive or negative number.

Consider the following true inequality: $5 < 8$ "5 is *less than* 8"

Multiply both sides by 3 $5 \cdot 3 \ldots 8 \cdot 3$

The inequality symbol remains unchanged $15 < 24$ "15 is *less than* 24"

Note: If both sides of an inequality are multiplied by the same positive number, the inequality symbol remains unchanged.

Consider the same true inequality: $5 < 8$ "5 is *less than* 8"

Multiply both sides by –3 $5(-3) \ldots 8(-3)$

The inequality symbol is reversed $-15 > -18$ "–15 is *greater than* –18 "

Note: If both sides of an inequality are multiplied by the same negative number, the inequality symbol must be reversed.

These two examples can be summarized in a general form as follows:

If $a < b$ then, $a \cdot c < b \cdot c$ if c is positive (c > 0).

If $a < b$ then, $a \cdot c > b \cdot c$ if c is negative (c < 0).

Note: The multiplication property holds for any inequality symbol ($<, \leq, >, \geq$).

Example 1

Solve and graph on the number line.

  $x - 5 < 3$

Solution

$$x - 5 < 3 \qquad \text{Addition property: add 5 to each side}$$
$$x - 5 + 5 < 3 + 5 \qquad \text{Simplify: combine like terms}$$
$$x < 8$$

This inequality has more than one solution. Any real number that is less than 8 satisfies this inequality and therefore is a solution.

The set of all real numbers that are solutions of this linear inequality can be represented in set builder notation as follows:

Solution set: $\{x \mid x < 8\}$ which is read "the set of all x such that x is less than eight"

To visualize the solution set, we can use the real number line to graph all the real numbers (solutions) that satisfy the inequality. The arrow indicates that any real number located to the left of 8 on the number line is a solution of the linear inequality.

The empty circle is used to indicate that 8 is not part of the solution set.

```
-------------- ← ° --------------
                8
```

Solution set: $\{x \mid x < 8\}$

Example 2

Solve and graph.

$$x + 8 \geq -2$$

Solution

$$x + 8 \geq -2 \qquad \text{Addition property: add } -8 \text{ to each side}$$
$$x + 8 + (-8) \geq -2 + (-8) \qquad \text{Simplify: combine like terms}$$
$$x \geq -10$$

Solution set: $\{x \mid x \geq -10\}$

Graph:
```
------------------------- • → -------------------------
                        -10
```

Note: The solid circle is used to indicate that -10 is a solution.

Example 3

Solve and write the solution in set notation.

$$\frac{1}{3}x - 4 > 5$$

Solution

$$\frac{1}{3}x - 4 + 4 > 5 + 4 \text{ Addition property: add 4 to each side}$$

$$\frac{1}{3}x > 9 \text{ Simplify: combine like terms}$$

$$3 \cdot \frac{1}{3}x > 3 \cdot 9 \text{ Multiplication property: multiply both sides by 3}$$

$$x > 27 \text{ Solution set: } \{x \mid x > 27\}$$

Example 4
___

Solve and graph.

$$7x + 1 \geq -20$$

Solution

$$7x + 1 + (-1) \geq -20 + (-1) \text{ Addition property: add } -1 \text{ to each side}$$

$$7x \geq -21 \text{ Simplify: combine like terms}$$

$$\frac{1}{7} \cdot 7x \geq \frac{1}{7}(-21) \text{ Multiplication property: multiply both sides by } \frac{1}{7}$$

$$x \geq -3$$

Solution set: $\{x \mid x \geq -3\}$

Graph:

```
----------------●→----------------
                -3
```

Note: The solid circle is used to graph the solution of an inequality that involves $\leq$ or $\geq$ and the empty circle is used to graph the solution of an inequality that involves $<$ or $>$.

Example 5
___

Solve and write the solution in set notation.

$$2(x + 3) - 5 \leq 5x - 8$$

Solution

$2x + 6 - 5 \leq 5x - 8$	Simplify: combine like terms
$2x + 1 \leq 5x - 8$	
$2x - 5x \leq -1 - 8$	Addition property
$-3x \leq -9$	Simplify: combine like terms
$\dfrac{-3x}{-3} \geq \dfrac{-9}{-3}$	Multiplication property: divide both sides by -3
$x \geq 3$	Reverse the inequality symbol because $-3 < 0$

Solution set: $\{x \mid x \geq 3\}$

Example 6

Solve and graph. Write the solution in set notation.

$$3(x - 1) + 5 > 8(x + 4)$$

Solution

$3(x - 1) + 5 > 8(x + 4)$	
$3x - 3 + 5 > 8x + 32$	Distributive property: remove parenthesis
$3x + 2 > 8x + 32$	Simplify: combine like terms
$3x - 8x > 32 - 2$	Addition property
$-5x > 30$	Simplify: combine like terms
$\dfrac{-5x}{-5} < \dfrac{30}{-5}$	Multiplication property: divide both sides by –5
$x < -6$	Reverse the inequality symbol because $-5 < 0$

Solution set: $\{x \mid x < -6\}$

Graph: ------------------------$\leftarrow \circ$ ---------------------
                            -6

Example 7

Solve and write the solution in set notation.

$$\frac{2}{3}(x + 4) - 5 \le \frac{1}{2}(x - 3) + 8$$

Solution

$$\frac{2}{3}(x + 4) - 5 \le \frac{1}{2}(x - 3) + 8$$

Step 1 Find LCD $= 6$

Step 2 Eliminate the denominators: multiply both sides by LCD $= 6$

$$6 \cdot \frac{2}{3}(x + 4) - 6 \cdot 5 \le 6 \cdot \frac{1}{2}(x - 3) + 6 \cdot 8$$

$$4(x + 4) - 30 \le 3(x - 3) + 48$$

$$4x + 16 - 30 \le 3x - 9 + 48$$

$$4x - 14 \le 3x + 39$$

$$4x - 3x \le 39 + 14$$

$$x \le 54$$

Solution set: $\{x \mid x \le 54\}$

Example 8

___

Solve and write the solution in set notation

$1.2(x - 2) + 0.9 > 0.4(2x + 5) - 3.1$

Solution

Eliminate the decimals: multiply both sides of the inequality by 10.

$12(x - 2) + 9 > 4(2x + 5) - 31$

$12x - 24 + 9 > 8x + 20 - 31$

$12x - 15 > 8x - 11$

$12x - 8x > 15 - 11$

$4x > 4$

$\dfrac{4x}{4} > \dfrac{4}{4}$

$x > 1$

Solution set: $\{x \mid x > 1\}$

Example 9

___

Solve and graph on the number line.

$5(x + 3) - 2 > 5x + 10$

Solution

$5(x + 3) - 2 > 5x + 10$

$5x + 15 - 2 > 5x + 10$

$5x + 13 > 5x + 10$

$5x - 5x > 10 - 13$

$0x > -3$ Solution: All real numbers

Since any real number that substituted for *x* will make the statement true, the solution is the set of all real numbers. For example $0(12) = 0 > -3$, $0(-20) = 0 > -3$, etc.

Graph:

Example 10

Solve and graph on the number line.

$$3(x - 1) - 12 > 5(x - 4) - 2x + 5$$

Solution

$$3(x - 1) - 12 > 5(x - 4) - 2x + 5$$

$$3x - 3 - 12 > 5x - 20 - 2x + 5$$

$$3x - 15 > 3x - 15$$

$$3x - 3x > 15 - 15$$

$$0x > 0$$

Solution: No solution

Since there is no real number that substituted for *x* will make the statement true, the inequality has no solution. For example $0(5) = 0$ which is not greater than zero.

Graph: ------------------------------------|------------------------------

☐ THREE-PART INEQUALITIES OR SIMULTANEOUS INEQUALITIES

Example 11

Solve and graph.

$$-3 < 2x - 5 < 15$$

Solution

This is called a three part inequality and it consists of two inequalities $-3 < 2x - 5$ and $2x - 5 < 15$ that will be solved simultaneously.

First isolate x by adding 5 to each part of the inequality.

$$-3 + 5 < 2x - 5 + 5 < 15 + 5$$

$$-3 + 5 < 2x < 15 + 5$$

The addition property allows us to move 5 from the middle part to the right and left part of the three part inequality in one step. If we simplify by combining like terms, we get

$$2 < 2x < 20$$

To obtain the solution, divide all three parts by 2.

$$\frac{2}{2} < \frac{2x}{2} < \frac{20}{2}$$

$$1 < x < 10$$

The solution consists of the set of all real numbers that lie between 1 and 10.

Solution set. $\{x \mid 1 < x < 10\}$

Graph:

1   10

Example 12

___

Solve and graph.

$$-11 \le 3(x-4) < 6$$

Solution

$-11 \le 3(x-4) < 6$	Remove parenthesis
$-11 \le 3x - 12 < 6$	Move -12 to the right and left part
$-11 + 12 \le 3x < 6 + 12$	Simplify: combine like terms
$1 \le 3x < 18$	Divide all three parts by 3
$\dfrac{1}{3} \le \dfrac{3x}{3} < \dfrac{18}{3}$	Simplify
$\dfrac{1}{3} \le x < 6$	

Solution set. $\{x \mid \dfrac{1}{3} \le x < 6\}$

Graph:

$$1/3 \qquad\qquad 6$$

Example 13

___

Solve and graph.

$$4 < 8 - 2x \le 20$$

Solution

$4 < 8 - 2x \le 20$	Move 8 to the right and left part
$4 - 8 < -2x \le 20 - 8$	Simplify: combine like terms
$-4 < -2x \le 12$	Divide all three parts by -2
$\dfrac{-4}{-2} > \dfrac{-2x}{-2} \ge \dfrac{12}{-2}$	Simplify
$2 > x \ge -6$	Reverse the inequality because $-2 < 0$
$\dfrac{1}{3} \le x < 6$	Rewrite the inequality in increasing order.

Solution set. $\{x \mid -6 \le x < 2\}$

Graph:

$$-6 \qquad\qquad 2$$

Example 14

Solve and graph.

$$-\frac{2}{3} \le \frac{x+9}{2} \le \frac{5}{6}$$

Solution

$$-\frac{2}{3} \le \frac{x+9}{2} \le \frac{5}{6}$$

Step 1 Find LCD $= 6$

Step 2 Eliminate the denominators: multiply both sides by LCD $= 6$

$$6\left(-\frac{2}{3}\right) \le 6 \cdot \frac{x+9}{2} \le 6 \cdot \frac{5}{6}$$

$$-4 \le 3(x+9) \le 5$$

$$-4 \le 3x + 27 \le 5$$

$$-4 - 27 \le 3x \le 5 - 27$$

$$-31 \le 3x \le -22$$

$$\frac{-31}{3} \le \frac{3x}{3} \le \frac{-22}{3}$$

$$-\frac{31}{3} \le x \le -\frac{22}{3}$$

Solution set. $\{x \mid -\frac{31}{3} \le x \le -\frac{22}{3}\}$

Graph:

$$-\frac{31}{3} \qquad\qquad -\frac{22}{3}$$

Remark: It is very important to understand the correct translation of the following:

1. 5 less than a number $\qquad$ $x - 5$
2. 5 is less than a number $\qquad$ $5 < x$
3. 5 more than a number $\qquad$ $x + 5$
4. 5 is more than a number $\quad$ $5 > x$

2.8 EXERCISES

Solve each inequality, write the solution in set notation and graph the solution set.

1. $a + 3 \geq 5$

2. $y - 1 \leq 8$

3. $x - 4 < -3$

4. $x + 12 > 3$

5. $x + 1 \geq 7$

6. $x - 2 \leq 5$

7. $2m + 4 < 26$

8. $3n - 6 \geq 15$

9. $-x + 6 < 10$

10. $-x - 3 > 8$

11. $-2a + 11 \leq 21$

12. $-3y + 9 \leq -3$

13. $20 - y > 1$

14. $5 - z < 15$

15. $4 - 7a < -10$

16. $1 - 4m > 9$

17. $6 \leq 3 - x$

18. $12 > 5 - x$

19. $4 > 7 + x$

20. $18 < 18 + x$

21. $4x \geq 12$

22. $3x \leq 15$

23. $\dfrac{x}{5} \leq 4$

24. $\dfrac{x}{8} > 2$

25. $-\dfrac{1}{3}x > 8$

26. $-\dfrac{1}{6}x < 3$

27. $-5x < 20$

28. $-7x > -21$

29. $\dfrac{2}{7}x \geq 10$

30. $\dfrac{3}{8}x \leq 24$

31. $-\dfrac{5}{6}x \leq -30$

32. $-\dfrac{3}{11}x \geq -6$

33. $2x - 5 > 11$

34. $3x + 4 < -11$

35. $-4x + 7 < 23$

36. $-6x - 8 > 4$

37. $3 - 5x \geq -12$

38. $15 - 2x \geq 9$

39. $8 < 3x + 6$

40. $24 < 9x - 3$

41. $2x + 7 > 3x - 4$

42. $6x - 1 > 7x + 10$

43. $x + 8 < -3x + 16$

44. $4x - 11 < -3x + 10$

45. $9x + 16 \geq 11x$

46. $23x + 6 \leq 27x - 4x$

47. $6x + 4 < 5(2x - 8)$

48. $2x + 44 > 6(3x + 2)$

49. $-4(7 - x) > 4(x - 9) + 36$

50. $-6(4 - 3x) < 9(2x - 5) + 40$

51. $2(5x + 3) \leq 4(x - 6) + 18$

52. $3(7x + 2) \geq 4(6x - 3) - 6$

53. $0.2(x - 2) > 0.1(x + 4) + 7$

54. $0.4(2x + 1) < 0.3(3x - 2) + 14$

55. $0.7(5 - 3x) < 0.4(7 - x) - 1$

56. $1.2(4 - x) > 2.1(1 - x) - 0.9$

57. $\dfrac{1}{2}(x+1) \le \dfrac{1}{3}(x+5) + \dfrac{1}{6}$

58. $\dfrac{3}{4}(3x+4) \le \dfrac{2}{3}(x-9) + \dfrac{13}{12}$

59. $\dfrac{1}{5}(2x-3) \ge \dfrac{1}{4}(4x-1) - \dfrac{1}{5}$

60. $\dfrac{4}{7}(x-4) \ge \dfrac{1}{3}(x+2) + \dfrac{1}{7}$

61. $\dfrac{3}{2}(x+7) - \dfrac{5}{4}(2x+6) \le \dfrac{1}{8}(x-21)$

62. $\dfrac{2}{5}(x+3) - \dfrac{x}{2} < \dfrac{1}{3}(14+x)$

63. $-6 < 4x - 10 \le 14$

64. $-9 \le 5x + 1 < 16$

65. $2 \le 7x - 12 < 9$

66. $3 < 6x - 15 \le 21$

67. $1 \le 5 - 2x \le 11$

68. $-8 \le 10 - 3x \le 25$

69. $-2 \le \dfrac{x+5}{4} < 3$

70. $-5 < \dfrac{2x+1}{3} \le 7$

71. $4 < \dfrac{3x+2}{2} \le \dfrac{11}{2}$

72. $6 \le \dfrac{4x-3}{3} \le \dfrac{25}{3}$

Problem Solving

73. The test scores of a student in an algebra class are 86, 92, and 95. What must she score on the fourth test to have an average score of a least 90?

74. The test scores of a student in an algebra class are 73, 84, 75, and 81. What must he score on the fifth test to have an average score of at least 80?

75. The parking rates at LAX are $3.00 for the first hour and $2.00 each 30 minutes or fraction thereof after the first hour. What is the maximum length of time you can park your car at LAX parking structure if you wish to pay no more than $9?

76. A downtown parking garage in Los Angeles charges $5.00 for the first hour and $3.00 each 30 minutes or fraction thereof after the first hour. What is the maximum length of time you can park in the garage if you wish to pay no more than $20?

77. A phone company charges for international calls $0.20 for the first minute and $0.10 for each additional minute. If the call cannot exceed $5.00, what is the maximum number of minutes available for the call?

78. International calling rates for a telephone company are $0.42 for the first minute and $0.23 for each additional minute. If the call cannot exceed $7.55, what is the maximum number of minutes available for the call?

CHAPTER 2 REVIEW EXERCISES

Simplify each expression.

1. $-4(3x - 5y + 2z) - 6(-x + y - 3z) + 12$

2. $3x^2 - y^2 - 5(x^2 - 2y^2) - 3x + 2y + x$

3. $5a - 8[a - 3(a - 3b) - 5b] + 10a - 12$

4. $-9m + 2[3m - 4(m - n) + 3n] - 25n$

Evaluate each expression when $x = -2$ and $y = 3$

5. $7x^2 - 2xy + 3y^2 - 12$

6. $3x^2 + 5xy - y^2 + 9$

7. $\dfrac{2x + 3y - xy + 7}{2x + y}$

8. $\dfrac{5x - 4y + 2xy + 30}{2(a + b)}$

Use the properties of equations to solve each equation.

9. $5x - 1 = 14 + 2x$

10. $4y + 8 = 24 + 2y$

11. $8z - 5 = 9 + z$

12. $11a - 3 = 19 - 11a$

13. $9x + 4 = -14 + 3x$

14. $9b - 5 = -17 + 6b$

15. $-2(y + 5) - 6(2 - y)) = 5(y - 6) + 4$

16. $-3(4x + 1) - 5(x - 8) = 8(x - 10) - 8$

17. $4m - 3[6m - 2(3m + 2)] = 30 - 2m$

18. $9 - 4[10a - (4a + 3) - 6] = 11a + 10$

19. $\dfrac{2}{3}(5x - 3) - \dfrac{3}{4}(3x - 2) = \dfrac{5}{12}(x + 2)$

20. $\dfrac{3}{5}(4y + 1) - \dfrac{5}{2}(y - 3) = \dfrac{7}{10}(y + 7)$

21. $\dfrac{1}{6}(3x - 2) - \dfrac{1}{8}(2x + 3) = \dfrac{5}{24}(4 - x)$

22. $\dfrac{1}{4}(6x - 1) - \dfrac{1}{6}(2x + 5) = \dfrac{1}{12}(17 + 8x)$

23. $0.5(8x - 3) - 0.7x = 0.9(x + 1)$

24. $0.3(4x + 9) + 0.2x = 0.1(5 + 3x)$

25. $0.14x + 0.07(5 - 2x) = 0.05(x - 1)$

26. $0.06(4x - 9) + 0.11x = 0.08(4 - x)$

Solve each proportion.

27. $\dfrac{y}{3} = \dfrac{y-5}{4}$

28. $\dfrac{12}{a} = \dfrac{7}{a+5}$

29. $\dfrac{x+15}{3} = \dfrac{2x}{7}$

30. $\dfrac{3x+1}{8} = \dfrac{4x-1}{11}$

31. $\dfrac{4y+7}{3} = \dfrac{3y-10}{2}$

32. $\dfrac{14}{5a+2} = \dfrac{2}{a+6}$

Solve each formula for the indicated variable.

33. $F = \dfrac{9}{5}C + 32$ for C

34. $A = \dfrac{1}{2}bh$ for b.

35. $P = 2L + 2W$ for L

Solve each inequality and graph. Write the solution in interval notation.

36. $3(2x+7) \le 3(x-8) + 12$

37. $5(x-3) \ge 2(x-5) - 9$

38. $1 \le 4x - 7 < 9$

39. Twelve less than two times an integer is the same as one less than the integer. Find the integer.

40. The sum of three consecutive even integers is 10 more than twice the largest integer. Find the integers.

41. The complement of an angle is 15° less than two times the measure of the angle. Find the measure of the angle, and its complement.

42. The supplement of an angle is 10° less than four times the measure of the angle. Find the measure of the angle, and its supplement.

43. One angle of a triangle is 8° more than twice the measure of the smallest angle. The third angle is 28° more than the measure of the smallest angle. Find the measure of each angle of the triangle.

44. If the length of a rectangle is 2 cm more than twice the width, and the perimeter of the rectangle is 46 cm, find the length and the width of the rectangle.

45. A car and a bus start from Los Angeles bus station and travel in opposite directions. The car travels 12 mph faster than the bus. In 2 hours the car and the bus are 224 mi apart. Find the average speed of the car and the average speed of the bus.

46. A car and a truck leave cities 244 mi apart at the same time, and travel toward each other. If the car travels 8 mph faster than the truck and they pass each other in 2 hours, find the average speed of the car and the average speed of the truck.

47. A teacher invested $15,000 in two saving accounts. Part was invested at 4% simple interest and the remainder at 5.5% simple interest for one year. If the total interest earned in one year was $735, how much was invested in each account?

48. How many pounds of regular coffee that sells for $5 per pound and how many pounds of gourmet coffee that sells for $8.50 per pound should be mixed to obtain 25 pounds of a blend that sells for $6.54 per pound?

49. How many liters of a 20% salt solution should be mixed with a 65% salt solution to obtain 75 liters of a 27.2% salt solution?

50. How many ounces of 45% acid solution should be mixed with 20 oz of water to obtain a 30% acid solution?

3 GRAPHING LINEAR EQUATIONS AND INEQUALITIES IN TWO VARIABLES

3.1 THE RECTANGULAR COORDINATE SYSTEM

In this section, an important part of our work will be related to graphing linear equations and inequalities in two variables. This cannot be done without a reference system called **The Rectangular Coordinate System** or **The Cartesian Coordinate System**, after the French mathematician Rene Descartes (1596–1650).

A rectangular coordinate system consists of two number lines that intersect at zero and are perpendicular to each other.

- The horizontal number line is usually called the *x*-axis
- The vertical number line is usually called the *y*-axis
- The point of intersection O of the two axes is called the origin.

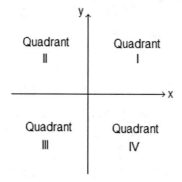

The *x*-axis together with the *y*-axis are called **the coordinate axes** and they determine a plane called the **coordinate plane**.

The coordinate axes divide the coordinate plane into four regions, called **quadrants**. The quadrants are numbered QI through QIV in a counterclockwise direction.

For each point in the plane, there is an ordered pair (x, y) corresponding to the point, where x and y are called the coordinates of the point. Also, for each ordered pair (x, y) there is a point in the plane corresponding to the ordered pair.

For example, to find (plot) the point P in the plane corresponding to the ordered pair (2, 3), start at the origin and move 2 units to the right along the *x*-axis and then move 3 units up parallel to the *y*-axis.

The point P (2, 3) with the *x*-coordinate 2 and *y*-coordinate 3 corresponding to the ordered pair (2, 3) is located in Quadrant I.

To plot the point Q corresponding to the ordered pair (–3, –1), start at the origin and move 3 units to the left along the *x*-axis and 1 unit down parallel to the *y*-axis.

To plot the point R corresponding to the ordered pair (0, 2), start at the origin and move 2 units up along the *y*-axis. The point R(0, 2) is located on the *y*-axis.

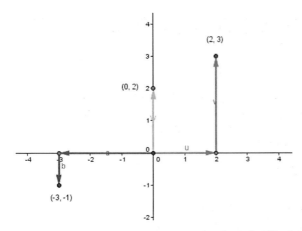

Note: If a point lies on the *x*-axis or *y*-axis, the point lies in none of the four quadrants.

Each ordered pair (*x, y*) is a solution of an equation in two variables *x* and *y*. For example, the ordered pair (1, 2) is a solution of $x + y = 3$ because if we substitute 1 for *x* and 2 for *y* we obtain a true numerical statement.

$x + y = 3$

$1 + 2 = 3$

$3 = 3$ True.

The equation $x + y = 3$ has an infinite number of solutions (ordered pairs). However, not every ordered pair is a solution of the equation $x + y = 3$. In other words, not every ordered pair satisfies the equation $x + y = 3$.

For example, (2, 4) is not a solution of $x + y = 3$ because if we substitute 2 for *x* and 4 for *y*, we obtain a false numerical statement.

$x + y = 3$

$2 + 4 = 3$

$6 = 3$ False

Example 1

Determine whether each ordered pair is a solution of the equation $2x + 3y = 6$.

a. (0, 2)

b. (–2 , 3)

Solution

a. To determine whether (0, 2) is a solution of the equation, substitute 0 for *x* and 2 for *y* into $2x + 3y = 6$.

$2x + 3y = 6$

$2(0) + 3(2) = 6$

$0 + 6 = 6$

$6 = 6$ True

Thus, (0, 2) is a solution of $2x + 3y = 6$.

b. $2x + 3y = 6$

$2(-2) + 3(3) = 6$

$-4 + 9 = 6$

$5 = 6$ False

Thus $(-2, 3)$ is not a solution of $2x + 3y = 6$

Example 2

Plot the following ordered pairs on a rectangular coordinate system.

$(-2, 3), (1, -2), (0, 4), (3, 0)$

Solution

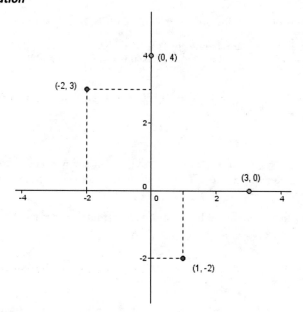

Example 3

Find the coordinates of each point.

Solution

A(2, 1)   B(−3, −1)   C(0, 3)   D(3, 0)   E(−2, 2)

Example 4

Complete each ordered pair that satisfies the equation $y = -x + 3$.

a. (2,)   d. (, 0)

b. (−1,)

c. (, 3)

Solution

a. In this ordered pair, the *x*-value is given, $x = 2$. To find the *y*-value, we substitute 2 for *x* in the equation

$y = -x + 3$

$y = -2 + 3$

$y = 1$

Thus, the ordered pair is (2, 1).

b. Again, the x-value is given, $x = -1$. To find the *y*-value, we substitute -1 for *x* in the equation

$y = -x + 3$

$y = -(-1) + 3$

$y = 1 + 3$

$y = 4$

Thus, the ordered pair is (−1, 4).

c. In this ordered pair the *y*-value is given, $y = 3$. To find the *x*-value, we substitute 3 for *y* in the equation

$y = -x + 3$

$3 = -x + 3$

$3 - 3 = -x$

$0 = -x$

$x = 0$

Thus, the ordered pair is (0, 3).

d. Again, the *y*-value is given, $y = 0$. To find the *x*-value, substitute 0 for *y* in the equation

$y = -x + 3$

$0 = -x + 3$

$-3 = -x$

$x = 3$

Thus, the ordered pair is (3, 0).

Example 5

Complete the table of values that satisfy the equation $2x + 3y = 5$. Write the results as ordered pairs.

x	y
1	
	−5
−2	

Solution

To complete the first ordered pair, substitute 1 for x in the equation to find the corresponding y-value.

$$2x+3y=5$$
$$2(1)+3y=5$$
$$2+3y=5$$
$$3y=5-2$$
$$3y=3$$
$$y=1$$

Thus, the first ordered pair is (1, 1).

To complete the second ordered pair, substitute –5 for y in the equation to find the corresponding x-value.

$$2x+3y=5$$
$$2x+3(-5)=5$$
$$2x-15=5$$
$$2x=5+15$$
$$2x=20$$
$$x=10$$

Thus, the second ordered pair is (10, –5).

To complete the third ordered pair, substitute –2 for x in the equation to find the corresponding y-value.

$$2x+3y=5$$
$$2(-2)+3y=5$$
$$-4+3y=5$$
$$3y=5+4$$
$$3y=9$$
$$y=3$$

Thus, the third ordered pair is (–2, 3). The table of values becomes

x	y
1	1
10	–5
–2	3

Example 6

Complete the table of values that satisfy the equation $x = -5$. Write the results as ordered pairs.

x	y
	3
	-5
	4

Solution

Since the x-value is always $x = -5$ for every value of y, to complete the ordered pairs, we can choose any values for y and the corresponding value for x is always $x = -5$.

In our case, if we choose $y = 3$, $y = -5$, and $y = 4$, the corresponding ordered pairs are $(-5, 3)$, $(-5, -5)$ and $(-5, 4)$, and the table of values becomes

x	y
-5	3
-5	-5
-5	4

Example 7

Complete the table of values that satisfy the equation $y = 4$.

x	y
0	
6	
-3	

Solution

Since the y-value is always $y = 4$ for every value of x, to complete the ordered pairs, we can choose any values for x and the corresponding value for y is always $y = 4$.

In our case, when we choose $x = 0$, $x = 6$, and $x = -3$ the corresponding ordered pairs are $(0, 4)$, $(6, 4)$, and $(-3, 4)$, and the table of values becomes

x	y
0	4
6	4
-3	4

3.1 EXERCISES

Determine whether the given ordered pair is a solution of the given equation.

1. $x + 3y = 5$ (2, 1)

2. $2x - y = 4$ (0, –4)

3. $3x + 2y = 7$ (1, 2)

4. $5x - 3y = 1$ (1, 1)

5. $4x - y = 3$ (–2, 3)

6. $5x + 2y = 10$ (4, –5)

7. $y = -6x$ (1, 6)

8. $x = 3y$ (1, 3)

9. $x + 5 = 0$ (–5, 2)

10. $y - 3 = 7$ (2, 10)

11. $y = \frac{1}{3}x + 4$ (0, 4)

12. $y = 4$ (4, 0)

13. $y = 1 - 5x$ (–1, 5)

14. $y = -\frac{2}{3}x$ (3, 2)

15. $2x + 3y - 1 = 0$ (1, –1)

Indicate the quadrant in which each point lies.

16. (3, –1)

17. (–4, 5)

18. (–1, –6)

19. (9, 11)

20. (–5, 3)

21. (4, –5)

22. (–8, –6)

23. (2, 7)

24. (15, –23)

Complete each ordered pair that satisfies the equation $3x - y = 1$.

25. (1,)

26. (, 5)

27. (0,)

28. (3,)

Complete each ordered pair for the equation $y = \frac{1}{2}x - 3$.

29. (2,)

30. (, 4)

31. (–4,)

32. (, –5)

Complete each table of values. Write the results as ordered pairs.

33. $2x + 4y = 8$

x	y
4	
	1
–2	

34. $x - 3y = 6$

x	y
–3	
	0
9	

35. $5x - y = 10$

x	y
	5
−2	
	0

36. $y = -\dfrac{2}{3}x + 1$

x	y
3	
	−3
0	

37. $y = \dfrac{3}{4}x - 2$

x	y
−4	
	1
0	

38. $x = 2y - 1$

x	y
	−3
5	
	2

39. $x = 3$

x	y
	5
	−8
	3

40. $y = -5$

x	y
−1	
0	
8	

41. $x + 1 = 0$

x	y
	4
	0
	−2

Plot each ordered pair in a rectangular coordinate system.

42. $(1, -3)$

43. $(-2, 4)$

44. $(-3, -2)$

45. $(2, 1)$

46. $(0, 2)$

47. $(-4, 0)$

48. $\left(\dfrac{1}{2}, 3\right)$

49. $\left(-\dfrac{3}{2}, -2\right)$

50. List the ordered pair corresponding to the points labeled A, B, C, D, E in the figure.

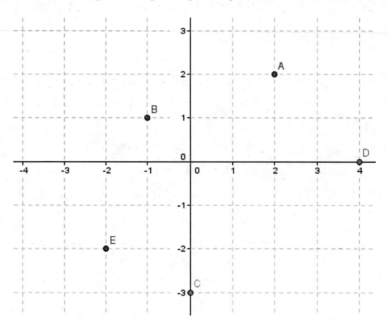

3.2 GRAPHING LINEAR EQUATIONS IN TWO VARIABLES

□ **Graphing Linear Equations by Plotting Points** □ **Graphing Linear Equations by Using the *X*- and *Y*-Intercepts**

The following are examples of linear equations in two variables:

$2x + 3y = 6, 5x + 6y = 30, 4x - y = 8, y = 3x - 1$

Definition

*A **linear equation** in two variables is an equation that can be written in the form ax + by = c where a, b, and c are real numbers and a and b are not both zero.*

The form $ax + by = c$ is referred to as *the standard form* of a linear equation in two variables. A solution to a linear equation in two variables x and y is an ordered pair of the form (x, y).

Regardless what variables are involved in a linear equation in two variables, the ordered pair corresponding to a solution is always written in alphabetical order: $(x, y), (a, b), (m, n), (p, q)$, etc.

We can choose any real number as a value for x or y, and then use the equation to find the corresponding value for y or x to generate as many ordered pairs as we desire.

Thus, a linear equation in two variables has an infinite number of solutions (ordered pairs). All the points in the plane corresponding to the solutions of a linear equation are located on a straight line.

Hence, the graph of a linear equation in two variables is a straight line.

In this section, we will discuss two ways used to graph a linear equation in two variables: graphing by plotting points and graphing by using the x- and y-intercepts.

□ GRAPHING LINEAR EQUATIONS BY PLOTTING POINTS

Graphing equations by plotting points is a very common method to graph linear equations and other basic nonlinear equations. First, we have to decide how many points are necessary to graph the line corresponding to a linear equation?

Since there are an infinite number of lines passing through a given point, we conclude that one point is not enough to graph the line corresponding to a linear equation in two variables. However, two distinct points determine a unique line. Therefore, to graph a linear equation in two variables we need at least two points corresponding to two distinct ordered pair solutions of the equation.

Usually, this can be accomplished by choosing two convenient (small and easy to plot) values for x and then substituting those values into the equation to find the corresponding values for *y.* Then, plot the points on a rectangular coordinate system, and draw a straight line passing through these points to obtain the graph.

Example 1

Graph.

$$y = 2x$$

Solution

We need two ordered pair solutions of the equation $y = 2x$.

First, we select two arbitrary values for x, and then substitute these values into $y = 2x$ to find the corresponding values for y. If we let $x = 0$, then $y = 2(0) = 0$.

The resulting ordered pair is $(0, 0)$.

If $x = 1$, then $y = 2(1) = 2$, gives the second ordered pair $(1, 2)$.

The values of x and y can be organized in a vertical table of values as shown below. Next, plot these two ordered pairs on a rectangular coordinate system, and draw a straight line through the corresponding points to obtain the graph of $y = 2x$.

Note: We can also choose arbitrary values for y, and then use the equation to find the corresponding values for x.

x	y
0	0
1	2

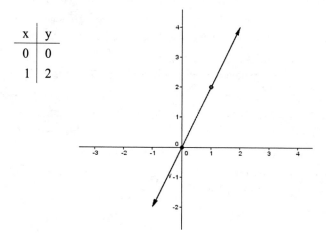

Example 2

Graph.

$$y = 3x - 1$$

Solution

We need two ordered pairs that satisfy the equation $y = 3x - 1$.

If $x = 0$, then $y = 3(0) - 1 = -1$.

If $x = 1$, then $y = 3(1) - 1 = 3 - 1 = 2$.

The results can be organized in a table of values as shown below. Then, plot the ordered pairs on the same rectangular coordinate system, and draw a straight line through these two points to obtain the graph of the equation $y = 3x - 1$.

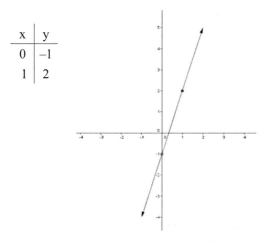

x	y
0	−1
1	2

Example 3

Graph.

$$x + 2y = 4$$

Solution

First, we solve the equation for y, and then we select two ordered pairs that satisfy the equation.

$$x + 2y = 4$$

$$2y = -x + 4$$

$$\frac{2y}{2} = \frac{-x}{2} + \frac{4}{2}$$

$$y = -\frac{1}{2}x + 2$$

To obtain integer values for y (avoid fractions) we select values for x that are multiples of 2 such as: 0, 2, −2, etc.

If $x = 0$, then $y = -\dfrac{1}{2}(0) + 2 = 0 + 2 = 2$.

If $x = 2$, then $y = -\dfrac{1}{2}(2) + 2 = -1 + 2 = 1$.

The results can be organized in a table of values as follows:

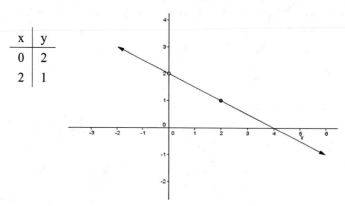

x	y
0	2
2	1

☐ GRAPHING LINEAR EQUATIONS BY USING THE *X*- AND *Y*-INTERCEPTS

So far, we can graph a linear equation in two variables by plotting two convenient random points. Another way to graph a linear equation is by choosing two special points, the *x*-intercept and the *y*-intercept.

> The ***x*-intercept** *(horizontal intercept) is the point where the graph crosses the x-axis and the **y-intercept** (vertical intercept) is the point where the graph crosses the y-axis.*

Since any point located on the *x*-axis has the *y*-coordinate zero, to find the *x*-intercept we set $y = 0$.

Also, any point located on the *y*-axis has the *x*-coordinate zero. Therefore, to find the *y*-intercept, set $x = 0$.

Example 4

Find the *x*- and *y*-intercepts and graph.

$$2x + 3y = 6$$

Solution

a. *x*-intercepts ($y = 0$):

$$2x + 3y = 6$$

$$2x + 3(0) = 6$$

$$2x = 6$$

$$x = 3$$

Thus, the x-intercept is: (3, 0)

b. *y*-intercept ($x = 0$):

$2x + 3y = 6$

$2(0) + 3y = 6$

$3y = 6$

$y = 2$

Thus, the *y*-intercept is: $(0, 2)$

To graph $2x + 3y = 6$, plot the points corresponding to the ordered pairs $(3, 0)$ and $(0, 2)$ and draw a straight line through those two points.

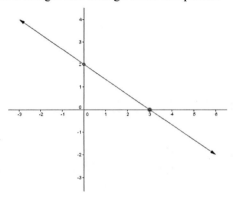

Example 5

Find the *x*- and *y*-intercepts and graph.

$x + 2y = 4$

Solution

a. *x*-intercept ($y = 0$):

$x + 2y = 4$

$x + 4(0) = 4$

$x = 4$

Thus, the *x*-intercept is: $(4, 0)$

b. *y*-intercept ($x = 0$):

$x + 2y = 4$

$0 + 2y = 4$

$2y = 4$

$y = 2$

Thus, the *y*-intercept is: $(0, 2)$

To graph $x + 2y = 4$, plot the points corresponding to (4, 0) and (0, 2) and draw the line passing through those two points.

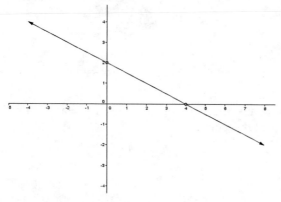

Example 6

Find the x-and y-intercepts and graph.

$$y = \frac{1}{2}x + 2$$

Solution

a. x-intercept ($y = 0$):

$$y = \frac{1}{2}x + 2$$

$$0 = \frac{1}{2}x + 2$$

$$-2 = \frac{1}{2}x \qquad \text{Multiply both sides by 2}$$

$$-2(2) = 2 \cdot \frac{1}{2}x$$

$$-4 = x$$

Therefore, the x-intercept is: $(-4, 0)$

b. y-intercept ($x = 0$):

$$y = \frac{1}{2}x + 2$$

$$y = \frac{1}{2}(0) + 2$$

$$y = 2$$

Therefore, the y-intercept is: (0, 2)

To graph $y = \dfrac{1}{2}x + 2$, plot the points corresponding to (−4, 0) and (0, 2) and draw the line through those two points.

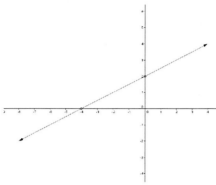

Example 7
_____

Find the *x*- and *y*-intercepts and graph. $3x - y = 0$.

Solution

a. *x*-intercept ($y = 0$):

$3x - y = 0$

$3x - 0 = 0$

$3x = 0$

$x = 0$

Thus, the *x*-intercept is: (0, 0)

b. *y*-intercept ($x = 0$):

$3x - y = 0$

$3(0) - y = 0$

$-y = 0$

$y = 0$

Thus, the *y*-intercept is: (0, 0)

Since the *x*- and *y*-intercept is the same point, and one point is not enough to graph the line we need one more order pair. If we let $x = 1$ for instance, the corresponding value for *y* is:

$3(1) - y = 0$

$3 - y = 0$

$3 = y$

So, the second ordered pair is: (1, 3). To graph $3x - y = 0$, plot the points corresponding to (0, 0) and (1, 3) and draw the line passing through those two points.

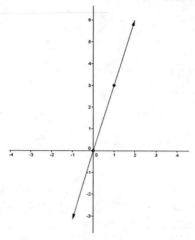

We know from the definition of a linear equation in two variables that a can be zero or b can be zero, but a and b cannot both be zero.

Case 1

If $a = 0$, the equation $ax + by = c$ becomes $0x + by = c$ or $by = c$.

Example 8

Graph.

$y = 2$, ($b = 1$, and $c = 2$)

Solution

To find two ordered pairs that are solutions of $y = 2$, we can choose any values for x, and the value of y is always 2. For example: (0, 2), (1, 2), (2, 2), etc.

The table of values and the graph are shown below.

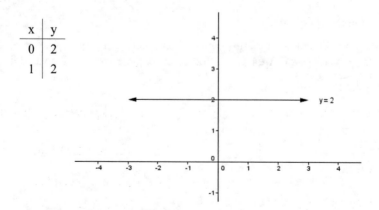

x	y
0	2
1	2

The graph of $y = 2$ is a horizontal line with the y-intercept (0,2).

Note: The graph of $y = k$ where k is a real number, is a horizontal line that intersects the y-axis at $(0, k)$. The horizontal line $y = 0$ is the x-axis.

Case 2

If $b = 0$, the equation $ax + by = c$ becomes $ax + 0y = c$, or $ax = c$.

Example 9

Graph

$$x = 3. \ (a = 1, \text{ and } c = 3)$$

Solution

When selecting ordered pairs that are solutions of $x = 3$, the value of x is always 3, regardless what values we choose for y. For example: (3, 0), (3, 1), (3, 2), etc.

The table of values and the graph are shown below.

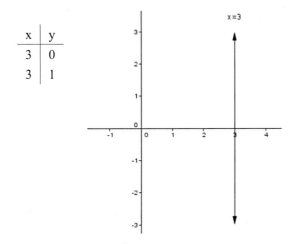

x	y
3	0
3	1

The graph of $x = 3$ is a vertical line with the x-intercept (3, 0).

Note: The graph of $x = k$, where k is a real number is a vertical line that intersects the x-axis at $(k, 0)$. The vertical line $x = 0$ is the y-axis.

3.2 EXERCISES

Complete the given ordered pairs. Then use the results to graph each equation by plotting the points.

1. $y = x$ (0,), (1,), (, −1)

2. $y = 2x$ (1,), (−1,), (,0)

3. $y = -\frac{1}{2}x$ (0,), (2,), (, 1)

4. $y = -x$ (0,), (−2,), (,1)

5. $y = 3x$ (−1,), (0,), (,3)

6. $y = \frac{1}{3}x$ (3,), (−3,), (,0)

7. $y = 2x - 1$ (0,), (1,), (,3)

8. $y = -3x + 1$ (0,), (1,), (, −2)

9. $y = \dfrac{3}{2}x - 1$ (2,), (0,), (,5)

10. $y = \dfrac{1}{2}x - 1$ (2,), (0,), (,1)

11. $2x - y = 4$ (1,), (2,), (,2)

12. $-x + 4y = 4$ (0,), (4,), (,0)

Graph each linear equation by plotting points.

13. $y = x - 2$

14. $y = -x + 5$

15. $y = x + 4$

16. $y = 3x - 1$

17. $y = 2x - 3$

18. $y = -4x + 2$

19. $y = 5x - 3$

20. $y = -3x + 2$

21. $y = -2x + 4$

22. $y = -\dfrac{2}{3}x + 4$

23. $y = \dfrac{3}{4}x - 2$

24. $y = \dfrac{1}{4}x + 2$

25. $y = -\dfrac{2}{5}x + 4$

26. $y = \dfrac{3}{2}x - 4$

27. $y = \dfrac{3}{5}x - 4$

28. $3x + 2y = -4$

29. $4x - 3y = 6$

30. $x + 2y = 4$

31. $3x + 4y = 8$

32. $5x - 2y = 4$

33. $6x + 3y = 12$

34. $5x - 3y = 15$

35. $x + 4y = 8$

36. $x = 3$

37. $x = -2$

38. $y = 2$

39. $y = -1$

Find the x- and y-intercepts and graph.

40. $x + y = 3$

41. $x - y = 2$

42. $x - 3y = 6$

43. $3x - 2y = 6$

44. $x - 2y = 4$

45. $5x + 2y = 10$

46. $20x - 50y = 100$

47. $4x + 5y = 20$

48. $2x + y = -4$

49. $0.2x - 0.3y = 0.6$

50. $3x + 4y = 12$

51. $3x - 5y = 15$

52. $6x - 9y = 18$

53. $40x + 30y = 120$

54. $0.5x + 0.2y = 1$

55. $4x - 3y = 12$

56. $x + 4y = 4$

57. $5x - y = 5$

58. $3x + y = 6$

59. $3x - y = 3$

60. $25x - 50y = 50$

61. $5x - 2y = -10$

62. $x + 2y = 4$

63. $3x + y = 6$

64. $2x + 4y = 8$

65. $4x - 2y = -8$

66. $3x + 2y = 6$

3.3 THE SLOPE OF A LINE

The slope of a line is a number that represents the measure of the **steepness** or the **slant** of a line. To find the slope of a line passing through $A(x_1, y_1)$ and $B(x_2, y_2)$ we compare the change in x and y values while moving along the line from A to B.

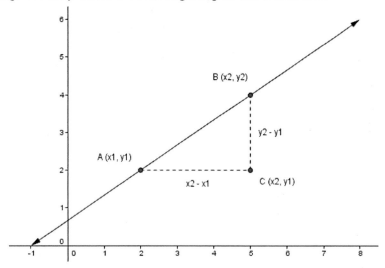

Definition

The **slope** of the line passing through $A(x_1, y_1)$ and $B(x_2 y_2)$ is defined by Slope $= m =$
$\dfrac{y_2 - y_1}{x_2 - x_1} = \dfrac{change..in..y}{change..in..x} = \dfrac{rise}{run}, (x_1 \neq x_2).$

Note: To find the slope of a line, we can use any two distinct points on the line.

Example 1

Find the slope of the line passing through $A(1,3)$ and $B(2,5)$. Then, graph the line.

Solution

If we label the coordinates of A: $x_1 = 1$ and $y_1 = 3$, and the coordinates of B: $x_2 = 2$ and $y_2 = 5$, the slope of the line is

$$m = \frac{y_2 - y_1}{x_2 - x_1} = \frac{5-3}{2-1} = \frac{2}{1} = 2$$

If we label the coordinates of A: $x_2 = 1$ and $y_2 = 3$, and the coordinates of B: $x_1 = 2$ and $y_1 = 5$ the slope of the line is

$$m = \frac{y_2 - y_1}{x_2 - x_1} = \frac{3-5}{1-2} = \frac{-2}{-1} = 2$$

Note: The slope of the line through any two points is the same regardless which point is labeled (x_1, y_1) and which one is labeled (x_2, y_2).

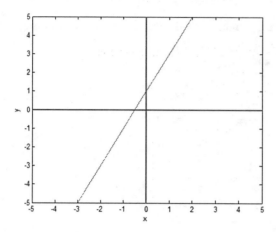

Example 2

Find the slope of the line through $A(-2,1)$ and $B(-3,3)$. Then, graph the line.

Solution

Let $x_1 = -2$, $y_1 = 1$, $x_2 = -3$ and $y_2 = 3$. The slope of the line is

$$m = \frac{y_2 - y_1}{x_2 - x_1} = \frac{3-1}{-3-(-2)} = \frac{2}{-3+2} = \frac{2}{-1} = -2$$

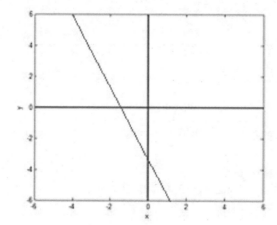

Example 3

___

Find the slope of the line through $P(-3,4)$ and $Q(3,4)$. Then, graph the line.

Solution

Let $x_1 = -3$, $y_1 = 4$, $x_2 = 3$, and $y_2 = 4$. The slope of the line is

$$m = \frac{y_2 - y_1}{x_2 - x_1} = \frac{4-4}{3-(-3)} = \frac{0}{3+3} = \frac{0}{6} = 0$$

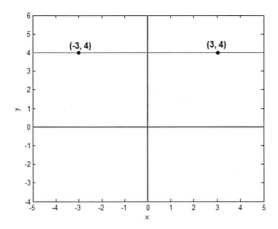

Example 4

___

Find the slope of the line through $P(2,-3)$ and $Q(2,-4)$. Then, graph the line.

Solution

Let $x_1 = 2$, $y_1 = -3$, $x_2 = 2$, and $y_2 = -4$. The slope of the line is

$$m = \frac{y_2 - y_1}{x_2 - x_1} = \frac{-4-(-3)}{2-2} = \frac{-4+3}{0} = \frac{-1}{0} = undefined$$

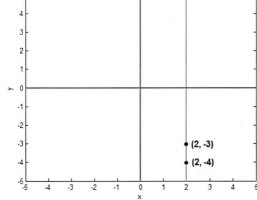

We can use examples 1 through 4 to classify the slopes of lines as follows:

a. *Positive Slope* (the line is slanted upward to the right).

b. *Negative Slope* (the line is slanted downward to the right).

c. *Zero Slope* (the line is horizontal).

d. *"No slope" or Undefined Slope* (the line is vertical).

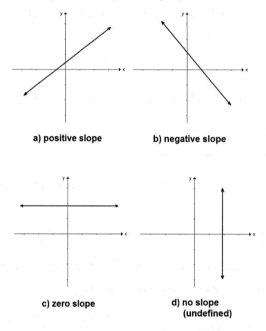

a) positive slope   b) negative slope

c) zero slope   d) no slope (undefined)

Example 5

Find the slope of each line.

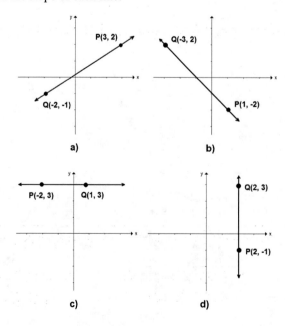

a)

b)

c)

d)

Solution

a. The coordinates of P are (3, 2), and the coordinates of Q are (−2, −1). Thus, the slope of the line is:

$$m = \frac{y_2 - y_1}{x_2 - x_1} = \frac{-1-2}{-2-3} = \frac{-3}{-5} = \frac{3}{5}$$

b. The coordinates of P are (1, −2), and the coordinates of Q are (−3, 2). So, the slope of the line is:

$$m = \frac{y_2 - y_1}{x_2 - x_1} = \frac{2+2}{-3-1} = \frac{4}{-4} = -1$$

c. The coordinates of P are (−2, 3), and the coordinates of Q are (1, 3). Thus, the slope of the line is:

$$m = \frac{y_2 - y_1}{x_2 - x_1} = \frac{3-3}{1+2} = \frac{0}{3} = 0$$

d. The coordinates of P are (2, −1), and the coordinates of Q are (2, 3). Thus, the slope of the line is:

$$m = \frac{y_2 - y_1}{x_2 - x_1} = \frac{3+1}{2-2} = \frac{4}{0} = \text{undefined}$$

Note: Two lines that lie in the same plane and do not intersect are called parallel lines.

a. If two lines are parallel they have the same slopes. $m_1 = m_2$

b. If two lines are perpendicular, their slopes are opposite reciprocal. $m_2 = m_2 = -\frac{1}{m_1}$ or $m_1 \cdot m_2 = -1$

Example 6
___

Determine whether the lines through the given pairs of points are parallel, perpendicular or neither.

a. L_1: (2, 5) and (3, 4)
   L_2: (6, −8) and (5, −7)

b. L_1: (6, −3) and (4, 5)
   L_2: (−2, 6) and (2, 7)

c. L_1: (4,7) and (−1, 8)
   L_2: (1, 6) and (3, 4)

Solution

In each case, find the slope of each line and compare the slopes.

a. $m_1 = \dfrac{y_2 - y_1}{x_2 - x_1} = \dfrac{4-5}{3-2} = \dfrac{-1}{1} = -1$

$m_2 = \dfrac{y_2 - y_1}{x_2 - x_1} = \dfrac{-7-(-8)}{5-6} = \dfrac{-7+8}{-1} = \dfrac{1}{-1} = -1$

Since the slopes $m_1 = m_2 = -1$, the lines are parallel.

b. $m_1 = \dfrac{y_2 - y_1}{x_2 - x_1} = \dfrac{5-(-3)}{4-6} = \dfrac{5+3}{-2} = \dfrac{8}{-2} = -4$

$m_2 = \dfrac{y_2 - y_1}{x_2 - x_1} = \dfrac{7-6}{2-(-2)} = \dfrac{1}{2+2} = \dfrac{1}{4}$

Since $m_2 = -\dfrac{1}{m_1}$, the lines are perpendicular.

c. $m_1 = \dfrac{y_2 - y_1}{x_2 - x_1} = \dfrac{8-7}{-1-4} = \dfrac{1}{-5} = -\dfrac{1}{5}$

$m_2 = \dfrac{y_2 - y_1}{x_2 - x_1} = \dfrac{4-6}{3-1} = \dfrac{-2}{2} = -1$

Since $m_1 \neq m_2$ and $m_2 \neq -\dfrac{1}{m_1}$, the lines are neither parallel nor perpendicular.

Example 7

Sketch the graph of a line through the point $(0, -3)$ having the slope $m = 0$.

Solution

Since the slope $m = 0$, this is a horizontal line with the y-intercept $(0, -3)$.

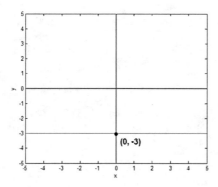

Example 8

Sketch the graph of a line through the point (1, 2) having the slope $m = 0$.

Solution

Since the slope $m = 0$, this is a horizontal line passing through (1, 2).

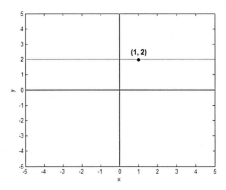

Example 9

Sketch the graph of a line through (2, 3) having the slope m undefined.

Solution

Since the slope m is undefined, this is a vertical line passing through (2, 3).

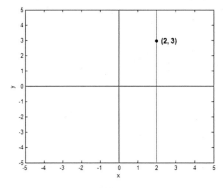

Example 10

Sketch the graph of a line through the point (1, 2) having the slope $m = \dfrac{1}{2}$.

Solution

To graph the line we need two points. Since only one point (1, 2) is given, we use the slope to find the second point.

$$m = \frac{1}{2} = \frac{change..in..y}{change..in..x}$$

Starting from the given point (1, 2), change the y-coordinate by moving 1 unit up parallel to y-axis, and change the x-coordinate by moving 2 units to the right, parallel to the x-axis.

The second point will have the coordinates (3, 3). Draw the line through (1, 2) and (3, 3) to obtain the graph.

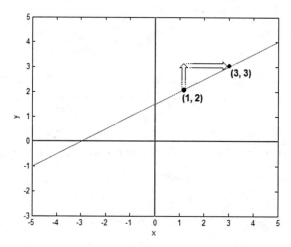

Example 11

Sketch the graph of a line through (–3, 3) having the slope $m = -\dfrac{2}{3}$.

Solution

Again, we use the slope to find the second point.

$$m = \frac{change..in..y}{change..in..x} = -\frac{2}{3} = \frac{-2}{3} = \frac{2}{-3}$$

Thus, we can use the negative sign for the change in y or change in x but not for both to obtain the second point. Since either one will give us the same line, let's use $m = \dfrac{-2}{3}$.

Starting from the given point (–3, 3), change the y-coordinate 2 units down parallel to the y-axis, and change the x-coordinate 3 units to the right, parallel to x-axis.

The second point will have the coordinates (0, 1). Draw the line through (–3, 3) and (0, 1) to obtain the graph.

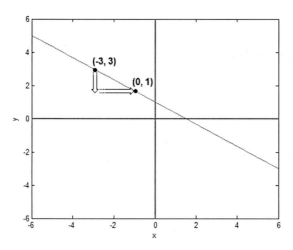

Example 12

Use the slope formula to find b if the line through (3, 5) and (–4, b) has the slope $m = \dfrac{4}{7}$.

Solution

First, use the slope formula to find the slope of the line passing through the given points. Then, substitute $\dfrac{4}{7}$ for m and solve the equation for b.

$$m = \frac{y_2 - y_1}{x_2 - x_1}$$

$$\frac{4}{7} = \frac{b-5}{-4-3}$$

$$\frac{4}{7} = \frac{b-5}{-7}$$ Multiply both sides by –7

$$(-7) \cdot \frac{4}{7} = (-7) \cdot \frac{b-5}{-7}$$

$$-4 = b - 5$$ Solve for b

$$-4 + 5 = b$$

$$b = 1$$

Example 13

Use the slope formula to find *a* if the line through (1, 4) and (*a*, 6) has the slope $m = \dfrac{2}{3}$.

Solution

First, use the slope formula to find the slope of the line passing through the given points. Then, substitute $\dfrac{2}{3}$ for *m* and solve the equation for *a*.

$$m = \frac{y_2 - y_1}{x_2 - x_1} \qquad\qquad \frac{2}{3} = \frac{6-4}{a-1} \qquad\qquad \frac{2}{3} = \frac{2}{a-1}$$

$$2(a - 1) = 2 \cdot 3 \qquad \text{Divide both sides by 2}$$

$$a - 1 = 3 \qquad\qquad \text{Solve for } a$$

$$a = 3 + 1$$

$$a = 4$$

3.3 EXERCISES

Find the slope of the line through the given points.

1. (4, 5) and (3, 7)

2. (–2, 3) and (3, 6)

3. (1, –3) and (–4, –7)

4. (5, 4) and (3, 8)

5. (–7, 3) and (2, –8)

6. (2, 5) and (4, 5)

7. (–3, –6) and (–1, –9)

8. (5, 6) and (5, –2)

9. (–8, –4) and (–8, 1)

10. (2, –4) and (0, 1)

11. (6, –5) and (–5, –5)

12. (3, 5) and (–6, 4)

13. $(1, \frac{1}{2})$ and $(4, -\frac{3}{2})$

14. $(\frac{4}{3}, 2)$ and $(\frac{5}{3}, 4)$

15. $(3, \frac{1}{4})$ and $(-\frac{1}{3}, -2)$

Use the indicated points to find the slope of each line.

16.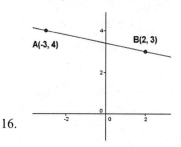

17.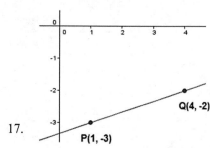

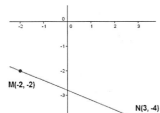

18.

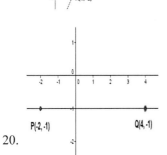

19.

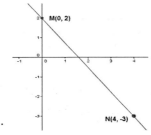

21.

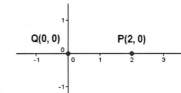

22.

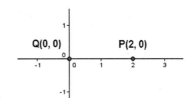

23.

20.

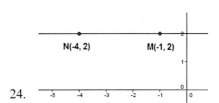

24.

Determine whether the lines through the given pairs of points are parallel, perpendicular or neither.

25. L_1: (2, 3) and (1, 4)

  L_2: (−1, 6) and (3, 10)

26. L_1: (−4, 5) and (2, −1)

  L_2: (3, 5) and (4, 4)

27. L_1: (−3, −2) and (5, 7)

  L_2: (1, 4) and (−2, −6)

28. L_1: (6, 4) and (−3, 4)

  L_2: (2, 8) and (2, −1)

29. L_1: (5, 6) and (5, −8)

  L_2: (−3, 2) and (4, 2)

30. L_1: (7, 1) and (3, 4)

  L_2: (2, 5) and (10, 2)

Graph the line with the given slope, passing through the given point.

31. Through (−1, 2) with $m = \dfrac{1}{2}$

32. Through $(2, 3)$ with $m = -\dfrac{2}{3}$

33. Through $(-3, 4)$ with $m = -3$

34. Through $(1, 4)$ with $m = 2$

35. Through $(0, 3)$ with $m = 0$

36. Through $(1, 2)$ with m undefined

37. Through $(4, 1)$ with m undefined

38. Through $(-2, 3)$ with $m = 0$

39. Through $(3, -1)$ with $m = -\dfrac{3}{2}$

40. Through $(-2, 1)$ with $m = \dfrac{1}{4}$

Use the slope formula to find the unknown coordinate such that the line through the points has the given slope.

41. $(2, 5)$ and $(4, y)$ slope $m = -2$

42. $(1, 6)$ and $(3, y)$ slope $m = -1$

43. $(5, -2)$ and $(1, y)$ slope $m = -\dfrac{5}{4}$

44. $(3, 4)$ and $(1, y)$ slope $m = -\dfrac{1}{2}$

45. $(6, 2)$ and $(x, 4)$ slope $m = -\dfrac{2}{3}$

46. $(-1, 4)$ and $(x, 7)$ slope $m = \dfrac{1}{2}$

47. $(3, -5)$ and $(x, 2)$ slope $m = \dfrac{7}{2}$

48. $(2, 1)$ and $(x, -4)$ slope $m = -\dfrac{5}{2}$

49. If the line that contains the points $(1, 5)$ and $(2, -3)$ is parallel to the line that contains the points $(2, 4)$ and $(x, -4)$, find x.

50. If the line that contains the points $(4, -5)$ and $(7, -1)$ is parallel to the line that contains the points $(2, 1)$ and $(5, y)$, find y.

51. If the line that contains the points $(3, 2)$ and $(-1, 4)$ is perpendicular to the line that contains the points $(4, -5)$ and $(x, 5)$, find x.

52. If the line that contains the points $(7, 1)$ and $(3, 2)$ is perpendicular to the line that contains the points $(1, 3)$ and $(5, y)$, find y.

53. A ladder leans against a wall and reaches a height of 8 ft. If the base of the ladder is 3 ft from the wall, find the slope of the ladder.

54. A ramp for disabled requires a horizontal run of 6 ft for every vertical rise of 6 in. Find the grade of the ramp.

3.4 EQUATIONS OF LINES

☐ **The Point-Slope Form of an Equation of a Line** ☐ **The Slope-Intercept Form of an Equation of a Line** ☐ **Equations of Lines**

If the equation of a line is given, we can find the slope of the line, x- and y-intercepts, and we can graph the line. In this section, our goal is to find the equation of a line given some information about the line.

☐ THE POINT-SLOPE FORM OF AN EQUATION OF A LINE

Objective: Find an equation of a line when a **point** on the line and the **slope** of the line is given.

Consider a nonvertical line passing through the *point* $P(x_1, y_1)$ that has a slope of m.

Our goal is to use the slope formula to find the equation of the line. To use the slope formula, we need two distinct points on the line.

Since only one point $P(x_1, y_1)$ is given, let $Q(x, y)$ be an arbitrary point on the line other than $P(x_1, y_1)$. Then, the slope of the line through the fixed point $P(x_1, y_1)$ and arbitrary point $Q(x, y)$ is given by the slope formula:

$$m = \frac{y - y_1}{x - x_1}$$

Multiply both sides of the equation by $(x - x_1)$.

$$m(x - x_1) = \frac{y - y_1}{x - x_1}(x - x_1)$$

Simplify.

$$m(x - x_1) = y - y_1 \text{ or}$$

$$y - y_1 = m(x - x_1)$$

which is the equation of a line in **point-slope form**.

Thus, the **equation of a line** passing through a point $P(x_1, y_1)$ with the slope m is given by

$$y - y_1 = m(x - x_1)$$

Example 1

Write an equation of the line through the point $P(2,5)$ with the slope $m = 3$.

Solution

Since we are given a point with the coordinates $(x_1, y_1) = (2,5)$ on the line and the slope of the line is $m = 3$, we can use the point-slope formula to find an equation of the line.

$$y - y_1 = m(x - x_1)$$

Substitute 2 for x_1, 5 for y_1, 3 for m, and solve for y.

$$y - 5 = 3(x - 2)$$

$$y - 5 = 3x - 6$$

$$y = 3x - 6 + 5$$

$$y = 3x - 1 \text{ (an equation of the line)}$$

Example 2

Write an equation of the line through the point $P(-3,1)$ with the slope $m = \dfrac{2}{3}$.

Solution

Substituting $(x_1, y_1) = (-3,1)$ and $m = \dfrac{2}{3}$ into the point-slope form we have:

$$y - y_1 = m(x - x_1)$$

$$y - 1 = \frac{2}{3}[x - (-3)]$$

$$y - 1 = \frac{2}{3}(x + 3)$$

$$y - 1 = \frac{2}{3}x + \frac{2}{3} \cdot 3$$

$$y - 1 = \frac{2}{3}x + 2$$

$$y = \frac{2}{3}x + 2 + 1$$

$$y = \frac{2}{3}x + 3$$

☐ THE SLOPE-INTERCEPT FORM OF AN EQUATION OF A LINE

Objective: Find an equation of a line when the **y-intercept** and the **slope** of the line is given.

Consider a nonvertical line with the **y-intercept** $P(0, b)$ and **slope** m.

Since the y-intercept $P(0, b)$ is a point on the line, and the slope m is given, we can use the point-slope formula to find an equation of the line.

$$y - y_1 = m(x - x_1)$$

Substitute $(x_1, y_1) = (0, b)$ into the formula and solve for y.

$$y - b = m(x - 0)$$

$$y - b = mx$$

$$y = mx + b$$

which is the equation of a line in **slope-intercept form.**

Thus, the **equation of line** with the y-intercept $P(0, b)$ and slope m is given by

$$y = mx + b$$

Example 3

Write an equation of the line with the y-intercept $P(0, 8)$ and slope $m = -\dfrac{2}{5}$.

Solution

Since the y-intercept $P(0, 8)$ and slope $m = -\dfrac{2}{5}$ is given, we can use the slope-intercept formula $y = mx + b$ with $(0, b) = (0, 8)$ and $m = -\dfrac{2}{5}$ to write an equation of the line.

$$y = mx + b$$

Substituting 8 for b and $m = -\dfrac{2}{5}$ into the slope-intercept formula, we have:

$$y = -\dfrac{2}{5}x + 8$$

Example 4

Write an equation of the line with the y-intercept $P(0, 0)$ and slope $m = 3$.

Solution

Since the y-intercept $P(0, 0)$ and slope $m = 3$ is given, we can use the slope-intercept formula to write an equation of the line.

$$y = mx + b$$

Substituting 0 for b and $m = 3$ into the slope-intercept formula, we have:

$$y = 3x + 0$$

$$y = 3x$$

Example 5

Find the slope and y-intercept of the line $x - 2y = 4$, and use them to graph the line.

Solution

To find the slope and y-intercept of the line $x - 2y = 4$, solve for y to rewrite the equation in slope-intercept form $y = mx + b$ where m is the slope and $(0, b)$ is the y-intercept.

$$x - 2y = 4$$

$$-2y = -x + 4$$

$$\frac{-2y}{-2} = \frac{-x}{-2} + \frac{4}{-2}$$

$$y = \frac{1}{2}x - 2$$

Thus, the slope of the line is $m = \dfrac{1}{2}$, and the y-intercept is $(0, -2)$.

To graph the line we need two points. First, we plot the y-intercept $(0, -2)$, and then we use the slope $m = \dfrac{1}{2}$ to find a second point. Since the change in y is positive 1 unit and the change in x is positive 2 units, start from $(0, -2)$ and move 1 unit up parallel to y-axis and 2 units to the right parallel to the x-axis to find the second point $(2, -1)$.

Then, draw a straight line through $(0, -2)$ and $(2, -1)$ to obtain the graph of the line.

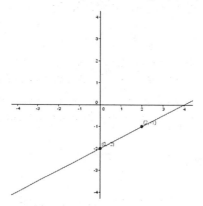

Note: The slope-intercept formula can be used to find an equation of a line even if the given point on the line is not the y-intercept.

Example 6

Use the slope-intercept formula to write an equation of the line through $P(-1, 5)$ with slope $m = -2$.

Solution

First, substitute $m = -2$ in the slope-intercept formula.

$$y = mx + b$$

$$y = -2x + b$$

Then, use the coordinates of $P(-1, 5)$ to find b. In other words, substitute 5 for y and -1 for x in $y = -2x + b$ to find b.

$$y = -2x + b$$

$$5 = -2(-1) + b$$

$$5 = 2 + b$$

$$5 - 2 = b$$

$$3 = b$$

Substitute 3 for b in $y = -2x + b$ to obtain the equation of the line.

$$y = -2x + 3$$

Note: Since $P(-1, 5)$ is not a y-intercept $(x \neq 0)$, do not substitute 5 for b in the slope-intercept formula.

Example 7

Write an equation of the line passing through the points $(2, 5)$ and $(3, -2)$.

Solution

To write the equation of a line we need a *point* on the line and the *slope* of the line. We can choose any one of the two points on the line. However, we don't have the slope of the line.

To find the slope of the line, we need two points on the line. Since two points on the line are given we can find the slope of the line and then use either one of the two points and the slope to write the equation of the line.

$$m = \frac{y_2 - y_1}{x_2 - x_1} = \frac{-2 - 5}{3 - 2} = \frac{-7}{1} = -7$$

Then, use for example the point $(2, 5)$ and $m = -7$ to write the equation of the line.

$$y = mx + b$$

$$y = -7x + b$$

Substitute 5 for y and 2 for x to find b.

$$5 = -7(2) + b$$

$$5 = -14 + b$$

$$5 + 14 = b$$

$$19 = b$$

Substitute 19 for b into $y = -7x + b$ to write the equation of the line.

$$y = -7x + 19$$

Example 8

Find an equation of the line with y-intercept $(0, 3)$ and x-intercept $(-2, 0)$.

Solution

Since the line contains two points $(0, 3)$ and $(-2, 0)$, we can find the slope of the line, and then use one point and the slope to write the equation of the line.

$$m = \frac{y_2 - y_1}{x_2 - x_1} = \frac{3 - 0}{0 - (-2)} = \frac{3}{2}$$

For this example, the y-intercept $(0, 3)$ is the best point to choose because we can use the slope-intercept formula $y = mx + b$ and we already know $b = 3$ and $m = \frac{3}{2}$.

$$y = mx + b$$

$$y = \frac{3}{2}x + 3$$

Example 9

Find an equation of the line passing through $A(3, -2)$ and parallel to the line $2x + y = 8$ (slope intercept form).

Solution

To write the equation of a line, we need a point on the line and the slope of the line. The point on the line $A(3, -2)$ is given, but we don't have the slope of the line yet. Since the lines are parallel, they have the same slope.

First, rewrite the original equation $2x + y = 8$ in slope-intercept form (solve for y) to find its slope, and then use this slope and the given point $A(3, -2)$ to write the equation of the line parallel to the original line.

$$2x + y = 8$$

Slope intercept form: $y = -2x + 8$ (slope $m = -2$)

The slope of the new line is the same as the slope of the original line, $m = -2$. Now, let's use the point-slope formula to write the equation of the line through $A(3, -2)$ with the slope $m = -2$.

$$y - y_1 = m(x - x_1)$$

$$y - (-2) = -2(x - 3)$$

$$y + 2 = -2x + 6$$

$$y = -2x + 6 - 2$$

$$y = -2x + 4$$

Example 10

Find an equation of the line passing through $(0, 3)$ and parallel to the x-axis.

Solution

Since the line is parallel to the x-axis, it's a horizontal line with the slope $m = 0$.

Now, use the slope-intercept formula to write the equation of the line with the y-intercept $(0, 3)$ and the slope $m = 0$.

$$y = mx + b$$

$$y = 0x + 3$$

$$y = 3$$

Example 11

Find an equation of the line passing through $B(-4, 2)$ and perpendicular to the line $x + 3y = 6$ (standard form).

Solution

First, rewrite the equation $x + 3y = 6$ in slope-intercept form (solve for y) to find the slope of the line.

$$3y = -x + 6$$

$$\frac{3y}{3} = \frac{-x}{3} + \frac{6}{3}$$

$$y = -\frac{1}{3}x + 2$$

The slope of this line is $m = -\dfrac{1}{3}$. A line perpendicular to the line $x + 3y = 6$ has the slope m = 3 (opposite reciprocal). Thus, an equation of the line through $B(-4, 2)$, perpendicular to the line $x + 3y = 6$, is

$$y - y_1 = m(x - x_1)$$

$$y - 2 = 3[x - (-4)]$$

$$y - 2 = 3(x + 4)$$

$$y - 2 = 3x + 12$$

$$y = 3x + 12 + 2$$

$$y = 3x + 14$$

Standard form: $-3x + y = 14$ or $3x - y = -14$ (ax + by = c)

□ EQUATIONS OF LINES

1. Equation of a line in point-slope form: $y - y_1 = m(x - x_1)$.
2. Equation of a line in slope-intercept form: $y = mx + b$.
3. Equation of a line in standard form: $ax + by = c$.
4. Equation of a horizontal line: $y = k$ (k = constant).
5. Equation of a vertical line: $x = k$ (k = constant).

3.4 EXERCISES

Use the point-slope form to write an equation of each line passing through the given point and having the given slope. Give the answer in slope-intercept form.

1. $(1, 3)$ $m = 2$
2. $(-4, 2)$ $m = 5$
3. 3. $(5, -1)$ $m = -3$
4. $(-3, -6)$ $m = -4$
5. $(-6, -1)$ $m = 3$
6. $(-2, 0)$ $m = -6$
7. $(4, 5)$ $m = -\dfrac{1}{2}$

8. $(-8, 3)$ $m = \dfrac{3}{4}$
9. $(2, -5)$ $m = \dfrac{5}{2}$
10. $(-4, -3)$ $m = -\dfrac{2}{3}$
11. $(-2, 5)$ m $= 0$
12. $(1, -2)$ $m = 0$

Use the slope-intercept form to write the equation of each line with the given y-intercept and having the given slope. Give the answer in standard form.

13. $(0, 2)$ $m = -3$
14. $(0, -3)$ $m = 6$
15. $(0, -5)$ $m = -2$
16. $(0, -9)$ $m = -\dfrac{2}{5}$
17. $(0, 7)$ $m = \dfrac{3}{2}$
18. $(0, 11)$ $m = -\dfrac{5}{7}$

19. $(0, \dfrac{1}{4})$ $m = \dfrac{4}{5}$
20. $(0, \dfrac{3}{4})$ m $= 0$
21. $(0, -\dfrac{2}{3})$ $m = 0$
22. $(0, 0)$ $m = -\dfrac{7}{8}$
23. $(0, -\dfrac{5}{6})$ $m = \dfrac{1}{6}$
24. $(0, -9)$ $m = -\dfrac{1}{2}$

Find the slope and y-intercept for each line, and use them to graph the line.

25. $2x - y = 1$
26. $x - y = 2$
27. $3x - 2y = 6$

28. $2x - 5y = 10$
29. $3x + 4y = 12$
30. $4x + y = 3$

31. $x = 2y + 6$ 34. $y = 3$

32. $x = -4y + 4$ 35. $y = -2$

33. $4x = 5y - 20$ 36. $y = 4x$

Write an equation for each line passing through the given points. Give the answer in slope-intercept form.

37. (3, 5) and (4, 8)   44. (-5, 0) and (0, -8)

38. (2, -4) and (6, 0)   45. (-6, -3) and (-2, 5)

39. (-1, 3) and (1, 7)   46. $\left(\dfrac{1}{2}, \dfrac{3}{4}\right)$ and $\left(\dfrac{3}{2}, \dfrac{1}{4}\right)$

40. (-3, -2) and (1, 6)

41. (-4, -5) and (-1, 5)   47. $\left(\dfrac{5}{6}, \dfrac{1}{6}\right)$ and $\left(-\dfrac{1}{6}, -\dfrac{5}{6}\right)$

42. (3, -4) and (0, 5)

43. (0, 3) and (4, 0)   48. $\left(-\dfrac{2}{3}, \dfrac{1}{5}\right)$ and $\left(\dfrac{1}{3}, \dfrac{6}{5}\right)$

49. Write an equation of the line passing through $A(-2, -4)$ and parallel to the line $3x + y = 5$ (standard form).

50. Write an equation of the line passing through $B(3, -1)$ and parallel to the line $4x - y = 1$ (slope-intercept form).

51. Write an equation of the line passing through $P(-1, -3)$ and perpendicular to the line $x + 2y = 6$ (slope intercept form).

52. Write an equation of the line passing through $Q(2, -5)$ and perpendicular to the line $2x - 3y = 6$ (standard form).

53. Write an equation of the line with the y-intercept $A(0, -2)$ and parallel to the line $4x + 2y = 8$ (standard form).

54. Write the equation of the line with the y-intercept $B(0, -3)$ and parallel to the line $5x + 3y = 3$ (slope intercept form).

55. Write an equation of the line passing through $M(-4, -3)$ and perpendicular to the line $4x + 3y = 12$ (slope intercept form).

56. Write an equation of the line passing through $N(-6, -4)$ and parallel to the line $x - 3y = 6$ (standard form).

57. Write an equation of the line passing through $P(2, -1)$ and parallel to the line with the x-intercept (1, 0) and y-intercept (0, -4).

58. Write an equation of the line passing through $Q(-1, 5)$ and perpendicular to the line with the x-intercept (-5, 0) and y-intercept (0, 1).

59. Write the equation of the line passing through $P(0, -1)$ and parallel to the x-axis.

60. Write the equation of the line passing through $Q(4, 0)$ parallel to the y-axis.

61. Write the equation of the line passing through $A(0, 8)$ and perpendicular to the y-axis.

62. Write the equation of the line passing through $B(-9, 0)$ and perpendicular to the x-axis.

3.5 GRAPHING LINEAR INEQUALITIES IN TWO VARIABLES

☐ **Graphing a Linear Inequality in Two Variables** ☐ **Alternative Method**

Examples of linear inequalities in two variables

a. $3x + y > 2$

b. $2x + 3y < 6$

c. $5x - 2y \le 10$

d. $x + y \ge 1$

> **Definition**
>
> *A **linear inequality in two variables** is an inequality that can be written in the form ax + by < c where a, b, and c are real numbers and a and b are not both zero.*

Note: The definition is true if the symbol < is replaced by any of the symbols >, ≥, or ≤.

A linear inequality in two variables is similar in form to a linear equation in two variables $ax + by = c$. A solution of a linear inequality is an ordered pair that satisfies the inequality.

Example 1

Graph.

$$y = -x + 1$$

Solution

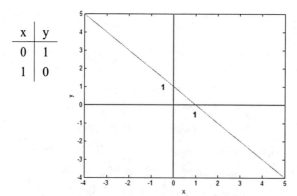

x	y
0	1
1	0

The line corresponding to $y = -x + 1$ divides the coordinate plane into three regions:

- The line itself
- The region above the line: upper half-plane
- The region below the line: lower half-plane

The graph of the equation $y = -x + 1$ represents the set of all points on the line (the line itself).

The graph of the inequality $y \le -x + 1$ represents the set of all points below the line and the points on the line.

This can be shown by drawing a solid line and shading the region below the line. The points on the line are part of the solution set because the inequality symbol includes the equal sign (less than or equal to). A solid line indicates that the line is part of the solution set.

Thus, any point located on the line or below the line belongs to the solution set. In other words, the coordinates of those points satisfies the inequality. For example, the origin is part of the solution set, and therefore (0, 0) should satisfy the inequality.

$$y \le -x + 1$$

$$0 \le -0 + 1$$

$$0 \le 1 \text{ True.}$$

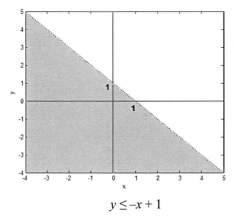

$$y \le -x + 1$$

The graph of the inequality $y < -x + 1$ represents the set of all points below the line.

Since the inequality symbol does not include the equal sign (less than), the points on the line are not part of the solution set. This can be shown by drawing a dashed line and shading the region below the line (lower half-plane).

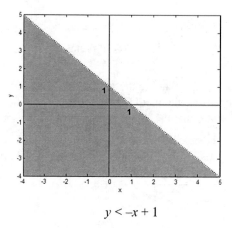

$$y < -x + 1$$

The graph of the inequality $y \geq -x + 1$ represents the set of all points above the line and the points on the line. The points on the line belong to the solution set because the inequality symbol includes the equal sign (greater than or equal to).

This can be shown by drawing a solid line and shading the region above the line (upper half-plane). Since the origin is not part of the solution set, $(0, 0)$ should not satisfy the inequality.

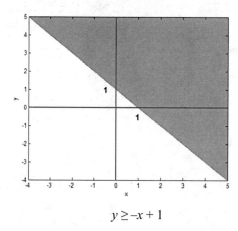

$$y \geq -x + 1$$

The graph of $y > -x + 1$ represents the set of all points above the line.

Since the inequality symbol does not include the equal sign (less than), the points on the line are not part of the solution set. This can be shown by drawing a dashed line and shading the region above the line (upper half-plane).

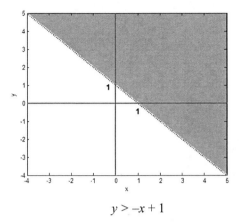

$$y > -x + 1$$

Note: The solution set of a linear inequality in two variables is an entire half-plane.

Let's summarize the steps used to graph a linear inequality in two variables.

☐ GRAPHING A LINEAR INEQUALITY IN TWO VARIABLES

Step 1 Solve the inequality for y.

- If $y > ax + b$ draw a dashed line and shade the region above the line.
- If $y < ax + b$ draw a dashed line and shade the region below the line.
- If $y \geq ax + b$ draw a solid line and shade the region above the line.
- If $y \leq ax + b$ draw a solid line and shade the region below the line.

Step 2 Graph the line.

$$(y = ax + b)$$

We can graph the line by plotting points, using x- and y-intercepts, or using the slope and y-intercept.

☐ ALTERNATIVE METHOD

First, graph an appropriate line (dashed or solid corresponding to the given inequality.

Then, use any point not on the line (usually the origin) as a test point. Substitute the coordinates of the point into the inequality. If a true statement results, shade the region containing the point. If a false statement results, shade the other region.

Example 1

Graph the linear inequality.

$$2x + y > 1$$

Solution

Step 1 Solve for y

$$y > -2x + 1$$

Since $y > ax + b$ we draw a dashed line and shade the region above the line.

Step 2 Graph the line $y = -2x + 1$

x	y
0	1
1	−1

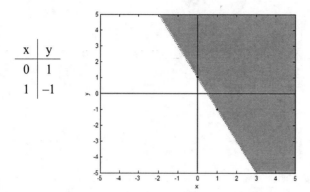

Example 2

Graph the linear inequality.

$$2x - 3y \geq 6$$

Solution

Step 1 Solve for y.

$$-3y \geq -2x + 6$$

$$\frac{-3y}{-3} \geq \frac{-2x}{-3} + \frac{6}{-3}$$

$$y \leq \frac{2}{3}x - 2$$

Since $y \leq ax + b$ we draw a solid line and shade the region below the line

Step 2 Graph the line

$$y = \frac{2}{3}x - 2$$

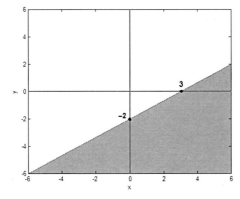

x	y
0	−2
3	0

Example 3

Graph the linear inequality.

$$x \geq -3y$$

Solution

Step 1 Solve for y

$$\frac{x}{-3} \geq \frac{-3y}{-3}$$

$$-\frac{1}{3}x \leq y \text{ or}$$

$$y \geq -\frac{1}{3}x$$

Since $y \geq ax + b$ we draw a solid line and shade the region above the line.

Step 2 Graph the line

$$y = -\frac{1}{3}x$$

x	y
0	0
3	−1

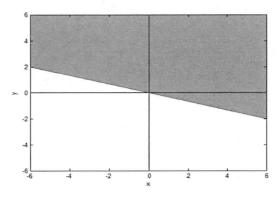

Example 4

Graph the linear inequality.

$x < 2$

Solution

For this example we cannot solve for y. The graph of $x = 2$ is a vertical line through $(2, 0)$. The points that satisfy the inequality $x < 2$ are located to the left of the line because any point lying in that region has the x-coordinate less than 2.

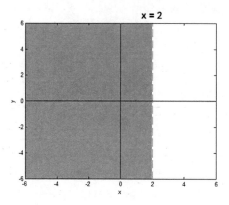

Example 5

Graph the linear inequality.

$y \geq -3$

Solution

The inequality is already solved for y. The graph of $y = -3$ is a horizontal line through $(0, -3)$. The points that satisfy the inequality $y \geq -3$ are located above the line because any point lying in that region has the y-coordinate greater than or equal to -3.

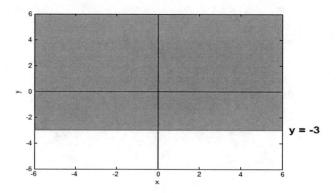

3.5 EXERCISES

Determine whether the given ordered pair is a solution of the given inequality.

1. $3x - y < 5$ (1, 2)
3. $4x - 3y \leq 12$ (4, 0)
5. $y < -3x$ (2, 6)

2. $2x + y \geq 3$ (1, 1)
4. $-x + 5y > 7$ (2, 1)

6. $y \geq \dfrac{2}{3}x$ (3, 4)

Graph each linear inequality.

7. $y > x + 3$
14. $x - y < -2$
23. $2x > 3y - 6$

8. $y \leq x - 2$
15. $3x - y < 5$

9. $y \leq \dfrac{1}{2}x$
16. $2x - y \geq 4$
24. $\dfrac{1}{2}x - \dfrac{1}{3}y \geq 1$

17. $x - 4y \leq 4$
25. $x > -2y$

10. $y \geq -x + 4$
18. $3x + 2y > 6$
26. $x \leq -3$

11. $y \leq -\dfrac{1}{3}x + 3$
19. $3x - 4y > 12$
27. $y < 2$

20. $-x + 5y > 5$
28. $-y + 2 < 0$

12. $y < -\dfrac{2}{5}x + 1$
21. $-x - 3y + 3 > 0$
29. $y - 6 \geq -7$

13. $x + y \geq 3$
22. $x < 2y + 4$
30. $x < 0$

3.6 INTRODUCTION TO FUNCTIONS

□ Relations □ Functions □ Evaluating Functions

□ RELATIONS

Examples of Relations:

a. {(1, 3), (2, 5), (7, 8), (7, 11), (15, 11)}

b. {(–1, 2), (–1, 3), (4, 5), (6, 7), (–6, 7)}

c. {(0, 4), (–2, –3), (3, –2), (8, 4)}

Definition

*A **relation** is any set of ordered pairs.*

Domain: The set of all x-coordinates in the set of ordered pairs of the form (x, y) that define a relation is called the domain of the relation.

Range: The set of all y-coordinates in the set of ordered pairs of the form (x, y) that define a relation is called the range of the relation.

For example, in the relation {(1, 3), (2, 5), (7, 8), (7, 11), (15, 11)} the domain and range are:

Domain: D = {1, 2, 7, 15}

Range: R = {3, 5, 8, 11}

Note: When writing the domain or range, repeated x- or y-coordinates are listed only once.

A diagram may be used for a graphical representation of a relation. An arrow is used to identify the y-coordinate associated with an x-coordinate in the set of ordered pairs.

For example, the graphical representation of the relation {(0, 4), (–2, –3), (3, –2), (8, 4)} is shown below.

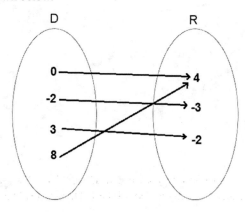

☐ FUNCTIONS

Consider the linear equation in two variables $y = x + 1$ and choose some random x-values to construct the following table of values:

x	0	1	2	3	4
y	1	2	3	4	5

The set of ordered pairs

$\{(0, 1), (1, 2), (2, 3), (3, 4), (4, 5)\}$

is a special relation called function because each x-value corresponds to exactly one y-value unlike the relation

$\{(1, 3), (2, 5), (7, 8), (7, 11), (15, 11)\}$

where $x = 7$ value corresponds to $y = 8$ and $y = 11$.

Thus, a special relation such as $\{(0, 1), (1, 2), (2, 3), (3, 4), (4, 5)\}$ is called function.

Definition

*A **function** is a set of ordered pairs (relation) in which every first coordinate corresponds to exactly one second coordinate.*

Note: Any function is a relation, but not every relation is a function.

The following is an alternative definition of a function.

Definition

*A **function** is a rule that assigns to each element of a set D (domain) exactly one element of a set R (range).*

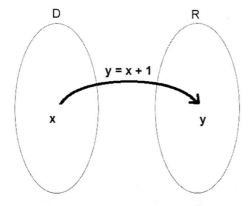

In the above example the rule is $y = x + 1$ (for every x-value in D, add 1 to obtain the corresponding y-value in R). The set D is called the domain and R is called the range of the function.

Domain: The set of all possible (allowable) x-values in the set of ordered pairs of the form (x, y) that defines a function is called the domain of the function.

Range: The set of all possible y-values in the set of ordered pairs of the form (x, y) that defines a function is called the range of the function.

If $y = \dfrac{1}{x}$, then the value $x = 0$ is not possible (allowable) in the domain. Also, for $y = x^2$, the value $y = -1$ is not possible in the range, regardless what values we choose for x.

For example, the domain and range of the following function

$$\{(1, 3), (4, 5), (6, 9), (7, 10), (8, 10)\}$$

are:

$$D = \{1, 4, 6, 7, 8 \} \text{ and } R = \{3, 5, 9, 10\}$$

The following diagrams will help us understand the definition of a function

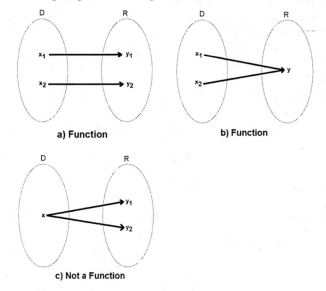

a) Function

b) Function

c) Not a Function

Example 1

Determine if each relation is a function. Then identify the domain and range.

a. $\{(-1, 2), (0, 3), (1, 4), (2, 5)\}$

b. $\{(4, 6), (7, 9), (9, 11), (4, 12)\}$

Solution

a. Notice that each x-value corresponds to exactly one y-value. Thus, the relation

$$\{(-1, 2), (0, 3), (1, 4), 2, 5)\}$$

is a function. $D = \{-1, 0, 1, 2\}$ and $R = \{2, 3, 4, 5\}$

b. The value $x = 4$ in the first ordered pair and the last ordered pair corresponds to $y = 6$ and $y = 12$, and therefore the set of ordered pairs

$$\{(4, 6), (7, 9), (9, 11), (4, 12)\}$$

is not a function (relation only). $D = \{4, 7, 9\}$ and $R = \{6, 9, 11, 12\}$

Thus, given a *set of ordered pairs*, the definition of a function helps us decide whether the set represents a function or not. To decide whether *a graph* represents a function, we can use the **vertical line test**, which is a consequence of the definition of a function.

Vertical Line Test

If no vertical line intersects the graph more than once, the graph represents a function.

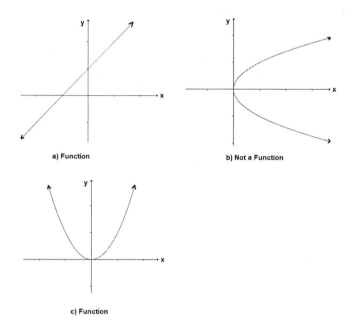

a) Function   b) Not a Function

c) Function

Note: By the vertical line test, every straight line represents a function except a vertical line.

Notation: In the table of values corresponding to $y = x + 1$, we can choose any x-value, but each y-value depends on a specific x-value. For this reason we call y a **dependent variable** and x an **independent variable**.

In other words,

   "y depends on x" or

   "y is a **function** of x"

which can be translated as: "$y = f(x)$" read "y equals f of x"

The term *function* was used for the first time in 1673 by the German mathematician G. W. Leibnitz. However, the Swiss mathematician L. Euler was the first one who used letters of the alphabet to describe functions. The most common notations for a function are: $y = f(x)$, $y = g(x)$, $y = h(x)$, etc.

Since $y = f(x)$, we can use either $y = x + 1$ to denote a linear equation, or $f(x) = x + 1$ to denote a linear function.

For example, the area of a circle $A = \pi R^2$ depends on the radius of the circle so that for every given radius R there is exactly one circle with the area A. Therefore, the area of a circle is a function of the radius of the circle: $A(R) = \pi R^2$ (read "A of R").

Also, the distance traveled by a car at a constant speed of 50 mph, $D = 50T$ depends on the time T so that at any given time T the distance traveled D is unique. Thus, the distance traveled is a function of time: $D(T) = 50T$ (read "D of T").

☐ EVALUATING FUNCTIONS

Sometimes we need to find the value of y in the range corresponding to a given value of x in the domain. The process is called "*evaluating a function*" and it can be accomplished by substituting the given value of x everywhere the variable x appears in the function.

Example 2

Evaluate.

$f(x) = 2x - 3$ at $x = 4$.

Solution

$$f(x) = 2x - 3$$

Substitute 4 for x: $f(4) = 2(4) - 3 = 8 - 3 = 5$

Thus, when $x = 4$, the corresponding y-value is $y = f(4) = 5$ or as an ordered pair is (4, 5).

Example 3

For the function $f(x) = 3x^2 - 4x + 2$ find,

a. $f(0)$

b. $f(-1)$

c. $f(2)$

Solution

a. Substitute 0 for x: $f(0) = 3(0)^2 - 4(0) + 2 = 0 - 0 + 2 = 2$

b. Substitute −1 for x: $f(-1) = 3(-1)^2 - 4(-1) + 2 = 3 \cdot 1 + 4 + 2 = 3 + 6 = 9$

c. Substitute 2 for x: $f(2) = 3(2)^2 - 4(2) + 2 = 3 \cdot 4 - 8 + 2 = 12 - 8 + 2 = 6$

Example 4

For the function $f(x) = |3x - 1|$ find

a. $f(0)$

b. $f(-4)$

c. $f(5)$

Solution

a. Substitute 0 for x: $f(0) = |3(0) - 1| = |0 - 1| = |-1| = 1$

b. Substitute −4 for x: $f(-4) = |3(-4) - 1| = |-12 - 1| = |-13| = 13$

c. Substitute 5 for x: $f(5) = |3(5) - 1| = |15 - 1| = |14| = 14$

Example 5

For the function $f(x) = \sqrt{x+5}$ find

  a.　$f(4)$

  b.　$f(-1)$

  c.　$f(-4)$

Solution

  a.　Substitute 4 for x:　　　$f(4) = \sqrt{4+5} = \sqrt{9} = 3$

  b.　Substitute -1 for x:　　$f(-1) = \sqrt{-1+5} = \sqrt{4} = 2$

  c.　Substitute -4 for x:　　$f(-4) = \sqrt{-4+5} = \sqrt{1} = 1$

3.6 EXERCISES

Determine whether the relation represents a function. Give the domain and range of each relation or function.

1. $\{(3, 2), (1, 5), (4, 6), (2, 9), (5, 1)\}$

2. $\{(1, 7), (2, 4), (3, 5), (1, 9), (4,11)\}$

3. $\{(2, 2), (3, 2), (4, 2), (5, 2), (6, 2)\}$

4. $\{(-1, 3), (-2, 4), (-3, 5), (-4,6)\}$

5. $\{(3, 4), (3, 5), (3, 6), (3, 7), (3, 8)\}$

6. $\{(0, 1), (1, 2), (2, 3), (3, 4), (1, 5)\}$

7. $\{(2, 0), (0, 2), (3, 1), (1, 3), (1, 4)\}$

8. $\{1, 1), (2,2), (3, 3), (4, 4), (5, 1)\}$

9. $\{(-1, -2), (-2, -3), (-3, -4), (-4, -5)\}$

10. $\{-6, -3), (-8, -4), (-10, -3)\}$

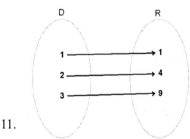

11.

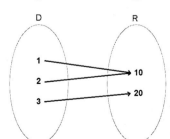

12.

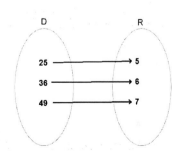

13.

14.

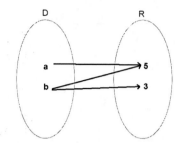

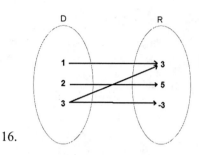

15.   16.

Use the vertical line test to determine whether each graph represents a function or a relation only. Then, give the domain and the range of each function or relation.

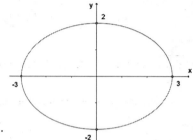

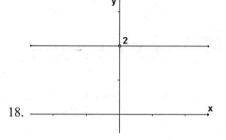

18.

17.

Evaluate each function at the indicated value.

19. $f(x) = 5x - 3$ find

    a. $f(0)$ b. $f(-1)$ c. $f(2)$

20. $f(x) = -4x + 2$ find

    a. $f(0)$ b. $f(3)$ c. $f(-2)$

21. $f(x) = -\dfrac{3}{2}x + 3$ find

    a. $f(0)$ b. $f(2)$ c. $f(-4)$

22. $f(x) = \dfrac{1}{3}x - 1$ find

    a. $f(3)$ b. $f(-3)$ c. $f(0)$

23. $f(x) = x^2 - 2$ find

    a. $f(1)$ b. $f(-1)$ c. $f(2)$

24. $f(x) = -x^2 + 3x - 2$ find

    a. $f(-1)$ b. $f(3)$ c. $f(0)$

25. $f(x) = |2x + 4|$ find

    a. $f(-2)$ b. $f\left(-\dfrac{1}{2}\right)$

                                                  c. $f(2)$

26. $f(x) = |4x - 5|$ find

    a. $f(1)$
    b. $f\left(\dfrac{1}{2}\right)$
    c. $f\left(-\dfrac{1}{4}\right)$

27. $f(x) = \sqrt{2x + 3}$ find

    a. $f(3)$
    b. $f(-1)$
    c. $f\left(-\dfrac{3}{2}\right)$

28. $f(x) = \sqrt{5x - 1}$ find

    a. $f(1)$
    b. $f(2)$
    c. $f\left(\dfrac{1}{5}\right)$

29. $f(x) = 2$ find

    a. $f(0)$
    b. $f(10)$
    c. $f(-4)$

30. Given $f(x) = -5x + 1$, find a number n in the domain of f such that $f(n) = 11$. Write the corresponding ordered pair of the function.

31. Given $f(x) = 7x - 2$, find a number m in the domain of f such that $f(m) = 5$. Write the corresponding ordered pair of the function.

CHAPTER 3 REVIEW EXERCISES

Determine whether the given ordered pair is a solution of the given equation.

1. $2x - y = 3$ $(1, -1)$

2. $2x + 3y = 5$ $(1, 1)$

3. $x - 4y = 6$ $(2, 1)$

4. $5x + 2y = -4$ $(-1, 3)$

5. $-3x + y = 4$ $(-1, 1)$

6. $6x + 7y = 13$ $(3, -1)$

For each equation, complete the given ordered pair. Then, use the results to graph the line.

7. $y = -4x + 1$ $(2,), (, 1), (0,)$

8. $y = -\dfrac{1}{2}x + 3$ $(0,), (2,), (, 4)$

9. $3x - 4y = 7$ $(, 2), (1,), (, -1)$

10. $5x + 3y = 8$ $(1,), (, 1), (4,)$

11. $x = -5$ $(, 6), (-5,), (-2,)$

12. $y = 7$ $(8,), (, 7), (3,)$

Find the slope of the line through the given pair of points.

13. $(5, -2)$ and $(6, 3)$

14. $(-1, 3)$ and $(6, 10)$

15. $(-3, -4)$ and $(-5, 2)$

16. $(7, -1)$ and $(7, 3)$

17. $(-4, 6)$ and $(2, 6)$

18. $\left(\dfrac{1}{5}, -5\right)$ and $\left(\dfrac{6}{5}, 2\right)$

For each of the following equations, find the slope and y-intercept. Then use the results to graph the line.

19. $y = \dfrac{2}{3}x + 1$

20. $y = -\dfrac{1}{3}x + 2$

21. $x + 2y = 4$

Decide whether each pair of lines is parallel, perpendicular, or neither.

22. $3x - y = 4$
$x + 3y = 6$

23. $y = \dfrac{1}{2}x + 3$
$2x - 4y = 5$

24. $5x + y = 1$
$5x - y = 6$

Find the x- and y-intercepts and graph.

25. $2x - 3y = 6$

26. $3x + y = -3$

27. $3x + 4y = 12$

28. $y = 2x - 4$

29. $x = 3y + 6$

30. $y = -\dfrac{1}{3}x + 1$

Write an equation of the line through the given points. Give the answer in slope intercept form.

31. $(2, 3)$ and $(3, -4)$

32. $(5, -4)$ and $(3, 8)$

33. $(-1, 6)$ and $(2, 0)$

34. $(-3, 2)$ and $(-4, -1)$

35. $(7, 3)$ and $(1, -3)$

36. $(2, 5)$ and $(6, 3)$

37. $(0, 4)$ and $(1, 0)$

38. $(0, -3)$ and $(-1, 0)$

39. $(0, 0)$ and $(-11, 11)$

Write an equation of the line through the given point parallel to the given line (standard form).

40. $(1, -3)$, $2x - y = 5$

41. $(3, -2)$, $3x = y + 2$

42. $(-4, 3)$ $4x - 2y = 1$

43. $(0, -4)$, $x + 2y = 3$

44. $(2, 0)$, $3x + 2y = -6$

45. $(-1, -5)$ $x = 8$

46. $(0, 0)$ $3x + 5y = 15$

47. $(2, -5)$ $y = 3$

48. $(1, 3)$ $x - y = 7$

Write an equation of the line through the given point perpendicular to the given line (slope-intercept form).

49. $(-2, -2)$, $x - 2y = 4$

50. $(6, -2)$, $3x + 6y = 18$

51. $(-1, 4)$, $x + y = 10$

52. $(0, 5)$, $2x + 4y = 8$

53. $(3, 0)$, $3x + y = 4$

54. $(2, 3)$ $y = -1$

55. $(0, 0)$ $5x - 3y = 15$

56. $(0, -1)$ $x = -7$

57. $(-4, 0)$ $y = 2$

Graph the following linear inequalities.

58. $y \leq -3x + 2$

59. $y > x + 4$

60. $2x - 3y \leq 6$

61. $x - 2y > 4$

62. $x \leq -2$

63. $y > 1$

64. $x \leq -y$

65. $x > 2y + 3$

66. $-x - y \leq 2$

Evaluate each function at the indicated value.

67. $f(x) = 3x - 2$ $f(5)$

68. $g(x) = 6x + 1$ $g(-2)$

69. $f(x) = x + 7$ $f(3)$

70. $h(x) = \sqrt{x + 6}$ $h(-2)$

71. $f(x) = 2x^2 - 1$ $f(-1)$

72. $g(x) = |4x - 1|$ $g(1)$

73. $f(x) = -x^2 + 3$ $f(-1)$

74. $h(x) = -|x + 8|$ $h(-8)$

75. $f(x) = \frac{3}{4}x + 1$ $f(4)$

4 SYSTEMS OF LINEAR EQUATIONS AND INEQUALITIES

4.1 SOLVING SYSTEMS OF LINEAR EQUATIONS BY GRAPHING

□ **Systems of Linear Equations** □ **The Graphing Method**

□ SYSTEMS OF LINEAR EQUATIONS

Examples of systems of linear equations

$$\begin{cases} y = 3x - 1 \\ x + y = 3 \end{cases} \qquad \begin{cases} 2x + 3y = 10 \\ 4x - y = 6 \end{cases} \qquad \begin{cases} x + y + z = 7 \\ 2x + y - z = 8 \\ x + 2y + 3z = 12 \end{cases}$$

Definition

*Two or more linear equations involving the same variables, considered together are called a **system of linear equations**.*

Throughout this chapter, our goal is to solve systems of two linear equations in two variables. If a system of two linear equations in two variables x and y has a solution, then the solution is an ordered pair of the form (x, y) that satisfies both equations.

In this chapter we will discuss three methods for solving systems of linear equations in two variables: the graphing method, the substitution method, and the addition (elimination) method.

□ THE GRAPHING METHOD

To solve a system of linear equations in two variables using the graphing method, graph each equation on the same coordinate axes, and if the graphs intersect, the solution is given by the ordered pair corresponding to their point of intersection.

In the previous chapter we learned that the graph of a linear equation in two variables is a straight line. If the lines intersect at one point, the system has a solution, which is the ordered pair corresponding to the point of intersection. Since the point of intersection lies on both lines, the ordered pair should satisfy both equations.

The **graphing method**, sometimes called the **geometric method**, is useful when the solution is an ordered pair containing integers. If the solution is an ordered pair containing fractions or decimals it is difficult to identify the coordinates of the point of intersection (solution). In this case we can only approximate the solution.

Example 1

Determine whether the ordered pair $(1, 3)$ is a solution of the system.

$$\begin{cases} 2x + y = 5 \\ 4x - y = 1 \end{cases}$$

Solution

The ordered pair $(1, 3)$ is a solution of the system if it satisfies each equation. In other words, if we substitute 1 for x and 3 for y and simplify, it should make each equation a true numerical statement.

$2x + y = 5$	$4x - y = 1$
$2(1) + 3 = 5$	$4(1) - 3 = 1$
$2 + 3 = 5$	$4 - 1 = 3$
$5 = 5$ True	$3 = 3$ True

The ordered pair $(1, 3)$ satisfies both equations, and therefore is the solution of the system.

Example 2

Solve by graphing.

$$\begin{cases} y = \dfrac{1}{2}x - 2 \\ y = -x + 1 \end{cases}$$

Solution

Graph each equation on the same coordinate system using two ordered pairs for each equation.

First, choose two convenient x-values for each equation and substitute those values into each equation to find the corresponding values for y. Plot the points corresponding to those ordered pairs and join the points to graph the lines.

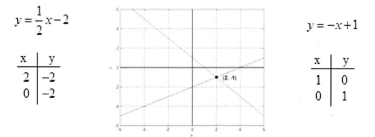

$y = \dfrac{1}{2}x - 2$

x	y
2	-2
0	-2

$y = -x + 1$

x	y
1	0
0	1

From the graph we can see that the lines intersect at the point whose coordinates are $(2, -1)$.

Thus, the ordered pair $(2, -1)$ is a possible solution for the system.

To check the solution, substitute 2 for x and -1 for y into each equation.

$$y = \frac{1}{2}x - 2 \qquad\qquad\qquad y = -x + 1$$

$$-1 = \frac{1}{2} \cdot 2 - 2 \qquad\qquad -1 = -2 + 1$$

$$-1 = 1 - 2 \qquad\qquad\qquad -1 = -1 \text{ True}$$

$$-1 = -1 \text{ True}$$

Since $(2, -1)$ satisfies both equations, the ordered pair $(2, -1)$ is the solution of the system.

Note: From this example we conclude that if the lines have different slopes ($m = \frac{1}{2}$, $m = -1$) they intersect in a single point. Therefore, the system has one solution.

Example 3

Solve by graphing.

$$\begin{cases} 2x + y = 5 \\ x + y = 3 \end{cases}$$

Solution

Graph both equations on the same coordinate system using two ordered pairs for each equation. First, write the equations in slope-intercept form by solving each equation for y. Then, choose two convenient ordered pairs for each equation, and determine their point of intersection (if any).

$$y = -2x + 5 \qquad\qquad\qquad y = -x + 3$$

x	y
2	1
3	-1

x	y
2	1
3	0

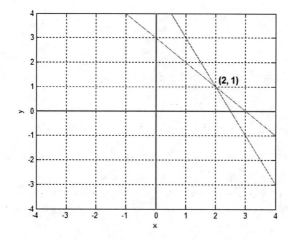

From the graph we can see that the lines intersect at the point whose coordinates are $(2, 1)$.

To check the solution, substitute 2 for x and 1 for y into each equation.

$y = -2x + 5$ $\qquad\qquad\qquad$ $y = -x + 3$

$1 = -2(2) + 5$ $\qquad\qquad\qquad$ $1 = -2 + 3$

$1 = -4 + 5$ $\qquad\qquad\qquad$ $1 = 1$ True

$1 = 1$ True

Since (2, 1) satisfies both equations, the ordered pair (2, 1) is the solution of the system.

Note: We can graph the lines using the x- and y-intercepts or the slope and y-intercept instead of random ordered pairs (table).

Example 4

Solve by graphing.

$$\begin{cases} 3x + 2y = 4 \\ x = 2 \end{cases}$$

Solution

The graph of $x = 2$ is a vertical line with x-intercept (2, 0). To graph the equation $3x + 2y = 4$ first, write the equation in slope-intersect form, then choose two convenient ordered pairs. Then determine their point of intersection.

$3x + 2y = 4$

$2y = -3x + 4$

$\dfrac{2y}{2} = -\dfrac{3}{2}x + \dfrac{4}{2}$

$y = -\dfrac{3}{2}x + 2$

x	y
0	2
2	-1

From the graph we can see that a possible solution for the system is the ordered pair (2, –1).

To check the solution, substitute 2 for x and –1 for y into each equation.

$x = 2$ $\qquad\qquad\qquad\qquad$ $3x + 2y = 4$

$2 = 2$ $\qquad$ True $\qquad\qquad$ $3(2) + 2(-1) = 4$

$\qquad\qquad\qquad\qquad\qquad\quad$ $6 - 2 = 4$

$\qquad\qquad\qquad\qquad\qquad\quad$ $4 = 4$ $\qquad\qquad$ True

The ordered pair (2, –1) satisfies both equations, therefore (2, –1) is a solution.

When we solve a system of linear equations by graphing, the solution depends on the relationship between the lines corresponding to the equations of the system. There are many ways to draw two lines in a plane (board, paper, etc) but all of them can be classified into three categories: intersecting lines, overlapping lines, and parallel lines.

- If the lines intersect at one point, the system has one solution.
- If the lines overlap (coincide), every point on the lines is a point of intersection and therefore the system has an infinite number of solutions (no unique solution).
- If the lines are parallel (do not intersect) there is no point of intersection and the system has no solution.

Note: A system that has a least one solution is called **consistent.**

A system that has no solution is called **inconsistent.**

If the equations have distinct graphs, the equations are called **independent.**

If the graphs of the equations coincide, the equations are called **dependent.**

The following graphs illustrate the possibilities listed above.

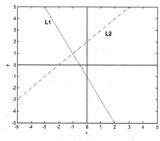 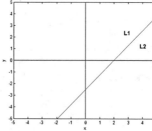 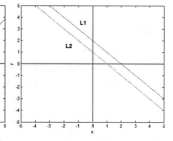

a. *Intersecting Lines*

Solution(s):
- One System
- Consistent Equations
- Independent

b. *Overlapping Lines*

Solution(s):
- Infinite Number of Solutions System
- Consistent Equations
- Dependent

c. *Parallel Lines*

Solution(s):
- No Solution System
- Inconsistent Equations
- Independent

Example 5

Solve by graphing.

$$\begin{cases} x + y = -4 \\ 2x + 2y = 6 \end{cases}$$

Solution

Graph each equation on the same coordinate system. First, write the equations in slope-intercept form (solve for y). Then choose two convenient ordered pairs for each equation, and determine the point of intersection.

$$x + y = -4$$
$$y = -x - 4$$

x	y
0	−4
−4	0

$$2x + 2y = 6$$
$$2y = -2x + 6$$
$$\frac{2y}{2} = \frac{-2x}{2} + \frac{6}{2}$$
$$y = -x + 3$$

$$y = -x + 3$$

x	y
−1	4
4	−1

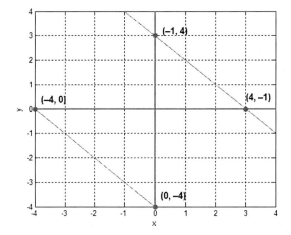

Because the lines are parallel (do not intersect), the system has no solution. Therefore, the system is inconsistent and the equations are independent.

Note: By inspection, from the slope intercept forms we can see that the lines have the same slope ($m = -1$) and different y-intercepts ($y = 3$, and $y = -4$). Hence, the lines are two distinct parallel lines. From this observation, we arrive to the same conclusion: the system is inconsistent (no solution) and the equations are independent.

Example 6

Solve by graphing.

$$\begin{cases} 4x - 2y = 6 \\ 2x - y = 3 \end{cases}$$

Solution

Write each equation in slope intercept form (solve for y).

$$4x - 2y = 6 \qquad\qquad 2x - y = 3$$
$$-2y = -4x + 6 \qquad\qquad -y = -2x + 3$$
$$\frac{-2y}{-2} = \frac{-4}{-2}x + \frac{6}{-2} \qquad\qquad y = 2x - 3$$
$$y = 2x - 3$$

From the slope intercept forms, we can see that the lines have the same slope ($m = 2$) and the same y-intercept ($y = -3$). In other words, the two equations are the same and therefore the corresponding lines coincide.

Without graphing the lines, we conclude that the system has an infinite number of solutions. Thus, the system is *consistent* and the equations are *dependent*.

If we graph those two equations on the same coordinate system, we can see that our conclusion is correct.

$y = 2x - 3$

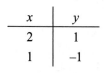

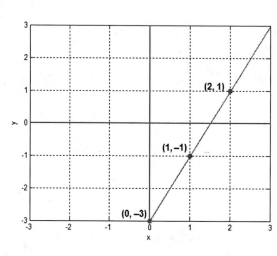

4.1 EXERCISES

Determine whether the given ordered pair is a solution of the system of equations.

1. $\begin{cases} x + 5y = 7 \\ 3x - 2y = 4 \end{cases}$ (2, 1)

2. $\begin{cases} 4x - 3y = 1 \\ 2x + y = 3 \end{cases}$ (1, 1)

3. $\begin{cases} x + y = 4 \\ 9x - 2y = 2 \end{cases}$ (1, 3)

4. $\begin{cases} 5x - 4y = 2 \\ x + 3y = 4 \end{cases}$ (1, 1)

5. $\begin{cases} 2x + 7y = 9 \\ 4x - 2y = 2 \end{cases}$ (2, 3)

6. $\begin{cases} 6x + y = 4 \\ -3x + 4y = 5 \end{cases}$ (-2, 8)

7. $\begin{cases} y = -x + 3 \\ x = 4 \end{cases}$ (4, -2)

8. $\begin{cases} y = 2 \\ -2y = x + 5 \end{cases}$ (0, 2)

9. $\begin{cases} y = \dfrac{1}{3}x - 1 \\ y = -2x \end{cases}$ (3, 1)

Solve each system of linear equations by graphing. Indicate whether the system is consistent or inconsistent and whether the equations are independent or dependent.

10. $\begin{cases} y = x - 3 \\ y = \dfrac{1}{2}x - 1 \end{cases}$

11. $\begin{cases} y = 2x + 1 \\ y = x + 2 \end{cases}$

12. $\begin{cases} y = -\dfrac{1}{3}x + 1 \\ y = x + 5 \end{cases}$

13. $\begin{cases} y = -\dfrac{1}{2}x \\ y = x - 3 \end{cases}$

14. $\begin{cases} 5x + 2y = 6 \\ 2x - 3y = -9 \end{cases}$

15. $\begin{cases} y = 3 \\ y = 4x - 1 \end{cases}$

16. $\begin{cases} 2x + y = 5 \\ 3x - y = 5 \end{cases}$

17. $\begin{cases} x + 2y = 2 \\ -x + 2y = 6 \end{cases}$

18. $\begin{cases} x + y = 5 \\ 3x - 2y = 0 \end{cases}$

19. $\begin{cases} x + y = -3 \\ x - y = -5 \end{cases}$

20. $\begin{cases} 5x + y = -6 \\ 2x - y = -1 \end{cases}$

21. $\begin{cases} 3x + 2y = 12 \\ 4x + y = 11 \end{cases}$

22. $\begin{cases} y = 3x - 1 \\ x = 1 \end{cases}$

23. $\begin{cases} 3x - 2y = 6 \\ 4x + y = 8 \end{cases}$

24. $\begin{cases} 2x + 7y = -1 \\ x + y = 2 \end{cases}$

25. $\begin{cases} x + 2y = 4 \\ 2x + 4y = 12 \end{cases}$

26. $\begin{cases} 3x - y = 5 \\ 6x - 2y = 6 \end{cases}$

27. $\begin{cases} x + 2y = 4 \\ 2x + 4y = 8 \end{cases}$

28. $\begin{cases} 3x + 2y = 2 \\ 6x + 4y = 8 \end{cases}$

29. $\begin{cases} 6x + 2y = -4 \\ 3x + y = -2 \end{cases}$

30. $\begin{cases} 10x + 5y = -5 \\ 2x + y = -1 \end{cases}$

31. $\begin{cases} 3x - y = -2 \\ x - 2y = 6 \end{cases}$

32. $\begin{cases} 2x + 3y = -3 \\ x - y = -4 \end{cases}$

33. $\begin{cases} x - 3y = 6 \\ y = \dfrac{1}{3}x + 2 \end{cases}$

34. $\begin{cases} 4x + y = -5 \\ 3x - y = -2 \end{cases}$

35. $\begin{cases} 2x - y = -3 \\ x + y = -6 \end{cases}$

36. $\begin{cases} x + 2y = 2 \\ 3x - 2y = 6 \end{cases}$

37. $\begin{cases} x = 2y + 4 \\ y = -\dfrac{1}{2}x \end{cases}$

38. $\begin{cases} y = \dfrac{1}{4}x \\ x + y = 0 \end{cases}$

39. $\begin{cases} 3x + 2y = -6 \\ 2x - y = 3 \end{cases}$

40. $\begin{cases} 5x + y = 3 \\ 10x + 2y = 6 \end{cases}$

41. $\begin{cases} x - 3y = 3 \\ 2x - 6y = 6 \end{cases}$

42. $\begin{cases} 0.2x - 0.1y = -0.4 \\ 0.4x + 0.1y = -0.2 \end{cases}$

43. $\begin{cases} 0.6x - 0,2y = -0.4 \\ 0.5x + 0.1y = -0.6 \end{cases}$

44. $\begin{cases} \dfrac{2}{3}x - \dfrac{1}{2}y = 1 \\ \dfrac{1}{4}x + \dfrac{1}{8}y = 1 \end{cases}$

45. $\begin{cases} \dfrac{1}{2}x + \dfrac{1}{4}y = 0 \\ \dfrac{1}{2}x - \dfrac{1}{2}y = 3 \end{cases}$

46. $\begin{cases} x = -2 \\ y = 3 \end{cases}$

47. $\begin{cases} x = 4 \\ y = -3 \end{cases}$

48. $\begin{cases} y = \dfrac{1}{2}x \\ y = 1 \end{cases}$

49. $\begin{cases} 2(x + 3) - (y - 1) = 8 \\ -4(x - 1) + 2(y + 2) = 6 \end{cases}$

50. $\begin{cases} 3(x + y) + 2(x - y) = 11 \\ 2(x + 2y) + 3(x - 2y) = 8 \end{cases}$

51. $\begin{cases} 0.1(x + y) + 0.2(x - y) = 0.2 \\ 0.4(x - y) + 0.3(x + y) = 1 \end{cases}$

52. $\begin{cases} 0.7(x + y) - 0.4(x + 2y) = -1.5 \\ 0.2(x + 3) + 0.1(y - 2) = -0.1 \end{cases}$

4.2 SOLVING SYSTEMS OF LINEAR EQUATIONS BY SUBSTITUTION

As we discussed in the previous section, the graphing method is not very useful when the solution involves fractions or decimals. For this reason we will introduce in the section an algebraic method called **substitution method.**

> The *substitution method* is used to find an exact solution of any system of linear equations in two variables if the system has a solution.

When solving systems by substitution, our goal is to eliminate one variable and change the system of two equations in two variables into a single equation in one variable.

The strategy used to solve a system of linear equations in two variables using the **substitution method** can be summarized as follows:

Step 1 Solve one of the equations of the system for one variable in terms of the other. The expression obtained is called *substitution*. To avoid fractions, choose one equation that contains a variable with the coefficient 1 or −1 (if possible) and solve for that variable.

Step 2 Substitute the expression obtained in step 1 into the other equation to eliminate one variable. The result is an equation in one variable.

Step 3 Solve the equation obtained in step 2 for the remaining variable.

Step 4 Substitute the solution from step 3 into the substitution from step 1 to find the value of the other variable.

Step 5 Write the solution as an ordered pair and check the solution.

Example 1

Solve the system of linear equations by substitution.

$$\begin{cases} 4x - 5y = -1 & (1) \\ 2x + y = 3 & (2) \end{cases}$$

Solution

Step 1 If possible, choose one equation that contains a variable with the coefficient 1 or −1 . In our case, we solve the second equation for y in terms of x.

$$y = 3 - 2x \quad (substitution) \quad (3)$$

Step 2 Substitute this expression for y into the first equation to eliminate y.

$$4x - 5(3 - 2x) = -1$$

Step 3 Simplify and solve the equation for the remaining variable x.

$$4x - 15 + 10x = -1$$

$$14x = 15 - 1$$

$$14x = 14$$

$$x = 1$$

Step 4 Substitute the solution $x = 1$ into the *substitution* (3) from step 1 to find y.

$$y = 3 - 2x$$

$$y = 3 - 2(1)$$

$$y = 3 - 2$$

$$y = 1$$

Step 5 A possible solution of the system is (1, 1).

To check the solution, substitute 1 for x and 1 for y into each original equation.

$4x - 5y = -1$	$2x + y = 3$
$4(1) - 5(1) = -1$	$2(1) + 1 = 3$
$4 - 5 = -1$	$2 + 1 = 3$
$-1 = -1$ True	$3 = 3$ True

Thus, the solution of the system is (1, 1). The solution can be written explicit as $\begin{cases} x = 1 \\ y = 1 \end{cases}$.

The system is *consistent* and the equations are *independent*.

Note: If the system contains variables other than x and y, the ordered pair is always written in alphabetical order. For example: (a, b), (m, n), (p, q), (r, s), etc.

Example 2

Solve the system of linear equations by substitution.

$$\begin{cases} 8x + 3y = -14 & (1) \\ y = 2x - 7 & (2) \end{cases}$$

Solution

Since the second equation is already solved for y, we can use that expression as our substitution.

$y = 2x - 7$　　(*substitution*)

Substitute $2x - 7$ for y into the first equation to eliminate y.

$8x + 3(2x - 7) = -14$

Simplify and solve for x.

$8x + 6x - 21 = -14$

$14x = -14 + 21$

$14x = 7$

$\dfrac{14x}{14} = \dfrac{7}{14}$

$x = \dfrac{1}{2}$

Substitute the solution $x = \dfrac{1}{2}$ into the substitution $y = 2x - 7$ to find y.

$y = 2(\dfrac{1}{2}) - 7$

$y = 1 - 7$

$y = -6$

A possible solution of the system is $(\dfrac{1}{2}, -6)$.

To check the solution, substitute $\dfrac{1}{2}$ for x and -6 for y into each equation.

$8x + 3y = -14$	$y = 2x - 7$
$8(\dfrac{1}{2}) + 3(-6) = -14$	$-6 = 2(\dfrac{1}{2}) - 7$
$4 - 18 = -14$	$-6 = 1 - 7$
$-14 = -14$　True	$-6 = -6$　　　　True

Therefore, the solution of the system is $(\dfrac{1}{2}, -6)$.

The system is *consistent* and the equations are *independent*.

Example 3

Solve the system of linear equations by substitution.

$$\begin{cases} x+2y = 4 & (1) \\ 2x+4y = 5 & (2) \end{cases}$$

Solution

Solve the first equation for x in terms of y.

$x = 4 - 2y$ (*substitution*)

Substitute this expression for x into the second equation.

$2(4 - 2y) + 4y = 5$

Simplify and solve for y.

$8 - 4y + 4y = 5$

$0y + 8 = 5$

$0y = 5 - 8$

$0y = -3$ or $0 = -3$

Since there is no real number y that multiplied by zero equals -3, the system has no solution. Thus, the system is *inconsistent* and the equations are *independent*.

Example 4

Solve the system of linear equations by substitution.

$$\begin{cases} 4x + y = 2 & (1) \\ 8x + 2y = 4 & (2) \end{cases}$$

Solution

Solve the first equation for y.

$y = 2 - 4x$ (*substitution*)

Substitute this expression for y into the second equation.

$8x + 2(2 - 4x) = 4$

$8x + 4 - 8x = 4$

$0x + 4 = 4$

$0x = 4 - 4$

$0x = 0$ or $0 = 0$

Since every real number x multiplied by zero equals zero, the system has an infinite number of solutions. Thus, the system is consistent and the equations are dependent.

4.2 EXERCISES

Solve each system of linear equations by the substitution method.

1. $\begin{cases} 6x - y = -4 \\ y = 4x + 2 \end{cases}$

2. $\begin{cases} x = 5y - 2 \\ 2x - y = 5 \end{cases}$

3. $\begin{cases} x + y = 4 \\ 3x - y = 4 \end{cases}$

4. $\begin{cases} x - y = 7 \\ 6x - y = 2 \end{cases}$

5. $\begin{cases} 2x - y = 4 \\ 4x - 3y = 0 \end{cases}$

6. $\begin{cases} 5x + 2y = -5 \\ 3x + y = -4 \end{cases}$

7. $\begin{cases} -6x + 2y = 4 \\ 4x - y = -4 \end{cases}$

8. $\begin{cases} x + 5y = 3 \\ 2x + 10y = 6 \end{cases}$

9. $\begin{cases} 8x - 2y = 4 \\ 4x - y = 2 \end{cases}$

10. $\begin{cases} x + 6y = 3 \\ 2x + 12y = 4 \end{cases}$

11. $\begin{cases} 7x - y = 4 \\ 14x - 2y = 5 \end{cases}$

12. $\begin{cases} 8x + y = 10 \\ -11x + 2y = 20 \end{cases}$

13. $\begin{cases} 2x - 4y = 2 \\ x - 2y = 1 \end{cases}$

14. $\begin{cases} 5x + y = 1 \\ 8x + 2y = 4 \end{cases}$

15. $\begin{cases} x + 6y = 3 \\ 2x + 4y = -2 \end{cases}$

16. $\begin{cases} 5x - 7y = 0 \\ 3x + y = 0 \end{cases}$

17. $\begin{cases} 8x + 10y = 0 \\ 2x - y = 0 \end{cases}$

18. $\begin{cases} -7x + y = 5 \\ 7x - y = -6 \end{cases}$

19. $\begin{cases} -x + 9y = 4 \\ x - 9y = -4 \end{cases}$

20. $\begin{cases} 3x + y = -9 \\ 4x + 3y = -2 \end{cases}$

21. $\begin{cases} y = \dfrac{1}{2}x + 3 \\ -3x + 2y = 2 \end{cases}$

22. $\begin{cases} x = \dfrac{3}{5}y - 1 \\ 5x + y = 15 \end{cases}$

23. $\begin{cases} 8x - 5y = 2 \\ -3x + y = 1 \end{cases}$

24. $\begin{cases} 3x + 2y = 2 \\ 2x + y = -2 \end{cases}$

25. $\begin{cases} 2x - 3y = 2 \\ x - 4y = 6 \end{cases}$

26. $\begin{cases} 4x + 8y = -4 \\ 2x + 5y = -1 \end{cases}$

27. $\begin{cases} 2x + y = 5 \\ 3x - y = 10 \end{cases}$

28. $\begin{cases} x - y = 1 \\ -2x + y = 5 \end{cases}$

29. $\begin{cases} 7x + y = 8 \\ 5x + 2y = 16 \end{cases}$

30. $\begin{cases} 10x - 3y = 1 \\ 4x + y = 7 \end{cases}$

31. $\begin{cases} x + 6y = 10 \\ 2x - 3y = 5 \end{cases}$

32. $\begin{cases} y = x - 6 \\ y = 2x - 13 \end{cases}$

33. $\begin{cases} x = y + 9 \\ x = -2y - 15 \end{cases}$

34. $\begin{cases} -6x + y = 2 \\ 6x - y = 3 \end{cases}$

35. $\begin{cases} 10x - y = 8 \\ -10x + y = 5 \end{cases}$

36. $\begin{cases} y = 2x + 3 \\ 4x - 2y = -6 \end{cases}$

37. $\begin{cases} x = 2y - 2 \\ y = 3x - 5 \end{cases}$

38. $\begin{cases} y = -2x - 1 \\ x = y + 7 \end{cases}$

39. $\begin{cases} 8x - 3y = 0 \\ 4x + y = 0 \end{cases}$

40. $\begin{cases} 2x + y = 7 \\ 3x + 2y = 3 \end{cases}$

41. $\begin{cases} 3x + 2y = 0 \\ 2x + y = -4 \end{cases}$

42. $\begin{cases} 5x + 3y = 1 \\ 3x + y = 3 \end{cases}$

43. $\begin{cases} \dfrac{1}{2}x + \dfrac{1}{5}y = 3 \\ \dfrac{5}{2}x + \dfrac{1}{10}y = 6 \end{cases}$

44. $\begin{cases} -\dfrac{1}{2}x + \dfrac{1}{3}y = -2 \\ \dfrac{1}{6}x - \dfrac{2}{3}y = -1 \end{cases}$

45. $\begin{cases} -\dfrac{1}{4}x + \dfrac{3}{2}y = -2 \\ \dfrac{5}{2}x - \dfrac{1}{2}y = -1 \end{cases}$

46. $\begin{cases} 0.2x + 0.7y = 0.1 \\ 0.1x - 0.6y = 1 \end{cases}$

49. $\begin{cases} x - y = 6 \\ 0.28x - 0.45y = 1 \end{cases}$

47. $\begin{cases} 0.5x + 0.2y = 0.1 \\ 0.4x + 0.1y = -0.4 \end{cases}$

50. $\begin{cases} 4(x + y) - 3(y - x) = 23 \\ 3(2x + y) + (x - 2y) = 23 \end{cases}$

48. $\begin{cases} x + y = 15 \\ 0.45x - 0.35y = 0.35 \end{cases}$

51. $\begin{cases} 5(x - y) + 4(x + y) = -32 \\ 7(x - y) - (x + y) = 8 \end{cases}$

4.3 SOLVING SYSTEMS OF LINEAR EQUATIONS BY ADDITION

In this section, we will solve systems of two linear equations in two variables using another algebraic method, called the **addition** or elimination method.

Like in the previous section, the main idea is to eliminate one variable and change a system of two linear equations in two variables into a single equation in one variable.

Using the addition method, we eliminate one variable by adding the equations. Most of the time, just adding the original equations does not eliminate one variable. So, before adding the equations we may need to change one or both equations.

The following steps could be useful to make the necessary changes in order to solve a system of linear equations using the **addition method**.

Step 1 If the equations are not in standard form, rewrite each equation in standard form ($ax + by = c$).

Step 2 Decide which variable is easier to eliminate.

Step 3 Multiply both sides of one or both equations by a proper nonzero constant so that the coefficients of the variable that will be eliminated are opposite numbers.

Step 4 Add the equations to eliminate one variable and obtain an equation in one variable.

Step 5 Solve the resulting equation.

Step 6 Substitute the value of the variable found in step 4 in one of the original equations and solve this equation to find the other variable.

Step 7 Write the solution as an ordered pair, and check the solution.

Note: If the equations contain fractions, multiply each equation by the LCD to clear the fractions.

If the equations contain decimals, multiply each equation as needed by 10, 100, etc. to clear the decimals.

Example 1

Solve by addition.

$$\begin{cases} y = -4x + 5 \\ 3x + 2y = 5 \end{cases}$$

Solution

Step 1 Write the top equation in standard form.

$$\begin{cases} 4x + y = 5 & (1) \\ 3x + 2y = 5 & (2) \end{cases}$$

Step 2 For this system it's easier to eliminate y. The coefficient of y in the second equation is 2, and the coefficient of y in the first equation is 1 and should be –2 (the opposite of 2). Thus, multiply both sides of the first equation by –2 and the second equation remain unchanged.

$$\begin{cases} -8x - 2y = -10 \\ 3x + 2y = 5 \end{cases}$$

Step 3 Add the equations to eliminate y.

$$\begin{cases} -8x - 2y = -10 \\ 3x + 2y = 5 \end{cases}$$

$$\overline{}$$

$$-5x = -5$$

Step 4 Solve the resulting equation.

$$-5x = -5$$

$$\frac{-5x}{-5} = \frac{-5}{-5}$$

$$x = 1$$

Step 5 Substitute 1 for x into the first equation to obtain y.

$$4x + y = 5$$

$$4(1) + y = 5$$

$$y = -4 + 5$$

$$y = 1$$

Step 6 Write the solution as an ordered pair and check the solution. The possible solution is (1, 1).

Check the solution:

$y = -4x + 5$	$3x + 2y = 5$
$1 = -4(1) + 5$	$3(1) + 2(1) = 5$
$1 = -4 + 5$	$3 + 2 = 5$
$1 = 1$ True	$5 = 5$ True

Thus, the solution is (1, 1). The system is *consistent* and the equations are *independent*.

Example 2

Solve by addition.

$$\begin{cases} 2x + 3y = 5 & (1) \\ 6x + 5y = 3 & (2) \end{cases}$$

Solution

Step 1 Both equations are in standard form.

Step 2 For this system it's easier to eliminate x, because we can change the coefficient of x in the first equation into -6, which is the opposite of the coefficient 6 of x in the second equation. This can be accomplished if we multiply both sides of the first equation by -3 and leave the second equation unchanged.

$$\begin{cases} -6x - 9y = -15 \\ 6x + 5y = 3 \end{cases}$$

Step 3 Add the equations to eliminate x.

$$\begin{cases} -6x - 9y = -15 \\ 6x + 5y = 3 \end{cases}$$
$$\overline{}$$
$$-4y = -12$$

Step 4 Solve the resulting equation.

$$-4y = -12$$

$$\frac{-4y}{-4} = \frac{-12}{-4}$$

$$y = 3$$

Step 5 Substitute 3 for y into the first equation.

$$2x + 3y = 5$$
$$\overline{}$$
$$2x + 3(3) = 5$$

$$2x + 9 = 5$$

$$2x = 5 - 9$$

$$2x = -4$$

$$x = -2$$

Step 6 Write the solution as an ordered pair and check the solution. The possible solution is
$(-2, 3)$.

Check the solution:

$2x + 3y = 5$	$6x + 5y = 3$
$2(-2) + 3(3) = 5$	$6(-2) + 5(3) = 3$
$-4 + 9 = 5$	$-12 + 15 = 3$
$5 = 5$ True	$3 = 3$ True

Thus, the solution is $(-2, 3)$. The system is *consistent* and the equations are *independent*.

Example 3

Solve by addition.

$$\begin{cases} 5x + 3y = 2 & (1) \\ 4x + 2y = 4 & (2) \end{cases}$$

Solution

For this system, we can eliminate either variable because the amount of work is about the same. However, we will eliminate y because it has smaller coefficients.

To eliminate y, we need to change the coefficients of y into opposite numbers. If we multiply the first equation by -2 and the second equation by 3, the coefficient of y in the first equation becomes -6 and the coefficient of y in the second equation becomes 6.

$$\begin{cases} -10x - 6y = -4 \\ 12x + 6y = 12 \end{cases}$$
$$2x = 8$$
$$x = 4$$

Substitute 4 for x into the second original equation.

$$4x + 2y = 4$$
$$4(4) + 2y = 4$$
$$16 + 2y = 4$$
$$2y = 4 - 16$$
$$2y = -12$$
$$y = -6$$

The solution is $(4, -6)$. The system is *consistent* and the equations are *independent*.

Note: If we substitute 4 for x into the first original equation, we will obtain the same value for y.

Example 4

Solve by addition.

$$\begin{cases} 2x + 4y = 6 & (1) \\ 3x + 6y = 9 & (2) \end{cases}$$

Solution

We can eliminate either x or y. To eliminate x, we divide the first equation by 2 and the second equation by -3.

$$\begin{cases} \dfrac{2x}{2} + \dfrac{4y}{2} = \dfrac{6}{2} \\ \dfrac{3x}{-3} + \dfrac{6y}{-3} = \dfrac{9}{-3} \end{cases}$$

Simplify.

$$\begin{cases} x + 2y = 3 \\ -x - 2y = -3 \end{cases}$$

$$\overline{0 = 0} \qquad \text{True}$$

In this case the graphs (lines) corresponding to those two equations coincide because the equations are the same.

Therefore, the system has an *infinite number* of *solutions*. We conclude that the system is *consistent* and the equations are *dependent*.

Example 5

Solve by addition.

$$\begin{cases} 6x - 4y = 2 & (1) \\ -9x + 6y = 5 & (2) \end{cases}$$

Solution

Again, we can eliminate either x or y. To eliminate y for example, the coefficients of y in the two equations must be opposite numbers. If we multiply the first equation by 3 and the second one by 2, the coefficient of y in the first equation will be -12 and the coefficient of y in the second equations will be 12.

$$\begin{cases} 18x - 12y = 6 \\ -18x + 12y = 10 \end{cases}$$

$$\overline{0x + 0y = 16 \text{ or } 0 = 16} \qquad \text{False}$$

Since there are no values x and y for which $0x + 0y = 16$, the system has *no solution*. Thus, the system is *inconsistent* and the equations are *independent*.

Example 6

Solve by addition.

$$\begin{cases} 0.03x + 0.04y = 0.08 \\ 0.02x - 0.06y = 0.01 \end{cases}$$

Solution

Multiply each equation by 100 to eliminate the decimals.

$$\begin{cases} 3x + 4y = 8 & (1) \\ 2x - 6y = 1 & (2) \end{cases}$$

To eliminate y, multiply the first equation by 3 and the second equation by 2.

$$\begin{cases} 9x + 12y = 24 \\ 4x - 12y = 2 \end{cases}$$

$$\overline{\hspace{3cm}}$$

$$13x = 26$$

$$x = 2$$

Substitute 2 for x in the simplified form of the first equation to find y.

$$3x + 4y = 8$$

$$3(2) + 4y = 8$$

$$6 + 4y = 8$$

$$4y = 8 - 6$$

$$4y = 2$$

$$\frac{4y}{4} = \frac{2}{4}$$

$$y = \frac{1}{2}$$

Thus, the solution is $\left(2, \dfrac{1}{2}\right)$. The system is *consistent* and the equations are *independent*.

Example 7

Solve by addition.

$$\begin{cases} \dfrac{3}{2}x + \dfrac{1}{4}y = \dfrac{5}{6} \\ \dfrac{1}{3}x + \dfrac{3}{2}y = \dfrac{2}{3} \end{cases}$$

Solution

Because the system contains fractions, multiply each fraction by the LCD to eliminate the fractions. Multiply the top equation by the LCD = 12 and the bottom equation by the LCD = 6.

$$\begin{cases} 12 \cdot \dfrac{3}{2}x + 12 \cdot \dfrac{1}{4}y = 12 \cdot \dfrac{5}{6} \\ 6 \cdot \dfrac{1}{3}x + 6 \cdot \dfrac{3}{2}y = 6 \cdot \dfrac{2}{3} \end{cases}$$

Simplify

$$\begin{cases} 18x + 3y = 10 \qquad (1) \\ 2x + 9y = 4 \qquad (2) \end{cases}$$

To eliminate x, multiply the second equation by -9 and leave the first equation unchanged.

$$\begin{cases} 18x + 3y = 10 \\ -18x - 81y = -36 \end{cases}$$

$$\overline{\qquad\qquad\qquad}$$

$$-78y = -26$$

$$\dfrac{-78y}{-78} = \dfrac{-26}{-78}$$

$$y = \dfrac{1}{3}$$

Substitute $\dfrac{1}{3}$ for y in the simplified form of the second equation to find x.

$$2x + 9y = 4$$

$$\overline{\qquad\qquad\qquad}$$

$$2x + 9 \cdot \dfrac{1}{3} = 4$$

$$2x + 3 = 4$$

$$2x = 4 - 3$$

$$2x = 1$$

$$\dfrac{2x}{2} = \dfrac{1}{2}$$

$$x = \dfrac{1}{2}$$

The solution is $\left(\dfrac{1}{2}, \dfrac{1}{3} \right)$. The system is consistent and the equations are independent.

4.3 EXERCISES

Solve each system of linear equations by the addition method.

1. $\begin{cases} 3x + y = 6 \\ 4x - y = 1 \end{cases}$

2. $\begin{cases} x + 5y = 3 \\ -x + 2y = 4 \end{cases}$

3. $\begin{cases} x + y = 6 \\ 5x - y = 6 \end{cases}$

4. $\begin{cases} x - y = -1 \\ x - 4y = 5 \end{cases}$

5. $\begin{cases} 2x + y = 3 \\ x + y = -1 \end{cases}$

6. $\begin{cases} 3x + y = 7 \\ 4x + y = 12 \end{cases}$

7. $\begin{cases} 4x - 3y = 2 \\ 3x + y = 8 \end{cases}$

8. $\begin{cases} x + 3y = 2 \\ 2x + 5y = 2 \end{cases}$

9. $\begin{cases} 2x + 7y = -3 \\ x + 6y = 1 \end{cases}$

10. $\begin{cases} 4x - 5y = 1 \\ 2x + 3y = -5 \end{cases}$

11. $\begin{cases} 6x - 5y = 2 \\ 3x - 2y = 2 \end{cases}$

12. $\begin{cases} 4x + 2y = -6 \\ 3x + 4y = 8 \end{cases}$

13. $\begin{cases} 10x - 5y = 15 \\ -2x + y = 3 \end{cases}$

14. $\begin{cases} 4x + y = 5 \\ 8x + 2y = 10 \end{cases}$

15. $\begin{cases} 5x + 2y = -1 \\ 10x + 3y = -9 \end{cases}$

16. $\begin{cases} 5x - 4y = 8 \\ 2x + 3y = 17 \end{cases}$

17. $\begin{cases} 3x + 7y = 15 \\ 2x + 5y = 10 \end{cases}$

18. $\begin{cases} 5x - 2y = 14 \\ 7x + 3y = -21 \end{cases}$

19. $\begin{cases} 4x - 3y = 1 \\ -8x + 6y = 5 \end{cases}$

20. $\begin{cases} 4x - 6y = 8 \\ 6x - 9y = 10 \end{cases}$

21. $\begin{cases} 3x + 2y = 9 \\ 4x + 3y = 8 \end{cases}$

22. $\begin{cases} 4x + 7y = 1 \\ 3x + 5y = 0 \end{cases}$

23. $\begin{cases} 6x + 3y = 5 \\ 4x - 9y = -4 \end{cases}$

24. $\begin{cases} 8x + 3y = 5 \\ 12x - 6y = 18 \end{cases}$

25. $\begin{cases} 2x = -y + 5 \\ y = -3x + 12 \end{cases}$

26. $\begin{cases} x = 5y - 7 \\ 3y = 2x - 7 \end{cases}$

27. $\begin{cases} y = 4x + 3 \\ 5x = 2y \end{cases}$

28. $\begin{cases} \dfrac{3}{4}x - \dfrac{2}{5}y = 3 \\ \dfrac{4}{3}x - \dfrac{11}{15}y = 5 \end{cases}$

29. $\begin{cases} \dfrac{5}{3}x - \dfrac{7}{8}y = 3 \\ \dfrac{3}{2}x - \dfrac{5}{8}y = 4 \end{cases}$

30. $\begin{cases} -\dfrac{1}{5}x + \dfrac{1}{4}y = 1 \\ \dfrac{3}{2}x - \dfrac{5}{6}y = 5 \end{cases}$

31. $\begin{cases} \dfrac{2}{3}x + \dfrac{1}{2}y = 0 \\ \dfrac{7}{4}x - \dfrac{1}{5}y = 0 \end{cases}$

32. $\begin{cases} \dfrac{1}{2}x - \dfrac{2}{3}y = 2 \\ -\dfrac{5}{4}x + \dfrac{4}{3}y = -3 \end{cases}$

33. $\begin{cases} 4x + \dfrac{1}{3}y = 2 \\ \dfrac{8}{5}x + \dfrac{1}{5}y = 1 \end{cases}$

34. $\begin{cases} x + y = 30 \\ 0.07x - 0.03y = 0.1 \end{cases}$

35. $\begin{cases} x - y = 10 \\ 0.2x - 0.3y = 2 \end{cases}$

36. $\begin{cases} 0.4x - 0.3y = 0.5 \\ -0.6x + 0.5y = 1.5 \end{cases}$

37. $\begin{cases} 0.04x + 0.03y = -0.01 \\ 0.05x + 0.04y = 0.01 \end{cases}$

38. $\begin{cases} 0.05x + 0.02y = 0.03 \\ 0.07x + 0.03y = 0.02 \end{cases}$

39. $\begin{cases} 7(x + 3y) - 4(x + y) = 5 \\ 3(x - 2y) + 5(x + 7y) = -3 \end{cases}$

40. $\begin{cases} 6(x - y) + 5(2x - y) = 37 \\ 2(x - 2y) + 3(x - y) = 8 \end{cases}$

4.4 GRAPHING SYSTEMS OF LINEAR INEQUALITIES

☐ **Systems of Linear Inequalities in Two Variables**

☐ SYSTEMS OF LINEAR INEQUALITIES IN TWO VARIABLES

A system of linear inequalities is a classic example of basic mathematics used in linear programming to solve real-life problems in business, science, etc . . .

Examples of systems of linear inequalities in two variables:

$$\begin{cases} 6x - y \le 4 \\ 3x + 2y > 6 \end{cases} \qquad \begin{cases} 4x - 3y \ge 12 \\ x + 8y < 16 \\ 2x + y > 3 \end{cases} \qquad \begin{cases} x + y > 2 \\ 5x - y < 1 \\ x \ge 0 \\ y \ge 0 \end{cases}$$

Definition

*Two or more linear inequalities involving the same variables, considered together, is called a **system of linear inequalities**.*

In chapter 3 we learned that the solution of a linear inequality in two variables is the set of ordered pairs corresponding to all the points contained in one of the following half-planes: lower half-plane (below the line), upper half-plane (above the line), right half-plane, or left half-plane.

The solution can be specified by shading the appropriate region. The points on the lines are included in the solution set if the linear inequalities contain the inequality symbols "is less than or equal to" or "is greater than or equal to." This can be illustrated by graphing a solid line. Otherwise, the graph is a dotted line.

The solution of a system of linear inequalities, if there is one, is the region where the shaded half-planes (solutions) corresponding to the linear inequalities overlap. Thus, the solution can be obtained if we graph both inequalities of the system on the same coordinate system, and then shade the proper regions.

Example 1

Graph the system of linear inequalities.

$$\begin{cases} y < x+3 \\ y \geq -2x+1 \end{cases}$$

Solution

First, we graph the lines either using the slopes and y-intercepts or two convenient ordered pairs for each line. The lines are given by the following equations:

$y = x+3$ $y = -2x+1$

Slope: $m = \dfrac{1}{1}$, y-intercept $(0, 3)$ Slope: $m = \dfrac{-2}{1}$, y-intercept $(0, 1)$

Since $y < x + 3$ contains the symbol "is less than", draw a dotted line and shade the region bellow the line. The inequality $y \geq -2x + 1$ contains the symbol "is greater than or equal to." Therefore, we draw a solid line and shade the region above the line.

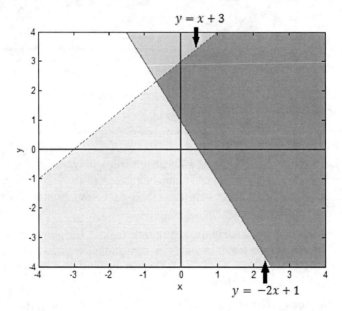

The solution of the system is the set of points located in the region where the shaded regions overlap.

Example 2

Graph the system of linear inequalities.

$$\begin{cases} 2x-3y \geq 6 \\ x+y < 1 \end{cases}$$

Solution

First, solve each inequality for y.

$$2x - 3y \geq 6 \qquad\qquad\qquad x + y < 1$$

$$\overline{-3y \geq -2x + 6} \qquad\qquad\qquad \overline{y < -x + 1}$$

$$\frac{-3y}{-3} \leq \frac{-2}{-3}x + \frac{6}{-3}$$

$$y \leq \frac{2}{3}x - 2$$

Since $y \leq \dfrac{2}{3}x - 2$ contains the inequality symbol $\leq$, we draw a solid line and shade the

region below the line.

The inequality $y < -x + 1$ contains the inequality symbol $<$. Therefore, we draw a dotted line and shade the region bellow the line.

Next, we graph the lines using two convenient ordered pairs for each line.

$$y = \frac{2}{3}x - 2 \qquad\qquad\qquad\qquad y = -x + 1$$

x	y
0	−2
3	0

x	y
1	0
0	1

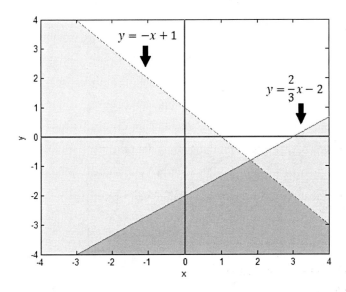

The solution of the system of inequalities is the set of points located in the region where the shaded regions overlap. The coordinates of a test point located in this region will satisfy both inequalities.

For example $(3, -3)$ is located in the darkest shaded region and it should satisfy both inequalities.

$y \leq \dfrac{2}{3}x - 2$

$-3 \leq \dfrac{2}{3}(3) - 2$

$-3 \leq 2 - 2$

$-3 \leq 0$ True

$y < -x + 1$

$-3 < -(3) + 1$

$-3 < -3 + 1$

$-3 < -2$ True

Example 3

Graph the system of linear inequalities.

$$\begin{cases} y \geq 2x + 3 \\ y \leq 2x - 1 \end{cases}$$

Solution

Since $y \geq 2x + 1$ contains the inequality symbol $\geq$, we draw a solid line and shade the region above the line. The inequality $y \geq 2x + 1$ contains the inequality symbol $\leq$. Therefore we draw a solid line and shade the region below the line.

Next, we draw the lines using the slopes and the y-intercepts.

$y \geq 2x + 3$ $y \leq 2x - 1$

Slope: $m = 2$, y-intercept $(0, 3)$ Slope: $m = 2$, y-intercept $(0, -1)$

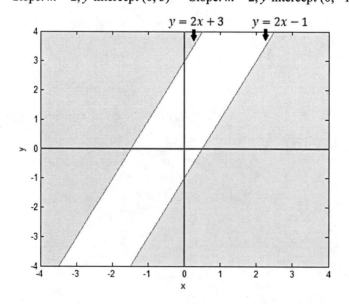

Since the shaded regions do not overlap, the system of linear inequalities has no solution.

Example 4

Solve the system of linear inequalities.

$$\begin{cases} x \geq -3 \\ y < 2 \end{cases}$$

Solution

The inequality $x \geq -3$ describes the half-plane on or to the right of the vertical line $x = -3$ because any point with the x-coordinate greater than or equal to -3 is located to the right of the line $x = -3$ (solid line, shade the right side).

The inequality $y < 2$ describes the half-plane below the horizontal line $y = 2$ because any point with the y-coordinate less than 2 is located bellow the line $y = 2$ (dotted line, shade bellow the line).

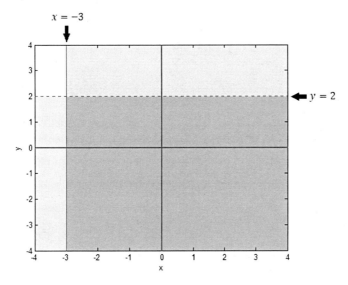

The solution of the system is the set of all the points in the region where the shaded regions overlap. Since the origin belongs to the solution, the test point (0, 0) should satisfy both inequalities.

$\underline{x \geq -3}$ $\underline{y < 2}$

$0 \geq -3$ True $0 < 2$ True

Example 5

Solve the system of linear inequalities.

$$\begin{cases} x+2y \le 4 \\ 3x+2y \le 6 \\ x \ge 0 \\ y \ge 0 \end{cases}$$

Solution

The inequality $x \ge 0$ describes the region on and to the right of y-axis. The inequality $y \ge 0$ describes the region on and above x-axis. From these two inequalities we conclude that the solution set is located in the first quadrant and the points on the coordinate axes belong to the solution set.

So, we just have to solve the first two inequalities for y and graph.

$$x+2y \le 4 \qquad\qquad 3x+2y \le 6$$

$$\overline{2y \le -x+4} \qquad\qquad \overline{2y \le -3x+6}$$

$$y \le -\frac{1}{2}x+2 \qquad\qquad y \le -\frac{3}{2}x+3$$

Slope: $m = -\dfrac{1}{2}$ y-intercept $(0, 2)$ Slope: $m = -\dfrac{3}{2}$, y-intercept $(0, 3)$

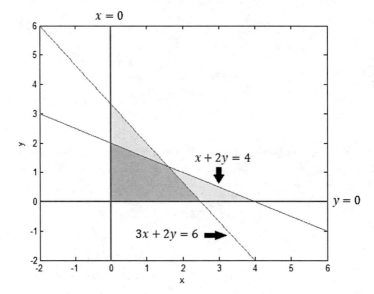

The solution is the set of all the points in the region where the shaded regions overlap.

Example 6
___

Solve the system of linear inequalities.

$$\begin{cases} -4 \le x < 3 \\ -1 < y \le 3 \end{cases}$$

Solution

The inequality $-4 \le x < 3$ describes the region between two vertical lines through $x = -4$ and $x = 3$. The inequality $-1 < y \le 3$ describes the region between two horizontal lines through $y = -1$ and $y = 3$.

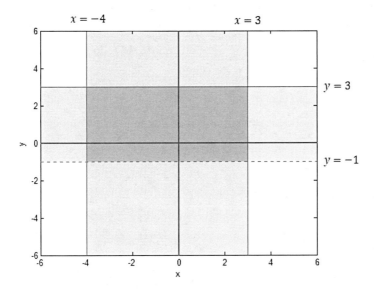

The solution of the system is the set of all the points in the region where the shaded regions overlap.

4.4 EXERCISES

Graph the solution of each system of linear inequalities.

1. $\begin{cases} y > x - 1 \\ y \le -2x + 3 \end{cases}$

2. $\begin{cases} y < x + 2 \\ y < 5x - 4 \end{cases}$

3. $\begin{cases} y \ge 3x - 2 \\ y \ge -x + 4 \end{cases}$

4. $\begin{cases} y \ge 4x - 1 \\ y - 1 < 4x \end{cases}$

5. $\begin{cases} y \geq \dfrac{1}{2}x - 1 \\ y - 1 < 2x \end{cases}$

6. $\begin{cases} 4x + y < +2 \\ y \leq \dfrac{1}{3}x - 2 \end{cases}$

7. $\begin{cases} y \leq \dfrac{3}{2}x - 3 \\ y \geq -\dfrac{1}{3}x + 1 \end{cases}$

8. $\begin{cases} y > \dfrac{4}{3}x - 4 \\ y \leq \dfrac{1}{2}x + 2 \end{cases}$

9. $\begin{cases} y \geq 4x - 2 \\ -2 < y \leq 1 \end{cases}$

10. $\begin{cases} y > -1 \\ y < x + 3 \end{cases}$

11. $\begin{cases} y \geq x - 2 \\ x < -2 \end{cases}$

12. $\begin{cases} y < \dfrac{2}{3}x + 1 \\ -1 < x \leq 3 \end{cases}$

13. $\begin{cases} y > 4x + 2 \\ y < 4x - 1 \end{cases}$

14. $\begin{cases} 2x + y \leq -3 \\ 2x + y > 2 \end{cases}$

15. $\begin{cases} x + y < 3 \\ -x - y \leq 1 \end{cases}$

16. $\begin{cases} x + 3y \geq 6 \\ 2x - y > 1 \end{cases}$

17. $\begin{cases} 2x + 3y < 6 \\ x - y \leq 2 \end{cases}$

18. $\begin{cases} 3x + y > 4 \\ 4x - 3y < 6 \end{cases}$

19. $\begin{cases} 5x + 3y \geq 9 \\ 3x - 2y < 4 \end{cases}$

20. $\begin{cases} 5x + 2y < 2 \\ y > x \end{cases}$

21. $\begin{cases} x - 5y \geq 5 \\ y < -x \end{cases}$

22. $\begin{cases} x + 4y \leq 4 \\ x + 3y < -3 \end{cases}$

23. $\begin{cases} 3x + 5y < 10 \\ 2x - 3y \leq 3 \end{cases}$

24. $\begin{cases} y + 4x > 3 \\ 2y - 3x < 2 \end{cases}$

25. $\begin{cases} x > -3 \\ y < -1 \end{cases}$

26. $\begin{cases} x \leq 2 \\ y < 3 \end{cases}$

27. $\begin{cases} -2 < x \le 3 \\ 1 \le y < 4 \end{cases}$

28. $\begin{cases} y \le -\dfrac{1}{3}x + 4 \\ x \ge 0 \\ y \ge 0 \end{cases}$

29. $\begin{cases} x + y < 3 \\ x \ge 0 \\ y \ge 0 \end{cases}$

30. $\begin{cases} 5x + 4y > 12 \\ x > 0 \\ y > 0 \end{cases}$

4.5 APPLICATIONS OF SYSTEMS OF LINEAR EQUATIONS

Most of the application problems in this section are the same type of word problems that we solved earlier in chapter 2. Then, one may ask what's different this time? Instead of using an equation in one variable, now we can use a **system of linear equations** in two variables to solve those problems. Indeed, when an application problem involves more than one unknown quantity, sometimes it is more convenient to use systems of linear equations to solve the problem.

The following example illustrates how a system of linear equations can be a very useful tool at your disposal when the situation calls for the use of systems.

Example 1

Tom invested $10,000 in two accounts. One account pays 3.5% annual simple interest and the other 5% annual simple interest. If the total interest earned from those two accounts after one year was $410, how much was invested at each rate?

Solution

Clearly this is an investment problem that involves two unknown quantities; the amount invested at 3.5% and the amount invested at 5%. Let x be the principal or the amount invested at 3.5% for instance. The most common mistake students make when using equations to solve this type of problem is to set the amount invested at 3.5% as x and the amount invested at 5% as $x - 10,000$ instead of $10,000 - x$.

So, if you are not sure, to avoid this dilemma, let y be the amount invested at 5%. Since two variables are involved, we need a system of linear equation to solve the problem.

Recall, the basic formula used to solve investment problems is $P \cdot r = I$ when $t = 1$ (principal × rate = interest earned). We can use the following chart to organize the information of the problem.

$$P \times r = I$$

		$P \times r = I$	
1st account	x	0.035	0.035x
2nd account	y	0.05	0.05y
	$10,000		$410

The system can be written as follows:

$$\begin{cases} x + y = 10,000 \\ 0.035x + 0.05y = 410 \end{cases}$$

First, multiply the bottom equation by 1,000 to avoid decimals.

$$\begin{cases} x + y = 10,000 \\ 35x + 50y = 410,000 \end{cases}$$

Now, we can solve the system by either the addition or substitution method. Since there is no obvious difference to use one method instead of the other for this system, we use the method of addition. To eliminate x, we multiply the top equation by -35 and the system becomes:

$$\begin{cases} -35x - 35y = -350,000 \\ 35x + 50y = 410,000 \end{cases}$$

$15y = 60,000$ (add the equations)

$y = 4,000$

To find x, we substitute 4,000 for y in the top original equation,

$x + 4,000 = 10,000$

$x = 10,000 - 4,000$

$x = 6,000$

So, the amount invested at 3.5% was $6,000 and the amount invested at 5% was $4,000.

Note: This problem can be solved using an equation in one variable if we set the amount invested at 5% as $10,000 - x$ instead of y.

Example 2

A motorboat can travel 24 mi with the current in 2 hours. On the return trip, against the current the same distance is traveled in 3 hours. Find the speed of the motorboat in still water and the speed of the current.

Solution

This is a motion problem and involves two unknown quantities: the speed of the boat in still water and the speed of the current. Let x = the speed of the motorboat in still water and y = the speed of the current. Since two variables are involved in this problem, we use a system of linear equations to solve the problem.

The speed of a boat traveling with the current is greater than the speed of a boat in calm water. Thus the speed of the boat traveling with the current is represented by $x + y$.

Using the same principle, the speed of the boat traveling against the current is $x - y$.

The basic formula used to solve motion problems is the distance formula $D = R \cdot T$ (Distance = Rate × Time).

Again, we use a chart to organize the information of the problem.

	R ×	T =	D
With	$x + y$	2	24
Against	$x - y$	3	24

The system can be written as follows:

$$\begin{cases} 2(x+y) = 24 \\ 3(x-y) = 24 \end{cases}$$

If we divide the top equation by 2 and the bottom equation by 3, the system becomes:

$$\begin{cases} x+y = 12 \\ x-y = 8 \end{cases}$$

The addition method is an obvious choice for this system.

$$\begin{cases} x+y = 12 \\ x-y = 8 \end{cases}$$

$2x / = 20$ (add the equations)

$x = 10$

Substitute 10 for x in $x + y = 12$ to obtain y.

$10 + y = 12$

$y = 12 - 10$

$y = 2$

Thus, the speed of the motorboat in still water was 10 mph and the speed of the current was 2 mph.

Example 3

A grocer wishes to mix chocolate raisins worth $4.49 per pound with chocolate buttons and peanuts worth $5.21 per pound to get 15 pounds of mixture that sells for $4.73 per pound. How many pounds of each should the grocer use to obtain the desire mixture?

Solution

This is a value mixture problem and involves two unknown quantities: the amount of chocolate raisins and the amount of chocolate buttons with peanuts. Let x = the amount of chocolate raisins and y = the amount of chocolate buttons with peanuts. The basic formula used to solve value mixture problems is $A \cdot C = V$ (Amount × Cost = Value).

The following chart can be used to organize the given information of the problem,

	A × C = V		
Chocolate Raisins	x	4.49	4.49x
Chocolate Buttons	y	5.21	5.21y
Mixture	15	4.73	(15)(4.73) = 70.95

The system can be written as follows:

$$\begin{cases} x+y=15 \\ 4.49x+5.21y=70.95 \end{cases}$$

To eliminate the decimals, multiply the bottom equation by 100.

$$\begin{cases} x+y=15 \\ 449x+521y=7095 \end{cases}$$

To avoid multiplying the top equation by large numbers (required by the addition method), we use the substitution method for this system. Solve for x from the top equation.

$x = 15 - y$ (substitution)

Substitute $15 - y$ for x in the bottom equation to eliminate x.

$449(15-y)+521y=7095$

$6735-449y+521y=7095$

$6735+72y=7095$

$72y=7095-6735$

$72y=360$

$y=5$

Substitute 5 for y in the substitution to obtain x.

$x=15-y$

$x=15-5$

$x=10$

Thus, the grocer uses 10 pounds of chocolate raisins and 5 pounds of chocolate buttons.

Example 4

How many gallons of a 28% antifreeze solution should be mixed with a 68% antifreeze solution to obtain 10 gallons of 45% antifreeze solution?

Solution

This is a percent mixture problem and involves two unknown quantities: the amount of 28% antifreeze solution and the amount of 68% antifreeze solution.

Let x = amount of 28% antifreeze solution and y = amount of 68% antifreeze solution.

The basic formula used to solve the percent mixture problems is $A \cdot r = Q$ (amount of solution × concentration rate = quantity of a substance). The following chart is very useful to organize the information of the problem.

	$A \times r = Q$		
28% solution	x	0.28	0.28x
68% solution	y	0.68	0.68y
Mixture	x + 3	0.45	(10)(0.45) = 4.5

The system can be written as follows:

$$\begin{cases} x+y=10 \\ 0.28x+0.68y=4.5 \end{cases}$$

Multiply the bottom equation by 100 to eliminate the decimals,

$$\begin{cases} x+y=10 \\ 28x+68y=450 \end{cases}$$

Again, let's use the substitution method. Solve x from the top equation.

$x=10-y$ (substitution)

Substitute $10-y$ for x in the bottom equation to eliminate x.

$$28(10-y)+68y=450$$
$$280-28y+68y=450$$
$$280+40y=450$$
$$40y=450-280$$
$$40y=170$$
$$y=4.25$$

Substitute 4.25 for y in the substitution to obtain x.

$$x=10-y$$
$$x=10-4.25$$
$$x=5.75$$

The amount of 28% antifreeze solution is 5.75 gallons and the amount of 68% antifreeze solution is 4.25 gallons.

Example 5

Four shirts and two ties cost $194 and two shirts and three ties cost $147. Find the cost of a shirt and the cost of a tie.

Solution

Let x = cost of a shirt and y = cost of a tie. The system can be written as follows:

$$\begin{cases} 4x+2y=194 \\ 2x+3y=147 \end{cases}$$

The addition method is an obvious choice for this system. Multiply the bottom equation by –2 to eliminate x.

$$\begin{cases} 4x+2y=194 \\ -4x-6y=-294 \end{cases}$$

$$/\,{-4y}=-100$$
$$y=25$$

Substitute 25 for y into the top equation to obtain x.

$4x + 2(25) = 194$

$4x + 50 = 194$

$4x = 194 - 50$

$4x = 144$

$x = 36$

Thus, a shirt cost $36 and a tie cost $25.

Example 6

A cash register contains $7.50 in dimes and nickels. If there are 105 coins in the register, how many dimes and how many nickels are in the cash register?

Solution

This is a coin problem and involves two unknown quantities: the number of dimes and the number of nickels. Let x = the number of dimes and y = the number of nickels in the cash register.

The system can be written as follows:

$$\begin{cases} x + y = 105 \\ 0.10x + 0.05y = 7.50 \end{cases}$$

Multiply the bottom equation by 100 to eliminate the decimals.

$$\begin{cases} x + y = 105 \\ 10x + 5y = 750 \end{cases}$$

For no specific reason, let's use the substitution method to solve the system.

Solve for y from the top equation.

$y = 105 - x$ (substitution)

Substitute $105 - x$ for y into the bottom equation to eliminate y.

$10x + 5(105 - x) = 750$

$10x + 525 - 5x = 750$

$5x = 750 - 525$

$5x = 225$

$x = 45$

Substitute 45 for x into the substitution to obtain y. $y = 105 - x = 105 - 45 = 60$. Thus, the cash register contains 45 dimes and 60 nickels.

4.5 EXERCISES

Investment Problems

1. A total of $15,000 was invested in two saving accounts. One account pays 4% annual simple interest and the other 6% annual simple interest. If the total interest earned after 1 year was $760, how much was invested at each rate?

2. John invested $6,000 in two saving accounts. One account pays 5% annual simple interest and the other 5.5% annual simple interest. If the total interest earned after 1 year was $320, how much did he invest at each rate?

3. A teacher invested $11,000 in two accounts. Part of the money was invested at 8% annual simple interest and the remainder at 6% annual simple interest. If the teacher received a total of $820 in interest after one year, how much did the teacher invest in each account?

4. Mary invested $30,000 in two bonds that pay 4.5% and 6.5% annual simple interest. If the total annual interest income from those two accounts after one year was $1590, how much was invested at each rate?

5. Susan invested $10,200 in two saving accounts. One account pays 3.5% annual simple interest and the other 5% annual simple interest. If the interest earned in one year from those two accounts was the same, how much did she invest in each account?

6. Bob invested three times as much at 8% annual simple interest as she did at 5% annual simple interest. If the total interest earned in one year from both accounts was $870, how much did he invest at each rate?

7. Jane invested twice as much at 4% annual simple interest as she did at 5%. If the total interest earned in one year from those two accounts was $260, how much did she invest at each rate?

8. A total of $20,000 was invested in two saving accounts. One account pays 3.9% annual simple interest and the other 4.5%. If the total interest earned in one year from those two accounts was the same, how much was invested at each rate?

Motion Problems

9. A boat can travel 18 miles against the current in 2 hours. On the return trip, the same distance is traveled in 1.2 hours. Find the speed of the boat in still water and the speed of the current.

10. It takes a boat 3 hours to travel 42 miles downstream, while it takes 4 hours longer to make the return trip upstream. Find the speed of the boat in still water and the speed of the current.

11. A small plane can fly 600 miles with the wind in 3 hours. On the return, flying against the wind the same distance is traveled in 4 hours. Find the speed of the plane in calm air and the speed of the wind.

12. An airplane flying with the wind can travel 2750 miles in 5 hours. The return trip against the wind takes 5.5 hours to travel the same distance. Find the speed of the plane in still air and the speed of the wind.

13. A car and a truck start at the same point and travel in opposite directions. The car travels 8 mi per hour faster than the truck. After 3 hours the car and the truck are 354 miles apart. Find the average speed of the car and the truck.

14. Two cars are 330 miles apart and travel toward each other. If they meet in 3 hours, and the difference of their speeds is 6 mph, find the average speed of each car.

Value Mixture Problems

15. John runs a coffee shop in downtown Seattle. He wants to mix coffee that sells for $6.50 per pound with coffee that sells for $7.90 per pound. How many pounds of each coffee should he use to get 42 pounds of mixture that sells for $7.00 per pound?

16. A shopkeeper sells regular coffee for $4.50 per pound and a gourmet coffee for $7.50 per pound. How many pounds of each coffee should the shopkeeper use to get 30 pounds of a blend that sells for $5.50 per pound?

17. A grocer wants to mix peanuts worth $4.90 per pound with hazelnuts worth $7.90 per pound to get 30 pounds of mixture that sells for $6.70 per pound. How many pounds of each should the grocer use?

18. Jane wants to mix almonds worth $6.99 per pound with cashews worth $8.99 per pound to get 50 pounds of mixture that sells for $389.50. How many pound of each should Jane use?

19. A merchant wishes to mix chocolate peanuts worth $4.99 per pound with chocolate raisins worth $4.49 per pound to get 20 pounds of mixture that sells for $95. How many pounds of each should the merchant use?

20. How many pounds of peppermint patties that sell for $1.45 per pound and how many pounds of lemon drops that sell for $1.85 per pound should be mixed to make 16 pounds of a mixture that sells for $1.60 per pound?

Percent Mixture Problems

21. How many ounces of a 35% acid solution should be mixed with a 60% acid solution to get 40 ounces of a 50% acid solution?

22. How many gallons of a 30% alcohol solution and how many gallons of a 70% alcohol solution should be mixed to get 10 gallons of 50% alcohol solution?

23. How many gallons of a 20% antifreeze solution and how many gallons of a 50% antifreeze solution should be mixed to get 30 gallons of a 40% antifreeze solution?

24. How many liters of a 25% hydrochloric acid solution should be mixed with a 65% hydrochloric acid solution to get 50 liters of a 45% hydrochloric acid solution?

25. How many liters of distilled water should be mixed with an 80% acid solution to get 20 liters of a 50% acid solution?

26. How many ounces of pure acid should be mixed with a 20% acid solution to get 40 ounces of a 65% acid solution?

Miscellaneous Problems

27. The tickets for a museum cost $8 for adults and $2.50 for children. How many tickets of each kind were sold in one weekend if altogether 200 tickets were sold for $775?

28. Three pairs of shoes and four pairs of socks cost $199, and two pairs of shoes and six pairs of socks cost $151. Find the cost of a pair of shoes and the cost of a pair of socks.

29. Tim has 40 dimes and quarters with a total value of $7.75. How many dimes and how many quarters does he have?

30. A coin collector has 65 nickels and quarters with a total value of $8.25. How many nickels and how many quarters does the coin collector have?

31. The sum of two positive integers is 35 and the difference between the larger and smaller integer is 7. Find the integers.

32. The sum of two integers is 29. If one integer is 7 more than the other, find the integers.

33. A stamp collection consists of 15-cent stamps and 40-cent stamps. There are 8 more 15-cent stamps than 40-cent stamps. If the total value of the stamps in the collection is $10, find the number of 15-cents stamps and 40-cent stamps.

34. A stamp collector has some 20-cent stamps and 35-cent stamps. The total value of the stamps in the collection is $19.50. If the collector has 75 stamps, find the number of 20-cent stamps and the number of 35-cent stamps.

CHAPTER 4 REVIEW EXERCISES

Solve each system of linear equations by the graphing method.

1. $\begin{cases} y = 3x - 2 \\ y = -\dfrac{1}{2}x + 5 \end{cases}$

2. $\begin{cases} y = x - 3 \\ 2x + y = 3 \end{cases}$

3. $\begin{cases} x + 2y = 4 \\ 3x - y = 5 \end{cases}$

4. $\begin{cases} x = y + 2 \\ 2x - 2y = 4 \end{cases}$

5. $\begin{cases} 2x + y = -6 \\ x = -2 \end{cases}$

6. $\begin{cases} x + 4y = 8 \\ y = 1 \end{cases}$

7. $\begin{cases} 4x - 3y = 6 \\ x - 3y = -3 \end{cases}$

8. $\begin{cases} x - 2y = 0 \\ 4x - y = -7 \end{cases}$

9. $\begin{cases} x + 4y = -4 \\ -x + y = -1 \end{cases}$

Solve each system of linear equations by the substitution method.

10. $\begin{cases} 3x + 2y = 7 \\ 2x + y = 4 \end{cases}$

11. $\begin{cases} x + 2y = 4 \\ 2x - y = 3 \end{cases}$

12. $\begin{cases} x - 2y = 0 \\ 3x - 4y = -2 \end{cases}$

13. $\begin{cases} 4x - y = 5 \\ -8x + 2y = 1 \end{cases}$

14. $\begin{cases} \dfrac{x}{4} + \dfrac{y}{3} = -\dfrac{1}{3} \\ x + 3y = 7 \end{cases}$

15. $\begin{cases} y = 5x - 1 \\ 10x - 2y = 2 \end{cases}$

16. $\begin{cases} 3x + 2y = -10 \\ x + 5y = 1 \end{cases}$

17. $\begin{cases} 4x + 3y = -1 \\ x + y = -2 \end{cases}$

18. $\begin{cases} 5x + 4y = 8 \\ x - y = 7 \end{cases}$

Solve each system of linear equations by the addition (elimination) method.

19. $\begin{cases} 5x + 2y = -1 \\ x - y = 4 \end{cases}$

20. $\begin{cases} 3x + 4y = 3 \\ 9x - 2y = 2 \end{cases}$

21. $\begin{cases} 4x + 5y = 3 \\ 3x - 2y = 8 \end{cases}$

22. $\begin{cases} 2x - 5y = 5 \\ -6x + 7y = 9 \end{cases}$

23. $\begin{cases} 4x - 10y = 5 \\ -2x + 5y = 1 \end{cases}$

24. $\begin{cases} x = 4y + 5 \\ 3x - 12y = 15 \end{cases}$

25. $\begin{cases} \dfrac{x}{3} + \dfrac{y}{4} = 4 \\ \dfrac{x}{2} + \dfrac{y}{8} = 4 \end{cases}$

26. $\begin{cases} 0.5x - 0.8y = 0.7 \\ 0.4x - 0.7y = 0.5 \end{cases}$

27. $\begin{cases} 4x + 3y = 1 \\ 12x - 15y = 8 \end{cases}$

Graph the solution of each system of linear inequalities.

28. $\begin{cases} y < \dfrac{1}{2}x + 3 \\ y \geq -x + 1 \end{cases}$

29. $\begin{cases} 2x + 3y \geq 6 \\ 3x - y > 1 \end{cases}$

30. $\begin{cases} y < -\dfrac{3}{2}x + 1 \\ x \geq 0 \\ y \geq 0 \end{cases}$

31. An investment club invested $10,000 into two simple interest accounts. On one account the annual simple interest rate is 4% , and on the other account the simple annual interest rate is 6%. If the total interest earned from the two accounts in one year is $440, find the amount invested into each account.

32. Tom invested $30,000 into two accounts. One account pays 3.5% annual simple interest, and the other account pays 4.5% annual simple interest. If the total interest earned from both accounts in one year is $1250, how much was invested into each account?

33. Two cars start from the same point at the same time and travel in opposite directions. The eastbound car is traveling 10 mph faster than the westbound car. In 3 hours the cars are 330 miles apart. Find the speed of each car.

34. A commercial plane flies 565 mph with the wind and 515 mph against the wind. Find the speed of the plane in still air and the speed of the wind.

35. A coffee merchant wishes to mix mocha coffee that sells for $8 per pound with Kona coffee that sells for $12 per pound to get 40 pounds of a blend that sells for $9.50 per pound. How many pounds of each coffee should the merchant use to obtain the desired blend?

36. How many ounces of pure silver that costs $19.40 per ounce and how many ounces of a silver alloy that costs $12.50 per ounce should be mixed to make 120 ounces of an alloy that costs $17.10 per ounce?

37. How many liters of a 72% alcohol solution, and how many liters of a 28% alcohol solution should be mixed to get 15 liters of a 36.8% alcohol solution?

38. How many liters of pure acid must be added to a 20% acid solution to make 8 liters of a 35% acid solution?

39. A coin bank contains 85 coins in nickels and quarters. If the total value of the coins is $9.25, find the number of nickels and quarters in the coin bank.

40. The sum of two positive integers is 63 and the difference between the larger and the smaller integer is 11. Find the integers.

5 EXPONENTS AND POLYNOMIALS

5.1 THE PRODUCT AND POWER RULES OF EXPONENTS

□ **Product Rule** □ **Power Rule** □ **Power Rule for a Product** □ **Power Rule for a Quotient**

In section 1.3 we learned that multiplication that involves a repeated factor can be written in a compact form called exponential form.

Example 1

$4 \cdot 4 \cdot 4 = 4^3$ where the number 4 is called the *base*, 3 is the *exponent*, and 4^3 is called *exponential expression* or *power term*.

□ PRODUCT RULE

In this section our main goal is to simplify algebraic expressions involving exponential expressions with integer exponents. This can be accomplished by using the rules of exponents.

Example 2

Use the definition of exponents to find the products.

a. $3^4 \cdot 3^2$ b. $x^2 \cdot x^3$ c. $a^m \cdot a^n$

Solution

a. $3^4 \cdot 3^2 = (3 \cdot 3 \cdot 3 \cdot 3)(3 \cdot 3) = 3 \cdot 3 \cdot 3 \cdot 3 \cdot 3 \cdot 3 = 3^6 = 3^{4+2}$

b. $x^2 \cdot x^3 = (x \cdot x)(x \cdot x \cdot x) = x \cdot x \cdot x \cdot x \cdot x = x^5 = x^{2+3}$

c. $a^m \cdot a^n = \underbrace{(a \cdot a \cdot a \cdots a)}_{(m)\,factors} \underbrace{(a \cdot a \cdot a \cdots a)}_{(n)\,factors} = \underbrace{a \cdot a \cdot a \cdots a}_{(m+n)\,factors} = a^{m+n}$

These examples can be summarized in a product rule for multiplying exponential expressions with the same base. The rule can be expressed in general form as follows:

Product Rule

$a^m \cdot a^n = a^{m+n}$ where a is a real number and m and n are positive integers.

Thus, to multiply exponential expressions with the same base, *add* the exponents and keep the common base.

☐ POWER RULE

Example 3

Use the product rule to multiply the following exponential expressions.

a. $7^3 \cdot 7^4$

c. $x^4 \cdot x^5$

b. $(-2)^5 \cdot (-2)^8$

d. $-2m^6 \cdot m^4$

e. $(3a^3)(4a^5)$

Solution

a. $7^3 \cdot 7^4 = 7^{3+4} = 7^7$

d. $-2m^6 \cdot m^4 = -2m^{6+4} = -2m^{10}$

b. $(-2)^5 \cdot (-2)^8 = (-2)^{5+8} = (-2)^{13}$

e. $(3a^3)(4a^5) = (3 \cdot 4)(a^3 \cdot a^5) = 12a^{3+5} = 12a^8$

c. $x^4 \cdot x^5 = x^{4+5} = x^9$

Example 4

Use the definition of exponents to simplify.

a. $\left(4^3\right)^2$

b. $\left(x^2\right)^4$

c. $\left(a^m\right)^n$

Solution

a. $(4^3)^2 = 4^3 \cdot 4^3 = (4 \cdot 4 \cdot 4)(4 \cdot 4 \cdot 4) = 4 \cdot 4 \cdot 4 \cdot 4 \cdot 4 \cdot 4 = 4^6 = 4^{(3)(2)}$

b. $(x^2)^4 = x^2 \cdot x^2 \cdot x^2 \cdot x^2 = (x \cdot x)(x \cdot x)(x \cdot x)(x \cdot x) = x \cdot x \cdot x \cdot x \cdot x \cdot x \cdot x \cdot x = x^8 = x^{(2)(4)}$

c. $\left(a^m\right)^n = \underset{(n)\,factors}{a^m \cdot a^m \cdot a^m \cdots a^m} = \underset{(m)\,factors}{(a \cdot a \cdot a \cdots a)}\underset{(m)\,factors}{(a \cdot a \cdot a \cdots a)} \cdots \underset{(m)\,factors}{(a \cdot a \cdot a \cdots a)} =$

$\underset{(n)\,groups..of..(m)\,factors}{(a \cdot a \cdot a \cdots a)(a \cdot a \cdot a \cdots a) \cdots (a \cdot a \cdot a \cdots a)} = \underset{(m \cdot n)\,factors}{(a \cdot a \cdot a \cdots a)} = a^{m \cdot n}$

These examples can be summarized in the following rule for exponents.

Power Rule

$(a^m)^n = a^{m \cdot n}$ where a is a real number and m and n are positive integers.

To raise an exponential expression to a power, *multiply* the exponents and keep the base.

☐ POWER RULE FOR A PRODUCT

Example 5

Use the power rule to simplify each exponential expression.

a. $(8^3)^5$

b. $((-2)^4)^6$

c. $(x^5)^2$

d. $((-m)^2)^4$

Solution

a. $(8^3)^5 = 8^{(3)(5)} = 8^{15}$

c. $(x^5)^2 = x^{(5)(2)} = x^{10}$

b. $((-2)^4)^6 = (-2)^{(4)(6)} = (-2)^{24}$

d. $((-m)^2)^4 = (-m)^{(2)(4)} = (-m)^8$

The power rule has two consequences: the power rule for a product and power rule for a quotient.

Example 6

Use the definition of exponents to simplify.

$(ab)^3$

Solution

$$(ab)^3 = (ab)(ab)(ab) = a \cdot b \cdot a \cdot b \cdot a \cdot b = (a \cdot a \cdot a)(b \cdot b \cdot b) = a^3b^3$$

This example suggests the following rule for the power of a product.

Power Rule for a Product

$(a \cdot b)^n = a^n \cdot b^n$ where a and b are real numbers and n is a positive integer.

When a product is raised to a power, each factor is raised to that power.

☐ POWER RULE FOR A QUOTIENT

Example 7

Use the power rule for a product to simplify each expression.

a. $(3x)^4$
b. $(-4x^2)^3$
c. $(2a^2b^3)^4$
d. $4(-3m^4n^5)^2$

Solution

a. $(3x)^4 = (3)^4(x)^4 = 81x^4$

b. $(-4x^2)^3 = (-4)^3(x^2)^3 = -64x^6$

c. $(2a^2b^3)^4 = (2)^4(a^2)^4(b^3)^4 = 16a^8b^{12}$

d. $4(-3m^4n^5)^2 = 4(-3)^2(m^4)^2(n^5)^2 = 4(9)m^8n^{10} = 36m^8n^{10}$

Example 8

Use the definition of exponents to simplify.

$\left(\dfrac{a}{b}\right)^3$

Solution

$$\left(\frac{a}{b}\right)^3 = \left(\frac{a}{b}\right)\left(\frac{a}{b}\right)\left(\frac{a}{b}\right) = \frac{a \cdot a \cdot a}{b \cdot b \cdot b} = \frac{a^3}{b^3}$$

This example suggests the following rule for the power of a quotient.

Power Rule for a Quotient

$$\left(\frac{a}{b}\right)^n = \frac{a^n}{b^n} \quad \text{where } a \text{ and } b \text{ are real numbers}$$

$(b \neq 0)$ and n is a positive integer.

When a quotient is raised to a power, both the numerator and denominator are raised to that power.

Example 7

Use the power rule for a quotient to simplify each expression.

a. $\left(\dfrac{3}{4}\right)^4$ b. $\left(\dfrac{x}{2}\right)^3$ c. $\left(\dfrac{x^2}{y^4}\right)^5$ d. $\left(\dfrac{5m^3}{2n^2}\right)^2$

Solution

a. $\left(\dfrac{3}{4}\right)^4 = \dfrac{3^4}{4^4} = \dfrac{81}{256}$

c. $\left(\dfrac{x^2}{y^4}\right)^5 = \dfrac{\left(x^2\right)^5}{\left(y^4\right)^5} = \dfrac{x^{10}}{y^{20}}$

b. $\left(\dfrac{x}{2}\right)^3 = \dfrac{x^3}{2^3} = \dfrac{x^3}{8}$

d. $\left(\dfrac{5m^3}{2n^2}\right)^2 = \dfrac{\left(5m^3\right)^2}{\left(2n^2\right)^2} = \dfrac{25m^6}{4n^4}$

Example 9

Simplify.

$$\left(-2x^3y^4\right)\left(6x^7y^5\right)$$

Solution

Use the product rule.

$$\left(-2x^3y^4\right)\left(6x^7y^5\right) = (-2 \cdot 6)x^3x^7y^4y^5 = -12x^{3+7}y^{4+5} = -12x^{10}y^9$$

Example 10

Simplify.

$$\left(-4ab^3\right)^2\left(3a^4b^5\right)$$

Solution

First, use the power rule to simplify $\left(-4ab^3\right)^2$, then use the product rule.

$$\left(-4ab^3\right)^2\left(3a^4b^5\right)=[(-4)^2\,a^2\,(b^3)^2](3a^4b^5)=16a^2b^6\cdot3a^4b^5=16\cdot3a^2a^4b^6b^5=48a^6b^{11}$$

Example 11

Simplify.

$$\left(5m^6n^2\right)^2\left(-m^3n^5\right)^3$$

Solution

Use the power rule to simplify $\left(5m^6n^2\right)^2$ and $\left(-m^3n^5\right)^3$ then use the product rule.

$$\left(5m^6n^2\right)^2\left(-m^3n^5\right)^3=[(5)^2(m^6)^2(n^2)^2][(-1)^3(m^3)^3(n^5)^3]=25m^{12}n^4(-1)m^9n^{15}=-25m^{21}n^{19}$$

Example 12

Simplify.

$$\left(\frac{2x^2y^3}{5a^7b^4}\right)^3$$

Solution

Use the power rule for a quotient to raise the numerator and denominator to the third power. Then use the power rule for a product to raise each factor to the third power.

$$\left(\frac{2x^2y^3}{5a^7b^4}\right)^3=\frac{(2x^2y^3)^3}{(5a^7b^4)^3}=\frac{2^3(x^2)^3(y^3)^3}{5^3(a^7)^3(b^4)^3}=\frac{8x^6y^9}{125a^{21}b^{12}}$$

To simplify this expression in one step, a combination of the power rule for a quotient and product can be used to raise each factor inside the parenthesis to the third power.

Example 13

Simplify.

$$\left(\frac{3a}{4b}\right)^3\left(\frac{-4a^2}{9b^3}\right)^2$$

Solution

$$\left(\frac{3a}{4b}\right)^3\left(\frac{-4a^2}{9b^3}\right)^2=\frac{(3a)^3}{(4b)^3}\cdot\frac{(-4a^2)^2}{(9b^3)^2}=\frac{27a^3}{64b^3}\cdot\frac{16a^4}{81b^6}=\frac{a^3a^4}{4b^3\cdot3b^6}=\frac{a^7}{12b^9}$$

5.1 EXERCISES

Evaluate each exponential expression.

1. 5^3

2. $(-5)^2$

3. -5^2

4. $(-2)^3$

5. $(-3)^4$

6. $(-1)^{10}$

7. $(-3)^3$

8. -3^3

9. $3^2 - 2^2$

Use the Product Rule for exponents to simplify each expression.

10. $2^2 \cdot 2^3$

11. $(-3) \cdot (-3)^3$

12. $(-4)(-4)^2$

13. $-5 \cdot 5^2$

14. $-2^4 \cdot 2^2$

15. $(-6)(-6)^8$

16. $(-3)^4 (-3)^5$

17. $(-5)^3 (-5)^7$

18. $7^3 \cdot 7 \cdot 7^4$

19. $x^4 \cdot x^7$

20. $y^3 \cdot y^9$

21. $-a^5 \cdot a^6$

22. $-m^3 \cdot m^{10}$

23. $(-x)^4 (-x)^3$

24. $(-y)^8 (-y)^2$

25. $(-5a^5)(4a^7)$

26. $(-10x^9)(-3x^4)$

27. $(11y^3)(-6y^4)$

28. $(-6x^2 y^3)(-4xy^6)$

29. $(3m^5 n^4)(7m^9 n)$

30. $(5a^2 b^3)^2$

31. $(-ab)(3a^2 bc^3)$

32. $9xy(-2x^3)(-y^4)$

33. $6m^2(-mn^3)(n^2)$

Use the Power Rule for exponents to simplify each expression.

34. $(2^3)^2$

35. $(7^4)^3$

36. $(5^8)^2$

37. $(9^5)^4$

38. $(x^3)^6$

39. $(y^4)^{10}$

40. $(m^7)^2$

41. $(3a^2)^3$

42. $(-4x^5)^2$

43. $(-5y^4)^3$

44. $(x^5 y^4)^6$

45. $(m^8 n^6)^5$

46. $(2x^2 y^3)^4$

47. $(4a^3 b^5)^3$

48. $(-5x^3 yz^2)^2$

49. $(-3mn^4)^3$

50. $(8a^6 b^7 c^2)^2$

51. $(-2x^8 y^4 z^3)^5$

52. $\left(\dfrac{xy}{z} \right)^8$

53. $\left(\dfrac{a}{bc} \right)^6$

54. $\left(\dfrac{x^5 y^4}{2} \right)^5$

55. $\left(\dfrac{xy^3}{9} \right)^2$

56. $\left(\dfrac{5x^2}{10y^3}\right)^5$

58. $\left(\dfrac{4a^3b^6}{c^8}\right)^2$

60. $\left(\dfrac{-m^5n^6}{x^7y^2}\right)^{10}$

57. $\left(\dfrac{3x^4y^8}{4ab^5}\right)^3$

59. $\left(\dfrac{-2x^8y^3}{5a^3b^4}\right)^3$

Simplify each exponential expression.

61. $(-4x)^2(-4x)$

62. $(-5x)(-5x)^3$

63. $(2x^2y^5)^3(x^4y)$

64. $(-3a^3b^3)^2(5ab^8)$

65. $(9m^5n^9)(-4m^2n^6)^2$

66. $(7xy^8)^2(-x^9y^4)$

67. $(4x^2y^5z)^3(-x^4z^6)^2$

68. $(-5m^4n^3)^2(m^3n)^5$

69. $(-a^6b^{10})^3(-a^4b^5)^4$

70. $(10x^9y^8)^2(-2xy^3)^3$

71. $(-a^5b^7c)^3(3a^2b^4)^4$

72. $(4x^4y^7)^2(x^8y^5)^3$

73. $\left(\dfrac{3m^3n^5}{a^7}\right)^4$

74. $\left(-\dfrac{2x^2y^3}{m^4}\right)^5$

75. $\left(-\dfrac{x^8}{9a^5b^8}\right)^2$

76. $\left(\dfrac{z^3}{3x^3y^6}\right)^4$

77. $\left(\dfrac{5a^3b^4}{2x^9y^7}\right)^3$

78. $\left(\dfrac{15m^5n^6}{25x^3y^2}\right)^2$

79. $\left(\dfrac{-x^{10}y^{12}}{2a^7b^4}\right)^3$

80. $\left(\dfrac{-m^3n^5}{3x^2y^8}\right)^4$

81. $\left(\dfrac{3x}{2y}\right)^3\left(\dfrac{4x}{y}\right)^2$

82. $\left(\dfrac{2a}{3b}\right)^4\left(\dfrac{a^5}{b^3}\right)^3$

83. $\left(\dfrac{x^3y^4}{ab^5}\right)^3\left(\dfrac{-xy^5}{4ab}\right)^2$

84. $\left(\dfrac{-mn^8}{3xy}\right)^2\left(\dfrac{m^2n^3}{x^4y}\right)^3$

5.2 ZERO EXPONENT, NEGATIVE EXPONENT, AND QUOTIENT RULES

□ Summary of the Rules of Exponents

Zero Exponent Rule

If $a \neq 0$, then $a^0 = 1$.

We can use the product rule from the previous section to understand why the zero exponent rule is true.

Use the product rule for exponents to simplify: $a^0 \cdot a = a^0 \cdot a^1 = a^{0+1} = a^1 = a$ $a \neq 0$

Thus, $a^0 \cdot a = a$ $a \neq 0$

Divide both sides by a: $a^0 = \dfrac{a}{a} = 1$ $a \neq 0$

Example 1

Evaluate each exponential expression. Assume $x \neq 0$.

  a. 4^0 c. -3^0 f. $(x+9)^0$

  b. $(-2)^0$ d. $(4x)^0$ g. $5(x-4)^0$

                                e. $4x^0$

Solution

  a. $4^0 = 1$ d. $(4x)^0 = 1$ f. $(x+9)^0 = 1$

  b. $(-2)^0 = 1$ e. $4x^0 = 4 \cdot 1 = 4$ g. $5(x-4)^0 = 5 \cdot 1 = 5$

  c. $-3^0 = -1 \cdot 3^0 = -1 \cdot 1 = -1$

Negative Exponent Rule

If $a \neq 0$, and n is a positive integer then $a^{-n} = \dfrac{1}{a^n}$.

Again, we can use the product rule and zero exponent rule to understand why the negative exponent rule true. $a^{-n} \cdot a^n = a^{-n+n} = a^0 = 1$ $a \neq 0$

Thus, $a^{-n} \cdot a^n = 1$ $a \neq 0$

    Divide both sides by a^n: $a^{-n} = \dfrac{1}{a^n}$ $a \neq 0$

)

Example 2

Evaluate each exponential expression. Assume $x \neq 0$.

a. 5^{-3}

b. $(-4)^{-2}$

c. -4^{-2}

d. $(5x)^{-3}$

e. $5x^{-3}$

f. $4^{-1} + 2^{-2}$

Solution

a. $5^{-3} = \dfrac{1}{5^3} = \dfrac{1}{125}$

b. $(-4)^{-2} = \dfrac{1}{(-4)^2} = \dfrac{1}{16}$

c. $-4^{-2} = -\dfrac{1}{4^2} = -\dfrac{1}{16}$

d. $(5x)^{-3} = \dfrac{1}{(5x)^3} = \dfrac{1}{5^3 x^3} = \dfrac{1}{125x^3}$

e. $5x^{-3} = 5\dfrac{1}{x^3} = \dfrac{5}{x^3}$

f. $4^{-1} + 2^{-2} = \dfrac{1}{4^1} + \dfrac{1}{2^2} = \dfrac{1}{4} + \dfrac{1}{4} = \dfrac{2}{4} = \dfrac{1}{2}$

Example 3

Simplify by writing with positive exponents $\dfrac{a^{-n}}{b^{-n}}$ and $\left(\dfrac{a}{b}\right)^{-n}$.

Assume $a \neq 0$, $b \neq 0$, and n is a positive integer.

Solution

Use the negative exponent rule. $\dfrac{a^{-n}}{b^{-n}} = \dfrac{\dfrac{1}{a^n}}{\dfrac{1}{b^n}} = \dfrac{1}{a^n} \cdot \dfrac{b^n}{1} = \dfrac{b^n}{a^n}$

First, use the power rule for a quotient. $\left(\dfrac{a}{b}\right)^{-n} = \dfrac{a^{-n}}{b^{-n}} = \dfrac{b^n}{a^n} = \left(\dfrac{b}{a}\right)^n$

Thus, we have the following consequences of the negative exponent rule:

Rule

If $a \neq 0$, $b \neq 0$, and n is a positive integer then, $\dfrac{a^{-n}}{b^{-n}} = \dfrac{b^n}{a^n}$ and $\left(\dfrac{a}{b}\right)^{-n} = \left(\dfrac{b}{a}\right)^n$

Example 4

Evaluate.

a. $\left(\dfrac{2}{5}\right)^{-3}$

b. $\left(\dfrac{1}{3}\right)^{-4}$

c. $\dfrac{8^{-2}}{4^{-3}}$

d. $\dfrac{4x^{-5}}{7y^{-8}}$

Solution

a. $\left(\dfrac{2}{5}\right)^{-3} = \left(\dfrac{5}{2}\right)^{3} = \dfrac{5^3}{2^3} = \dfrac{125}{8}$

c. $\dfrac{8^{-2}}{4^{-3}} = \dfrac{4^3}{8^2} = \dfrac{64}{64} = 1$

b. $\left(\dfrac{1}{3}\right)^{-4} = \left(\dfrac{3}{1}\right)^{4} = \dfrac{3^4}{1^4} = \dfrac{81}{1} = 81$

d. $\dfrac{4x^{-5}}{7y^{-8}} = \dfrac{4y^8}{7x^5}$ $(x \neq 0, y \neq 0)$

Example 5

Simplify.

$(5^{-1}x^3y^{-4})^{-2}$.

Assume $x \neq 0, y \neq 0$.

Solution 1

First, use the power rule then the negative exponent rule.

$$(5^{-1}x^3y^{-4})^{-2} = 5^{(-1)(-2)}x^{3(-2)}y^{(-4)(-2)} = 5^2x^{-6}y^8 = \dfrac{25y^8}{x^6}$$

Solution 2

First, use the negative exponent rule then the power rule.

$$(5^{-1}x^3y^{-4})^{-2} = \dfrac{1}{(5^{-1}x^3y^{-4})^2} = \dfrac{1}{5^{(-1)(2)}x^{(3)(2)}y^{(-4)(2)}} = \dfrac{1}{5^{-2}x^6y^{-8}} = \dfrac{5^2y^8}{x^6} = \dfrac{25y^8}{x^6}$$

Example 6

Simplify.

$(4x^{-2}y)^3(2m^3n^{-4})^{-2}$.

Write the answer with positive exponents. Assume $x, m, n \neq 0$.

Solution 1

First, use the negative exponent rule and then the power rule .

$$(4x^{-2}y)^3(2m^3n^{-4})^{-2} = \dfrac{(4x^{-2}y)^3}{(2m^3n^{-4})^2} = \dfrac{4^3x^{(-2)(3)}y^3}{2^2m^{(3)(2)}n^{(-4)(2)}} = \dfrac{64x^{-6}y^3}{4m^6n^{-8}} = \dfrac{16x^{-6}y^3}{m^6n^{-8}} = \dfrac{16y^3n^8}{m^6x^6}$$

Solution 2

First, use the power rule and then the negative exponent rule.

$$(4x^{-2}y)^3(2m^3n^{-4})^{-2} = [4^3x^{-6}y^3][2^{-2}m^{(3)(-2)}n^{(-4)(-2)}] = [64x^{-6}y^3][2^{-2}m^{-6}n^8] = \dfrac{64y^3n^8}{2^2x^6m^6} = \dfrac{16y^3n^8}{x^6m^6}$$

> **Quotient Rule**
>
> If $a \neq 0$ and m and n are positive integers, then $\dfrac{a^m}{a^n} = a^{m-n}$

To divide exponential expressions with the same base, subtract the exponents and keep the base.

Example 7

Use the quotient rule to simplify. Write the answer with positive exponents.

a. $\dfrac{5^9}{5^3}$

b. $\dfrac{4^2}{4^5}$

c. $\dfrac{m^{15}}{m^7}$

d. $\dfrac{x^3}{x^8}$

e. $\dfrac{a^4}{a^{-6}}$

f. $\dfrac{y^{-5}}{y^7}$

g. $\dfrac{5^2}{3^2}$

Solution

Assume all variables represent nonzero real numbers.

a. $\dfrac{5^9}{5^3} = 5^{9-3} = 5^6$

b. $\dfrac{4^2}{4^5} = 4^{2-5} = 4^{-3} = \dfrac{1}{4^3}$

c. $\dfrac{m^{15}}{m^7} = m^{15-7} = m^8$

d. $\dfrac{x^3}{x^8} = x^{3-8} = x^{-5} = \dfrac{1}{x^5}$

e. $\dfrac{a^4}{a^{-6}} = a^{4-(-6)} = a^{4+6} = a^{10}$

f. $\dfrac{y^{-5}}{y^7} = y^{-5-7} = y^{-12} = \dfrac{1}{y^{12}}$

g. $\dfrac{5^2}{3^2} = \dfrac{25}{9}$ (the quotient rule cannot be applied because they have different bases)

Example 8

Simplify. Write the answer with positive exponents.

$$\dfrac{12a^5b^8c}{9ab^3}$$

Solution

Assume $a, b \neq 0$.

$$\dfrac{12a^5b^8c}{9ab^3} = \dfrac{4a^{5-1}b^{8-3}c}{3} = \dfrac{4a^4b^5c}{3}$$

Example 9

Simplify.

Write the answer with positive exponents.

$$\frac{6x^3y^{-7}}{8x^{-4}y^5} \quad (x\,,y \neq 0)$$

Solution 1

First, apply the quotient rule and then the negative exponent rule.

$$\frac{6x^3y^{-7}}{8x^{-4}y^5} = \frac{3x^{3-(-4)}y^{-7-5}}{4} = \frac{3x^{3+4}y^{-12}}{4} = \frac{3x^7}{4y^{12}}$$

Solution 2

First, apply the negative exponent rule and then the product rule.

$$\frac{6x^3y^{-7}}{8x^{-4}y^5} = \frac{6x^3x^4}{8y^5y^7} = \frac{3x^{3+4}}{4y^{5+7}} = \frac{3x^7}{4y^{12}}$$

Example 10

Simplify.

Write the answer with positive exponents.

$$\frac{(3a^5b^{-3})^2}{(a^{-1}b^3)^3} \quad (a\,,b \neq 0)$$

Solution 1

First, apply the power rule then the quotient rule and the negative exponent rule.

$$\frac{(3a^5b^{-3})^2}{(a^{-1}b^3)^3} = \frac{3^2\,a^{(5)(2)}b^{(-3)(2)}}{a^{(-1)(3)}b^{(3)(3)}} = \frac{9a^{10}b^{-6}}{a^{-3}b^9} = \frac{9a^{10-(-3)}b^{-6-9}}{1} = \frac{9a^{10+3}b^{-15}}{1} = \frac{9a^{13}}{b^{15}}$$

Solution 2

First, apply the power rule then the negative exponent rule and the product rule.

$$\frac{(3a^5b^{-3})^2}{(a^{-1}b^3)^3} = \frac{9a^{10}b^{-6}}{a^{-3}b^9} = \frac{9a^{10}a^3}{b^9b^6} = \frac{9a^{10+3}}{b^{9+6}} = \frac{9a^{13}}{b^{15}}$$

□ SUMMARY OF THE RULES OF EXPONENTS

If $a \neq 0$, $b \neq 0$ and m, n are positive integers then:

1. **Product Rule:** $a^m \cdot a^n = a^{m+n}$

2. **Power Rule:** $\left(a^m\right)^n = a^{m \cdot n}$ $\begin{cases} (a \cdot b)^n = a^n \cdot b^n \\ \left(\dfrac{a}{b}\right)^n = \dfrac{a^n}{b^n} \end{cases}$

3. **Quotient Rule:** $\dfrac{a^m}{a^n} = a^{m-n}$

4. **Zero Exponent Rule:** $a^0 = 1$

5. **Negative Exponent Rule:** $a^{-n} = \dfrac{1}{a^n}$

5.2 EXERCISES

Evaluate. Assume all variables represent nonzero real numbers.

1. 9^0

2. $(-7)^0$

3. $(-10)^0$

4. -6^0

5. -2^0

6. $4(8x)^0$

7. $-2(3x)^0$

8. $8x^2y^0$

9. $3x^0y^3$

10. $(-4a)^0$

11. $(-6a)^0$

12. $-4a^0$

13. $-6a^0$

14. $(x+y)^0$

15. $x^0 - y^0$

16. $\left(\dfrac{3}{5}\right)^0$

Simplify. Write the answer with positive exponents. Assume all variables represent nonzero real numbers.

17. 4^{-3}

18. -11^{-2}

19. $(-5)^{-3}$

20. $(-9)^{-2}$

21. m^{-5}

22. x^{-8}

23. $-y^{-8}$

24. $(-a)^{-7}$

25. $7ab^{-4}$

26. $-3m^{-6}n^2$

27. $\dfrac{1}{8^{-2}}$

28. $\dfrac{2}{15^{-2}}$

29. $\dfrac{3x^5}{y^{-4}}$

30. $\dfrac{4a}{3b^{-1}}$

31. $\dfrac{6m^{-3}}{5n}$

32. $\dfrac{11x^{-8}}{12y^3}$

33. $\dfrac{a^{-7}}{b^{-3}}$

34. $\dfrac{m^{-11}}{n^{-9}}$

35. $\dfrac{2x^{-4}}{5y^{-5}}$

36. $\dfrac{9ab^{-3}}{5mn^{-6}}$

37. $\left(\dfrac{2x}{y^2}\right)^{-4}$

38. $\left(\dfrac{x^3}{3y}\right)^{-3}$

39. $\left(\dfrac{x^{-2}y^2}{z^{-3}}\right)^{-7}$

40. $\left(\dfrac{a^4b^{-3}}{m^{-4}n}\right)^{-2}$

41. $\dfrac{4^{10}}{4^7}$

42. $\dfrac{5^8}{5^6}$

43. $\dfrac{3^2}{3^5}$

44. $\dfrac{8^5}{8^7}$

45. $\dfrac{m^{10}}{m^4}$

46. $\dfrac{x^9}{x^3}$

47. $\dfrac{y^2}{y^7}$

48. $\dfrac{n^3}{n^4}$

49. $\dfrac{2x^7}{3x^3}$

50. $\dfrac{8a^6}{10a^{15}}$

51. $\dfrac{24x^8y^3}{16x^2y^7}$

52. $\dfrac{11a^3b^5}{55a^9b^2}$

53. $\dfrac{9x^4y^5}{6x^3y^8}$

54. $\dfrac{12m^3n^6}{32m^9n^{10}}$

55. $\dfrac{18a^{12}b^5}{27a^3b^2}$

56. $\dfrac{15xy^3}{35x^5y^2}$

57. $\left(\dfrac{6x^{-3}y^5}{8x^4y^{-1}}\right)^3$

58. $\left(\dfrac{2m^5n^{-4}}{10m^{-3}n^2}\right)^2$

59. $\dfrac{(5x^{-6}y^7)^3}{(10x^{-4}y^{10})^2}$

60. $\dfrac{(-a^4b^{-2}c)^7}{(3a^8b^{-5})^3}$

61. $\dfrac{(x^{-3}y^4z)^3}{(x^5y^{-2}z^2)^{-2}}$

62. $\dfrac{(xy^{-6}z^2)^4}{(x^{-2}y^3z)^{-3}}$

63. $\dfrac{(ab^2c^{-1})^{-5}}{(a^2b^{-2}c^3)^{-1}}$

64. $\dfrac{(a^{-1}b^5c^4)^{-2}}{(a^{-3}bc^{-1})^{-4}}$

65. $\left(\dfrac{x^3y^{-2}}{x^4y}\right)^{-5}$

66. $\left(\dfrac{a^5b^4}{a^{-2}b^3}\right)^{-3}$

67. $\left(\dfrac{21x^4y^6}{14xy^3}\right)^{-2}$

68. $\left(\dfrac{12m^2n^{-3}}{18m^{-1}n^4}\right)^{-4}$

69. $\dfrac{(ab^2)^3(a^4b^{-1})^{-2}}{(2a^3b^{-2})^2}$

70. $\dfrac{(x^3y^{-2})^4(x^{-4}y^2)^{-3}}{(x^2y^3)^{-1}}$

71. $\dfrac{(m^{-2}n^{-3})^{-4}(m^2n^2)^{-3}}{(m^{-3}n^{-4})^2}$

5.3 APPLICATIONS: SCIENTIFIC NOTATION

Often in science, such as physics, chemistry or biology, we have to deal with very large or very small numbers, which is a cumbersome task. For example the speed of light is approximately 300,000,000 m/s, the distance from planet Earth to our Sun is about 150,000,000,000 mi and the radius of an electron is 0.0000000000000028179 mi. Exponents can provide a shorthand form called Scientific Notation to write these numbers. Scientific notation changes only the form of the number and not the value of the number.

> **Definition**
>
> *A number N is written in **scientific notation** when N is expressed in the form $N = a \times 10^n$, where $1 \le |a| < 10$ and n is an integer.*

If the number N is greater than or equal to 10 ($N \ge 10$), to find "a" move the decimal point to the left. In this case the exponent "n" is positive and equal to the number of places the decimal point was moved over.

Example 1

Write 123,000,000 in scientific notation.

Solution

Since the number is greater than 10, to find the number a ($1 \le |a| < 10$), the decimal point must be moved 8 places to the left. Then, $a = 1.23$ is a number between 1 and 10, and n is positive, $n = 8$.

Thus, the number can be written in scientific notation as follows:

$$123,000,000 = 1.23 \times 10^8$$

Example 2

Write 11 in scientific notation.

Solution

The number is greater than 10. To find the number a ($1 \le |a| < 10$), the decimal point must be moved one place to the left. Then $a = 11$ and n is positive, $n = 1$.

So, the number can be written in scientific notation as follows:

$$11 = 1.1 \times 10^1$$

If the number N is less than 1 ($N < 1$), to find "a" move the decimal point to the right of the first nonzero digit. In this case the exponent "n" is negative and equal to the number of places the decimal point was moved over.

Example 3

Write 0.000,987 in scientific notation.

Solution

Since the number is less than 1, to find the number a ($1 \le |a| < 10$), move the decimal point to the right four places (9 is the first nonzero digit). Then, $a = 9.87$ and n is negative, $n = -4$.

Thus, the number can be written in scientific notation as follows:

$$0.000987 = 9.87 \times 10^{-4}$$

If the number N is between 1 and 10, $1 \le N < 10$, then $a = N$ and $n = 0$.

Example 4

Write 7 in scientific notation.

Solution

Since $1 \le 7 < 10$, $a = 7$ and $n = 0$. Therefore, $7 = 7 \times 10^0$

Sometimes, we need to convert a number written in scientific notation to standard form (decimal form). If the exponent is positive, move the decimal point to the right. The number of places is given by the exponent. If there are not enough digits to complete the number of places, add zeros.

Example 5

Write the number in standard form (without exponents).

$$3.57 \times 10^5$$

Solution

Since the exponent is positive ($n = 5$), move the decimal point over 5 places to the right. Then, add three more zeros to complete the number of places. Thus,

$$3.57 \times 10^5 = 375,000$$

If the exponent is negative, move the decimal point to the left. The number of places is given by the exponent. Again, if there are not enough digits to complete the number of places, add zeros.

Example 6

Write the number in standard form (without exponents).

$$1.56 \times 10^{-6}$$

Solution

Since the exponent is negative ($n = -6$), move the decimal point 6 places to the left. Then, add 5 more zeros to complete the number of places. Thus,

$$1.56 \times 10^{-6} = 0.00000156$$

Example 7

Multiply and write the answer in scientific notation.

$(3 \times 10^8)(5 \times 10^6)$

Solution

$(3 \times 10^8)(5 \times 10^6) = (3)(5) \times 10^{8+6} = 15 \times 10^{14} = (1.5 \times 10^1) \times 10^{14} = 1.5 \times 10^{1+14} = 1.5 \times 10^{15}$

Example 8

Multiply and write the answer in scientific notation.

$(4 \times 10^4)(6 \times 10^{-9})$

Solution

$(4 \times 10^4)(6 \times 10^{-9}) = (4)(6) \times 10^{4-9} = 24 \times 10^{-5} =$
$(2.4 \times 10^1) \times 10^{-5} = 2.4 \times 10^{1-5} = 2.4 \times 10^{-4}$

Example 9

Divide and write the answer in standard form (without exponents).

$\dfrac{8 \times 10^{14}}{2 \times 10^9}$

Solution

$\dfrac{8 \times 10^{14}}{2 \times 10^9} = 4 \times 10^{14-9} = 4 \times 10^5 = 400,000$

Example 10

Divide and write the answer in standard form (without exponents).

$\dfrac{8.4 \times 10^5}{2.1 \times 10^9}$

Solution

$\dfrac{8.4 \times 10^5}{2.1 \times 10^9} = 4 \times 10^{5-9} = 4 \times 10^{-4} = 0.0004$

Example 11

Simplify and write the answer in scientific notation.

$\dfrac{(6.3 \times 10^6)(7 \times 10^{-4})}{2.1 \times 10^7}$

Solution

$$\frac{(6.3\times10^6)(7\times10^{-4})}{2.1\times10^7} = \frac{(3\times10^6)(7\times10^{-4})}{10^7} = \frac{21\times10^{6-4}}{10^7} = \frac{21\times10^2}{10^7} = 21\times10^{2-7} = 21\times10^{-5} = $$

$$(2.1\times10^1)x10^{-5} = 2.1\times10^{1-5} = 2.1\times10^{-4}$$

5.3 EXERCISES

Determine whether each number is in scientific notation.

1. 5.29×10^8

2. 8.25×10^{-4}

3. 12×10^{-3}

4. 0.9×10^{12}

5. 4.0×10^2

6. 1×10^{-15}

7. 22×10^3

8. -8×10^5

9. 0.1×10^4

10. 8×10^0

11. 3.768×10^{-27}

12. 5×10

Write each number in scientific notation.

13. 631,000,000

14. 0.00008143

15. 5239.23

16. 613.907

17. 12,000,000,000

18. 21

19. 0.000405

20. 2350.1

21. 3572

22. 21,000

23. 0.003120

24. 30,000

25. −1,005.23

26. 0.0000000216

27. −21,000

28. 0.23×10^5

29. 126.4×10^{-6}

30. 0.06×10^4

Write each number in standard form (without exponents).

31. 1.97×10^5

32. 9.687×10^6

33. 4.009×10^{-3}

34. 3.4×10^{-6}

35. 6.81×10^{-5}

36. 3.00×10^5

37. 7.9305×10^1

38. -8.41×10^{-4}

39. -5×10^{-5}

40. 5.34009×10^4

41. 9.99999×10^3

42. -4.361×10^4

Perform each indicated operation. Write the answer in scientific notation.

43. $(1.0 \times 10^4)(9.21 \times 10^{-6})$

44. $(2.0 \times 10^{-8})(3.15 \times 10^{10})$

45. $(4.0 \times 10^2)(8.0 \times 10^5)$

46. $(5.2 \times 10^{-15})(5.0 \times 10^{27})$

47. $(2.5 \times 10^{16})(2.5 \times 10^{-23})$

48. $(6.0 \times 10^4)(5.0 \times 10^{-10})$

Perform each indicated operation. Write the answer in standard form (without exponents.)

49. $\dfrac{6.3 \times 10^{18}}{2.1 \times 10^{15}}$

50. $\dfrac{9.6 \times 10^{-5}}{3.2 \times 10^{-8}}$

51. $\dfrac{2.0 \times 10^{-9}}{8.0 \times 10^{-7}}$

52. $\dfrac{(5.6 \times 10^5)(1.5 \times 10^{-10})}{4.2 \times 10^{-3}}$

53. $\dfrac{(7.2 \times 10^{12})(4.5 \times 10^{-6})}{8.1 \times 10^4}$

54. $\dfrac{(3.0 \times 10^{10})(2.0 \times 10^{-2})}{1.5 \times 10^6}$

55. $\dfrac{(4.2x10^{-4})(2.5x10^8)}{2.1x10^{10}}$

56. In 2010, there were about 8.3 million automobiles registered in Texas. Write the number in scientific notation.

57. The estimated number of galaxies in the observable universe is about 200,000,000,000. Write the number in scientific notation.

58. The Bohr radius (physics) is a constant, approximately equal to 5.29×10^{-11}. Write the number in standard form (without exponents).

5.4 ADDITION AND SUBTRACTION OF POLYNOMIALS

☐ **Polynomials** ☐ **Addition of Polynomials (horizontal format)** ☐ **Addition of Polynomials (vertical format)** ☐ **Subtraction of Polynomials (horizontal format)** ☐ **Subtraction of Polynomials (vertical format)**

☐ POLYNOMIALS

Consider the following variable expression: $5x^3 + x^2 + 3x + 2$, which is also an example of polynomial in x. This polynomial has four terms and each term is of the form ax^n where a is a real number and n is a whole number: 0, 1, 2, 3, . . .

Term	a	n	
$5x^3$	$a = 5$	$n = 3$	
x^2	$a = 1$	$n = 2$	
$3x$	$a = 3$	$n = 1$	
2	$a = 2$	$n = 0$	$(2 = 2 \cdot 1 = 2 \cdot x^0)$

Definition

A *polynomial* in x is a sum of a finite number of terms of the form ax^n where a is a real number and n is a whole number.

The following are variable expressions that are not polynomials:

a. $3x^4 + 2x^{-2} + 8$ The exponent $n = -2$ is not a whole number

b. $x^3 + 5x^{\frac{1}{2}} - 2$ The exponent $n = \frac{1}{2}$ is not a whole number

c. $x^2 + \frac{1}{x} + 1$ $\frac{1}{x} = x^{-1}$, the exponent $n = -1$ is not a whole number

With respect to the number of terms, polynomials can be classified as follows:

a. monomials: $2x^2$, $3x$, 5, $7x^2y$ (polynomial with one term)

b. binomials: $2x + 3$, $x + 4$, $y^2 - 4$ (polynomial with two terms)

c. trinomials: $x^2 + 7x + 4$, $x^2 + xy + y^2$ (polynomial with three terms)

Note: A polynomial that has more than three terms is called simply polynomial.

Recall from chapter 1, that the degree of a term containing one variable is given by the exponent of the variable.

$5x^3$ degree 3

$4x$ degree 1

6   degree 0 $(6 = 6x^0)$

If a term has more than one variable, the degree of the term is given by the sum of the exponents.

$3x^5y^3z$ degree $5 + 3 + 1 = 9$

The **degree of a polynomial** is given by the degree of the term with the highest degree in the polynomial.

Example: The degree of the polynomial $x^2 + 9x^4 - 3x + 4$ is 4 and is given by the term with the highest degree: $9x^4$.

A polynomial in x is written in **descending order** when the exponents of x are decreasing from left to right. If a polynomial contains more than one variable, it can be written in descending order with respect to one of the variables in the polynomial.

For example, the polynomial $4x^3y + 3x^2y^3 + 2xy^2 + 7$ is written in descending order with respect to x. When a polynomial in one variable is written in descending order, the degree of the polynomial is given by the degree of the leading term.

The polynomial $7x^3 - 4x^2 + 3x - 9$ is written in descending order. The degree of this polynomial is 3 and is given by the degree of the leading term $7x^3$ which has the highest degree.

☐ ADDITION OF POLYNOMIALS (HORIZONTAL FORMAT)

To add two or more polynomials, in horizontal format, remove the parenthesis (if any) and combine the like terms.

Example 1

Add.

$$(5x^2 - 2x + 6) + (-x^2 + 3x + 4)$$

Solution

$$(5x^2 - 2x + 6) + (-x^2 + 3x + 4) = 5x^2 - 2x + 6 - x^2 + 3x + 4 = 4x^2 + x + 10$$

Example 2

Add.

$$(y^2 + 4y - 8) + (4y^2 - y + 3) + (-2y^2 + 3y + 4)$$

Solution

$$(y^2 + 4y - 8) + (4y^2 - y + 3) + (-2y^2 + 3y + 4) = y^2 + 4y - 8 + 4y^2 - y + 3 - 2y^2 + 3y + 4 =$$
$$3y^2 + 6y - 1$$

Example 3

Add.

$$(6x^2y^2 + 3xy + 5) + (2x^2y^2 - 5xy + 2y)$$

Solution

$$(6x^2y^2 + 3xy + 5) + (2x^2y^2 - 5xy + 2y) = 6x^2y^2 + 3xy + 5 + 2x^2y^2 - 5xy + 2y =$$
$$8x^2y^2 - 2xy + 2y + 5$$

☐ ADDITION OF POLYNOMIALS (VERTICAL FORMAT)

To add two or more polynomials in vertical format, line up the like terms, and add the terms in each column.

Example 4

Use the vertical format to add.

$$(3x^2 + x + 7) + (2x^2 - 4x - 2)$$

Solution

$$
\begin{array}{r}
3x^2 + \ x + 7 \\
\underline{2x^2 - 4x - 2} \\
5x^2 - 3x + 5
\end{array}
$$

Example 5

Use the vertical format to add.

$$(x^3 + 6x - 2) + (2x^3 - 9x^2 + 8)$$

Solution

$$
\begin{array}{r}
x^3 \qquad\ \ + 6x - 2 \\
\underline{2x^3 - 9x^2 \qquad + 8} \\
3x^3 - 9x^2 + 6x + 6
\end{array}
$$

Example 6

Use the vertical format to add.

$$(6x^2 - 4x + 3) + (2x^2 - x + 7) + (x^2 + 8x - 7)$$

Solution

$$
\begin{array}{r}
6x^2 - 4x + 3 \\
2x^2 - \ x + 7 \\
\underline{x^2 + 8x - 9} \\
9x^2 + 3x + 1
\end{array}
$$

☐ SUBTRACTION OF POLYNOMIALS (HORIZONTAL FORMAT)

To subtract two or more polynomials in horizontal format, remove the parenthesis (if any) and combine the like terms. When removing parenthesis preceded by a negative sign, change the signs for all the terms inside the parenthesis.

Example 7

Subtract.

$$(2x^2 - x + 4) - (x^2 - 6x + 2)$$

Solution

$$(2x^2 - x + 4) - (x^2 - 6x + 2) = 2x^2 - x + 4 - x^2 + 6x - 2 = x^2 + 5x + 2$$

Example 8

Subtract.

$-4x^2 + 3x + 7$ from $3x^2 - 5x + 8$.

Solution

$$(3x^2 - 5x + 8) - (-4x^2 + 3x + 7) = 3x^2 - 5x + 8 + 4x^2 - 3x - 7 = 7x^2 - 8x + 1$$

Example 9

Add or subtract.

$$(9x^2 - 2x + 6) - (5x^2 + 3x - 4) + (x^2 + 7x - 5)$$

Solution

$$(9x^2 - 2x + 6) - (5x^2 + 3x - 4) + (x^2 + 7x - 5) =$$

$$9x^2 - 2x + 6 - 5x^2 - 3x + 4 + x^2 + 7x - 5 =$$

$$5x^2 + 2x + 5$$

□ SUBTRACTION OF POLYNOMIALS (VERTICAL FORMAT)

To subtract two or more polynomials in vertical format, line up the like terms and subtract the terms in each column.

Example 10

Use the vertical format to subtract.

$$(5x^2 - 9x + 3) - (4x^2 - 6x + 8)$$

Solution

$$5x^2 - 9x + 3$$
$$-(4x^2 - 6x + 8)$$

To make the subtraction easier, change the signs of $4x^2 - 6x + 8$, and write the polynomials in vertical format again. Then **add** the like terms in each column.

$$5x^2 - 9x + 3$$
$$-4x^2 + 6x - 8$$
$$\overline{x^2 - 3x - 5}$$

Example 11

Use the vertical format to subtract $3x^2 - 2x + 5$ from $6x^2 - 4x + 9$

Solution

$$6x^2 - 4x + 9$$
$$-(3x^2 - 2x + 5)$$

Change the signs of $3x^2 - 2x + 5$ and add the like terms in each column.

$$6x^2 - 4x + 9$$
$$-3x^2 + 2x - 5$$
$$\overline{3x^2 - 2x + 4}$$

So far we can add and subtract polynomials. Also, polynomials can be evaluated for a given value for the variable.

Example 12

Evaluate.

$$2x^2 + 6x - 3 \text{ for } x = 2.$$

Solution

We can evaluate this polynomial as a variable expression.

$$2x^2 + 6x - 3 = 2(2)^2 + 6(2) - 3 = 2 \cdot 4 + 12 - 3 = 8 + 12 - 3 = 17$$

We can make this process easier to understand by using function notation to label a polynomial in x as P(x).

This notation will connect polynomials with the concept of functions discussed in Chapter 3 where we learned how to evaluate functions.

Example 13
_____

Evaluate.

$$P(x) = 5x^2 - 3x + 12 \text{ for } x = -1.$$

Solution

$$P(-1) = 5(-1)^2 - 3(-1) + 12 = 5 \cdot 1 + 3 + 12 = 5 + 3 + 12 = 20$$

5.4 EXERCISES

Determine whether each expression is a polynomial. If the expression is not a polynomial explain why not.

1. $2x + 3$

2. $x^2 + 2x^{-1} + 3$

3. $3x^2 + \dfrac{1}{x} + 9$

4. $4x^4 - 9x^{\frac{2}{3}} + 1$

5. -4

6. $2x + \dfrac{3}{x} - 5x^2$

7. $6x^{\frac{1}{2}} + 3x$

8. $8x^3$

9. $x^3 - 1$

Identify each polynomial as a monomial, binomial or trinomial. Give the degree of each polynomial.

10. $5y^2 + 7y - 1$

11. $6x^4 - 2x$

12. $8x^7$

13. -15

14. $7x - 2$

15. $x^3 + 2x^6 - 4$

16. $x^4 - 1$

17. $3y^5 + 2y^4 + y^3$

18. $-12x^{15}$

19. $4x^2y^2 + 5y^3 + 1$

20. $7x^3y^3 + xy^4 - y$

21. $3x^2y^5 + x^6$

Write each polynomial in descending order of the variable x.

22. $2x^2 - 1 + 3x + 4x^3$

23. $5x + 3x^2 - 4$

24. $x^2 + 5x^4 - 9$

25. $x^2y^2 + xy^3 + x^3y$

26. $x^2 + x^3y + xy^2 + 11$

27. $x - y^2x^2 + y^4$

28. $x^3 + 3x^2 - 5x^4 + 8x - 2$

29. $x^2y^2 + x^4y^5 + 7$

30. $-3 + x^2 - 9x$

Evaluate each polynomial at the given value.

31. If $P(x) = 3x^2 - 5x + 2$, find $P(-2)$

32. If $P(x) = x^2 + 8x - 3$, find $P(3)$

33. If $P(x) = x^3 - 2x^2 + 4x - 1$, find $P(-1)$

34. If $P(x) = x^3 - x - 8$, find $P(-3)$

35. If $P(x) = 8x^2 - 6x + 3$, find $P\left(\dfrac{1}{2}\right)$

36. If $P(x) = 6x^2 - \dfrac{1}{2}x + 5$, find $P(4)$

Use the horizontal format to add or subtract.

37. $(5x + 3) + (-2x + 7)$

38. $(4x + 12) + (-x + 8)$

39. $(8x - 3) - (-4x + 5)$

40. $(10x + 8) - (6x - 5)$

41. $(3x - 4) + (5x^2 - 8x + 7)$

42. $(9x - 3) + (7x^2 - 8x + 10)$

43. $(6x - 8) - (-14x^2 - 5x + 2)$

44. $(-x + 4) - (-2x^2 - 7x + 8)$

45. $(4x^2 - 5x + 9) + (-7x^2 + 9x - 4)$

46. $(7x^2 - 4x + 2) + (x^2 - 9x - 6)$

47. $(-5x^2 + 8x - 7) - (-8x^2 + 6x - 4)$

48. $(2x^2 - 7x - 1) - (6x^2 - x - 11)$

49. $(2a^4 - 7a^2 + 5) + (-6a^4 + 9a^2 - 8)$

50. $(8a^4 + 3a^2 - 5) + (a^4 - 11a^2 + 10)$

51. $(-3a^3 + 4a - 1) - (-9a^3 + a - 6)$

52. $(-2a^3 - a + 9) - (-4a^3 - 5a + 7)$

53. $(y^3 - 3y^2 + 5y - 3) + (2y^2 - y + 9)$

54. $(4y^3 + y^2 - 3y + 4) + (y^3 - 2y - 1)$

55. $(3x^2 + 4y^2 - 6xy) + (-x^2 + 4y^2 + xy)$

56. $(9x^2 - 5y^2 + xy) - (x^2 - y^2 - 8xy)$

57. $(2x^2y - 5xy^2 + xy) - (x^2y - 8xy^2 + 2)$

58. $(8x^2y^2 - 2xy + 4) - (5x^2y^2 - xy + 8)$

59. $(3x^{2n} + 8x^n - 4) - (-8x^{2n} - 2x^n - 5)$

60. $(4x^{2n} + 11x^n + 9) + (7x^{2n} - 6x^n + 2)$

61. $(-5y^{4n} + 9y^{2n} - 12) + (10y^{4n} - y^{2n} + 8)$

62. $(y^{4n} + 3y^{2n} - 5) - (6y^{4n} - y^{2n} - 7)$

63. $(\dfrac{5}{4}y^3 + 6y^2 - 4y + \dfrac{8}{3}) - (\dfrac{1}{4}y^3 - y^2 - \dfrac{1}{3})$

64. $(-\dfrac{2}{7}y^3 + y^2 - y + \dfrac{8}{5}) - (-\dfrac{9}{7}y^3 - y + \dfrac{3}{5})$

65. $(4x^2 - 10x + 8) - (-3x^2 - 8x + 4) + (x^2 + 6x - 3)$

66. $(2.8x^2 - 3.8x + 0.4) - (0.8x^2 + 1.2x - 8.6) + (x^2 - 5x + 2)$

67. $(1.5x^2 + 4.6x - 9.1) + (2.5x^2 - 1.6x - 0.9) - (2x^2 + 7x - 5)$

68. $(14x^3 - 3x^2 + 5x - 9) + (x^3 + 8x^2 - 2x + 8) - (10x^3 - 12x^2 - 4x + 15)$

69. $(9a^3 + 4a^2 - 8a + 3) - (-11a^3 - 16a^2 + 5a - 8) + (-10a^3 - 10a^2 + 12a - 13)$

70. $[(8x^2 +3x-5)-(6x^2 -4x-9)]+[(11x^2 -8x+6)-(7x^2 -5x+18)]$

71. $[(16x^2 -7x+14)-(14x^2 -10x+9)]-[(20x^2 +8x-5)-(18x^2 +x-15)]$

Use the vertical format to add or subtract.

72. $(11x^2 -15x+9)+(8x^2 +12x-6)$

73. $(16x^2 -8x+14)-(12x^2 +10x-7)$

74. $(18x^2 +10x-11)-(15x^2 +6x-20)$

75. $(3x^2 -5x+9)+(7x^2 +10x-3)$

76. $(6x^3 -4x+3)-(-9x^2 -6x-5)$

77. $(8x^3 +7x^2 -6)+(x^3 +3x+8)$

78. $(12x^4 -9x^2 +14)+(5x^4 +11x^2 -9)$

79. $(x^4 +18x^2 -12)-(-6x^4 +10x^2 -8)$

80. Subtract $6x^2 -5x+10$ from $8x^2 -12x+15$

81. Subtract $4x^2 -11x-8$ from $14x^2 -15x+10$

82. Subtract $x^3 -5x^2 +3x-4$ from $19x^3 -16x^2 +6x-9$

83. Subtract $-7x^3 +4x^2 -10x+14$ from $21x^3 +9x^2 -6x+8$

84. Find an expression for the perimeter of a rectangle with the length $L = 2x^2 +5x-3$ and the width $W = 4x^2 -2x+8$.

85. Find an expression for the perimeter of a square with the side $s = 4x^3 -5x^2 -9x+8$.

86. Find an expression for the perimeter of a triangle with the sides: $a = 21x^2 +7x-14$, $b = 12x^2 -18x+7$, and $c = -18x^2 +3x-1$.

5.5 MULTIPLICATION OF POLYNOMIALS

□ **Multiplying Monomials** □ **Multiplying a Monomial by a Polynomial** □ **Multiplying a Binomial by a Polynomial** □ **Multiplying a Trinomial by a Polynomial**

□ MULTIPLYING MONOMIALS

> **Rule**
>
> *When multiplying two or more monomials, multiply the coefficients and then use the product rule for exponents to multiply the variables.*

Example 1

Multiply.

a. $(3x^2)(5x^3)$ b. $(-2x^4y^3)(8xy^2)$ c. $(-6a^3b^4c)(-8a^5b^2c^3)$

Solution

First, multiply the coefficients then multiply the variables.

a. $(3x^2)(5x^3) = (3)(5)x^2 \cdot x^3 = 15x^{2+3} = 15x^5$

b. $(-2x^4y^3)(8xy^2) = (-2)(8)x^4 \cdot x \cdot y^3 \cdot y^2 = -16x^{4+1}y^{3+2} = -16x^5y^5$

c. $(-6a^3b^4c)(-8a^5b^2c^3) = (-6)(-8)a^3 \cdot a^5 \cdot b^4 \cdot b^2 \cdot c \cdot c^3 = 48a^{3+5}b^{4+2}c^{1+3} = 48a^8b^6c^4$

Example 2

Multiply.

$$\left(-\frac{3}{4}x^5y^7z^2\right)\left(\frac{12}{15}x^4y^3z^9\right)$$

Solution

$$\left(-\frac{3}{4}x^5y^7z^2\right)\left(\frac{12}{15}x^4y^3z^9\right) = \left(-\frac{3}{4}\right)\left(\frac{12}{15}\right)x^5 \cdot x^4 \cdot y^7 \cdot y^3 \cdot z^2 \cdot z^9 =$$

$$\left(-\frac{3}{4}\cdot\frac{12}{15}\right)x^{5+4}y^{7+3}z^{2+9} = -\frac{3}{5}x^9y^{10}z^{11}$$

☐ MULTIPLYING A MONOMIAL BY A POLYNOMIAL

> **Rule**
>
> *When multiplying a monomial by a polynomial, first apply the distributive property (multiply the monomial by each term of the polynomial), and then use the previous rule to simplify.*

Example 3

Multiply.

   a. $5x(4x^2 + 10)$
                                        b. $4y^3(2y^2 + 6y - 5)$

Solution

Apply the distributive property.

   a. $5x(4x^2 + 10) = (5x)(4x^2) + (5x)(10) = 20x^3 + 50x$

   b. $4y^3(2y^2 + 6y - 5) = (4y^3)(2y^2) + (4y^3)(6y) + (4y^3)(-5) = 8y^5 + 24y^4 - 20y^3$

Example 4

Multiply.

   a. $-8x^2 y(5xy^3 + 3x^2 y^2 - 2xy)$

   b. $\dfrac{1}{2}a^5(6a^3 - 4a^2 + 8a - 2)$

Solution

Apply the distributive property.

   a. $-8x^2 y(5xy^3 + 3x^2 y^2 - 2xy) = (-8x^2 y)(5xy^3) + (-8x^2 y)(3x^2 y^2) + (-8x^2 y)(-2xy) =$

      $-40x^3 y^4 - 24x^4 y^3 + 16x^3 y^2$

   b. $\dfrac{1}{2}a^5(6a^3 - 4a^2 + 8a - 2) = \left(\dfrac{1}{2}a^5\right)(6a^3) + \left(\dfrac{1}{2}a^5\right)(-4a^2) + \left(\dfrac{1}{2}a^5\right)(8a) + \left(\dfrac{1}{2}a^5\right)(-2) =$

      $\dfrac{1}{2} \cdot 6a^8 + \dfrac{1}{2} \cdot (-4)a^7 + \dfrac{1}{2}8a^6 + \dfrac{1}{2} \cdot (-2)a^5 = 3a^8 - 2a^7 + 4a^6 - a^5$

□ MULTIPLYING A BINOMIAL BY A POLYNOMIAL

Rule

To multiply a binomial by a polynomial, multiply each term of the binomial by each term of the polynomial and then combine the like terms if possible.

Example 5

Multiply.

$$(3x+4)(5x+2)$$

Solution

Multiply each term of the first binomial by each term of the second binomial (in any order) and combine like terms.

However, if we multiply the terms of the first binomial by the terms of the second binomial in a specific order, this method is called FOIL.

$(3x+4)(5x+2) = 3x(5x+2) + 4(5x+2) =$ Distributive property

$$\underbrace{(3x)(5x)}_{\text{Firsts}} + \underbrace{(3x)(2)}_{\text{Outers}} + \underbrace{(4)(5x)}_{\text{Inners}} + \underbrace{(4)(2)}_{\text{Lasts}} = \quad \text{Distributive property}$$

$15x^2 + 6x + 20x + 8 =$ Multiply

$15x^2 + 26x + 8$ Combine like terms

Thus, $(3x+4)(5x+2) = 15x^2 + 26x + 8$

Example 6

Use the FOIL method to multiply.

$$(5x+6y)(4x-3y)$$

Solution

$(5x+6y)(4x-3y) = (5x)(4x) + (5x)(-3y) + (6y)(4x) + (6y)(-3y) =$

$20x^2 - 15xy + 24xy - 18y^2 =$

$20x^2 + 9xy - 18y^2$

Note: To eliminate confusion when combining like terms, the product of two terms should always be written in alphabetical order (xy instead of yx).

Example 7

Multiply.

$$(7m-4)(8m^2+5m+3)$$

Solution

Multiply each term of the binomial by each term of the trinomial and then combine the like terms.

$$(7m-4)(8m^2+5m+3) =$$

$$7m(8m^2+5m+3)-4(8m^2+5m+3) =$$

$$(7m)(8m^2)+(7m)(5m)+(7m)(3)+(-4)(8m^2)+(-4)(5m)+(-4)(3) =$$

$$56m^3+35m^2+21m-32m^2-20m-12 =$$

$$56m^3+3m^2+m-12$$

Example 8

Multiply.

$$(2a+3)(5a^3-9a^2+7a-6)$$

Solution

Multiply each term of the binomial by each term of the polynomial and then combine the like terms.

$$(2a+3)(5a^3-9a^2+7a-6) =$$

$$(2a)(5a^3)+(2a)(-9a^2)+(2a)(7a)+(2a)(-6)+$$

$$(3)(5a^3)+(3)(-9a^2)+(3)(7a)+(3)(-6) =$$

$$10a^4-18a^3+14a^2-12a+15a^3-27a^2+21a-18 =$$

$$10a^4-3a^3-13a^2+9a-18$$

☐ MULTIPLYING A TRINOMIAL BY A POLYNOMIAL

> **Rule**
>
> *To multiply a trinomial by a polynomial, multiply each term of the trinomial by each term of the polynomial, and then combine the like terms if possible.*

Example 9

Multiply.

$$(3y^2 + 6y - 2)(5y^2 - 2y + 4)$$

Solution

Multiply each term of the first trinomial by each term of the second trinomial and combine like terms.

$$(3y^2 + 6y - 2)(5y^2 - 2y + 4) =$$

$$(3y^2)(5y^2) + (3y^2)(-2y) + (3y^2)(4) +$$

$$(6y)(5y^2) + (6y)(-2y) + (6y)(4) +$$

$$(-2)(5y^2) + (-2)(-2y) + (-2)(4) =$$

$$15y^4 - 6y^3 + 12y^2 + 30y^3 - 12y^2 + 24y - 10y^2 + 4y - 8 =$$

$$15y^4 + 24y^3 - 10y^2 + 28y - 8$$

Note: In general, to multiply a polynomial by a polynomial, multiply each term of the first polynomial by each term of the second polynomial, and then combine the like terms if possible.

5.5 EXERCISES

Multiply.

1. $(2xy)(3x^2y^3)$

2. $(4x^2y)(8x^3y^5)$

3. $(-5a^5b^7)(4a^3b)$

4. $(-12m^8n^2)(10m^3n^6)$

5. $(-6x^4y^5)(-3x^5y^4z)$

6. $(-5mn^6)(-7m^8n)$

7. $\left(\dfrac{5}{4}a^3b^4\right)(8ab^5)$

8. $\left(6m^2n^5\right)\left(\dfrac{2}{3}m^4n^4\right)$

9. $\left(\dfrac{3}{5}xy^2\right)\left(\dfrac{10}{3}x^3y\right)$

10. $3x(4x-6)$

11. $9a(2a+10)$

12. $-2m^2(6m+8)$

13. $-15m^3(2m+1)$

14. $3ab(a^2+b^2)$

15. $5x^2y(xy-y^2)$

16. $4a(3a^2+2a+5)$

17. $3m^2(6m^3+4m+7)$

18. $-8x(x^4-x^2+2)$

19. $-3x^2y^3(x^2+4xy+y^2)$

20. $-6y^4(2y^3+4y-9)$

21. $4m^7(m^5-m^3+8)$

22. $6a^3(4a^4-9a^3+3a^2-4a+5)$

23. $10x^5(6x^6-8x^4-5x^2+4)$

24. $-2x^2y^2(3x^2+4x^2y+7xy^2-5y^2-6)$

25. $-4ab(4a^2-5ab^2+9a^2b-8b^2+3)$

26. $(x+5)(x+7)$

27. $(a+8)(a-4)$

28. $(m+9)(m-10)$

29. $(y+7)(y-2)$

30. $(x-9)(x+1)$

31. $(a-5)(a+6)$

32. $(2x+1)(3x+2)$

33. $(4a+5)(6a+3)$

34. $(7m-3)(2m+5)$

35. $(3m-4)(3m+4)$

36. $(5n+3)(5n-3)$

37. $(2a+5)(2a+5)$

38. $(6x+2)(6x-2)$

39. $(5m-4n)(5m+4n)$

40. $(3x+2y)(3x-2y)$

41. $(2a-3)(2a-3)$

42. $(4x+3)(2-5x)$

43. $(a+b)^3$

44. $(2x+1)^2$

45. $(4x-3)^2$

46. $(a-b)^3$

47. $(x+0.5)(x-0.6)$

48. $\left(x+\dfrac{1}{2}\right)\left(x-\dfrac{1}{2}\right)$

49. $\left(x+\dfrac{3}{4}\right)\left(x-\dfrac{3}{4}\right)$

50. $(x+6)(2x^2+3x+1)$

51. $(x-2)(4x^2+5x-3)$

52. $(x+y)(x^2+2xy+y^2)$

53. $(x-y)(x^2-2xy+y^2)$

54. $(a+b)(a^2-ab+b^2)$

55. $(a-b)(a^2+ab+b^2)$

56. $(6x+4)(2x^2-5x+8)$

57. $(3m-2n)(m^2+4mn+5n^2)$

58. $(5a+3b)(2a^2+3ab+b^2)$

59. $(4x+5y)(6x^2+xy+8y^2)$

60. $(4m^2+8m+2)(5m-3)$

61. $(5a^2+3a-4)(3a+2)$

62. $(6a+3b)(a^4+3a^2b+4ab^2-b^4)$

63. $(3x+4y)(x^4-x^3y+xy^3-y^4)$

64. $(a^2+2ab+b^2)(a^2-2ab+b^2)$

65. $(m^2+mn+n^2)(m^2-mn+n^2)$

66. $(x-y)(x+y)(x^2+y^2)$

67. $(m^2+n^2)(m+n)(m-n)$

5.6 SPECIAL PRODUCTS

□ **The Square of a Binomial** □ **The Product of the Sum and Difference of Two Terms** □ **Summary of Special Products Formulas**

In this section we will introduce three formulas that represent shortcuts used to find the product of some special binomials directly (mentally).

□ THE SQUARE OF A BINOMIAL

Example 1

Use the FOIL method to expand.

$(a+b)^2$

Solution

$$(a+b)^2 = (a+b)(a+b) = a^2 + ab + ab + b^2 = a^2 + 2ab + b^2$$

Thus, $(a+b)^2 = a^2 + 2ab + b^2$

In words: *The square of a binomial = (the square of the first term) + (twice the product of the two terms) + (the square of the second term).*

Example 2

Use the square of a binomial formula to expand.

a. $(x+2)^2$ b. $(m+3)^2$ c. $(\frac{3}{2}n+5)^2$ d. $(4x+3y)^2$

Solution

a. $(x+2)^2 = x^2 + 2(x)(2) + 2^2 = x^2 + 4x + 4$

b. $(m+3)^2 = m^2 + 2(m)(3) + 3^2 = m^2 + 6m + 9$

c. $(\frac{3}{2}n+5)^2 = (\frac{3}{2}n)^2 + 2(\frac{3}{2}n)(5) + 5^2 = \frac{9}{4}n^2 + 15n + 25$

d. $(4x+3y)^2 = (4x)^2 + 2(4x)(3y) + (3y)^2 = 16x^2 + 24xy + 9y^2$

Example 3

Use the FOIL method to expand.

$(a-b)^2$

Solution

$$(a-b)^2 = (a-b)(a-b) = a^2 - ab - ab + b^2 = a^2 - 2ab + b^2$$

Thus, $(a-b)^2 = a^2 - 2ab + b^2$

In words: *The square of a binomial = (the square of the first term) – (twice the product of the two terms) + (the square of the second term).*

Example 4

Use the square of a binomial formula to expand.

   a. $(a-5)^2$ b. $(x-4)^2$ c. $(5m-3)^2$ d. $(2m+5n)^2$

Solution

   a. $(a-5)^2 = a^2 - 2(a)(5) + 5^2 = a^2 - 10a + 25$

   b. $(x-4)^2 = x^2 - 2(x)(4) + 4^2 = x^2 - 8x + 16$

   c. $(3n-2)^2 = (3n)^2 - 2(3n)(2) + 2^2 = 9n^2 - 12n + 4$

   d. $(2m-5n)^2 = (2m)^2 - 2(2m)(5n) + (5n)^2 = 4m^2 - 20mn + 25n^2$

Example 5

Use the square of a binomial formula to expand.

   a. $(9x+4y)^2$ c. $(2x^2 + \frac{3}{2})^2$

   b. $(6m-4n)^2$ d. $(2y-7x^3)$

Solution

   a. $(9x+4y)^2 = (9x)^2 + 2(9x)(4y) + (4y)^2 = 81x^2 + 72xy + 16y^2$

   b. $(6m-8n)^2 = (6m)^2 - 2(6m)(8n) + (8n)^2 = 36m^2 - 96mn + 64n^2$

   c. $(2x^2 + \frac{3}{2}y)^2 = (2x^2)^2 + 2(2x^2)(\frac{3}{2}y) + (\frac{3}{2}y)^2 = 4x^4 + 6x^2y + \frac{9}{4}y^2$

   d. $(2y-7x^3)^2 = (2y)^2 - 2(2y)(7x^3) + (7x^3)^2 = 4y^2 - 28x^3y + 49x^6$

☐ THE PRODUCT OF THE SUM AND DIFFERENCE OF TWO TERMS

Example 6

Use the FOIL method to multiply.

   $(a+b)(a-b)$

Solution

$$(a+b)(a-b) = a^2 - ab + ab + b^2 = a^2 - b^2$$

Thus, $(a+b)(a-b = a^2 - b^2)$

In words: (*The product of the sum and difference of the same two terms*) = (*the square of the first term*) − (*the square of the second term*).

Note: This formula will be used very often in the next chapter when factoring a difference of squares of the form $a^2 - b^2$.

Example 7

Use the product of a sum and a difference formula to multiply.

a. $(x+6)(x-6)$

b. $(m-10)(m+10)$

c. $(a^2 - 5)(a^2 + 5)$

d. $(2n-3m)(2n+3m)$

Solution

a. $(x+6)(x-6) = x^2 - 6^2 = x^2 - 36$

b. $(m-10)(m+10) = m^2 - 10^2 = m^2 - 100$

c. $(a^2 - 5)(a^2 + 5) = (a^2)^2 - 5^2 = a^4 - 25$

d. $(2n-3m)(2n+3m) = (2n)^2 - (3m)^2 = 4n^2 - 9m^2$

Example 8

Use the product of a sum and a difference formula to multiply.

a. $\left(y+\dfrac{1}{3}\right)\left(y-\dfrac{1}{3}\right)$

b. $\left(\dfrac{m}{2}+\dfrac{n}{5}\right)\left(\dfrac{m}{2}-\dfrac{n}{5}\right)$

c. $(5x^3 + 4y^3)(5x^3 - 4y^3)$

d. $[(m+n)+3][(m+n)-3]$

e. $[(2x+1)-y][(2x+1)+y]$

Solution

a. $\left(y+\dfrac{1}{3}\right)\left(y-\dfrac{1}{3}\right) = y^2 - \left(\dfrac{1}{3}\right)^2 = y^2 - \dfrac{1}{9}$

b. $\left(\dfrac{m}{2}+\dfrac{n}{5}\right)\left(\dfrac{m}{2}-\dfrac{n}{5}\right) = \left(\dfrac{m}{2}\right)^2 - \left(\dfrac{n}{5}\right)^2 = \dfrac{m^2}{4} - \dfrac{n^2}{25}$

c. $(5x^3 + 4y^3)(5x^3 - 4y^3) = (5x^3)^2 - (4y^3)^2 = 25x^6 - 16y^6$

d. $[(m+n)+3][(m+n)-3] = (m+n)^2 - 3^2 = m^2 + 2mn + n^2 - 9$

e. $[(2x+1)-y][(2x+1)+y] = (2x+1)^2 - y^2 = 4x^2 + 4x + 1 - y^2$

□ SUMMARY OF SPECIAL PRODUCTS FORMULAS

1. $(a+b)^2 = a^2 + 2ab + b^2$

3. $(a-b)(a+b) = a^2 - b^2$

2. $(a-b)^2 = a^2 - 2ab + b^2$

5.6 EXERCISES

Use the special products formulas to square each binomial.

1. $(x+8)^2$

2. $(m+6)^2$

3. $(n-3)^2$

4. $(y-9)^2$

5. $(2x+3)^2$

6. $(5x-2)^2$

7. $(4y-5)^2$

8. $(3a+7)^2$

9. $(x+3y)^2$

10. $(a+5b)^2$

11. $(m-10n)^2$

12. $(x-11y)^2$

13. $(2a+3b)^2$

14. $(7a-2b)^2$

15. $(3x-4y)^2$

16. $(4m+5n)^2$

17. $(9x+2y)^2$

18. $(6m+5n)^2$

19. $(5a-8b)^2$

20. $(2a-11b)^2$

21. $(x^2+2)^2$

22. $(y^2-4)^2$

23. $(3-a^3)^2$

24. $(6+m^3)^2$

25. $3(1-y^4)^2$

26. $5(1+x^4)^2$

27. $(3x^2-8y)^2$

28. $(5m-3n^2)^2$

29. $(x+3)^3$

30. $(a-5)^3$

31. $(2m+5)^3$

32. $(3n-2)^3$

33. $[(x+y)-3]^2$

34. $[(a-b)+4]^2$

35. $\left(m+\dfrac{5}{2}\right)^2$

36. $\left(\dfrac{3}{4}-n\right)^2$

Use the product of a sum and a difference formula to find each product.

37. $(x+3)(x-3)$

38. $(a-5)(a+5)$

39. $(y+9)(y-9)$

40. $(m+8)(m-8)$

41. $(2a-5)(2a+5)$

42. $(3x+11)(3x-11)$

43. $(4a+3)(4a-3)$

44. $(6x+1)(6x-1)$

45. $(5x - 8y)(5x + 8y)$

46. $(10x + 11y)(10x - 11y)$

47. $\left(a + \dfrac{3}{4}\right)\left(a - \dfrac{3}{4}\right)$

48. $\left(x + \dfrac{7}{9}\right)\left(x - \dfrac{7}{9}\right)$

49. $(2x^3 + 1)(2x^3 - 1)$

50. $(0.5a - 0.2)(0.5a + 0.2)$

51. $(0.9 + x)(0.9 - x)$

52. $[(x + y) - 5][(x + y) + 5]$

53. $[(m + n) - 7][(m + n) + 7]$

54. $[(2a - b) + 6][(2a - b) - 6]$

55. $[(x + 3y) - 8][(x + 3y) + 8]$

5.7 DIVISION OF POLYNOMIALS

☐ Dividing a Polynomial by a Monomial ☐ Dividing a Polynomial by a Polynomial (Long Division)

☐ DIVIDING A POLYNOMIAL BY A MONOMIAL

To divide a polynomial by a monomial we will use the following properties:

$$\frac{a+b}{c} = \frac{a}{c} + \frac{b}{c} \quad \text{OR} \quad \frac{a-b}{c} = \frac{a}{c} - \frac{b}{c}$$

> In words: *To divide a polynomial by a monomial, divide each term of the polynomial by the monomial*

Example 1

Divide.

$$\frac{15x^4 - 6x^3 + 3x^2 - 9x}{3x}$$

Solution

$$\frac{15x^4 - 6x^3 + 3x^2 - 9x}{3x} = \frac{15x^4}{3x} - \frac{6x^3}{3x} + \frac{3x^2}{3x} - \frac{9x}{3x} = 5x^3 - 2x^2 + x - 3$$

Note: $15x^4 - 6x^3 + 3x^2 - 9x$ is called the **dividend**, $3x$ the **divisor**, and $5x^3 - 2x^2 + x - 3$ the **quotient**.

Example 2

Divide.

$$\frac{16m^3 - 4m^2 - 12m + 4}{-2m}$$

Solution

$$\frac{16m^3 - 4m^2 - 12m + 4}{-2m} = \frac{16m^3}{-2m} - \frac{4m^2}{-2m} - \frac{12m}{-2m} + \frac{4}{-2m} = -8m^2 + 2m + 6 - \frac{2}{m}$$

Example 3

Divide.

$$\frac{14a^3 + 21a^2 - 35a + 2}{7a^2}$$

Solution

$$\frac{14a^3 + 21a^2 - 35a + 2}{7a^2} = \frac{14a^3}{7a^2} + \frac{21a^2}{7a^2} - \frac{35a}{7a^2} + \frac{2}{7a^2} = 2a + 3 - \frac{5}{a} + \frac{2}{7a^2}$$

Example 4

Divide.

$$(12y^2 + 5 - 24y^3 - 18y) \div (-6y)$$

Solution.

$$(12y^2 + 5 - 24y^3 - 18y) \div (-6y) = \frac{-24y^3 + 12y^2 - 18y + 5}{-6y} =$$

$$\frac{-24y^3}{-6y} + \frac{12y^2}{-6y} - \frac{18y}{-6y} + \frac{5}{-6y} =$$

$$4y^2 - 2y + 3 - \frac{5}{6y}$$

☐ DIVIDING A POLYNOMIAL BY A POLYNOMIAL (LONG DIVISION)

To divide a polynomial by a polynomial we will use the Long Division format, which is very common in arithmetic for dividing whole numbers.

$$\frac{Quotient}{Divisor \overline{)Dividend}}$$

Example 5

Use Long Division to divide.

$$(3x^2 + 11x - 4) \div (3x - 1)$$

Solution

First, write the dividend and the divisor in descending order. In this example, the dividend is $3x^2 + 11x - 4$ and the divisor is $3x - 1$ and both are written in descending order. Next, write the dividend and the divisor in the Long Division format.

$$3x - 1 \overline{)3x^2 + 11x - 4}$$

Step 1 To find the first term of the quotient, divide the first term $3x^2$ of the dividend by the first term $3x$ of the divisor

$$\frac{3x^2}{3x} = x$$

and place x in the quotient (above the dividend).

$$\begin{array}{r} x \phantom{{}+11x-4} \\ 3x-1{\overline{\smash{\big)}\,3x^2+11x-4}} \end{array}$$

Step 2 Multiply the first term of the quotient x by the divisor $3x-1$: $x(3x-1)=3x^2-x$ and write this product under the dividend $3x^2+11x$ to be subtracted. Since $-(3x^2-x)=-3x^2+x$ we can write $-3x^2+x$ instead of $-(3x^2-x)$ under $3x^2+11x$ and then **add the like terms**.

$$\begin{array}{r} x \phantom{{}+11x-4} \\ 3x-1{\overline{\smash{\big)}\,3x^2+11x-4}} \\ \underline{-3x^2+x\phantom{{}-4}} \\ 12x \phantom{{}-4} \end{array}$$

Drop –4 and repeat the process.

$$\begin{array}{r} x \phantom{{}+11x-4} \\ 3x-1{\overline{\smash{\big)}\,3x^2+11x-4}} \\ \underline{-3x^2+x\phantom{{}-4}} \\ 12x-4 \end{array}$$

Step 3 To find the second term of the quotient, divide the first term $12x$ of the new dividend $12x - 4$ to the first term $3x$ of the divisor $3x - 1$.

$$\frac{12x}{3x} = 4$$

and place 4 in the quotient.

$$\begin{array}{r} x+4 \\ 3x-1{\overline{\smash{\big)}\,3x^2+11x-4}} \\ \underline{-3x^2+x\phantom{{}-4}} \\ 12x-4 \end{array}$$

Step 4 Multiply 4 by the divisor $3x-1$ and write the product $4(3x-1)=12x-4$ under the new dividend $12x - 4$ to be subtracted. **Change the signs**: $-(12x-4)=-12x+4$ and write this product under the new dividend $12x-4$. Then add the like terms.

$$\begin{array}{r} x+4 \\ 3x-1{\overline{\smash{\big)}\,3x^2+11x-4}} \\ \underline{-3x^2+x\phantom{{}-4}} \\ 12x-4 \\ \underline{-12x+4} \\ 0\quad 0 \end{array}$$

Thus, the quotient is $x + 4$ and there is no remainder. The division process is completed and the answer can be written as follows:

$$(3x^2 + 11x - 4) \div (3x - 1) = x + 4$$

To check the answer, use the general rule:

Dividend = (divisor) × (quotient) + remainder

In our case, $3x^2 + 11x - 4 = (3x - 1)(x + 4) + 0 = 3x^2 + 12x - x - 4 = 3x^2 + 11x - 4$. True.

Example 6

Use Long Division to divide.

$$\frac{2x^3 + 11x^2 + 22x + 15}{2x + 3}$$

Solution

First, make sure that both polynomials are written in descending order. Next, write the dividend and divisor in the Long Division format.

$$
\begin{array}{r}
x^2 \\
2x+3\overline{)2x^3 + 11x^2 + 22x + 15} \\
\underline{-2x^3 - 3x^2} \\
8x^2 + 22x
\end{array}
$$

Divide $2x^3 / 2x = x^2$ and place x^2 in the quotient.

Multiply $x^2(2x + 3) = 2x^3 + 3x^2$ and **change the signs**: $-2x^3 - 3x^2$. Write this product under $2x^3 + 11x^2$ and **add the like terms**. Then, drop $22x$.

Repeat the process with a new dividend $8x^2 + 22x$.

$$
\begin{array}{r}
x^2 + 4x \\
2x+3\overline{)2x^3 + 11x^2 + 22x + 15} \\
\underline{-2x^3 - 3x^2} \\
8x^2 + 22x \\
\underline{-8x^2 - 12x} \\
10x + 15
\end{array}
$$

Divide $8x^2 / 2x = 4x$ and place $4x$ in the quotient.

Multiply $4x(2x + 3) = 8x^2 + 12x$ and **change the signs**: $-8x^2 - 12x$. Write this product under $8x^2 + 22x$ and **add the like terms**. Then, drop 15.

Repeat the process again with the dividend $10x + 15$.

$$
\begin{array}{r}
x^2 + 4x + 5 \\
2x+3\overline{)2x^3 + 11x^2 + 22x + 15} \\
\underline{-2x^3 - 3x^2} \\
8x^2 + 22x \\
\underline{-8x^2 - 12x} \\
10x + 15 \\
\underline{-10x - 15} \\
0 \ 0
\end{array}
$$

Divide $10x / 2x = 5$ and place 5 in the quotient.

Multiply $5(2x + 3) = 10x + 15$ and **change the signs**: $-10x - 15$. Place this product under $10x + 15$ and **add**.

Thus, $(2x^3 + 11x^2 + 22x + 15) \div (2x + 3) = x^2 + 4x + 5$.

Check:

$2x^3 + 11x^2 + 22x + 15 = (2x + 3)(x^2 + 4x + 5) = 2x^3 + 8x^2 + 10x + 3x^2 + 12x + 15 =$

$2x^3 + 11x^2 + 22x + 15$ True.

Example 7

Use Long Division to divide.

$$\frac{12x^3 + 14x + 5x^2 - 6}{4x - 1}$$

Solution

First, write the dividend in descending order: $12x^3 + 5x^2 + 14x - 6$. Then, write the dividend and divisor in the Long Division format.

$$
\begin{array}{r}
3x^2 \\
4x-1\overline{\smash{\big)}\,12x^3 + 5x^2 + 14x - 6} \\
\underline{-12x^3 - 3x^2} \\
8x^2 + 14x
\end{array}
$$

Divide $12x^3 / 4x = 3x^2$ and place $3x^2$ in the quotient.

Multiply $3x^2(4x - 1) = 12x^3 - 3x^2$ and **change the signs**: $-12x^3 + 3x^2$. Write this product under $12x^3 + 5x^2$ and **add the like terms**. Then, drop $14x$.

Repeat the process with the new dividend $8x^2 + 14x$.

$$
\begin{array}{r}
3x^2 + 2x \\
4x-1\overline{\smash{\big)}\,12x^3 + 5x^2 + 14x - 6} \\
\underline{-12x^3 - 3x^2} \\
8x^2 + 14x \\
-8x^2 + 2x \\
16x - 6
\end{array}
$$

Divide $8x^2 / 4x = 2x$ and place $2x$ in the quotient.

Multiply $2x(4x - 1) = 8x^2 - 2x$ and **change the signs**: $-8x^2 + 2x$. Write this product under $8x^2 + 14x$ and **add the like terms**. Then drop -6.

Repeat the process with the dividend $16x - 6$.

$$
\begin{array}{r}
3x^2 + 2x + 4 \\
4x-1\overline{\smash{\big)}\,12x^3 + 5x^2 + 14x - 6} \\
\underline{-12x^3 - 3x^2} \\
8x^2 + 14x \\
-8x^2 + 2x \\
16x - 6 \\
-16x + 4 \\
-2
\end{array}
$$

Divide $16x / 4x = 4$ and place 4 in the quotient.

Multiply $4(4x - 1) = 16x - 4$ and **change the signs**: $-16x + 4$. Write this product under $16x - 6$ and **add the like terms**.

Since the degree of –2 is zero, which is less than the degree of one of the divisor $4x - 1$, the division process is completed and therefore –2 is the remainder. The answer can be written as follows:

$$\frac{12x^3 + 5x^2 + 14x - 6}{4x - 1} = 3x^2 + 2x + 4 - \frac{2}{4x - 1}$$

To check the answer, multiply both sides by $4x - 1$.

$$(4x - 1)\frac{12x^3 + 5x^2 + 14x - 6}{4x - 1} = (4x - 1)(3x^2 + 2x + 4) - (4x - 1)\left(\frac{2}{4x - 1}\right)$$

$$12x^3 + 5x^2 + 14x - 6 = (4x - 1)(3x^2 + 2x + 4) - 2 =$$

$$12x^3 + 8x^2 + 16x - 3x^2 - 2x - 4 - 2 =$$

$$12x^3 + 5x^2 + 14x - 6 \text{ True.}$$

Example 8

Use Long Division to divide.

$$(x^4 - 1) \div (x + 1)$$

Solution

Since the terms in x^3, x^2, and x in the dividend are missing, there is no place to line up like terms for subtraction. Thus, we should fill the places of the missing terms with zero coefficient terms: $0x^3$, $0x^2$, and $0x$.

$$\begin{array}{r} x^3 - x^2 + x - 1 \\ x+1\overline{)x^4 + 0x^3 + 0x^2 + 0x - 1} \\ \underline{-x^4 - x^3} \\ -x^3 + 0x^2 \\ \underline{-x^3 + x^2} \\ x^2 + 0x \\ \underline{-x^2 - x} \\ -x - 1 \\ \underline{x + 1} \\ 0\ 0 \end{array}$$

Divide $x^4 / x = x^3$ and place x^3 in the quotient. Multiply $x^3(x+1) = x^4 + x^3$ and **change the signs:** $-x^4 - x^3$. Write $-x^4 - x^3$ under $x^4 + 0x^3$ and **add the like terms.** Then, drop $0x^2$. Divide $-x^3 / x = -x^2$ and place $-x^2$ in the quotient. Multiply $-x^2(x+1) = -x^3 - x^2$ and **change the signs:** $x^3 + x^2$. Write $x^3 + x^2$ under $-x^3 + 0x^2$ and **add the like terms.** Then, drop $0x$. Divide $x^2 / x = x$ and write x in the quotient. Multiply $x(x+1) = x^2 + x$ and **change the signs:** $-x^2 - x$. Write $-x^2 - x$ under $x^2 + 0x$ and **add the like terms.** Drop -1. Divide $-x / x = -1$ and write -1 in the quotient. Multiply $-1(x+1) - x - 1$ and **change the signs:** $x + 1$. Write $x + 1$ under $-x - 1$and **add the like terms.** There is no remainder.

The answer is: $(x^4 - 1) \div (x + 1) = x^3 - x^2 + x - 1$.

5.7 EXERCISES

Divide.

1. $\dfrac{6x^2 - 18x + 9}{3}$

2. $\dfrac{16x^3 - 24x^2 + 8x}{8x}$

3. $\dfrac{9a^4 + 27a^2 - 18a}{9a}$

4. $\dfrac{20m^3 - 40m^2 + 60m}{10m}$

5. $\dfrac{12y^6 + 48y^4 - 36y^2}{12y^2}$

6. $\dfrac{15a^8 - 45a^6 + 30a^4}{15a^4}$

7. $\dfrac{4x^3 - 20x + 5}{4x}$

8. $\dfrac{18n^8 + 45n^6 - 10n^4}{9n^5}$

9. $\dfrac{35x^5 + 28x^4 + 6x^3}{7x^4}$

10. $\dfrac{-5x^7 + 40x^5 - 8x^3}{5x^3}$

11. $\dfrac{18x^{12} + 54x^{10} - 90x^8}{-18x^{10}}$

12. $\dfrac{20m^5 - 12m^4 - 36m^3}{4m^4}$

13. $\dfrac{22m^2n^3 + 14mn^2 - 26mn - 42m^3n^2}{-2mn}$

14. $\dfrac{-64x^4y^5 - 48x^3y^6 + 80x^2y^8 + 16xy}{16xy}$

Use Long Division to divide.

15. $\dfrac{x^2 + 8x + 15}{x + 3}$

16. $\dfrac{x^2 + 5x - 6}{x + 6}$

17. $\dfrac{x^2 - x - 56}{x - 8}$

18. $\dfrac{x^2 + 5x - 36}{x - 4}$

19. $\dfrac{x^2 - 3x - 42}{x + 5}$

20. $\dfrac{x^2 - 5x - 18}{x + 2}$

21. $\dfrac{3x^2 + 19x + 21}{x + 5}$

22. $\dfrac{2x^2 - 9x - 18}{x - 6}$

23. $\dfrac{6x^2 + 13x - 8}{3x - 1}$

24. $\dfrac{6x^2 - x - 12}{2x - 3}$

25. $\dfrac{20x^2 + 11x - 5}{5x + 4}$

26. $\dfrac{12x^2 - 29x - 10}{3x - 8}$

27. $\dfrac{2m^2 + 13m + 15}{2m + 3}$

28. $\dfrac{3m^2 + 19m - 41}{3m - 5}$

29. $\dfrac{7y^2 + 41y + 35}{7y + 6}$

30. $\dfrac{22a + 5 + 8a^2}{4a + 1}$

31. $\dfrac{2a + 15 - 8a^2}{-2a + 3}$

32. $\dfrac{20 - 22a - 12a^2}{-6a + 4}$

33. $\dfrac{2x^3 + 5x^2 + 8x + 5}{x + 1}$

34. $\dfrac{4x^3 - 7x^2 - 17x + 9}{x - 3}$

35. $\dfrac{15y^3 - 7y^2 - 14y + 9}{3y - 2}$

36. $\dfrac{12x^3 - 5x^2 + 13x - 10}{3x - 2}$

37. $\dfrac{15x^3 - 17x^2 + 6x + 4}{5x + 1}$

38. $\dfrac{14x^3 + 29x^2 - 29x + 1}{7x - 3}$

39. $\dfrac{20x^3 + 18x + 23x^2 + 9}{4x + 3}$

40. $\dfrac{21x^3 + 38x + 29x^2 + 20}{7x + 5}$

41. $\dfrac{10x^3 - 11x - 38 + 23x^2}{5x + 9}$

42. $\dfrac{15y^3 - 16y^2 + 10}{5y + 3}$

43. $\dfrac{x^3 + 27}{x + 3}$

44. $\dfrac{14m^3 + 24m^2 - 43m + 10}{7m - 2}$

45. $\dfrac{y^3 - 8}{y - 2}$

46. $\dfrac{6x^4 + 23x^3 + 18x^2 - x + 8}{2x + 5}$

47. $\dfrac{a^4 - 81}{a + 3}$

48. $\dfrac{8y^4 + 20y^3 - 10y^2 + 5y - 5}{4y^2 + 1}$

49. $\dfrac{m^4 - 1}{m^2 + 1}$

50. $\dfrac{x^5 + x^4 + x^3 + x^2 + x + 1}{x^2 + x + 1}$

51. $\dfrac{n^5 - 32}{n - 2}$

CHAPTER 5 REVIEW EXERCISES

Simplify.

1. $(-5x^2y^4)^2$

2. $(4m^3n^5)^3$

3. $(-2a^6b^5c^3)^4$

4. $(2a^4)^2(-3a^2)^2$

5. $(-4x^2)^2(x^5)^4$

6. $(-m^3)^3(-5m^2)^2$

7. $(5x^4y^5)^2(-2x^3y^4)^3$

8. $(-2a^2b^3c^2)^3(3a^5b^2c)^2$

9. $(4m^4n^5)^2(-m^3n^2)^5$

10. $\left(\dfrac{6a^4c}{2a^2b^3}\right)^3$

11. $\left(\dfrac{3x^2y^2}{4x^5y^3}\right)^2$

12. $\left(\dfrac{18a^3b^4}{12a^5b^2}\right)^3$

13. $\left(\dfrac{-3x^2}{6y^3}\right)^4\left(\dfrac{2x^3}{y^5}\right)^0$

14. $\left(\dfrac{a^3b^3}{x^4y^5}\right)^2\left(\dfrac{-x^3y^5}{3a^2b^2}\right)^3$

15. $\left(\dfrac{-9mn^3}{3a^2b^4}\right)^2\left(\dfrac{a^3b^2}{m^2n^2}\right)^3$

16. $\dfrac{(x^2y^{-3})^4(x^3b^{-5})^{-2}}{(2x^{-4}y^{-1})^3}$

17. $\dfrac{(a^2b^{-4})^2(a^{-3}b^{-4})^{-1}}{(a^4b^{-3})^{-2}}$

18. $\dfrac{(m^{-1}n^2)^{-3}(m^{-6}n^3)^2}{(m^5n^{-1})^4}$

Write each number in scientific notation.

19. 136,000,000

20. 541,200,000,000

21. 0.000,000,123

22. 0.000,017

23. 0.3

24. 17

Perform each indicated operation. Write the answer in scientific notation.

25. $(2.0 \times 10^8)(2.5 \times 10^{-6})$

26. $(5.0 \times 10^{-3})(4.6 \times 10^8)$

Perform each indicated operation. Write the answer in standard form (without exponents)

27. $\dfrac{4.2 \times 10^{12}}{2.1 \times 10^8}$

28. $\dfrac{10.2 \times 10^{-3}}{3.4 \times 10^{-6}}$

29. $\dfrac{2.0 \times 10^{-11}}{6.0 \times 10^{-8}}$

Add or Subtract.

30. $(3x^2 - 5x + 1) + (x^2 + 4x - 3)$

31. $(6x^2 + 4x - 8) + (-x^2 + 3x + 6)$

32. $(2y^2 - y + 7) - (-3y^2 + 4y - 2)$

33. $(-7m^2 + 3m - 5) - (2m^2 - 4m - 8)$

34. $[(4a^2 - 6a + 1) - (-2a^2 + 3a - 5)] + [(7a^2 + 2a - 4) - (5a^2 - 8a + 2)]$

35. $[(-x^3 + 3x^2 - 4x + 10) - (-5x^3 - 2x^2 + 3x - 1)] - [(5x^3 - 2x^2 + 8x - 3) - (x^3 - x + 4)]$

Multiply.

36. $-3x(2x^2 + 6x - 5)$

37. $5x(4x^2 - 7x + 3)$

38. $8x^2 y(x^2 y - xy + xy^2)$

39. $(2x + 3y)(5x - 4y)$

40. $(3a - 2b)(a + 8b)$

41. $(5m - 3n)(2m - 6n)$

42. $(4x + 3)^2$

43. $(5y - 8)^2$

44. $(5a - 4b)(5a + 4b)$

45. $(2x - 5)(3x^2 - 7x + 2)$

46. $(3y + 2)(5y^2 + 4y - 2)$

47. $(2m + 3n)^2$

48. $(2x^2 + 3x - 6)(4x^2 - 5x + 2)$

49. $(3x - 2y)^3$

Divide.

50. $\dfrac{24x^3 y^2 + 16x^2 y^2 - 20x^2 y^3}{4xy}$

51. $\dfrac{9a^3 + 12a^2 - 6a + 1}{2a}$

52. $\dfrac{18m^3 n^2 + 24m^2 n - 30mn^2 - 42m^2 n^3}{-3mn}$

53. $\dfrac{-32x^4 y^5 + 64x^3 y^4 - 80x^2 y^2 + xy}{8xy}$

54. $\dfrac{2x^2 + 14x + 24}{x + 3}$

55. $\dfrac{12m^2 + 29m + 10}{4m + 3}$

56. $\dfrac{20y^2 - 7y - 6}{5y + 2}$

57. $\dfrac{24x^2 + 23x - 10}{3x + 4}$

58. $\dfrac{8x^2 + 37x - 15}{x + 5}$

59. $\dfrac{6x^2 - 25x - 10}{2x - 9}$

60. $\dfrac{8x^3 - 45x^2 - 16x - 12}{x - 6}$

61. $\dfrac{14x^3 + 13x - 37x^2 - 18}{2x - 5}$

62. $\dfrac{9x^3 + 8x + 132}{3x + 7}$

63. $\dfrac{8x^3 + 27x^2 - 17x + 12}{x + 4}$

64. $\dfrac{18y^3 - 3y^2 + 23y + 6}{6y + 1}$

65. $\dfrac{27x^3 - 6x^2 + 20 + 37x}{9x + 4}$

66. $\dfrac{8x^3 + 6x - 4}{2x + 3}$

67. $\dfrac{x^3 + 2x^2 + 2x + 1}{x^2 + x + 1}$

68. $\dfrac{20x^4 - 5x^2 + 2}{4x^2 - 1}$

6 FACTORING POLYNOMIALS

6.1 FACTORING A MONOMIAL FROM A POLYNOMIAL AND FACTORING BY GROUPING

□ **The Greatest Common Factor (GCF)** □ **Factoring a Monomial from a Polynomial** □ **Factoring a Binomial from a Polynomial** □ **Factoring by Grouping**

To factor a polynomial means to write the polynomial as a product of two or more polynomial factors, if possible. In particular, factoring a monomial from a polynomial is the process that reverses the distributive property (distributive property in reverse).

For example:

Distributive property: $2x(x+1) = 2x^2 + 2x$

Factor a monomial from a polynomial: $2x^2 + 2x = 2x(x+1)$

The monomial $2x$ is called the greatest common factor (GCF) of $2x^2$ and $2x$.

□ THE GREATEST COMMON FACTOR (GCF)

The above example suggests that in order to factor a monomial from a polynomial, we need the greatest common factor of all the terms of the polynomial.

Since every term of a polynomial is a monomial, first we need to discuss how to find the greatest common factor of two or more monomials.

Sometimes, the coefficient of a monomial is a number other than one. Thus, we will begin our discussion with the greatest common factor of two or more numbers.

In chapter 1 we introduced the following rule that was used to find the greatest common factor of two or more numbers.

Rule

To find the GCF of two or more numbers:

Step 1 Write each number as a product of its prime factors (prime factorization). Repeated factors should be written in exponential form.

Step 2 Choose only factors common to each number with the lowest exponent.

Step 3 Multiply the factors from Step 2 to find the GCF.

Example 1

Find the greatest common factor (GCF) of: 12 and 90.

Solution

$$12 = 2^2 \cdot 3$$
$$90 = 2 \cdot 3^2 \cdot 5$$
$$\overline{\text{GCF} = 2 \cdot 3 = 6}$$

Recall, the GCF of two or more numbers is the largest number that is a factor of all the numbers or the largest number that will exactly divide each number.

Now, we will extend this rule to find the greatest common factor of two or more monomials.

Rule

To find the GCF of two or more monomials:

Step 1 Write the coefficient of each monomial as a product of its prime factors (in exponential form) followed by the variable part of the monomial.

Step 2 Choose only common factors (numbers and variables) of the monomials with the lowest exponent.

Step 3 Multiply the factors from Step 2 to find the GCF.

Example 2

Find the greatest common factor of: $18x^3y^4z^2$ and $60x^5y^2$.

Solution

$$18x^3y^4z^2 = 2 \cdot 3^2 \qquad x^3y^4z^3$$
$$60x^5y^2 = 2^2 \cdot 3 \cdot 5 \ \ x^5y^2$$
$$\overline{\text{GCF} = 2 \cdot 3 \cdot \qquad x^3y^2 = 6x^3y^2}$$

Example 3

Find the greatest common factor of: $5m^2n^3$, $15m^4n^2$, $20m^3n^4p$.

Solution

$$5m^2n^3 = \qquad\quad 5m^2n^3$$
$$15m^4n^2 = \qquad 3 \cdot 5m^4n^2$$
$$20m^3n^4p = 2^2 \qquad \cdot 5m^3n^4p$$
$$\overline{\text{GCF} = \qquad\quad 5m^2n^2}$$

☐ FACTORING A MONOMIAL FROM A POLYNOMIAL

> **Rule**
>
> To factor a monomial from a polynomial, factor out the greatest common monomial factor from each term of the polynomial.

Note: The greatest common monomial factor of a polynomial is the largest monomial that divides exactly each term of the polynomial

When the coefficients of the monomials are small numbers, the GCF can be identified by inspection. For example, the GCF for $12x + 18$ is 6 because 6 is the largest number that is a factor of $12x$ and 18.

The following example illustrates the significance of the GCF when factoring a monomial from a polynomial.

Example 4

Factor.

$$12x + 18$$

Solution

Since 2 is a common factor of $12x$ and 18, we can factor out 2.

$$12x + 18 = 2(6x + 9)$$

The terms of the binomial $6x + 9$ can be found by dividing $12x \div 2 = 6x$ and $18 \div 2 = 9$.

The binomial $6x + 9$ is not factored completely because $6x$ and 9 have 3 as a common factor and therefore $6x + 9$ can be factored again.

Also, 3 is a common factor of $12x$ and 18. So, we can factor out 3.

$$12x + 18 = 3(4x + 6)$$

Again, $4x + 6$ is not factored completely because $4x$ and 6 have 2 as a common factor.

From the above discussion, we already know that 6 is the GCF of $12x$ and 18. If we factor out 6,

$$12x + 18 = 6(2x + 3)$$

the polynomial $12x + 18$ is factored completely because $2x + 3$ cannot be factored again (prime factor).

We conclude that by factoring the GCF from all the terms of a polynomial the factoring process was completed in one step. To check the answer, apply the distributive property.

Note: In general, a polynomial is in factored form when the polynomial is written as a product of its factors. A polynomial is factored completely when the polynomial is written as a product of its prime factors.

Example 5

Factor out the GCF.

a. $16x + 24$

b. $14a^3 + 21a^2$

c. $24m^2n - 40mn^2$

Solution

a. By inspection the $GCF = 8$. The other factor can be obtained by dividing each term of the polynomial $16x + 24$ by 8: $16x \div 8 = 2x$, $24 \div 8 = 3$. Therefore,

$$16x + 24 = 8(2x + 3)$$

b. By inspection the $GCF = 7a^2$. Divide each term of the polynomial $14a^3 + 21a^2$ by the $GCF = 7a^2$ to find the terms of the second factor.

$$14a^3 + 21a^2 = 7a^2(2a + 3)$$

c. By inspection the $GCF = 8mn$. Divide each term of the polynomial $24m^2n - 40mn^2$ by the $GCF = 8mn$ to find the terms of the second factor.

$$24m^2n - 40mn^2 = 8mn(3m - 5n)$$

Example 6

Factor out the GCF.

a. $21x^4 + 7x^3 + 49x^2$

b. $15a^3b^2 - 20a^2b^2 + 35a^2b^3$

Solution

a. By inspection, the $GCF = 7x^2$. To find the terms of the second factor, divide each term of the polynomial $21x^4 + 7x^3 + 49x^2$ by the $GCF = 7x^2$.

$$21x^4 \div 7x^2 = 3x^2, \ 7x^3 \div 7x^2 = x, \ 49x^2 \div 7x^2 = 7$$

Therefore, $21x^4 + 7x^3 + 49x^2 = 7x^2(3x^2 + x + 7)$

b. By inspection the $GCF = 5a^2b^2$. Divide each term of the polynomial $15a^3b^2 - 20a^2b^2 + 35a^2b^3$ by the $GCF = 5a^2b^2$.

$$15a^3b^2 \div 5a^2b^2 = 3a, \ -20a^2b^2 \div 5a^2b^2 = -4, \ 35a^2b^3 \div 5a^2b^2 = 7b$$

Thus, $15a^3b^2 - 20a^2b^2 + 35a^2b^3 = 5a^2b^2(3a - 4 + 7b)$

Example 7

Factor out a negative monomial.

$$-45m^8 - 72m^6 + 18m^4$$

Solution

By inspection, the $GCF = -9m^4$. Divide each term of the polynomial $-45m^8 - 72m^6 + 18m^4$ by the $GCF = -9m^4$.

$$-45m^8 \div (-9m^4) = 5m^4, \ -72m^6 \div (-9m^4) = 8m^2, \ 18m^4 \div (-9m^4) = -2$$

Thus, $-45m^8 - 72m^6 + 18m^4 = -9m^4(5m^4 + 8m^2 - 2)$

☐ FACTORING A BINOMIAL FROM A POLYNOMIAL

If the GCF of all the terms of a polynomial is a binomial instead of a monomial, we can factor out a binomial.

For example, the greatest common factor for all the terms of the polynomial $(x+y)a + (x+y)b$ is a binomial $GCF = x + y$.

So, we factor out the binomial $(x+y)$, and then we divide each term of the polynomial by $x+y$ to find the terms of the second factor.

$$(x+y)a + (x+y)b = (x+y)(a+b)$$

Example 8

Factor.

a. $y(x-5) + 3(y-5)$

b. $5a(3x+2y) - 2b(3x+2y)$

Solution

a. $y(x-5) + 3(x-5) = (x-5)(y+3)$

b. $5a(3x+2y) - 2b(3x+2y) = (3x+2y)(5a-2b)$

Example 9

Factor.

a. $2m(n-4) + 5(4-n)$

b. $7x(3a-5b) - 3y(5b-3a)$

Solution

a. Since $4-n = -n+4 = -(n-4)$ we can rewrite the polynomial as follows:

$$2m(n-4) + 5(4-n) = 2m(n-4) + 5[-(n-4)] = 2m(n-4) - 5(n-4) = (n-4)(2m-5)$$

b. Similarly, $5b-3a = -3a+5b = -(3a-5b)$. Thus,

$$7x(3a-5b) - 3y(5b-3a) = 7x(3a-5b) - 3y[-(3a-5b)] = 7x(3a-5b) + 3y(3a-5b) =$$
$$(3a-5b)(7x+3y)$$

☐ FACTORING BY GROUPING

Example 10

Factor.

$$2mx + 2my + 3nx + 3ny$$

Solution

There is no factor common to all the terms of the polynomial. However, if we group the first two terms and the last two terms, then each group has a common factor.

$$(2mx + 2my) + (3nx + 3ny)$$

By inspection, the greatest common factor for the first group is $GCF = 2m$ and for the second group $GCF = 3n$. Factor out $2m$ for the first group and $3n$ for the second group.

$$2m(x+y)+3n(x+y)$$

Now, there is a common binomial factor $(x+y)$ which is the greatest common factor for all the terms of the polynomial. If we factor out the $GCF = x+y$, and then divide each term of the polynomial $2m(x+y)+3n(x+y)$ by $(x+y)$ the result is:

$$2m(x+y)+3n(x+y)=(x+y)(2m+3n)$$

Note: We can group the first with the third term and the second with the last term to obtain the same result. *This process is called factoring by grouping.*

Example 11

Factor.

a. $m^2 + m - 3m - 3$　　　　　　　b. $6xy - 8x - 9y + 12$

Solution

a. Group the first two terms and the last two terms.

$$(m^2 + m)+(-3m-3)$$

Factor m from the first group and -3 from the last group.

$$m(m+1)-3(m+1)$$

Factor $(m+1)$ from both terms. $m(m+1)-3(m+1)=(m+1)(m-3)$

b. Group the first with the third term and the second with the last terms.

$$(6xy-9y)+(-8x+12)$$

Factor out $3y$ from the first group, and -4 from the second group.

$$3y(2x-3)-4(2x-3)$$

Factor $(2x-3)$ from both terms. $3y(2x-3)-4(2x-3)=(2x-3)(3y-4)$

Note: When factoring by grouping, most of the time we can combine any two terms of the polynomial. The sign and the coefficient of each term leads to the best combination.

6.1 EXERCISES

Find the greatest common factor for each group of monomials.

1. m^5, m^3

2. $-x^9$, x^4

3. $14a^3$, $28a^2$

4. $18y^6$, $24y^8$

5. $42x^3y^2$, $49xy^4$

6. $72a^4b^5$, $45a^3b^7c$

7. $9x^2y^3z^4$, $15x^5y^2$, $75x^3y^4z^2$

8. $60m^2n^2$, $48m^3n$, $66mn^4$

9. $52a^3b^5c^2$, $39a^4b^2c$, $65a^2b^3c^8$

10. $24x^2y^2$, $72x^4y^3$, $96x^3y^3$

Factor each polynomial completely.

11. $5x + 20$

12. $6x + 18$

13. $16a + 20$

14. $12a + 30$

15. $14m^2 + 21m$

16. $10x^3 - 25x^2$

17. $9y - 12y^4$

18. $5a^4 + 7a^2$

19. $11m^6 - 15m^4$

20. $4x^4y - 5x^3y^2$

21. $8a^3b^4 + 9a^4b^3$

22. $12y^3 - 27y^2$

23. $16m^2n^2 - 20m^3n^3$

24. $48x^5y^4 - 72x^4y^5$

25. $15x^3y^2z + 35xy^2z^3$

26. $26a^4b^2c^3 - 39a^3b^3c^4$

27. $n^3 + 5n^2 - 3n$

28. $y^5 - 3y^2 + 8y$

29. $x^3 + 4x^2 - 9x$

30. $b^6 - 8b^4 - 6b^2$

31. $2a^3 + 6a^2 - 24a$

32. $5n^4 + 20n^3 - 15n^2$

33. $4x^3 - 20x^2 - 16x$

34. $24a^4 + 40a^2 - 8a^3$

35. $6m^5 - 18m^3 + 48m$

36. $8x^4 - 32x^2 + 24x$

37. $16y^3 + 24y^2 - 64y$

38. $a^2b^2 - 3a^2b + 5a^2$

39. $m^3n^2 - 5m^2n^2 + 8m^2n^3$

40. $4a^2b^3 + 36a^5b^4 - 16a^4b^2$

41. $9x^2y^2 - 27x^3y^2 + 45x^2y^3$

42. $5x^3y^3 + 20x^2y^2 - 35xy$

43. $12a^4b^4 - 36a^3b^2 + 72a^2b^3$

Factor a binomial from a polynomial.

44. $x(y + 4) + 5(y + 4)$

45. $m(n - 3) + 6(n - 3)$

46. $4a(x - y) + b(x - y)$

47. $2x(3y + 2) + 5(3y + 2)$

48. $8m(5n - 1) - 6(5n - 1)$

49. $3x(2y + 3) - 12(2y + 3)$

50. $a^2(2x + 5y) + b^2(2x + 5y)$

51. $m^4(4a + 7b) + n^4(4a + 7b)$

52. $2x(4a - b) + (4a - b)$

53. $8y(2x + 1) + (2x + 1)$

54. $5m(3n - 2) - (3n - 2)$

55. $4x(6y - 1) - (6y - 1)$

56. $3a(2x - 3y) + 4(3y - 2x)$

57. $11b(6m - 5n) + 8(5n - 6m)$

58. $a^2(x + 4) + a(x + 4)$

59. $x^3(2y + 3) - x^2(2y + 3)$

60. $(a + 1)(x + 5) + a(x + 5)$

61. $(x - 2)(m + 3) + 4(m + 3)$

Factor by Grouping.

62. $ab - b + 3a - 3$

63. $mn + n + 6m + 6$

64. $x^2 + 6x + 2x + 12$

65. $x^2 + 3x + 4x + 12$

66. $x^2 - 3x - 5x + 15$

67. $x^2 - 2x - 7x + 14$

68. $2x^2 + 12x - 3x - 18$

69. $3x^2 + 15x - 4x - 20$

70. $5y^3 + 2y^2 - 15y - 6$

71. $4m^3 - 3m^2 + 8m - 6$

72. $8a^2 - 14a + 12a - 21$

73. $4n^2 - 32n + 5n - 40$

74. $10a^2 - 2ab + 5ab - b^2$

75. $6x^2 - 3xy + 4xy - 2y^2$

76. $3x^3 - 5x^2 + 12x - 20$

77. $15x^3 + 20x^2 + 3x + 4$

78. $x^2 - 3x - x + 3$

79. $x^3 - 5x^2 + x - 5$

80. $y^4 + 2y^2 + y^2 + 2$

81. $x^4 + 3x^2 - 5x^2 - 15$

82. $14ab - 6a + 28b - 12$

83. $8xy + 10x - 12y - 15$

84. $20x^3 - 8x^2 + 15x^2 - 6x$

85. $x^3 - x^2z + xy - yz$

86. $12xy - 16x + 18y - 24$

87. $18x^2 - 45xy + 24xy - 60y^2$

6.2 FACTORING TRINOMIALS OF THE FORM: $x^2 + bx + c = 0$

In this section, our goal is to factor trinomials of the form $ax^2 + bx + c$, where $a = 1$.

In other words, we will develop a factoring technique that helps us express a trinomial of the form $x^2 + bx + c$ as a product of its prime factors (if the trinomial is not prime).

In general, a trinomial of this form is the result of multiplying (FOIL) two binomials.

For example: $(x + 2)(x + 3) = x^2 + 3x + 2x + 6 = x^2 + 5x + 6$

Thus, factoring trinomials of the form $x^2 + bx + c$ is the reverse process of FOIL learned in the previous chapter. From the above example, $x^2 + 5x + 6 = (x + 2)(x + 3)$

Now, can we find the factors $(x + 2)$ and $(x + 3)$ without doing the product first (FOIL)?

First, let's find a general rule to guess the unknown numbers such as 2 and 3 involved in these factors, needed to factor a trinomial of this form. Suppose that the unknown numbers we are looking for are m and n. Then,

$$x^2 + bx + c = (x + m)(x + n)$$

$$x^2 + bx + c = x^2 + nx + mx + mn$$

$$x^2 + bx + c = x^2 + (m + n)x + mn$$

If we compare the coefficients of the left-hand and the right-hand side of the last two identical polynomials,

$$x^2 + bx + c = x^2 + (m + n)x + mn$$

we observe the following relationship between the coefficients of the trinomial $x^2 + bx + c$ and the numbers m and n.

$b = m + n$ (the coefficients of x)

$c = m \cdot n$ (the constant terms)

This can be summarized in the following rule:

Rule

To factor a trinomial of the form $x^2 + bx + c$, we must find two numbers with the product equal to the constant term c, and the sum equal to the coefficient b of x in the middle term.

Since the coefficient of x^2 is one, it's easy to guess what terms of those two factors we have to multiply to obtain x^2.

$$x^2 + 5x + 6 = (x\ \ )(x\ \ )$$

Next, we must find the numbers 2 and 3 and their signs to complete each factor.

In our example, we must find two numbers with the product 6 and the sum 5. Obviously, the numbers are 2 and 3 ($2 \cdot 3 = 6$, and $2 + 3 = 5$).

Thus, $x^2 + 5x + 6 = (x+2)(x+3)$

So far, we can guess the numbers m and n but we still don't know their signs. Next, we will use basic knowledge from chapter 1 to determine the signs of the numbers m and n.

CASE 1

If the product c of those two numbers is negative, then one number is positive and the other number is negative $(+ \cdot - = -)$.

To decide which one is positive and which one is negative, we have to look at the sum b.

If the sum b is positive, the larger number in absolute value is positive.

For example: $+7 - 3 = +4$ (positive sum).

If the sum b is negative, the larger number in absolute value is negative.

For example: $-7 + 3 = -4$ (negative sum).

CASE 2

If the product c of those two numbers is positive, then the numbers are either both positive or both negative $(+ \cdot + = +$ and $- \cdot - = +)$.

Again, we have to look at the sum b of the two numbers to decide if they are positive or negative.

If the sum is positive, both numbers are positive.

For example: $+3 + 4 = +7$ (positive sum).

If the sum is negative, both numbers are negative.

For example: $-3 - 4 = -7$ (negative sum).

Example 1

Factor.

$$x^2 + 9x + 20$$

Solution

According to the rule, to factor this trinomial, we must find two numbers whose product is $+20$ and whose sum is $+9$. Since the product is positive, both numbers can be positive or both numbers can be negative. Since the sum is positive, both numbers are positive.

Thus, $x^2 + 9x + 20 = (x + ?)(x + ?)$

To find the unknown numbers, try all the possibilities to write the product $+20$ using positive factors.

$$1 \cdot 20 = 20, \ 2 \cdot 10 = 20, \text{ and } 4 \cdot 5 = 20$$

The only possible combination that gives the product 20 and the sum 9 is: 5 and 4.

Thus, $x^2 + 9x + 20 = (x+5)(x+4)$

To check the answer, FOIL : $(x+5)(x+4) = x^2 + 4x + 5x + 20 = x^2 + 9x + 20$,   True.

Example 2

Factor.

$$x^2 - 8x + 12$$

Solution

To factor $x^2 - 8x + 12$, we must find two numbers whose product is +12 and whose sum is –8. Since the product is positive, the numbers can be both positive or both negative. Since the sum is negative, the numbers are both negative.

Thus, $x^2 - 8x + 12 = (x - ?)(x - ?)$

To find the numbers, find out how many ways you can write the product +12 using negative factors.

$$(-3)(-4) = +12, \ (-2)(-6) = +12, \ (-1)(-12) = +12$$

The only possible combination that gives the product +12 and the sum –8 is: –2 and –6.

Thus, $x^2 - 8x + 12 = (x - 2)(x - 6)$

Example 3

Factor.

$$x^2 + 2x - 35$$

Solution

To factor $x^2 + 2x - 35$, we need to find two numbers whose product is –35 and whose sum is +2. Since the product is negative, one number must be negative and the other one positive.

Thus, $x^2 + 2x - 35 = (x - ?)(x + ?)$

Since the sum is positive, the larger number in absolute value is positive. To guess the numbers, find out how many ways you can you write the product –35 so that the larger factor is positive.

$$-5 \cdot 7 = -35, \ -1 \cdot 35 = -35$$

The only possible combination that gives the product –35 and the sum +2 is: 7 and –5.

Thus, $x^2 + 2x - 35 = (x + 7)(x - 5)$

Example 4

Factor.

$$x^2 - 5x - 24$$

Solution

To factor $x^2 - 5x - 24$, we need to find two numbers whose product is –24 and whose sum is –5.

Since the product is negative, one number must be negative and the other number positive.

Thus, $x^2 - 5x - 24 = (x - ?)(x + ?)$

Since the sum is negative, the larger number in absolute value is negative. To guess the numbers, find out how many ways you can write the product –24, so that the larger factor is negative.

$$1(-24) = -24, \ 2(-12) = -24, \ 3(-8) = -24, \ 4(-6) = -24$$

The only possible combination that gives the product –24 and the sum –5 is: –8 and 3.

Thus, $x^2 - 5x - 24 = (x-8)(x+3)$

Example 5

Factor.

$$-x^2 + 3x + 28$$

Solution

First, we factor out –1, to obtain a trinomial of the form $x^2 + bx + c$.

$$-x^2 + 3x + 28 = -1(x^2 - 3x - 28)$$

Next, we use the strategy introduced in this section to factor the trinomial $x^2 - 3x - 28$.

To factor this trinomial, we need two numbers whose product is –28 and whose sum is –3. Since the product is negative, the numbers have opposite signs.

$$x^2 - 3x - 28 = (x - ?)(x + ?)$$

Since the sum is negative, the larger number in absolute value is negative. To guess the numbers, find out how many ways you can write the product –28 so that the larger factor is negative.

$$1(-28) = -28, \ 2(-14) = -28, \ 4(-7) = -28$$

The only possible combination that gives the product –28 and the sum –3 is: –7 and 4.

Thus, $-x^2 + 3x + 28 = -(x - 7)(x + 4)$

Example 6

Factor.

$$x^2 + 4xy - 45y^2$$

Solution

This trinomial is different because it contains two variables. We can ignore the second variable y if we write the variables of the trinomial as follows:

$$x^2 + 4xy - 45y^2 = (x \quad y)(x \quad y)$$

Now, we can apply the same technique to find two numbers whose product is –45 and whose sum is 4. Following the same procedures, we can find the numbers 9 and –5 with the product $9(-5) = -45$ and the sum $9 - 5 = 4$.

Thus, $x^2 + 4xy - 45y^2 = (x + 9y)(x - 5y)$

Example 7

Factor completely.

$$3x^2 + 3x - 18$$

Solution

Again, this trinomial is different because the leading coefficient $a = 3 \neq 1$.

We can change the trinomial $3x^2 + 3x - 18$ if we factor out 3.

$$3x^2 + 3x - 18 = 3(x^2 + x - 6)$$

Next, apply the same technique to factor the trinomial $x^2 + x - 6$. We need two numbers whose product is –6 and whose sum is 1. By inspection, the numbers are –2 and 3.

$$3(-2) = -6 \text{ and } 3 - 2 = 1$$

Thus, $3x^2 + 3x - 18 = 3(x + 3)(x - 2)$

6.2 EXERCISES

Factor each trinomial completely. If a trinomial cannot be factored (prime) state so.

1. $x^2 + 6x + 8$

2. $x^2 + 8x + 7$

3. $x^2 + 9x + 18$

4. $30 + 11x + x^2$

5. $x^2 + 4x - 21$

6. $x^2 + 3x - 10$

7. $x^2 + 2x - 24$

8. $x^2 + 6x - 27$

9. $x^2 - 3x - 4$

10. $x^2 - 2x - 8$

11. $x^2 - 3x - 28$

12. $x^2 - 11x + 18$

13. $14 + 9x + x^2$

14. $x^2 - 14x + 33$

15. $2 - 3x + x^2$

16. $x^2 - 5x - 14$

17. $x^2 - 8x - 20$

18. $x^2 - x + 1$

19. $x^2 + 2x - 8$

20. $x^2 - x - 12$

21. $x^2 + x - 6$

22. $x^2 - x - 6$

23. $x^2 - 12x + 36$

24. $x^2 - 6x + 9$

25. $x^2 + 8x + 16$

26. $x^2 + 16x + 64$

27. $y^2 + 12y - 2$

28. $x^2 - 3xy - 18y^2$

29. $a^2 - ay - 20y^2$

30. $m^2 + 11mn + 30n^2$

31. $x^2 - 3xy - 40y^2$

32. $x^2 + 5xy + 6y^2$

33. $a^2 + 4ab - 21b^2$

34. $m^2 + 6mn - 16n^2$

35. $x^2 - 3xy - 70y^2$

36. $x^2 + 9xy + 14y^2$

37. $-x^2 + x + 30$

38. $-a^2 + 5a + 24$

39. $-x^2 - 8x + 20$

40. $-x^2 + 18x - 81$

41. $-x^2 + 10xy - 25y^2$

42. $-x^2 + 14xy - 48y^2$

43. $3x^2 + 18x + 24$

44. $2x^2 + 14x - 36$

45. $2x^2 - 12x - 80$

46. $10x^2 - 30x + 20$

47. $5x^2 + 5xy - 100y^2$

48. $2x^3 - 4x^2 - 48x$

49. $45y + 14xy + x^2 y$

50. $a^2 b^2 - ab - 6$

51. $2m^2 n^2 + 2mn - 24$

52. $(a+b)x^2 + 5(a+b)x - 6(a+b)$

53. $(m-n)y^2 - 4(m-n)y - 12(m-n)$

54. $(x+2y)a^2 - 13(x+2y)a + 30(x+2y)$

55. $(3a-1)x^2 - 9(3a-1)x + 20(3a-1)$

6.3 FACTORING TRINOMIALS OF THE FORM: $ax^2 + bx + c$ ($a \neq 1$)

□ Trial and Error Method □ Factoring by Grouping Method

□ TRIAL AND ERROR METHOD

When factoring trinomials of the form $x^2 + bx + c$ ($a = 1$), it's obvious what terms of the binomial factors we have to multiply to obtain x^2.

$$x^2 + bx + c = (x \quad)(x \quad)$$

If $a \neq 1$, the factoring becomes more complicated because there are more possibilities to obtain ax^2.

Example 1

Factor.

$$6x^2 + 17x + 12$$

Solution

Since the first term of the trinomial is $6x^2$, there are two possibilities $(3x)(2x)$ or $(6x)(1x)$ for the first terms of the binomial factors (trial factors) to obtain the product $6x^2$.

Thus, $6x^2 + 17x + 12 = (3x + ?)(2x + ?)$

or

$6x^2 + 17x + 12 = (6x + ?)(x + ?)$

To determine the missing terms for each binomial factor, we need two numbers whose product is 12. Since $a > 0$, $b > 0$, and $c > 0$ we choose only positive factors of 12.

12: $1 \cdot 12, 2 \cdot 6, 3 \cdot 4$

Now, substitute these numbers into each binomial factor and list all possible trial factors.

$6x^2 + 17x + 12 = (3x + ?)(2x + ?)$	$6x^2 + 17x + 12 = (6x + ?)(x + ?)$
$12 = 1 \cdot 12$ $6x^2 + 17x + 12 = (3x + 1)(2x + 12)$	$6x^2 + 17x + 12 = (6x + 1)(x + 12)$
$6x^2 + 17x + 12 = (3x + 12)(2x + 1)$	$6x^2 + 17x + 12 = (6x + 12)(x + 1)$
$12 = 2 \cdot 6$ $6x^2 + 17x + 12 = (3x + 2)(2x + 6)$	$6x^2 + 17x + 12 = (6x + 2)(x + 6)$
$6x^2 + 17x + 12 = (3x + 6)(2x + 2)$	$6x^2 + 17x + 12 = (6x + 6)(x + 2)$
$12 = 3 \cdot 4$ $6x^2 + 17x + 12 = (3x + 3)(2x + 4)$	$6x^2 + 17x + 12 = (6x + 3)(x + 4)$
$6x^2 + 17x + 12 = (3x + 4)(2x + 3)$	$6x^2 + 17x + 12 = (6x + 4)(x + 3)$

To determine which factoring is correct, either FOIL each factoring or check the middle term $17x$ of the trinomial for each factoring.

The middle term can be obtained if we add the products of the inner and outer terms for each factoring.

Consider the factoring $(x+1)(2x+12)$ for example. The middle term is:

$$\underset{outers}{(x)(12)} + \underset{inners}{(1)(2x)} = 12x + 2x = 14x \neq 17x$$

So, this is not the correct factoring.

By checking the middle terms for all factorings (products), we found that the product $(3x+4)(2x+3)$ is the only one factoring that was correct: $(3x)(3)+(4)(2x)=17x$.

Thus, $6x^2 +17x+12 = (3x+4)(2x+3)$

Note: If a trial factor has a common factor itself, it need not be tried. For example $3x+12$, or $2x+4$, or $6x+6$ etc., have common factors and therefore need not be tried.

Trial and error method is not a very practical method to factor trinomials of the form $ax^2 + bx + c$ especially if the trinomial has large coefficients or after all these trials you will find out that the trinomial is not factorable (prime). Therefore, we introduce an alternative method that is shorter than the trial and error method and it's used very often when factoring trinomials of the form $ax^2 + bx + c$.

☐ FACTORING BY GROUPING METHOD

Example 2

Factor by grouping.

$$6x^2 - 8x + 15x - 20$$

Solution

Group the first two and the last two terms.

$$(6x^2 - 8x) + (15x - 20)$$

Factor out $2x$ from the first group and 5 from the second group.

$$2x(3x-4) + 5(3x-4)$$

Factor $3x-4$ from both terms. $(3x-4)(2x+5)$

Thus, $6x^2 - 8x + 15x - 20 = (3x-4)(2x+5)$

Example 3

Factor by grouping.

$$6x^2 + 17x + 12$$

Solution

To factor this trinomial, we will use factoring by grouping, a technique introduced in section 1. But, factoring by grouping requires an even number of terms and this trinomial has only three terms.

So, our goal is to change this trinomial into a polynomial with four terms. This can be accomplished if we rewrite the middle term $17x$ as the sum or a difference of two terms. However, there are many pairs of terms with the sum or difference $17x$.

For example $10x + 7x = 17x$, $16x + x = 17x$, $20x - 3x = 17x$, etc.

Thus, we need to find a technique that helps us guess the two numbers needed to rewrite the middle term as a sum or difference of two terms. Suppose,

$$ax^2 + bx + c = (mx + p)(nx + q) = mnx^2 + mqx + npx + pq = mnx^2 + (mq + np)x + pq$$

To find the numbers **mq** and **np** needed to rewrite the middle term as a sum or a difference of two terms **mqx + npx**, we compare the coefficients of two identical polynomials:

$$ax^2 + bx + c = mnx^2 + (mq + np)x + pq$$

$mn = a$

$mq + np = b$

$pq = c$

The product of the two numbers is $P = (mq)(np) = (mn)(pq) = ac$ and sum

$$S = mq + np = b$$

Hence, the only pair of numbers that help us factor a trinomial of the form $ax^2 + bx + c$ by grouping are two integers whose product is $P = a \cdot c$ and the sum $S = b$.

In our case, we need two integers with the product $P = a \cdot c = 6 \cdot 12 = 72$ and the sum $S = b = 17$.

By inspection, the integers are 9 and 8: ($9 + 8 = 17$, and $9 \cdot 8 = 72$). Use this pair of integers to rewrite the middle term: $17x = 9x + 8x$. Then the trinomial becomes:

$$6x^2 + 17x + 12 = 6x^2 + 9x + 8x + 12 = (6x^2 + 9x) + (8x + 12) = 3x(2x + 3) + 4(2x + 3) =$$

$$(2x + 3)(3x + 4)$$

Thus, $6x^2 + 17x + 12 = (2x + 3)(3 + 4)$

Example 4

Factor.

a. $15x^2 - x - 2$ b. $12x^2 + 29x - 8$ c. $20x^2 - 7xy - 3y^2$

Solution

a. We need to find two integers whose sum is $S = b = -1$ and whose product is $P = a \cdot c = (15)(-2) = -30$. By inspection, the integers are 5 and –6.

Use these two integers to rewrite the middle term $-x$ of the trinomial as $-x = 5x - 6x$.

Then, the trinomial becomes:

$15x^2 - x - 2 = 15x^2 + 5x - 6x - 2 = (15x^2 + 5x) + (-6x - 2) =$

$5x(3x + 1) - 2(3x + 1) = (3x + 1)(5x - 2)$

Thus, $15x^2 - x - 2 = (3x + 1)(5x - 2)$

b. We need to find two integers whose product is $P = a \cdot c = (12)(-8) = -96$ and whose sum is $S = b = 29$. By inspection the integers are 32 and –3.

Then, we can use these integers to rewrite the middle term of the trinomial: $29x = -3x + 32x$. The trinomial becomes:

$12x^2 + 29x - 8 = 12x^2 - 3x + 32x - 8 = (12x^2 - 3x) + (32x - 8) =$

$3x(4x - 1) + 8(4x - 1) = (4x - 1)(3x + 8)$

Thus, $12x^2 + 29x - 8 = (4x - 1)(3x + 8)$

c. The trinomial $20x^2 - 7xy - 3y^2$ has two variables. Ignore the second variable y, and apply the same technique used to factor trinomials of the form $ax^2 + bx + c$ in one variable.

We need to find two integers whose product is $P = a \cdot c = 20 \cdot (-3) = -60$ and whose sum is $S = b = -7$. By inspection, the integers are 5 and –12:

$(5)(-12) = -60$, and $5 - 12 = -7$.

Use the integers to rewrite the middle term of the trinomial $-7xy$ as: $-7xy = 5xy - 12xy$.

Then, the trinomial becomes:

$20x^2 - 7xy - 3y^2 = 20x^2 + 5xy - 12xy - 3y^2 = (20x^2 + 5xy) + (-12xy - 3y^2) =$

$5x(4x + y) - 3y(4x + y) = (4x + y)(5x - 3y)$

Example 5

Factor by grouping.

a. $-24x^2 - 44xy + 28y^2$ b. $2x^4 + 11x^3 - 40x^2$

Solution

a. First, factor out –4: $-24x^2 - 44xy + 28y^2 = -4(6x^2 + 11xy - 7y^2)$

Then, factor the trinomial: $6x^2 + 11xy - 7y^2$. We need to find two integers whose product is $P = a \cdot c = 6(-7) = -42$ and the sum $S = b = 11$. By inspection the integers are 14 and –3. Use these integers to rewrite the middle term of the trinomial $11xy$ as:

$11xy = -3xy + 14xy$

Then the trinomial becomes:

$-24x^2 - 44xy + 28y^2 = -4(6x^2 + 11xy - 7y^2) = -4(6x^2 - 3xy + 14xy - 7y^2) =$

$-4[(6x^2 - 3xy) + (14xy - 7y^2)] = -4[3x(2x - y) + 7y(2x - y)] = -4(2x - y)(3x + 7y)$

Thus, $-24x^2 - 44xy + 28y^2 = -4(2x - y)(3x + 7y)$

b. First, factor out x^2: $2x^4 + 11x^3 - 40x^2 = x^2(2x^2 + 11x - 40)$

Then factor the trinomial: $2x^2 + 11x - 40$. We need to find two integers whose product is $P = a \cdot c = 2(-40) = -80$ and whose sum is $S = b = 11$. By inspection, the integers are 16 and –5. Use these integers to rewrite the middle term of the trinomial $11x$ as: $11x = 16x - 5x$.

Then, the trinomial becomes: $2x^2 + 11x - 40 = 2x^2 + 16x - 5x - 40$.

Now, we can factor by grouping.

$2x^2 + 11x - 40 = 2x^2 + 16x - 5x - 40 = (2x^2 + 16x) + (-5x - 40) = 2x(x + 8) - 5(x + 8) = (x + 8)(2x - 5)$

Thus, $2x^4 + 11x^3 - 40x^2 = x^2(x + 8)(2x - 5)$

6.3 EXERCISES

Use the trial and error method to complete each factorization.

1. $6x^2 + 5x + 1 = (3x + 1)(........)$

2. $8x^2 + 2x - 3 = (2x - 1)(........)$

3. $4x^2 - 3x - 10 = (4x + 5)(........)$

4. $9x^2 + 38x + 8 = (x + 4)(........)$

5. $10x^2 + 19xy - 15y^2 = (5x - 3y)(........)$

6. $14x^2 + 60x + 16 = (2x + 8)(........)$

7. $12x^2 + 5x - 3 = (3x - 1)(........)$

8. $15x^2 - xy - 6y^2 = (5x + 3y)(........)$

Factor each trinomial completely. If the trinomial is prime, so state.

9. $2y^2 + 7y + 3$

10. $3x^2 - 11x - 4$

11. $5m^2 - 3m - 2$

12. $8x^2 + 2x - 1$

13. $6m^2 + 7m + 2$

14. $10x^2 - 3x - 1$

15. $12a^2 + 5a - 2$

16. $6x^2 + 13x + 6$

17. $12x^2 - 5x - 3$

18. $18x^2 - 5x - 2$

19. $14x^2 + x - 3$

20. $6b^2 + 19b + 10$

21. $16x^2 + 2x - 3$

22. $20y^2 - 28y - 3$

23. $15x^2 + x - 2$

24. $36c^2 - 12c + 1$

25. $16x^2 + 16x + 4$

26. $81x^2 + 18x + 1$

27. $9x^2 - 12x + 4$

28. $12y^2 - y - 6$

29. $8a^2 + 2a - 15$

30. $15x^2 + 23xy + 4y^2$

31. $10x^2 + 11xy + 3y^2$

32. $10a^2 + 3ab - 4b^2$

33. $18m^2 - 5mn - 2n^2$

34. $20x^2 + 16xy + 3y^2$

35. $24a^2 + 19ab + 2b^2$

36. $6x^2 - x - 1$

37. $8m^2 - 10m - 1$

38. $12y^2 + 4y - 1$

39. $30x^2 - 7x - 2$

40. $40a^2 - 11a - 2$

41. $45x^2 - 9x - 2$

42. $4x^2 + 3xy + y^2$

43. $24x^3 + x^2 - 3x$

44. $15m^2 + 14m - 8$

45. $12x^2 + 20xy + 3y^2$

46. $14x^2 + 33xy - 5y^2$

47. $60x^2 - 50xy + 10y^2$

48. $40a^2 - 18ab + 2b^2$

49. $80m^2 - 60mn - 20n^2$

50. $10y^3 - 99y^2z - 10yz^2$

51. $25m^4 + 30m^3 + 9m^2$

52. $36a^4 + 60a^3 + 25a^2$

53. $32m^3 - 48m^2 + 18m$

54. $20x^3y - 20x^2y + 5xy$

55. $-12x^4y + 2x^3y + 2x^2y$

56. $-12x^4y^2 + 21x^3y^2 - 9x^2y^2$

6.4 SPECIAL FACTORING FORMULAS

□ **Factoring the Difference of Two Squares** □ **Factoring Perfect Square Trinomials** □ **Factoring the Sum and Difference of Two Cubes**

In the previous chapter we introduced the following special products formulas:

$$(a+b)(a-b) = a^2 - b^2$$

$$(a+b)^2 = a^2 + 2ab + b^2$$

$$(a-b)^2 = a^2 - 2ab + b^2$$

Since factoring is the reverse process of multiplication, by reversing these formulas we obtain the following special factoring formulas:

$$a^2 - b^2 = (a+b)(a-b)$$

$$a^2 + 2ab + b^2 = (a+b)^2$$

$$a^2 - 2ab + b^2 = (a-b)^2$$

□ FACTORING THE DIFFERENCE OF TWO SQUARES

Examples of difference of squares: $x^2 - 36$, $y^2 - 81$, $4a^2 - 25$, $16m^2 - 49n^2$

> To factor a difference of two squares, we will use *the difference of two squares formula.*
>
> $a^2 - b^2 = (a + b)(a - b)$

Example 1

Factor.

a. $x^2 - 49$

b. $m^2 - 4n^2$

c. $9x^2 - 16y^2$

d. $n^2 - \dfrac{16}{25}$

Solution

First, rewrite each binomial explicitly as a difference of squares. Then, identify *a* and *b* and substitute their values in the difference of squares formula.

$$a^2 - b^2 = (a+b)(a-b)$$

a. $x^2 - 49 = x^2 - 7^2 = (x+7)(x-7)$ $\qquad\qquad$ ($a = x$ and $b = 7$)

b. $m^2 - 4n^2 = m^2 - (2n)^2 = (m+2n)(m-2n)$ $\qquad$ ($a = m$ and $b = 2n$)

c. $9x^2 - 16y^2 = (3x)^2 - (4y)^2 = (3x+4y)(3x-4y)$ $\quad$ ($a = 3x$ and $b = 4y$)

d. $n^2 - \dfrac{16}{25} = n^2 - \left(\dfrac{4}{5}\right)^2 = \left(n+\dfrac{4}{5}\right)\left(n-\dfrac{4}{5}\right)$ $\qquad$ ($a = n$ and $b = \dfrac{4}{5}$)

Example 2

Factor.

a. $4 - 9x^6$ $\qquad\qquad$ b. $x^4 - 16$ $\qquad\qquad$ c. $2y^2 - 50$ $\qquad\qquad$ d. $x^2 + 36$

Solution

Write each binomial explicitly as a difference of squares. Then, identify *a* and *b* and substitute their value in the difference of squares formula.

a. $4 - 9x^6 = 2^2 - (3x^3)^2 = (2-3x^3)(2+3x^3)$

b. $x^4 - 16 = (x^2)^2 - 4^2 = (x^2-4)(x^2+4) = [x^2-(2)^2](x^2+4) = (x-2)(x+2)(x^2+4)$

c. $2y^2 - 50 = 2(y^2-25) = 2[y^2-(5)^2] = 2(y-5)(y+5)$

d. $x^2 + 36$ prime (cannot be factor over the integers because it's a sum of two squares).

Note: $x^2 + 36 \neq (x+6)(x-6)$ because $(x+6)(x-6) = x^2 - 36$

$\qquad\quad x^2 + 36 \neq (x+6)(x+6)$ because $(x+6)(x+6) = x^2 + 12x + 36$

$\qquad\quad x^2 + 36 \neq (x-6)(x-6)$ because $(x-6)(x-6) = x^2 - 12x + 36$

☐ FACTORING PERFECT SQUARE TRINOMIALS

Examples of perfect square trinomials: $x^2 + 6x + 9$, $x^2 + 10x + 25$, $x^2 - 14x + 49$

To factor perfect square trinomials we will use one of the following special factoring formulas:

$$a^2 + 2ab + b^2 = (a+b)^2$$
$$a^2 - 2ab + b^2 = (a-b)^2$$

How do we recognize perfect square trinomials?

- Two terms of the trinomial (usually the first and the last term) must be perfect squares. Both terms must be either positive or negative.

- The third term must be either plus or minus twice the product of the positive square root of the two perfect square terms. Thus, the third term can be either positive or negative.

Note: A perfect square trinomial can be factored as the square of a binomial. The sign of the second term in the squared binomial is the same as the sign of the term that is not a perfect square in the trinomial.

For example, $x^2 + 10x + 25$ is a perfect square trinomial because:

- The first term x^2 is a perfect square: x^2 is the square of x $[(x)^2 = x^2]$.
- The last term 25 is a perfect square: 25 is the square of 5 $[(5)^2 = 25]$.
- Both perfect squares terms are positive.
- The middle term is twice the product of $x = \sqrt{x^2}$ and $5 = \sqrt{25}$: $10x = 2(x)(5)$.
- Thus, $x^2 + 10x + 25 = (x+5)^2$

Note: The sign of the second term in the squared binomial is positive because the sign of middle term $10x$ in the trinomial is positive.

Example 3

Factor.

$$x^2 - 14x + 49$$

Solution

Since the first term $x^2 = (x)^2$ is a perfect square, and the last term $49 = 7^2$ is a perfect square, the trinomial $x^2 - 14x + 49$ might be a perfect square trinomial. So far we identified $a = x$ and $b = 7$. Now, we have to check the middle term, $2ab = 2(x)(7) = 14x$ True.

Since the middle term is negative, the trinomial $x^2 - 14x + 49$ can be factored as:

$$x^2 - 14x + 49 = (x - 7)^2$$

Example 4

Factor.

$$4y^2 + 12y + 9$$

Solution

Since the first term $4y^2 = (2y)^2$ is a perfect square, and $9 = (3)^2$ is a perfect square, the trinomial $4y^2 + 12y + 9$ might be a perfect square trinomial.

In this case, $a = 2y$ and $b = 3$. The middle term is $2ab = 2(2y)(3) = 12y$ True.

Since the middle term is positive, the trinomial $4y^2 + 12y + 9$ can be factored as:
$4y^2 + 12y + 9 = (2y + 3)^2$

Example 5

Factor.

   a. $16x^2 + 70xy + 81y^2$ b. $-36m^3 + 84m^2 - 49m$ c. $x^2 - 4x + 3$

Solution

a. Since the first term $16x^2 = (4x)^2$ is a perfect square, and $81y^2 = (9y)^2$ is a perfect square, the trinomial $16x^2 + 72xy + 81y^2$ might be a perfect square.

To find out if it's a perfect square or not, we have to check the middle term.

$$2ab = 2(4x)(9y) = 72xy \neq 70xy \qquad\qquad \text{False.}$$

Therefore, the trinomial $16x^2 + 72xy + 81y^2$ is not a perfect square trinomial.

b. First, factor out $-m$.

$$-36m^3 + 84m^2 - 49m = -m(36m^2 - 84m + 49)$$

Since the first term $36m^2 = (6m)^2$ is a perfect square, and the last term $49 = (7)^2$ is a perfect square, the trinomial $36m^2 - 84m + 49$ might be a perfect square. Again, to find out, identify $a = 6m$, $b = 7$ and check the middle term.

$$2ab = 2(6m)(7) = 84m \qquad\qquad \text{True.}$$

Since the middle term of the trinomial $36m^2 - 84m + 49$ is negative, the trinomial can be factored as follows: $-36m^3 + 84m^2 - 49m = -m(36m^2 - 84m + 49) = -m(6m - 7)^2$

c. The trinomial $x^2 - 4x + 3$ is not a perfect square because 3 is not a perfect square.

Example 6

Factor completely.

a. $y^2 + \dfrac{8}{9}y + \dfrac{16}{81}$

   b. $x^2 + 6x - 9$

Solution

a. Since the first term $y^2 = (y)^2$ is a perfect square, and the second term $\dfrac{16}{81} = \left(\dfrac{4}{9}\right)^2$ is a perfect square, the trinomial $-36m^3 + 84m^2 - 49m$ might be a perfect square trinomial. To find out, identify $a = y$, $b = \dfrac{4}{9}$ and check the middle term.

$$2ab = 2(y)\left(\dfrac{4}{9}\right) = \dfrac{8}{9}y \qquad\qquad \text{True.}$$

Since the middle term of the trinomial $y^2 + \dfrac{8}{9}y + \dfrac{16}{81}$ is positive, the trinomial can be factored as follows:

$$y^2 + \dfrac{8}{9}y + \dfrac{16}{81} = \left(y + \dfrac{4}{9}\right)^2$$

b. The trinomial $x^2 + 6x - 9$ is not a perfect square because one perfect square term (x^2) is positive and the other perfect square term (-9) is negative.

☐ FACTORING THE SUM AND DIFFERENCE OF TWO CUBES

The sum and difference of two cubes can be factored using the following formulas:

Sum of Cubes: $a^3 + b^3 = (a + b)(a^2 - ab + b^2)$

Difference of Cubes: $a^3 - b^3 = (a-b)(a^2 + ab + b^2)$

Example 7

Factor.

$$x^3 + 27$$

Solution

First, express the binomial as a sum of two cubes: $x^3 + 3^3$

Then, identify $a = x$ and $b = 3$ and substitute their values into the appropriate formula.

$$a^3 + b^3 = (a+b)(a^2 - ab + b^2)$$
$$x^3 + 3^3 = (x+3)(x^2 - 3x + 9)$$

Example 8

Factor.

$$y^3 - 125$$

Solution

First, express the binomial as a difference of two cubes: $y^3 - 5^3$

Next, identify $a = y$ and $b = 5$ and substitute their values into the difference of cubes formula.

$$a^3 - b^3 = (a-b)(a^2 + ab + b^2)$$
$$y^3 - 5^3 = (y-5)(y^2 + 5y + 25)$$

Example 9

Factor.

$$27m^3 + 64n^3$$

Solution

Express the binomial as a sum of two cubes: $(3m)^3 + (4n)^3$

Identify $a = 3m$ and $n = 4n$ and substitute their values into the sum of cubes formula.

$$a^3 + b^3 = (a+b)(a^2 - ab + b^2)$$
$$(3m)^3 + (4n)^3 = (3m+4n)[(3m)^2 - (3m)(4n) + (4n)^2]$$
$$= (3m+4n)(9m^2 - 12mn + 16n^2)$$

Example 10

Factor.

$$4c^3 - 32$$

Solution

$$4c^3 - 32 = 4(c^3 - 8) = 4(c^3 - 2^3) = 4(c-2)(c^2 + 2c + 4)$$

Example 11

Factor.

$$(z+2)^3 - 1$$

Solution

$$(z+2)^3 - 1 = (z+2)^3 - 1^3$$

Identify $a = z + 2$ and $b = 1$ and substitute these values into the difference of squares formula.

$$a^3 - b^3 = (a-b)(a^2 + ab + b^2)$$

$$(z+2)^3 - 1 = [(z+2)-1][(z+2)^2 + 1 \cdot (z+2) + 1^2]$$

$$= (z+2-1)(z^2 + 4z + 4 + z + 2 + 1)$$

$$= (z+1)(z^2 + 5z + 7)$$

6.4 EXERCISES

Factor each difference of two squares completely.

1. $x^2 - 36$

2. $x^2 - 81$

3. $y^2 - 100$

4. $m^2 - 121$

5. $n^2 - 9$

6. $c^2 - 144$

7. $x^2 + 4$

8. $y^2 - 64$

9. $9a^2 - 4$

10. $25 - 16y^2$

11. $64 - 9x^2$

12. $100 - 36x^2$

13. $1 - 49m^2$

14. $1 - 169n^2$

15. $81x^2 - 4y^2$

16. $16m^2 - 25n^2$

17. $0.09x^2 - 0.49y^2$

18. $36a^2 - 121b^2$

19. $4n^2 - 9m^4$

20. $0.25x^2 - 0.64y^2$

21. $x^4 - 25$

22. $y^6 - 100$

23. $m^8 - 4$

24. $n^{10} - 81$

25. $x^2 - \dfrac{4}{25}$

26. $y^2 - \dfrac{9}{16}$

27. $m^2 - \dfrac{1}{49}$

28. $n^2 - \dfrac{1}{64}$

29. $\dfrac{16}{25} - x^2$

30. $\dfrac{81}{100} - y^2$

31. $\dfrac{36}{49} - m^2$

32. $\dfrac{169}{121} - n^2$

33. $18 - 50x^2$

34. $2y^3 - 32y$

35. $5m^3 - 45m$

36. $8x^2 - 32$

37. $81x^4 - 16$

38. $25y^4 - 100$

39. $64 - 4m^4$

40. $1 - 81x^4$

41. $(x-1)^2 - y^2$

42. $(y+2)^2 - 9$

43. $36 - (m+5)^2$

44. $169 - (n+3)^2$

Factor each perfect square trinomial completely.

45. $x^2 + 6x + 9$

46. $y^2 + 16y + 64$

47. $m^2 - 2m + 1$

48. $49 - 14x + x^2$

49. $121 + 22m + m^2$

50. $9 - 6n + n^2$

51. $9x^2 + 48x + 64$

52. $49y^2 - 72y + 25$

53. $x^2 + \dfrac{2}{3}x + \dfrac{1}{9}$

54. $x^2 - 3x + 2.25$

55. $16x^2 + 8xy + y^2$

56. $-32x^3 + 48x^2 - 18x$

Factor each sum or difference of cubes.

57. $x^3 + 8$

58. $x^3 + 64$

59. $z^3 - 27$

60. $c^3 - 1$

61. $64x^3 + 1$

62. $1 - 216z^3$

63. $64y^3 - 125z^3$

64. $8x^3 - 27y^3$

65. $2z^3 + 250$

66. $81x^3 + 24y^3$

67. $x^6 - y^6$

68. $(m-5)^3 - 8$

69. $x^3(y^2 - 4) + 27(y^2 - 4)$

70. $x^3y^3 + 125$

71. $(x+y)^3 + 1000$

6.5 GENERAL REVIEW OF FACTORING

Factor each polynomial completely. If the polynomial is prime, so state.

1. $12x^2 + 24x$

2. $7y^2 + 28y^3$

3. $5x^2y - 35xy^2$

4. $8x^2y^3 + 12xy^2$

5. $4x^3y + 8x^2y - 12xy$

6. $5m^3n^2 - 10m^2n^3 - 40m^2n^2$

7. $8x^2 - 10x + 12x - 15$

8. $x^2 + 6x + 9 - y^2$

9. $27x^2 - 36x - 6x + 8$

10. $30x^2 - 35x - 18x + 21$

11. $12x^2 + 20xy - 3xy - 5y^2$

12. $56x^2 + 16xy - 21xy - 6y^2$

13. $x^2 - 2x - 15$

14. $x^2 + 3x - 18$

15. $x^2 + x - 72$

16. $x^2 - 16x + 64 - z^2$

17. $x^2 - xy - 20y^2$

18. $x^2 - 6xy - 27y^2$

19. $x^2 + 13xy + 40y^2$

20. $x^2 - 20xy + 99y^2$

21. $6x^2 - x - 2$

22. $15x^2 + 7x - 2$

23. $20x^2 - 11x - 3$

24. $6x^2 + 13x - 8$

25. $3x^2 + xy - 10y^2$

26. $8x^2 + 18xy - 5y^2$

27. $18x^2 + 9xy - 2y^2$

28. $21x^2 - 2xy - 3y^2$

29. $64m^2 - 49$

30. $9x^2 - 64y^2$

31. $y^4 - 125y$

32. $m^4 - 64m$

33. $5n^4 - 5$

34. $81x^5 - x$

35. $a^4b - 16b^5$

36. $x^2(y^2 - 4) - 36(y^2 - 4)$

37. $25x^2 + 30x + 9$

38. $49x^2 - 112x + 64$

39. $100x^2 + 20x + 1$

40. $81y^2 + 198y + 121$

41. $x^4 - 81$

42. $x^4 - 16$

43. $3y^4 - 48$

44. $2y^4 - 162$

45. $a^2(b^3 + 1) - 81(b^3 + 1)$

46. $a^7 - a$

47. $m^5n^3 - m^2n^6$

48. $2x^3 - 32x^5$

49. $27x^3 - 1000y^3$

50. $x^4 - 121x^2$

51. $6x^2 - 8xb + 3ax - 4ab$

52. $12mx + 8my - 3nx - 2ny$

53. $6x^2 + x - 12$

54. $8a^2 - 14a - 15$

55. $x^2 - 4x - 77$

56. $y^2 - 2y - 80$

57. $6a^3b - 20a^2b - 16ab$

58. $10ab^3 + 28ab^2 - 6ab$

59. $50 + 15x - 5x^2$

60. $36 - 3y - 3y^2$

61. $a^2 + 10ab + 21b^2$

62. $x^2 + 12xy + 27y^2$

63. $(x^2 + 6x + 9) - y^2$

64. $(m^2 + 4mn + 4n^2) - 36$

65. $8ax - 10ay + 12bx - 15by$

66. $4a^4b - 28a^3b + 49a^2b$

6.6 SOLVING QUADRATIC EQUATIONS BY FACTORING

□ Quadratic Equations □ Zero Factor Property

□ QUADRATIC EQUATIONS

Examples of quadratic equations: $2x^2 + 4x + 3 = 0$, $6x^2 + 10x + 1 = 0$, $x^2 + 6x + 2 = 0$

Definition

A **quadratic equation** or second degree equation is an equation that can be written in the form $ax^2 + bx + c = 0$ where a, b, and c are real numbers and $a \neq 0$.

Note: The form $ax^2 + bx + c = 0$, $a \neq 0$ is called the **standard form** of a quadratic equation.

Some quadratic equations can be solved by factoring. To solve a quadratic equation by factoring, we introduce a property that allows us to separate a quadratic equation into two linear equations equivalent to the quadratic equation, and then solve each linear equation. To understand such property, consider the following products:

$a \cdot 0 = 0$

$0 \cdot b = 0$

$0 \cdot 0 = 0$

In each case, the product equals zero because at least one factor is zero. This can be summarized in the following property:

□ ZERO FACTOR PROPERTY

If $a \cdot b = 0$, then $a = 0$ or $b = 0$ for any real numbers a and b.

Example 1

Solve.

$$(x + 1)(x - 3) = 0$$

Solution

$$(x + 1)(x - 3) = 0$$

Use the Zero Factor Property to set each factor equal to zero.

$$x + 1 = 0 \text{ or } x - 3 = 0$$

Solve each linear equation. $x = -1$ or $x = 3$

Check each solution. $(-1 + 1)(-1 - 3) = 0$, $(0)(-4) = 0$, $0 = 0$ True.

$(3 + 1)(3 - 3) = 0$ $(4)(0) = 0$, $0 = 0$ True.

Thus, the solutions are $x = -1$ and $x = 3$.

Strategy for Solving Quadratic Equations by Factoring

Step 1 Write the equation in standard form.

Step 2 Factor completely.

Step 3 Use the Zero Factor Property to set each variable factor equal to zero.

Step 4 Solve the resulting linear equations.

Step 5 Check each solution.

Example 2

Solve by factoring.

$$x^2 + x = 20$$

Solution

Step 1 Write the equation in standard form. $x^2 + x - 20 = 0$

Step 2 Factor completely. $(x + 5)(x - 4) = 0$

Step 3 Use the Zero Factor Property to set each factor equal to zero. $x + 5 = 0$ or $x - 4 = 0$

Step 4 Solve the resulting equations. $x = -5$ or $x = 4$

Step 5 Check the solutions by substituting each solution in the original equation.

$$x^2 + x - 20 = 0 \qquad\qquad x^2 + x - 20 = 0$$
$$(-5)^2 + (-5) - 20 = 0 \qquad\qquad (4)^2 + 4 - 20 = 0$$
$$25 - 5 - 20 = 0 \qquad\qquad 16 + 4 - 20 = 0$$
$$0 = 0 \quad \text{True.} \qquad\qquad 0 = 0 \quad \text{True.}$$

Thus, the solutions are $x = -5$ and $= 4$

Example 3

Solve.

$$x^2 = 12x - 36$$

Solution

Step 1 Write the equation in standard form.

$$x^2 - 12x + 36 = 0$$

Step 2 Factor completely.

$$(x - 6)(x - 6) = 0$$

Step 3 Use the Zero Factor Property to set each factor equal to zero and solve the resulting equations. Since the factors are the same, set only one of them equal to zero.

$$x - 6 = 0$$

$$x = 6$$

Step 4 Check the solution by substituting $x = 6$ in the original equation.

$$x^2 = 12x - 36$$

$$(6)^2 = 12(6) - 36$$

$$36 = 72 - 36$$

$$36 = 36 \text{ True.}$$

Thus, the solution is $x = 6$. The equation has two solutions, but they are equal.

Example 4

Solve by factoring.

$$x(6x + 1) = 12$$

Solution

Step 1 Write the equation in standard form.

$$x(6x + 1) = 12$$

$$6x^2 + x = 12$$

$$6x^2 + x - 12 = 0$$

Step 2 Factor completely (by grouping).

$$6x^2 - 8x + 9x - 12 = 0$$

$$2x(3x - 4) + 3(3x - 4) = 0$$

$$(2x + 3)(3x - 4) = 0$$

Step 3 Use the Zero Factor Property to set each factor equal to zero.

$$2x + 3 = 0 \text{ or } \qquad\qquad 3x - 4 = 0$$

Step 4 Solve the resulting linear equations.

$$2x = -3 \qquad\qquad 3x = 4$$

$$x = -\frac{3}{2} \text{ or} \qquad\qquad x = \frac{4}{3}$$

Step 5 Check the solutions by substituting each solution into the original equation.

$$6x^2 + x - 12 = 0 \qquad\qquad 6x^2 + x - 12 = 0$$

$$6\left(-\frac{3}{2}\right)^2 - \frac{3}{2} - 12 = 0 \qquad\qquad 6\left(\frac{4}{3}\right)^2 + \frac{4}{3} - 12 = 0$$

$$6\left(\frac{9}{4}\right) - \frac{3}{2} - 12 = 0 \qquad\qquad 6\left(\frac{16}{9}\right) + \frac{4}{3} - 12 = 0$$

$$\frac{27}{2} - \frac{3}{2} - 12 = 0 \qquad\qquad \frac{32}{3} + \frac{4}{3} - 12 = 0$$

$$\frac{24}{2} - 12 = 0 \qquad\qquad \frac{36}{3} - 12 = 0$$

$$12 - 12 = 0 \qquad\qquad 12 - 12 = 0$$

$$0 = 0 \text{ True.} \qquad\qquad 0 = 0 \text{ True.}$$

Thus, the solutions are $x = -\frac{3}{2}$ and $x = \frac{4}{3}$.

Example 5

Solve by factoring.

$$4x^2 = 9$$

Solution

Step 1 Write the equation in standard form.

$$4x^2 - 9 = 0$$

Step 2 Factor completely (a difference of squares).

$$(2x + 3)(2x - 3) = 0$$

Step 3 Use the Zero Factor Property to set each factor equal to zero.

$$2x + 3 = 0 \text{ or} \qquad\qquad 2x = -3$$

Step 4 Solve the resulting linear equations.

$$2x = -3 \text{ or} \qquad\qquad 2x = 3$$

$$x = -\frac{3}{2} \text{ or} \qquad\qquad x = \frac{3}{2}$$

Step 5 Check the solutions by substituting each solution into the original equation.

$$4x^2 - 9 = 0 \qquad\qquad 4x^2 - 9 = 0$$

$$4\left(-\frac{3}{2}\right)^2 - 9 = 0 \qquad\qquad 4\left(\frac{3}{2}\right)^2 - 9 = 0$$

$$4\left(\frac{9}{4}\right) - 9 = 0 \qquad\qquad 4\left(\frac{9}{4}\right) - 9 = 0$$

$$9 - 9 = 0 \qquad\qquad 9 - 9 = 0$$

$$0 = 0 \text{ True.} \qquad\qquad 0 = 0 \text{ True.}$$

Thus, the solutions are $x = -\frac{3}{2}$ and $x = \frac{3}{2}$.

Example 6

Solve by factoring.

$$2x^2 = 6x$$

Solution

Step 1 Write the equation in standard form.

$$2x^2 - 6x = 0$$

Step 2 Factor completely.

$$2x(x - 3) = 0$$

Step 3 Use the Zero Factor Property to set each factor equal to zero.

Since $2 \neq 0$ (not a variable term), $x = 0$ or $x - 3 = 0$

Step 4 Solve the resulting linear equations. $x = 0$ or $x = 3$

Step 5 Check the solutions by substituting each solution into the original equation.

$$2x^2 = 6x \qquad\qquad 2x^2 = 6x$$

$$2(0)^2 = 6(0) \qquad\qquad 2(3)^2 = 6(3)$$

$$0 = 0 \text{ True.} \qquad\qquad 2(9) = 18$$

$$\qquad\qquad\qquad\qquad 18 = 18 \text{ True.}$$

Thus, the solutions are $x = 0$ and $x = 3$.

Note: The Zero Factor Property can be used only when the product of the factors is equal to zero.

Example 7

Solve by factoring.

$$(x+8)(x+1) = -10$$

Solution

Step 1 Write the equation in standard form.

$$(x+8)(x+1) = -10$$

$$x^2 + x + 8x + 8 = -10$$

$$x^2 + 9x + 8 + 10 = 0$$

$$x^2 + 9x + 18 = 0$$

Step 2 Factor completely.

$$(x+6)(x+3) = 0$$

Step 3 Use the Zero Factor Property to set each factor equal to zero.

$$x + 6 = 0 \text{ or } \qquad x + 3 = 0$$

Step 4 Solve the resulting equations. $x = -6$ or $x = -3$

Step 5 Check the solutions by substituting each solution into the original equation.

$(-6+8)(-6+1) = -10$	$(-3+8)(-3+1) = -10$
$(2)(-5) = -10$	$(5)(-2) = -10$
$-10 = -10$ True.	$-10 = -10$ True.

Thus, the solutions are $x = -6$ and $x = -3$.

6.6 EXERCISES

Solve each quadratic equation by factoring.

1. $(x+3)(x-8) = 0$

2. $(x-5)(x+2) = 0$

3. $(4x+1)(3x-2) = 0$

4. $(6x-5)(7x+4) = 0$

5. $x^2 + 4x = 0$

6. $x^2 - 11x = 0$

7. $2x^2 = 6x$

8. $7x^2 = 21x$

9. $3x^2 - 5x = 0$

10. $5x^2 + 8x = 0$

11. $x^2 - 36 = 0$

12. $x^2 - 121 = 0$

13. $x^2 = 49$

14. $x^2 = 169$

15. $x^2 = 25$

16. $3x^2 = 48$

17. $2x^2 = 32$

18. $5x^2 = 500$

19. $4x^2 - 9 = 0$

20. $9y^2 - 25 = 0$

21. $x^2 - x - 6 = 0$

22. $x^2 - 3x - 40 = 0$

23. $x^2 + 7x + 12 = 0$

24. $x^2 - 2x - 35 = 0$

25. $x^2 - 7x - 18 = 0$

26. $x^2 + 6x - 40 = 0$

27. $x^2 - 11x + 30 = 0$

28. $x^2 = 24 - 5x$

29. $x^2 = 9x - 20$

30. $x^2 + 4x = 12$

31. $x^2 - 5x = 24$

32. $x(x + 2) = 15$

33. $x(x - 4) = 32$

34. $x(x - 7) = 18$

35. $x(x + 14) = -40$

36. $x(2 - x) = -15$

37. $(x + 2)^2 = 16$

38. $(x - 5)^2 = 4$

39. $(x - 8)^2 = 25$

40. $(x + 3)^2 = 49$

41. $12x^2 + 10x - 2 = 0$

42. $12x^2 + 23x + 5 = 0$

43. $3x^2 - 17x - 6 = 0$

44. $5x^2 - 34x - 7 = 0$

45. $6x^2 - 49x + 8 = 0$

46. $6x^2 - x - 2 = 0$

47. $16x^2 + 14x + 3 = 0$

48. $20x^2 + 16x + 3 = 0$

49. $30x^2 + 7x - 2 = 0$

50. $8x^2 - 18x - 5 = 0$

51. $30x^2 + 17x + 2 = 0$

52. $(x + 3)(x - 4) = 18$

53. $(x + 5)(x + 1) = 32$

54. $(x + 7)(x - 2) = 10$

55. $(2x - 3)^2 = 9$

56. $(4x + 1)^2 = 16$

57. $(5x + 3)^2 = 36$

58. $(18x - 27)(x + 2) = -52$

59. $(4x - 1)(2x + 3) = 22$

60. $(2x + 3)(3x + 1) = 5$

6.7 APPLICATIONS OF QUADRATIC EQUATIONS

□ **Integer Problems** □ **Geometry Problems**

□ INTEGER PROBLEMS

Recall the set of integers is $z = \{\ldots -3, -2, -1, 0, 1, 2, 3, \ldots\}$

Example 1

The product of two integers is 40. If one integer is 3 less than the other, find the integers.

Solution

If we let x represent the first integer, then the second integer is $x - 3$.

$$\begin{array}{ll} \text{1st} & x \\ \text{2nd} & x - 3 \end{array}$$

Since their product is 40, we can write the equation,

$$x(x - 3) = 40$$

$$x^2 - 3x = 40$$

$$x^2 - 3x - 40 = 0$$

$$(x - 8)(x + 5) = 0$$

$$x - 8 = 0 \text{ or } x + 5 = 0$$

$$x = 8 \text{ or } x = -5$$

Thus, the integers are:

$$\begin{array}{llll} \text{1st} & 8 & \text{or} & \text{1st} & -5 \\ \text{2nd} & 8 - 3 = 5 & & \text{2nd} & -5 - 3 = -8 \end{array}$$

Example 2

If the product of two consecutive odd integers is 143, find the integers.

Solution

First, set up two consecutive odd integers.

   1st x

   2nd $x + 2$

Since their product is 143, we can write the equation:

   $x(x+2) = 143$

   $x^2 + 2x = 143$

   $x^2 + 2x - 143 = 0$

   $(x+13)(x-11) = 0$

   $x + 13 = 0$ or $x - 11 = 0$

   $x = -13$ or $x = 11$

Thus, the solution is:

   1st -13 or   1st   11

   2nd $-13 + 2 = 11$ 2nd $11 + 2 = 13$

Example 3

If the product of two consecutive positive even integers is 168, find the integers.

Solution

Set up two consecutive even integers:

   1st x

   2nd $x + 2$

The equation is: $x(x+2) = 168$

   $x^2 + 2x - 168 = 0$

   $(x+14)(x-12) = 0$

   $x + 14 = 0$ or $x - 12 = 0$

   $x = -14$ or $x = 12$

Since we need positive even integers, the solution is:

   1st   12

   2nd $12 + 2 = 14$

□ GEOMETRY PROBLEMS

Pythagorean Theorem

In a right triangle, the square of the hypotenuse is equal to the sum of the squares of the two legs.

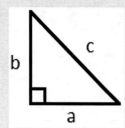

$(leg)^2 + (leg)^2 = (hypotenuse)^2$

$a^2 + b^2 = c^2$ (Pythagorean Formula)

Example 4

If the lengths of the sides of a right triangles are given by three consecutive even integers, find the lengths of the two legs and the length of the hypotenuse.

Solution

Let x be the length of the shortest leg (1st leg). Then,

1st	x
2nd	$x + 2$
hypotenuse	$x + 4$

If we apply the Pythagorean Formula,

$(leg)^2 + (leg)^2 = (hypotenuse)^2$

$$x^2 + (x+2)^2 = (x+4)^2$$
$$x^2 + x^2 + 4x + 4 = x^2 + 8x + 16$$
$$2x^2 + 4x + 4 - x^2 - 8x - 16 = 0$$
$$x^2 - 4x - 12 = 0$$
$$(x+2)(x-6) = 0$$
$$x + 2 = 0 \text{ or } x - 6 = 0$$
$$x = -2 \text{ or } x = 6$$

Since the side of a triangle can not have negative length, the solution is $x = 6$.

Thus,

1st leg	$= 6$
2nd leg	$= 6 + 2 = 8$
hypotenuse	$= 6 + 4 = 10$

Example 5

The diagonal of a rectangle is 20 cm². If the width is 4 less than the length, find the dimensions of the rectangle.

Solution

If x represents the length of the rectangle, then $x - 4$ represents the width. If we apply the Pythagorean Formula,

$$x^2 + (x-4)^2 = 20^2$$

$$x^2 + x^2 - 8x + 16 = 400$$

$$2x^2 - 8x + 16 - 400 = 0$$

$$2x^2 - 8x - 384 = 0$$

Divide the equation by 2,

$$x^2 - 4x - 192 = 0$$

$$(x-16)(x+12) = 0$$

$$x - 16 = 0 \text{ or } x + 12 = 0$$

$$x = 16 \text{ or } x = -12$$

Since the length of a rectangle cannot be a negative number, the solution is $x = 16$.

Thus, the length of the rectangle is L = 16 cm and the width W = 16 − 4 = 12 cm.

Example 6

The area of a rectangle is 54 in². If the length of the rectangle is 3 more than the width, find the dimensions of the rectangle.

Solution

Let x represent the width of the rectangle. Then, $x + 3$ represents the length of the rectangle. The area of a rectangle is given by the formula,

Area = length × width

Using this formula, the equation can be written as follows:

$$x(x+3) = 54$$

$$x^2 + 3x = 54$$

$$x^2 + 3x - 54 = 0$$

$$(x+9)(x-6) = 0$$

$$x + 9 = 0 \text{ or } x - 6 = 0$$

$$x = -9 \text{ or } x = 6$$

Since the dimension of a rectangle cannot be negative, the solution is $x = 6$.

Thus, the width of the rectangle is W = 6 in and the length L = 6 + 3 = 9 in.

Example 7

If the length of each side of a square is extended by 5 m, the area of the resulting square is 81 m^2. Find the length of the side of the original square.

Solution

Let x = the length of the side of the original square. Then, the length of the side of the new square is $x + 5$. The area of a square is given by the formula $A = s^2$ where s is the length of the side of the square. Using this formula, the equation is:

$$(x+5)(x+5) = 81$$

$$x^2 + 5x + 5x + 25 = 81$$

$$x^2 + 10x + 25 - 81 = 0$$

$$x^2 + 10x - 56 = 0$$

$$(x+14)(x-4) = 0$$

$$x+14 = 0 \text{ or } x-4 = 0$$

$$x = -14 \text{ or } x = 4$$

Since the length of the side of the square cannot be negative, the solution is $x = 4$.

Thus, the length of the side of the original square is $x = 4$ m.

Example 8

The area of a triangle is 15 cm². If the length of the base is 1 cm more than the length of the height, find the base and height of the triangle.

Solution

Let x = height of the triangle. Then $x + 1$ represents the base of the triangle.

The area of a triangle is given by the formula $A = \dfrac{1}{2}b \cdot h$ where b is the length of the base and h is the length of the height of the triangle. Using this formula, the equation can be written as follows:

$$\frac{1}{2}x(x+1) = 15$$

Multiply the equation by 2.

$$x(x+1) = 30$$

$$x^2 + x - 30 = 0$$

$$(x+6)(x-5) = 0$$

$$x+6 = 0 \text{ or } x-5 = 0$$

$$x = -6 \text{ or } x = 5$$

Since the height of a triangle cannot be a negative number, the solution is $x = 5$.

Thus, the height of the triangle is $h = 5$ cm and the base $b = 6 + 7 = 7$cm.

Example 9

An object is thrown upward from a cliff 192 ft above the ground with an initial velocity of 64 ft/sec. The height (in feet) of the object at any given time t (in seconds) is given by the equation:

$$h(t) = -16t^2 + 64t + 192$$

Find the time t for the object to reach the ground.

Solution

The object reaches the ground when the height of the object is zero: $h(t) = 0$.

$$-16t^2 + 64t + 192 = 0$$

Divide the equation by -16.

$$t^2 - 4t - 12 = 0$$
$$(t - 6)(t + 2) = 0$$
$$t - 6 = 0 \text{ or } t + 2 = 0$$
$$t = 6 \text{ or } t = -2$$

Since the time cannot be a negative number, the solution is $t = 6$.

Thus, the object reaches the ground after 6 seconds.

6.7 EXERCISES

1. The product of two positive integers is 50. If one integer is 5 more than the other, find the integers.

2. The product of two integers is 14. If one integer is 3 less than twice the other, find the integers.

3. One integer is 7 more than 2 times another. If their product is 85, find the integers.

4. One integer is 5 less than 3 times another. If their product is 100, find the integers.

5. The product of two consecutive even integers is 120. Find the integers.

6. The product of two consecutive positive odd integers is 420. Find the integers.

7. The difference of two integers is 8, and the product of the two integers is 180. Find the integers.

8. The difference of two integers is 13, and the product of the two integers is 300. Find the two integers.

9. The sum of two integers is 15, and their product is 56. Find the integers.

10. The sum of two integers is 24, and their product is 80. Find the integers.

11. The diagonal of a rectangle is 25 cm. If the length is 5 cm more than the width, find the dimensions of the rectangle.

12. The diagonal of a rectangle is 40 cm. If the width is 8 cm less than the length, find the dimensions of the rectangle.

13. If the lengths of the sides of a right triangle are given by three consecutive odd integers, find the lengths of the two legs.

14. The hypotenuse of a right triangle is 30 in. If one leg is 6 in. longer than the other, find the lengths of the two legs.

15. The length of a rectangle is 12 cm more than the width. If the area of the rectangle is 220 cm², find the dimensions of the rectangle.

16. The length of a rectangle is 8 ft more than twice the width. If the area of the rectangle is 280 ft², find the dimensions of the rectangle.

17. The width of a rectangle is 5 m less than the length. If the area of the rectangle is 500 m², find the dimensions of the rectangle.

18. The width of a rectangle is 4 in. less than 3 times the length. If the area of the rectangle is 55 in², find the dimensions of the rectangle.

19. The length of each side of a square is extended 3 m. The area of the resulting square is 100 m². Find the length of the side of the original square.

20. The length of each side of a square is extended by 7 in. The area of the resulting square is 169 in². Find the length of the side of the original square.

21. The base of a triangle is three times the height. If the area of the triangle is 54 cm², find the base and the height of the triangle.

22. The height of a triangle is 6 cm more than the base. If the area of the triangle is 80 cm², find the base and the height of the triangle.

23. An object is dropped from a cliff 256 feet above the ground. The height (in feet) of the object at any given time t (in seconds) is given by the equation: $h(t) = -16t^2 + 256$. Find the time for the object to reach the ground.

24. An object is thrown upward from the top of a building that is 288 feet tall. If the height (in feet) of the object at any given time t (in seconds) is given by: $h(t) = -16t^2 + 48t + 288$, find the time for the object to reach the ground.

CHAPTER 6 REVIEW EXERCISES

Find the greatest common factor (GCF).

1. $15xy^3$, $35x^2y^4$, $50x^5y^2$

2. $18a^3b^2$, $24a^2b^2$, $34a^4b^3$

Factor completely. If an expression is prime, so state.

3. $15x^2 - 12x$

4. $16a^2b + 48ab^2$

5. $8m^2n^3 - 24m^3n^2$

6. $10x^3y^4 + 30x^2y^3 - 50x^4y^2$

7. $14a^2b^3 - 21a^4b^2 + 35a^5b$

8. $3x(y+4) + 2(y+4)$

9. $a(2b+1) - (2b+1)$

Factor by grouping.

10. $5x^2 + 10x + 3x + 6$

11. $6a^2 - 24a - 5a + 20$

12. $2x^2 + 6x - xy - 3y$

13. $3x^2 + 6xy + 4xy + 8y^2$

14. $12a^2 + 8ab - 21ab - 14b^2$

15. $xy - 5x - 4y + 20$

16. $5x^3 + 5xy^2 - 4x^2y - 4y^3$

17. $10ax + 6ay + 35bx + 21by$

Factor completely. If a trinomial is prime, so state.

18. $x^2 - 5x - 24$

19. $a^2 + 3a - 28$

20. $m^2 - 5m - 36$

21. $n^2 + 6n - 16$

22. $x^2 + 4x - 45$

23. $a^2 - 11a + 28$

24. $x^2 + 3xy - 10y^2$

25. $2x^2 - 22xy + 60y^2$

26. $x^3 + 7x^2 + 12x$

27. $6x^2 + 11x + 4$

28. $15a^2 + 11ab + 2b^2$

29. $6x^2 + 13x - 15$

30. $12x^2 - 5xy - 2y^2$

31. $12a^2 + 17ab - 5b^2$

32. $9x^2 - 12xy + 4y^2$

Factor completely.

33. $a^2 - 49$

34. $x^2 - 144$

35. $100 - b^2$

36. $25x^2 - 1$

37. $4 - 81m^2$

38. $36a^2 - 49b^2$

39. $x^2 - \dfrac{4}{9}$

40. $y^2 - \dfrac{25}{16}$

41. $\dfrac{1}{4} - a^2$

42. $a^4 - 16$

43. $3x^5 - 3x$

44. $m^4 - n^4$

45. $x^3 - 64$

46. $8b^3 + 27$

47. $2m^3 + 16$

Solve.

48. $x^2 - 11x = 0$

49. $a^2 + 4a = 0$

50. $5x^2 - 35x = 0$

51. $x^2 - 6x - 27 = 0$

52. $x^2 - 10x + 24 = 0$

53. $m^2 - 8m = 9$

54. $2x^2 - 5x - 3 = 0$

55. $15x^2 + x = 2$

56. $8n^2 - 2n = 3$

57. $x^2 - 8x + 16 = 0$

58. $4a^2 + 12a + 9 = 0$

59. $4x^2 - 81 = 0$

60. $(x+2)(x+3) = 12$

61. $(x+1)(x-5) = 7$

62. $6x^2 - 12 = x$

63. $(x-5)^2 = 36$

64. $(2a-1)^2 = 4$

65. $(3y+4)^2 = 81$

66. The product of two consecutive even integers is 168. Find the two integers.

67. One leg of a right triangle is 3 in more than the other leg. The hypotenuse is 6 in longer than the shortest leg. Find the lengths of the three sides of the triangle.

68. The length of a rectangle is 5 in longer than the width. If the area of the rectangle is 176 in², find the length and width of the rectangle.

69. An object is dropped from a cliff 400 feet above the ground. The height (in feet) of the object at any given time t (in seconds) is given by the equation: $h(t) = -16t^2 + 400$. Find the time for the object to reach the ground.

70. The height of a triangle is 11 cm less than the base. If the area of the triangle is 121 cm², find the base and the height of the triangle.

7 RATIONAL EXPRESSIONS AND EQUATIONS

7.1 SIMPLIFYING RATIONAL EXPRESSIONS

□ **Rational Expressions** □ **Finding the Values that Make a Rational Expression Undefined** □ **Evaluating Rational Expressions** □ **Simplifying Rational Expressions**

☐ RATIONAL EXPRESSIONS

Examples of Rational Expressions:

a. $x^2 \dfrac{x^2-2x+1}{x^3-1}$

b. $\dfrac{2x+3}{2x^2+x-3}$

c. $\dfrac{x^2-1}{x-1}$

Definition

A **rational expression** is an expression of the form $\dfrac{P}{Q}$, where P and Q are polynomials and $Q \neq 0$.

Note: Because division by zero cannot be defined, when $Q=0$, a rational expression is undefined. When $P=0$, and $Q \neq 0$ the rational expression is equal to zero $\left(\dfrac{0}{Q}=0\right)$.

☐ FINDING THE VALUES THAT MAKE A RATIONAL EXPRESSION UNDEFINED

Example 1

Determine the values of the variable for which the rational expression is undefined.

a. $\dfrac{3x+4}{x-2}$

b. $\dfrac{x^2-1}{x^2-x-6}$

c. $\dfrac{x+5}{x^2+1}$

d. $\dfrac{x^2-9}{5}$

Solution

a. The rational expression $\dfrac{3x+4}{x-2}$ is undefined when the denominator $x-2$ is zero.

Step 1 Set the denominator equal to zero: $x-2=0$

Step 2 Solve for x: $x=2$

Answer: The rational expression is undefined for $x=2$.

b. The rational expression $\dfrac{x^2-1}{x^2-x-6}$ is undefined when the denominator x^2-x-6 is zero.

Step 1 Set the denominator equal to zero: $x^2-x-6=0$

Step 2 Solve for x:

$$(x-3)(x+2)=0$$

$$x-3=0 \text{ or } x+2=0$$

$$x=3 \text{ or } x=-2$$

Answer: The rational expression is undefined for $x=3$ and $x=-2$.

c. The rational expression $\dfrac{x+5}{x^2+1}$ is undefined when the denominator x^2+1 is zero.

Since x^2 is positive and 1 is positive, there is no value x that will make the sum x^2+1 zero. Thus, there is no value x that will make the denominator equal to zero.

Answer: None

d. The rational expression $\dfrac{x^2-9}{5}$ is undefined when the denominator equals zero.

Since $5 \neq 0$, there is no value that will make the denominator equal to zero and the rational expression undefined.

Answer: None

☐ EVALUATING RATIONAL EXPRESSIONS

We can evaluate a rational expression for any value that will not make the denominator equal to zero. To evaluate a rational expression for a given value, substitute the value for the variable and simplify the numerical expression.

Example 2

Evaluate.

$\dfrac{3x+1}{x-3}$ for

a. $x=0$ b. $x=-2$ c. $x=4$

Solution

a. $\dfrac{3x+1}{x-3}=\dfrac{3\cdot 0+1}{0-3}=\dfrac{1}{-3}=-\dfrac{1}{3}$

b. $\dfrac{3x+1}{x-3}=\dfrac{3(-2)+1}{-2-3}=\dfrac{-6+1}{-5}=\dfrac{-5}{-5}=1$

c. $\dfrac{3x+1}{x-3}=\dfrac{3\cdot 4+1}{4-3}=\dfrac{12+1}{1}=\dfrac{13}{1}=13$

☐ SIMPLIFYING RATIONAL EXPRESSIONS

We can also simplify rational expressions. A rational expression is simplified or in lowest terms when the numerator and denominator have no common factors other than one.

Fundamental Property of Rational Expressions

If P, Q and R are polynomials such that $Q \neq 0$ and $R \neq 0$, then $\dfrac{P \cdot R}{Q \cdot R} = \dfrac{P}{Q}$.

In other words, if the numerator and denominator have a common factor, we can cancel the common factor.

Example 3

Simplify.

$$\frac{12x^2 y}{20x}$$

Solution

$$\frac{12x^2 y}{20x} = \frac{3xy \cdot 4x}{5 \cdot 4x} = \frac{3xy}{5}$$

Strategy for Simplifying Rational Expressions

Step 1 Factor the numerator and denominator completely.

Step 2 Use the fundamental property of rational expressions to cancel any common non-zero factors.

Example 4

Simplify.

$$\frac{x^2 - 9}{x^2 + x - 6}$$

Solution

Factor both the numerator and denominator and apply the fundamental property of rational expressions.

$$\frac{x^2 - 9}{x^2 + x - 6} = \frac{(x-3)(x+3)}{(x+3)(x-2)} = \frac{x-3}{x-2}$$

Example 5

Simplify.

$$\frac{x^2 + 5x}{x^2 - 2x - 35}$$

Solution

$$\frac{x^2 + 5x}{x^2 - 2x - 35} = \frac{x(x+5)}{(x-7)(x+5)} = \frac{x}{x-7}$$

Example 6

Simplify.

$$\frac{x^2 - 6x - 16}{x^2 + 6x + 8}$$

Solution

$$\frac{x^2 - 6x - 16}{x^2 + 6x + 8} = \frac{(x-8)(x+2)}{(x+4)(x+2)} = \frac{x-8}{x+4}$$

Example 7

Simplify.

$$\frac{x^2 + 3xy + 2y^2}{x^2 - y^2}$$

Solution

$$\frac{x^2 + 3xy + 2y^2}{x^2 - y^2} = \frac{(x+2y)(x+y)}{(x-y)(x+y)} = \frac{x+2y}{x-y}$$

Example 8

Simplify.

$$\frac{2-a}{a^2-4}$$

Solution

$$\frac{2-a}{a^2-4} = \frac{-(a-2)}{(a+2)(a-2)} = \frac{-1}{a+2} = -\frac{1}{a+2}$$

Example 9

___

Simplify.

$$\frac{x^3 - 4x}{x^3 - 8}$$

Solution

$$\frac{x^3 - 4x}{x^3 - 8} = \frac{x(x^2 - 4)}{(x - 2)(x^2 + 2x + 4)} = \frac{x(x - 2)(x + 2)}{(x - 2)(x^2 + 2x + 4)} = \frac{x(x + 2)}{x^2 + 2x + 4}$$

Example 10

___

Simplify.

$$\frac{ax + ay + bx + by}{ax - ay + bx - by}$$

Solution

$$\frac{ax + ay + bx + by}{ax - ay + bx - by} = \frac{a(x + y) + b(x + y)}{a(x - y) + b(x - y)} = \frac{(x + y)(a + b)}{(x - y)(a + b)} = \frac{x + y}{x - y}$$

Example 11

___

Simplify.

$$\frac{x^2(a + 1) - 3x(a + 1) - 70(a + 1)}{x^2(a + 1) + 10x(a + 1) + 21(a + 1)}$$

Solution

$$\frac{x^2(a + 1) - 3x(a + 1) - 70(a + 1)}{x^2(a + 1) + 10x(a + 1) + 21(a + 1)} = \frac{(a + 1)(x^2 - 3x - 70)}{(a + 1)(x^2 + 10x + 21)} =$$

$$\frac{(a + 1)(x - 10)(x + 7)}{(a + 1)(x + 3)(x + 7)} = \frac{x - 10}{x + 3}$$

7.1 EXERCISES

Determine the values of the variable for which each expression is undefined.

1. $\dfrac{2x+1}{x}$

2. $\dfrac{x-4}{3x}$

3. $\dfrac{3x-5}{x-3}$

4. $\dfrac{x^2+1}{x+5}$

5. $\dfrac{x}{x^2-9}$

6. $\dfrac{5}{x^2-16}$

7. $\dfrac{4x+3}{x^2+2x-15}$

8. $\dfrac{2-x}{x^2-5x-24}$

9. $\dfrac{3x}{x^2+4}$

10. $\dfrac{5x+7}{x^2+9}$

11. $\dfrac{3x-2}{5}$

12. $\dfrac{x+8}{12}$

Simplify.

13. $\dfrac{15ab^3}{12a^2b^2}$

14. $\dfrac{24x^2y^3}{32xy}$

15. $\dfrac{9xy^2}{27x^3y^3}$

16. $\dfrac{8x}{2x+10}$

17. $\dfrac{18x}{6x+24}$

18. $\dfrac{x+9}{x^2-81}$

19. $\dfrac{a-2}{a^2-4}$

20. $\dfrac{2x-8}{x^2-16}$

21. $\dfrac{3x+15}{x^2-25}$

22. $\dfrac{x+7}{x^2+4x-21}$

23. $\dfrac{x-4}{x^2+6x-40}$

24. $\dfrac{x^2+6x-16}{x+8}$

25. $\dfrac{x^2+5x-14}{x-2}$

26. $\dfrac{x^2+x-56}{x^2-4x-21}$

27. $\dfrac{x^2+9x+20}{x^2+6x+5}$

28. $\dfrac{x^2+2x-15}{x^2+9x-36}$

29. $\dfrac{x^2+11x+10}{x^2+8x-20}$

30. $\dfrac{x^2-15x+56}{x^2-12x+32}$

31. $\dfrac{x^2+6xy+8y^2}{x^2+7xy+10y^2}$

32. $\dfrac{x^2+4xy-21y^2}{x^2-13xy+30y^2}$

33. $\dfrac{x^2-4}{x^3-8}$

34. $\dfrac{3x+6y}{x^2-4y^2}$

35. $\dfrac{2x+1}{2x^2+7x+3}$

36. $\dfrac{3x+2}{3x^2+17x+10}$

37. $\dfrac{x^2+4x+4}{4x^2+11x+6}$

38. $\dfrac{5x^2+14x-3}{x^2-9}$

39. $\dfrac{x^2-2x-15}{6x^2-29x-5}$

40. $\dfrac{12x^2+5x-2}{4x^2+19x-5}$

41. $\dfrac{6x^2+x-2}{8x^2+2x-3}$

42. $\dfrac{3x^2+19x+20}{3x^2+x-4}$

43. $\dfrac{x-3}{3-x}$

44. $\dfrac{a-6}{6-a}$

45. $\dfrac{y-3}{9-y^2}$

46. $\dfrac{x^3-27}{9-x^2}$

47. $\dfrac{x^2-8x-9}{18+7x-x^2}$

48. $\dfrac{21-4x-x^2}{x^2+x-12}$

49. $\dfrac{x^2+5x}{x^2+8x+15}$

50. $\dfrac{x^2-4x-32}{x^2-8x}$

51. $\dfrac{-x^2-8x}{x^2-64}$

52. $\dfrac{2x^2-xy-y^2}{3x^2-xy-2y^2}$

53. $\dfrac{4x^2+3xy-y^2}{8x^2+9xy+y^2}$

54. $\dfrac{x^3-a^3}{a^2-x^2}$

55. $\dfrac{xy+5x+5y+25}{xy-3x+5y-15}$

56. $\dfrac{ab+8a-5b-40}{ab-5b+2a-10}$

57. $\dfrac{x^3 - 4x^2}{x^3 - 64}$

58. $\dfrac{y^3 - 8}{y^2 + 2y + 4}$

59. $\dfrac{a^2b + a^2d + bc^2 + c^2d}{a^2b - a^2d + bc^2 - c^2d}$

60. $\dfrac{ab - 3a + 3b - 9}{ab + 3b - 4a - 12}$

61. $\dfrac{x^2 - y^2 + 3x + 3y}{5x - 5y + 15}$

62. $\dfrac{(x-2)(x+1) + (x-2)(x-3)}{(x-1)(x-4) + (x-1)(x+2)}$

63. $\dfrac{x^2(x+5) - 4(x+5)}{x^4 - 16}$

64. $\dfrac{y^2(m+2n) - 2y(m+2n) - 8(m+2n)}{y^2(m+2n) + 3y(m+2n) - 28(m+2n)}$

65. $\dfrac{x^2(z+3) + 3x(z+3) - 40(z+3)}{z^2(x+8) + 4z(x+8) + 3(x+8)}$

66. Evaluate $\dfrac{3x+2}{x^2 + 2x + 5}$ for $x = 0$ and $x = 1$.

67. Evaluate $\dfrac{5x-3}{x^2 - 3x + 4}$ for $x = 0$ and $x = -1$.

68. Evaluate. $\dfrac{x^2 - 2x + 3}{x^2 + 4x - 1}$ for $x = 2$ and $x = 3$.

69. Evaluate. $\dfrac{2x^2 - x + 4}{3x^2 + x - 6}$ for $x = 1$ and $x = 2$.

7.2 MULTIPLYING AND DIVIDING RATIONAL EXPRESSIONS

☐ **Multiplying Rational Expressions** ☐ **Dividing Rational Expressions**

☐ MULTIPLYING RATIONAL EXPRESSIONS

> **Rule**
>
> If $\dfrac{P}{Q}$ and $\dfrac{R}{S}$ are rational expressions, then $\dfrac{P}{Q} \cdot \dfrac{R}{S} = \dfrac{P \cdot R}{Q \cdot S}$.
>
> In other words, when multiplying rational expressions, multiply their numerators, multiply their denominators, and write the quotient in simplest form. If the numerators and denominators have some common factors, cancel those factors before multiplying.

Example 1

Multiply.

a. $\dfrac{5x}{7y} \cdot \dfrac{14xy}{10x}$

b. $\dfrac{3ab}{2a^2} \cdot \dfrac{4ab^3}{6a^2b^2}$

c. $\dfrac{18x^5y^8}{24x^6y^4} \cdot \dfrac{8xy}{9x^2y^3}$

Solution

a. $\dfrac{5x}{7y} \cdot \dfrac{14xy}{10x} = \dfrac{(5x \cdot 2 \cdot 7y)x}{7y \cdot 2 \cdot 5x} = \dfrac{x}{1} = x$

b. $\dfrac{3ab}{2a^2} \cdot \dfrac{4ab^3}{6a^2b^2} = \dfrac{12a^2b^4}{12a^4b^2} = \dfrac{(12a^2b^2)b^2}{(12a^2b^2)a^2} = \dfrac{b^2}{a^2}$

c. $\dfrac{18x^5y^8}{24x^6y^4} \cdot \dfrac{8xy}{9x^2y^3} = \dfrac{9 \cdot 2 \cdot 8x^6y^9}{8 \cdot 3 \cdot 9x^8y^7} = \dfrac{2(x^6y^7)y^2}{3(x^6y^7)x^2} = \dfrac{2y^2}{3x^2}$

Example 2

Multiply.

a. $\dfrac{5x+5y}{10x(x+3)} \cdot \dfrac{x^2+3x}{x^2-y^2}$

b. $\dfrac{x^2-4x}{x+6} \cdot \dfrac{x^2+8x+12}{x^2-2x-8}$

Solution

a. $\dfrac{5x+5y}{10x(x+3)} \cdot \dfrac{x^2+3x}{x^2-y^2} = \dfrac{5(x+y)}{10x(x+3)} \cdot \dfrac{x(x+3)}{(x+y)(x-y)} = \dfrac{5x(x+3)(x+y)}{2[5x(x+3)(x+y)](x-y)} = \dfrac{1}{2(x-y)}$

b. $\dfrac{x^2-4x}{x+6} \cdot \dfrac{x^2+8x+12}{x^2-2x-8} = \dfrac{x(x-4)}{x+6} \cdot \dfrac{(x+6)(x+2)}{(x-4)(x+2)} = \dfrac{x}{1} = x$

Example 3

Multiply.

a. $\dfrac{4-x^2}{x^2+3x-10} \cdot \dfrac{x^2+9x+20}{x^2+6x+8}$

b. $\dfrac{x^2-16}{(x-4)^2} \cdot \dfrac{x^3-64}{x^2+5x+4}$

Solution

a. $\dfrac{4-x^2}{x^2+3x-10} \cdot \dfrac{x^2+9x+20}{x^2+6x+8} = \dfrac{(2-x)(2+x)}{(x+5)(x-2)} \cdot \dfrac{(x+5)(x+4)}{(x+2)(x+4)} = \dfrac{2-x}{x-2} = \dfrac{-1(x-2)}{x-2} = -1$

b. $\dfrac{x^2-16}{(x-4)^2} \cdot \dfrac{x^3-64}{x^2+5x+4} = \dfrac{(x-4)(x+4)}{(x-4)^2} \cdot \dfrac{x^3-4^3}{(x+4)(x+1)} = $

$\dfrac{x+4}{x-4} \cdot \dfrac{(x-4)(x^2+4x+16)}{(x+4)(x+1)} = \dfrac{x^2+4x+16}{x+1}$

Example 4

Multiply.

$\dfrac{x^2+4xy-12y^2}{x^2+6xy-16y^2} \cdot \dfrac{x^2+7xy-8y^2}{x^2+7xy+6y^2}$

Solution

$\dfrac{x^2+4xy-12y^2}{x^2+6xy-16y^2} \cdot \dfrac{x^2+7xy-8y^2}{x^2+7xy+6y^2} = \dfrac{(x+6y)(x-2y)}{(x+8y)(x-2y)} \cdot \dfrac{(x+8y)(x-y)}{(x+6y)(x+y)} = \dfrac{x-y}{x+y}$

Example 5

Multiply.

$$\frac{2x^2+7x+3}{3x^2+7x-6}\cdot\frac{4x^2+x-3}{2x^2+3x+1}$$

Solution

$$\frac{2x^2+7x+3}{3x^2+7x-6}\cdot\frac{4x^2+x-3}{2x^2+3x+1}=\frac{2x^2+6x+x+3}{3x^2+9x-2x-6}\cdot\frac{4x^2+4x-3x-3}{2x^2+2x+x+1}=$$

$$\frac{(2x^2+6x)+(x+3)}{(3x^2+9x)+(-2x-6)}\cdot\frac{(4x^2+4x)+(-3x-3)}{(2x^2+2x)+(x+1)}=$$

$$\frac{2x(x+3)+1(x+3)}{3x(x+3)-2(x+3)}\cdot\frac{4x(x+1)-3(x+1)}{2x(x+1)+1(x+1)}=$$

$$\frac{(x+3)(2x+1)}{(x+3)(3x-2)}\cdot\frac{(x+1)(4x-3)}{(x+1)(2x+1)}=\frac{4x-3}{3x-2}$$

☐ DIVIDING RATIONAL EXPRESSIONS

Rule

If $\dfrac{P}{Q}$ and $\dfrac{R}{S}$ are rational expressions, then $\dfrac{P}{Q}\div\dfrac{R}{S}=\dfrac{P}{Q}\cdot\dfrac{S}{R}=\dfrac{P\cdot S}{Q\cdot R}$ *,* $(R\neq 0)$

In other words, when dividing rational expressions, multiply the first rational expression by the reciprocal of the second one.

Note: If the numerators and denominators have some common factors *do not cancel* those factors before you change the division to an equivalent multiplication.

Example 6

Divide.

$$\frac{2ab^3}{5a^2}\div\frac{6ab}{20a^3}$$

Solution

$$\frac{2ab^3}{5a^2} \div \frac{6ab}{20a^3} = \frac{2ab^3}{5a^2} \cdot \frac{20a^3}{6ab} = \frac{2 \cdot 5 \cdot 4a^4 b^3}{5 \cdot 2 \cdot 3a^3 b} = \frac{4}{3}\frac{2}{2}\frac{5}{5}\frac{a^4}{a^3} \cdot \frac{b^3}{b} = \frac{4}{3} \cdot \frac{a}{1} \cdot \frac{b^2}{1} = \frac{4ab^2}{3}$$

Example 7

Divide.

$$\frac{3x}{x+5} \div \frac{3x^2 - 6x}{x^2 - 25}$$

Solution

$$\frac{3x}{x+5} \div \frac{3x^2 - 6x}{x^2 - 25} = \frac{3x}{x+5} \cdot \frac{x^2 - 25}{3x^2 - 6x} = \frac{3x}{x+5} \cdot \frac{(x-5)(x+5)}{3x(x-2)} = \frac{x-5}{x-2}$$

Example 8

Divide.

$$\frac{x^2 - 2x + 1}{8} \div (x-1)^3$$

Solution

$$\frac{x^2 - 2x + 1}{8} \div (x-1)^3 = \frac{(x-1)^2}{8} \cdot \frac{1}{(x-1)^3} = \frac{1}{8(x-1)}$$

Example 9

Divide.

$$\frac{x^2 + 5x - 14}{x^2 + 11x + 24} \div \frac{x^2 + 2x - 35}{x^2 - 2x - 15}$$

Solution

$$\frac{x^2 + 5x - 14}{x^2 + 11x + 24} \div \frac{x^2 + 2x - 35}{x^2 - 2x - 15} = \frac{x^2 + 5x - 14}{x^2 + 11x + 24} \cdot \frac{x^2 - 2x - 15}{x^2 + 2x - 35} =$$

$$\frac{(x+7)(x-2)}{(x+8)(x+3)} \cdot \frac{(x-5)(x+3)}{(x+7)(x-5)} = \frac{x-2}{x+8}$$

Example 10

Divide.

$$\frac{xy-2x+4y-8}{xy-2x-5y+10} \div \frac{x^2-16}{x^3-125}$$

Solution

$$\frac{xy-2x+4y-8}{xy-2x-5y+10} \div \frac{x^2-16}{x^3-125} = \frac{xy-2x+4y-8}{xy-2x-5y+10} \cdot \frac{x^3-125}{x^2-16} =$$

$$\frac{(xy-2x)+(4y-8)}{(xy-2x)+(-5y+10)} \cdot \frac{x^3-5^3}{x^2-4^2} = \frac{x(y-2)+4(y-2)}{x(y-2)-5(y-2)} \cdot \frac{(x-5)(x^2+5x+25)}{(x-4)(x+4)} =$$

$$\frac{(y-2)(x+4)}{(y-2)(x-5)} \cdot \frac{(x-5)(x^2+5x+25)}{(x-4)(x+4)} = \frac{x^2+5x+25}{x-4}$$

Example 11

Divide.

$$\frac{2x^2+3xy+y^2}{2x^2+7xy+3y^2} \div \frac{x^2-y^2}{x^2-9y^2}$$

Solution

$$\frac{2x^2+3xy+y^2}{2x^2+7xy+3y^2} \div \frac{x^2-y^2}{x^2-9y^2} = \frac{2x^2+3xy+y^2}{2x^2+7xy+3y^2} \cdot \frac{x^2-9y^2}{x^2-y^2} =$$

$$\frac{2x^2+2xy+xy+y^2}{2x^2+6xy+xy+3y^2} \cdot \frac{x^2-9y^2}{x^2-y^2} = \frac{2x(x+y)+y(x+y)}{2x(x+3y)+y(x+3y)} \cdot \frac{x^2-9y^2}{x^2-y^2} =$$

$$\frac{(x+y)(2x+y)}{(x+3y)(2x+y)} \cdot \frac{(x-3y)(x+3y)}{(x-y)(x+y)} = \frac{x-3y}{x-y}$$

Example 12

Perform the indicated operations and write the answer in simplest form.

$$\frac{x^2+5x-6}{x^2-7x+12} \cdot \frac{x^2+7x-30}{x^2+7x+6} \div \frac{x^2+5x-50}{x^2-9x+20}$$

Solution

$$\frac{x^2+5x-6}{x^2-7x+12}\cdot\frac{x^2+7x-30}{x^2+7x+6}\div\frac{x^2+5x-50}{x^2-9x+20}=\frac{x^2+5x-6}{x^2-7x+12}\cdot\frac{x^2+7x-30}{x^2+7x+6}\cdot\frac{x^2-9x+20}{x^2+5x-50}=$$

$$\frac{(x+6)(x-1)}{(x-4)(x-3)}\cdot\frac{(x+10)(x-3)}{(x+6)(x+1)}\cdot\frac{(x-5)(x-4)}{(x+10)(x-5)}=\frac{x-1}{x+1}$$

7.2 EXERCISES

Multiply.

1. $\dfrac{9x^2}{15y}\cdot\dfrac{20xy}{36x^3}$

2. $\dfrac{4ab^2}{18a^2}\cdot\dfrac{12a}{8b}$

3. $\dfrac{25x^3y^3}{21x^2y}\cdot\dfrac{7x}{10xy^2}$

4. $16ab\cdot\dfrac{2a^2b^2}{24a^3b^4}$

5. $\dfrac{6x^2y^3}{27x^4y^4}\cdot 18y$

6. $\dfrac{-3a^3b^5}{8ab}\cdot\dfrac{32a^2b}{12a^4b^4}$

7. $\dfrac{3-x}{10x}\cdot\dfrac{25x^2}{x^2-9}$

8. $\dfrac{2x+1}{7xy}\cdot\dfrac{14x^2}{4x+2}$

9. $\dfrac{a^2-4}{a+3}\cdot\dfrac{2a+6}{a^2-3x-10}$

10. $\dfrac{5x-x^2}{x+7}\cdot\dfrac{x^2+10x+21}{x^3-2x^2-15x}$

11. $\dfrac{x^4-y^4}{x^2+y^2}\cdot\dfrac{5}{(x-y)^2}$

12. $\dfrac{a^3+b^3}{a^2-b^2}\cdot\dfrac{a+b}{a^2-ab+b^2}$

13. $\dfrac{a^2+10a+16}{a^2-64}\cdot\dfrac{a^2-11a+24}{a^2-7a-18}$

14. $\dfrac{a^2+12a+35}{a^2+11a+28}\cdot\dfrac{a^2+6a+8}{a^2-25}$

15. $\dfrac{x^2+7x+12}{x^2+12x+27}\cdot\dfrac{x^2+10x+9}{x^2+15x+44}$

16. $\dfrac{x^2+9x-10}{x^2+13x+30}\cdot\dfrac{x^2+9x+18}{x^2+11x-12}$

17. $\dfrac{x^2+5xy+6y^2}{x^2+12xy+27y^2}\cdot\dfrac{x^2+13xy+36y^2}{x^2+5xy+4y^2}$

18. $\dfrac{x^2+2xy-15y^2}{x^2-10xy+21y^2}\cdot\dfrac{x^2-6xy-7y^2}{x^2+7xy+10y^2}$

19. $\dfrac{2x^2+7x+3}{x^2+7x+12} \cdot \dfrac{x^2-16}{4x^2-1}$

20. $\dfrac{3x^2+14x+8}{5x^2+19x-4} \cdot \dfrac{5x^2+4x-1}{3x^2+11x+6}$

Divide.

21. $\dfrac{2x^2}{3y^3} \div \dfrac{8x^3}{9y^2}$

22. $\dfrac{7a^2b}{6ab^2} \div \dfrac{21a^2}{18b^2}$

23. $\dfrac{15x^3y^5}{14x^4y^2} \div \dfrac{35x^2y^2}{28xy}$

24. $\dfrac{18ab^3}{5ab} \div 6ab^2$

25. $14x^5y^8 \div \dfrac{42x^6y^4}{9xy}$

26. $\dfrac{27a^3b^2}{14ab^4} \div \dfrac{54a^2b}{35ab^2}$

27. $\dfrac{3x+6}{5x^3} \div \dfrac{x^2-4}{15x^4}$

28. $\dfrac{18xy}{4x+12} \div \dfrac{27x^2y^2}{x^2+3x}$

29. $\dfrac{x^3-27}{x+3} \div \dfrac{x^2+3x+9}{x^2-9}$

30. $\dfrac{x^2-5x-36}{x^2+7x-8} \div \dfrac{x^2-4x-45}{x^2+13x+40}$

31. $\dfrac{x^2+9x-22}{x^2+14x+33} \div \dfrac{x^2+7x+10}{x^2+8x+15}$

32. $\dfrac{x^2+9x+20}{x^2+3x-10} \div \dfrac{x^2-16}{x^3-8}$

33. $\dfrac{x^3+27}{9x^2-1} \div \dfrac{(x+3)^2}{(3x-1)^2}$

34. $\dfrac{x^2-xy-20y^2}{x^2+3xy-40y^2} \div \dfrac{x^2+5xy+4y^2}{x^2+7xy-8y^2}$

35. $\dfrac{x^2+13xy+30y^2}{x^2+6xy-40y^2} \div \dfrac{x^2-8xy-20y^2}{x^2-14xy+40y^2}$

36. $\dfrac{6x^2+4x+3xy+2y}{8x^2-2x+4xy-y} \div \dfrac{3x^2+17x+10}{4x^2+11x-3}$

37. $\dfrac{5x^2+14x-3}{2x^2+13x+20} \div \dfrac{25x^2-10x+1}{5x^2+19x-4}$

38. $\dfrac{3x^2+2x-1}{x^2+13x+12} \div \dfrac{x^2-4x+3}{x^2+11x-12}$

39. $\dfrac{4x^2+11x+6}{x^2+22x+40} \div \dfrac{x^2-14x-15}{x^2+21x+20}$

Perform the indicated operations.

40. $\dfrac{x^2+10x+16}{x^2+10x+24} \cdot \dfrac{x^2+11x+30}{x^2+13x+40} \div \dfrac{x^3+8}{x^2-16}$

41. $\dfrac{4a+6}{a^2-5a-50} \cdot \dfrac{a^2+10a+25}{2a^2+13a+15} \div \dfrac{2a^3-8a}{a^4-16}$

42. $\dfrac{y^2-100}{x^2-25} \div \dfrac{y^2(x-3)+6y(x-3)-40(x-3)}{x^2(y-4)+2x(y-4)-15(y-4)}$

7.3 FINDING THE LEAST COMMON DENOMINATOR (LCD)

□ **Finding the Least Common Denominator (LCD)**
□ **Writing Rational Expressions in Terms of the LCD of Their Denominators**

In this section, our goal is to review the preliminary steps used for addition and subtraction of rational expressions. There are two steps to follow before adding and subtracting rational expressions with different denominators:

Step 1 Find the least common denominator (LCD).

Step 2 Rewrite each rational expression in terms of the common denominator.

□ FINDING THE LEAST COMMON DENOMINATOR (LCD)

In section 1.6 we discussed in detail how to find the least common denominator (LCD) when adding or subtracting fractions involving numbers. In this section, we will expand the same procedure to add or subtract rational expressions.

> **Strategy for finding the least common denominator of two or more rational expressions:**
>
> **Step 1** Factor each denominator completely and write repeated factors in exponential form.
>
> **Step 2** Choose common and uncommon factors with the largest exponents.
>
> **Step 3** Multiply those factors to obtain the LCD.

Note: The least common denominator (LCD) contains all the factors of each denominator.

Example 1
___

Find the LCD.

$$\frac{1}{12xy^3z}, \quad \frac{1}{18x^2y}$$

Solution

$$12xy^3z = 2^2 \cdot 3 \cdot x \cdot y^3 \cdot z$$

$$18x^2y = 2 \cdot 3^2 \cdot x^2 \cdot y$$
___
$$LCD = 2^2 \cdot 3^2 \cdot x^2 \cdot y^3 = 36x^2y^3z$$

Example 2

Find the LCD.

$$\frac{8}{x}, \frac{9}{2x+1}$$

Solution

$$x = x$$
$$2x + 1 = 2x + 1$$
$$\overline{\text{LCD} = x(2x + 1)}$$

Example 3

Find the LCD.

$$\frac{15x}{x+2}, \frac{x+7}{x^2+7x+10}$$

Solution

$$x + 2 = x + 2$$
$$x^2 + 7x + 10 = (x + 2)(x + 5)$$
$$\overline{\text{LCD} = (x + 2)(x + 5)}$$

Example 4

Find the LCD.

$$\frac{2xy}{x^2-4}, \frac{3x^2}{x^2-4x+4}$$

Solution

$$x^2 - 4 = (x - 2)(x + 2)$$
$$x^2 - 4x + 4 = (x - 2)^2$$
$$\overline{\text{LCD} = (x - 2)^2(x + 2)}$$

Example 5

Find the LCD.

$$\frac{3a+7}{a^2+10a+24}, \frac{5a}{a^2+6a+8}$$

Solution

$$a^2 + 10a + 24 = (a + 4)(a + 6)$$
$$a^2 + 6a + 8 = (a + 4)(a + 2)$$
$$\overline{\text{LCD} = (a + 4)(a + 2)(a + 6)}$$

Example 6

Find the LCD.

$$\frac{x+9}{x^2+3x} \ , \quad \frac{2x+1}{x^2+10x+21} \ , \quad \frac{x^2+4}{x^2-49}$$

Solution

$$x^2+3x = x(x+3)$$
$$x^2+10x+21 = (x+3)(x+7)$$
$$\underline{x^2-49 = \qquad (x+7)(x-7)}$$
$$LCD = x(x+3)(x+7)(x-7)$$

Example 7

Find the LCD.

$$\frac{1}{a-2} \ , \quad \frac{11}{2-a}$$

Solution

$$a-2 = a-2$$
$$\underline{2-a = -(a-2)}$$
$$LCD = a-2$$

Note: The negative sign is an uncommon factor and should be taken. However, using the property $\dfrac{a}{-b} = \dfrac{-a}{b} = -\dfrac{a}{b}$, the negative sign from the denominator can be placed in front of the fraction bar and the fractions become $\dfrac{1}{a-2}$, $-\dfrac{11}{a-2}$.
It is obvious that the least common denominator for the last two fractions written in this form is $LCD = a-2$

Example 8

Find the LCD.

$$\frac{4x+1}{1-2x} \ , \quad \frac{x+5}{2x^2+5x-3}$$

Solution

$$1-2x = -(2x-1)$$
$$\underline{2x^2+5x-3 = (2x-1)(x+3)}$$
$$LCD = (2x-1)(x+3)$$

The next step before adding and subtracting rational expressions is to rewrite each rational expression as an equivalent rational expression with the least common denominator.

☐ WRITING RATIONAL EXPRESSIONS IN TERMS OF THE LCD OF THEIR DENOMINATORS

Example 9

Write each rational expression with the indicated denominator.

a. $\dfrac{a}{a-3} = \dfrac{?}{2(a-3)(a+2)}$ b. $\dfrac{3}{5x} = \dfrac{?}{15x^3}$ c. $\dfrac{5x}{x+1} = \dfrac{?}{x^2+5x+4}$

Solution

a. Compare the denominators $a-3$ and $2(a-3)(a+2)$ to find out what factors are missing in the first denominator.

The missing factors can be found by inspection or dividing $\dfrac{2(a-3)(a+2)}{a-3} = 2(a+2)$.

Next, multiply the fraction $\dfrac{a}{a-3}$ by $\dfrac{2(a+2)}{2(a+2)} = 1$.

$$\dfrac{a}{a-3} \cdot \dfrac{2(a+2)}{2(a+2)} = \dfrac{2a(a+2)}{2(a-3)(a+2)}$$

b. Then, factor the denominator $15x^3 = 3 \cdot 5 \cdot x^3$.

Next, compare the denominators $5x$ and $3 \cdot 5 \cdot x^3$ to decide what factors are missing in the denominator $5x$.

$$\dfrac{3 \cdot 5 \cdot x^3}{5x} = 3x^2$$

So, the missing factors are $3x^2$. Then, multiply the fraction $\dfrac{3}{5x}$ by $\dfrac{3x^2}{3x^2} = 1$.

$$\dfrac{3}{5x} \cdot \dfrac{3x^2}{3x^2} = \dfrac{9x^2}{15x^3}$$

c. Factor $x^2 + 5x + 4 = (x+1)(x+4)$. Compare the denominators $x+1$ and $(x+1)(x+4)$ to decide what factors are missing. By inspection, we can see that the factor $x+4$ is missing. Then, multiply $\dfrac{5x}{x+1}$ by $\dfrac{x+4}{x+4}$ to obtain:

$$\dfrac{5x}{x+1} \cdot \dfrac{x+4}{x+4} = \dfrac{5x(x+4)}{(x+1)(x+4)} = \dfrac{5x(x+4)}{x^2+5x+4}$$

Example 10

Write each rational expression with the indicated denominator.

a. $\dfrac{12x}{5x-15}=\dfrac{?}{10x^2-30x}$

b. $\dfrac{11x+1}{x^2+11x+28}=\dfrac{?}{(x+4)(x+7)(x+1)}$

Solution

a. Factor each denominator: $5x-15=5(x-3)$, $10x^2-30x=10x(x-3)=2\cdot5\cdot x(x-3)$. Compare the denominators $5(x-3)$ and $2\cdot5\cdot x(x-3)$ to decide what factors are missing.

By inspection we can see that the factor $2x$ is missing. Multiply $\dfrac{12x}{5x-15}$ by $\dfrac{2x}{2x}$.

$$\dfrac{12x}{5x-15}\cdot\dfrac{2x}{2x}=\dfrac{12x}{5(x-3)}\cdot\dfrac{2x}{2x}=\dfrac{24x}{10x(x-3)}=\dfrac{24x}{10x^2-30x}$$

b. Factor $x^2+11x+28=(x+7)(x+4)$ and compare with $(x+7)(x+4)(x+1)$. The missing factor is $x+1$. Thus, multiply $\dfrac{11x+1}{x^2+11x+28}$ by $\dfrac{x+1}{x+1}$.

$$\dfrac{11x+1}{x^2+11x+28}\cdot\dfrac{x+1}{x+1}=\dfrac{(11x+1)(x+1)}{(x^2+11x+28)(x+1)}=\dfrac{(11x+1)(x+1)}{(x+7)(x+4)(x+1)}$$

Example 11

Write each rational expression with the given denominator.

a. $\dfrac{2a+3}{a^2-2a+4}=\dfrac{?}{a^3+8}$

b. $\dfrac{-x}{2x^2+11x+12}=\dfrac{?}{(2x+3)(x+4)(x-5)}$

Solution

a. Factor $a^3+8=a^3+2^3=(a+2)(a^2-2a+4)$ and compare with a^2-2a+4. The missing factor is $a+2$. So, multiply $\dfrac{2a+3}{a^2-2a+4}$ by $\dfrac{a+2}{a+2}$.

$$\dfrac{2a+3}{a^2-2a+4}\cdot\dfrac{a+2}{a+2}=\dfrac{(2a+3)(a+2)}{(a^2-2a+4)(a+2)}=\dfrac{(2a+3)(a+2)}{a^3+8}$$

b. Factor $2x^2+11x+12=2x^2+8x+3x+12=2x(x+4)+3(x+4)=(2x+3)(x+4)$. Compare the denominators $(2x+3)(x+4)$ and $(2x+3)(x+4)(x-5)$ to decide what factors are missing.

The missing factor is $x-5$. Then, multiply $\dfrac{-x}{2x^2+11x+12}$ by $\dfrac{x-5}{x-5}$.

$$\dfrac{-x}{2x^2+11x+12}\cdot\dfrac{x-5}{x-5}=\dfrac{-x(x-5)}{(2x^2+11x+12)(x-5)}=\dfrac{-x(x-5)}{(2x+3)(x+4)(x-5)}$$

Example 12

Write the rational expression with the given denominator.

$$\frac{10}{x-4} = \frac{?}{4-x}$$

Solution

Since $4-x = -1(x-4)$ the missing factor is -1. Multiply $\dfrac{10}{x-4}$ by $\dfrac{-1}{-1}$.

$$\frac{10}{x-4} \cdot \frac{-1}{-1} = \frac{-10}{-1(x-4)} = \frac{-10}{-x+4} = \frac{-10}{4-x} = -\frac{10}{4-x}$$

7.3 EXERCISES

Find the LCD.

1. $\dfrac{5}{21x}, \dfrac{9}{14x^2}$

2. $\dfrac{2}{9x^2}, \dfrac{-4}{15x^3}$

3. $\dfrac{1}{8a^4b}, \dfrac{6}{40b^2}$

4. $\dfrac{-3}{12ab}, \dfrac{11}{20a^2c}$

5. $\dfrac{7}{18x^2y^3}, \dfrac{13}{24x^3yz^2}$

6. $\dfrac{17}{10xy^2z}, \dfrac{19}{14x^3yz^2}$

7. $\dfrac{4x}{x+3}, \dfrac{5}{2x+6}$

8. $\dfrac{x-1}{x-2}, \dfrac{x^2}{x^2-2x}$

9. $\dfrac{14}{3a-6}, \dfrac{15x}{12a-24}$

10. $\dfrac{2a}{a^2-1}, \dfrac{a-5}{a^2+2a-3}$

11. $\dfrac{x+1}{x^2-4}, \dfrac{x-1}{x^2-4x+4}$

12. $\dfrac{2x}{x^2+3x}, \dfrac{x^3}{x^2+7x+12}$

13. $\dfrac{7}{a+2}, \dfrac{9}{a+5}$

14. $\dfrac{a+1}{a-3}, \dfrac{a-1}{3-a}$

15. $\dfrac{-1}{2a-5}, \dfrac{-3}{10-4a}$

16. $\dfrac{1}{x^2-5x}, \dfrac{x+2}{x^2-7x+10}$

17. $\dfrac{6}{x^2+13x+30}, \dfrac{x}{x^2+6x+9}$

18. $\dfrac{2x-1}{x^2+9x+20}$, $\dfrac{2x+1}{x^2-2x-24}$

21. $\dfrac{a}{a^2-25}$, $\dfrac{2a+3}{a^2-10a+25}$

19. $\dfrac{3a}{a^2+5a-36}$, $\dfrac{a^3}{a^2+10a+9}$

22. $\dfrac{2}{x^2-9}$, $\dfrac{-3}{x^3+27}$

20. $\dfrac{1}{a^2-16}$, $\dfrac{1}{a^2-6a+8}$

23. $\dfrac{x+10}{x^2-2x+4}$, $\dfrac{x+6}{x^3+8}$

24. $\dfrac{5x+1}{x^2+3x+2}$, $\dfrac{4x}{x^2+5x+6}$, $\dfrac{x+5}{x^2+4x+3}$

25. $\dfrac{x-3}{x^2-3x-10}$, $\dfrac{x+1}{x^2+10x+16}$, $\dfrac{9x}{x^2+3x-40}$

26. $\dfrac{a+15}{a^2+7a-8}$, $\dfrac{a-4}{a^2-4a+3}$, $\dfrac{a^2-1}{a^2+5a-24}$

27. $\dfrac{8}{2a^2+7a-4}$, $\dfrac{12}{3a^2+14a+8}$, $\dfrac{16}{6a^2+a-2}$

Write each rational expression with the indicated denominator.

28. $\dfrac{3}{2x}=\dfrac{?}{16x}$

29. $\dfrac{4}{5a}=\dfrac{?}{15a}$

30. $\dfrac{-1}{7x}=\dfrac{?}{21x^3}$

31. $\dfrac{-5}{4x^2}=\dfrac{?}{32x^4}$

32. $\dfrac{2a}{3a+6}=\dfrac{?}{15a+30}$

33. $\dfrac{a-1}{2a+10}=\dfrac{?}{10a+50}$

34. $\dfrac{5}{2-x}=\dfrac{?}{3(x-2)}$

35. $\dfrac{x}{3x-2}=\dfrac{?}{4-6x}$

36. $\dfrac{11x}{x+4}=\dfrac{?}{5(x+4)^2}$

37. $\dfrac{21x}{x^2+3x}=\dfrac{?}{x(x+3)(x-1)}$

38. $\dfrac{15x}{x^2-7x}=\dfrac{?}{x(x-7)(x+4)}$

39. $\dfrac{x-4}{x^2-8x+15} = \dfrac{?}{(x-5)(x-3)(x+1)}$

40. $\dfrac{3x+5}{x^2-8x+12} = \dfrac{?}{(x-2)(x-6)(x+2)}$

41. $\dfrac{6x-1}{x^2+6x-16} = \dfrac{?}{(x-2)(x+8)(x+5)}$

42. $\dfrac{x^2+3}{x^2+12x+32} = \dfrac{?}{(x+4)(x-1)(x+8)}$

43. $\dfrac{2x}{x^2+x+1} = \dfrac{?}{x^3-1}$

44. $\dfrac{x+2}{x^2-1} = \dfrac{?}{x^4-1}$

45. $\dfrac{a}{a^2-5a} = \dfrac{?}{a^3-25a}$

46. $\dfrac{10a^2}{a^2+3a} = \dfrac{?}{a^3+6a^2+9a}$

47. $\dfrac{x+y}{x^2-4xy+3y^2} = \dfrac{?}{(x-y)(x-3y)(x+2y)}$

48. $\dfrac{3x+2y}{x^2+5xy-14y^2} = \dfrac{?}{(x-2y)(x+7y)(x+y)}$

49. $\dfrac{x+9}{2x^2+11x+12} = \dfrac{?}{(2x+3)(x+4)(x-5)}$

50. $\dfrac{x+1}{3x^2+14x-5} = \dfrac{?}{(3x-1)(x+5)(x+8)}$

51. $\dfrac{x-y}{4x^2+3xy-y^2} = \dfrac{?}{(4x-y)(x+y)(x-y)}$

7.4 ADDITION AND SUBTRACTION OF RATIONAL EXPRESSIONS

□ **Adding and Subtracting Rational Expressions with the Same Denominator** □ **Adding and Subtracting Rational Expressions with Different Denominators**

□ ADDING AND SUBTRACTING RATIONAL EXPRESSIONS WITH THE SAME DENOMINATOR

> **Rule**
>
> If $\dfrac{P}{Q}$ and $\dfrac{R}{Q}$ are rational expressions, then $\dfrac{P}{Q}+\dfrac{R}{Q}=\dfrac{P+R}{Q}$ and $\dfrac{P}{Q}-\dfrac{R}{Q}=\dfrac{P-R}{Q}$.
>
> In other words, to add or subtract rational expressions with the same denominator, add or subtract their numerators and keep the common denominator.

Example 1

Add or subtract.

a. $\dfrac{5}{6x}+\dfrac{7}{6x}$

b. $\dfrac{11}{2a^2}-\dfrac{5}{2a^2}$

Solution

a. $\dfrac{5}{6x}+\dfrac{7}{6x}=\dfrac{5+7}{6x}=\dfrac{12}{6x}=\dfrac{6\cdot 2}{6x}=\dfrac{2}{x}$

b. $\dfrac{11}{2a^2}-\dfrac{5}{2a^2}=\dfrac{11-5}{2a^2}=\dfrac{6}{2a^2}=\dfrac{2\cdot 3}{2a^2}=\dfrac{3}{a^2}$

Example 2

Add or subtract.

a. $\dfrac{4x}{2x+1}+\dfrac{2}{2x+1}$

b. $\dfrac{2a}{a^2-25}-\dfrac{10}{a^2-25}$

Solution

a. $\dfrac{4x}{2x+1}+\dfrac{2}{2x+1}=\dfrac{4x+2}{2x+1}=\dfrac{2(2x+1)}{2x+1}=2$

b. $\dfrac{2a}{a^2-25}-\dfrac{10}{a^2-25}=\dfrac{2a-10}{a^2-25}=\dfrac{2(a-5)}{(a-5)(a+5)}=\dfrac{2}{a+5}$

Example 3

Add or subtract.

a. $\dfrac{x^2+3x+5}{x^2+9x+20}+\dfrac{5x+10}{x^2+9x+20}$

b. $\dfrac{x^2}{x^2-6x+8}-\dfrac{16}{x^2-6x+8}$

Solution

a. $\dfrac{x^2+3x+5}{x^2+9x+20}+\dfrac{5x+10}{x^2+9x+20}=\dfrac{x^2+3x+5+5x+10}{x^2+9x+20}=\dfrac{x^2+8x+15}{x^2+9x+20}=$

$\dfrac{(x+5)(x+3)}{(x+5)(x+4)}=\dfrac{x+3}{x+4}$

b. $\dfrac{x^2}{x^2-6x+8}-\dfrac{16}{x^2-6x+8}=\dfrac{x^2-16}{x^2-6x+8}=\dfrac{(x-4)(x+4)}{(x-4)(x-2)}=\dfrac{x+4}{x-2}$

Example 4

Add or subtract.

$$\dfrac{x^2+7x-4}{x^2+4x-12}+\dfrac{x^2+x-3}{x^2+4x-12}-\dfrac{x^2+x-13}{x^2+4x-12}$$

Solution

$$\dfrac{x^2+7x-4}{x^2+4x-12}+\dfrac{x^2+x-3}{x^2+4x-12}-\dfrac{x^2+x-13}{x^2+4x-12}=$$

$$\dfrac{(x^2+7x-4)+(x^2+x-3)-(x^2+x-13)}{x^2+4x-12}=$$

$$\dfrac{x^2+7x-4+x^2+x-3-x^2-x+13}{x^2+4x-12}=$$

$$\dfrac{x^2+7x+6}{x^2+4x-12}=\dfrac{(x+6)(x+1)}{(x+6)(x-2)}=\dfrac{x+1}{x-2}$$

□ ADDING AND SUBTRACTING RATIONAL EXPRESSIONS WITH DIFFERENT DENOMINATORS

Strategy for adding or subtracting rational expressions with different denominators:

Step 1 Factor each denominator completely.

Step 2 Find the least common denominator (LCD).

Step 3 Rewrite each rational expression as an equivalent rational expression whose denominator is the LCD.

Step 4 Add or subtract the numerators and keep the common denominator.

Step 5 Write the answer in simplest form.

Example 5

Add or subtract.

a. $\dfrac{5}{2x^2y} + \dfrac{1}{7xy^2}$

b. $\dfrac{2}{5a} - \dfrac{3}{10a^2}$

Solution

a. $\dfrac{5}{2x^2y} + \dfrac{1}{7xy^2}$

Step 1 Find the LCD.

$$2x^2y = 2x^2y$$
$$7xy^2 = 7xy^2$$
$$\overline{LCD = 2 \cdot 7 \cdot x^2 \cdot y^2 = 14x^2y^2}$$

Step 2 Rewrite each rational expression in terms of the $LCD = 14x^2y^2$.

First, compare each denominator with the LCD to decide what factors are missing.

If we compare $2x^2y$ and $LCD = 14x^2y^2$, the missing factor is $\dfrac{14x^2y^2}{2x^2y} = 7y$.

If we compare $7xy^2$ and $LCD = 14x^2y^2$, the missing factor is $\dfrac{14x^2y^2}{7xy^2} = 2y$.

Then, $\dfrac{5}{2x^2y} \cdot \dfrac{7y}{7y} + \dfrac{1}{7xy^2} \cdot \dfrac{2y}{2y} = \dfrac{5(7y) + 1(2y)}{14x^2y^2}$

Steps 3 and 4   Add and simplify the answer if possible.

$$\dfrac{5}{2x^2y} + \dfrac{1}{7xy^2} = \dfrac{5(7y) + 1(2y)}{14x^2y^2} = \dfrac{35y + 2y}{14x^2y^2} = \dfrac{37y}{14x^2y^2} = \dfrac{37}{14x^2y}$$

b. $\dfrac{2}{5a} - \dfrac{3}{10a^2}$

Step 1 Find the LCD.

Step 2 Rewrite each rational expression in terms of $LCD = 10a^2$.

Compare each denominator with the LCD to decide what factors are missing.

The missing factor for the first fraction is $\dfrac{10a^2}{5a} = 2a$.

The missing factor for the second fraction is $\dfrac{10a^2}{10a^2} = 1$.

Then, $\dfrac{2}{5a} - \dfrac{3}{10a^2} = \dfrac{2}{5a} \cdot \dfrac{2a}{2a} - \dfrac{3}{10a^2} \cdot \dfrac{1}{1} = \dfrac{2(2a) - 3 \cdot 1}{10a^2}$

Steps 3 and 4   Subtract and simplify (if possible).

$$\dfrac{2}{5a} - \dfrac{3}{10a^2} = \dfrac{2}{5a} \cdot \dfrac{2a}{2a} - \dfrac{3}{10a^2} \cdot \dfrac{1}{1} = \dfrac{2(2a) - 3 \cdot 1}{10a^2} = \dfrac{4a - 3}{10a^2}$$

Example 6

___

Add or subtract.

a. $\dfrac{x}{x+1} + \dfrac{1}{x-1}$

b. $\dfrac{4x-8}{2x-3} - \dfrac{2}{3-2x}$

Solution

a. $\dfrac{x}{x+1} + \dfrac{1}{x-1}$

By inspection, the $LCD = (x+1)(x-1)$.

Multiply each numerator by the missing factor and write the sum as a single fraction with the denominator $LCD = (x+1)(x-1)$.

$$\dfrac{x}{x+1} + \dfrac{1}{x-1} = \dfrac{x(x-1) + 1(x+1)}{(x+1)(x-1)} = \dfrac{x^2 - x + x + 1}{(x+1)(x-1)} = \dfrac{x^2 + 1}{x^2 - 1}$$

b. $\dfrac{4x-8}{2x-3} - \dfrac{2}{3-2x}$

First, rewrite the denominator $3-2x = -1(2x-3)$.

The rational expression becomes: $\dfrac{4x-8}{2x-3} - \dfrac{2}{-1(2x-3)}$

Then, use the property $\dfrac{a}{-b} = \dfrac{-a}{b} = -\dfrac{a}{b}$ to place the negative sign in front of the fraction bar and apply the double negative property $-(-a) = a$ to change the subtraction into addition.

$$\dfrac{4x-8}{2x-3} - \dfrac{2}{-1(2x-3)} = \dfrac{4x-8}{2x-3} - \left(-\dfrac{2}{2x-3}\right) = \dfrac{4x-8}{2x-3} + \dfrac{2}{2x-3} = \dfrac{4x-8+2}{2x-3} =$$

$$\dfrac{4x-6}{2x-3} = \dfrac{2(2x-3)}{2x-3} = 2$$

Example 7

Add.

$$\dfrac{x+1}{x^2+5x+6} + \dfrac{3x}{x^2-2x-8}$$

Solution

Factor each denominator if possible.

$$\dfrac{x+1}{x^2+5x+6} + \dfrac{3x}{x^2-2x-8} = \dfrac{x+1}{(x+2)(x+3)} + \dfrac{3x}{(x+2)(x-4)}$$

By inspection, the $LCD = (x+2)(x+3)(x-4)$

Multiply each numerator by the missing factors and write the sum as a single fraction with the denominator $LCD = (x+2)(x+3)(x-4)$

$$\dfrac{(x+1)(x-4)+3x(x+3)}{(x+2)(x+3)(x-4)} = \dfrac{x^2-4x+x-4+3x^2+9x}{(x+2)(x+3)(x-4)} =$$

$$\dfrac{4x^2+6x-4}{(x+2)(x+3)(x-4)} = \dfrac{2(2x^2+3x-2)}{(x+21)(x+3)(x-4)} = \dfrac{2(2x^2+4x-x-2)}{(x+2)(x+3)(x-4)} =$$

$$\dfrac{2[2x(x+2)-1(x+2)]}{(x+2)(x+3)(x-4)} = \dfrac{2[(x+2)(2x-1)]}{(x+2)(x+3)(x-4)} = \dfrac{2(2x-1)}{(x+3)(x-4)}$$

Example 8

Subtract.

$$\frac{3x-6}{x^2-4} - \frac{2x}{x^2+4x+4}$$

Solution

Factor each denominator if possible.

$$\frac{3x-6}{(x-2)(x+2)} - \frac{2x}{(x+2)(x+2)} = \frac{3x-6}{(x-2)(x+2)} - \frac{2x}{(x+2)^2}$$

By inspection, the $LCD = (x-2)(x+2)^2$

Multiply each numerator by the missing factors and write the sum as a single fraction with the denominator $LCD = (x-2)(x+2)^2$

$$\frac{(3x-6)(x+2)-2x(x-2)}{(x-2)(x+2^2} = \frac{3x^2+6x-6x-12-2x^2+4x}{(x-2)(x+2)^2} =$$

$$\frac{x^2+4x-12}{(x-2)(x+2)^2} = \frac{(x-2)(x+6)}{(x-2)(x+2)^2} = \frac{x+6}{(x+2)^2}$$

Example 9

Simplify.

$$\frac{x+4}{x+2} + \frac{x+1}{x-2} - \frac{12}{x^2-4}$$

Solution

Factor each denominator if possible.

$$\frac{x+4}{x+2} + \frac{x+1}{x-2} - \frac{12}{x^2-4} = \frac{x+4}{x+2} + \frac{x+1}{x-2} - \frac{12}{(x+2)(x-2)}$$

By inspection, the $LCD = (x+2)(x-2)$.

Multiply each numerator by the missing factors and write the sum as a single fraction with the denominator $LCD = (x+2)(x-2)$.

$$\frac{(x+4)(x-2)+(x+1)(x+2)-12}{(x+2)(x-2)} = \frac{x^2-2x+4x-8+x^2+2x+x+2-12}{(x-2)(x+2)} =$$

$$\frac{2x^2+5x-18}{(x-2)(x+2)} = \frac{2x^2-4x+9x-18}{(x-2)(x+2)} = \frac{2x(x-2)+9(x-2)}{(x-2)(x+2)} = \frac{(x-2)(2x+9)}{(x-2)(x+2)} = \frac{2x+9}{x+2}$$

Example 10

Simplify.

$$\frac{x+2}{x+3} + \frac{3}{x-4} - \frac{21}{x^2-x-12}$$

Solution

Factor each denominator, if possible.

$$\frac{x+2}{x+3} + \frac{3}{x-4} - \frac{21}{x^2-x-12} = \frac{x+2}{x+3} + \frac{3}{x-4} - \frac{21}{(x-4)(x+3)}$$

By inspection, the $LCD = (x-4)(x+3)$

Multiply each numerator by the missing factors and write the sum and difference as a single fraction with the denominator $LCD = (x-4)(x+3)$.

$$\frac{(x+2)(x-4)+3(x+3)-21}{(x-4)(x+3)} = \frac{x^2-4x+2x-8+3x+9-21}{(x-4)(x+3)} =$$

$$\frac{x^2+x-20}{(x-4)(x+3)} = \frac{(x+5)(x-4)}{(x-4)(x+3)} = \frac{x+5}{x+3}$$

7.4 **EXERCISES**

Add or subtract. Write each answer in simplest form.

1. $\dfrac{2}{x^2} + \dfrac{3}{x^2}$

2. $\dfrac{4}{y} - \dfrac{1}{y}$

3. $\dfrac{5}{3x} - \dfrac{8}{3x}$

4. $\dfrac{11}{4a} + \dfrac{9}{4a}$

5. $\dfrac{x-3}{x-2} + \dfrac{1}{x-2}$

6. $\dfrac{x+5}{x+7} + \dfrac{2}{x+7}$

7. $\dfrac{x^2}{x-3} - \dfrac{9}{x-3}$

8. $\dfrac{a^2}{a+5} - \dfrac{25}{a+5}$

9. $\dfrac{2a+3}{a-4} - \dfrac{a+7}{a-4}$

10. $\dfrac{5y-4}{y+6} + \dfrac{y+40}{y+6}$

11. $\dfrac{x^2+6x}{x+3} + \dfrac{9}{x+3}$

12. $\dfrac{x^2-10x}{x-5} + \dfrac{25}{x-5}$

13. $\dfrac{y^2}{y^2+3y+2} - \dfrac{y+6}{y^2+3y+2}$

14. $\dfrac{y^2-5}{y^2+6y+5}+\dfrac{3y-5}{y^2+6y+5}$

15. $\dfrac{x^2-3x+4}{x^2-7x+12}+\dfrac{x^2+x-1}{x^2-7x+12}-\dfrac{x^2-7x+27}{x^2-7x+12}$

16. $\dfrac{x^2-x+8}{x^2+8x+15}-\dfrac{x^2+2x-5}{x^2+8x+15}+\dfrac{x^2+15x+22}{x^2+8x+15}$

Simplify.

17. $\dfrac{x+4}{3}+\dfrac{x+1}{6}$

18. $\dfrac{3x-1}{6}-\dfrac{2x-4}{4}$

19. $\dfrac{2x+3}{2x}-\dfrac{3x+4}{3x}$

20. $\dfrac{4y+1}{12y}+\dfrac{3y+12}{18y}$

21. $\dfrac{2}{3x^3y^2}+\dfrac{6}{4xy^3}$

22. $\dfrac{7}{6xy}-\dfrac{12}{8x^2}$

23. $\dfrac{x-1}{x+2}-\dfrac{2}{x+3}$

24. $\dfrac{x+3}{x-1}+\dfrac{2-x}{x+4}$

25. $\dfrac{x+5}{x+8}-\dfrac{x}{x+3}$

26. $\dfrac{x+1}{x-2}+\dfrac{x-1}{x+2}$

27. $\dfrac{x}{x+4}+\dfrac{4}{x-4}$

28. $\dfrac{2x-5}{x-8}+\dfrac{x+3}{8-x}$

29. $\dfrac{3x+1}{x-1}-\dfrac{x-5}{1-x}$

30. $\dfrac{x+1}{3x+4}-\dfrac{5x+6}{6x+8}$

31. $\dfrac{x+11}{2x-1}+\dfrac{2x-24}{4x-2}$

32. $\dfrac{x+2}{x-6}-\dfrac{10x+36}{x^2-36}$

33. $\dfrac{12x+28}{x^2-49}+\dfrac{x+3}{x+7}$

34. $\dfrac{x^2+1}{x-3}-\dfrac{24+x-3x^2}{x^2-6x+9}$

35. $\dfrac{8-2x^2}{x^2+4x+4}+\dfrac{x^2}{x+2}$

36. $\dfrac{5}{x^2-25}-\dfrac{4}{x^2-2x-15}$

37. $\dfrac{6}{x^2-1}+\dfrac{3}{x^2-3x+2}$

38. $\dfrac{14}{x^2-2x-48}-\dfrac{3}{x^2+9x+18}$

39. $\dfrac{8}{x^2-5x+6} - \dfrac{2}{x^2-x-2}$

40. $\dfrac{x}{x^2+x-6} - \dfrac{3}{5(x^2+7x+12)}$

41. $\dfrac{x+6}{x^2-9x+20} + \dfrac{2-x}{x^2-5x+4}$

42. $\dfrac{3x+4}{3x^2+2x-5} - \dfrac{x}{x^2+3x-4}$

43. $\dfrac{2x-1}{x^2+3x+2} - \dfrac{x-2}{x^2-3x-4}$

44. $\dfrac{x+1}{x-3} + \dfrac{x}{x+3} + \dfrac{10x+12}{x^2-9}$

45. $\dfrac{x-2}{x+4} + \dfrac{3}{x-4} - \dfrac{24}{x^2-16}$

46. $\dfrac{x+2}{x+6} + \dfrac{2}{x-6} - \dfrac{24}{x^2-36}$

47. $\dfrac{x+5}{x+1} - \dfrac{2}{x-1} + \dfrac{4}{x^2-1}$

48. $\dfrac{x-4}{x+2} - \dfrac{3}{x+3} - \dfrac{3}{x^2+5x+6}$

49. $\dfrac{x+10}{x+6} - \dfrac{4}{x+5} + \dfrac{4}{x^2+11x+30}$

50. $\dfrac{x+6}{x+9} - \dfrac{x}{x-4} - \dfrac{39}{x^2+5x-36}$

51. $\dfrac{x+7}{x+3} + \dfrac{x}{x+8} - \dfrac{20}{x^2+11x+24}$

52. $\dfrac{x+3}{x-5} + \dfrac{x-1}{x+1} + \dfrac{10x-2}{x^2-4x-5}$

53. $\dfrac{x-7}{x+10} + \dfrac{x+1}{x-2} + \dfrac{22x+16}{x^2+8x-20}$

54. $\dfrac{x+4}{x-3} - \dfrac{x+5}{x-4} + \dfrac{3x-2}{x^2-7x+12}$

55. $\dfrac{x+6}{x-7} + \dfrac{x+7}{x-6} - \dfrac{x^2+7x-85}{x^2-13x+42}$

56. $\dfrac{x+1}{2x-1} - \dfrac{x+3}{3x+2} + \dfrac{x^2-17x+3}{6x^2+x-2}$

57. $\dfrac{x+y}{x+3y} + \dfrac{2x-y}{x-4y} + \dfrac{4xy-2y^2}{x^2-xy-12y^2}$

58. $\dfrac{5}{x^2-2x-3} - \dfrac{3}{x^2+5x+4} + \dfrac{7}{x^2+x-12}$

59. $\dfrac{4}{x^2+x-6} - \dfrac{8}{x^2-2x-15} + \dfrac{3}{x^2-7x+10}$

7.5 COMPLEX FRACTIONS

Examples of complex fractions:

a. $\dfrac{\dfrac{1}{x}+\dfrac{1}{y}}{x^2-y^2}$
b. $\dfrac{2x}{\dfrac{1}{x+1}+\dfrac{1}{x-1}}$,
c. $\dfrac{x+\dfrac{1}{x}}{x-\dfrac{1}{x}}$

Definition

A complex fraction is a fraction that contains one or more fractions in its numerator or denominator or both numerator and denominator.

In this section, our goal is to simplify complex fractions. To simplify a complex fraction, simplify the numerator and denominator (if possible) and write the numerator and denominator as single fractions, and then apply the following rule used to divide fractions:

$$\frac{\dfrac{A}{B}}{\dfrac{C}{D}}=\frac{A}{B}\div\frac{C}{D}=\frac{A}{B}\cdot\frac{D}{C}=\frac{AD}{BC}$$

Example 2

Simplify.

$$\frac{1+\dfrac{1}{a}}{1-\dfrac{1}{a^2}}$$

Solution.

The method used in the previous section to add or subtract rational expressions can be used to simplify both the numerator and denominator. The least common denominator for the numerator is $LCD = a$ and for the denominator the $LCD = a^2$.

$$\frac{1+\dfrac{1}{a}}{1-\dfrac{1}{a^2}}=\frac{\dfrac{1}{1}+\dfrac{1}{a}}{\dfrac{1}{1}-\dfrac{1}{a^2}}=\frac{\dfrac{1\cdot a+1}{a}}{\dfrac{1\cdot a^2-1}{a^2}}=\frac{\dfrac{a+1}{a}}{\dfrac{a^2-1}{a^2}}=\frac{a+1}{a}\cdot\frac{a^2}{a^2-1}=\frac{a+1}{a}\cdot\frac{a^2}{(a-1)(a+1)}=\frac{a}{a-1}$$

Example 3

Simplify.

$$\frac{\dfrac{1}{x}+\dfrac{1}{y}}{\dfrac{x^2-y^2}{x}}$$

Solution

By inspection, the least common denominator for the numerator is $LCD = xy$.

$$\frac{\dfrac{1}{x}+\dfrac{1}{y}}{\dfrac{x^2-y^2}{x}}=\frac{\dfrac{1\cdot y+1\cdot x}{xy}}{\dfrac{x^2-y^2}{x}}=\frac{\dfrac{y+x}{xy}}{\dfrac{x^2-y^2}{x}}=\frac{x+y}{xy}\cdot\frac{x}{x^2-y^2}=\frac{x+y}{xy}\cdot\frac{x}{(x-y)(x+y)}=\frac{1}{y(x-y)}$$

Example 4

Simplify.

$$\frac{\dfrac{2}{3}+\dfrac{1}{4}}{\dfrac{2}{5}-\dfrac{1}{2}}$$

Solution

By inspection, the least common denominator for the numerator is LCD = 12 and for the denominator is LCD = 10.

$$\frac{\dfrac{2}{3}+\dfrac{1}{4}}{\dfrac{2}{5}-\dfrac{1}{2}}=\frac{\dfrac{2\cdot4+1\cdot3}{12}}{\dfrac{2\cdot2-1\cdot5}{10}}=\frac{\dfrac{8+3}{12}}{\dfrac{4-5}{10}}=\frac{\dfrac{11}{12}}{\dfrac{-1}{10}}=\frac{11}{12}\cdot\frac{10}{-1}=-\frac{110}{12}=-\frac{55}{6}$$

Example 5

Simplify.

$$\frac{1+\dfrac{8}{x}+\dfrac{15}{x^2}}{1+\dfrac{3}{x}-\dfrac{10}{x^2}}$$

Solution

There is another way (shortcut) to simplify a complex fraction. This method works best when the fractions contained in the numerator have the same common denominator as the fractions contained in the denominator. In our case the $LCD = x^2$ for both.

If we multiply and divide the complex fraction by the $LCD = x^2$, the complex fraction becomes:

$$\frac{1+\dfrac{8}{x}+\dfrac{15}{x^2}}{1+\dfrac{3}{x}-\dfrac{10}{x^2}}\cdot\frac{x^2}{x^2} = \frac{\left(1+\dfrac{8}{x}+\dfrac{15}{x^2}\right)x^2}{\left(1+\dfrac{3}{x}-\dfrac{10}{x^2}\right)x^2} = \frac{1\cdot x^2+\dfrac{8}{x}\cdot x^2+\dfrac{15}{x^2}\cdot x^2}{1\cdot x^2+\dfrac{3}{x}\cdot x^2-\dfrac{10}{x^2}\cdot x^2} = \frac{x^2+8x+15}{x^2+3x-10} = \frac{(x+5)(x+3)}{(x+5)(x-2)} =$$

$$\frac{x+3}{x-2}$$

Example 6

Simplify.

$$\frac{\dfrac{1}{x-1}+\dfrac{1}{x+1}}{\dfrac{2}{x-1}-\dfrac{1}{x+1}}$$

Solution 1

By inspection, the common denominator for the fractions contained in the numerator and denominator is $LCD = (x-1)(x+1)$.

First, multiply each fraction by the missing factor.

$$\frac{\dfrac{1}{x-1}+\dfrac{1}{x+1}}{\dfrac{2}{x-1}-\dfrac{1}{x+1}} = \frac{\dfrac{1(x+1)+1(x-1)}{(x-1)(x+1)}}{\dfrac{2(x+1)-1(x-1)}{(x-1)(x+1)}} = \frac{\dfrac{x+1+x-1}{(x-1)(x+1)}}{\dfrac{2x+2-x+1}{(x-1)(x+1)}} = \frac{\dfrac{2x}{(x-1)(x+1)}}{\dfrac{x+3}{(x-1)(x+1)}} =$$

$$\frac{2x}{(x+1)(x-1)}\cdot\frac{(x-1)(x+1)}{x+3} = \frac{2x}{x+3}$$

Solution 2

Since the common denominator of the fractions contained in the numerator is the same as the common denominator of the fractions contained in denominator, multiply and divide the complex fraction by the $LCD = (x-1)(x+1)$.

$$\frac{\dfrac{1}{x-1}+\dfrac{1}{x+1}}{\dfrac{2}{x-1}-\dfrac{1}{x+1}}\cdot\frac{(x+1)(x-1)}{(x+1)(x-1)} = \frac{\dfrac{1}{x-1}(x+1(x-1)+\dfrac{1}{x+1}(x-1)(x+1)}{\dfrac{2}{x-1}(x-1)(x+1)-\dfrac{1}{x+1}(x-1)(x+1)} =$$

$$\frac{1(x+1)+1(x-1)}{2(x+1)-1(x-1)} = \frac{x+1+x-1}{2x+2-x+1} = \frac{2x}{x+3}$$

Example 7

Simplify.

$$\frac{\dfrac{x+1}{x^2+7x+12}}{\dfrac{x^2-1}{x^2+9x+20}}$$

Solution

$$\frac{\dfrac{x+1}{x^2+7x+12}}{\dfrac{x^2-1}{x^2+9x+20}}=\frac{x+1}{x^2+7x+12}\cdot\frac{x^2+9x+20}{x^2-1}=\frac{x+1}{(x+3)(x+4)}\cdot\frac{(x+4)(x+5)}{(x-1)(x+1)}=$$

$$\frac{x+5}{(x+3)(x-1)}$$

Example 8

Simply.

$$\frac{x^{-1}+x^{-2}}{x^{-1}-x^{-2}}$$

Solution

First, apply the negative exponents rule for exponents: $a^{-n}=\dfrac{1}{a^n}$.

In our case $x^{-1}=\dfrac{1}{x}$ and $x^{-2}=\dfrac{1}{x^2}$. Thus, the complex fraction becomes,

$$\frac{x^{-1}+x^{-2}}{x^{-1}-x^{-2}}=\frac{\dfrac{1}{x}+\dfrac{1}{x^2}}{\dfrac{1}{x}-\dfrac{1}{x^2}}=\frac{\dfrac{1\cdot x+1}{x^2}}{\dfrac{1\cdot x-1}{x^2}}=\frac{\dfrac{x+1}{x^2}}{\dfrac{x-1}{x^2}}=\frac{x+1}{x^2}\cdot\frac{x^2}{x-1}=\frac{x+1}{x-1}$$

Example 9

Simplify.

$$1+\frac{1}{1-\dfrac{1}{3}}$$

Solution

$$1+\frac{1}{1-\dfrac{1}{3}}=1+\frac{1}{\dfrac{1\cdot3-1}{3}}=1+\frac{1}{\dfrac{3-1}{3}}=1+\frac{1}{\dfrac{2}{3}}=1+\frac{1}{\dfrac{2}{3}}=1+\frac{1}{3}\cdot\frac{3}{2}=1+\frac{3}{2}=\frac{1\cdot2+3}{2}=\frac{2+3}{2}=\frac{5}{2}$$

7.5 EXERCISES

Simplify each complex fraction.

1. $\dfrac{\dfrac{6}{5}}{\dfrac{18}{30}}$

2. $\dfrac{\dfrac{8}{7}}{\dfrac{4}{21}}$

3. $\dfrac{\dfrac{3x}{2y}}{\dfrac{x^2}{6y^3}}$

4. $\dfrac{\dfrac{5a^2}{3b}}{\dfrac{15a}{12b^2}}$

5. $\dfrac{\dfrac{1}{2}+\dfrac{3}{4}}{\dfrac{1}{4}+\dfrac{2}{8}}$

6. $\dfrac{\dfrac{3}{2}-\dfrac{6}{5}}{\dfrac{3}{5}-\dfrac{1}{10}}$

7. $\dfrac{\dfrac{5}{x+1}}{\dfrac{y}{x^2-1}}$

8. $\dfrac{\dfrac{4}{x+2}}{\dfrac{x-2}{x^2-4}}$

9. $\dfrac{\dfrac{x+1}{y^2-16}}{\dfrac{x^2-1}{y+4}}$

10. $\dfrac{\dfrac{x^2+7x+10}{x^2+4x+3}}{\dfrac{x^2+4x-5}{x^2+2x-3}}$

11. $\dfrac{\dfrac{x^2-2x-8}{x^2+4x-12}}{\dfrac{x^2-5x+4}{x^2+5x-6}}$

12. $\dfrac{\dfrac{x^2-9}{x^2-y^2}}{\dfrac{x^3-27}{x+y}}$

13. $\dfrac{1-\dfrac{1}{x}}{x-\dfrac{1}{x}}$

14. $\dfrac{\dfrac{1}{16}-\dfrac{1}{x^2}}{\dfrac{1}{4}-\dfrac{1}{x}}$

15. $\dfrac{\dfrac{1}{a}-2}{\dfrac{1}{a^2}-4}$

16. $\dfrac{\dfrac{1}{a^2}-9}{\dfrac{1}{a}-3}$

17. $\dfrac{\dfrac{36}{x}-x}{\dfrac{6}{x}+1}$

18. $\dfrac{\dfrac{2}{x^2}-\dfrac{1}{x}}{\dfrac{4}{x^2}-1}$

19. $\dfrac{\dfrac{1}{x}-\dfrac{1}{y}}{\dfrac{1}{x^2}-\dfrac{1}{y^2}}$

20. $\dfrac{\dfrac{1}{x}+\dfrac{1}{y}}{\dfrac{x^2-y^2}{xy}}$

21. $\dfrac{\dfrac{2}{x}-\dfrac{1}{x+1}}{\dfrac{x^2-4}{x+1}}$

22. $\dfrac{1+\dfrac{1}{x+1}}{2-\dfrac{x}{x+1}}$

23. $\dfrac{1-\dfrac{5}{x^2-4}}{1-\dfrac{1}{x-2}}$

24. $\dfrac{\dfrac{2}{x+2}-\dfrac{1}{x}}{\dfrac{1}{x-6}+\dfrac{1}{x+2}}$

25. $\dfrac{x - \dfrac{6}{x+1}}{x - \dfrac{3}{x+2}}$

31. $\dfrac{\dfrac{1}{x+5} - \dfrac{1}{x+6}}{\dfrac{1}{x+5} - \dfrac{1}{x+7}}$

37. $\dfrac{\dfrac{x}{x+y} + \dfrac{y}{x-y}}{\dfrac{x^2 + y^2}{x^2 - y^2}}$

26. $\dfrac{x - \dfrac{24}{x+2}}{x - \dfrac{12}{x+4}}$

32. $\dfrac{\dfrac{4}{x+4} - \dfrac{3}{x+3}}{\dfrac{4}{x+4} - \dfrac{5}{x+5}}$

38. $\dfrac{5x^{-1} - 4x^{-2}}{25 - 16x^{-2}}$

27. $\dfrac{\dfrac{2}{x} - \dfrac{1}{x+1}}{\dfrac{1}{x} + \dfrac{1}{x+1}}$

33. $\dfrac{\dfrac{2x}{x+6} - \dfrac{x}{x+3}}{\dfrac{3x}{x+3} - \dfrac{2x}{x+2}}$

39. $\dfrac{2x^{-1} - 3x^{-2}}{4 - 9x^{-2}}$

40. $\dfrac{1 + x^{-1} - 56x^{-2}}{1 + 5x^{-1} - 24x^{-2}}$

28. $\dfrac{\dfrac{3}{2x} - \dfrac{1}{x+1}}{\dfrac{3}{x} - \dfrac{1}{2x+1}}$

34. $\dfrac{\dfrac{x-1}{x+1} - \dfrac{x+1}{x-1}}{\dfrac{x-1}{x+1} + \dfrac{x+1}{x-1}}$

41. $2 + \dfrac{2}{2 + \dfrac{1}{2}}$

29. $\dfrac{\dfrac{2}{x+2} - \dfrac{1}{x+1}}{\dfrac{1}{x+2} + \dfrac{1}{x-2}}$

35. $\dfrac{1 + \dfrac{11}{x} + \dfrac{24}{x^2}}{1 + \dfrac{4}{x} - \dfrac{32}{x^2}}$

42. $\dfrac{x - \dfrac{x}{1 - \dfrac{1}{x}}}{}$

30. $\dfrac{\dfrac{3}{x+4} - \dfrac{2}{x+3}}{\dfrac{4}{x-7} + \dfrac{1}{x+3}}$

36. $\dfrac{1 + \dfrac{1}{x} - \dfrac{30}{x^2}}{1 + \dfrac{8}{x} + \dfrac{12}{x^2}}$

43. $\dfrac{\dfrac{1}{x^2 - x - 2} - \dfrac{1}{x^2 + x - 6}}{\dfrac{1}{x^2 + 4x + 3} + \dfrac{1}{x^2 + x - 6}}$

44. $\dfrac{\dfrac{1}{x^2 - 2x - 8} - \dfrac{1}{x^2 - x - 12}}{\dfrac{1}{x^2 + 5x + 6} - \dfrac{1}{x^2 + 6x + 9}}$

7.6 SOLVING RATIONAL EQUATIONS

□ Rational Equations

□ RATIONAL EQUATIONS

Examples of rational equations:

a. $\dfrac{1}{x-1} + \dfrac{4}{x+2} = 2$

c. $\dfrac{x}{x-2} + \dfrac{4}{x+2} = \dfrac{5x+4}{x^2-4}$

b. $\dfrac{x+1}{x+3} - \dfrac{1}{x+4} = \dfrac{x+5}{x^2+7x+12}$

Definition

A **rational equation** is an equation that contains one or more rational expressions.

Strategy for solving a rational equation:

Step 1 Find the least common denominator (LCD).

Step 2 Clear denominators. Multiply both sides of the equation by the LCD.

Step 3 Solve the resulting equation.

Step 4 Check the solution(s).

Example 1

Solve.

$$\dfrac{2x+1}{2} - \dfrac{x}{3} = \dfrac{x-3}{6}$$

Solution

Step 1 Find the LCD. By inspection the LCD = 6.

Step 2 Clear denominators. Multiply both sides of the equation by the LCD = 6.

$$6 \cdot \dfrac{2x+1}{2} - 6 \cdot \dfrac{x}{3} = 6 \cdot \dfrac{x-3}{6} \qquad \text{Simplify.}$$

$$3(2x+1) - 2x = x - 3 \qquad \text{Apply the distributive property.}$$

Step 3 Solve the resulting equation.

$\quad\quad 6x + 3 - 2x = x - 3$ Simplify

$\quad\quad 4x + 3 = x - 3$ Use the addition property to isolate x

$\quad\quad 4x - x = -3 - 3$ Simplify

$\quad\quad 3x = -6$ Divide both sides of the equation by 3

$\quad\quad \dfrac{3x}{3} = \dfrac{-6}{3}$

$\quad\quad x = -2$

Step 4 Check the solution.

$\quad\quad \dfrac{2(-2)+1}{2} - \dfrac{-2}{3} = \dfrac{-2-3}{6}$

$\quad\quad \dfrac{-4+1}{2} + \dfrac{2}{3} = \dfrac{-5}{6},\quad \dfrac{-3}{2} + \dfrac{2}{3} = \dfrac{-5}{6},\quad \dfrac{-9}{6} + \dfrac{4}{6} = \dfrac{-5}{6},$

$\quad\quad \dfrac{-5}{6} = \dfrac{-5}{6}$ True.

The solution is $x = -2$

Example 2

Solve.

$$\frac{x}{x-1} + \frac{3}{x+1} = \frac{4x+1}{x^2-1}$$

Solution

Step 1 Find the LCD. First, factor each denominator if possible.

$$\frac{x}{x-1} + \frac{3}{x+1} = \frac{4x+1}{(x-1)(x+1)}$$

By inspection the $LCD = (x-1)(x+1)$

Step 2 Clear denominators. Multiply both sides by the $LCD = (x-1)(x+1)$ and simplify.

$$\frac{x}{x-1}(x-1)(x+1) + \frac{3}{x+1}(x-1)(x+1) = \frac{4x+1}{(x-1)(x+1)}(x-1)(x+1)$$

$$x(x+1) + 3(x-1) = 4x+1$$

Step 3 Solve the resulting equation.

$$x(x+1)+3(x-1)=4x+1 \quad \text{Apply the distributive property}$$

$$x^2+x+3x-3=4x+1 \quad \text{Simplify}$$

$$x^2+4x-3=4x+1 \quad \text{Write the equation in Standard Form}$$

$$x^2+4x-3-4x-1=0 \quad \text{Simplify}$$

$$x^2-4=0 \quad \text{Factor}$$

$$(x-2)(x+2)=0 \quad \text{Apply the Zero Factor Property}$$

$$x-2=0 \text{ or } x+2=0 \quad \text{Solve for } x$$

$$x=2 \text{ or } x=-2$$

Step 4 Check the solutions.

$$\frac{2}{2-1}+\frac{3}{2+1}=\frac{4\cdot2+1}{2^2-1} \text{ , } \frac{2}{1}+\frac{3}{3}=\frac{8+1}{4-1} \text{ , } 2+1=\frac{9}{3} \text{ , } 3=3 \qquad \text{True}$$

$$\frac{-2}{-2-1}+\frac{3}{-2+1}=\frac{4(-2)+1}{(-2)^2-1}, \frac{-2}{-3}+\frac{3}{-1}=\frac{-8+1}{4-1}, \frac{2}{3}-\frac{3}{1}=\frac{-7}{3}$$

$$\frac{2}{3}-\frac{9}{3}=-\frac{7}{3}, \quad -\frac{7}{3}=-\frac{7}{3} \qquad \text{True}$$

The solutions are: $x=2$ and $x=-2$.

Note: Step 4 can be simplified if we use the following restriction: exclude (do not check) the value(s) that makes the denominator zero.

Example 3

Solve.

$$\frac{x+3}{x+1}-\frac{x}{x+2}=\frac{6x}{x^2+3x+2} \quad (x\neq-1,\ x\neq-2)$$

Solution

Step 1 Find the LCD. First, factor each denominator if possible.

$$\frac{x+3}{x+1}-\frac{x}{x+2}=\frac{6x}{(x+1)(x+2)}$$

By inspection the $LCD=(x+1)(x+2)$

Step 2 Clear denominators. Multiply both sides by the LCD.

$$\frac{x+3}{x+1}(x+1)(x+2)-\frac{x}{x+2}(x+1)(x+2)=\frac{6x}{(x+1)(x+2)}(x+1)(x+2)$$

$$(x+3)(x+2)-x(x+1)=6x$$

Step 3 Solve the resulting equation.

$$(x+3)(x+2)-x(x+1)=6x$$

$$x^2+2x+3x+6-x^2-x=6x$$

$$4x+6=6x$$

$$4x-6x=-6$$

$$-2x=-6$$

$$x=3$$

Step 4 Check the solution. Since $x=3$ is not a restricted value, $x=3$ is a possible solution.

$$\frac{3+3}{3+1}-\frac{3}{3+2}=\frac{6(3)}{3^2+3(3)+2}\;,\;\;\frac{6}{4}-\frac{3}{5}=\frac{18}{20}\;,\;\;\frac{30-12}{20}=\frac{18}{20}\;,\;\;\frac{18}{20}=\frac{18}{20}\qquad\text{True.}$$

Thus, the solution is x = 3.

Example 4

Solve.

$$\frac{x+2}{x+5}+\frac{x-1}{x+3}=\frac{x^2+5x+6}{x^2+8x+15}\quad(x\neq-5,\quad x\neq-3)$$

Solution

Step 1 Find the LCD. Factor each denominator if possible.

$$\frac{x+2}{x+5}+\frac{x-1}{x+3}=\frac{x^2+5x+6}{(x+5)(x+3)}$$

By inspection $LCD=(x+5)(x+3)$

Step 2 Clear denominators. Multiply both sides by the $LCD=(x+5)(x+3)$.

$$\frac{x+2}{x+5}(x+5)(x+3)+\frac{x-1}{x+3}(x+5)(x+3)=\frac{x^2+5x+6}{(x+5)(x+3)}(x+5)(x+3)$$

Simplify.

$$(x+2)(x+3)+(x-1)(x+5)=x^2+5x+6$$

Step 3 Solve the resulting equation.

$$x^2 + 3x + 2x + 6 + x^2 + 5x - x - 5 = x^2 + 5x + 6$$

$$2x^2 + 9x + 1 = x^2 + 5x + 6$$

$$2x^2 + 9x + 1 - x^2 - 5x - 6 = 0$$

$$x^2 + 4x - 5 = 0$$

$$(x + 5)(x - 1) = 0$$

$$x + 5 = 0 \quad \text{or} \quad x - 1 = 0$$

$$x = -5 \quad \text{or} \quad x = 1$$

Step 4 Check the solutions. Since $x = -5$ is a restricted value, the only possible solution is $x = 1$.

$$\frac{1+2}{1+5} + \frac{1-1}{1+3} = \frac{1^2 + 5(1) + 6}{1^1 + 8(1) + 15} \ , \ \frac{3}{6} + 0 = \frac{12}{24} \ , \ \frac{1}{2} = \frac{1}{2} \qquad \text{True.}$$

Thus, the solution is x = 1.

Example 5

Solve.

$$2 - \frac{x+1}{x-2} = \frac{4}{x+3} \quad (x \neq 2, -3)$$

Solution

Step 1 Find the LCD. By inspection $LCD = (x - 2)(x + 3)$

Step 2 Clear denominators. Multiply both sides by the $LCD = (x - 2)(x + 3)$.

$$2(x-2)(x+3) - \frac{x+1}{x-2}(x-2)(x+3) = \frac{4}{x+3}(x-2)(x+3)$$

Simplify.

$$2(x-2)(x+3) - (x+1)(x+3) = 4(x-2)$$

Step 3 Solve the resulting equation.

$$2(x-2)(x+3) - (x+1)(x+3) = 4(x-2)$$

$$2(x^2 + 3x - 2x - 6) - (x^2 + 3x + x + 3) = 4x - 8$$

$$2x^2 + 6x - 4x - 12 - x^2 - 3x - x - 3 = 4x - 8$$

$$2x^2 + 2x - 12 - x^2 - 4x - 3 - 4x + 8 = 0$$

$$x^2 - 6x - 7 = 0$$

$$(x-7)(x+1) = 0$$

$$x - 7 = 0 \ \text{ or } \ x + 1 = 0$$

$$x = 7 \ \text{ or } \ x = -1$$

Step 4   Check the solutions. Since $x = 7$ and $x = -1$ are not restricted values, $x = 7$ and $x = -1$ are possible solutions.

$$2 - \frac{7+1}{7-2} = \frac{4}{7+3}, \ 2 - \frac{8}{5} = \frac{4}{10}, \ \frac{10-8}{5} = \frac{4}{10}, \ \frac{2}{5} = \frac{2}{5} \qquad \text{True.}$$

$$2 - \frac{-1+1}{-1-2} = \frac{4}{-1+3}, \ 2 - 0 = \frac{4}{2}, \ 2 = 2 \qquad \text{True.}$$

Thus, the solutions are $x = 7$ and $x = -1$.

Example 6

Solve.

$$x - \frac{8}{x} = 7 \quad (x \neq 0)$$

Solution

Step 1   Find the LCD. By inspection the LCD $= x$.

Step 2   Clear denominators. Multiply both sides of the equation by LCD $= x$.

$$x \cdot x - x \cdot \frac{8}{x} = x \cdot 7$$

$$x^2 - 8 = 7x$$

Step 3   Solve the resulting equation.

$$x^2 - 7x - 8 = 0$$

$$(x-8)(x+1) = 0$$

$$x + 8 = 0 \ \text{ or } \ x + 1 = 0$$

$$x = 8 \ \text{ or } \ x = -1$$

Step 4   Check the solutions. Since $x = 8$ and $x = -1$ are not restricted values, the possible solutions are $x = 8$ and $x = -1$.

$$8 - \frac{8}{8} = 7, \ 8 - 1 = 7, \ 7 = 7 \text{ True} \quad -1 - \frac{8}{-1} = 7, \ -1 + 8 = 7, \ 7 = 7 \text{ True.}$$

Thus the solutions are $x = 8$ and $x = -1$.

Example 7

Solve.

$$\frac{x}{x^2 - 6x + 8} = \frac{x+2}{x^2 + x - 6} - \frac{x+4}{x^2 - x - 12}$$

Solution

Step 1 Find the LCD. First, factor each denominator if possible.

$$\frac{x}{(x-4)(x-2)} = \frac{x+2}{(x+3)(x-2)} - \frac{x+4}{(x-4)(x+3)} \quad (x \neq 2, -3, 4)$$

By inspection the $LCD = (x-2)(x+3)(x-4)$

Step 2 Clear denominators. Multiply both sides by the $LCD = (x-2)(x+3)(x-4)$.

$$\frac{x}{(x-4)(x-2)}(x-2)(x+3)(x-4) = \frac{x+2}{(x+3)(x-2)}(x-2)(x+3)(x-4) -$$

$$\frac{x+4}{(x-4)(x+3)}(x-2)(x+3)(x-4)$$

Simplify.

$$x(x+3) = (x+2)(x-4) - (x+4)(x-2)$$

Step 3 Solve the resulting equation.

$$x(x+3) = (x+2)(x-4) - (x+4)(x-2)$$

$$x^2 + 3x = x^2 - 2x - 8 - x^2 + 2x - 4x + 8$$

$$x^2 + 3x = -4x$$

$$x^2 + 3x + 4x = 0$$

$$x^2 + 7x = 0$$

$$x(x+7) = 0$$

$$x = 0 \quad \text{or} \quad x + 7 = 0$$

$$x = 0 \quad \text{or} \quad x = -7$$

Step 4 Check the solutions. Since $x = 0$ and $x = -7$ are not restricted values, the possible solutions are $x = 0$ and $x = -7$.

$$\frac{0}{8} = \frac{2}{-6} - \frac{4}{-12}, \ 0 = -\frac{1}{3} + \frac{1}{3}, \ 0 = 0 \qquad\qquad \text{True.}$$

$$\frac{-7}{(-7)^2 - 6(-7) + 8} = \frac{-7+2}{(-7)^2 - 7 - 6} - \frac{-7+4}{(-7)^2 - (-7) - 12}, \ \frac{-7}{99} = \frac{-5}{36} - \frac{-3}{44}, \ \frac{-7}{99} = \frac{-55+27}{396}$$

$$\frac{-7}{99} = \frac{-28}{396} \ , \ \frac{-7}{99} = \frac{-7}{99} \ ,$$ True.

Thus, the solutions are $x = 0$ and $x = -7$

Example 8

In the following example, we will emphasize the similarities and differences between ***simplifying rational expressions*** and ***solving rational equations***.

The most common mistake the students make is to clear the denominators when simplifying rational expressions and keep the denominators when solving rational equations.

Rational Expression	**Rational Equation**
Simplify $\dfrac{x}{x-5}+\dfrac{3}{x+5}-\dfrac{9x+5}{x^2-25}$	**Solve** $\dfrac{x}{x-5}+\dfrac{3}{x+5}=\dfrac{9x+5}{x^2-25}$

Solution

1. Find the LCD.

   Factor each denominator if possible.

   $$\frac{x}{x-5}+\frac{3}{x+5}-\frac{9x+5}{(x-5)(x+5)}$$

   By inspection the $LCD=(x-5)(x+5)$

2. Multiply each numerator by the missing factor and write the sum as a single fraction with the denominator $LCD=(x-5)(x+5)$

   $$\frac{x(x+5)+3(x-5)-(9x+5)}{(x-5)(x+5)}=$$

   $$\frac{x^2+5x+3x-15-9x-5}{(x-5)(x+5)}=$$

   $$\frac{x^2-x-20}{(x-5)(x+5)}=\frac{(x-5)(x+4)}{(x-5)(x+5)}=$$

   $$\frac{x+4}{x-5}$$

   Warning: Keep the denominators.

Solution

1. Find the LCD.

   Factor each denominator if possible.

   $$\frac{x}{x-5}+\frac{3}{x+5}-\frac{9x+5}{(x-5)(x+5)}$$

   By inspection the $LCD=(x-5)(x+5)$

2. **Clear the denominators.**

   Multiply both sides by $LCD=(x+5)(x-5)$

   $$\frac{x}{x-5}(x-5)(x+5)+\frac{3}{x+5}(x-5)(x+5)=$$

   $$\frac{9x+5}{(x-5)(x+5)}(x-5)(x+5)$$

3. Solve the resulting equation.

   $$x^2+5x+3x-15=9x+5$$

   $$x^2+8x-15=9x+5$$

   $$x^2+8x-15-9x-5=0$$

   $$x^2-x-20=0$$

   $$(x-5)(x+4)=0$$

   $$x-5=0 \text{ or } x+4=0$$

   $$x=5 \text{ or } x=-4$$

4. Check the solutions.

   Since $x = 5$ makes the denominator $x - 5 =$ zero, it must be excluded.

   $$\frac{-4}{-4-5}+\frac{3}{-4+5}=\frac{9(-4)+5}{(-4)^2-25}$$

   $$\frac{-4}{-9}+\frac{3}{1}=\frac{-36+5}{16-25}$$

   $$\frac{4}{9}+\frac{27}{9}=\frac{-31}{-9}$$

   $$\frac{31}{9}=\frac{31}{9} \quad \text{True.}$$

   The solution is $x = -4$

7.6 EXERCISES

Solve each rational equation and check the solution.

1. $\dfrac{x}{3} + \dfrac{4}{5} = \dfrac{x}{15}$

2. $\dfrac{x}{2} - \dfrac{x}{12} = \dfrac{5}{6}$

3. $\dfrac{3}{4} - \dfrac{x}{5} = \dfrac{3}{20}$

4. $\dfrac{13x}{18} - \dfrac{2}{3} = \dfrac{7}{9}$

5. $8 + \dfrac{5}{x} = 3$

6. $10 - \dfrac{3}{x} = 7$

7. $x - \dfrac{2}{x} = 1$

8. $x + \dfrac{6}{x} = -5$

9. $\dfrac{11}{x-2} = \dfrac{9}{x-4}$

10. $\dfrac{3}{x+1} = \dfrac{5}{x+3}$

11. $\dfrac{x}{x+4} = \dfrac{1}{x-2}$

12. $\dfrac{x}{x+5} = \dfrac{3}{x+1}$

13. $\dfrac{x}{x-1} - \dfrac{2}{x+1} = \dfrac{4}{x^2-1}$

14. $\dfrac{1}{x-4} - \dfrac{x}{x+4} = \dfrac{4}{x^2-16}$

15. $\dfrac{x+1}{x-2} - \dfrac{x}{x+2} = \dfrac{12}{x^2-4}$

16. $\dfrac{x-2}{x+3} + \dfrac{x}{x-3} = \dfrac{10}{x^2-9}$

17. $\dfrac{x+3}{x+4} - \dfrac{2}{x+1} = 1$

18. $\dfrac{x+4}{x+2} + \dfrac{8}{x-1} = 4$

19. $\dfrac{2}{x-1} + \dfrac{3}{x+4} = \dfrac{15}{x^2+3x-4}$

20. $\dfrac{8}{x+8} - \dfrac{5}{x+7} = \dfrac{1}{x^2+15x+56}$

21. $\dfrac{x-1}{x+3} - \dfrac{x}{x-4} = \dfrac{5x+17}{x^2-x-12}$

22. $\dfrac{x+6}{x+1} - \dfrac{x}{x+5} = \dfrac{20x}{x^2+6x+5}$

23. $\dfrac{x+8}{x-2} + \dfrac{x}{x+1} = \dfrac{x+4}{x^2-x-2}$

24. $\dfrac{x+4}{x-5} + \dfrac{x}{x+6} = \dfrac{9x+54}{x^2+x-30}$

25. $\dfrac{x-1}{x+4} + \dfrac{x+1}{x-3} = \dfrac{x^2+4x+17}{x^2+x-12}$

26. $\dfrac{x-7}{x+6} + \dfrac{x-4}{x-8} = \dfrac{x^2-7x+48}{x^2-2x-48}$

27. $\dfrac{3}{x^2+x-2} + \dfrac{1}{x^2-x-6} = \dfrac{1}{x^2-4x+3}$

28. $\dfrac{4}{x^2-3x-4} - \dfrac{1}{x^2+6x+5} = \dfrac{x}{x^2+x-20}$

29. $\dfrac{x+2}{x^2+2x-15} - \dfrac{x+1}{x^2+3x-18} = \dfrac{4x-1}{x^2+11x+30}$

7.7 APPLICATIONS OF RATIONAL EQUATIONS

□ **Work Problems** □ **Problems Involving Unknown Numbers**
□ **Uniform Motion Problems**

□ WORK PROBLEMS

To solve work problems, first we need to understand the concept of rate of work. For example, if one person can complete a job in 3 hours, then in 1 hour the person can complete $\frac{1}{3}$ of the job. |_____|_____|_____|

$$\frac{1}{3} \qquad \frac{1}{3} \qquad \frac{1}{3}$$

In other words, the rate of work or the speed of that person is 1/3 of the job per hour (assuming that the person works at a constant rate).

If another person can complete a different job in 20 minutes, then in 1 minute the person can complete 1/20 of the job. Thus, the rate of work for this person is 1/20.

Definition

*The **Rate of Work** is defined as the part of a job completed in one unit of time.*

If a person can complete a job in 5 hours, the rate of work for that person is 1/5. If that person works for 3 hours and then the person quits, the job will not be completed. Then, the part of the job completed by that person in 3 hours is:

$$\text{Part of the job completed} = \frac{1}{5} + \frac{1}{5} + \frac{1}{5} = \frac{1}{5} \cdot 3 = \frac{1}{5} \cdot \frac{3}{1} = \frac{3}{5}$$

Since 1/5 represents the rate of work and 3 hours is the time worked, this example suggests the basic equation used to solve work problems:

(Rate of work) × (Time working together) = Part of the job completed

or

R × T = P

In our case: $\frac{1}{5} \cdot 3 = \frac{3}{5}$

Note: If two people working together can complete a job in 5 hours, we cannot determine the rate of work for each person. Only individual time can be used to determine the rate of work.

Example 1

John can wash his car in 30 min and his younger brother Paul can wash the same car in 40 min. How long will it take them to wash the car if they work together?

Solution

Let x be the time it takes John and his brother Paul to wash the car, working together. Since John can complete the job in 30 min, his rate of work is 1/30. His brother's rate of work is 1/40.

This can be summarized in the following table:

	Rate of work	x	Time working together	=	Part of the job completed
John	$\dfrac{1}{30}$		x		$\dfrac{1}{30} \cdot x = \dfrac{x}{30}$
Paul	$\dfrac{1}{40}$		x		$\dfrac{1}{40} \cdot x = \dfrac{x}{40}$

Since John and Paul work towards the same goal, the part of the job completed by John and the part of the job completed by Paul add up to one whole like 3/3, 7/7, 11/11, etc. which is always equal to 1 (job completed).

This leads to the following rational equation:

$$\frac{x}{30} + \frac{x}{40} = 1$$

By inspection LCD = 120. If we multiply both sides of the equation by the LCD = 120, the resulting equation is:

$$120 \cdot \frac{x}{30} + 120 \cdot \frac{x}{40} = 120 \cdot 1$$

$$4x + 3x = 120$$

$$7x = 120$$

$$\frac{7x}{7} = \frac{120}{7}$$

$$x = 17.1 \ \text{min}$$

So, it takes John and Paul working together about 17 min to wash the car.

Example 2

A large pump can fill a swimming pool in 5 hours, and a smaller pump can fill the same swimming pool in 8 hours. How long will it take the two pumps working together to fill the pool?

Solution

Let x = time it takes the two pumps to fill the pool, working together.

The rate of work for the large pump is $\dfrac{1}{5}$ and the rate of work for the smaller pump is $\dfrac{1}{8}$.

	Rate of work	x Time working together	= Part of the job completed
Large Pump	$\dfrac{1}{5}$	x	$\dfrac{x}{5}$
Small Pump	$\dfrac{1}{8}$	x	$\dfrac{x}{8}$

Since the two pumps are working towards the same goal, the equation can be written as follows: $\dfrac{x}{5} + \dfrac{x}{8} = 1$

By inspection LCD = 40. If we multiply both sides of the equation by the LCD = 40, the equation becomes:

$$40 \cdot \frac{x}{5} + 40 \cdot \frac{x}{8} = 40 \cdot 1$$

$$8x + 5x = 40$$

$$13x = 40$$

$$\frac{13x}{13} = \frac{40}{13}$$

$$x = 3.1 \quad \text{hours}$$

Thus, it takes the two pumps about 3 hours to fill the pool, working together.

Example 3

An inlet pipe can fill a water tank in 3 hours. An outlet pipe can empty the same tank in 4 hours. If both pipes are open at the same time, how long would it take to fill the tank?

Solution

Let x = time the two pipes are open.

The rate of work for the inlet pipe is $\dfrac{1}{3}$ and the rate of work for the outlet pipe is $\dfrac{1}{4}$.

	Rate of work	x Time working together	= Part of the job completed
Inlet pipe	$\dfrac{1}{3}$	x	$\dfrac{x}{3}$
Outlet pipe	$\dfrac{1}{4}$	x	$\dfrac{x}{4}$

In this case the pipes are working *against* each other. The inlet pipe is doing the job (filling the tank), and the outlet pipe is doing the damage (emptying the tank). Thus, we subtract the part of the damage done by the outlet pipe from the part of the job completed by the inlet pipe, and the difference is equal to one because sooner or later the job will be completed (full tank) by the inlet pipe.

Then, the equation can be written as follows:

$$\frac{x}{3} - \frac{x}{4} = 1$$

By inspection, LCD = 12. If we multiply both sides of the equation by the LCD = 12, the equation becomes:

$$12 \cdot \frac{x}{3} - 12 \cdot \frac{x}{4} = 12 \cdot 1$$

$$4x - 3x = 12$$

$$x = 12$$

So, it takes 12 hours to fill the tank.

Note: If the question is "how long would it take to empty the tank?" then the outlet pipe is doing the job and the inlet pipe is doing the damage.

Example 4

A hot-water faucet can fill a sink in 8 minutes while the cold-water faucet takes 6 minutes to fill the same sink. If the drain can empty the sink in 12 minutes, how long would it take to fill the sink if, by mistake, both faucets and the drain are open at the same time?

Solution

Let x = the time the two faucets and the drain are open.

	Rate of work	x	Time worked together	=	Part of the job completed
H.W. Faucet	$\frac{1}{8}$		x		$\frac{x}{8}$
C.W. Faucet	$\frac{1}{6}$		x		$\frac{x}{6}$
Drain	$\frac{1}{12}$		x		$\frac{x}{12}$

In this example, the hot-water and the cold-water faucets are doing the job and the drain is doing the damage. Hence, the equation can be written as follows:

$$\frac{x}{8} + \frac{x}{6} - \frac{x}{12} = 1$$

By inspection, the LCD = 24. If we multiply both sides of the equation by the LCD = 24 the equation becomes:

$$24 \cdot \frac{x}{8} + 24 \cdot \frac{x}{6} - 24 \cdot \frac{x}{12} = 24 \cdot 1$$

$$3x + 4x - 2x = 24$$

$$5x = 24$$

$$\frac{5x}{5} = \frac{24}{5}$$

$x = 4.8$

So, it takes 4.8 minutes to fill the sink.

Example 5

A large printer can print the payroll of a corporation in 36 minutes and together with a smaller printer can print the same payroll in 24 minutes. How long would it take the smaller printer to print the payroll by itself?

Solution

Let x = time it takes the smaller printer to print the payroll. Then, the rate of work for the smaller printer is $\frac{1}{x}$ and the rate of work for the larger printer is $\frac{1}{36}$.

	Rate of work	x	Time working together	=	Part of the job completed
Large Printer	$\frac{1}{36}$		24		$\frac{24}{36}$
Smaller Printer	$\frac{1}{x}$		24		$\frac{24}{x}$

$$\frac{24}{36} + \frac{24}{x} = 1$$

$$\frac{2}{3} + \frac{24}{x} = 1$$

By inspection, the LCD = 3x. If we multiply both sides of the equation by the LCD = 3x, the equation becomes:

$$(3x) \cdot \frac{2}{3} + (3x) \cdot \frac{24}{x} = (3x) \cdot 1$$

$$2x + 72 = 3x$$

$$72 = 3x - 2x$$

$$72 = x$$

Hence, it takes the smaller printer 72 minutes to print the payroll by itself.

□ PROBLEMS INVOLVING UNKNOWN NUMBERS

Example 6

What number subtracted from the numerator and multiplied by the denominator of the fraction $\frac{4}{7}$ makes the resulting fraction $\frac{1}{7}$?

Solution

Let x be the number. The equation is:

$$\frac{4-x}{7x} = \frac{1}{7}$$

By inspection LCD = $7x$. If we multiply both sides of the equation by the LCD = $7x$, the equation becomes:

$$(7x) \cdot \frac{4-x}{7x} = (7x) \cdot \frac{1}{7}$$

$$4 - x = x$$

$$4 = x + x$$

$$4 = 2x$$

$$\frac{4}{2} = \frac{2x}{2}$$

$$2 = x$$

So, the unknown number is $x = 2$.

Example 7

The sum of the reciprocal of two consecutive odd integers is $\dfrac{12}{35}$. Find the two integers.

Solution

First, we set up two consecutive odd integers.

1st integer $= x$

2nd integer $= x + 2$

The sum of their reciprocals is $\dfrac{1}{x} + \dfrac{1}{x+2}$. So, the equation can be written as follows:

$$\frac{1}{x} + \frac{1}{x+2} = \frac{12}{35}$$

By inspection, the LCD $= 35x(x + 2)$. Multiplying both sides of the equation by the LCD,

$$35x(x+2) \cdot \frac{1}{x} + 35x(x+2) \cdot \frac{1}{x+2} = 35x(x+2) \cdot \frac{12}{35}$$

$$35(x+2) + 35x = 12x(x+2)$$

$$35x + 70 + 35x = 12x^2 + 24x$$

$$70x + 70 = 12x^2 + 24x$$

$$0 = 12x^2 + 24x - 70x - 70$$

$$0 = 12x^2 - 46x - 70$$

or

$$12x^2 - 46x - 70 = 0$$

Divide both sides of the equation by 2.

$$6x^2 - 23x - 35 = 0$$

To factor by grouping, we need four terms. We rewrite the middle term as the sum of two numbers with the product $P = 6(-35) = -210$ and the sum $S = -23$. By inspection, the numbers are -30 and 7.

$$6x^2 - 30x + 7x - 35 = 0$$

$$6x(x-5) + 7(x-5) = 0$$

$$(x-5)(6x+7) = 0$$

$$x - 5 = 0 \quad \text{or} \quad 6x + 7 = 0$$

$$x = 5 \quad \text{or} \quad x = -\frac{7}{6}$$

Since $x = -\dfrac{7}{6}$ is not an integer, the only solution for the problem is $x = 5$. So, the integers are:

1st integer = 5

2nd integer = $x + 2$ = 7

□ UNIFORM MOTION PROBLEMS

In chapter 2 we have learned that the distance formula Distance = Rate × Time is the basic equation used to solve uniform motion problems. There are two alternatives of this equation that can be found by solving the equation for rate or time.

$$Rate = \frac{D}{T}, \quad Time = \frac{D}{R}$$

Example 8

A freight train travels 100 mi in the same amount of time it takes a passenger train to travel 125 mi. If the rate of the passenger train is 10 mph greater than the rate of the freight train, find the rate of each train.

Solution

Let x = the rate of the freight train. Then, the rate of the passenger train is:

$x + 10$. Since we know the distance and the rate for each train, we can use the formula $T = \dfrac{D}{R}$ to find the time for each train.

Freight Train: $T = \dfrac{D}{R} = \dfrac{100}{x}$

Passenger Train: $T = \dfrac{D}{R} = \dfrac{125}{x+10}$

This can be summarized in the following table:

	Rate	x	Time	=	Distance
Freight Train	x		$\dfrac{100}{x}$		100
Passenger Train	$x+10$		$\dfrac{125}{x+10}$		125

Since the amount of time for each train is the same, the equation is:

$$\frac{125}{x+10} = \frac{100}{x}$$

By inspection LCD = $x(x + 10)$. If we multiply both sides of the equation by the LCD = $x(x + 10)$, the equation becomes:

$$x(x+10) \cdot \frac{125}{x+10} = x(x+10) \cdot \frac{100}{x}$$

$$125x = 100(x+10)$$

$$125x = 100x + 1000$$

$$125x - 100x = 1000$$

$$25x = 1000$$

$$\frac{25x}{25} = \frac{1000}{25}$$

$$x = 40$$

So, the rate of the freight train is $x = 40$ mph and the rate of the passenger train is $x + 10 = 40 + 10 = 50$ mph.

Note: This rational equation can be solved as a proportion. Using the property of proportions, which states that in a proportion the cross products are equal,

$$125x = 100(x+10)$$

which is the same equation.

Example 9

A small plane flew 300 mi with the wind in the same amount of time it flew 200 mi against the wind. If the speed of the plane in calm air is 200 mph, find the speed of the wind.

Solution

Let x = rate of the wind. When the plane flies with the wind, the plane travels faster (the wind pushes the plane). So the rate of the plane with the wind is $R = 200 + x$.

When the plane flies against the wind, the plane travels slower (the wind slows down the plane). So, the rate of the plane against the wind is $R = 200 - x$. Since we know the distance and the rate of the plane we can use the formula $T = \dfrac{D}{R}$ to find the time.

With the wind: $T = \dfrac{D}{R} = \dfrac{300}{200 + x}$

Against the wind: $T = \dfrac{D}{R} = \dfrac{200}{200 - x}$

We can summarize this in the following table:

Since the amount of time flying with the wind and flying against the wind is the same, the equation is:

$$\frac{300}{200 + x} = \frac{200}{200 - x}$$

This rational equation can be solved as a proportion.

$300(200 - x) = 200(200 + x)$

$60{,}000 - 300x = 40{,}000 + 200x$

$60{,}000 - 40{,}000 = 200x + 300x$

$20{,}000 = 500x$

$\dfrac{20{,}000}{500} = \dfrac{500x}{500}$

$x = 40$

So, the rate of the wind is 40 mph.

7.7 EXERCISES

1. A bricklayer can build a brick wall in 2 days. His apprentice needs 3 days to build the same wall. How long would it take them to build the wall if they work together?

2. An experienced roofer can put a new roof on a house in 12 hours. His brother Joe can do the same job in 14 hours. How long would it take them working together to install the new roof?

3. A cabinetmaker can make a set of kitchen cabinets in 15 hours. His partner can make the same set of kitchen cabinets in 20 hours. How long would it take them working together to make the set of kitchen cabinets?

4. A small printer can print the payroll for a company in 35 min. A larger printer can print the same payroll in 14 min. How long would it take to print the payroll if both printers are used?

5. One large pump can fill a swimming pool in 7 hours. A smaller pump takes 9 hours to fill the same swimming pool. How long would it take the two pumps working together to fill the swimming pool?

6. A hot-water faucet can fill a sink in 6 min, and a cold-water faucet can fill the same sink in 9 min. How long will it take to fill the sink if both faucets are open?

7. Two pipes are used to fill a water tank. The smaller pipe can fill the water tank in 14 hours and the larger pipe can fill the same tank in 12 hours. How long will it take the two pipes working together to fill the water tank?

8. A milk tank has two inlet pipes and one outlet pipe. The two inlet pipes can fill the tank in 10 and 15 hours respectively. The outlet pipe can empty the tank in 20 hours. If the tank is empty, how long will it take to fill the tank when all three pipes are open?

9. The hot-water faucet can fill a bathtub in 9 min and the cold-water faucet can fill the bathtub in 12 min. The drain can empty the bathtub in 18 min. If the bathtub is empty, how long will it take to fill the bathtub if both hot and cold faucets are on and the drain is open?

10. Mike can wash his truck in 30 min. Together with his brother Jeff they can wash the same truck in 20 min. How long will it take Jeff to wash the car by himself?

11. Joe can clean his room in 24 min. Together with his sister Mary they can clean the room in 16 min. How long will it take Mary to clean the room by herself?

12. When a number is added to the numerator and subtracted from the denominator of the fraction $\frac{5}{8}$, the resulting fraction is $\frac{8}{5}$. Find the number.

13. When a number is subtracted from the numerator and multiplied by the denominator of the fraction $\frac{5}{11}$, the resulting fraction is $\frac{3}{22}$. Find the number.

14. The sum of the reciprocals of two positive consecutive even integers is $\frac{7}{24}$. Find the integers.

15. The sum of the reciprocals of two consecutive integers is $\frac{5}{6}$. Find the integers.

16. A tour boat can travel 10 mph in still water. Traveling with the current, the boat can travel 24 miles in the same amount of time it takes to travel 8 miles against the current. Find the speed of the current.

17. A small plane can fly 285 mph in calm air. Traveling with the wind the plane flew 350 mi in the same amount of time as it takes to fly 315 mi against the wind. Find the speed of the wind.

18. A passenger train travels 10 mph faster than a freight train. If the passenger train travels 180 mi in the same amount of time it takes the freight train to travel 150 mi, find the rate of each train.

19. The distance from Los Angeles to San Diego is about 116 mi. A tour bus leaves Los Angeles at 8:00 a.m. Because of the freeway conditions, the speed of the bus for the first 26 mi was 8 mi per hour less than the speed of the bus for the last 90 mi. If the entire trip took 2 hours, what was the speed of the bus for the first 26 mi?

CHAPTER 7 REVIEW EXERCISES

Determine the values of the variable for which the rational expression is undefined.

1. $\dfrac{5x-3}{x+4}$

2. $\dfrac{x-3}{x^2-3x-10}$

3. $\dfrac{2x+1}{x^2+9}$

4. $\dfrac{x^2+x+1}{8}$

Simplify.

5. $\dfrac{x^2-2x}{x^2-6x+8}$

8. $\dfrac{x-2}{4-x^2}$

6. $\dfrac{x^2+2x-15}{x^2-7x+12}$

9. $\dfrac{x^2+6xy+8y^2}{x^2-xy-6y^2}$

7. $\dfrac{x^2-9}{x^3-27}$

10. $\dfrac{12x^2-9xy+8xy-6y^2}{3x^2-18xy+2xy-12y^2}$

Multiply.

11. $\dfrac{3x^2y}{5x^5y^3}\cdot\dfrac{15xy^3}{18x^2y^2}$

14. $\dfrac{3x^2-5xy-2y^2}{3x^2+13xy+4y^2}\cdot\dfrac{2x^2+9xy+4y^2}{2x^2-9xy-5y^2}$

12. $\dfrac{x^2-9}{x^2-36}\cdot\dfrac{x^2-2x-24}{x^2+7x+12}$

15. $\dfrac{x^2+7x-8}{x^2+5x-24}\cdot\dfrac{x^2+3x-18}{x^2+14x+48}$

13. $\dfrac{x-5}{8y}\cdot\dfrac{24y^3}{5-x}$

16. $\dfrac{6x^2+17x+12}{8x^2+10x-3}\cdot\dfrac{4x^2+19x-5}{3x^2-11x-20}$

Divide.

17. $\dfrac{7x^3y^2}{9xy^4}\div\dfrac{21x^5y}{27xy}$

20. $\dfrac{x^2-x-30}{x^2+3x}\div\dfrac{2x^2+4x-30}{2x^2-18}$

18. $\dfrac{x^2-4x-21}{(x+3)^2}\div\dfrac{x^2-15x+56}{x^2-7x-8}$

21. $(x^3-8)\div\dfrac{x^2+2x+4}{2x}$

19. $\dfrac{x^2-9y^2}{3x+4y}\div\dfrac{x^2+4xy+3y^2}{3x^2+7xy+4y^2}$

22. $\dfrac{4x^2+5x-6}{4x^2+x-3}\div\dfrac{x^2-5x-14}{x^2-8x-9}$

Multiply or divide.

23. $\dfrac{x^2+2x-8}{x^2+7x+12} \div \dfrac{x^2+x-30}{x^2-2x-15} \cdot \dfrac{x^2-36}{x^2-4}$

24. $\left(\dfrac{x^2-5x-24}{3x^2+8x-3} \cdot \dfrac{x^2-4x-45}{x^2-7x-8}\right) \div \dfrac{x^2+3x-10}{3x^2+2x-1}$

Add or subtract.

25. $\dfrac{x^2+5}{x^2+8x+15} + \dfrac{8x+10}{x^2+8x+15}$

26. $\dfrac{2x^2-5}{2x-3} - \dfrac{2-x}{3-2x}$

Simplify.

27. $\dfrac{x+1}{x-3} - \dfrac{x}{x+2} + \dfrac{x^2-7x-8}{x^2-x-6}$

28. $\dfrac{x-5}{x-4} - \dfrac{x+6}{x+4} + \dfrac{8}{x^2-16}$

29. $\dfrac{x+2}{x^2+4x-5} + \dfrac{x+6}{x^2+2x-15} - \dfrac{x-2}{x^2-4x+3}$

30. $\dfrac{x-\dfrac{3}{x+2}}{1-\dfrac{3}{x+2}}$

31. $\dfrac{\dfrac{1}{4}-\dfrac{1}{x^2}}{\dfrac{1}{2}+\dfrac{1}{x}}$

Solve.

32. $\dfrac{x+8}{x-3} + \dfrac{x-2}{x+4} = \dfrac{x^2+4x+42}{x^2+x-12}$

33. $\dfrac{x}{x-5} + \dfrac{3}{x+5} = \dfrac{8x+1}{x^2-25}$

34. $\dfrac{x+1}{x^2-3x+2} + \dfrac{x+5}{x^2+2x-3} = \dfrac{5x+1}{x^2+x-6}$

35. Two pipes are used to fill a water tank. The smaller pipe can fill the tank in 7 hours, and the larger pipe can fill the same water tank in 3 hours. How long will it take the two pipes working together to fill the water tank?

36. A small plane can fly 320 mph in calm air. Traveling with the wind, the plane flew 680 mi in the same amount of time it takes to fly 600 mi against the wind. Find the speed of the wind.

37. When a number is multiplied by the numerator, and added to the denominator of the fraction $\frac{3}{8}$, the resulting fraction is $\frac{9}{11}$. Find the number.

38. The sum of the reciprocals of two positive consecutive odd integers is $\frac{12}{35}$. Find the integers.

8 RADICAL EXPRESSIONS AND EQUATIONS

8.1 ROOTS AND RADICALS

□ Radicals □ Classifying Square Roots □ Applications of Radicals

For every mathematical operation, there is another operation that can be used to reverse (undo) the first one. For example, addition can be reversed by subtraction, multiplication by division, etc. In this section, our goal is to introduce an operation that will be used to reverse the power of a number.

The following example illustrates the need for such reverse operation.

Example 1

Suppose the length of the side of a square is $s = 8$. Using the formula $A = s^2$, we can find the area of the square:

$$A = s^2 = 8^2 = 64$$

If we know the area of the square, in order to find the length of the side we need a reverse operation that helps us undo the squaring operation (second power). In other words, this reverse operation will take 64 back to 8.

In our example $8^2 = 64$, the number 64 is *"the square of 8"* and 8 is *"the square root of 64."* Since $(-8)^2 = 64$, we conclude that –8 is also a square root of 64.

Therefore, the positive real number 64 has two square roots, one positive (8) and one negative (–8).

Remark

Any *positive* real number has two real square roots, one positive square root and one negative square root.

Note: Zero has two equal square roots because $+0 = -0 = 0$ and a negative real number such as –9 has no real square roots because there is no real number that squared gives –9.

Example 2

Find the square roots of each number.

    a. 25   b. 16   c. 1

Solution

    a. 25 has two square roots: 5 because $5^2 = 25$ and –5 because $(-5)^2 = 25$.

    b. 16 has two square roots: 4 because $4^2 = 16$ and –4 because $(-4)^2 = 16$.

    c. 1 has two square roots: 1 because $1^2 = 1$ and –1 because $(-1)^2 = 1$.

The above examples suggest the following conclusion: *A number a is the real square root of a positive real number N if $a^2 = N$.*

☐ RADICALS

For any positive real number, the symbol $\sqrt{}$ called radical sign or square root is used to indicate the **nonnegative** (≥ 0) **or principal square root** of the number, and $-\sqrt{}$ is used to indicate the **negative square root** of the number.

The expression $\sqrt{a}$ is read "the square root of a."

Example 3

Evaluate each square root.

a. $\sqrt{81} = 9$ and $-\sqrt{81} = -9$

b. $\sqrt{36} = 6$ and $-\sqrt{36} = -6$

c. $\sqrt{16} = 4$ and $-\sqrt{16} = -4$

d. $\sqrt{0} = 0$ and $-\sqrt{0} = -0 = 0$

To reverse (undo) the higher-order powers, there is a need to expand the concept of square root to higher-order roots:

$\sqrt{}$ square root (2nd root)

$\sqrt[3]{}$ cube root (3rd root)

$\sqrt[4]{}$ 4th root

$\sqrt[5]{}$ 5th root

....

$\sqrt[n]{}$ nth root (n is an integer $n \geq 2$)

In general

A number a is the nth root (n is an integer $n \geq 2$) of a real number N if $a^n = N$.

In the expression $\sqrt[n]{a}$, the symbol $\sqrt{}$ is called **radical sign**, n is a natural number, $n \geq 2$ and is called the **index** (order), a is called **radicand**, and the expression $\sqrt[n]{a}$ is called **radical expression**.

For example, if we know the volume of a cube $V = s^3$, to find the length of its side s we need the cube root to undo the third power: $\sqrt[3]{V} = \sqrt[3]{s^3} = s$.

Note: For the square root, the index 2 is omitted $\sqrt[2]{a} = \sqrt{a}$ just like 1 is omitted for $a^1 = a$.

Example 4

Find each root, if possible.

a. $\sqrt[3]{8}$ b. $\sqrt[5]{-32}$ c. $\sqrt[4]{81}$ d. $\sqrt[6]{-1}$

Solution

a. $\sqrt[3]{8} = 2$ because $2^3 = 8$

b. $\sqrt[5]{-32} = -2$ because $(-2)^5 = -32$

c. $\sqrt[4]{81} = 3$ because $(3)^4 = 81$

d. $\sqrt[6]{-1}$ is not a real number because there is no real number that raised to the 6th power gives -1 (This is always true if the radicand is negative and the index is even.)

For example $1^6 = 1$ and $(-1)^6 = 1$, neither one gives -1.

The above examples suggest the following conclusion:

If N is a real number and n is an integer $n \geq 2$, then $\sqrt[n]{N} = a$ *if* $a^n = N$.

Since a^2 is a positive real number for any real number $a \neq 0$ and $\sqrt{a^2}$ denotes the positive or principal square root of a^2, we must use the absolute value symbol to make sure that the principal root is positive:

$$\sqrt{a^2} = |a|$$

Note: $\sqrt{a^2} \neq a$

The following example illustrates the need for absolute value. When $a = -3$, then $\sqrt{(-3)^2} \neq -3$. The correct answer is: $\sqrt{(-3)^2} = \sqrt{9} = 3 = |-3|$

Example 5

Use absolute value to evaluate.

a. $\sqrt{(-5)^2}$ c. $\sqrt{(2x-1)^2}$ e. $\sqrt{7^2}$

b. $\sqrt{81x^2}$ d. $\sqrt{x^2 + 4x + 4}$ f. $\sqrt{y^2}$

Solution

a. $\sqrt{(-5)^2} = |-5| = 5$ d. $\sqrt{x^2 + 4x + 4} = \sqrt{(x+2)^2} = |x+2|$

b. $\sqrt{81x^2} = |9x|$ e. $\sqrt{7^2} = |7| = 7$

c. $\sqrt{(2x-1)^2} = |2x-1|$ f. $\sqrt{y^2} = |y|$

Note: When a rational number is multiplied by itself, the product is a *perfect square*.

For example, $1, 4, 81, 0.36, \dfrac{4}{25}$, etc. are perfect squares because, $1 = 1 \cdot 1$, $4 = 2 \cdot 2$, $81 = 9 \cdot 9$, $0.36 = (0.6)(0.6)$, $\dfrac{4}{25} = \dfrac{2}{5} \cdot \dfrac{2}{5}$

☐ CLASSIFYING SQUARE ROOTS

a. The square root of a rational number that is a perfect square is a *rational number*.

For example, $\sqrt{81} = 9$, $\sqrt{0.36} = 0.6$, $\sqrt{\dfrac{4}{25}} = \dfrac{2}{5}$ are rational numbers.

b. The square root of a positive real number that is not a perfect square is an *irrational number*.

For example, $\sqrt{3} = 1.73....$, $\sqrt{12} = 3.46...$ are irrational numbers.

c. The square root of a negative real number is *not a real number*.

For example, $\sqrt{-4}$ is not a real number because there is no real number whose square is -4.

But, $\sqrt[3]{-8} = -2$ because $(-2)^3 = -8$ (This is always possible if the index is odd.)

Example 6

Classify each square root.

a. $\sqrt{0.04}$ b. $\sqrt{20}$ c. $-\sqrt{9}$ d. $\sqrt{-25}$ e. $\sqrt{\dfrac{9}{64}}$

Solution

a. $\sqrt{0.04} = 0.2$ rational number

b. $\sqrt{20} = 4.47...$ irrational number

c. $-\sqrt{9} = -3$ rational number

d. $\sqrt{-25}$ not a real number

e. $\sqrt{\dfrac{9}{64}} = \dfrac{3}{8}$ rational number

The following table illustrates the relationship between the "square" of a number and the positive "square root" of the number.

$1^2 = 1$	$\sqrt{1} = 1$	$1^3 = 1$	$\sqrt[3]{1} = 1$	$1^4 = 1$	$\sqrt[4]{1} = 1$	$1^5 = 1$	$\sqrt[5]{1} = 1$
$2^2 = 4$	$\sqrt{4} = 2$	$2^3 = 8$	$\sqrt[3]{8} = 2$	$2^4 = 16$	$\sqrt[4]{16} = 2$	$2^5 = 32$	$\sqrt[5]{32} = 2$
$3^2 = 9$	$\sqrt{9} = 3$	$3^3 = 27$	$\sqrt[3]{27} = 3$	$3^4 = 81$	$\sqrt[4]{81} = 3$	·················	
$4^2 = 16$	$\sqrt{16} = 4$	$4^3 = 64$	$\sqrt[3]{64} = 4$	·················			
$5^2 = 25$	$\sqrt{25} = 5$	$5^3 = 125$	$\sqrt[3]{125} = 5$				
$6^2 = 36$	$\sqrt{36} = 6$	·················					
$7^2 = 49$	$\sqrt{49} = 7$						
·················							

☐ APPLICATIONS OF RADICALS

Pythagorean Theorem

In a right triangle, the sum of the squares of the two legs is equal to the square of the hypotenuse.

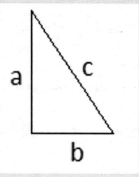

$$a^2 + b^2 = c^2$$

Pythagorean Formula

Example 7

Find the hypotenuse c of a right triangle whose legs are $a = 3$ cm and $b = 4$ cm.

Solution

$$a^2 + b^2 = c^2$$

$$3^2 + 4^2 = c^2$$

$$9 + 16 = c^2$$

$$25 = c^2$$

$$c = \sqrt{25} = 5$$

Thus, the hypotenuse of the triangle is 5 cm.

Example 8

Use the Pythagorean Theorem to find the missing leg a if the leg $b = 6$ cm, and the hypotenuse $c = 10$ cm.

Solution

$$a^2 + b^2 = c^2$$

$$a^2 + 6^2 = 10^2$$

$$a^2 + 36 = 100$$

$a^2 = 100 - 36$

$a^2 = 64$

$a = \sqrt{64} = 8$

Thus, the missing leg of the right triangle is 8 cm.

Distance Formula

The distance between two points (x_1, y_1) and (x_2, y_2) is given by the distance formula

$d = \sqrt{(x_2 - x_1)^2 + (y_2 - y_1)^2}$

Example 9
_____

Find the distance between the points (3, –4) and (9, 4).

Solution

$d = \sqrt{(x_2 - x_1)^2 + (y_2 - y_1)^2} =$

$\sqrt{(9-3)^2 + (4-(-4))^2} =$

$\sqrt{6^2 + (4+4)^2} =$

$\sqrt{36 + 8^2} =$

$\sqrt{36 + 64} = \sqrt{100} = 10$

Thus, the distance between the two points is 10 units.

8.1   EXERCISES

Find all square roots of each number.

1. 49	6. 0	11. $\dfrac{1}{25}$
2. 100	7. 4	
3. 9	8. 121	12. $\dfrac{16}{49}$
4. 1	9. 0.81	
5. 36	10. 0.01	

Classify the square root of each number as rational, irrational or not a real number.

13. $\sqrt{1}$

14. $\sqrt{169}$

15. $\sqrt{24}$

16. $\sqrt{40}$

17. $-\sqrt{4}$

18. $-\sqrt{25}$

19. $\sqrt{-81}$

20. $\sqrt{-15}$

21. $\sqrt{\dfrac{4}{9}}$

22. $-\sqrt{\dfrac{1}{64}}$

23. $\sqrt{0.9}$

24. $\sqrt{-0.49}$

Evaluate each square root, if possible.

25. $\sqrt{16}$

26. $\sqrt{400}$

27. $\sqrt{121}$

28. $\sqrt{81}$

29. $\sqrt{49}$

30. $\sqrt{225}$

31. $\sqrt{81}$

32. $\sqrt{36}$

33. $-\sqrt{100}$

34. $-\sqrt{196}$

35. $-\sqrt{0.81}$

36. $-\sqrt{0.0121}$

37. $\sqrt{\dfrac{81}{100}}$

38. $\sqrt{\dfrac{4}{49}}$

39. $-\sqrt{\dfrac{9}{25}}$

40. $-\sqrt{\dfrac{1}{169}}$

41. $\sqrt{0.64}$

42. $\sqrt{0.16}$

43. $-\sqrt{0.0144}$

44. $-\sqrt{0.49}$

45. $\sqrt{-9}$

46. $\sqrt{-0.01}$

47. $-\sqrt{-36}$

48. $-\sqrt{-25}$

49. $-\sqrt{\dfrac{49}{121}}$

50. $\sqrt{-\dfrac{16}{81}}$

51. $-\sqrt{-0.04}$

52. $-\sqrt{-\dfrac{25}{64}}$

Find each root, if possible.

53. $\sqrt[3]{-27}$

54. $\sqrt[5]{32}$

55. $-\sqrt[4]{81}$

56. $\sqrt[3]{125}$

57. $\sqrt[3]{\dfrac{8}{27}}$

58. $\sqrt[4]{\dfrac{16}{625}}$

59. $\sqrt[4]{-81}$

60. $\sqrt[5]{-1}$

61. $\sqrt{-36}$

62. $\sqrt[3]{-\dfrac{8}{27}}$

63. $\sqrt[6]{64}$

64. $\sqrt[5]{0}$

65. $\sqrt[4]{16}$

66. $\sqrt[6]{-1}$

67. $\sqrt{\dfrac{81}{144}}$

68. $\sqrt[3]{\dfrac{27}{1000}}$

Use the absolute value to evaluate.

69. $\sqrt{(x-4)^2}$

72. $\sqrt{(3x+4)^2}$

75. $\sqrt{y^2+2x+1}$

70. $\sqrt{y^2+8y+16}$

73. $\sqrt{x^2-10x+25}$

76. $\sqrt{16(x+2)^2}$

71. $\sqrt{x^2+6x+9}$

74. $\sqrt{4x^2-4x+1}$

77. Use the Pythagorean Theorem to find the missing leg b of a right triangle, if a = 12 cm and c = 13 cm.

78. Use the Pythagorean Theorem to find the hypotenuse c of a right triangle if a = 6 in. and $b = \sqrt{13}$ in.

79. The diagonal of a rectangle is 15 in. If the width of the rectangle is 9 in., find the length of the rectangle.

80. Mary is flying a kite on 50 ft of string. If the distance along a horizontal line between Mary's hand and the vertical line from the kite to the ground is 40 ft, how high is the kite above her hand?

81. Use the Distance Formula to find the distance between the points $(-4,5)$ and $(8,-4)$.

82. Use the Distance Formula to find the distance between $(-6,-7)$ and $(0,-15)$.

8.2 SIMPLIFYING RADICAL EXPRESSIONS

☐ **Simplifying Radical Expressions Containing Numbers** ☐ **Simplifying Radical Expressions Containing Variables** ☐ **Simplifying Higher Order Radical Expressions**

☐ SIMPLIFYING RADICAL EXPRESSIONS CONTAINING NUMBERS

A square root expression is simplified (in simplest radical form) if the radicand contains no perfect square factors other than 1.

When simplifying radical expressions, our goal is to remove the entire radicand or as much as possible from under the radical sign.

This can be accomplished by using the following two rules of radicals:

Product Rule for Square Roots

If $a \geq 0$ or $b \geq 0$, then $\sqrt{a}\sqrt{b} = \sqrt{a \cdot b}$

The product of the square roots is equal to the square root of the product.

Example 1

$$\sqrt{3} \cdot \sqrt{12} = \sqrt{3 \cdot 12} = \sqrt{36} = 6$$

Example 2

$$\sqrt{50} = \sqrt{25 \cdot 2} = \sqrt{25}\sqrt{2} = 5\sqrt{2}$$

Quotient Rule for Square Roots

If $a \geq 0$ or $b > 0$, then $\dfrac{\sqrt{a}}{\sqrt{b}} = \sqrt{\dfrac{a}{b}}$

The quotient of the square roots is equal to the square root of the quotient.

Example 3

$$\frac{\sqrt{32}}{\sqrt{2}} = \sqrt{\frac{32}{2}} = \sqrt{16} = 4 \text{ and } \sqrt{\frac{16}{9}} = \frac{\sqrt{16}}{\sqrt{9}} = \frac{4}{3}$$

If the radicand is a perfect square, then the entire radicand can be removed from under the radical.

For example, $\sqrt{25} = 5$, $\sqrt{16} = 4$, $\sqrt{169} = 13$, $\sqrt{\dfrac{25}{121}} = \dfrac{5}{11}$, $\sqrt{0.49} = 0.7$ etc.

If the radicand is not a perfect square, first write the radicand as a product of the largest perfect square factor in the radicand and a factor that is not a perfect square, and does not contain a perfect square factor other than one. Then using the product rule in the form

$\sqrt{a \cdot b} = \sqrt{a} \cdot \sqrt{b}$, remove the largest perfect square from the radicand.

For example, $\sqrt{20} = \sqrt{4 \cdot 5} = \sqrt{4}\sqrt{5} = 2\sqrt{5}$ (4 is the largest perfect square and 5 is not a perfect square). The radical expression $2\sqrt{5}$ is in simplest form because the radicand $5 = 5 \cdot 1$ contains no perfect squares factors other than 1.

If the radicand is a relatively small number, by inspection you can identify the largest perfect square, otherwise the radical is not completely simplified after one step.

For example, $\sqrt{32} = \sqrt{4 \cdot 8} = \sqrt{4}\sqrt{8} = 2\sqrt{8}$. The radical expression $2\sqrt{8}$ is not in simplest form because the radicand $8 = 4 \cdot 2$ contains a perfect square factor 4 other than one. This result is a consequence of the fact that the factor 4 was not the maximum perfect square.

Thus, we need to continue a few more steps to simplify the radical expression completely

$$\sqrt{32} = \sqrt{4 \cdot 8} = \sqrt{4}\sqrt{8} = 2\sqrt{8} =$$

$$2\sqrt{4 \cdot 2} = 2\sqrt{4}\sqrt{2} = 2 \cdot 2\sqrt{2} = 4\sqrt{2}$$

If we can identify the largest perfect square from the beginning, the radical expression could be simplified in one step.

$$\sqrt{32} = \sqrt{16 \cdot 2} = \sqrt{16}\sqrt{2} = 4\sqrt{2}$$

Example 4

Simplify.

a. $\sqrt{18}$ b. $\sqrt{50}$ c. $3\sqrt{48}$

Solution

a. $\sqrt{18} = \sqrt{9 \cdot 2} = \sqrt{9}\sqrt{2} = 3\sqrt{2}$

b. $\sqrt{50} = \sqrt{25 \cdot 2} = \sqrt{25}\sqrt{2} = 5\sqrt{2}$

c. $3\sqrt{48} = 3\sqrt{16 \cdot 3} = 3\sqrt{16}\sqrt{3} = 3 \cdot 4\sqrt{3} = 12\sqrt{3}$

If the radicand is a large number, use prime factorization to write the number in prime factored form and then identify all the *pair factors*. The product of those pair factors gives the largest perfect square.

Example 5

___

Simplify.

$$\sqrt{252}$$

252	2
126	2
63	3
21	3
7	7
1	1

The number 252 contains two pairs $2 \cdot 2 = 4$ and $3 \cdot 3 = 9$.

Their product $4 \cdot 9 = 36$ is the largest perfect square.

Then $\sqrt{252} = \sqrt{36 \cdot 7} = \sqrt{36}\sqrt{7} = 6\sqrt{7}$, which is the simplest form.

Example 6

___

Simplify.

$$\sqrt{392}.$$

392	2
196	2
98	2
49	7
7	7
1	1

The number 392 contains two pairs $2 \cdot 2 = 4$ and $7 \cdot 7 = 49$. Their product $49 \cdot 4 = 196$ is the largest perfect square. Thus $\sqrt{392} = \sqrt{196 \cdot 2} = \sqrt{196}\sqrt{2} = 14\sqrt{2}$ which is in simplest form

☐ SIMPLIFYING RADICAL EXPRESSIONS CONTAINING VARIABLES

Note: When a variable is multiplied by itself, the product is a perfect square.

For example, a^2, x^4, y^6, m^{14} etc. are perfect squares because $a^2 = a \cdot a$, $x^4 = x^2 \cdot x^2$, $y^6 = y^3 \cdot y^3$, and $m^{14} = m^7 \cdot m^7$.

The above examples suggest that a variable written in exponential form is a perfect square when the exponent is even. Thus, a^{10} and m^6 are perfect squares, while x^7, and y^{15} are not perfect squares.

In this section, when simplifying radical expressions containing variables, we assume that all the variables represent nonnegative numbers.

Example 7

___

Simplify.

a. $\sqrt{x^4}$ b. $\sqrt{y^6}$ c. $\sqrt{9m^{14}}$ d. $8\sqrt{16a^2b^8}$

Solution

a. $\sqrt{x^4} = x^2$

b. $\sqrt{y^6} = y^3$

c. $\sqrt{9m^{14}} = \sqrt{9}\sqrt{m^{14}} = 3m^7$

d. $8\sqrt{16a^2b^8} = 8\sqrt{16}\sqrt{a^2}\sqrt{b^8} = 8 \cdot 4ab^4 = 32ab^4$

If the radicand contains variables that are not perfect squares, write each variable as a product of the largest perfect square factor in the variable and a factor that is not a perfect square.

For example,

$x^9 = x^8 \cdot x$ (x^8 is the largest perfect square because it
             has the largest even exponent smaller than 9)

$y^{15} = y^{14} \cdot y$ (y^{14} is the largest perfect square)

$n^5 = n^4 \cdot n$ (n^4 is the largest perfect square)

Example 8

Simplify.

a. $\sqrt{x^9}$ b. $\sqrt{x^{10}y^{15}}$ c. $\sqrt{25b^{11}}$ d. $\sqrt{45x^3y^7}$

Solution

a. $\sqrt{x^9} = \sqrt{x^8 \cdot x} = \sqrt{x^8}\sqrt{x} = x^4\sqrt{x}$

b. $\sqrt{x^{10}y^{15}} = \sqrt{x^{10}y^{14} \cdot y} = \sqrt{x^{10}}\sqrt{y^{14}}\sqrt{y} = x^5y^7\sqrt{y}$

c. $\sqrt{25b^{11}} = \sqrt{25b^{10}b} = \sqrt{25}\sqrt{b^{10}}\sqrt{b} = 5b^5\sqrt{b}$

d. $\sqrt{45x^3y^7} = \sqrt{9 \cdot 5x^2xy^6y} = \sqrt{9x^2y^6}\sqrt{5xy} = 3xy^3\sqrt{5xy}$

Example 9

Simplify.

a. $2x\sqrt{40x^{21}y^{19}z}$ b. $5x^2y\sqrt{128x^{17}y^{13}}$ c. $6ab^2c^3\sqrt{12a^3b^2c^5}$

Solution

a. $2x\sqrt{40x^{21}y^{19}z} = 2x\sqrt{4 \cdot 10x^{20}xy^{18}yz} = 2x\sqrt{4x^{20}y^{18}}\sqrt{10xyz} =$
    $2x(2x^{10}y^9)\sqrt{10xyz} = 4x^{11}y^9\sqrt{10xyz}$

b. $5x^2y\sqrt{128x^{17}y^{13}} = 5x^2y\sqrt{64 \cdot 2x^{16}xy^{12}y} = 5x^2y\sqrt{64x^{16}y^{12}}\sqrt{2xy} =$
    $5x^2y(8x^8y^6)\sqrt{2xy} = 40x^{10}y^7\sqrt{2xy}$

c. $6ab^2c^3\sqrt{12a^3b^2c^5} = 6ab^2c^3\sqrt{4\cdot 3a^2ab^2c^4c} = 6ab^2c^3\sqrt{4a^2b^2c^4}\sqrt{3ac} =$

$6ab^2c^3(2abc^2)\sqrt{3ac} = 12a^2b^3c^5\sqrt{3ac}$

☐ SIMPLIFYING HIGHER ORDER RADICAL EXPRESSIONS

Product Rule for Cube Roots

If a and b are real numbers then, $\sqrt[3]{a}\cdot\sqrt[3]{b} = \sqrt[3]{a\cdot b}$. *The product of the cube roots is equal to the cube root of the products.*

Example 9

$\sqrt[3]{2}\cdot\sqrt[3]{4} = \sqrt[3]{8} = 2$

Quotient Rule for Cube Roots

If a and b are real numbers and $b \neq 0$ *then,* $\dfrac{\sqrt[3]{a}}{\sqrt[3]{b}} = \sqrt[3]{\dfrac{a}{b}}$. *The quotient of the cube roots is equal to the cube root of the quotient.*

Example 10

Simplify.

$\dfrac{\sqrt[3]{54}}{\sqrt[3]{2}}$

Solution

$$\frac{\sqrt[3]{54}}{\sqrt[3]{2}} = \sqrt[3]{\frac{54}{2}} = \sqrt[3]{27} = 3$$

Note: When a rational number is multiplied by itself three times, the product is a perfect cube.

For example: 1, 8, 27, −64, 0.001, $\dfrac{64}{125}$, are perfect cubes because $1 = 1\cdot 1\cdot 1$, $8 = 2\cdot 2\cdot 2$, $27 =$

$3\cdot 3\cdot 3$, $-64 = (-4)(-4)(-4)$, $0.001 = 0.1\cdot 0.1\cdot 0.1$, $\dfrac{64}{125} = \dfrac{4}{5}\cdot\dfrac{4}{5}\cdot\dfrac{4}{5}$

When simplifying cube roots, if the radicand is a perfect cube, then the entire radicand can be removed from under the radical.

For example, $\sqrt[3]{1} = 1$, $\sqrt[3]{8} = 2$, $\sqrt[3]{27} = 3$, $\sqrt[3]{0.001} = 0.1$, $\sqrt[3]{\dfrac{64}{125}} = \dfrac{4}{5}$, $\sqrt[3]{x^3} = x$.

If the radicand is not a perfect cube, first write the radicand as a product of the largest perfect cube and a factor that is not a perfect cube and does not contain a perfect cube other than one. Then using the rules of radicals, remove the largest perfect cube from the radicand.

For example,

$56 = 8 \cdot 7$ $8 = 2 \cdot 2 \cdot 2$ is the largest perfect cube.

$135 = 27 \cdot 5$ $27 = 3 \cdot 3 \cdot 3$ is the largest perfect cube.

$x^7 = x^6 \cdot x$ $x^6 = x^2 \cdot x^2 \cdot x^2$ is the largest perfect cube.

$x^{11} = x^9 \cdot x^2$ $x^9 = x^3 \cdot x^3 \cdot x^3$ is the largest perfect cube.

Example 11

Simplify.

$\sqrt[3]{81}$

Solution

$$\sqrt[3]{81} = \sqrt[3]{27 \cdot 3} = \sqrt[3]{27} \cdot \sqrt[3]{3} = 3\sqrt[3]{3}$$

If the radicand is a large number, use prime factorization to write the number in prime factored form and then identify all triple factors. The product of those triple factors gives the larges perfect cube.

Example 12

Simplify.

$\sqrt[3]{108}$

108	2
54	2
27	3
9	3
3	3
1	1

The number 108 contains one triple $3 \cdot 3 \cdot 3 = 27$.

Then, $\sqrt[3]{108} = \sqrt[3]{27 \cdot 4} = \sqrt[3]{27} \cdot \sqrt[3]{4} = 3\sqrt[3]{4}$.

Example 13

Simplify.

a. $\sqrt[3]{64x^6}$

b. $\sqrt[3]{125x^{10}}$

c. $\sqrt[3]{40x^9y^{14}}$

Solution

a. $\sqrt[3]{64x^6} = \sqrt[3]{4 \cdot 4 \cdot 4 \cdot x^2 \cdot x^2 \cdot x^2} = \sqrt[3]{4^3(x^2)^3} = 4x^2$

b. $\sqrt[3]{125x^{10}} = \sqrt[3]{5^3x^9x} = \sqrt[3]{5^3(x^3)^3x} = 5x^3 \cdot \sqrt[3]{x}$

c. $\sqrt[3]{40x^{15}y^{14}} = \sqrt[3]{8 \cdot 5 \cdot x^{15}y^{12}y^2} = \sqrt[3]{8(x^5)^3(y^4)^3 \cdot 5y^2} = 2x^5y^4 \cdot \sqrt[3]{5y^2}$

General Rule:

If a and b are real numbers, then $\sqrt[n]{a} \cdot \sqrt[n]{b} = \sqrt[n]{ab}$ for n odd ($n \geq 3$).

If $a \geq 0$ or $b \geq 0$, then $\sqrt[n]{a} \cdot \sqrt[n]{b} = \sqrt[n]{ab}$ for n even ($n \geq 2$).

If a and b are real numbers and $b \neq 0$, then $\dfrac{\sqrt[n]{a}}{\sqrt[n]{b}} = \sqrt[n]{\dfrac{a}{b}}$ for n odd ($n \geq 3$)

If $a \geq 0$ or $b > 0$, then $\dfrac{\sqrt[n]{a}}{\sqrt[n]{b}} = \sqrt[n]{\dfrac{a}{b}}$ for n even ($n \geq 2$)

8.2 EXERCISES

Simplify each radical expression completely. Assume all variables are nonnegative real numbers.

1. $\sqrt{40}$

2. $\sqrt{24}$

3. $\sqrt{27}$

4. $\sqrt{75}$

5. $\sqrt{48}$

6. $\sqrt{500}$

7. $\sqrt{80}$

8. $\sqrt{63}$

9. $\sqrt{125}$

10. $\sqrt{162}$

11. $\sqrt{60}$

12. $\sqrt{28}$

13. $\sqrt{45}$

14. $\sqrt{98}$

15. $\sqrt{200}$

16. $\sqrt{800}$

17. $\sqrt{245}$

18. $\sqrt{250}$

19. $-4\sqrt{50}$

20. $-3\sqrt{18}$

21. $8\sqrt{20}$

22. $7\sqrt{162}$

23. $\dfrac{1}{4}\sqrt{128}$

24. $\dfrac{1}{6}\sqrt{108}$

25. $11\sqrt{44}$

26. $\sqrt{x^8}$

27. $\sqrt{a^{12}}$

28. $\sqrt{16y^4}$

29. $\sqrt{81x^{10}}$

30. $\sqrt{x^7}$

31. $\sqrt{y^5}$

32. $\sqrt{63x^5}$

33. $\sqrt{72x^3}$

34. $\sqrt{8x^6y^9}$

35. $\sqrt{12x^4y^5}$

36. $\sqrt{90x^{17}y^{11}}$

37. $2x^3\sqrt{96x^{16}y^{21}}$

38. $5b\sqrt{300a^2b^7c}$

39. $3xy^2\sqrt{32x^3y^7}$

40. $4ab\sqrt{500a^{12}b^5c}$

41. $-5x^2y^3\sqrt{21x^2y^3}$

42. $-8xy\sqrt{15xy^5}$

43. $2m^2n\sqrt{180m^5n^{11}}$

44. $\frac{3}{4}a^3b^2\sqrt{112a^8b^7}$

45. $\frac{4}{7}mn\sqrt{294m^3n^{15}}$

46. $\sqrt{\dfrac{64x^2}{25}}$

47. $\sqrt{\dfrac{16x^4}{y^8}}$

48. $\sqrt{\dfrac{45x^3}{100}}$

49. $\sqrt{\dfrac{90x^{10}}{49}}$

50. $\sqrt{\dfrac{20x^6y^8}{z^4}}$

51. $\sqrt{\dfrac{32a^4b^{20}}{169}}$

52. $\sqrt{\dfrac{242x^4y^6}{25x}}$

53. $\sqrt{\dfrac{192a^5b^7c}{36ab^2}}$

54. $\sqrt{\dfrac{147m^9n^{10}}{121m^5n^3}}$

55. $\sqrt[3]{-27}$

56. $\sqrt[3]{-1}$

57. $\sqrt[3]{216}$

58. $\sqrt[3]{40}$

59. $\sqrt[3]{128}$

60. $\sqrt[3]{81}$

61. $\sqrt[3]{-64a^6b^9}$

62. $4m\cdot\sqrt[3]{216m^{12}n^{15}}$

63. $-3y\cdot\sqrt[3]{-108x^7y^{10}}$

64. $\sqrt[3]{-125x^4}$

65. $\sqrt[3]{1000x^5y^{15}}$

66. $\sqrt[3]{48x^7y^{16}}$

67. $\sqrt[3]{\dfrac{16x^3}{27}}$

68. $\sqrt[3]{\dfrac{54x^9}{125}}$

69. $\sqrt[3]{\dfrac{250a^7}{343}}$

70. $\sqrt[3]{\dfrac{81m^4n^6}{8m}}$

71. $\sqrt[3]{\dfrac{-48a^2b^8}{6a^5}}$

72. $\sqrt[3]{\dfrac{-24m^7n^{12}}{3m}}$

73. $\sqrt[4]{16x^4}$

74. $\sqrt[5]{-a^5b^6}$

8.3 ADDING AND SUBTRACTING RADICAL EXPRESSIONS

□ **Like Terms** □ **Like Radicals** □ **Unlike Radicals**

□ LIKE TERMS

In chapter 5 we added and subtracted polynomial like terms such as $2x + 4x = 6x$. This identity is true for any value assigned to the variable x. If we let $x = \sqrt{2}$, and substitute $\sqrt{2}$ for x we get $2\sqrt{2} + 4\sqrt{2} = 6\sqrt{2}$. The radical expressions $2\sqrt{2}$ and $4\sqrt{2}$ are called like radicals.

□ LIKE RADICALS

Radicals that have the same index, same radicand, and the same variables with the same exponents, outside the radical (if any) are called like radicals.

For example: $7x^2\sqrt{5}$, $-2x^2\sqrt{5}$, $11x^2\sqrt{5}$, $x^2\sqrt{5}$ are like radicals because they have the same index (2), same radicand (5), and the same variable with the same exponent outside the radical (x^2).

□ UNLIKE RADICALS

If at least one condition required for like radicals fails, the radicals are called unlike radicals.

For example,

$8\sqrt{3}$, $2\sqrt{6}$, $\sqrt{7}$	unlike radicals because they have different radicand.
$2\sqrt[3]{5}$, $\sqrt{5}$	unlike radicals because they have different indices.
$4\sqrt{2}$, $\sqrt[3]{3}$	unlike radicals because they have different indices and different radicand .
$2x\sqrt{6}$, $y\sqrt{6}$, $x^2\sqrt{6}$	unlike radicals because they have different variables outside or the variables have different exponents .

Note: Like radicals can be combined the same way we combine like terms. Unlike radicals cannot be combined.

Example 1

Simplify each radical expression, if possible, by combining like radicals.

a. $5\sqrt{3}+8\sqrt{3}$

b. $4\sqrt{7}-2\sqrt{7}+\sqrt{2a}-3\sqrt{2a}$

c. $\sqrt[3]{3x}+6-8\sqrt[3]{3x}-1$

d. $2\sqrt{5}+5\sqrt{2}$

Solution

a. $5\sqrt{3}+8\sqrt{3}=13\sqrt{3}$

b. $4\sqrt{7}-2\sqrt{7}+\sqrt{2a}-3\sqrt{2a}=2\sqrt{7}-2\sqrt{2a}$

c. $\sqrt[3]{3x}+6-8\sqrt[3]{3x}-1=5-7\sqrt[3]{3x}$

d. $2\sqrt{5}+5\sqrt{2}$ cannot be combined (unlike radicals).

To determine whether radicals with the same index are like or unlike radicals, each radical should be in simplest form.

Example 2

Simplify each radical expression, if possible, by combining like radicals.

a. $\sqrt{20x}+\sqrt{45x}-\sqrt{80x}$

b. $\sqrt{12xy^2}+\sqrt{8xy^2}+\sqrt{50xy^2}$

Solution

First, write each radicand as a product of the largest perfect square and a factor that is not a perfect square, then use the product rule to simplify.

a. $\sqrt{20x}+\sqrt{45x}-\sqrt{80x}=\sqrt{4\cdot5x}+\sqrt{9\cdot5x}-\sqrt{16\cdot5x}=2\sqrt{5x}+3\sqrt{3x}-4\sqrt{5x}=\sqrt{5x}$

b. $\sqrt{12xy^2}+\sqrt{8xy^2}+\sqrt{50xy^2}=\sqrt{4y^2\cdot3x}+\sqrt{4y^2\cdot2x}+\sqrt{25y^2\cdot2x}=$

$=2y\sqrt{3x}+2y\sqrt{2x}+5y\sqrt{2x}=2y\sqrt{3x}+7y\sqrt{2x}$

Example 3

Simplify each radical expression, if possible, by combining like radicals.

a. $3\sqrt{8}+5\sqrt{18}$

b. $\sqrt{75}-\sqrt{48}+4\sqrt{27}$

c. $2x\sqrt{24x^3}-3x^2\sqrt{6x}$

Solution

a. $3\sqrt{8}+5\sqrt{18}=3\sqrt{4\cdot2}+5\sqrt{9\cdot2}=3\sqrt{4}\sqrt{2}+5\sqrt{9}\sqrt{2}=3\cdot2\sqrt{2}+5\cdot3\sqrt{2}=$

$6\sqrt{2}+15\sqrt{2}=21\sqrt{2}$

b. $\sqrt{75}-\sqrt{48}+4\sqrt{27}=\sqrt{25\cdot3}-\sqrt{16\cdot3}+4\sqrt{9\cdot3}=5\sqrt{3}-4\sqrt{3}+4\cdot3\sqrt{3}=$

$5\sqrt{3}-4\sqrt{3}+12\sqrt{3}=\sqrt{3}+12\sqrt{3}=13\sqrt{3}$

c. $2x\sqrt{24x^3}-3x^2\sqrt{6x}=2x\sqrt{4\cdot6\cdot x^2\cdot x}-3x^2\sqrt{6x}=2x\cdot2\cdot x\sqrt{6x}-3x^2\sqrt{6x}=$

$$4x^2\sqrt{6x} - 3x^2\sqrt{6x} = x^2\sqrt{6x}$$

Example 4

Simplify each radical expression, if possible, by combining like radicals.

a. $8a\sqrt{20a^5b^3} - 3b\sqrt{45a^7b}$

b. $2y\sqrt{32x^2y} + 3x\sqrt{50y^3}$

Solution

a. $8a\sqrt{20a^5b^3} - 3b\sqrt{45a^7b} = 8a\sqrt{4\cdot5\cdot a^4 \cdot a\cdot b^2 \cdot b} - 3b\sqrt{9\cdot5\cdot a^6 \cdot a\cdot b} =$

$8a\cdot2a^2b\sqrt{5ab} - 3b\cdot3a^3\sqrt{5ab} = 16a^3b\sqrt{5ab} - 9a^3b\sqrt{5ab} = 7a^3b\sqrt{5ab}$

b. $2y\sqrt{32x^2y} + 3x\sqrt{50y^3} = 2y\sqrt{16\cdot2x^2y} + 3x\sqrt{25\cdot2y^2y} =$

$2y\cdot4x\sqrt{2y} + 3x\cdot5y\sqrt{2y} = 8xy\sqrt{2y} + 15xy\sqrt{2y} = 23xy\sqrt{2y}$

Example 5

Simplify.

a. $2\sqrt[3]{27x^3} + 4x\sqrt[3]{64}$

b. $15\cdot\sqrt[3]{8a^3b^4} - 3ab\cdot\sqrt[3]{125b}$

Solution

Write each radicand as a product of the largest perfect cube and a factor that is not a perfect cube and does not contain a perfect cube other than one, then use the product rule to simplify.

a. $2\cdot\sqrt[3]{27x^3} + 4x\cdot\sqrt[3]{64} = 2\cdot3x + 4x\cdot4 = 6x + 16x = 22x$

b. $15\cdot\sqrt[3]{8a^3b^4} - 3ab\cdot\sqrt[3]{125b} = 15\cdot\sqrt[3]{8a^3b^3b} - 3ab\cdot\sqrt[3]{125b} = 15\cdot2ab\cdot\sqrt[3]{b} - 3ab\cdot5\sqrt[3]{b} =$

$30ab\cdot\sqrt[3]{b} - 15ab\cdot\sqrt[3]{b} = 15ab\cdot\sqrt[3]{b}$

Example 6

Simplify.

$11\cdot\sqrt[3]{32x^4y^5} - xy\cdot\sqrt[3]{500xy^2}$

Solution

$11\cdot\sqrt[3]{32x^4y^5} - xy\cdot\sqrt[3]{500xy^2} = 11\cdot\sqrt[3]{8\cdot4x^3xy^3y^2} - xy\cdot\sqrt[3]{125\cdot4xy^2} =$

$11\cdot2xy\cdot\sqrt[3]{4xy^2} - xy\cdot5\cdot\sqrt[3]{4xy^2} = 22xy\cdot\sqrt[3]{4xy^2} - 5xy\cdot\sqrt[3]{4xy^2} = 17xy\cdot\sqrt[3]{4xy^2}$

8.3 EXERCISES

Simplify each radical expression.

1. $2\sqrt{3} + 5\sqrt{3}$

2. $4\sqrt{7} - 8\sqrt{7}$

3. $3\sqrt{5} + 11\sqrt{5}$

4. $10\sqrt{a} + 5\sqrt{a} - 7\sqrt{a}$

5. $6\sqrt{x} - \sqrt{x} + 9\sqrt{x}$

6. $3a\sqrt{2b} + 5a\sqrt{2b}$

7. $-5\sqrt{6x} - 3\sqrt{6x}$

8. $8\sqrt{11} - 12\sqrt{11}$

9. $2\sqrt{y} - \sqrt{y} + 4 + \sqrt{x}$

10. $2\sqrt{15} + 4\sqrt{3} - \sqrt{15} + \sqrt{3}$

11. $4\sqrt{y} - 3 + 5\sqrt{y} - 1$

12. $3\sqrt{12} + 5\sqrt{27} + \sqrt{48}$

13. $\sqrt{32} + \sqrt{18} + \sqrt{50}$

14. $2\sqrt{45} + 3\sqrt{20} + \sqrt{125}$

15. $4\sqrt{28} + 5\sqrt{63} + \sqrt{7}$

16. $6\sqrt{48} - 2\sqrt{75} + 5\sqrt{12}$

17. $\sqrt{50} + \sqrt{72} + \sqrt{100}$

18. $2\sqrt{90} - 3\sqrt{160}$

19. $3\sqrt{80} - \sqrt{180} + 4\sqrt{20}$

20. $-2\sqrt{24} + 7\sqrt{54} - \sqrt{96}$

21. $8\sqrt{40} - 4\sqrt{90} + 2\sqrt{10}$

22. $-5\sqrt[3]{24} + 6\sqrt[3]{81}$

23. $2\sqrt[3]{16} - \sqrt[3]{128}$

24. $11\sqrt[3]{40} - \sqrt[3]{135}$

25. $-4\sqrt[3]{48} - 5\sqrt[3]{162}$

26. $10\sqrt[3]{7} - 2\sqrt[3]{56}$

27. $3\sqrt[3]{80} + \sqrt[3]{270}$

28. $20\sqrt{8} + 8\sqrt{12} - 3\sqrt{32} - 9\sqrt{27}$

29. $10\sqrt{20} - 2\sqrt{28} - 4\sqrt{80} + \sqrt{112}$

30. $3\sqrt{44} + 2\sqrt{90} - 3\sqrt{99} - 2\sqrt{40}$

31. $12\sqrt{60} - 4\sqrt{63} + 2\sqrt{135} + 8\sqrt{112}$

32. $x\sqrt{12xy^3} + \sqrt{75x^3y^3} - xy\sqrt{3xy}$

33. $ab\sqrt{32a^3b^2} - a^2\sqrt{8ab^4} + a^2b^2\sqrt{2a}$

34. $5a^2\sqrt{3ab} + 6\sqrt{27a^5b} + a\sqrt{300a^3b}$

35. $3y\sqrt{18x^2} - 4x\sqrt{128y^2} + xy\sqrt{8}$

36. $4ab\sqrt{48a^3b} - 3a^2\sqrt{3ab^3}$

37. $2x\sqrt{28x^3y^4} + 10x^2y^2\sqrt{7x}$

38. $x\sqrt{8x^3y^5} - y\sqrt{50x^5y^3} + xy\sqrt{2x^3y^3}$

39. $a^2b\sqrt{20ab^3} + ab^2\sqrt{45a^3b} - a^2b^2\sqrt{5ab}$

40. $\sqrt{50a^5b^7} - 4ab^2\sqrt{72a^3b^3} + ab\sqrt{18a^3b^5}$

41. $x^2\sqrt{32xy^5} - y\sqrt{200x^5y^3} - x^2y^2\sqrt{8xy}$

42. $2x^2 \cdot \sqrt[3]{40x} + \sqrt[3]{5x^7}$

43. $a^4 \cdot \sqrt[3]{32a^3b} - \sqrt[3]{4a^{15}b}$

44. $2x^2 \cdot \sqrt[3]{16x^4} - 5x^3 \cdot \sqrt[3]{54x} + \sqrt[3]{2x^{10}}$

45. $\sqrt[3]{27x^3y^4} + \sqrt[3]{64x^4y^3} - \sqrt[3]{125x^3y^3}$

8.4 MULTIPLYING RADICAL EXPRESSIONS

In this section, we will use the Product Rule ($\sqrt[n]{a} \cdot \sqrt[n]{b} = \sqrt[n]{ab}$ for appropriate a and b) in combination with the Distributive Property, Foil, etc. to multiply radical expressions. The result should always be written in simplest form. The multiplication of radical expressions is similar to the multiplication of polynomials.

Example 1
___

Multiply.

a. $\sqrt{12} \cdot \sqrt{6}$ 　　　　 b. $3\sqrt{2} \cdot \sqrt{14}$ 　　　　 c. $5\sqrt{3x^3} \cdot x\sqrt{21x}$ 　　　　 d. $\sqrt[3]{9x^2} \cdot \sqrt[3]{6x^4}$

Solution

a. $\sqrt{12} \cdot \sqrt{6} = \sqrt{12 \cdot 6} = \sqrt{72} = \sqrt{36 \cdot 2} = 6\sqrt{2}$ or
$\sqrt{12} \cdot \sqrt{6} = \sqrt{2 \cdot 6} \cdot \sqrt{6} = \sqrt{2} \cdot \sqrt{6} \cdot \sqrt{6} = \sqrt{2} \cdot \sqrt{36} = 6\sqrt{2}$

b. $3\sqrt{2} \cdot \sqrt{14} = 3\sqrt{2 \cdot 14} = 3\sqrt{28} = 3\sqrt{4 \cdot 7} = 3 \cdot 2\sqrt{7} = 6\sqrt{7}$ or
$3\sqrt{2} \cdot \sqrt{14} = 3\sqrt{2} \cdot \sqrt{2 \cdot 7} = 3\sqrt{2} \cdot \sqrt{2} \cdot \sqrt{7} = 3\sqrt{4} \cdot \sqrt{7} = 3 \cdot 2\sqrt{7} = 6\sqrt{7}$

c. $5\sqrt{3x^3} \cdot x\sqrt{21x} = 5x\sqrt{3x^3 \cdot 21x} = 5x\sqrt{63x^4} = 5x\sqrt{9 \cdot 7x^4} = 5x \cdot 3x^2\sqrt{7} = 15x^3\sqrt{7}$

d. $\sqrt[3]{9x^2} \cdot \sqrt[3]{6x^4} = \sqrt[3]{9x^2 \cdot 6x^4} = \sqrt[3]{54x^6} = \sqrt[3]{27 \cdot 2x^6} = 3x^2 \cdot \sqrt[3]{2}$

Example 2
___

Multiply.

a. $\sqrt{10}\left(\sqrt{2} + \sqrt{5}\right)$ 　　　　 b. $\sqrt{6}\left(\sqrt{3} - \sqrt{8}\right)$ 　　　　 c. $\sqrt{2}\left(\sqrt{8} + 3\right)$

Solution

a. $\sqrt{10}\left(\sqrt{2} + \sqrt{5}\right) = \sqrt{10} \cdot \sqrt{2} + \sqrt{10} \cdot \sqrt{5} =$ 　　　 Distributive Property

$\sqrt{10 \cdot 2} + \sqrt{10 \cdot 5} = \sqrt{20} + \sqrt{50} =$ 　　　 Product Rule

$\sqrt{4 \cdot 5} + \sqrt{25 \cdot 2} = 2\sqrt{5} + 5\sqrt{2}$ 　　　 Simplify

b. $\sqrt{6}\left(\sqrt{3} - \sqrt{8}\right) = \sqrt{6} \cdot \sqrt{3} - \sqrt{6} \cdot \sqrt{8} =$ 　　　 Distributive Property

$\sqrt{6 \cdot 3} - \sqrt{6 \cdot 8} = \sqrt{18} - \sqrt{48} =$ 　　　 Product Rule

$\sqrt{9 \cdot 2} - \sqrt{16 \cdot 3} = 3\sqrt{2} - 4\sqrt{3}$ 　　　 Simplify

c. $\sqrt{2}\left(\sqrt{8}+3\right)=\sqrt{2}\cdot\sqrt{8}+3\sqrt{2}=$ Distributive Property

$\sqrt{2\cdot8}+3\sqrt{2}=\sqrt{16}+3\sqrt{2}=$ Product Rule

$4+3\sqrt{2}$ Simplify

Example 3

Multiply.

a. $2\sqrt{3}\left(5\sqrt{6}-3\sqrt{12}\right)$

c. $4x\sqrt{2x}\left(3x\sqrt{10x}+\sqrt{40x^3}\right)$

b. $-6\sqrt{8}\left(3\sqrt{5}-4\right)$

Solution

Apply the distributive property. First, multiply the coefficients and then the radicands.

a. $2\sqrt{3}\left(5\sqrt{6}-3\sqrt{12}\right)=\left(2\sqrt{3}\right)\left(5\sqrt{6}\right)-\left(2\sqrt{3}\right)\left(3\sqrt{12}\right)=$ Distributive Property

$2\cdot5\sqrt{3\cdot6}-2\cdot3\sqrt{3\cdot12}=10\sqrt{18}-6\sqrt{36}=$ Product Rule

$10\sqrt{9\cdot2}-6\cdot6=10\cdot3\sqrt{2}-36=30\sqrt{2}-36$ Simplify

b. $-6\sqrt{8}\left(3\sqrt{5}-4\right)=\left(-6\sqrt{8}\right)\left(3\sqrt{5}\right)-\left(-6\sqrt{8}\right)\left(4\right)=$ Distributive Property

$-6\cdot3\sqrt{8\cdot5}+6\cdot4\sqrt{8}=-18\sqrt{40}+24\sqrt{8}=$ Product Rule

$-18\sqrt{4\cdot10}+24\sqrt{4\cdot2}=-18\cdot2\sqrt{10}+24\cdot2\sqrt{2}=-36\sqrt{10}+48\sqrt{2}$ Simplify

c. $4x\sqrt{2x}\left(3x\sqrt{10x}+\sqrt{40x^3}\right)=\left(4x\sqrt{2x}\right)\left(3x\sqrt{10x}\right)+\left(4x\sqrt{2x}\right)\left(\sqrt{40x^3}\right)=$ Distributive Property

$4x\cdot3x\sqrt{2x\cdot10x}+4x\sqrt{2x\cdot40x^3}=12x^2\sqrt{20x^2}+4x\sqrt{80x^4}=$ Product Rule

$12x^2\sqrt{4\cdot5x^2}+4x\sqrt{16\cdot5x^4}=12x^2\cdot2x\sqrt{5}+4x\cdot4x^2\sqrt{5}=$ Simplify

$24x^3\sqrt{5}+16x^3\sqrt{5}=40x^3\sqrt{5}$

Example 4

Multiply.

a. $\left(\sqrt{5}+\sqrt{8}\right)\left(\sqrt{10}+3\right)$

b. $\left(2\sqrt{6}+\sqrt{12}\right)\left(4\sqrt{3}-\sqrt{12}\right)$

Solution

a.

$$\left(\sqrt{5}+\sqrt{8}\right)\left(\sqrt{10}+3\right)=\sqrt{5}\sqrt{10}+3\sqrt{5}+\sqrt{8}\sqrt{10}+3\sqrt{8}=\text{ FOIL}$$

$$\sqrt{5\cdot10}+3\sqrt{5}+\sqrt{8\cdot10}+3\sqrt{8}=\sqrt{50}+3\sqrt{5}+\sqrt{80}+3\sqrt{8}=\text{ Product Rule}$$

$$\sqrt{25\cdot2}+3\sqrt{5}+\sqrt{16\cdot5}+3\sqrt{4\cdot2}=5\sqrt{2}+3\sqrt{5}+4\sqrt{5}+3\cdot2\sqrt{2}=\text{ Simplify}$$

$$5\sqrt{2}+3\sqrt{5}+4\sqrt{5}+6\sqrt{2}=11\sqrt{2}+7\sqrt{5}$$

b.

$$\left(2\sqrt{6}+\sqrt{12}\right)\left(4\sqrt{3}-\sqrt{12}\right)=\text{ FOIL}$$

$$\left(2\sqrt{6}\right)\left(4\sqrt{3}\right)-\left(2\sqrt{6}\right)\left(\sqrt{12}\right)+\left(\sqrt{12}\right)\left(4\sqrt{3}\right)-\left(\sqrt{12}\right)\left(\sqrt{12}\right)=$$

$$2\cdot4\sqrt{6\cdot3}-2\sqrt{6\cdot12}+4\sqrt{12\cdot3}-\sqrt{12\cdot12}=\text{ Product Rule}$$

$$8\sqrt{18}-2\sqrt{72}+4\sqrt{36}-\sqrt{144}=$$

$$8\sqrt{9\cdot2}-2\sqrt{36\cdot2}+4\cdot6-12=8\cdot3\sqrt{2}-2\cdot6\sqrt{2}+24-12=\text{ Simplify}$$

$$24\sqrt{2}-12\sqrt{2}+24-12=12\sqrt{2}+12$$

Example 5

Multiply.

a. $\left(3\sqrt{2x^3}-\sqrt{y}\right)\left(\sqrt{x}+4\sqrt{xy}\right)$

b. $\left(2\sqrt{2a}+\sqrt{8}\right)^2$

Solution

a.

$$\left(3\sqrt{2x^3}-\sqrt{y}\right)\left(\sqrt{x}+4\sqrt{xy}\right)=$$

$$3\sqrt{2x^3}\cdot\sqrt{x}+\left(3\sqrt{2x^3}\right)\left(4\sqrt{xy}\right)-\sqrt{y}\cdot\sqrt{x}-\sqrt{y}\left(4\sqrt{xy}\right)=$$

$$3\sqrt{2x^3\cdot x}+3\cdot4\sqrt{2x^3\cdot xy}-\sqrt{xy}-4\sqrt{y\cdot xy}=$$

$$3\sqrt{2x^4}+12\sqrt{2x^4y}-\sqrt{xy}-4\sqrt{xy^2}=$$

$$3x^2\sqrt{2}+12x^2\sqrt{2y}-\sqrt{xy}-4y\sqrt{x}$$

b.
$$\left(2\sqrt{2a}+\sqrt{8}\right)^2 = \left(2\sqrt{2a}+\sqrt{8}\right)\left(2\sqrt{2a}+\sqrt{8}\right)= \text{ FOIL}$$

$$\left(2\sqrt{2a}\right)\left(2\sqrt{2a}\right)+\left(2\sqrt{2a}\right)\sqrt{8}+\sqrt{8}\left(2\sqrt{2a}\right)+\sqrt{8}\sqrt{8}=$$

$$2\cdot2\sqrt{2a\cdot2a}+2\sqrt{2a\cdot8}+2\sqrt{8\cdot2a}+\sqrt{8\cdot8}= \text{ Product Rule}$$

$$4\sqrt{4a^2}+2\sqrt{16a}+2\sqrt{16a}+\sqrt{64}=$$

$$4\cdot2a+2\cdot4\sqrt{a}+2\cdot4\sqrt{a}+8= \text{ Simplify}$$

$$8a+8\sqrt{a}+8\sqrt{a}+8=8a+16\sqrt{a}+8$$

Radical expressions of the form $\sqrt{a}+\sqrt{b}$ and $\sqrt{a}-\sqrt{b}$ are called *conjugate radicals*.
For example $\sqrt{3}+\sqrt{2}$ is the conjugate of $\sqrt{3}-\sqrt{2}$ and $\sqrt{3}-\sqrt{2}$ is the conjugate of $\sqrt{3}+\sqrt{2}$.
Note: When multiplying conjugates, the radicals are always eliminated from the product.
This property is very useful when dividing radical expressions.

Example 6

Multiply.

a. $\left(\sqrt{3}+\sqrt{2}\right)\left(\sqrt{3}-\sqrt{2}\right)$ b. $\left(\sqrt{7}+\sqrt{5}\right)\left(\sqrt{7}-\sqrt{5}\right)$ c. $\left(\sqrt{6}-2\right)\left(\sqrt{6}+2\right)$

Solution

a.
$$\left(\sqrt{3}+\sqrt{2}\right)\left(\sqrt{3}-\sqrt{2}\right)=\sqrt{3}\cdot\sqrt{3}-\sqrt{3}\cdot\sqrt{2}+\sqrt{2}\cdot\sqrt{3}-\sqrt{2}\cdot\sqrt{2}= \text{ FOIL}$$

$$\sqrt{3\cdot3}-\sqrt{3\cdot2}+\sqrt{2\cdot3}-\sqrt{2\cdot2}=\sqrt{9}-\sqrt{6}+\sqrt{6}-\sqrt{4}= \text{ Product Rule}$$

$$3-2=1 \text{ Simplify}$$

b.
$$\left(\sqrt{7}+2\sqrt{5}\right)\left(\sqrt{7}-2\sqrt{5}\right)=\sqrt{7}\cdot\sqrt{7}-2\sqrt{7}\cdot\sqrt{5}+2\sqrt{5}\cdot\sqrt{7}-4\sqrt{5}\cdot\sqrt{5}= \text{ FOIL}$$

$$\sqrt{7\cdot7}-2\sqrt{7\cdot5}+2\sqrt{5\cdot7}-4\sqrt{5\cdot5}=\sqrt{49}-2\sqrt{35}+2\sqrt{35}-4\sqrt{25}= \text{ Product Rule}$$

$$7-4\cdot5=7-20=-13 \text{ Simplify}$$

c.
$$\left(\sqrt{8}-2\right)\left(\sqrt{8}+2\right)=\sqrt{8}\cdot\sqrt{8}+2\sqrt{8}-2\sqrt{8}-2\cdot2= \text{ FOIL}$$

$$\sqrt{8\cdot8}+2\sqrt{8}-2\sqrt{8}-4=\sqrt{64}-4= \text{ Product Rule}$$

$$8-4=4 \text{ Simplify}$$

Also, we can use the special product formula $(a+b)(a-b) = a^2 - b^2$ to multiply conjugate radicals.

a. $\left(\sqrt{3}+\sqrt{2}\right)\left(\sqrt{3}-\sqrt{2}\right) = \left(\sqrt{3}\right)^2 - \left(\sqrt{2}\right)^2 = 3-2 = 1$

b. $\left(\sqrt{7}+2\sqrt{5}\right)\left(\sqrt{7}-2\sqrt{5}\right) = \left(\sqrt{7}\right)^2 - \left(2\sqrt{5}\right)^2 = 7-4\cdot5 = 7-20 = -13$

c. $\left(\sqrt{8}-2\right)\left(\sqrt{8}+2\right) = \left(\sqrt{8}\right)^2 - (2)^2 = 8-4 = 4$

Example 7

Multiply.

$$\left(\sqrt[3]{2}+\sqrt[3]{9}\right)\left(\sqrt[3]{4}-\sqrt[3]{3}\right)$$

Solution

a.

$$\left(\sqrt[3]{2}+\sqrt[3]{9}\right)\left(\sqrt[3]{4}-\sqrt[3]{3}\right) = \sqrt[3]{2}\cdot\sqrt[3]{4}-\sqrt[3]{2}\cdot\sqrt[3]{3}+\sqrt[3]{9}\cdot\sqrt[3]{4}-\sqrt[3]{9}\cdot\sqrt[3]{3} = \text{ FOIL}$$

$$\sqrt[3]{2\cdot4}-\sqrt[3]{2\cdot3}+\sqrt[3]{9\cdot4}-\sqrt[3]{9\cdot3} = \sqrt[3]{8}-\sqrt[3]{6}+\sqrt[3]{36}-\sqrt[3]{27} = \text{ Product Rule}$$

$$2-\sqrt[3]{6}+\sqrt[3]{36}-3 = \sqrt[3]{36}-\sqrt[3]{6}-1 \text{ Simplify}$$

8.4 EXERCISES

Multiply and simplify.

1. $\sqrt{2}\sqrt{6}$

2. $\sqrt{3}\sqrt{8}$

3. $\sqrt{5}\sqrt{10}$

4. $\sqrt{7}\sqrt{7}$

5. $\sqrt{3}\sqrt{18}$

6. $\sqrt{6}\sqrt{12}$

7. $\sqrt{20}\sqrt{8}$

8. $\sqrt{2}\sqrt{27}$

9. $\sqrt{15}\sqrt{3}$

10. $\left(-2\sqrt{5}\right)\left(4\sqrt{15}\right)$

11. $\left(3\sqrt{2}\right)\left(-5\sqrt{32}\right)$

12. $\left(2\sqrt{7}\right)^2$

13. $\left(-4x\sqrt{6}\right)\left(6x\sqrt{12}\right)$

14. $\left(2a\sqrt{3}\right)\left(5a^2\sqrt{18}\right)$

15. $\left(xy\sqrt{2}\right)\left(7x\sqrt{20}\right)$

16. $\sqrt[3]{2}\sqrt[3]{4}$

17. $\sqrt[3]{3}\sqrt[3]{9}$

18. $\sqrt[3]{4}\sqrt[3]{20}$

19. $\sqrt{a^3b}\sqrt{ab}$

20. $\sqrt{2xy}\sqrt{8x^3y^3}$

21. $3\sqrt{x^3y^5}\sqrt{27x^5y}$

22. $-5\sqrt{3x^2y} \cdot 4\sqrt{xy^2}$

23. $10\sqrt{3ab} \cdot 2\sqrt{6a^2b^2}$

24. $\sqrt{5x^3y^3} \cdot \sqrt{10x^2y}$

25. $\sqrt{5}\left(\sqrt{15}-\sqrt{8}\right)$

26. $\sqrt{3}\left(\sqrt{6}+\sqrt{12}\right)$

27. $\sqrt{2}\left(\sqrt{12}-\sqrt{10}\right)$

28. $\sqrt{6}\left(\sqrt{2}+\sqrt{3}\right)$

29. $\sqrt{10}\left(\sqrt{5}-\sqrt{2}\right)$

30. $\sqrt{27}\left(\sqrt{6}-\sqrt{3}\right)$

31. $\sqrt{7}\left(\sqrt{7}+3\right)$

32. $\sqrt[3]{2}\left(\sqrt[3]{32}-5\right)$

33. $\sqrt[3]{5}\left(\sqrt[3]{25}+8\right)$

34. $\sqrt{6a}\left(\sqrt{2a}+\sqrt{3a^3}\right)$

35. $\sqrt{x}\left(\sqrt{75x}-\sqrt{48x}\right)$

36. $-\sqrt{a^3}\left(\sqrt{27a}-\sqrt{18a}\right)$

37. $\sqrt{2x}\left(\sqrt{24x^5}+\sqrt{2x^3}\right)$

38. $\sqrt{a^5}\left(\sqrt{125a}+\sqrt{a}\right)$

39. $\sqrt{3xy}\left(\sqrt{8x^3y}+5\right)$

40. $\left(\sqrt{2}+\sqrt{5}\right)\left(\sqrt{2}-\sqrt{10}\right)$

41. $\left(\sqrt{2}+\sqrt{3}\right)\left(\sqrt{8}-\sqrt{6}\right)$

42. $\left(\sqrt{3}-\sqrt{15}\right)\left(\sqrt{6}-\sqrt{3}\right)$

43. $\left(\sqrt{3}+\sqrt{8}\right)\left(\sqrt{12}+\sqrt{3}\right)$

44. $\left(2\sqrt{14}-5\sqrt{2}\right)\left(4\sqrt{2}+\sqrt{7}\right)$

45. $\left(6\sqrt{5}+5\sqrt{6}\right)\left(2\sqrt{8}-8\sqrt{2}\right)$

46. $\left(6\sqrt{x}+5\sqrt{y}\right)\left(2\sqrt{x}-\sqrt{8y}\right)$

47. $\left(a+\sqrt{3b}\right)\left(2a-\sqrt{15b}\right)$

48. $\left(\sqrt{6}+\sqrt{8}\right)^2$

49. $\left(\sqrt{5}-\sqrt{10}\right)^2$

50. $\left(\sqrt{2}+\sqrt{12}\right)^2$

51. $\left(\sqrt{3}+\sqrt{15}\right)^2$

52. $\left(\sqrt{11}-\sqrt{7}\right)\left(\sqrt{11}+\sqrt{7}\right)$

53. $\left(\sqrt{19}+\sqrt{17}\right)\left(\sqrt{19}-\sqrt{17}\right)$

54. $\left(2\sqrt{5}+\sqrt{3}\right)\left(2\sqrt{5}-\sqrt{3}\right)$

55. $\left(\sqrt{6}+\sqrt{10}\right)\left(\sqrt{6}-\sqrt{10}\right)$

56. $\left(\sqrt{12}-3\right)\left(\sqrt{12}+3\right)$

57. $\left(5\sqrt{3}-2\right)\left(5\sqrt{3}+2\right)$

58. $\left(\sqrt{2x}-\sqrt{y}\right)\left(\sqrt{2x}+\sqrt{y}\right)$

59. $\left(\sqrt{7a}+\sqrt{b}\right)\left(\sqrt{7a}-\sqrt{b}\right)$

60. $\left(2\sqrt{x}+3y\right)\left(2\sqrt{x}-3y\right)$

61. $\left(\sqrt{3a}+2b\right)\left(\sqrt{3a}-2b\right)$

62. $\left(\sqrt[3]{2}+\sqrt[3]{3}\right)\left(\sqrt[3]{4}-\sqrt[3]{9}\right)$

63. $\left(\sqrt[3]{5}-\sqrt[3]{6}\right)\left(\sqrt[3]{25}-\sqrt[3]{8}\right)$

64. $\left(\sqrt[3]{2}-\sqrt[3]{3}\right)\left(\sqrt[3]{4}+\sqrt[3]{6}+\sqrt[3]{9}\right)$

8.5 DIVIDING RADICAL EXPRESSIONS

In this section we will use the Quotient Rule introduced in section 8.2 to divide radical expressions.

$$\frac{\sqrt[n]{a}}{\sqrt[n]{b}} = \sqrt[n]{\frac{a}{b}} \text{ (for appropriate } a \text{ and } b)$$

Example 1

Divide.

a. $\dfrac{\sqrt{75}}{\sqrt{3}}$

b. $\dfrac{\sqrt{48x^3}}{\sqrt{2x}}$

c. $\sqrt{\dfrac{20a}{9b^2}}$

d. $\sqrt{\dfrac{12x^5}{49y^4}}$

Solution

a. $\dfrac{\sqrt{75}}{\sqrt{3}} = \sqrt{\dfrac{75}{3}} = \sqrt{25} = 5$

b. $\dfrac{\sqrt{48x^3}}{\sqrt{2x}} = \sqrt{\dfrac{48x^3}{2x}} = \sqrt{24x^2} = \sqrt{4 \cdot 6x^2} = 2x\sqrt{6}$

c. $\sqrt{\dfrac{20a}{9b^2}} = \dfrac{\sqrt{20a}}{\sqrt{9b^2}} = \dfrac{\sqrt{4 \cdot 5a}}{3b} = \dfrac{2\sqrt{5a}}{3b}$

d. $\sqrt{\dfrac{12x^5}{49y^4}} = \dfrac{\sqrt{12x^5}}{\sqrt{49y^4}} = \dfrac{\sqrt{4 \cdot 3x^4 x}}{\sqrt{49y^4}} = \dfrac{2x^2\sqrt{3x}}{7y^2}$

Note: In example a) and b) we used the quotient rule forward because the resulting radicand could be simplified, otherwise the quotient rule will make no difference.

A fraction containing radical expression(s) in its denominator is considered simplified when the denominator contains no radical(s).

The process used to eliminate the radical(s) from the denominator of a fraction involving radical(s) in the denominator is called "**rationalizing the denominator**."

Thus, dividing radical expressions or simplifying quotients involving radicals in the denominator or rationalizing the denominator refers to the same process: eliminating any radical expressions from denominator.

When simplifying fractions containing radical expression(s) in their denominators, in general there are two cases:

1. The denominator contains a single radical expression.

2. The denominator contains a sum or a difference of two radical expressions.

CASE 1

If the denominator contains a single radical expression, to rationalize the denominator, multiply both the numerator and denominator of the fraction by the same **appropriate** radical expression. If the denominator contains a square root, multiply and divide the fraction by the same square root.

Example 2

Rationalize.

a. $\dfrac{7}{\sqrt{5}}$
b. $\dfrac{\sqrt{3}}{3\sqrt{2}}$
c. $\dfrac{\sqrt{8x}}{\sqrt{3y}}$
d. $\dfrac{\sqrt[3]{2}}{\sqrt[3]{x}}$

Solution

a. $\dfrac{7}{\sqrt{5}}\cdot\dfrac{\sqrt{5}}{\sqrt{5}}=\dfrac{7\sqrt{5}}{\sqrt{25}}=\dfrac{7\sqrt{5}}{5}$

b. $\dfrac{\sqrt{3}}{3\sqrt{2}}\cdot\dfrac{\sqrt{2}}{\sqrt{2}}=\dfrac{\sqrt{3\cdot2}}{3\sqrt{2\cdot2}}=\dfrac{\sqrt{6}}{3\sqrt{4}}=\dfrac{\sqrt{6}}{3\cdot2}=\dfrac{\sqrt{6}}{6}$

c. $\dfrac{\sqrt{8x}}{\sqrt{3y}}\cdot\dfrac{\sqrt{3y}}{\sqrt{3y}}=\dfrac{\sqrt{8x\cdot3y}}{\sqrt{3y\cdot3y}}=\dfrac{\sqrt{24xy}}{\sqrt{9y^2}}=\dfrac{\sqrt{4\cdot6xy}}{3y}=\dfrac{2\sqrt{6xy}}{3y}$

d. $\dfrac{\sqrt[3]{2}}{\sqrt[3]{x}}\cdot\dfrac{\sqrt[3]{x^2}}{\sqrt[3]{x^2}}=\dfrac{\sqrt[3]{2x^2}}{\sqrt[3]{x^3}}=\dfrac{\sqrt[3]{2x^2}}{x}$

In the last example, the radicand of the denominator is x. To eliminate the radical from the denominator, the radicand should be x^3. Thus, the appropriate radical expression is $\sqrt[3]{x^2}$.

If the radicand is a fraction, first apply the quotient rule, then simplify the radical expression from the denominator before you rationalize the denominator.

Example 3

Simplify.

a. $\sqrt{\dfrac{ab}{12}}$
b. $\sqrt{\dfrac{5ab^3}{48a^2b}}$
c. $\dfrac{\sqrt{15}}{\sqrt{32x^3y^2}}$
d. $\dfrac{\sqrt{8a^3b}}{\sqrt{3ab^2}}$

Solution

a. $\sqrt{\dfrac{ab}{12}}=\dfrac{\sqrt{ab}}{\sqrt{12}}=\dfrac{\sqrt{ab}}{\sqrt{4\cdot3}}=\dfrac{\sqrt{ab}}{2\sqrt{3}}\cdot\dfrac{\sqrt{3}}{\sqrt{3}}=\dfrac{\sqrt{3ab}}{2\sqrt{3\cdot3}}=\dfrac{\sqrt{3ab}}{2\sqrt{9}}=\dfrac{\sqrt{3ab}}{2\cdot3}=\dfrac{\sqrt{3ab}}{6}$

b. $\sqrt{\dfrac{5ab^3}{48a^2b}}=\sqrt{\dfrac{5b^2}{48a}}=\dfrac{\sqrt{5b^2}}{\sqrt{48a}}=\dfrac{b\sqrt{5}}{\sqrt{16\cdot3a}}=\dfrac{b\sqrt{5}}{4\sqrt{3a}}\cdot\dfrac{\sqrt{3a}}{\sqrt{3a}}=\dfrac{b\sqrt{5\cdot3a}}{4a\sqrt{3a\cdot3a}}=$

$\dfrac{b\sqrt{15a}}{4a\sqrt{9a^2}}=\dfrac{b\sqrt{15a}}{4a\cdot3a}=\dfrac{b\sqrt{15a}}{12a^2}$

c. $\dfrac{\sqrt{15}}{\sqrt{32x^3y^2}} = \dfrac{\sqrt{15}}{\sqrt{16 \cdot x^2 \cdot x \cdot y^2}} = \dfrac{\sqrt{15}}{4xy\sqrt{x}} \cdot \dfrac{\sqrt{x}}{\sqrt{x}} = \dfrac{\sqrt{15x}}{4xy\sqrt{x \cdot x}} = \dfrac{\sqrt{15x}}{4xy\sqrt{x^2}} = \dfrac{\sqrt{15x}}{4xy \cdot x} = \dfrac{\sqrt{15x}}{4x^2y}$

d. $\dfrac{\sqrt{8a^3b}}{\sqrt{3a^5b^2}} = \sqrt{\dfrac{8a^3b}{3a^5b^2}} = \sqrt{\dfrac{8}{3a^2b}} = \dfrac{\sqrt{8}}{\sqrt{3a^2b}} = \dfrac{\sqrt{8}}{a\sqrt{3b}} \cdot \dfrac{\sqrt{3b}}{\sqrt{3b}} = \dfrac{\sqrt{8 \cdot 3b}}{a\sqrt{3b \cdot 3b}} = \dfrac{\sqrt{24b}}{a\sqrt{9b^2}} = $

$\dfrac{\sqrt{4 \cdot 6b}}{a \cdot 3b} = \dfrac{2\sqrt{6b}}{3ab}$

CASE 2

In the previous section we learned that the product of conjugate radicals contains no radicals.
For example, $\left(\sqrt{5}+\sqrt{2}\right)\left(\sqrt{5}-\sqrt{2}\right) = \left(\sqrt{5}\right)^2 - \left(\sqrt{2}\right)^2 = 5-2 = 3$
This property can be used to rationalize the denominator. When the denominator contains a sum or a difference of two radical expressions, multiply both the numerator and the denominator by the conjugate of the denominator.

Example 4

Rationalize.

a. $\dfrac{\sqrt{8}}{\sqrt{3}+\sqrt{2}}$
b. $\dfrac{\sqrt{5}}{\sqrt{7}-2}$
c. $\dfrac{\sqrt{x}+\sqrt{y}}{\sqrt{x}-\sqrt{y}}$

Solution

a. The conjugate of $\sqrt{3}+\sqrt{2}$ is $\sqrt{3}-\sqrt{2}$. Multiply both the numerator and the denominator of the fraction by $\sqrt{3}-\sqrt{2}$ and simplify.

$\dfrac{\sqrt{8}}{\sqrt{3}+\sqrt{2}} \cdot \dfrac{\sqrt{3}-\sqrt{2}}{\sqrt{3}-\sqrt{2}} = \dfrac{\sqrt{8}(\sqrt{3}-\sqrt{2})}{\left(\sqrt{3}+\sqrt{2}\right)\left(\sqrt{3}-\sqrt{2}\right)} = \dfrac{\sqrt{8}\sqrt{3}-\sqrt{8}\sqrt{2}}{\left(\sqrt{3}\right)^2-\left(\sqrt{2}\right)^2} = \dfrac{\sqrt{24}-\sqrt{16}}{3-2} = $

$\dfrac{\sqrt{4 \cdot 6}-4}{1} = \dfrac{2\sqrt{6}-4}{1} = 2\sqrt{6}-4$

b. The conjugate of $\sqrt{7}-2$ is $\sqrt{7}+2$. Multiply both the numerator and the denominator of the fraction by $\sqrt{7}+2$.

$\dfrac{\sqrt{5}}{\sqrt{7}-2} \cdot \dfrac{\sqrt{7}+2}{\sqrt{7}+2} = \dfrac{\sqrt{5}\left(\sqrt{7}+2\right)}{\left(\sqrt{7}-2\right)\left(\sqrt{7}+2\right)} = \dfrac{\sqrt{5}\sqrt{7}+2\sqrt{5}}{\left(\sqrt{7}\right)^2-2^2} = \dfrac{\sqrt{35}+2\sqrt{5}}{7-4} = \dfrac{\sqrt{35}+2\sqrt{5}}{3}$

c. The conjugate of $\sqrt{x}-\sqrt{y}$ is $\sqrt{x}+\sqrt{y}$. Multiply both the numerator and the denominator of the fraction by $\sqrt{x}+\sqrt{y}$.

$$\frac{\sqrt{x}+\sqrt{y}}{\sqrt{x}-\sqrt{y}}\cdot\frac{\sqrt{x}+\sqrt{y}}{\sqrt{x}+\sqrt{y}}=\frac{\left(\sqrt{x}+\sqrt{y}\right)\left(\sqrt{x}+\sqrt{y}\right)}{\left(\sqrt{x}-\sqrt{y}\right)\left(\sqrt{x}+\sqrt{y}\right)}=\frac{\sqrt{x}\sqrt{x}+\sqrt{x}\sqrt{y}+\sqrt{y}\sqrt{x}+\sqrt{y}\sqrt{y}}{\left(\sqrt{x}\right)^{2}-\left(\sqrt{y}\right)^{2}}=$$

$$\frac{\sqrt{x^{2}}+\sqrt{xy}+\sqrt{xy}+\sqrt{y^{2}}}{x-y}=\frac{x+2\sqrt{xy}+y}{x-y}$$

Example 5

Rationalize the denominator.

a. $\dfrac{\sqrt{12}}{3\sqrt{2}+\sqrt{3}}$

b. $\dfrac{\sqrt{6}+2}{7-\sqrt{8}}$

Solution

a. $\dfrac{\sqrt{12}}{3\sqrt{2}+\sqrt{3}}\cdot\dfrac{3\sqrt{2}-\sqrt{3}}{3\sqrt{2}-\sqrt{3}}=\dfrac{\sqrt{12}\left(3\sqrt{2}-\sqrt{3}\right)}{\left(3\sqrt{2}+\sqrt{3}\right)\left(3\sqrt{2}-\sqrt{3}\right)}=\dfrac{3\sqrt{12}\sqrt{2}-\sqrt{12}\sqrt{3}}{\left(3\sqrt{2}\right)^{2}-\left(\sqrt{3}\right)^{2}}=\dfrac{3\sqrt{24}-\sqrt{36}}{9\cdot2-3}=$

$\dfrac{3\sqrt{4\cdot6}-6}{18-3}=\dfrac{3\cdot2\sqrt{6}-6}{15}=\dfrac{6\sqrt{6}-6}{15}=\dfrac{3\left(2\sqrt{6}-2\right)}{15}=\dfrac{2\sqrt{6}-2}{5}$

b. $\dfrac{\sqrt{6}+2}{7-\sqrt{8}}\cdot\dfrac{7+\sqrt{8}}{7+\sqrt{8}}=\dfrac{\left(\sqrt{6}+2\right)\left(7+\sqrt{8}\right)}{\left(7-\sqrt{8}\right)\left(7+\sqrt{8}\right)}=\dfrac{7\sqrt{6}+\sqrt{6}\sqrt{8}+2\cdot7+2\sqrt{8}}{7^{2}-\left(\sqrt{8}\right)^{2}}=$

$\dfrac{7\sqrt{6}+\sqrt{48}+14+2\sqrt{8}}{49-8}=\dfrac{7\sqrt{6}+\sqrt{16\cdot3}+14+2\sqrt{4\cdot2}}{41}=\dfrac{7\sqrt{6}+4\sqrt{3}+14+4\sqrt{2}}{41}$

8.5 **EXERCISES**

Simplify.

1. $\dfrac{\sqrt{18x}}{\sqrt{49x^{3}}}$

2. $\dfrac{\sqrt{12xy^{2}}}{\sqrt{25x}}$

3. $\dfrac{\sqrt{20ab}}{\sqrt{81ab^{3}}}$

4. $\dfrac{\sqrt{75x^{3}y^{3}}}{\sqrt{16xy}}$

5. $\dfrac{\sqrt{33a}}{\sqrt{44ab^{2}}}$

6. $\dfrac{\sqrt{6x^{2}y^{3}}}{\sqrt{27y}}$

7. $\sqrt{\dfrac{38a^{3}b}{18ab^{3}}}$

8. $\sqrt{\dfrac{48a^{2}b^{5}}{75b^{3}}}$

9. $\sqrt{\dfrac{32x^{2}y^{2}}{98x}}$

Rationalize the denominator.

10. $\dfrac{2}{\sqrt{6}}$

11. $\dfrac{5}{\sqrt{10}}$

12. $\dfrac{1}{\sqrt{8}}$

13. $\dfrac{3}{\sqrt{12}}$

14. $\dfrac{4}{\sqrt{7}}$

15. $\dfrac{15}{\sqrt{50}}$

16. $\dfrac{3}{\sqrt{27}}$

17. $\dfrac{5}{\sqrt{125}}$

18. $\dfrac{20}{\sqrt{75}}$

19. $\sqrt{\dfrac{3}{8}}$

20. $\sqrt[3]{\dfrac{5}{15x^2}}$

21. $\dfrac{8}{\sqrt[3]{4x}}$

22. $\dfrac{\sqrt[3]{16}}{\sqrt[3]{9}}$

23. $\dfrac{\sqrt{6}}{\sqrt{27}}$

24. $\dfrac{x}{\sqrt{8x^3}}$

25. $\sqrt{\dfrac{11a^3}{33ab}}$

26. $\sqrt{\dfrac{3xy}{24xy^2}}$

27. $\sqrt{\dfrac{15a^3b^2}{50ab^3}}$

28. $\dfrac{4}{\sqrt{6}-\sqrt{2}}$

29. $\dfrac{9}{\sqrt{14}-\sqrt{11}}$

30. $\dfrac{\sqrt{8}}{\sqrt{5}-\sqrt{2}}$

31. $\dfrac{\sqrt{12}}{\sqrt{6}+\sqrt{3}}$

32. $\dfrac{\sqrt{5}+\sqrt{10}}{\sqrt{8}+\sqrt{2}}$

33. $\dfrac{2\sqrt{6}-\sqrt{18}}{\sqrt{10}-\sqrt{3}}$

34. $\dfrac{x+\sqrt{27}}{x-\sqrt{2}}$

35. $\dfrac{\sqrt{2x}+3}{\sqrt{2x}-3}$

36. $\dfrac{8+\sqrt{5}}{5-\sqrt{5}}$

37. $\dfrac{15}{3+\sqrt{6}}$

38. $\dfrac{\sqrt{3}}{\sqrt{8}-2}$

39. $\dfrac{\sqrt{12}+4}{\sqrt{3}-1}$

40. $\dfrac{\sqrt{6}+8}{\sqrt{10}-2}$

41. $\dfrac{\sqrt{2x}+1}{\sqrt{2x}-1}$

42. $\dfrac{\sqrt{y}-4}{\sqrt{y}+4}$

43. $\dfrac{2\sqrt{3}+3\sqrt{2}}{4\sqrt{6}}$

44. $\dfrac{4\sqrt{8}-6\sqrt{2}}{5\sqrt{10}}$

45. $\dfrac{6\sqrt{5}-5\sqrt{6}}{\sqrt{5}-\sqrt{6}}$

46. $\dfrac{\sqrt{8}+\sqrt{3}}{\sqrt{8}-\sqrt{3}}$

47. $\dfrac{\sqrt{12}-\sqrt{2}}{\sqrt{12}+\sqrt{2}}$

48. $\dfrac{3\sqrt{6}}{\sqrt{8}-\sqrt{6}}$

49. $\dfrac{5\sqrt{2}-2\sqrt{6}}{5\sqrt{2}+2\sqrt{6}}$

50. $\dfrac{x\sqrt{3}+y\sqrt{8}}{x\sqrt{3}-y\sqrt{8}}$

51. $\dfrac{\sqrt{a}-\sqrt{b}}{\sqrt{a}+\sqrt{b}}$

8.6 RADICAL EQUATIONS

Examples of radical equations: $\sqrt{x} = 2$, $\sqrt{x-1} - 2 = 3$, $\sqrt{2x+3} = \sqrt{x-4}$, $\sqrt[3]{x+1} = 2$.

The equations $x\sqrt{3} = 5$ and $x + \sqrt{2} = 4$ are not radical equations because the variable x is not contained in the radicand. The above examples give us an idea of a radical equation.

Definition

An equation containing one or more radicals with the variable(s) in the radicand of a least one radical is called **radical equation**.

To solve radical equations that involve square roots, we use the following property:

The Squaring Property

If a and b are real numbers and a = b, then $a^2 = b^2$.

Note: If $a^2 = b^2$ it does not necessarily mean $a = b$. For example $(-5)^2 = (5)^2$ but $-5 \neq 5$.

In general, the squaring property produces an equation that contains more solutions than the original equation. Some of these solutions do not satisfy the original equation, and are called **extraneous solutions**. Therefore, when solving radical equations we must check all possible solutions and reject any extraneous solutions.

Strategy for Solving Radical Equations Containing Square Roots

Step 1 Isolate the radical on one side of the equation and simplify the other side.

Step 2 Square both sides of the equation (The Squaring Property).

Step 3 If the equation still contains a radical, repeat Steps 1 and 2, otherwise solve the squared equation for the variable.

Step 4 Check the solution(s) in the original equation, and reject any extraneous solutions.

Example 1

Solve.

a. $\sqrt{x} = 4$ 　　　　 b. $\sqrt{x+3} = 2$ 　　　 c. $\sqrt{3x+1} = \sqrt{x+5}$ 　　 d. $\sqrt{x-5} + 3 = 7$

Solution

a. $\sqrt{x} = 4$

$\left(\sqrt{x}\right)^2 = 4^2$ Square both sides

$x = 16$ Solve for x

Check: $\sqrt{x} = 4$, $\sqrt{16} = 4$, $4 = 4$.   True.

Thus, the solution is $x = 16$.

b. $\sqrt{x+3} = 2$

$\left(\sqrt{x+3}\right)^2 = 2^2$ Square both sides

$x + 3 = 4$ Solve for x

$x = 4 - 3$

$x = 1$

Check: $\sqrt{x+3} = 2$, $\sqrt{1+3} = 2$, $\sqrt{4} = 2$, $2 = 2$ True.

Thus, the solution is $x = 1$.

c. $\sqrt{3x+1} = \sqrt{x+5}$

$\left(\sqrt{3x+1}\right)^2 = \left(\sqrt{x+5}\right)^2$ Square both sides

$3x + 1 = x + 5$ Solve for x.

$3x - x = 5 - 1$

$2x = 4$

$\dfrac{2x}{2} = \dfrac{4}{2}$

$x = 2$

Check: $\sqrt{3x+1} = \sqrt{x+5}$, $\sqrt{3 \cdot 2 + 1} = \sqrt{2+5}$, $\sqrt{6+1} = \sqrt{7}$, $\sqrt{7} = \sqrt{7}$ True.

Thus, the solution is $x = 2$

d. $\sqrt{x-5} + 3 = 7$

$\sqrt{x-5} = 7 - 3$ Isolate the radical and simplify

$\sqrt{x-5} = 4$

$\left(\sqrt{x-5}\right)^2 = 4^2$ Square both sides

$x - 5 = 16$ Solve for x

$x = 16 + 5$

$x = 21$

Check: $\sqrt{x-5} + 3 = 7$, $\sqrt{21-5} + 3 = 7$, $\sqrt{16} + 3 = 7$, $4 + 3 = 7$, $7 = 7$ True.

Thus, the solution is $x = 21$.

In example d) we isolated the radical before applying the squaring property. If we skip this step, the equation becomes more complicated and the radical will not be eliminated even after we square both sides of the equation, as we can see from the following:

$$\left(\sqrt{x-5}+3\right)^2 = 7^2$$

If we apply $(a+b)^2 = a^2 + 2ab + b^2$, the equation becomes:

$$\left(\sqrt{x-5}\right)^2 + 2\cdot 3 \cdot \sqrt{x-5} + 3^2 = 49$$

$$x-5+6\sqrt{x-5}+9 = 49$$

which is more complicated than the original equation and the radical is still part of the equation.

Example 2

Solve.

$$\sqrt{3x+4} - 1 = 3$$

Solution

$\sqrt{3x+4} - 1 = 3$	Isolate the radical.
$\sqrt{3x+4} = 3+1$	Simplify the left-hand side.
$\sqrt{3x+4} = 4$	
$\left(\sqrt{3x+4}\right)^2 = 4^2$	Square both sides.
$3x+4 = 16$	Solve for x.
$3x = 16-4$	
$3x = 12$	
$\dfrac{3x}{3} = \dfrac{12}{3}$	
$x = 4$	

Check:

$$\sqrt{3x+4} - 1 = 3$$

$$\sqrt{3\cdot 4+4} - 1 = 3$$

$$\sqrt{12+4} - 1 = 3$$

$$\sqrt{16} - 1 = 3$$

$$4-1 = 3$$

$$3 = 3 \qquad\qquad\qquad \text{True.}$$

Thus, the solution is $x = 4$.

If a radical equation contains the variable x outside the radical, when both sides of the equation are squared, x becomes x^2. In general, this is one of the cases when we end up with an extraneous solution.

Example 3

Solve.

$$\sqrt{2x-1}+2=x$$

Solution

$$\sqrt{2x-1}+2=x$$

$$\sqrt{2x-1}=x-2 \qquad \text{Isolate the radical}$$

$$\left(\sqrt{2x-1}\right)^2=(x-2)^2 \qquad \text{Square both sides}$$

If we apply $(a-b)^2=a^2-2ab+b^2$, the equation becomes

$$2x-1=x^2-4x+4 \qquad \text{Write the equation in standard form}$$

$$0=x^2-4x+4-2x+1$$

$$0=x^2-6x+5$$

$$0=(x-5)(x-1) \qquad \text{Factor}$$

$$x-5=0 \ \text{ or } \ x-1=0 \quad \text{Solve for } x$$

$$x=5 \ \text{ or } \ x=1$$

Check:

$$\sqrt{2x-1}+2=x \qquad\qquad\qquad \sqrt{2x-1}+2=x$$

$$\sqrt{2\cdot5-1}+2=5 \qquad\qquad\quad \sqrt{2\cdot1-1}+2=1$$

$$\sqrt{10-1}+2=5 \qquad\qquad\qquad \sqrt{2-1}+2=1$$

$$\sqrt{9}+2=5 \qquad\qquad\qquad\quad \sqrt{1}+2=1$$

$$3+2=5 \qquad\qquad\qquad\qquad 1+2=1$$

$$5=5 \ \text{True.} \qquad\qquad\qquad\quad 3=1 \ \text{False.}$$

Since $x=1$ does not check the original equation it is called an extraneous solution and must be rejected. Thus, the solution is $x=5$.

Example 4

Solve.

$$2\sqrt{4x-3}-3=x$$

Solution

$$2\sqrt{4x-3}-3=x$$

$$2\sqrt{4x-3}=x+3$$

$$\left(2\sqrt{4x-3}\right)^2=(x+3)^2$$

$$4(4x-3)=x^2+6x+9$$

$$16x-12=x^2+6x+9$$

$$0=x^2+6x+9-16x+12$$

$$0=x^2-10x+21$$

$$0=(x-7)(x-3)$$

$$x-7=0 \text{ or } x-3=0$$

$$x=7 \text{ or } x=3$$

Check:

$2\sqrt{4x-3}-3=x$	$2\sqrt{4x-3}-3=x$
$2\sqrt{4\cdot7-3}-3=7$	$2\sqrt{4\cdot3-3}-3=3$
$2\sqrt{28-3}-3=7$	$2\sqrt{12-3}-3=3$
$2\sqrt{25}-3=7$	$2\sqrt{9}-3=3$
$2\cdot5-3=7$	$2\cdot3-3=3$
$10-3=7$	$6-3=3$
$7=7$ True.	$3=3$ True.

Thus, the solutions are $x=7$ and $x=3$.

Example 5

Solve.

$$\sqrt{x^2+x-7}=x$$

Solution

$$\sqrt{x^2+x-7}=x$$

$$\left(\sqrt{x^2+x-7}\right)^2=x^2 \qquad \text{Square both sides.}$$

$$x^2+x-7=x^2 \qquad \text{Solve for } x.$$

$$x^2+x-7-x^2=0$$

$$x-7=0$$

$$x=7$$

Check:

$$\sqrt{x^2 + x - 7} = x$$

$$\sqrt{7^2 + 7 - 7} = 7$$

$$\sqrt{49} = 7$$

$$7 = 7 \quad \text{True.}$$

Thus, the solution is $x = 7$.

Example 6

Solve.

$$\sqrt{x + 8} = -3$$

Solution

$$\sqrt{x + 8} = -3$$

Since the left-hand side is the principal square root, which is always positive, and the right-hand side is negative, this radical equation has no real solution. If we solve the equation (by mistake) following the standard steps, we will arrive at the same conclusion.

$$\left(\sqrt{x + 8}\right)^2 = (-3)^2 \qquad \text{Square both sides.}$$

$$x + 8 = 9 \qquad\qquad \text{Solve for } x.$$

$$x = 9 - 8$$

$$x = 1$$

Check:

$$\sqrt{x + 8} = -3$$

$$\sqrt{1 + 8} = -3$$

$$\sqrt{9} = -3$$

$$3 = -3 \qquad\qquad\qquad\qquad\qquad\qquad\qquad \text{False.}$$

So, the radical equation has no solution.

If a radical equation contains two radicals, isolate the most complicated radical on one side of the equation and then apply the squaring property.

Example 7

Solve

$$\sqrt{3x + 1} + \sqrt{x + 3} = 4$$

Solution

$$\sqrt{3x+1} + \sqrt{x+3} = 4$$

$$\sqrt{3x+1} = 4 - \sqrt{x+3} \qquad \text{Isolate one radical.}$$

$$\left(\sqrt{3x+1}\right)^2 = \left(4 - \sqrt{x+3}\right)^2 \qquad \text{Square both sides}$$

$$3x+1 = 4^2 - 2 \cdot 4 \cdot \sqrt{x+3} + \left(\sqrt{x+3}\right)^2$$

$$3x+1 = 16 - 8\sqrt{x+3} + x + 3 \qquad \text{Isolate the radical .}$$

$$8\sqrt{x+3} = 16 + x + 3 - 3x - 1 \qquad \text{Simplify the left-hand side.}$$

$$8\sqrt{x+3} = 18 - 2x \qquad \text{Divide both sides by 2.}$$

$$\left(4\sqrt{x+3}\right)^2 = (9-x)^2 \qquad \text{Square both sides.}$$

$$16(x+3) = 81 - 18x + x^2 \qquad \text{Simplify.}$$

$$16x + 48 = 81 - 18x + x^2 \qquad \text{Write the equation in standard form.}$$

$$0 = 81 - 18x + x^2 - 16x - 48$$

$$0 = x^2 - 34x + 33$$

$$0 = (x-33)(x-1) \qquad \text{Factor.}$$

$$x - 33 = 0 \ \text{ or } \ x - 1 = 0 \qquad \text{Solve for } x.$$

$$x = 33 \ \text{ or } \ x = 1$$

Check:

$$\sqrt{3x+1} + \sqrt{x+3} = 4 \qquad\qquad \sqrt{3x+1} + \sqrt{x+3} = 4$$

$$\sqrt{3 \cdot 33 + 1} + \sqrt{33+3} = 4 \qquad\qquad \sqrt{3 \cdot 1 + 1} + \sqrt{1+3} = 4$$

$$\sqrt{99+1} + \sqrt{36} = 4 \qquad\qquad \sqrt{3+1} + \sqrt{4} = 4$$

$$\sqrt{100} + 6 = 4 \qquad\qquad \sqrt{4} + 2 = 4$$

$$10 + 6 = 4 \qquad\qquad 2 + 2 = 4$$

$$16 = 4 \ \text{False.} \qquad\qquad 4 = 4 \ \text{True.}$$

Thus, the solution is $x = 1$, and $x = 33$ is an extraneous solution and must be rejected.

Now, we can extend the concept of square root equations to cube root equations.

Example 8

Solve.

$$\sqrt[3]{x+1} = 3$$

Solution

To eliminate the cube root, we cube both sides of the equation.

$$\left(\sqrt[3]{x+1}\right)^3 = 3^3$$

$$x+1 = 27$$

$$x = 27 - 1$$

$$x = 26$$

Check:

$$\sqrt[3]{x+1} = 3$$

$$\sqrt[3]{26+1} = 3$$

$$\sqrt[3]{27} = 3$$

$$3 = 3 \qquad\qquad\qquad\qquad \text{True.}$$

The solution is $x = 26$.

Example 9

Solve.

$$\sqrt[3]{5x+3} + 8 = 5$$

Solution

$$\sqrt[3]{5x+3} + 8 = 5 \qquad \text{Isolate the radical.}$$

$$\sqrt[3]{5x+3} = 5 - 8 \qquad \text{Simplify the left-hand side.}$$

$$\sqrt[3]{5x+3} = -3$$

$$\left(\sqrt[3]{5x+3}\right)^3 = (-3)^3 \qquad \text{Cube both sides.}$$

$$5x+3 = -27 \qquad \text{Solve for } x.$$

$$5x = -27 - 3$$

$$5x = -30$$

$$x = -6$$

Check:

$$\sqrt[3]{5x+3}+8=5$$

$$\sqrt[3]{5(-6)+3}+8=5$$

$$\sqrt[3]{-30+3}+8=5$$

$$\sqrt[3]{-27}+8=5$$

$$-3+8=5$$

$$5=5 \qquad\qquad\qquad\qquad\qquad\qquad\qquad\qquad\text{True.}$$

Thus, the solution is $x=-6$.

8.6 EXERCISES

Solve each radical equation. Check all possible solutions.

1. $\sqrt{x}=4$

2. $\sqrt{y}=9$

3. $\sqrt{x}=11$

4. $\sqrt{a}=6$

5. $\sqrt{x}=-3$

6. $-\sqrt{y}=10$

7. $\sqrt{5x}+1=6$

8. $\sqrt{8x}-3=1$

9. $\sqrt{3x}+7=9$

10. $\sqrt{x+5}=3$

11. $\sqrt{x-8}=2$

12. $\sqrt{2x-3}=3$

13. $\sqrt{3x+9}=6$

14. $\sqrt{x+3}-2=2$

15. $\sqrt{x-11}+4=7$

16. $\sqrt{4x+5}+8=13$

17. $\sqrt{5x-6}+2=10$

18. $\sqrt{8x-1}=\sqrt{2x+5}$

19. $\sqrt{10x+4}=\sqrt{7x+10}$

20. $\sqrt{x+11}=\sqrt{9x-5}$

21. $\sqrt{2-3x}=\sqrt{2x-8}$

22. $2\sqrt{4x-3}-1=5$

23. $4\sqrt{6x-1}+5=13$

24. $\sqrt{x^2-3x+6}=4$

25. $\sqrt{x^2+2x+56}=8$

26. $\sqrt{x^2-x+7}=7$

27. $\sqrt{2x^2-5x+13}=4$

28. $\sqrt{x^2-5x+35}=x$

29. $\sqrt{x^2+3x-24}=x$

30. $\sqrt{2x^2-4x-5}=x$

31. $\sqrt{4x^2+3x+2}=2x+1$

32. $\sqrt{x^2-6x+8}=x-3$

33. $\sqrt{9x^2 - x - 7} = 3x - 2$

34. $\sqrt{x+7} - 1 = x$

35. $\sqrt{x+15} + 5 = x$

36. $\sqrt{x+9} = x + 7$

37. $\sqrt{2x+5} - 1 = x$

38. $\sqrt{3x-2} + 2 = x$

39. $\sqrt{4x+13} - 2 = x$

40. $5\sqrt{x} = x + 4$

41. $5\sqrt{x} = x + 6$

42. $2\sqrt{x} = \sqrt{9x+5}$

43. $\sqrt[3]{x+3} = 2$

44. $\sqrt[3]{2x-1} = 3$

45. $\sqrt[3]{3x+4} = 4$

46. $\sqrt[3]{5x+1} = 6$

47. $\sqrt[3]{8x-2} = 2$

48. $\sqrt[3]{x+9} = 7$

49. $\sqrt{x+1} + \sqrt{5x+1} = 6$

50. $\sqrt{6x+1} - \sqrt{x+5} = 2$

51. $\sqrt{x+4} - \sqrt{x-1} = 1$

52. $\sqrt{9x-2} - \sqrt{4x+1} = 1$

53. $\sqrt{4x-3} - \sqrt{x-2} = 2$

54. $\sqrt{x-6} + \sqrt{x-3} = 3$

8.7 COMPLEX NUMBERS

□ Addition and Subtraction of Complex Numbers □ Multiplication of Complex Numbers □ Division of Complex Numbers

In the previous sections we learned that the principal or positive square root of $x^2 = -1$ is $\sqrt{x^2} = \sqrt{-1}$. But, $\sqrt{-1}$ is not a real number because there is no real number that squared equals -1. Since numbers such as $\sqrt{-1}$ are not real numbers, the great mathematician Rene Descartes called them imaginary numbers. However, Euler was the first mathematician who used the letter "i" to represent the imaginary number $\sqrt{-1}$. If the imaginary number $i = \sqrt{-1}$, then $i^2 = -1$.

Now, we can use $i = \sqrt{-1}$ and the product rule for square roots to evaluate the square root of a negative number as follows:

$$\sqrt{-4} = \sqrt{4(-1)} = \sqrt{4}\sqrt{-1} = 2i$$

$$\sqrt{-9} = \sqrt{9(-1)} = \sqrt{9}\sqrt{-1} = 3i$$

$$\sqrt{-16} = \sqrt{16(-1)} = \sqrt{16}\sqrt{-1} = 4i$$

$$\sqrt{-12} = \sqrt{12(-1)} = \sqrt{-1}\sqrt{12} = i\sqrt{4\cdot 3} = i\sqrt{4}\sqrt{3} = 2i\sqrt{3}$$

Thus, the imaginary unit $i = \sqrt{-1}$ is the building block for a new set of numbers "C" called complex numbers.

Definition

*A **complex number** is a number that can be written in the form z = a + bi, where a and b are real numbers and $i = \sqrt{-1}$. The form z = a + bi is called the standard form or rectangular form of a complex number.*

For example, $z = 2 + 3i$, $z = 4 - 5i$, $z = -1 + 2i$, and $z = 10i$ are complex numbers.

The real number a is called the real part and b is called the imaginary part of the complex number $z = a + bi$. If the real part $a = 0$, the complex number $z = bi$ is called pure imaginary number. If the imaginary part $b = 0$, the number $z = a$ is called the pure real number.

For example $z = 5i$ is a pure imaginary number and $z = 8$ is a the pure real number.

□ ADDITION AND SUBTRACTION OF COMPLEX NUMBERS

We add and subtract complex numbers in the same way we add and subtract polynomials, by combining like terms. In other words, we add the real part and add the imaginary part for addition and we subtract the real part and subtract the imaginary part for subtraction.

$$(a+bi)+(c+di)=(a+c)+(b+d)i$$

$$(a+bi)-(c+di)=(a-c)+(b-d)i$$

Example 1

Add or subtract.

   a. $(2+3i)+(4-5i)$ b. $(-1+6i)-(3-7i)$

Solution

   a. $(2+3i)+(4-5i)=$ Remove the parentheses.

      $2+3i+4-5i=$ Combine like terms.

      $(2+4)+(3i-5i)=$ Simplify.

      $6-2i$

   b. $(-1+6i)-(3-7i)=$ Remove the parentheses.

      $-1+6i-3+7i=$ Combine like terms.

      $(-1-3)+(6i+7i)$ Simplify.

      $-4+13i$

Example 2

Add or subtract.

   a. $(-3-4i)+(-5+8i)$ b. $(1-2i)-(-10+11i)$

Solution

   a. $(-3-4i)+(-5+8i)=$ Remove the parentheses.

      $-3-4i-5+8i=$ Combine like terms.

      $(-3-5)+(-4i+8i)=$ Simplify.

      $-8+4i$

   b. $(1-2i)-(-10+11i)=$ Remove the parentheses.

      $1-2i+10-11i=$ Combine like terms.

      $(1+10)+(-2i-11i)=$ Simplify.

      $11-13i$

☐ MULTIPLICATION OF COMPLEX NUMBERS

We multiply complex numbers the same way we would multiply polynomials.

When multiplying complex numbers, we need to substitute -1 for i^2 in order to simplify the product.

Example 3

Multiply, and write the product in standard form.

a. $4 \cdot 5i$ b. $(-2i)(7i)$ c. $3(4 + 2i)$ d. $6i(5 - i)$

Solution

a. $4 \cdot 5i = 20i = 0 + 20i$

b. $(-2i)(7i) = -14i^2 = (-14)(-1) = 14 = 14 + 0i$

c. $3(4 + 2i) = 12 + 6i$

d. $6i(5 - i) = 30i - 6i^2 = 30i - 6(-1) = 30i + 6 = 6 + 30i$

Example 4

Multiply.

a. $\sqrt{-8}\sqrt{-8}$ b. $\sqrt{-12}\sqrt{-3}$ c. $\sqrt{-5}\sqrt{-8}$

Solution

a. $\sqrt{-8}\sqrt{-8} = (i\sqrt{8})(i\sqrt{8}) = i^2\sqrt{64} = 8i^2 = -8$

b. $\sqrt{-12}\sqrt{-3} = (i\sqrt{12})(i\sqrt{3}) = i^2\sqrt{36} = 6i^2 = -6$

c. $\sqrt{-5}\sqrt{-8} = (i\sqrt{5})(i\sqrt{8}) = i^2\sqrt{40} = -\sqrt{4 \cdot 10} = -2\sqrt{10}$

Note: The product rule for radicals $\sqrt{a}\sqrt{b} = \sqrt{a \cdot b}$ does not hold if both a and b are negative numbers.

For example,

$$\sqrt{-4}\sqrt{-9} = \sqrt{(-4)(-9)} = \sqrt{36} = 6 \text{ (wrong)}$$

$$\sqrt{-4}\sqrt{-9} = 2i \cdot 3i = 6i^2 = 6(-1) = -6 \text{ (right)}$$

Example 5

Multiply, and write the product in standard form.

$(2 + 5i)(8 - 3i)$

Solution

$(2 + 5i)(8 - 3i) =$	FOIL
$2 \cdot 8 - 2 \cdot 3i + 5i \cdot 8 + (5i)(-3i) =$	Simplify
$16 - 6i + 40i - 15i^2 =$	Replace i^2 with -1 and combine like terms
$16 + 34i - 15(-1) =$	
$16 + 34i + 15 =$	Write the product in standard form
$31 + 34i$	

Example 6

Multiply, and write the product in standard form.

$$(3+2i)^2$$

Solution

$$(3+2i)^2 = (3+2i)(3+2i) = \qquad \text{FOIL}$$

$$3 \cdot 3 + 3 \cdot 2i + 2i \cdot 3 + (2i)(2i) = \qquad \text{Simplify}$$

$$9 + 6i + 6i + 4i^2 = \qquad \text{Replace } i^2 \text{ with } -1 \text{ and combine like terms}$$

$$9 + 12i + 4(-1) =$$

$$9 + 12i - 4 = \qquad \text{Standard form}$$

$$5 + 12i$$

The complex numbers $z = a + bi$ and $\bar{z} = a - bi$ are called **complex conjugates** of each other.

The product of complex conjugates is always a real number.

$$(a+bi)(a-bi) = a \cdot a - a \cdot bi + bi \cdot a + bi(-bi) = a^2 - abi + abi - b^2 i^2 = a^2 - b^2(-1) = a^2 + b^2$$

Thus, $(a+bi)(a-bi) = a^2 + b^2$

Example 7

Multiply.

a. $(3+2i)(3-2i)$

b. $(-4+i)(-4-i)$

c. $(2+10i)(2-10i)$

Solution

a. $(3+2i)(3-2i) = 3^2 + 2^2 = 9 + 4 = 13$

b. $(-4+i)(-4-i) = (-4)^2 + 1^2 = 16 + 1 = 17$

c. $(2+10i)(2-10i) = 2^2 + 10^2 = 4 + 100 = 104$

Example 8

Simplify.

a. i^{24}

b. i^{63}

Solution

a. $i^{24} = (i^2)^{12} = (-1)^{12} = 1$

b. $i^{63} = i^{62} \cdot i = (i^2)^{31} \cdot i = (-1)^{31} i = -1 \cdot i = -i$

□ DIVISION OF COMPLEX NUMBERS

When a fraction contains a complex number in its denominator, it's very common in algebra to write the fraction with no i in the denominator. The process of eliminating i from the denominator is called "***rationalizing the denominator***."

If the denominator contains a complex number of the form $z = bi$ it can be rationalized by multiplying both the numerator and denominator by i.

Example 9
___

Rationalize the denominator and write the answer in standard form. $\dfrac{6+7i}{3i}$

Solution

To rationalize the denominator, multiply both the numerator and denominator by i.

$$\frac{6+7i}{3i}\cdot\frac{i}{i}=\frac{(6+7i)i}{3i\cdot i}=\frac{6i+7i^2}{3i^2}=\frac{6i+7(-1)}{3(-1)}=\frac{6i-7}{-3}=\frac{-7}{-3}+\frac{6i}{-3}=\frac{7}{3}-2i$$

Example 10
___

Rationalize the denominator, and write the answer in standard form.

$$\frac{16-20i}{-2i}$$

Solution
___

Multiply both the numerator and the denominator by i.

$$\frac{16-20i}{-2i}\cdot\frac{i}{i}=\frac{(16-20i)i}{-2i\cdot i}=\frac{16i-20i^2}{-2i^2}=\frac{16i-20(-1)}{-2(-1)}=\frac{16i+20}{2}=\frac{20}{2}+\frac{16i}{2}=10+8i$$

If the denominator contains a complex number of the form $a + bi$ or $a - bi$, multiply both the numerator and the denominator by the complex conjugate of the denominator.

Example 11
___

Rationalize the denominator and write the answer in standard form.

$$\frac{3i}{5+2i}$$

Solution
___

The complex conjugate of the denominator $5 + 2i$ is $5 - 2i$. Thus, multiply both the numerator and the denominator by $5 - 2i$.

$$\frac{3i}{5+2i}\cdot\frac{5-2i}{5-2i}=\frac{3i(5-2i)}{(5+2i)(5-2i)}=\frac{15i-6i^2}{5^2+2^2}=\frac{15i-6(-1)}{25+4}=\frac{15i+6}{29}=\frac{6}{29}+\frac{15}{29}i$$

Example 12

Rationalize the denominator, and write the answer in standard form.

$$\frac{4+3i}{3+2i}$$

Solution

The complex conjugate of the denominator $3+2i$ is $3-2i$.

$$\frac{4+3i}{3+2i}\cdot\frac{3-2i}{3-2i}=\frac{(4+3i)(3-2i)}{(3+2i)(3-2i)}=\frac{4\cdot3-4\cdot2i+3i\cdot3+(3i)(-2i)}{3^2+2^2}=\frac{12-8i+9i-6i^2}{9+4}=$$

$$\frac{12+i-6(-1)}{13}=\frac{12+i+6}{13}=\frac{18+i}{13}=\frac{18}{13}+\frac{1}{13}i$$

Example 13

Rationalize, and write the answer in standard form. $\dfrac{5+\sqrt{-4}}{4-\sqrt{-9}}$

Solution

First, write the numerator and denominator as a complex number in standard form ($a+bi$). Then, rationalize the denominator.

$$\frac{5+\sqrt{-4}}{4-\sqrt{-9}}=\frac{5+2i}{4-3i}\cdot\frac{4+3i}{4+3i}=\frac{(5+2i)(4+3i)}{(4-3i)(4+3i)}=\frac{5\cdot4+5\cdot3i+2i\cdot4+(2i)(3i)}{4^2+3^2}=$$

$$\frac{20+15i+8i+6i^2}{16+9}=\frac{20+23i+6(-1)}{25}=\frac{20+23i-6}{25}=\frac{14+23i}{25}=\frac{14}{25}+\frac{23}{25}i$$

8.7 EXERCISES

Write each imaginary number in terms of i and simplify.

1. $\sqrt{-64}$ 4. $\sqrt{-49}$ 7. $\sqrt{-20}$

2. $\sqrt{-36}$ 5. $\sqrt{-32}$ 8. $\sqrt{-28}$

3. $\sqrt{-81}$ 6. $\sqrt{-48}$ 9. $\sqrt{-50}$

Write each complex number in standard form: $a+bi$

10. $2+\sqrt{-16}$ 13. $-6+\sqrt{-24}$ 16. $-1-2\sqrt{-8}$

11. $4-\sqrt{-25}$ 14. $5-3\sqrt{-75}$ 17. $10+4\sqrt{-6}$

12. $1+\sqrt{-18}$ 15. $-8+5\sqrt{-72}$ 18. $-2+3\sqrt{-80}$

Add or subtract the following complex numbers.

19. $(5+2i)+(-3+i)$

20. $(-4+3i)+(2-8i)$

21. $(11+5i)+(6-4i)$

22. $(2-7i)+(-3+4i)$

23. $(-5+8i)+(4-7i)$

24. $(1+3i)+(-10+i)$

25. $(8+i)-(-2+3i)$

26. $(2+6i)-(3-4i)$

27. $(-4+17i)-(-8+11i)$

28. $(-5+3i)-(15+2i)$

29. $(10-2i)-(4-3i)$

30. $(-1+i)-(12-14i)$

31. $6-(18-15i)$

32. $(5+7i)-11i$

33. $21i+(3-18i)$

Multiply the following complex numbers.

34. $(-2i)(10i)$

35. $(3i)(-4i)$

36. $(-2i)(-11i)$

37. $4(-12i)$

38. $(-5)(8i)$

39. $(3i)^2$

40. $(-5i)^2$

41. $-2(3+7i)$

42. $4(-1+6i)$

43. $6i(-3+11i)$

44. $\dfrac{1}{2}i(8-20i)$

45. $-5i(4+5i)$

46. $-i(-1-i)$

47. $(3-2i)(2+5i)$

48. $(-2+9i)(1-4i)$

49. $(5-3i)(-4+6i)$

50. $(11+2i)(-1+3i)$

51. $(3-10i)(5-2i)$

52. $(2+4i)^2$

53. $(2-8i)^2$

54. $(6-i)^2$

55. $(2+\sqrt{-9})(-3+\sqrt{-4})$

56. $(-1+\sqrt{-36})(4-i)$

57. $(1+3i)(2+\sqrt{-16})$

58. $(4+5i)(4-5i)$

59. $(11+2i)(11-2i)$

60. $(2+7i)(2-7i)$

61. $(5+3i)(5-3i)$

62. $(10+5i)(10-5i)$

63. $(-4+6i)(-4-6i)$

64. $\sqrt{-15}\sqrt{-15}$

65. $\sqrt{-2}\sqrt{-32}$

66. $\sqrt{-8}\sqrt{-6}$

67. $\sqrt{-2}(\sqrt{-8}+\sqrt{-32})$

68. $\sqrt{-6}(\sqrt{-2}-\sqrt{-12})$

69. $\sqrt{-3}(\sqrt{-12}+\sqrt{-18})$

Rationalize the denominators and write the answer in standard form.

70. $\dfrac{4}{5i}$

77. $\dfrac{-5}{6-4i}$

84. $\dfrac{1+2i}{1-2i}$

71. $\dfrac{2}{7i}$

78. $\dfrac{2i}{3-2i}$

85. $\dfrac{2+\sqrt{-25}}{3+\sqrt{-49}}$

72. $\dfrac{2+3i}{4i}$

79. $\dfrac{-8i}{6+i}$

86. $\dfrac{1+\sqrt{-8}}{2+3i}$

73. $\dfrac{5+2i}{-3i}$

80. $\dfrac{4+i}{5-2i}$

87. $\dfrac{6+7i}{1-\sqrt{-9}}$

74. $\dfrac{6+8i}{-2i}$

81. $\dfrac{-1+3i}{10+3i}$

88. $\dfrac{2-\sqrt{-81}}{2+\sqrt{-81}}$

75. $\dfrac{5}{\sqrt{-16}}$

82. $\dfrac{7-i}{4+5i}$

89. $\dfrac{2}{1+i}-\dfrac{1}{1-i}$

76. $\dfrac{4}{8+3i}$

83. $\dfrac{5-6i}{-3+8i}$

90. $\dfrac{i+1}{2+i}-\dfrac{i}{2-i}$

Simplify.

91. i^{42}

93. i^{102}

95. $(-i)^{25}$

92. i^{71}

94. i^{18}

96. $(-i)^{17}$

CHAPTER 8 REVIEW EXERCISES

Simplify each radical completely.

1. $\sqrt{44}$

2. $\sqrt{128}$

3. $\sqrt{45}$

4. $\sqrt[3]{32}$

5. $\sqrt[3]{54}$

6. $\sqrt[3]{128}$

7. $\sqrt{72x^2y^3}$

8. $\sqrt{48m^5n^6}$

9. $\sqrt{50a^3b^9}$

10. $\sqrt[3]{16x^3y^4}$

11. $\sqrt[3]{81a^5b^6}$

12. $\sqrt[3]{40m^7n^8}$

13. $\sqrt{\dfrac{8x^2y^7}{3x^4b^9}}$

14. $\sqrt{\dfrac{5x^3y^5}{8xy}}$

15. $\sqrt{\dfrac{2ab^6}{18a^5b}}$

Add or subtract.

16. $\sqrt{2}+\sqrt{18}+\sqrt{72}$

17. $\sqrt{20}-\sqrt{45}+\sqrt{80}$

18. $\sqrt{24}+\sqrt{54}-\sqrt{216}$

19. $5\sqrt{28}-3\sqrt{63}+2\sqrt{112}$

20. $2\sqrt{40}+6\sqrt{90}-8\sqrt{160}$

21. $y\sqrt{27x^3y}+x\sqrt{48xy^3}-\sqrt{75x^3y^3}$

22. $ab\sqrt{5a^3b^5}-a^2\sqrt{20ab^7}+b^2\sqrt{45a^5b^3}$

23. $\sqrt[3]{16}+\sqrt[3]{54}-\sqrt[3]{250}$

24. $x\sqrt[3]{3xy^4}-y\sqrt[3]{24x^4y}-\sqrt[3]{81x^4y^4}$

Multiply.

25. $\sqrt{3x^3y^4}\sqrt{12xy^6}$

26. $2\sqrt{18xy^7}\sqrt{8x^3y}$

27. $\left(\sqrt[3]{2ab^2}\right)\left(\sqrt[3]{4a^2b}\right)$

28. $\left(3\sqrt[3]{5x^4y}\right)\left(-4\sqrt[3]{25x^2y^2}\right)$

29. $\sqrt{3x^5y}\left(\sqrt{6xy^4}-\sqrt{8x^2y^3}\right)$

30. $\sqrt{5ab}\left(\sqrt{20a^3b^3}+\sqrt{5a^5b^7}\right)$

31. $\left(\sqrt{18}+3\right)\left(\sqrt{2}+5\right)$

32. $\left(2\sqrt{5}+\sqrt{8}\right)\left(\sqrt{5}-3\sqrt{6}\right)$

33. $\left(\sqrt{11}+\sqrt{7}\right)\left(\sqrt{11}-\sqrt{7}\right)$

34. $\left(\sqrt{x}+2\sqrt{y}\right)\left(\sqrt{x}-2\sqrt{y}\right)$

35. $\left(\sqrt[3]{2}-1\right)\left(\sqrt[3]{2}+1\right)$

36. $\left(4\sqrt[3]{3}+\sqrt[3]{2}\right)\left(\sqrt[3]{9}-3\sqrt[3]{4}\right)$

Divide.

37. $\dfrac{\sqrt{25}}{\sqrt{49}}$

38. $\dfrac{\sqrt{169}}{\sqrt{121}}$

39. $\dfrac{\sqrt{24x^3y^2}}{\sqrt{50x^5y^6}}$

40. $\dfrac{\sqrt{18ab^3}}{\sqrt{225a^3b}}$

Solve each radical equation.

41. $\sqrt{x} = 5$

42. $\sqrt[3]{x-1} = 2$

43. $\sqrt{2x+1} = 3$

44. $\sqrt{3x-2} = 4$

45. $\sqrt{x-3} = -2$

46. $\sqrt{x^2 - 5x + 1} = -3$

47. $\sqrt{x-2} + 4 = x$

48. $\sqrt{x+5} + 1 = x$

49. $\sqrt{2x^2 + 3x - 1} = \sqrt{x^2 + 4x + 5}$

50. $\sqrt{x^2 + x - 3} = x + 1$

51. $2\sqrt{x+1} - x = -2$

52. $\sqrt{x+3} + \sqrt{x-2} = 5$

Add or subtract.

53. $(3 + 5i) + (-2 + 8i)$

54. $(7 - 3i) + (-5 - 4i)$

55. $(2 + 3i) - (-6 + 7i)$

56. $(-8 + i) - (-3 + 6i)$

Multiply.

57. $2i(3 + 4i)$

58. $-5i(-3 + 6i)$

59. $\sqrt{-4}\left(\sqrt{-9} + \sqrt{-81}\right)$

60. $\sqrt{-5}\left(\sqrt{-20} - \sqrt{45}\right)$

61. $(4 + 5i)(-2 + 6i)$

62. $(-1 - 7i)(4 - 5i)$

63. $(5 + 3i)(5 - 3i)$

64. $(9 + 2i)(9 - 2i)$

Rationalize the denominator and write the answer in standard form.

65. $\dfrac{2}{3i}$

66. $\dfrac{4}{5i}$

67. $\dfrac{6}{3+i}$

68. $\dfrac{-3}{4-3i}$

69. $\dfrac{2+i}{5+3i}$

70. $\dfrac{4-3i}{4+3i}$

71. $\dfrac{3+\sqrt{-16}}{4-\sqrt{-9}}$

72. $\dfrac{5-\sqrt{-4}}{3+\sqrt{-25}}$

73. $\dfrac{1}{3+i} + \dfrac{i}{3-i}$

Simplify.

74. i^{102}

75. i^{52}

76. $(-i)^{18}$

77. Use the Distance Formula to find the distance between $(-3, 5)$ and $(3, 3)$.

78. Use Pythagorean Formula to find the hypotenuse of a right triangle with the legs $a = 12$ and $b = 16$.

9 QUADRATIC EQUATIONS

9.1 SOLVING QUADRATIC EQUATIONS BY THE SQUARE ROOT PROPERTY

□ Square Root Property

Recall that a quadratic equation is an equation that can be written in the form $ax^2 + bx + c = 0$, where a, b, and c are real numbers and $a \neq 0$. A quadratic equation in this form is said to be in *standard form*. In chapter 6 we learned how to solve quadratic equations by factoring. Since most quadratic equations cannot be factored, our goal in this chapter is to introduce some new techniques for solving quadratic equations.

Example 1

Solve by factoring

$$x^2 = 16.$$

Solution

$x^2 - 16 = 0$	Write the equation in standard form.
$(x-4)(x+4) = 0$	Factor.
$x - 4 = 0$ or $x + 4 = 0$	Apply zero factor property.
$x = 4$ or $x = -4$	Solve each equation for x.

The solutions 4 and –4 represent the positive and negative square roots of 16. The positive square root of 16 is $+\sqrt{16} = +4$ and the negative square root of 16 is $-\sqrt{16} = -4$. If we combine the square roots of 16, we have $\pm\sqrt{16} = \pm 4$. We conclude that if $x^2 = 16$ then, $x = \pm\sqrt{16} = \pm 4$.

This can be summarized in the following property.

Square Root Property

If k is a real number and $x^2 = k$, then $x = \pm\sqrt{k}$.

Example 2

Use the square root property to solve.

$$x^2 = 49$$

Solution

$$x = \pm\sqrt{49}$$
$$x = \pm 7$$

The solutions are $x = 7$ and $x = -7$.

Example 3

Use the square root property to solve.

$$x^2 = 12$$

Solution

$$x = \pm\sqrt{12}$$
$$x = \pm\sqrt{4 \cdot 3}$$
$$x = \pm 2\sqrt{3}$$

Thus, the solutions are $2\sqrt{3}$ and $-2\sqrt{3}$.

Example 4

Use the square root property to solve.

$$x^2 - 27 = 0$$

Solution

$$x^2 = 27$$
$$x = \pm\sqrt{27}$$
$$x = \pm\sqrt{9 \cdot 3}$$
$$x = \pm 3\sqrt{3}$$

Thus, the solutions are $x = 3\sqrt{3}$ and $x = -3\sqrt{3}$.

Example 5

Use the square root property to solve.

$$8x^2 - 2 = 0.$$

Solution

$$8x^2 = 2$$
$$x^2 = \frac{2}{8}$$
$$x^2 = \frac{1}{4}$$
$$x = \pm\sqrt{\frac{1}{4}}$$
$$x = \pm\frac{1}{2}$$

Thus, the solutions are $\frac{1}{2}$ and $-\frac{1}{2}$.

Example 6

Use the square root property to solve.

$$(x-1)^2 = 81$$

Solution

$$x-1 = \pm\sqrt{81}$$
$$x-1 = \pm 9$$
$$x = 1 \pm 9$$
$$x = 1+9 = 10 \text{ and } x = 1-9 = -8$$

Thus, the solutions are $x = 10$ and $x = -8$.

Example 7

Use the square root property to solve.

$$(x+5)^2 - 8 = 0$$

Solution

$$(x+5)^2 = 8$$
$$x+5 = \pm\sqrt{8}$$
$$x = -5 \pm 2\sqrt{2}$$

Thus, the solutions are $x = -5 + 2\sqrt{2}$ and $x = -5 - 2\sqrt{2}$.

Example 8

Use the square root property to solve.

$$(2x+3)^2 - 20 = 0$$

Solution

$$(2x+3)^2 = 20$$
$$2x+3 = \pm\sqrt{20}$$
$$2x = -3 \pm 2\sqrt{5}$$
$$x = \frac{-3 \pm 2\sqrt{5}}{2}$$

Thus, the solutions are $x = \dfrac{-3+2\sqrt{5}}{2}$ and $x = \dfrac{-3-2\sqrt{5}}{2}$.

Example 9

Use the square root property to solve.

$$(3x+6)^2 - 2 = 43$$

Solution

$$(3x+6)^2 = 43+2$$

$$(3x+6)^2 = 45$$

$$3x+6 = \pm\sqrt{45}$$

$$3x = -6 \pm 3\sqrt{5}$$

$$x = \frac{-6 \pm 3\sqrt{5}}{3} = \frac{3(-2 \pm \sqrt{5})}{3} = -2 \pm \sqrt{5}$$

Thus, the solutions are $x = -2+\sqrt{5}$ and $x = -2-\sqrt{5}$.

Example 10

Use the square root property to solve.

$$x^2 + 16 = 0$$

Solution

$$x^2 = -16$$

$$x = \pm\sqrt{-16}$$

$$x = \pm i\sqrt{16}$$

$$x = \pm 4i$$

Thus, the solutions are $x = 4i$ and $x = -4i$

Example 11

The length of a rectangle is three times its width. Find the length and the width of the rectangle if the area is 48 in^2.

Solution

The area of a rectangle is $A = L \cdot W$. Let the width be $W = x$. Then the length is $L = 3x$. Substituting W and L, into the formula $A = L \cdot W$ we have the equation:

$$3x \cdot x = 48$$

$$3x^2 = 48 \qquad \text{Divide the equation by 3.}$$

$$x^2 = 16$$

$$x = \pm\sqrt{16}$$

$$x = \pm 4$$

Since the length and width of a rectangle cannot be negative, we choose $x = 4$. Thus, the width of the rectangle is $W = x = 4$ in and the length is $L = 3x = 3(4) = 12$ in.

Example 12

The product of two positive integers is 75. Determine the two integers if the larger integer is five times the smaller integer.

Solution

Let x be the smaller integer. Then the larger integer is $5x$. The product of the two integers is,

$$5x \cdot x = 75$$

$$5x^2 = 75 \qquad \text{Divide the equation by 5.}$$

$$x^2 = 25$$

$$x = \pm\sqrt{25}$$

$$x = \pm 5$$

Since the integers are positive, we choose $x = 5$. Thus, the smaller integer is $x = 5$ and the larger integer is $5x = 5(5) = 25$.

Example 13

The side of a square is $s = (x-1)$ in. If the area of the square is 36 in^2, find the length of each side of the square.

Solution

The area of square is $A = s^2$. Substituting the side s,

$$(x-1)^2 = 36$$

$$x-1 = \pm 6$$

$$x = 1 \pm 6$$

$$x = 1+6 = 7 \text{ and } x = 1-6 = -5$$

Since the side of a square cannot be negative, we choose $x = 7$. Thus, the length of each side of the square is $s = 7$ in.

9.1 EXERCISES

Solve each quadratic equation by the square root property.

1. $x^2 = 4$

2. $x^2 = 81$

3. $x^2 = 64$

4. $x^2 = 121$

5. $x^2 = 18$

6. $x^2 = 54$

7. $2x^2 = 50$

8. $5x^2 = 125$

9. $4x^2 = 9$

10. $25x^2 = 36$

11. $x^2 - 32 = 0$

12. $x^2 - 50 = 0$

13. $2x^2 - 5 = 0$

14. $5x^2 - 6 = 0$

15. $(x-2)^2 = 9$

16. $(x+5)^2 = 36$

17. $3(x+3)^2 = 48$

18. $5(x-8)^2 = 45$

19. $(x-1)^2 - 5 = 0$

20. $(x-4)^2 - 11 = 0$

21. $(x+7)^2 - 6 = 30$

22. $(x-9)^2 + 3 = 52$

23. $(2x-3)^2 = 100$

24. $(3x+1)^2 = 49$

25. $(4x+5)^2 = 36$

26. $(9x-1)^2 = 121$

27. $(5x-2)^2 = 15$

28. $(7x-3)^2 = 17$

29. $(2x+4)^2 = 24$

30. $(5x+10)^2 = 50$

31. $(4x+8)^2 = 32$

32. $(2x+6)^2 = 8$

33. $\left(x+\dfrac{1}{2}\right)^2 = \dfrac{1}{4}$

34. $\left(x-\dfrac{3}{5}\right)^2 = \dfrac{16}{25}$

35. $(x+\dfrac{2}{3})^2 = \dfrac{7}{9}$

36. $(x+\dfrac{5}{6})^2 = \dfrac{11}{36}$

37. $9(x-1)^2 = 16$

38. $4(x+8)^2 = 81$

39. $x^2 = 0.09$

40. $x^2 = 0.25$

41. $x^2 + 9 = 0$

42. $x^2 + 1 = 0$

43. $0 = (2x-5)^2 - 16$

44. $0 = (7x-11)^2 - 169$

45. $6 = (3x+4)^2 - 10$

46. $11 = (5x-1)^2 - 14$

47. $(3x+7)^2 + 2 = 26$

48. $(4x-9)^2 - 5 = 40$

49. $(11x+1)^2 - 4 = 32$

50. $(8x+3)^2 + 7 = 8$

51. The length of a rectangle is three times its width. Find the length and the width of the rectangle if the area is 75 cm².

52. The width of a rectangle is $\dfrac{1}{3}$ its length. Find the length and the width of the rectangle if the area is 27 in².

53. The product of two positive integers is 54. Determine the two integers if the larger integer is six times the smaller integer.

54. The product of two positive integers is 32. Determine the two integers if the smaller integer is $\dfrac{1}{2}$ the larger integer.

55. The side of a square is $s = (x+3)$ in . If the area of the square is 100 in², find the length of each side of the square.

56. The side of a square is $s = (x-5)$ ft. If the area of the square is 169 ft², find the length of each side of the square.

57. The height h (in feet) of an object dropped from a cliff 144 ft high is given by $h = 144 - 16t^2$, where t is the time (in seconds). How long does it take for the object to reach the ground?

58. The height of an object dropped from a tower 256 m high is given by $h = 256 - 16t^2$, where t is the time (in seconds). How long does it take for the object to reach the ground?

9.2 SOLVING QUADRATIC EQUATION BY COMPLETING THE SQUARE

The method introduced in the previous section was used to solve quadratic equations in standard form $ax^2 + bx + c = 0$, $a \neq 0$ when the coefficient $b = 0$ and quadratic equations in the form $(px + q)^2 = r$ as illustrated in the following examples:

Example 1

Solve by the square root property.

$$2x^2 - 18 = 0 \quad (b = 0)$$

Solution

$\quad 2x^2 = 18 \qquad$ Divide the equation by 2.

$\quad x^2 = 9$

$\quad x = \pm\sqrt{9}$

$\quad x = \pm 3$

Thus, the solutions are $x = 3$ and $x = -3$.

Example 2

Solve by the square root property.

$$(2x + 5)^2 = 14$$

Solution

$\quad 2x + 5 = \pm\sqrt{14}$

$\quad 2x = -5 \pm \sqrt{14}$

$\quad x = \dfrac{-5 \pm \sqrt{14}}{2}$

Thus, the solutions are $x = \dfrac{-5 + \sqrt{14}}{2}$ and $x = \dfrac{-5 - \sqrt{14}}{2}$.

The technique from example 1 can be used to solve any quadratic equation with the coefficient $b = 0$. In this section, we will expand the method used in example 2 to solve any quadratic equation by rewriting the equation as an equivalent equation of the form $(px + q)^2 = r$ that can be solved by the square root property.

Thus, if the quadratic equation is not written in the form $(px + q)^2 = r$, then our goal is to rewrite the quadratic equation $ax^2 + bx + c = 0$, $a \neq 0$ in the form $(px + q)^2 = r$, and then use the square root property to solve for x. This task can be simplified if the leading coefficient

$a = 1$. If $a \neq 1$, we can divide the equation by $a \neq 0$ to change the leading coefficient to 1. We can accomplish our goal by first rewriting the trinomial $x^2 + bx + c$ $(a = 1)$ as the square of a binomial:

$$x^2 + bx + c = (x + q)^2$$

Definition

*A trinomial that can be written as the square of a binomial is called a **perfect square trinomial.***

Examples of perfect square trinomials:

$$x^2 + 6x + 9 = (x + 3)^2$$

$$x^2 - 4x + 4 = (x - 2)^2$$

$$x^2 + 8x + 16 = (x + 4)^2$$

Since most trinomials are not perfect square trinomials, we introduce a new technique called **completing the square** that helps us rewrite any trinomial as a perfect square trinomial.

In any perfect square trinomial written in descending order with the leading coefficient $a = 1$, the leading term and the constant term are always perfect squares with the same sign. In the above examples, the leading term x^2 and the constant terms $9 = 3^2$, $4 = 2^2$, $16 = 4^2$ are perfect squares, and have the same sign.

Usually, trinomials with the leading term x^2 are not perfect square trinomials either because the constant term is not a perfect square or the constant term is not the proper perfect square or has a sign different than the sign of x^2.

For example: $x^2 + 6x + 5$ is not a perfect square trinomial because the constant term 5 is not a perfect square. Also, the trinomial $x^2 + 6x + 4$ is not a perfect square trinomial because 4 is not the proper perfect square.

The trinomial $x^2 + 10x - 25$ is not a perfect square trinomial because x^2 is positive and -25 is negative. Thus, a very important step in the process of completing the square is to find the appropriate perfect square constant term.

From the expansion $(x + k)^2 = x^2 + 2kx + k^2$, we can see that the unknown constant term k^2 is related to the coefficient of x which is $2k$ Thus, to find the constant term k^2, first divide the coefficient of x by 2 ($2k \div 2 = k$) then, square the result to obtain k^2.

This can be expressed in the following rule:

$$\text{Constant term} = \left(\frac{coefficient\ of\ x}{2} \right)^2$$

Example 3

Solve by completing the square.

$$x^2 + 6x + 5 = 0$$

Solution

Since 5 is not a perfect square, remove 5 to the right-hand side (add –5 to each side of the equation) .

$$x^2 + 6x = -5$$

To find the appropriate constant term, divide the coefficient of x by 2 ($6 \div 2 = 3$) then square the result ($3^2 = 9$).

Now, we are ready to complete the square: add 9 to both sides of the equation.

$$x^2 + 6x + 9 = -5 + 9$$

Then, write the perfect square trinomial from the left-hand side as the square of a binomial.

$$(x + 3)^2 = 4$$

Apply the square root property.

$$x + 3 = \pm 2$$

Solve for x.

$$x = -3 \pm 2$$

Thus, the solutions are: $x = -3 + 2 = -1$ and $x = -3 - 2 = -5$.

We will summarize this example by listing the steps to follow when solving a quadratic equations of the form $x^2 + bx + c = 0$ by completing the square:

Strategy for Solving Quadratic Equations by Completing the Square

Step 1 Write the quadratic equation $x^2 + bx + c = 0$ in the form $x^2 + bx = -c$.

Step 2 Find the appropriate constant term: divide the coefficient of x by 2, then square the result. The sign of the coefficient of x is irrelevant because it will be squared.

Step 3 Complete the square: add the constant term from Step 2 to each side of the equation.

Step 4 Write the perfect square trinomial from the left-hand side as the square of a binomial.

Step 5 Apply the square root property.

Step 6 Solve for x, and check the solutions.

Note: If the coefficient a of x^2 is not 1, first divide both sides of the equation by a.

Example 4

Solve by completing the square.

$$x^2 - 8x + 15 = 0$$

Solution

Remove 15 to the right-hand side (add −15 to each side).	$x^2 - 8x = -15$
Find the constant term.	$8 \div 2 = 4,\ 4^2 = 16$
Add 16 to each side of the equation.	$x^2 - 8x + 16 = -15 + 16$
Rewrite the left-hand side as the square of a binomial.	$(x - 4)^2 = 1$
Apply the square root property.	$x - 4 = \pm 1$
Solve for x.	$x = 4 \pm 1$

The solutions are: $x = 4 + 1 = 5$ and $x = 4 - 1 = 3$

Example 5

Solve by completing the square.

$$x^2 + 10x - 7 = 0$$

Solution

Remove −7 to the right-hand side (add 7 to each side).	$x^2 + 10x = 7$
Find the constant term.	$10 \div 2 = 5,\ 5^2 = 25$
Add 25 to each side of the equation.	$x^2 + 10x + 25 = 7 + 25$
Rewrite the left-hand side as the square of a binomial.	$(x + 5)^2 = 32$
Apply the square root property.	$x + 5 = \pm\sqrt{32}$
Solve for x.	$x = -5 \pm 4\sqrt{2}$

The solutions are: $x = -5 + 4\sqrt{2}$ and $x = -5 - 4\sqrt{2}$

Example 6

Solve by completing the square.

$$x^2 - 4x + 13 = 0$$

Solution

Remove 13 to the right-hand side.	$x^2 - 4x = -13$
Find the constant term.	$4 \div 2 = 2,\ 2^2 = 4$
Add 4 to each side of the equation.	$x^2 - 4x + 4 = -13 + 4$
Rewrite the left-hand side as the square of a binomial.	$(x-2)^2 = -9$
Apply the square root property.	$(x-2)^2 = -9$
Solve for x.	$x = 2 \pm 3i$

Thus, the solutions are: $x = 2 + 3i$ and $x = 2 - 3i$

Example 7

Solve by completing the square.

$$x^2 + 3x - 4 = 0$$

Solution

Remove 4 to the right-hand side.	$x^2 + 3x = 4$
Find the constant term.	$3 \div 2 = \dfrac{3}{2},\ \left(\dfrac{3}{2}\right)^2 = \dfrac{9}{4}$
Add $\dfrac{9}{4}$ to each side of the equation.	$x^2 + 3x + \dfrac{9}{4} = 4 + \dfrac{9}{4}$
Rewrite the left-hand side as the square of a binomial.	$\left(x + \dfrac{3}{2}\right)^2 = \dfrac{16}{4} + \dfrac{9}{4} = \dfrac{25}{4}$
Apply the square root property.	$x + \dfrac{3}{2} = \pm\dfrac{5}{2}$
Solve for x.	$x = -\dfrac{3}{2} \pm \dfrac{5}{2}$

The solutions are: $x = -\dfrac{3}{2} + \dfrac{5}{2} = \dfrac{2}{2} = 1$ and $x = -\dfrac{3}{2} - \dfrac{5}{2} = -\dfrac{8}{2} = -4$

Example 8

Solve by completing the square.

$$2x^2 + 8x + 6 = 0$$

Solution

Since the coefficient of x^2 is not 1, divide both sides by 2.	$x^2 + 4x + 3 = 0$
Remove 3 to the right-hand side.	$x^2 + 4x = -3$
Find the constant term.	$4 \div 2 = 2, \ 2^2 = 4$
Add 4 to each side of the equation.	$x^2 + 4x + 4 = -3 + 4$
Rewrite the left-hand side as the square of a binomial.	$(x + 2)^2 = 1$
Apply the square root property.	$x + 2 = \pm 1$
Solve for x.	$x = -2 \pm 1$

The solutions are: $x = -2 + 1 = -1$ and $x = -2 - 1 = -3$.

Example 9

Solve by completing the square.

$$3x^2 + 4x - 2 = 0$$

Solution

Since the coefficient of x^2 is not 1, divide both sides by 3.	$x^2 + \dfrac{4}{3}x - \dfrac{2}{3} = 0$
Remove $-\dfrac{2}{3}$ to the right-hand side.	$x^2 + \dfrac{4}{3}x = \dfrac{2}{3}$
Find the constant term.	$\dfrac{4}{3} \div 2 = \dfrac{4}{3} \cdot \dfrac{1}{2} = \dfrac{2}{3}, \ \left(\dfrac{2}{3}\right)^2 = \dfrac{4}{9}$
Add $\dfrac{4}{9}$ to each side of the equation.	$x^2 + \dfrac{4}{3}x + \dfrac{4}{9} = \dfrac{2}{3} + \dfrac{4}{9}$
Rewrite the left-hand side as the square of a binomial.	$\left(x + \dfrac{2}{3}\right)^2 = \dfrac{6}{9} + \dfrac{4}{9}$
Simplify the right-hand side.	$\left(x + \dfrac{2}{3}\right)^2 = \dfrac{10}{9}$
Apply the square root property.	$x + \dfrac{2}{3} = \pm\sqrt{\dfrac{10}{9}}$
Solve for x.	$x = -\dfrac{2}{3} \pm \dfrac{\sqrt{10}}{3}$

Thus, the solutions are: $x = \dfrac{-2+\sqrt{10}}{3}$ and $x = \dfrac{-2-\sqrt{10}}{3}$

Example 10

Solve by completing the square.

$$(5x+3)(x-1) = 3$$

Solution

Write the equation in standard form.

$$5x^2 - 5x + 3x - 3 = 3$$
$$5x^2 - 2x - 3 - 3 = 0$$
$$5x^2 - 2x - 6 = 0$$

Since the coefficient of x^2 is not 1, divide both sides by 5.

$$x^2 - \frac{2}{5}x - \frac{6}{5} = 0$$

Remove $-\dfrac{6}{5}$ to the right-hand side.

$$x^2 - \frac{2}{5}x = \frac{6}{5}$$

Find the constant term.

$$\frac{2}{5} \div 2 = \frac{2}{5} \cdot \frac{1}{2} = \frac{2}{10} = \frac{1}{5}$$
$$\left(\frac{1}{5}\right)^2 = \frac{1}{25}$$

Add $\dfrac{1}{25}$ to each side of the equation.

$$x^2 - \frac{2}{5}x + \frac{1}{25} = \frac{6}{5} + \frac{1}{25}$$

Rewrite the left-hand side as the square of a binomial.

$$\left(x - \frac{1}{5}\right)^2 = \frac{30}{25} + \frac{1}{25}$$

Apply the square root property.

$$x - \frac{1}{5} = \pm\sqrt{\frac{31}{25}}$$

Solve for x.

$$x = \frac{1}{5} \pm \frac{\sqrt{31}}{5}$$

The solutions are: $x = \dfrac{1+\sqrt{31}}{5}$ and $x = \dfrac{1-\sqrt{31}}{5}$

Example 11

The length of a rectangle is 6 cm more than its width. If the area of the rectangle is 27 cm², find the length and width of the rectangle.

Solution

The area of a rectangle is given by $A = L \cdot W$. Let the width be $W = x$.

Then the length is $L = x + 6$. Substituting L, W, and A into $A = L \cdot W$,

$$x(x+6) = 27$$

$$x^2 + 6x = 27$$

$$x^2 + 6x + 9 = 27 + 9$$

$$(x+3)^2 = 36$$

$$x + 3 = \pm 6$$

$$x = -3 \pm 6$$

The solutions are, $x = -3 + 6 = 3$ and $x = -3 - 6 = -9$

Since the dimensions of a rectangle cannot be a negative number, we choose $x = 3$.

Thus, $W = x = 3$ cm and $L = x + 6 = 9$ cm.

Example 12

The product of two integers is 64. If the smaller integer is 12 less than the larger integer, find the two integers.

Solution

Let x be the larger integer. Then, the smaller integer is $x - 12$. Their product is,

$$x(x-12) = 64$$

$$x^2 - 12x = 64$$

$$x^2 - 12x + 36 = 64 + 36$$

$$(x-6)^2 = 100$$

$$x - 6 = \pm 10$$

$$x = 6 \pm 10$$

$$x = 6 + 10 = 16 \text{ and } x = 6 - 10 = -4$$

Since both 16 and –4 are integers, the problem has two solutions.

1st: If the larger integer is 16 and the smaller integer is $16 - 12 = 4$, Check: $16 \cdot 4 = 64$.

2nd: If the larger integer is –4 and the smaller integer is $-4 - 12 = -16$, $(-16)(-4) = 64$.

9.2 EXERCISES

Solve each equation by completing the square.

1. $x^2 + 6x - 16 = 0$

2. $x^2 - 2x - 35 = 0$

3. $x^2 - 4x - 45 = 0$

4. $x^2 + 12x + 11 = 0$

5. $x^2 - 6x - 7 = 0$

6. $x^2 - 10x + 16 = 0$

7. $x^2 - 8x - 48 = 0$

8. $x^2 - 14x + 24 = 0$

9. $x^2 - 12x + 20 = 0$

10. $x^2 + 8x - 20 = 0$

11. $x^2 + 2x - 5 = 0$

12. $x^2 + 4x - 1 = 0$

13. $x^2 + 10x - 7 = 0$

14. $x^2 - 18x + 1 = 0$

15. $x^2 - 2 = 6x$

16. $x^2 + 5 = 10x$

17. $x^2 = 10x - 25$

18. $x^2 = 20x - 100$

19. $x^2 + 3x - 10 = 0$

20. $x^2 - 5x - 24 = 0$

21. $x^2 + x - 2 = 0$

22. $x^2 + 7x - 8 = 0$

23. $x^2 + 3 = 5x$

24. $x^2 + 1 = 9x$

25. $x^2 = 11x - 10$

26. $x^2 = 13x - 11$

27. $4x^2 - 8x - 10 = 0$

28. $5x^2 + 10x - 5 = 0$

29. $2x^2 + 6x + 4 = 0$

30. $6x^2 + 12x - 18 = 0$

31. $2x^2 + x - 3 = 0$

32. $3x^2 - 5x - 2 = 0$

33. $8x^2 - 2x - 3 = 0$

34. $6x^2 - 5x - 6 = 0$

35. $3x^2 - 10x - 8 = 0$

36. $4x^2 + 5x - 6 = 0$

37. $5x^2 - 4x - 3 = 0$

38. $2x^2 - 7x - 1 = 0$

39. $(2x - 3)(x + 4) = -10$

40. $(5x - 1)(x + 2) = 3$

41. $\dfrac{1}{2}x^2 + \dfrac{3}{4}x = 1$

42. $\dfrac{2}{3}x^2 + \dfrac{5}{6}x = 1$

43. $3x^2 - 6x = 0$

44. $4x^2 - 12x = 0$

45. $3x^2 - 7x = 0$

46. $2x^2 - 5x = 0$

47. The length of a rectangle is 4 in more than its width. If the area of the rectangle is 32 in², find the length and width of the rectangle.

48. The width of a rectangle is 8 m less than its length. If the area of the rectangle is 33 m², find the length and width of the rectangle.

49. The product of two integers is 56. If the smaller integer is 10 less than the larger, find the two integers.

50. The product of two positive integers is 45. If their sum is 18, find the two integers.

51. The product of two integers is 63. If their difference is 18, find the two integers.

52. The product of two integers is 51. If the larger integer is 14 more than the smaller, find the two integers.

53. Find two consecutive integers such that the sum of their squares is 61.

54. Find two consecutive odd integers such that the sum of their squares is 164.

55. Find two consecutive even integers such that the difference of their squares is 52.

9.3 SOLVING QUADRATIC EQUATIONS BY THE QUADRATIC FORMULA

In this section we will introduce the most common method used to solve quadratic equations. This method involves the famous Quadratic Formula, which can be obtained by completing the square a quadratic equation in standard form $ax^2 + bx + c = 0$, $a \neq 0$.

First, let's consider an example to recall the steps used to solve a quadratic equation by completing the square.

Example 1

Solve by completing the square.

$$3x^2 + 4x + 1 = 0$$

Solution

$3x^2 + 4x + 1 = 0$ Remove 1 to the right-hand side.

$3x^2 + 4x = -1$ Divide each side by 3.

$$\frac{3x^2}{3} + \frac{4}{3}x = -\frac{1}{3}$$

$$x^2 + \frac{4}{3}x = -\frac{1}{3}$$ Find the constant term to complete the square.

$$\frac{4}{3} \div 2 = \frac{4}{3} \cdot \frac{1}{2} = \frac{4}{6} = \frac{2}{3}, \left(\frac{2}{3}\right)^2 = \frac{4}{9}$$ Add the constant term $\frac{4}{9}$ to both sides.

$$x^2 + \frac{4}{3}x + \frac{4}{9} = -\frac{1}{3} +$$ Rewrite the left-hand side as a binomial square, and find the common denominator for the right side.

$$x^2 + \frac{4}{3}x + \frac{4}{9} = -\frac{1}{3} +$$

$$\left(x + \frac{2}{3}\right)^2 = -\frac{3}{9} + \frac{4}{9}$$

$$\left(x + \frac{2}{3}\right)^2 = \frac{1}{9}$$ Apply the square root property.

$$x + \frac{2}{3} = \pm\sqrt{\frac{1}{9}}$$

$$x = -\frac{2}{3} \pm \frac{1}{3}$$ Solve for x.

$$x = -\frac{2}{3} + \frac{1}{3} = -\frac{1}{3}$$

$$x = -\frac{2}{3} - \frac{1}{3} = -\frac{3}{3} =$$

Thus, the solution are: $x = -\dfrac{1}{3}$ and $x = -1$

Now, let's follow the same steps to solve a quadratic equation in standard form by completing the square.

Example 2

Solve by completing the square.

$$ax^2 + bx + c = 0, \quad a \neq 0$$

Solution

$$ax^2 + bx + c = 0, \quad a \neq 0$$

$$ax^2 + bx = -c$$

Remove c to the right-hand side.

$$x^2 + \frac{b}{a}x = -\frac{c}{a}$$

Divide each side by $a \neq 0$.

$$\frac{b}{a} \div 2 = \frac{b}{a} \cdot \frac{1}{2} = \frac{b}{2a}, \quad \left(\frac{b}{2a}\right)^2 = \frac{b^2}{4a^2}$$

Find the constant term.

$$x^2 + \frac{b}{a}x + \frac{b^2}{4a^2} = \frac{b^2}{4a^2} - \frac{c}{a}$$

Add the constant term $\dfrac{b^2}{4a^2}$ to both sides to complete the square.

$$\left(x + \frac{b}{2a}\right)^2 = \frac{b^2}{4a^2} - \frac{4ac}{4a^2}$$

Rewrite the left-hand side as the square of a binomial. Find the common denominator for the right-hand side.

$$\left(x + \frac{b}{2a}\right)^2 = \frac{b^2 - 4ac}{4a^2}$$

Rewrite the right-hand side with a common denominator.

$$x + \frac{b}{2a} = \pm\sqrt{\frac{b^2 - 4ac}{4a^2}}$$

Apply the square root property.

$$x + \frac{b}{2a} = \pm\frac{\sqrt{b^2 - 4ac}}{\sqrt{4a^2}}$$

Simplify the radical expression.

$$x = -\frac{b}{2a} \pm \frac{\sqrt{b^2 - 4ac}}{2a}$$

Solve for x.

$$x = \frac{-b \pm \sqrt{b^2 - 4ac}}{2a}$$

The Quadratic Formula.

Thus, the solutions are: $x = \dfrac{-b + \sqrt{b^2 - 4ac}}{2a}$ and $x = \dfrac{-b - \sqrt{b^2 - 4ac}}{2a}$

Strategy for Solving a Quadratic Equation by the Quadratic Formula

Step 1 Write the equation in standard form: $ax^2 + bx + c = 0$, $a \neq 0$.

Step 2 Identify the coefficients a, b, and c.

Step 3 Substitute the values for a, b, and c into the quadratic formula.

Step 4 Simplify the radical expression to write the solution in simplest form.

Step 5 Check the answers.

Example 3

Solve by using the quadratic formula.

$$x^2 + 5x = 6$$

Solution

First, write the equation in standard form. $x^2 + 5x - 6 = 0$

Next, identify $a = 1$, $b = 5$, and $c = -6$.

Then, substitute these values into the quadratic formula.

$$x = \frac{-b \pm \sqrt{b^2 - 4ac}}{2a} =$$

$$\frac{-5 \pm \sqrt{5^2 - 4(1)(-6)}}{2(1)} =$$

$$\frac{-5 \pm \sqrt{25 + 24}}{2} =$$

$$\frac{-5 \pm \sqrt{49}}{2} = \frac{-5 \pm 7}{2}$$

The solutions are: $x = \dfrac{-5 + 7}{2} = \dfrac{2}{2} = 1$ and $x = \dfrac{-5 - 7}{2} = \dfrac{-12}{2} = -6$.

Example 4

Solve by using the quadratic formula.

$$x^2 + 4x + 4 = 0$$

Solution

$a = 1$, $b = 4$, and $c = 4$.

$$x = \frac{-b \pm \sqrt{b^2 - 4ac}}{2a} =$$

$$\frac{-4 \pm \sqrt{4^2 - 4(1)(4)}}{2(1)} =$$

$$\frac{-4 \pm \sqrt{16 - 16}}{2} =$$

$$\frac{-4 \pm \sqrt{0}}{2} = \frac{-4 \pm 0}{2}$$

Thus, the solution are: $x = \dfrac{-4 + 0}{2} = \dfrac{-4}{2} = -2$ and $x = \dfrac{-4 - 0}{2} = \dfrac{-4}{2} = -2$.

Example 5

Solve by the quadratic formula.

$$5x^2 + 6x + 5 = 0$$

Solution

$a = 5$, $b = 6$, and $c = 5$.

$$x = \frac{-b \pm \sqrt{b^2 - 4ac}}{2a} =$$

$$\frac{-6 \pm \sqrt{6^2 - 4(5)(5)}}{2(5)} =$$

$$\frac{-6 \pm \sqrt{36 - 100}}{10} =$$

$$\frac{-6 \pm \sqrt{-64}}{10} = \frac{-6 \pm 8i}{10} =$$

$$\frac{2(-3 \pm 4i)}{10} = \frac{-3 \pm 4i}{5}$$

Thus, the solutions are: $x = \dfrac{-3 + 4i}{5}$ and $x = \dfrac{-3 - 4i}{5}$.

From the last three examples we can draw a very important conclusion regarding the type and the number of solutions to a quadratic equation.

The radicand $b^2 - 4ac$ (the expression inside the square root sign) is called the **discriminant** and it's the deciding factor.

For instance, the equation in example 3 has two real solutions: $x = 1$, and $x = -6$, and the discriminant is $b^2 - 4ac = 49 > 0$ (positive).

The equation in example 4 has one real solution: $x = -2$, and the discriminant is $b^2 - 4ac = 0$ (zero), and the equation in example 5 has two complex solutions: $x = \dfrac{-3 + 4i}{5}$, $x = \dfrac{-3 - 4i}{2}$, and the discriminant is $b^2 - 4ac = -64 < 0$ (negative).

This can be summarized as follows:

1. If $b^2 - 4ac > 0$, the quadratic equation has two distinct real solutions.

2. If $b^2 - 4ac = 0$, the quadratic equation has one real solution.

3. If $b^2 - 4ac < 0$, the quadratic equation has two complex solutions (no real solutions).

Thus, the discriminant can be used to determine the type and number of solutions of a quadratic equation without solving the equation.

Example 6

Use the discriminant to determine the number and type of solutions to the quadratic equation.

$$x^2 + 3x + 4 = 0$$

Solution

$a = 1$, $b = 3$, and $c = 4$. Then,

$$b^2 - 4ac = 3^2 - 4(1)(4) = 9 - 16 = -7 < 0$$

Since the discriminant is negative, the quadratic equation has **two complex solutions.**

Example 7

Determine the number and type of solutions to the following equation without solving the equation.

$$x^2 + 6x + 9 = 0$$

Solution

$a = 1$, $b = 6$, and $c = 9$. Then,

$$b^2 - 4ac = 6^2 - 4(1)(9) = 36 - 36 = 0$$

Since the discriminant is zero, the quadratic equation has **one real solution**.

9.3 EXERCISES

Use the discriminant $b^2 - 4ac$ to determine the type and number of solutions for each quadratic equation.

1. $x^2 - 4x + 3 = 0$

2. $3x^2 - 2x + 1 = 0$

3. $2x^2 - x + 5 = 0$

4. $x^2 + 10x = -25$

5. $x^2 - 6x + 9 = 0$

6. $5x^2 - 10x + 4 = 0$

7. $4x^2 + 8x = 3$

8. $x^2 + x + 1 = 0$

Use the quadratic formula to solve each quadratic equation.

9. $x^2 - 4x + 3 = 0$

10. $x^2 + 8x + 7 = 0$

11. $x^2 + 3x - 10 = 0$

12. $x^2 - 5x - 14 = 0$

13. $x^2 - x - 2 = 0$

14. $x^2 + 8x - 16 = 0$

15. $x^2 - 10x + 25 = 0$

16. $x^2 + 12x + 20 = 0$

17. $2x^2 - 5 = 0$

18. $4x^2 - 3 = 0$

19. $3x^2 - 4x = 0$

20. $6x^2 + 5x = 0$

21. $6x^2 - 7x - 3 = 0$

22. $4x^2 + 13x - 12 = 0$

23. $5x^2 + 14x - 3 = 0$

24. $6x^2 - x - 12 = 0$

25. $x(3x + 11) = 20$

26. $x(6x + 13) = 15$

27. $4x^2 = x + 5$

28. $2x^2 = 7x - 3$

29. $x^2 - x + 1 = 0$

30. $x^2 + 2x + 3 = 0$

31. $3x^2 + 3x - 1 = 0$

32. $5x^2 + 3x - 1 = 0$

33. $2x^2 + 5x - 3 = 0$

34. $7x^2 - 8x - 2 = 0$

35. $(2x + 1)(3x - 2) = 3$

36. $(4x - 3)(4x + 5) = -14$

37. $0.2x^2 - 0.4x = 0.1$

38. $0.3x^2 + 0.6x = 0.4$

39. $0.01x^2 - 0.08x + 0.15 = 0$

40. $0.02x^2 - 0.06x - 0.1 = 0$

41. $\frac{1}{3}x^2 + 2x - 1 = 0$

42. $\frac{1}{4}x^2 + \frac{1}{3}x - 1 = 0$

43. $\frac{1}{7}x^2 + 2x + 7 = 0$

44. $\frac{1}{3}x^2 - \frac{3}{4}x - 1 = 0$

45. $5x(x + 1) = 2x + 8$

46. $9x(x - 2) = 10x - 3$

47. The area of a rectangle is 50 in². If the width is 15 inches less than twice the length, find the length and width of the rectangle.

48. The area of a rectangle is 40 cm². If the width is 19 cm less than three times the length, find the width and length of the rectangle.

49. The product of two integers is 55. If the larger integer is 39 more than four times the smaller integer, find the two integers.

50. The product of two positive integers is 72. If the smaller integer is 10 less than twice the larger integer, find the two integers.

51. An object is thrown upward from a cliff 72 ft above the ground. The height h of the object t seconds after it is thrown is $h = -16t^2 + 48t + 72$. Find the time when the object is 8 ft above the ground.

52. An object is dropped from a tower 128 ft above the ground. The height of the object t seconds after it is dropped is $h = -16t^2 - 32t + 128$. Find the time when the object hits the ground.

53. The hypotenuse of a right triangle is 20 cm. If the shorter leg is 4 cm less than the longer leg, find the length of each leg of the triangle.

54. The length of the shorter leg of a right triangle is 6 in. If the hypotenuse is 14 in less than three times the longer leg, find the length of the hypotenuse.

9.4 SOLVING EQUATIONS QUADRATIC IN FORM

□ **Equations Quadratic in Form**

□ EQUATIONS QUADRATIC IN FORM

Examples:

$$4x^4 - 3x^2 - 1 = 0$$

$$x^{\frac{2}{5}} + 6x^{\frac{1}{5}} + 5 = 0$$

$$x^{-2} - 3x^{-1} - 4 = 0$$

$$2x + 4x^{\frac{1}{2}} - 3 = 0$$

$$x^{\frac{2}{3}} - x^{\frac{1}{3}} - 12 = 0$$

$$(x+1)^4 + 2(x+1)^2 - 3 = 0$$

Definition

*An equation that can be written in the form $au^{2n} + bu^n + c = 0$, where a, b, and c are real numbers ($a \neq 0$), u is a variable (expression) and n is a rational number is called an **equation quadratic in form**.*

Note: A quadratic equation is a particular case of equation quadratic in form with $n = 1$.

How do we recognize equation quadratic in form? If the equation is written in descending order, the exponent of u in the leading term is always twice the exponent of u in the middle term.

For example, if the exponent of u in the middle term is $\dfrac{1}{3}$, the exponent of u in the leading term is $2 \cdot \left(\dfrac{1}{3}\right) = \dfrac{2}{3}$.

Usually, to solve an equation quadratic in form, we make a substitution of the form $y = u^n$. Then, $y^2 = \left(u^n\right)^2 = u^{2n}$, and the equation quadratic in form $au^{2n} + bu^n + c = 0$, becomes a quadratic equation $ay^2 + by + c = 0$ which can be solved by factoring or any other method discussed in this chapter.

Example 1

Solve.

$$x^{\frac{2}{3}} - x^{\frac{1}{3}} - 12 = 0$$

Solution

Let $y = x^{\frac{1}{3}}$. Then, $(y)^2 = \left(x^{\frac{1}{3}}\right)^2 = x^{\frac{2}{3}}$. Substituting, the original equation becomes a quadratic equation.

$$y^2 - y - 12 = 0$$

$$(y-4)(y+3) = 0$$

$$y - 4 = 0 \text{ or } y + 3 = 0$$

$$y = 4 \text{ or } y = -3$$

Since the original equation was written in terms of x, we replace y with $x^{\frac{1}{3}}$, and then solve for x: $x^{\frac{1}{3}} = 4$ or $x^{\frac{1}{3}} = -3$ which can be written in radical form $\sqrt[3]{x} = 4$ or $\sqrt[3]{x} = -3$

Cubing both sides of each equation, we have: $\left(\sqrt[3]{x}\right)^3 = 4^3 = 64$ or $\left(\sqrt[3]{x}\right)^3 = (-3)^3 = -27$. Thus, the possible solutions are $x = 64$ and $x = -27$.

Also, cubing each exponential expression $\left(x^{\frac{1}{3}}\right)^3 = 4^3 = 64$ or $\left(x^{\frac{1}{3}}\right)^3 = (-3)^3 = -27$ we obtain the same solutions: $x = 64$ or $x = -27$.

Note: To solve for x, we can use the power rule for rational exponents or radicals.

Example 2

Solve.

$$x^4 - 10x^2 + 9 = 0$$

Solution

Let $y = x^2$. Then, $(y)^2 = \left(x^2\right)^2 = x^4$. Substituting, the original equation becomes a quadratic equation.

$$y^2 - 10y + 9 = 0$$

$$(y-9)(y-1) = 0$$

$$y - 9 = 0 \text{ or } y - 1 = 0$$

$$y = 9 \text{ or } y = 1$$

Since the original equation was written in x, we replace y with x^2, and then solve for x.

$$x^2 = 9 \text{ or } x^2 = 1$$

Apply the square root property to each equation to get

$$x = \pm 3 \text{ or } x = \pm 1$$

Note: The original equation can also be solved by factoring.

$$x^4 - 10x^2 + 9 = 0$$

$$(x^2 - 9)(x^2 - 1) = 0$$

$$x^2 - 9 = 0 \text{ or } x^2 - 1 = 0$$

$$x^2 = 9 \text{ or } x^2 = 1$$

$$x = \pm 3 \text{ or } x = \pm 1$$

Thus, the possible solutions are $x = \pm 3$ or $x = \pm 1$.

Example 3

Solve.

$$x^{-2} - x^{-1} - 42 = 0$$

Solution

Let $y = x^{-1}$. Then $(y)^2 = \left(x^{-1}\right)^2 = x^{-2}$. Substituting, the original equation becomes a quadratic equation.

$$y^2 - y - 42 = 0$$

$$(y - 7)(y + 6) = 0$$

$$y - 7 = 0 \text{ or } y + 6 = 0$$

$$y = 7 \text{ or } y = -6$$

Now, we replace y with x^{-1}, and then solve for x.

$$x^{-1} = 7 \text{ or } x^{-1} = -6$$

$$\frac{1}{x} = \frac{7}{1} \text{ or } \frac{1}{x} = -\frac{6}{1}$$

Multiply across $7x = 1$ or $-6x = 1$

Thus, the possible solutions are: $x = \dfrac{1}{7}$ or $x = -\dfrac{1}{6}$.

Example 4

Solve.

$$6x + 5x^{\frac{1}{2}} - 4 = 0$$

Solution

Let $y = x^{\frac{1}{2}}$. Then, $y^2 = \left(x^{\frac{1}{2}}\right)^2 = x$. Substituting, the original equation becomes a quadratic equation.

$$6y^2 + 5y - 4 = 0$$

$$y = \frac{-b \pm \sqrt{b^2 - 4ac}}{2a} = \frac{-5 \pm \sqrt{25 - 4(6)(-4)}}{2(6)} =$$

$$\frac{-5 \pm \sqrt{25+96}}{12} = \frac{-5 \pm \sqrt{121}}{12} =$$

$$\frac{-5 \pm 11}{12}$$

The solutions are $y = \dfrac{-5+11}{12} = \dfrac{6}{12} = \dfrac{1}{2}$ and $y = \dfrac{-5-11}{12} = -\dfrac{16}{12} = -\dfrac{4}{3}$

Replace y with $x^{\frac{1}{2}}$ and solve for x.

$$x^{\frac{1}{2}} = \frac{1}{2} \text{ and } x^{\frac{1}{2}} = -\frac{4}{3} \text{ (not possible)}$$

Since, $x^{\frac{1}{2}} = \sqrt{x} = -\dfrac{4}{3}$ is not possible, because the square root always gives the positive root, we can reject this case. If you miss this observation, and proceed with the normal routine, you will find the mistake when you check the solutions.

Let's assume the worst case, and continue to solve both equations. Squaring both sides gives:

$$\left(x^{\frac{1}{2}}\right)^2 = \left(\frac{1}{2}\right)^2 \text{ and } \left(x^{\frac{1}{2}}\right)^2 = \left(-\frac{4}{3}\right)^2$$

Thus, the possible solution are: $x = \dfrac{1}{4}$ and $x = \dfrac{16}{9}$.

Any time we squared both sides to find x, there is a possibility that one of the solutions is extraneous.

Check.

$$6\left(\frac{1}{4}\right)+5\left(\frac{1}{4}\right)^{\frac{1}{2}}-4=0 \qquad\qquad 6\left(\frac{16}{9}\right)+5\left(\frac{16}{9}\right)^{\frac{1}{2}}-4=0$$

$$\frac{6}{4}+5\left(\frac{1}{2}\right)-4=0 \qquad\qquad 2\left(\frac{16}{3}\right)+5\left(\frac{4}{3}\right)-4=0$$

$$\frac{6}{4}+\frac{5}{2}-4=0 \qquad\qquad \frac{32}{3}+\frac{20}{3}-4=0$$

$$\frac{6}{4}+\frac{10}{4}-4=0 \qquad\qquad \frac{52}{3}-4=0$$

$$\frac{16}{4}-4=0 \qquad\qquad \frac{52}{3}-\frac{12}{3}=0$$

$$4-4=0$$

$$0=0 \text{ True.} \qquad\qquad \frac{40}{3}=0 \text{ False.}$$

So, the only solutions is $x = \dfrac{1}{4}$.

Example 5

Solve.

$$x^4 + 2x^2 - 15 = 0$$

Solution

Let $y = x^2$. Then $y^2 = x^4$. Substituting, the equation becomes:

$$y^2 + 2y - 15 = 0$$

$$(y+5)(y-3) = 0$$

$$y + 5 = 0 \text{ or } y - 3 = 0$$

$$y = -5 \text{ or } y = 3$$

Replace y with x^2, and solve for x.

$$x^2 = -5 \text{ or } x^2 = 3$$

$$x = \pm\sqrt{-5} \text{ or } x = \pm\sqrt{3}$$

The solutions are: $x = \pm i\sqrt{5}$ or $x = \pm\sqrt{3}$.

Example 6

Solve.

$$6(x-2)^{-2} + 5(x-2)^{-1} - 6 = 0$$

Solution

Let $y = (x-2)^{-1}$. Then, $y^2 = \left((x-2)^{-1}\right)^2 = (x-2)^{-2}$. Substituting, the equation becomes:
$6y^2 + 5y - 6 = 0$

$$y = \frac{-b \pm \sqrt{b^2 - 4ac}}{2a} = \frac{-5 \pm \sqrt{25 - 4(6)(-6)}}{2(6)} =$$

$$\frac{-5 \pm \sqrt{25 + 144}}{12} = \frac{-5 \pm \sqrt{169}}{12} =$$

$$\frac{-5 \pm 13}{12}$$

The solutions are: $x = \dfrac{-5+13}{12} = \dfrac{8}{12} = \dfrac{2}{3}$ and $x = \dfrac{-5-13}{12} = \dfrac{-18}{12} = -\dfrac{3}{2}$

Replace y with $(x-2)^{-1}$, and solve for x.

$$(x-2)^{-1} = \frac{2}{3} \text{ and } (x-2)^{-1} = -\frac{3}{2}$$

$$\frac{1}{x-2} = \frac{2}{3} \text{ and } \frac{1}{x-2} = -\frac{3}{2}$$

Multiply across, $2(x-2)=3$ and $3(x-2)=-2$

$$2x-4=3 \text{ and } 3x-6=-2$$

$$2x=3+4 \text{ and } 3x=-2+6$$

$$2x=7 \text{ and } 3x=4$$

$$x=\frac{7}{2} \text{ and } x=\frac{7}{2}$$

Thus, the possible solutions are $x=\frac{7}{2}$ and $x=\frac{4}{3}$.

9.4 EXERCISES

Solve each equation.

1. $x-8x^{\frac{1}{2}}+12=0$

2. $x-8x^{\frac{1}{2}}+15=0$

3. $x-5x^{\frac{1}{2}}+4=0$

4. $x-3x^{\frac{1}{2}}+2=0$

5. $x-3x^{\frac{1}{2}}-10=0$

6. $x-5x^{\frac{1}{2}}-24=0$

7. $x^{\frac{2}{3}}+2x^{\frac{1}{3}}-8=0$

8. $x^{\frac{2}{3}}-6x^{\frac{1}{3}}=-5$

9. $2x^{\frac{2}{3}}+5x^{\frac{1}{3}}=3$

10. $3x^{\frac{2}{3}}+14x^{\frac{1}{3}}-5=0$

11. $3x^{\frac{2}{3}}-13x^{\frac{1}{3}}+4=0$

12. $4x^{\frac{2}{3}}+17x^{\frac{1}{3}}=15$

13. $x^{\frac{2}{5}}-3x^{\frac{1}{5}}=-2$

14. $6x^{\frac{2}{5}}-5x^{\frac{1}{5}}+1=0$

15. $x^{\frac{2}{5}}-5x^{\frac{1}{5}}+6=0$

16. $2x^{\frac{2}{5}}-5x^{\frac{1}{5}}+2=0$

17. $x^4-5x^2=-4$

18. $x^4-6x^2+8=0$

19. $x^4-13x^2+36=0$

20. $x^4-8x^2=9$

21. $x^4-17x^2+16=0$

22. $x^4-19x^2+48=0$

23. $6x^{-2}+13x^{-1}=5$

24. $6x^{-2}-11x^{-1}+4=0$

25. $x^{-2}-9x^{-1}+18=0$

26. $x^{-2}-9x^{-1}+14=0$

27. $x^{-2}-4x^{-1}-21=0$

28. $x^{-2}+4x^{-1}=32$

29. $x^4-16=0$

30. $x^4-81=0$

31. $(x+1)^4-10(x+1)^2+9=0$

32. $(x+2)^4-26(x+2)^2+25=0$

33. $x-\sqrt{x}-6=0$

34. $x-\sqrt{x}-12=0$

35. $x-\sqrt{4x}-15=0$

36. $x+\sqrt{25x}-6=0$

9.5 GRAPHING QUADRATIC EQUATIONS IN TWO VARIABLES

☐ **Quadratic Equations in Two Variables**

☐ QUADRATIC EQUATIONS IN TWO VARIABLES

Examples:

$$y = 2x^2 + 3x + 5$$

$$y = -4x^2 + 2x + 9$$

$$y = x^2 + 6x$$

$$y = 5x^2 - 9$$

Definition

An equation that can be written in the form $y = ax^2 + bx + c$, *where a, b, and c are real numbers and* $a \neq 0$ *is called a* **quadratic equation in two variables**.

The graph of a quadratic equation in two variables is called *parabola* (U shape curve). If the leading coefficient *a* is positive ($a > 0$) the parabola opens upward. If *a* is negative ($a < 0$), the parabola opens downward.

One method used to graph quadratic equations in two variables is by plotting points (ordered pairs) and then connect the points with a smooth U shape curve to obtain a parabola.

Example 1

Graph.

$$y = x^2$$

Solution

Because the graph is not a straight line, we need more than two ordered pairs.

$x = -2$	$y = (-2)^2 = 4$
$x = -1$	$y = (-1)^2 = 1$
$x = 0$	$y = 0^2 = 0$
$x = 1$	$y = 1^2 = 1$
$x = 2$	$y = 2^2 = 4$

x	y	(x, y)
−2	4	(−2, 4)
−1	1	(−1, 1)
0	0	(0, 0)
1	1	(1, 1)
2	4	(2, 4)

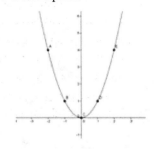

Note: Since $a = 1 > 0$, as we expected, the parabola opens upward.

The lowest point (0,0) on this parabola is called the **vertex**. The graph is symmetric about the vertical line $x = 0$ (y-axis) through the vertex.

This line is called the **line (axis) of symmetry**.

Example 2

Graph.

$$y = x^2 + x - 6$$

Solution

The graph is a parabola that opens up ($a = 1 > 0$).

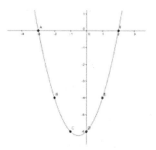

$x = -3$	$y = (-3)^2 - 3 - 6 = 0$
$x = -2$	$y = (-2)^2 - 2 - 6 = -4$
$x = -1$	$y = (-1)^2 - 1 - 6 = -6$
$x = 0$	$y = 0^2 - 0 - 6 = -6$
$x = 1$	$y = 1^2 + 1 - 6 = -4$
$x = 2$	$y = 2^2 + 2 - 6 = 0$

x	y	(x, y)
−3	0	(−3, 0)
−2	−4	(−2, −4)
−1	−6	(−1, −6)
0	−6	(0, −6)
1	−4	(1, −4)
2	0	(2, 0)

Example 3

Graph.

$$y = -x^2 + 2x + 3$$

Solution

$x = -2$	$y = -(-2)^2 + 2(-2) + 3 = -5$
$x = -1$	$y = -(-1)^2 + 2(-1) + 3 = 0$
$x = 0$	$y = -0^2 + 2(0) + 3 = 3$
$x = 1$	$y = -(1)^2 + 2(1) + 3 = 4$
$x = 2$	$y = -(2)^2 + 2(2) + 3 = 3$
$x = 3$	$y = -(3)^2 + 2(3) + 3 = 0$
$x = 4$	$y = -(4)^2 + 2(4) + 3 = -5$

x	y	(x, y)
−2	−5	(−2, −5)
−1	0	(−1, 0)
0	3	(0, 3)
1	4	(0, 4)
2	3	(2, 3)
3	0	(3, 0)
4	−5	(4, −5)

In the last example, we selected $x = 3$ and $x = 4$ but did not even consider $x = -3$ and $x = -4$. Is there anything wrong with these x-values? No, we can choose any x-values.

However, we have to make sure that the corresponding y-values are small numbers otherwise we have to plot large numbers which is an inconvenience that we try to avoid.

For instance, in example 3 if we choose $x = -4$, the corresponding y-value is: $y = -(-4)^2 + 2(-4) + 3 = -21$ which requires a large coordinate system (grid) in order to plot. We can avoid this guess work if we know the location of the vertex. Once we know the coordinates of the vertex, we choose two or three points to the right of the vertex and two or three points to the left.

The x-coordinate of the vertex of a parabola given by $y = ax^2 + bx + c$ can be found using the formula $x = -\dfrac{b}{2a}$. To find the y-coordinate, substitute the x-value in the equation $y = ax^2 + bx + c$.

In the last example $y = -x^2 + 2x + 3$, with $a = -1$, $b = 2$, and $c = 3$ the x-coordinate of the vertex is $x = -\dfrac{b}{2a} = -\dfrac{2}{2(-1)} = -\dfrac{2}{-2} = 1$.

The y-coordinate is $y = -(1)^2 + 2(1) + 3 = 4$.

So, the vertex is located at (1, 4). When we selected the x-values, the reference value was the x-coordinate $x = 1$ of the vertex, and then we selected three values to the left $x = 0$, $x = -1$, $x = -2$ and three values to the right $x = 2$, $x = 3$, and $x = 4$.

Example 4

___

Graph

$$y = 2x^2 - 8x, (a = 2, b = -8, c = 0)$$

Solution

The graph is a parabola that opens up ($a = 2 > 0$).

First, we find the x-coordinate of the vertex: $x = -\dfrac{b}{2a} = -\dfrac{-8}{2(2)} = \dfrac{8}{4} = 2$.

Next, we choose two values to the left of $x = 2$ ($x = 1$, $x = 0$) and two values to the right, $x = 3$ and $x = 4$. Then, we find the corresponding y-values,

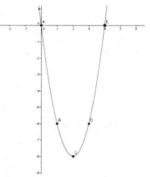

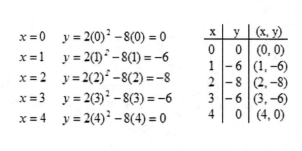

$x = 0$	$y = 2(0)^2 - 8(0) = 0$
$x = 1$	$y = 2(1)^2 - 8(1) = -6$
$x = 2$	$y = 2(2)^2 - 8(2) = -8$
$x = 3$	$y = 2(3)^2 - 8(3) = -6$
$x = 4$	$y = 2(4)^2 - 8(4) = 0$

x	y	(x, y)
0	0	(0, 0)
1	-6	(1, -6)
2	-8	(2, -8)
3	-6	(3, -6)
4	0	(4, 0)

The line of symmetry is $x = 2$.

Another method used to graph quadratic equations in two variables is by plotting the main features of a parabola: the x-intercepts, y-intercept, and the vertex instead of plotting some random points.

Example 5

___

Graph.

$$y = x^2 - 4x + 3, (a = 1, b = -4, \text{ and } c = 3)$$

Solution

a. **x-intercepts** (set $y = 0$)

$$x^2 - 4x + 3 = 0$$

$$(x - 3)(x - 1) = 0$$

$$x - 3 = 0 \text{ or } x - 1 = 0$$

$$x = 3 \text{ or } x = 1$$

$$(3, 0) \, (1, 0)$$

b. **y-intercept** (set $x = 0$)

$$y = 0^2 - 4(0) + 3 = 3$$

$$y = 3$$

$$(0, 3)$$

c. **Vertex**

$$x = -\frac{b}{2a} = -\frac{-4}{2(1)} = \frac{4}{2} = 2$$

$$y = 2^2 - 4(2) + 3 = -1$$

$$V(2, -1 \,)$$

d. **Line of symmetry**

$$x = 2$$

e. **Graph**

The graph is a parabola that opens up $(a = 1 > 0)$.

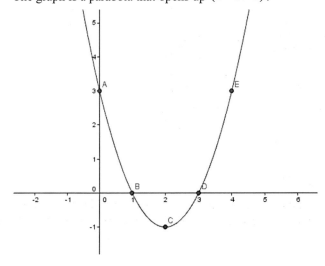

Example 6

Find the x and y-intercepts, vertex, and line of symmetry. Then graph the equation.

$$y = x^2 - 4, (a = 1, \ b = 0, \text{ and } c = -4)$$

Solution

a. **x-intercepts** (set $y = 0$)

$$x^2 - 4 = 0$$
$$(x - 2)(x + 2) = 0$$
$$x = 2 \text{ or } x = -2$$
$$(2, 0), \ (-2, 0)$$

b. **y-intercept** (set $x = 0$)

$$y = 0^2 - 4 = -4$$
$$(0, -4)$$

c. **Vertex**

$$x = -\frac{b}{2a} = -\frac{0}{2(1)} = 0$$
$$y = 0^2 - 4 = -4$$
$$V(0, -4)$$

d. **Line of Symmetry**

$$x = 0 \ (y\text{-axis})$$

e. **Graph**

The graph is a parabola that opens up $(a = 1 > 0)$.

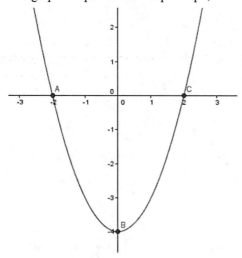

Example 7

Find the x and y-intercepts, vertex, and line of symmetry. Then graph the equation.

$$y = -x^2 + 2x - 1 \ (a = -1, \ b = 2, \text{ and } c = -1)$$

Solution

    a. ***x*-intercept** (set $y = 0$)

$$-x^2 + 2x - 1 = 0$$

$$x^2 - 2x + 1 = 0$$

$$(x-1)(x-1) = 0$$

$$x = 1, \text{ or } x = 1$$

$$(1, 0)$$

    b. ***y*-intercept** (set $x = 0$)

$$y = -0^2 + 2(0) - 1 = -1$$

$$(0, -1)$$

    c. **Vertex**

$$x = -\frac{b}{2a} = -\frac{2}{2(-1)} = -\frac{2}{-2} = 1$$

$$y = -(1)^2 + 2(1) - 1 = 0$$

$$V(1, 0)$$

    d. **Line of Symmetry**

$$x = 1$$

    e. **Graph**

The graph is a parabola that opens downward $(a = -1 < 0)$.

Since there are only two point to plot $(1, 0)$ and $(0, -1)$, in order to draw a smooth curve, we need to select at least one more point. An obvious choice would be the symmetric of the y-intercept $(0, -1)$ with respect to the line of symmetry $x = 1$ which is the point with the coordinates $(2, -1)$.

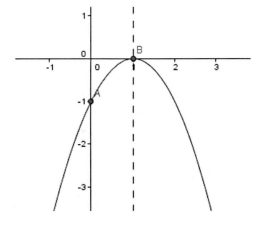

Example 8

Find the x and y-intercepts, vertex, and line of symmetry. Then graph the equation.

$$y = x^2 + 2x + 3 \ (a = 1, \ b = 2, \text{ and } c = 3)$$

Solution

a. **x-intercept** (set $y = 0$)

$$x^2 + 2x + 3 = 0$$

$$x = \frac{-b \pm \sqrt{b^2 - 4ac}}{2a} =$$

$$\frac{-2 \pm \sqrt{2^2 - 4(1)(3)}}{2(1)} =$$

$$\frac{-2 \pm \sqrt{4 - 12}}{2} =$$

$$\frac{-2 \pm \sqrt{-8}}{2} = \frac{-2 \pm 2i\sqrt{2}}{2} =$$

$$\frac{2(-1 \pm i\sqrt{2})}{2} = -1 \pm i\sqrt{2}$$

Since the x-intercepts are imaginary numbers, the graph does not intersect the x-axis (no x-intercepts).

b. **y-intercept** (set $x = 0$)

$$y = 0^2 + 2(0) + 3 = 3$$

$$y = 3$$

$$(0, 3)$$

c. **Vertex:**

$$x = -\frac{b}{2a} = -\frac{2}{2(1)} = -\frac{2}{2} = -1$$

$$y = (-1)^2 + 2(-1) + 3 = 2$$

$$V(-1, 2)$$

d. **Line of symmetry**

$$x = -1$$

e. **Graph.**

The graph is a parabola that opens up ($a = 1 > 0$). Again, there are only two points available, (0, 3) and $V(-1, 2)$. The third point could be the point symmetric with the y-intercept (0, 3) with respect to the line of symmetry $x = -1$ which is the point with the coordinates $(-2, 3)$.

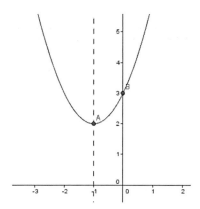

If a parabola opens downward, the vertex is the highest point on the graph. In other words, the y-coordinate has the largest (maximum) value at the vertex.

If the parabola opens upward, the vertex is the lowest point on the graph. Thus, the y-coordinate has the smallest (minimum) value at the vertex.

Example 9
_____

A ball is thrown upward from a height of 6 feet above the ground. The height y (in feet) of the ball above the ground at time x (in seconds) is given by $y = -16x^2 + 32x + 6$.

a. How long does it take for the ball to reach the maximum height?

b. What is the maximum height reached by the ball?

Solution

The equation $y = -16x^2 + 32x + 6$ is a quadratic equation in two variables. Since $a = -16$, the graph is a parabola that opens downward.

The maximum height of the ball occurs at the highest point on the graph which is the vertex. The x-coordinate of the vertex corresponds to the time when the ball reaches the maximum height and the y-coordinate corresponds to the maximum height reached by the ball.

a. $x = -\dfrac{b}{2a} = -\dfrac{32}{2(-16)} = -\dfrac{32}{-32} = 1$. So, the ball reaches the maximum height after 1 sec.

b. $y = -16(1)^2 + 32(1) + 6 = -16 + 32 + 6 = 22\,ft$. The maximum height reached by the ball is 22 feet.

Example 10
_____

The monthly profit of y dollars a small business earns by selling x items, is given by $y = -0.01x^2 + 80x - 2000$.

a. Find the number of items the business must sell each month to obtain the maximum profit.

b. Find the maximum profit.

Solution

The monthly profit equation is a quadratic equation in two variables. Since $a = -0.01 < 0$, the graph is a parabola that opens down. The maximum profit occurs at the highest point on the graph which is the vertex.

The x-coordinate of the vertex corresponds to the number of items the business must sell to obtain the maximum profit. The y-coordinate of the vertex corresponds to maximum profit.

a. $x = -\dfrac{b}{2a} = -\dfrac{80}{2(-0.01)} = -\dfrac{80}{-0.02} = -\dfrac{8000}{-2} = 4000$. So, the business must sell 4,000 items.

b. $y = -0.01(4000)^2 + 80(4000) - 2000 = -0.01(16,000,000) + 320,000 - 2000 = 158,000$
The maximum profit for a month is $158,000.

9.5 EXERCISES

Determine whether the parabola opens downward or upward.

1. $y = 2x^2 - 4x + 5$

2. $y = 7x^2 + x - 3$

3. $y = -x^2 + 3x - 1$

4. $y = -3x^2 - 2x + 8$

5. $y = 6 + 10x^2$

6. $y = -2 - 11x^2$

7. $y = 2x - 9x^2$

8. $y = x + 5x^2$

9. $y = -\dfrac{3}{4}x^2$

Graph each quadratic equation by plotting points.

10. $y = -\dfrac{1}{2}x^2$

11. $y = \dfrac{1}{4}x^2$

12. $y = 2x^2$

13. $y = 3x^2$

14. $y = x^2 - 1$

15. $y = x^2 + 2$

16. $y = 2x^2 + 1$

17. $y = 3x^2 - 4$

18. $y = -x^2 + 3$

19. $y = -x^2 + 2$

20. $y = -x^2 - 3x$

21. $y = -3x^2 + 6x$

22. $y = x^2 - 4x + 4$

23. $y = -2x^2 + 8x - 1$

24. $y = \dfrac{3}{2}x^2 + 1$

Find the x- and y-intercepts, vertex, and axis of symmetry for each parabola. Then sketch the graph.

25. $y = x^2 - 4x + 3$

26. $y = x^2 - 2x - 3$

27. $y = -x^2 - 2x + 8$

28. $y = -x^2 + 3x + 4$

29. $y = x^2 + 6x + 5$

30. $y = -x^2 - x + 6$

31. $y = x^2 + 2x - 3$

32. $y = x^2 + 6x - 7$

33. $y = -2x^2 - 3x + 2$

34. $y = 4x^2 - 8x - 5$

35. $y = x^2 + 4x - 5$

36. $y = x^2 - 4x + 3$

37. $y = -4x^2 + 1$

38. $y = -4x^2 + 9$

39. $y = \frac{1}{4}x^2 - 1$

40. $y = \frac{1}{9}x^2 - 1$

41. $y = x^2 - 4x$

42. $y = 2x^2 - 4x$

43. $y = 3x^2 - 6x$

44. $y = -x^2 + 6x$

45. $y = -x^2 + 4x - 4$

46. $y = -x^2 + 6x - 9$

47. $y = x^2 - 4$

48. $y = -x^2 + 1$

49. An object is projected upward from the top of a building 80 ft above the ground. The height h (in feet) of the object above the ground at any time t (in seconds) is given by $y = -16t^2 + 64t + 80$.

   a. How long does it take for the object to reach the maximum height?

   b. What is the maximum height reached by the object?

50. A projectile is fired upward from a height of 10 ft above the ground. The height h (in feet) of the projectile at any time t (in seconds) is given by $h = -16t^2 + 480t + 10$.

   a. How long does it take for the projectile to reach the maximum height?

   b. What is the maximum height reached by the projectile?

51. The monthly profit of y dollars a small store earns by selling x items is given by $y = -0.2x^2 + 60x - 300$.

   a. Find the number of items the store must sell each month to obtain the maximum profit.

   b. Find the maximum profit.

52. The monthly profit of y dollars a manufacturer earns by selling x items is given by $y = -0.003x + 1200x - 5000$.

   a. Find the number of items the manufacturer must sell each month to obtain the maximum profit.

   b. Find the maximum profit.

CHAPTER 9 REVIEW EXERCISES

Use the square root property to solve each quadratic equation.

1. $x^2 = 64$

2. $y^2 = 121$

3. $x^2 = 12$

4. $a^2 = 20$

5. $2x^2 - 1 = 5$

6. $7b^2 + 3 = 59$

7. $8m^2 - 50 = 0$

8. $9x^2 = 25$

9. $(x+3)^2 = 16$

10. $(y-5)^2 = 36$

11. $(2a+1)^2 - 12 = 0$

12. $(3y-2)^2 - 48 = 0$

13. $2(x-4)^2 = 8$

14. $3(4a-1)^2 = 27$

15. $4(x+8)^2 = 9$

16. $32(x-1)^2 = 50$

Solve each quadratic equation by completing the square.

17. $a^2 - 12a = 0$

18. $y^2 + 6y = 0$

19. $x^2 - 3x = 0$

20. $x^2 - 4x - 5 = 0$

21. $x^2 + 2x - 48 = 0$

22. $x^2 - 6x + 8 = 0$

23. $x^2 + 4x = -3$

24. $x^2 + 2x = 1$

25. $y^2 + 10y = 11$

26. $a^2 + 8a + 4 = 0$

27. $m^2 + 12m - 4 = 0$

28. $x^2 - 4x - 20 = 0$

29. $2b^2 - 8b - 12 = 0$

30. $3y^2 - 6y - 15 = 0$

31. $x^2 + 3x - 4 = 0$

32. $n^2 - 5n + 1 = 0$

33. $2y^2 - y - 3 = 0$

34. $3x^2 - 11x - 4 = 0$

35. $5x^2 - 7x - 6 = 0$

36. $6a^2 - a - 2 = 0$

37. $3y^2 + 5y - 12 = 0$

Use the discriminant to determine the nature and number of solutions for each quadratic equation.

38. $x^2 - 3x - 4 = 0$

39. $2x^2 + 3x - 5 = 0$

40. $x^2 - 8x + 16 = 0$

41. $x^2 + x + 1 = 0$

42. $5y^2 - y - 3 = 0$

43. $x^2 + 6x + 9 = 0$

44. $4x^2 - 5x + 3 = 0$

45. $x^2 - 10x = -25$

46. $3m^2 - 4m + 5 = 0$

Use the Quadratic Formula to solve each quadratic equation.

47. $x^2 - 5x + 4 = 0$

48. $a^2 - a - 30 = 0$

49. $6y^2 + 5y - 6 = 0$

50. $3m^2 + 11m - 4 = 0$

51. $4x^2 - 5x - 6 = 0$

52. $4x^2 - 9 = 0$

53. $5x^2 + 2x + 2 = 0$

54. $x^2 + 12x + 36 = 0$

55. $4x^2 - 12x + 9 = 0$

56. $x^2 - 2x + 17 = 0$

57. $(x + 3)(2x + 5) = 10$

58. $(2x - 5)^2 + 3 = 4$

Solve each equation quadratic in form.

59. $x^4 - 13x^2 + 36 = 0$

60. $x^4 - 17x^2 + 16 = 0$

61. $x^{\frac{2}{3}} - 7x^{\frac{1}{3}} - 8 = 0$

62. $x^{\frac{2}{3}} - 26x^{\frac{1}{3}} - 27 = 0$

63. $y^{\frac{2}{5}} + 33y^{\frac{1}{5}} + 32 = 0$

64. $a^{\frac{2}{5}} - 63a^{\frac{1}{5}} - 64 = 0$

65. $6x^{-2} + x^{-1} - 1 = 0$

66. $12x^{-2} + 5x^{-1} - 2 = 0$

67. $x - 2x^{\frac{1}{2}} - 15 = 0$

68. $2x + 5x^{\frac{1}{2}} - 3 = 0$

69. $(x + 3)^2 - (x + 3) - 12 = 0$

70. $2x^{\frac{2}{3}} + 11x^{\frac{1}{3}} + 5 = 0$

Graph each quadratic equation in two variables by plotting points.

71. $y = x^2 + 1$

72. $y = x^2 - 2$

73. $y = -3x^2 + 6x$

74. $y = -2x^2 + 8x$

75. $y = x^2 - x - 6$

76. $y = x^2 + 2x - 3$

77. $y = -x^2 + 3x - 4$

78. $y = -x^2 + x + 2$

79. $y = 2x^2 - 7x - 4$

Find the x- and y-intercepts, vertex, line of symmetry and graph.

80. $y = x^2 - 4x$

81. $y = -x^2 + 2x$

82. $y = -x^2 - 6x$

83. $y = x^2 - 4x + 3$

84. $y = x^2 + 3x - 4$

85. $y = -x^2 - 2x + 3$

86. $y = 2x^2 + 5x - 3$

87. $y = 3x^2 - 8x - 3$

88. $y = 4x^2 + 2x - 2$

89. $y = -2x^2 + 8$

90. $y = -3x^2 + 3$

91. $y = 2x^2 - 3x - 5$

92. The area of a rectangle is 90 in². If the width is 9 in less than the length, find the width and length of the rectangle.

93. The width of a rectangle is 3 cm less than the length. If the diagonal of the rectangle is 15 cm, find the width and length of the rectangle.

94. An object is dropped from a tower 240 ft above the ground. The height of the object t seconds after it was dropped is $h = -16t^2 - 32t + 240$. Find the time when the object hits the ground.

ANSWERS TO ODD-NUMBERED PROBLEMS

CHAPTER 1

SECTION 1.1

1. $\{-2, -1, 0, 1, 2, 3\}$ **3.** $\{1, 2, 3, 4, 5\}$ **5.** $\{\ \}$ **7.** $\{0, 1, 2, 3, 4\}$ **9.** True **11.** False **13.** True **15.** False

17. a) $1, 17, 80$ b) $0, 1, 17, 80$ c) $-10, -3, 0, 1, 17, 80$ d) $-10, -3, -\frac{3}{2}, 0, 0.\overline{23}, \frac{5}{7}, 2.53, 4\frac{2}{5}, 17, 80$

e) $\sqrt{2}, \pi$ f) all

19.

21. -16 **23.** 5 **25.** $-1\frac{1}{8}$ **27.** 12 **29.** $\frac{11}{2}$ **31.** -1.23 **33.** 35 **35.** -17 **37.** -0.6 **39.** $-8 < -5$
41. $-14 < \frac{3}{8}$ **43.** $\left|\frac{2}{3}\right| = \left|-\frac{2}{3}\right|$ **45.** $-|-2| < |-2|$ **47.** $3.8 > 3.79$ **49.** $\frac{1}{2} < \frac{3}{4}$ **51.** $-3.22, -3.21, 0, 3, \frac{7}{3}, 4, |-11|$ **53.** $x \le 0$ **55.** $\{x \,|\, x \le 7, x \text{ is a natural number}\}$, $\{1, 2, 3, 4, 5, 6, 7\}$ **57.** $\{x \,|\, -3 < x < 3, x \text{ is an integer}\}$, $\{-2, -1, 0, 1, 2\}$

SECTION 1.2

1.

3.

5.

7. 9 **9.** 5 **11.** -13 **13.** -12 **15.** -50 **17.** -44 **19.** 60 **21.** 0 **23.** -20 **25.** -7 **27.** 13 **29.** -5 **31.** 11
33. -91 **35.** 10 **37** -12 **39.** 25 **41.** 10 **43.** 0 **45.** -9 **47.** 9 **49.** 27 **51.** -12 **53.** -24 **55.** 39 **57.** 17
59. -46 **61.** 0 **63.** -164 **65.** 40 **67.** -13 **69.** -15 **71.** -30 **73.** 60 **75.** 43 **77.** 13 **79.** 93 **81.** -6
83. -8 **85** 18 **87.** 78 **89.** 10 **91.** -13 **93.** -22 **95.** 13 **97.** $4,170,000$ **99.** $\$2,097$ **101.** $17°$

SECTION 1.3

1. 20 **3.** -30 **5.** -90 **7.** 120 **9.** -100 **11.** -1600 **13.** 16 **15.** 0 **17.** 81 **19.** -40 **21.** -24 **23.** 150
25. -128 **27.** -120 **29.** -800 **31.** negative **33.** negative **35.** positive **37.** negative **39.** positive **41.** 3
43. -4 **45.** -3 **47.** 4 **49.** -20 **51.** 6 **53.** -7 **55.** -9 **57.** 0 **59.** undefined **61.** -8 **63.** 1 **65.** 16
67. -81 **69.** 125 **71.** -1 **73.** 27 **75.** 81 **77.** $\$6,000$ **79.** $3,000$ **81.** $\$12.50$

SECTION 1.4

1. a) 1, 2, 3, 4, 6, 9, 12, 18, 36   **b)** 1, 3, 5, 15   **c)** 1, 2, 4, 5, 8, 10, 20, 40   **3. a)** 1, 3, 5, 9, 15, 45   **b)** 1, 2, 3,

4, 6, 12   **c)** 1, 2, 5, 10, 25, 50   **5. a)** composite   **b)** neither   **c)** prime   **7. a)** $(2)(2)(5)(5) = 2^2 \cdot 5^2$

b) $(2)(3)(5)(7)$ **c)** $(2)(3^2)(5)$ **9. a)** $(2^3)(11)$ **b)** $(2)(7)(11)$ **c)** $(1)(17)$ **11. a)** 18   **b)** 6   **c)** 6   **13. a)** $\frac{3}{10}$

b) $\frac{7}{9}$ **c)** $\frac{3}{7}$ **15. a)** $\frac{3}{5}$ **b)** $\frac{11}{19}$ **c)** $\frac{21}{32}$ **17. a)** $\frac{18}{120}$ **b)** $\frac{3}{10}$ **c)** $\frac{7}{9}$ **19. a)** proper   **b)** improper $1\frac{3}{18} = 1\frac{1}{6}$

c) improper $1\frac{0}{14} = 1$ **21. a)** improper $1\frac{6}{19}$ **b)** improper $1\frac{1}{3}$ **c)** proper   **23. a)** $-1\frac{5}{11}$ **b)** $4\frac{2}{3}$ **c)** $1\frac{1}{12}$

SECTION 1.5

1. a) $\frac{23}{6}$ **b)** $-\frac{95}{11}$ **c)** $\frac{21}{9}$ **3. a)** $\frac{74}{3}$ **b)** $\frac{53}{9}$ **c)** $\frac{36}{31}$ **5. a)** $\frac{3}{7}$ **b)** $\frac{1}{3}$ **c)** $\frac{7}{16}$ **7. a)** $-\frac{77}{1}$ **b)** 1   **c)** $-\frac{10}{21}$

9. a) $\frac{7}{3}$ **b)** $\frac{2}{3}$ **c)** $\frac{8}{5}$ **11. a)** –3   **b)** $\frac{6}{5}$ **c)** $-\frac{1}{24}$ **13. a)** –42   **b)** $\frac{21}{2}$ **c)** $\frac{3}{4}$ **15. a)** 9   **b)** 30   **c)** $-\frac{9}{2}$

17. a) 4   **b)** $-\frac{69}{13}$ **c)** $\frac{40}{27}$ **19.** 18 cups   **21.** A: 7, B: 12   A's and B's 19

SECTION 1.6

1. a) LCM = 48   **b)** LCM = 144   **c)** LCM = 140   **3. a)** LCD = 60   **b)** LCD = 120   **c)** LCD = 140

5. a) LCD = 192   **b)** LCD = 72   **c)** LCD = 34   **7. a)** $\frac{15}{18}$ **b)** $\frac{9}{21}$ **c)** $\frac{6}{45}$ **9. a)** $\frac{8}{60}$ **b)** $\frac{12}{54}$ **c)** $\frac{21}{56}$ **11. a)** $\frac{1}{2}$

b) $\frac{2}{3}$ **c)** $\frac{1}{12}$ **13. a)** $\frac{1}{4}$ **b)** $\frac{1}{6}$ **c)** $\frac{7}{9}$ **15. a)** $\frac{37}{54}$ **b)** $\frac{19}{24}$ **c)** $\frac{29}{80}$ **17. a)** $\frac{37}{5}$ **b)** $\frac{5}{4}$ **c)** $-\frac{45}{8}$ **19. a)** $-\frac{3}{17}$ **b)** $\frac{185}{36}$

c) $\frac{113}{63}$ **21. a)** $6\frac{3}{8}$ **b)** $4\frac{5}{19}$ **c)** $10\frac{1}{2}$ **23. a)** $4\frac{2}{17}$ **b)** $1\frac{67}{90}$ **c)** $11\frac{29}{60}$ **25. a)** $5\frac{91}{264}$ **b)** $1\frac{53}{50} = 2\frac{3}{50}$ **c)** $4\frac{1}{6}$

27. $3\frac{3}{4}$ hrs.   **29.** $8\frac{11}{20}$ in   **31.** $\frac{8}{3} = 2\frac{2}{3}$

SECTION 1.7

1. a) commutative (addition)   **b)** identity (addition)   **c)** associative (multiplication)   **3. a)** associative (addition)

b) distributive   **c)** commutative (addition)   **5. a)** inverse (addition)   **b)** inverse (multiplication)   **c)** distributive

7. $4 + (x + 2)$ **9.** $12p + 12q$ **11.** $4x$ **13.** m(np)   **15.** $11x + 33$ **17.** –1   **19.** 22   **21.** 14   **23.** –34   **25.** –105

27. 52   **29.** 14   **31.** 9   **33.** –63   **35.** –18   **37.** –5   **39.** 2   **41.** –10

CHAPTER 2

SECTION 2.1

1.
Term	Coefficient
$4x^2$	4
$5x$	5
$-y$	-1
3	3

3.
Term	Coefficient
12mn	12
m	1
$-n$	-1
6	6

5. like **7.** unlike **9.** $-4x + 7$ **11.** $9x + 30$ **13.** $11x - 11$ **15.** $2x + 13$ **17.** $-2x + 21$ **19.** $6x + 2$

21. $-4a + 11b - 2$ **23.** $13x^2y + 2xy^2 - 3xy$ **25.** $-m - 9$ **27.** $8x + 4y + 10z$ **29.** $-2x + 18$ **31.** $-2m - 5$

33. $\frac{4}{5}x + \frac{1}{6}$ **35.** 9 **37.** 6 **39.** 1 **41.** -19 **43.** 143 **45.** 20 **47.** 2 **49.** $-\frac{29}{6}$ **51.** $5x + 16$ **53.** $2x - 4$

55. $\frac{x+4}{5}$ **57.** $3 - (x - 8) = 11 - x$ **59.** $\frac{18+x}{9-x}$ **61.** $6 + \frac{x}{2}$ **63.** $3(x - 10)$

SECTION 2.2

1. expression **3.** equation **5.** expression **7.** yes **9.** yes **11.** no **13.** $x = 10$ **15.** $y = -17$ **17.** $x = 6$

19. $z = -7$ **21.** $x = 12$ **23.** $y = -11$ **25.** $y = 9$ **27.** $y = 2$ **29.** $a = -16$ **31.** $y = -9$ **33.** $b = 3$ **35.** $y = -10$

37. $a = -6$ **39.** $m = 1$ **41.** $y = \frac{3}{7}$ **43.** $x = \frac{3}{2}$ **45.** $y = -\frac{11}{8}$ **47.** $y = 7$ **49.** $x = 0$ **51.** $x = 30$ **53.** $y = -11$

55. $x = 11.7$ **57.** $y = 11.8$ **59.** $y = 3$ **61.** $x = -8$ **63.** $x = 8$ **65.** $m = 5$ **67.** $x = -3$ **69.** $x = -4$ **71.** $z = -8$

73. $z = 11$ **75.** $x = -4$ **77.** $x = -20$ **79.** $x = 10$ **81.** $a = -30$ **83.** $x = -32$ **85.** $x = 12$ **87.** $y = 20$ **89.** $x = 1$

91. $x = 10.5$ **93.** $m = 4$ **95.** $x = -16.8$ **97.** $x = 3$ **99.** $z = 2$ **101.** $x = -1$ **103.** $x = -2$ **105.** $m = 2$ **107.** $x = -9$

109. $y = -3$ **111.** $a = 2$ **113.** $x = 3$ **115.** $a = -15$ **117.** $m = 28$ **119.** $x = 12$ **121.** $x = 5$ **123.** $x = -8$ **125.** $y = 3$

127. $x = 6$ **129.** $x = 3$

SECTION 2.3

1. $x = 2$ **3.** $x = -5$ **5.** $x = -3$ **7.** $x = 7$ **9.** All real numbers **11.** $a = -2$ **13.** $x = -4$ **15.** no solution **17.** $x = 6$

19. All real numbers **21.** $x = 3$ **23.** No solution **25.** $x = 6$ **27.** $x = 0$ **29.** $x = 3$ **31.** $x = 13$ **33.** $x = 2$

35. $x = 1$ **37.** $x = 4$ **39.** $x = 2$ **41.** $x = 8$ **43.** $x = 2$ **45.** $x = 1$ **47.** $x = 4$ **49.** $y = 12$ **51.** $x = 3$ **53.** $x = -5$

55. $x = -1$ **57.** $x = 9$ **59.** $x = 4$ **61.** $x = 6$ **63.** $x = 62$ **65.** No solution

SECTION 2.4

1. 27, 29   **3.** 11, 12, 13   **5.** 7, 9, 11   **7.** −1, 0, 1   **9.** 10, 12   **11.** −19, −17, −15   **13.** −8, −7   **15.** 6, 23

17. 7, 37   **19.** − 6   **21.** angle = 20°, complement = 70° **23.** angle = 50°, supplement = 130° **25.** angle = 35°

complement = 55°, supplement = 145° **27.** 15°, 60°, 105° **29.** 38°, 59°, 83° **31.** 13°,   **33.** 40.25°, 139.75°

35. angle = 83° complement = 7°.

SECTION 2.5

1. P = 38 in   **3.** C = 9 ft   **5.** R = 50 mph   **7.** m = 3   **9.** B = 6 cm   **11.** w = $\frac{P-2L}{2}$ **13.** P = $\frac{I}{rt}$ **15.** R = $\frac{C}{2\pi}$

17. F = $\frac{9}{5}$ C + 32   **19.** c = P − a − b   **21.** m = $\frac{y-b}{x}$ **23.** P = 3x − m − n   **25.** x = 5   **27.** x = 33   **29.** s = 24cm

31. C = 31.4 in   **33.** x = 40 mph and 65 mph   **35.** 11:00 a.m.   **37.** 2 hrs @ 45 mph,   **39.** 2 hrs and 5 hrs   **41.** 0.5 hrs

43. 377 m

SECTION 2.6

1. $5,000 @ 5%, $7,000 @ 7.5%   **3.** $10,000 @5.5%, $18,000 @ 6%   **5.** $4,000 @ 8%, $12,000 @ 11

7. $6,000 @ 6%, $9,000 @ 4%   **9.** 12 lb, 12 lb   **11.** 31 lb, 10 lb   **13.** 8.7 lb, 6.3 lb   **15.** 22.4 lb   **17.** 5 gal

19. 48 L   **21.** x = 3 L   **23.** 9 qts and 3 qts   **25.** 10%

SECTION 2.7

1. $\frac{3}{7}$ **3.** $\frac{15}{8}$ **5.** $\frac{7}{36}$ **7.** True   **9.** True   **11.** True   **13.** True   **15.** 55 oz @ $4.99   **17.** 48 oz @ $7.39   **19.** 46 oz

@ $3.49   **21.** m = 7   **23.** a = 3   **25.** y = 6   **27.** x = 84   **29.** y = −1   **31.** $280   **33.** x = 2   **35.** 3,300 mi

37. $9,350   **39.** 40 gal   **41.** x = 1 ft, y = 3 ft   **43.** x = 6 cm, y = 4 cm

SECTION 2.8

1. $\{a|a \geq 2\}$ ——●—→ (2)

3. $\{x|x < 1\}$ ←○—— (1)

5. $\{x|x \geq 6\}$ ——●—→ (6)

7. $\{m|m < 11\}$ ←○—— (11)

9. $\{x|x > -4\}$ ——○—→ (-4)

11. $\{a|a \geq -5\}$ ——●—→ (-5)

13. $\{y|y < 19\}$ ←○—— (19)

15. $\{a|a > 2\}$ ——○—→ (2)

17. $\{x|x \leq -3\}$ ←——●—— (-3)

19. $\{x|x < -3\}$ ←○—— (-3)

21. $\{x|x \geq 3\}$ ——●—→ (3)

23. $\{x|x \leq 20\}$ ←——●—— (20)

25. $\{x|x < -24\}$ ←○—— (-24)

27. $\{x|x > -4\}$ ——○—→ (-4)

29. $\{x|x \geq 35\}$ ——●—→ (35)

31. $\{x \mid x \geq 36\}$ ——●—→ (36)

33. $\{x|x > 8\}$ ——○—→ (8)

35. $\{x|x > -4\}$ ——○—→ (-4)

37. $\{x|x \leq 3\}$ ←——●—— (3)

39. $\left\{x \Big| x > \dfrac{2}{3}\right\}$ ——○—→ (2/3)

41. $\{x|x < 11\}$ ←——●—— (11)

43. $\{x|x < 2\}$ ←○—— (2)

45. $\{x|x \leq 8\}$ ←——●—— (8)

47. $\{x|x > 11\}$ ——○—→ (11)

49. *No Sol.* ———————

51. $\{x \mid x \leq -2\}$ ←——●—— (2)

53. $\{x|x > 78\}$ ——○—→ (78)

55. $\{x|x > 1\}$ ——○—→ (1)

57. $\{x|x \leq 8\}$ ←——●—— (8)

59. $\left\{x \Big| x \leq -\dfrac{1}{4}\right\}$ ←——●—— (1/4)

61. $\{x \mid x > 5\}$ ------○→---------- (5)

63. $\{x \mid 1 < x < 6\}$ ——○——○—— (1)(6)

65. $\{x \mid 2 \leq x < 3\}$ ——●——○—— (2)(3)

67. $\{x \mid -3 \leq x \leq 2\}$ ——●——●—— (-3)(2)

69. $\{x \mid -13 \leq x < 7\}$ ——●——○—— (-13)(7)

71. $\{x \mid 2 < x \leq 3\}$ ——○——●—— (2)(3)

73. *at least 87*

75. *2.5 hrs*

77. 49 min

CHAPTER 3

SECTION 3.1

1. Yes **3.** Yes **5.** No **7.** No **9.** Yes **11.** Yes **13.** No **15.** No **17.** Q II **19.** Q I **21.** Q IV **23.** Q I

25. $(1, 2)$ **27.** $(0, -1)$ **29.** $(2, -2)$ **31.** $(-4, -5)$ **33.** $(4, 0), (2, 1), (-2, 3)$ **35.** $(4, 5), (-2, -10), (2, 0)$

37. $(-4, -5), (4, 1), (0, -2)$ **39.** $(3, 5), (3, -8), (3, 3)$ **41.** $(-1, 4), (-1, 0), (-1, -2)$

43.

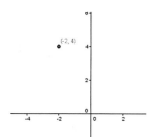

45.

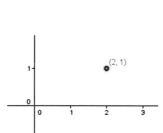

47.

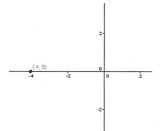

49.

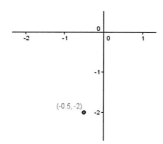

SECTION 3.2

1. $(0, 0), (1, 1), (-1, -1)$

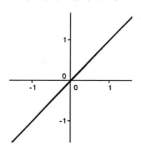

3. $(0, 0), (2, -1), (-2, 1)$

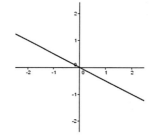

5. $(-1, -3), (0, 0), (1, 3)$

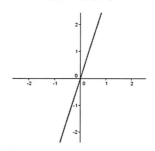

7. $(0, -1), (1, 1), (2, 3)$

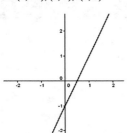

9. $(2, 2), (0, -1), (4, 5)$

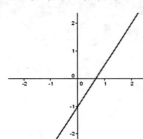

11. $(1, -2), (2, 0), (3, 2)$

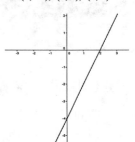

13. $y = x - 2$

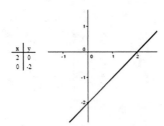

15. $y = x + 4$

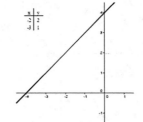

17. $y = 2x - 3$

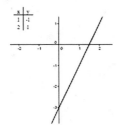

19. $y = 5x - 3$

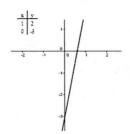

21. $y = -2x + 4$

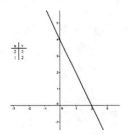

23. $y = \frac{3}{4} x - 2$

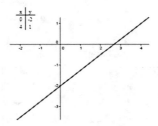

25. $y = -\frac{2}{5}x + 4$

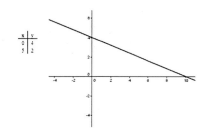

27. $y = \frac{3}{5}x - 4$

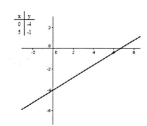

29. $4x - 3y = 6$

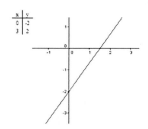

31. $3x + 4y = 8$

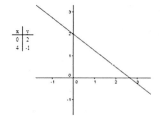

33. $6x + 3y = 12$

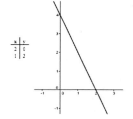

35. $x + 4y = 8$

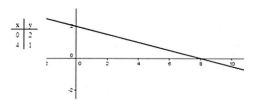

37. $x = -2$

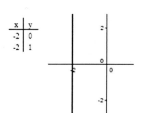

39. $y = -1$

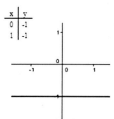

41. x-int. (2, 0), y-int. (0, −2)

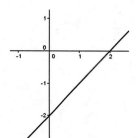

43. x-int. (2, 0), y-int. (0, −3)

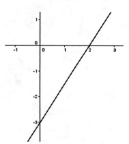

45. x-int. (2, 0), y-int. (0, 5)

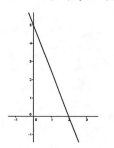

47. x-int. (5, 0), y-int. (0, 4)

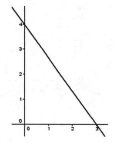

49. x-int. (3, 0), y-int. (0, −2)

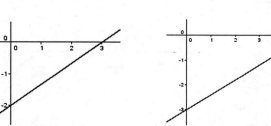

51. x-int. (5, 0), y-int. (0, −3)

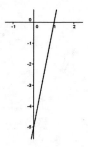

53. x-int. (3, 0), y-int. (0, 4)

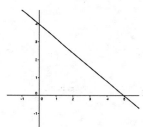

55. x-int. (3, 0), y-int. (0, −4)

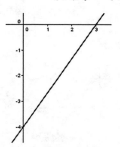

57. x-int. (1, 0), y-int. (0, −5)

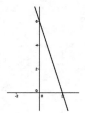

59. x-int. (1, 0), y-int. (0, −3)

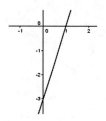

61. x-int. (− 2, 0), y-int. (0, 5)

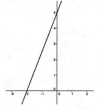

63. x-int. (2, 0), y-int. (0, 6)

65. x-int. (–2, 0), y-int. (0, 4)

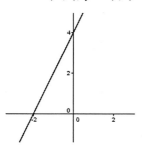

SECTION 3.3

1. m = –2   **3.** m = $\frac{4}{5}$ **5.** m = $-\frac{11}{9}$ **7.** m = $-\frac{3}{2}$ **9.** undefined   **11.** m = 0   **13.** m = $-\frac{2}{3}$ **15.** m = $\frac{27}{40}$

17. m = $\frac{1}{3}$ **19.** m = $\frac{8}{3}$ **21.** m = $-\frac{5}{4}$ **23.** undefined   **25.** perpendicular   **27.** neither   **29.** perpendicular

31. y = $\frac{x+5}{2}$ **33.** y = –3x – 5   **35.** y = 3

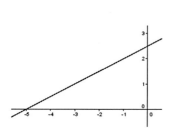

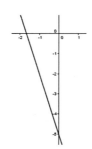

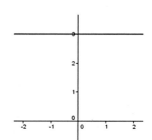

37. x = 4   **39.** y = $\frac{-3x+7}{2}$

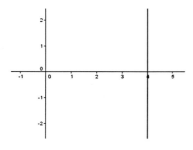

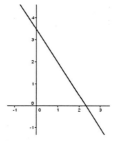

41. y = 1   **43.** y = 3   **45.** x = 3   **47.** x = 5   **49.** x = 3   **51.** x = 9   **53.** m = $\frac{8}{3}$

SECTION 3.4

1. $y = 2x + 1$ **3.** $y = -3x + 14$ **5.** $y = 3x + 17$ **7.** $y = -\frac{1}{2}x + 7$ **9.** $y = \frac{5}{2}x - 10$ **11.** $y = 0x + 5$

13. $3x + y = 2$ **15.** $2x + y = -5$ **17.** $3x - 2y = -14$ **19.** $16x - 20y = -5$ **21.** $0x + 3y = -2$ **23.** $x - 6y = 5$

25. $m = 2$, $(0, -1)$ **27.** $m = \frac{3}{2}$, $(0, -3)$ **29.** $m = -\frac{3}{4}$, $(0, 3)$ **31.** $m = \frac{1}{2}$, $(0, -3)$ **33.** $m = \frac{4}{5}$, $(0, 4)$

35. $m = 0$, $(0, -2)$ **37.** $y = 3x - 4$ **39.** $y = 2x + 5$ **41.** $y = \frac{10}{3}x + \frac{25}{3}$ **43.** $y = -\frac{3}{4}x + 3$ **45.** $y = 2x + 9$

47. $y = \frac{3x-2}{3}$ **49.** $3x + y = -10$ **51.** $y = 2x - 1$ **53.** $2x + y = -2$ **55.** $y = \frac{3}{4}x + 0$ **57.** $y = 4x - 9$

59. $y = -1$ **61.** $y = 8$

SECTION 3.5

1. Yes **3.** No **5.** No

7. $y > x + 3$

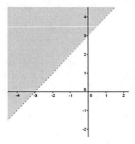

9. $y \leq \frac{1}{2}x$

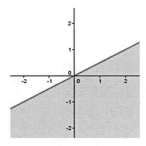

11. $y < -\frac{1}{3}x + 3$

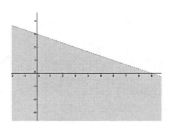

13. $y \geq -x + 3$

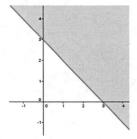

15. $y > 3x - 5$

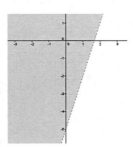

17. $y \geq \frac{1}{4}x - 1$

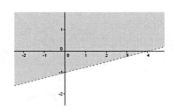

19. $y < \frac{3}{4}x - 3$ **21.** $y < -\frac{1}{3}x + 1$ **23.** $y < \frac{2}{3}x + 2$

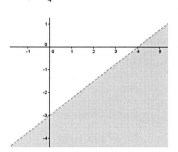   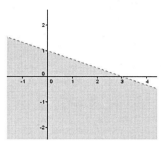   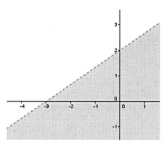

25. $y > -\frac{1}{2}x$ **27.** $y < 2$ **29.** $y \geq -1$

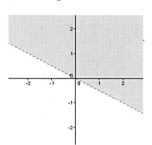   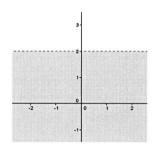   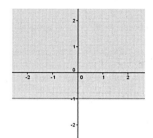

SECTION 3.6

1. Function, D = {1, 2, 3, 4, 5}, R = {1, 2, 5, 6, 9}   **3.** Function, D = {2, 3, 4, 5, 6}, R = {2}

5. Not a function, D = {3}, R = {4, 5, 6, 7, 8}   **7.** Not a function, D = {0, 1, 2, 3}, R = {0, 1, 2, 3, 4}

9. Function, D = {–4, –3, –2, –1}, R = {–5, –4, –3, –2}   **11.** Function, D = {1, 2, 3}, R = {1, 4, 9}

13. Not a function, D = {4, 9}, R = {–3, –2, 2, 3}   **15.** Not a function, D = {a, b}, R = {5, 3}

17. Relation, D = {x | –3 ≤ x ≤ 3}, R = {y | –2 ≤ y ≤ 2}   **19.** a) f(0) = –3   b) f(–1) = –8   c) f(2) = 7

21. a) f(0) = 3   b) f(2) = 0   c) f(–4) = 9   **23.** a) f(1) = –1   b) f(–1) = –1   c) f(2) = 2   **25.** a) f(–2) = 0

b) $f\left(-\frac{1}{2}\right) = 3$ c) f(2) = 8   **27.** a) f(3) = 3   b) f(–1) = 1   c) $f\left(-\frac{3}{2}\right) = 0$ **29.** a) f(0) = 2   b) f(10) = 2

c) f(–4) = 2   **31.** m = 1

CHAPTER 4

SECTION 4.1

1. Yes **3.** No **5.** No **7.** No **9.** No **11.** $(1, 3)$ consistent, independent **13.** $(2, -1)$ consistent, independent

15. $(1, 3)$ consistent, independent **17.** $(-2, 2)$ consistent, independent **19.** $(-4, 1)$ consistent, independent

21. $(2, 3)$ consistent, independent **23.** $(2, 0)$ consistent, independent **25.** No solution, inconsistent, independent

27. Infinite number of solutions, consistent, dependent **29.** Infinite number of solutions, consistent, dependent

31. $(-2, -4)$ consistent, independent **33.** No solutions, inconsistent, independent **35.** $(-3, -3)$ consistent,

independent **37.** $(2, -1)$ consistent, independent **39.** $(0, -3)$ consistent, independent **41.** infinite

number of solutions, consistent, dependent **43.** $(-1, -1)$ consistent, independent **45.** $(2, -4)$ consistent,

independent **47.** $(4, -3)$ consistent, independent **49.** infinite number of solutions, consistent, dependent

51. $(2, 4)$ consistent, independent

SECTION 4.2

1. $(-1, -2)$ **3.** $(2, 2)$ **5.** $(6, 8)$ **7.** $(-2, -4)$ **9.** infinite number of solutions **11.** No solution **13.** infinite

number of solutions **15.** $(-3, 1)$ **17.** $(0, 0)$ **19.** infinite number of solutions **21.** $(2, 4)$ **23.** $(-1, -2)$

25. $(-2, -2)$ **27.** $(3, -1)$ **29.** $(0, 8)$ **31.** $(4, 1)$ **33.** $(1, -8)$ **35.** No solution **37.** $(\frac{12}{5}, \frac{11}{5})$ **39.** $(0, 0)$

41. $(-8, 12)$ **43.** $(2, 10)$ **45.** $(-\frac{20}{29}, -\frac{42}{29})$ **47.** $(-3, 8)$ **49.** $(10, 4)$ **51.** $(-4, -4)$

SECTION 4.3

1. $(1, 3)$ **3.** $(2, 4)$ **5.** $(4, -5)$ **7.** $(2, 2)$ **9.** $(-5, 1)$ **11.** $(2, 2)$ **13.** No solution **15.** $(-3, 7)$ **17.** $(5, 0)$

19. No solution **21.** $(11, -12)$ **23.** $(\frac{1}{2}, \frac{2}{3})$ **25.** $(7, -9)$ **27.** $(-2, -5)$ **29.** $(6, 8)$ **31.** $(0, 0)$ **33.** $(\frac{1}{4}, 3)$

35. $(10, 0)$ **37.** $(-7, 9)$ **39.** $(-4, 1)$

SECTION 4.4

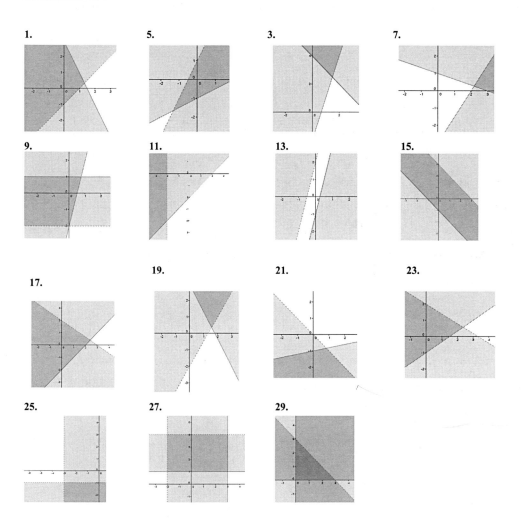

1.   **5.**   **3.**   **7.**

9.   **11.**   **13.**   **15.**

19.   **21.**   **23.**

17.

25.   **27.**   **29.**

SECTION 4.5

1. $7,000 @ 4% and $8,000 @ 6%   **3.** $8,000 @ 8% and $3,000 @ 6%   **5.** $6,000 @ 3.5% and $4,200 @ 5%

7. $4,000 @ 4% and $2,000 @ 5%   **9.** speed of the boat: 12 mph, speed of the current: 3 mph   **11.** speed of the

plane: 175 mph, speed of the wind: 25 mph   **13.** truck: 55 mph, car: 63 mph   **15.** 27 lb of $6.50 and 15 lb of $7.90

17. 12 lb of $4.90 and 18 lb of $7.90   **19.** 10.4 lb of $4.99 and 9.6 lb of %4.49   **21.** 35%: 16 oz 60%: 24 oz

23. 20%: 10 gal and 50%: 20 gal   **25.** distilled water: 7.5 L and 80%: 12.5 L   **27.** adults: 50 tickets, children: 150

tickets   **29.** dimes: 15, quarters: 25   **31.** 21 and 14   **33.** $0.40 stamps: 16 and $0.15 stamps: 24

CHAPTER 5

SECTION 5.1

1. 125 **3.** –25 **5.** 81 **7.** –27 **9.** 5 **11.** $(-3)^4 = 81$ **13.** $-5^3 = -125$ **15.** $(-6)^9$ **17.** $(-5)^{10}$ **19.** x^{11}

21. $-a^{11}$ **23.** $(-x)^7$ **25.** $-20a^{12}$ **27.** $-66y^7$ **29.** $21m^{14}n^5$ **31.** $-3a^3b^2c^3$ **33.** $-6m^3n^5$ **35.** 7^{12}

37. 9^{20} **39.** y^{40} **41.** $27a^6$ **43.** $-125y^{12}$ **45.** $m^{40}n^{30}$ **47.** $64a^9b^{15}$ **49.** $-27m^3n^{12}$ **51.** $-32x^{40}y^{20}z^{15}$

53. $\frac{a^6}{b^6c^6}$ **55.** $\frac{x^2y^6}{81}$ **57.** $\frac{27x^{12}y^{24}}{64a^3b^{15}}$ **59.** $\frac{-8x^{24}y^9}{125a^9b^{12}}$ **61.** $-64x^3$ **63.** $8x^{10}y^{16}$ **65.** $144m^9n^{21}$

67. $64x^{14}y^{15}z^{15}$ **69.** $-a^{34}b^{50}$ **71.** $-81a^{23}b^{37}c^3$ **73.** $\frac{81m^{12}n^{20}}{a^{28}}$ **75.** $\frac{x^{16}}{81a^{10}b^{16}}$ **77.** $\frac{125a^9b^{12}}{8x^{27}y^{21}}$ **79.** $-\frac{x^{30}y^{36}}{8a^{21}b^{12}}$

81. $\frac{54x^5}{y^5}$ **83.** $\frac{x^{11}y^{22}}{16a^5b^{17}}$

SECTION 5.2

1. 1 **3.** 1 **5.** –1 **7.** –2 **9.** $3y^3$ **11.** 1 **13.** –6 **15.** 0 **17.** $\frac{1}{64}$ **19.** $-\frac{1}{125}$ **21.** $\frac{1}{m^5}$ **23.** $-\frac{1}{y^8}$

25. $\frac{7a}{b^4}$ **27.** 64 **29.** $3x^5y^4$ **31.** $\frac{6}{5m^3n}$ **33.** $\frac{b^3}{a^7}$ **35.** $\frac{2y^5}{5x^4}$ **37.** $\frac{y^8}{16x^4}$ **39.** $\frac{x^{14}}{y^{14}z^{21}}$ **41.** 64 **43.** $\frac{1}{27}$ **45.** m^6

47. $\frac{1}{y^5}$ **49.** $\frac{2x^4}{3}$ **51.** $\frac{3x^6}{2y^4}$ **53.** $\frac{3x}{2y^3}$ **55.** $\frac{2a^9b^3}{3}$ **57.** $\frac{27y^{18}}{64x^{21}}$ **59.** $\frac{5y}{4x^{10}}$ **61.** xy^8z^7 **63.** $\frac{c^8}{a^3b^{12}}$ **65.** x^5y^{15}

67. $\frac{4}{9x^6y^6}$ **69.** $\frac{b^{12}}{4a^{11}}$ **71.** m^8n^{14}

SECTION 5.3

1. Yes **3.** No **5.** Yes **7.** No **9.** No **11.** Yes **13.** 6.31×10^8 **15.** 5.23923×10^3 **17.** 1.2×10^{10}

19. 4.05×10^{-4} **21.** 3.572×10^3 **23.** 3.12×10^{-3} **25.** -1.00523×10^3 **27.** -2.1×10^4 **29.** 1.264×10^{-4}

31. 197,000 **33.** 0.004009 **35.** 0.0000681 **37.** 79.305 **39.** –0.00005 **41.** 9999.99 **43.** 9.21×10^{-2}

45. 3.2×10^8 **47.** 6.25×10^{-7} **49.** 3,000 **51.** 0.0025 **53.** 400 **55.** 0.000005 **57.** 2×10^{11}

SECTION 5.4

1. Yes **3.** No, negative exponent **5.** Yes **7.** No, fraction exponent **9.** Yes **11.** binomial, degree 4

13. monomial, degree 0 **15.** trinomial, degree 6 **17.** trinomial, degree 5 **19.** trinomial, degree 4 **21.** binomial,

degree 7 **23.** $3x^2 + 5x - 4$ **25.** $x^3y + x^2y^2 + xy^3$ **27.** $-y^2x^2 + x + y^4$ **29.** $x^4y^5 + x^2y^2 + 7$

31. $P(-2) = 24$ **33.** $P(-1) = -8$ **35.** $P(\frac{1}{2}) = 2$ **37.** $3x + 10$ **39.** $12x - 8$ **41.** $5x^2 - 5x + 3$ **43.** $14x^2 + 11x -$

10 **45.** $-3x^2 + 4x + 5$ **47.** $3x^2 + 2x - 3$ **49.** $-4a^4 + 2a^2 - 3$ **51.** $6a^3 + 3a + 5$ **53.** $y^3 - y^2 + 4y + 6$

55. $2x^2 + 8y^2 - 5xy$ **57.** $x^2y + 3xy^2 + xy - 2$ **59.** $11x^{2n} + 10x^n + 1$ **61.** $5y^{4n} + 8y^{2n} - 4$ **63.** $y^3 + 7y^2 -$

$4y + 3$ **65.** $8x^2 + 4x + 1$ **67.** $2x^2 - 4x - 5$ **69.** $10a^3 + 10a^2 - a - 2$ **71.** $-4x - 5$ **73.** $4x^2 - 18x + 21$

75. $10x^2 + 5x + 6$ **77.** $9x^3 + 7x^2 + 3x + 2$ **79.** $7x^4 + 8x^2 - 4$ **81.** $10x^2 - 4x + 18$ **83.** $28x^3 + 5x^2 + 4x - 6$

85. $16x^3 - 20x^2 - 36x + 32$

SECTION 5.5

1. $6x^3y^4$ **3.** $-20a^8b^8$ **5.** $18x^9y^9z$ **7.** $10a^4b^9$ **9.** $2x^4y^3$ **11.** $18a^2 + 90a$ **13.** $-30m^4 - 15m^3$

15. $5x^3y^2 - 5x^2y^3$ **17.** $18m^5 + 12m^3 + 21m^2$ **19.** $-3x^4y^3 - 12x^3y^4 - 3x^2y^5$ **21.** $4m^{12} - 4m^{10} + 32m^7$

23. $60x^{11} - 80x^9 - 50x^7 + 40x^5$ **25.** $-16a^3b + 20a^2b^3 - 36a^3b^2 + 32ab^3 - 12ab$ **27.** $a^2 + 4a - 32$ **29.** $y^2 +$

$5y - 14$ **31.** $a^2 + a - 30$ **33.** $24a^2 + 42a + 15$ **35.** $9m^2 - 16$ **37.** $4a^2 + 20a + 25$ **39.** $25m^2 - 16n^2$

41. $4a^2 - 12a + 9$ **43.** $a^3 + 3a^2b + 3ab^2 + b^3$ **45.** $16x^2 - 24x + 9$ **47.** $x^2 - 0.1x - 0.3$ **49.** $x^2 - \frac{9}{16}$

51. $4x^3 - 3x^2 - 13x + 6$ **53.** $x^3 - 3x^2y + 3xy^2 - y^3$ **55.** $a^3 - b^3$ **57.** $3m^3 + 10m^2n + 7mn^2 - 10n^3$

59. $24x^3 + 34x^2y + 37xy^2 + 40y^3$ **61.** $15a^3 + 19a^2 - 6a - 8$ **63.** $3x^5 + x^4y + xy^4 + 3x^2y^3 - 4x^3y^2 - 4y^5$

65. $m^4 + m^2n^2 + n^4$ **67.** $m^4 - n^4$

SECTION 5.6

1. $x^2 + 16x + 64$ **3.** $n^2 - 6n + 9$ **5.** $4x^2 + 12x + 9$ **7.** $16y^2 - 40y + 25$ **9.** $x^2 + 6xy + 9y^2$ **11.** $m^2 - 20mn +$

$100n^2$ **13.** $4a^2 + 12ab + 9b^2$ **15.** $9x^2 - 24xy + 16y^2$ **17.** $81x^2 + 36xy + 4y^2$ **19.** $25a^2 - 80ab + 64b^2$

21. $x^4 + 4x^2 + 4$ **23.** $9 - 6a^3 + a^6$ **25.** $3 - 6y^4 + 3y^8$ **27.** $9x^4 - 48x^2y + 64y^2$ **29.** $x^3 + 9x^2 + 27x + 27$

31. $8m^3 + 60m^2 + 150m + 125$ **33.** $x^2 + y^2 + 2xy - 6x - 6y + 9$ **35.** $m^2 + 5m + \frac{25}{4}$ **37.** $x^2 - 9$ **39.** $y^2 - 81$

41. $4a^2 - 25$ **43.** $16a^2 - 9$ **45.** $25x^2 - 64y^2$ **47.** $a^2 - \frac{9}{16}$ **49.** $4x^6 - 1$ **51.** $0.81 - x^2$ **53.** $m^2 + 2mn +$

$n^2 - 49$ **55.** $x^2 + 6xy + 9y^2 - 64$

SECTION 5.7

1. $2x^2 - 6x + 3$ **3.** $a^3 + 3a - 2$ **5.** $y^4 + 4y^2 - 3$ **7.** $x^2 - 5 + \frac{5}{4x}$ **9.** $5x + 4 + \frac{6}{7x}$ **11.** $-x^2 - 3 + \frac{5}{x^2}$

13. $-11mn^2 - 7n + 13 + 21m^2n$ **15.** $x + 5$ **17.** $x + 7$ **19.** $x - 8 - \frac{2}{x+5}$ **21.** $3x + 4 + \frac{1}{x+5}$ **23.** $2x + 5 -$

$\frac{3}{3x-1}$ **25.** $4x - 1 - \frac{1}{5x+4}$ **27.** $m + 5$ **29.** $y + 5 + \frac{5}{7y+6}$ **31.** $4a + 5$ **33.** $2x^2 + 3x + 5$ **35.** $5y^2 + y - 4 +$

$\frac{1}{3y-2}$ **37.** $3x^2 - 4x + 2 + \frac{2}{5x+1}$ **39.** $5x^2 + 2x + 3$ **41.** $2x^2 + x - 4 - \frac{2}{5x+9}$ **43.** $x^2 - 3x + 9$ **45.** $y^2 + 2y + 4$

47. $a^3 - 3a^2 + 9a - 27$ **49.** $m^2 - 1$ **51.** $n^4 + 2n^3 + 4n^2 + 8n + 16$

CHAPTER 6

SECTION 6.1

1. $GCF = m^3$ **3.** $GCF = 14a^2$ **5.** $GCF = 7xy^2$ **7.** $GCF = 3x^2y^2$ **9.** $GCF = 13a^2b^2c$ **11.** $5(x+4)$

13. $4(4a+5)$ **15.** $7m(2m+3)$ **17.** $3y(3-4y^3)$ **19.** $m^4(11m^2-15)$ **21.** $a^3b^3(8b+9a)$

23. $4m^2n^2(4-5mn)$ **25.** $5xy^2z(3x^2+7z^2)$ **27.** $n(n^2+5n-3)$ **29.** $x(x^2+4x-9)$ **31.** $2a(a^2+3a-12)$

33. $4x(x^2-5x-4)$ **35.** $6m(m^4-3m^2+8)$ **37.** $8y(2y^2+3y-8)$ **39.** $m^2n^2(m-5+8n)$ **41.** $9x^2y^2(1-3x+5y)$ **43.** $12a^2b^2(a^2b^2-3a+6b)$ **45.** $(n-3)(m+6)$ **47.** $(3y+2)(2x+5)$ **49.** $3(2y+3)(x-4)$

51. $(4a+7b)(m^4+n^4)$ **53.** $(2x+1)(8y+1)$ **55.** $(6y-1)(4x-1)$ **57.** $(6m-5n)(11b+8)$ **59.** $x^2(2y+3)(x-1)$

61. $(m+3)(x+2)$ **63.** $(m+1)(n+6)$ **65.** $(x+3)(x+4)$ **67.** $(x-2)(x-7)$ **69.** $(x+5)(3x-4)$ **71.** $(4m-3)(m^2+2)$ **73.** $(n-8)(4n+5)$ **75.** $(2x-y)(3x+2y)$ **77.** $(3x+4)(5x^2+1)$ **79.** $(x-5)(x^2+1)$ **81.** $(x^2+3)(x^2-5)$ **83.** $(4y+5)(2x-3)$ **85.** $(x-z)(x^2+y)$ **87.** $3(2x-5y)(3x+4y)$

SECTION 6.2

1. $(x+4)(x+2)$ **3.** $(x+6)(x+3)$ **5.** $(x+7)(x-3)$ **7.** $(x+6)(x-4)$ **9.** $(x-4)(x+1)$ **11.** $(x-7)(x+4)$

13. $(x+7)(x+2)$ **15.** $(x-2)(x-1)$ **17.** $(x-10)(x+2)$ **19.** $(x+4)(x-2)$ **21.** $(x+3)(x-2)$ **23.** $(x-6)^2$

25. $(x+4)^2$ **27.** prime **29.** $(a-5y)(a+4y)$ **31.** $(x-8y)(x+5y)$ **33.** $(a+7b)(a-3b)$ **35.** $(x-10y)(x+7y)$

37. $-(x-6)(x+5)$ **39.** $-(x+10)(x-2)$ **41.** $-(x-5y)(x-5y)$ **43.** $3(x+4)(x+2)$ **45.** $2(x-10)(x+4)$

47. $5(x+5y)(x-4y)$ **49.** $y(x+9)(x+5)$ **51.** $2(mn+4)(mn-3)$ **53.** $(m-n)(y-6)(y+2)$

55. $(3a-1)(x-5)(x-4)$

SECTION 6.3

1. $(3x+1)(2x+1)$ **3.** $(4x+5)(x-2)$ **5.** $(5x-3y)(2x+5y)$ **7.** $(3x-1)(4x+3)$ **9.** $(2y+1)(y+3)$ **11.** $(5m+2)(m-1)$ **13.** $(2m+1)(3m+2)$ **15.** $(4a-1)(3a+2)$ **17.** $(3x+1)(4x-3)$ **19.** $(2x+1)(7x-3)$

21. $(2x+1)(8x-3)$ **23.** $(3x-1)(5x+2)$ **25.** $4(2x+1)(2x+1)$ **27.** $(3x-2)(3x-2)$ **29.** $(2a+3)(4a-5)$

31. $(2x+y)(5x+3y)$ **33.** $(2m-n)(9m+2n)$ **35.** $(8a+b)(3a+2b)$ **37.** prime **39.** $(6x+1)(5x-2)$

41. $(3x-1)(15x+2)$ **43.** $x(3x-1)(8x+3)$ **45.** $(6x+y)(2x+3y)$ **47.** $10(2x-y)(3x-y)$ **49.** $20(m-n)(4m+n)$

51. $m^2(5m+3)(5m+3)$ **53.** $2m(4m-3)(4m-3)$ **55.** $-2x^2y(2x-1)(3x+1)$

SECTION 6.4

1. $(x-6)(x+6)$ **3.** $(y-10)(y+10)$ **5.** $(n-3)(n+3)$ **7.** prime   **9.** $(3a-2)(3a+2)$ **11.** $(8-3x)(8+3x)$

13. $(1-7m)(1+7m)$ **15.** $(9x-2y)(9x+2y)$ **17.** $(0.3x-0.7y)(0.3x+0.7y)$ **19.** $(2n-3m^2)(2n+3m^2)$

21. $(x^2-5)(x^2+5)$ **23.** $(m^4-2)(m^4+2)$ **25.** $(x-\frac{2}{5})(x+\frac{2}{5})$ **27.** $(m-\frac{1}{7})(m+\frac{1}{7})$ **29.** $(\frac{4}{5}-x)(\frac{4}{5}+x)$

31. $(\frac{6}{7}-m)(\frac{6}{7}+m)$ **33.** $2(3-5x)(3+5x)$ **35.** $5m(m+3)(m-3)$ **37.** $(3x-2)(3x+2)(9x^2+4)$

39. $4(2-m)(2+m)(4+m^2)$ **41.** $(x-1-y)(x-1+y)$ **43.** $(1-m)(11+m)$ **45.** $(x+3)^2$ **47.** $(m-1)^2$

49. $(11+m)^2$ **51.** $(3x+8)^2$ **53.** $(x+\frac{1}{3})^2$ **55.** $(4x+y)^2$ **57.** $(x+2)(x^2-2x+4)$ **59.** $(z-3)(z^2+3z+9)$

61. $(4x+1)(16x^2-4x+1)$ **63.** $(4y-5z)(16y^2+20yz+25z^2)$ **65.** $2(z+5)(z^2-5z+25)$ **67.** $(x-y)$
$(x+y)(x^2+xy+y^2)(x^2-xy+y^2)$ **69.** $(y-2)(y+2)(x+3)(x^2-3x+9)$ **71.** $(x+y+10)$
$(x^2+y^2+2xy-10x-10y+100)$

SECTION 6.5

1. $12x(x+2)$ **3.** $5xy(x-7y)$ **5.** $4xy(x+3)(x-1)$ **7.** $(4x-5)(2x+3)$ **9.** $(3x-4)(9x-2)$ **11.** $(3x+5)(4x-y)$

13. $(x-5)(x+3)$ **15.** $(x+9)(x-8)$ **17.** $(x-5y)(x+4y)$ **19.** $(x+8y)(x+5y)$ **21.** $(2x+1)(3x-2)$ **23.** $(5x+1)$
$(4x-3)$ **25.** $(x+2y)(3x-5y)$ **27.** $(6x-y)(3x+2y)$ **29.** $(8m-7)(8m+7)$ **31.** $y(y-5)(y^2+5y+25)$

33. $5(n^2+1)(n-1)(n+1)$ **35.** $b(a^2+4b^2)(a-2b)(a+2b)$ **37.** $(5x+3)^2$ **39.** $(10x+1)^2$ **41.** $(x^2+9)(x-3)$
$(x+3)$ **43.** $3(y^2+4)(y+2)(y-2)$ **45.** $(b+1)(b^2-b+1)(a-9)(a+9)$ **47** $m^2n^3(m-n)(m^2+mn+n^2)$

49. $(3x-10y)(9x^2+30xy+100y^2)$ **51.** $(3x-4b)(2x+a)$ **53.** $(2x+3)(3x-4)$ **55.** $(x-11)(x+7)$

57. $2ab(a-4)(3a+2)$ **59.** $-5(x-5)(x+2)$ **61.** $(a+7b)(a+3b)$ **63.** $(x+3-y)(x+3+y)$ **65.** $(4x-5y)$
$(2a+3b)$

SECTION 6.6

1. $\{-3,8\}$ **3.** $\{-\frac{1}{4},\frac{2}{3}\}$ **5.** $\{-4,0\}$ **7.** $\{0,3\}$ **9.** $\{0,\frac{5}{3}\}$ **11.** $\{-6,6\}$ **13.** $\{-7,7\}$ **15.** $\{-5,5\}$

17. $(-4,4)$ **19.** $\{-\frac{3}{2},\frac{3}{2}\}$ **21.** $(-2,3)$ **23.** $\{-4,-3\}$ **25.** $\{-2,9\}$ **27.** $\{5,6\}$ **29.** $\{4,5\}$ **31.** $\{-3,8\}$

33. $\{-4,8\}$ **35.** $\{-10,-4\}$ **37.** $\{-6,2\}$ **39.** $\{3,13\}$ **41.** $\{-1,\frac{1}{6}\}$ **43.** $\{-\frac{1}{3},6\}$ **45.** $\{\frac{1}{6},8\}$

47. $\{-\frac{3}{8},-\frac{1}{2}\}$ **49.** $\{-\frac{2}{5},\frac{1}{6}\}$ **51.** $\{-\frac{2}{5},-\frac{1}{6}\}$ **53.** $\{-9,3\}$ **55.** $\{0,3\}$ **57.** $\{-\frac{9}{5},\frac{3}{5}\}$ **59.** $\{-\frac{5}{2},\frac{5}{4}\}$

SECTION 6.7

1. {5, 10}   **3.** {5, 17}   **5.** {– 12, –10}, {10, 12}   **7.** {–18, –10}, {10, 18}   **9.** {7, 8}   **11.** w = 15cm, L = 20cm

13. {6, 8, 10}   **15.** w = 10cm, L = 22cm   **17.** w = 20m, L = 25m   **19.** s = 7m   **21.** b = 18cm, h = 6cm

23. t = 4 sec

CHAPTER 7

SECTION 7.1

1. $x = 0$ **3.** $x = 3$ **5.** $x = 3$, $x = -3$,   **7.** $x = -5$, $x = 3$ **9.** None   **11.** None   **13.** $\frac{5b}{4a}$ **15.** $\frac{1}{3x^2y}$ **17.** $\frac{3x}{x+4}$

19. $\frac{1}{a+2}$ **21.** $\frac{3}{x-5}$ **23.** $\frac{1}{x+10}$ **25.** $x + 7$ **27.** $\frac{x+4}{x+1}$ **29.** $\frac{x+1}{x-2}$ **31.** $\frac{x+4y}{x+5y}$ **33.** $\frac{x+2}{x^2+x+4}$ **35.** $\frac{1}{x+3}$ **37.** $\frac{x+2}{4x+3}$

39. $\frac{x+3}{6x+1}$ **41.** $\frac{3x+2}{4x+3}$ **43.** -1 **45.** $-\frac{1}{y+3}$ **47.** $-\frac{x+1}{x+2}$ **49.** $\frac{x}{x+3}$ **51.** $-\frac{x}{x-8}$ **53.** $\frac{4x-y}{8x+y}$ **55.** $\frac{y+5}{y-3}$

57. $\frac{x^2}{x^2+4x+16}$ **59.** $\frac{b+d}{b-d}$ **61.** $\frac{x+y}{5}$ **63.** $\frac{x+5}{x^2+4}$ **65.** $\frac{x-5}{z+1}$ **67.** $-\frac{3}{4}$ and -1 **69.** $-\frac{5}{2}$ and $\frac{5}{4}$

SECTION 7.2

1. $\frac{1}{3}$ **3.** $\frac{5x}{6}$ **5.** $\frac{4}{x^2}$ **7.** $-\frac{5x}{2(x+3)}$ **9.** $\frac{2(a-2)}{a-5}$ **11.** $\frac{5(x+y)}{x-y}$ **13.** $\frac{a-3}{a-9}$ **15.** $\frac{x+1}{x+11}$ **17.** $\frac{x+2y}{x+y}$ **19.** $\frac{x-4}{2x-1}$ **21.** $\frac{3}{4xy}$

23. $\frac{6y^2}{7x^2}$ **25.** $3y^5$ **27.** $\frac{9x}{x-2}$ **29.** $(x-3)^2$ **31.** $\frac{x-2}{x+2}$ **33.** $\frac{(3x-1)(x^2-3x+9)}{(3x+1)((x+3)}$ **35.** $\frac{x+3y}{x+2y}$ **37.** $\frac{x+3}{2x+5}$ **39.** $\frac{4x+3}{x-15}$

41. $\frac{a^2+4}{a(a-10)}$

SECTION 7.3

1. $42x^2$ **3.** $40a^4b^2$ **5.** $72x^3y^3z^2$ **7.** $2(x+3)$ **9.** $12(a-2)$ **11.** $(x+2)(x-2)^2$ **13.** $(a+2)(a+5)$

15. $2(2a-5)$ **17.** $(x+10)(x+3)^2$ **19.** $(a+9)(a+1)(a-4)$ **21.** $(a+5)(a-5)^2$ **23.** $(x+2)(x^2-2x+4)$

25. $(x+8)(x-5)(x+2)$ **27.** $(3a+2)(2a-1)(a+4)$ **29.** $\frac{12}{15a}$ **31.** $-\frac{40x^2}{32x^4}$ **33.** $\frac{5(a-1)}{10a+50}$ **35.** $-\frac{2x}{4-6x}$

37. $\frac{21x(x-1)}{x(x+3)(x-1)}$ **39.** $\frac{(x-4)(x+1)}{(x-5)(x-3)(x+1)}$ **41.** $\frac{(6x-1)(x+5)}{(x-2)(x+8)(x+5)}$ **43.** $\frac{2x(x-1)}{x^3-1}$ **45.** $\frac{a(a+5)}{a^3-25a}$ **47.** $\frac{(x+y)(x+2y)}{(x-y)(x-3y)(x+2y)}$

49. $\frac{(x+9)(x-5)}{(2x+3)(x+4)(x-5)}$ **51.** $\frac{(x-y)^2}{(4x-y)(x+y)(x-y)}$

SECTION 7.4

1. $\frac{5}{x^2}$ **3.** $\frac{-1}{x}$ **5.** 1 **7.** $x+3$ **9.** 1 **11.** $x+3$ **13.** $\frac{y-3}{y+1}$ **15.** $\frac{x+8}{x-4}$ **17.** $\frac{x+3}{2}$ **19.** $\frac{1}{6x}$ **21.** $\frac{9x^2+4y}{6x^3y^3}$

23. $\frac{x^2-7}{(x+2)(x+3)}$ **25.** $\frac{15}{(x+3)(x+8)}$ **27.** $\frac{x^2+16}{x^2-16}$ **29.** 4 **31.** 1 **33.** $\frac{x+1}{x-7}$ **35.** $\frac{x^2-2x+4}{x+2}$ **37.** $\frac{9}{(x-2)(x+1)}$

39. $\frac{6x+4}{(x-3)(x-2)(x+1)}$ **41.** $\frac{12x-16}{(x-4)(x-1)(x-5)}$ **43.** $\frac{(x-8)(x-1)}{(x-4)(x+1)(x+2)}$ **45.** $\frac{x+1}{x+4}$ **47.** $\frac{x+3}{x+1}$ **49.** 1 **51.** $\frac{2(x+6)}{x+8}$

53. $\frac{2(x+2)}{x-2}$ **55.** $\frac{x}{x-6}$ **57.** $\frac{3(x-y)}{x-4y}$ **59.** $-\frac{1}{(x+3)(x-2)}$

SECTION 7.5

1. 2 **3.** $\frac{9y^2}{x}$ **5.** $\frac{5}{2}$ **7.** $\frac{5(x-1)}{y}$ **9.** $\frac{1}{(x-1)(y-4)}$ **11.** $\frac{x+2}{x-2}$ **13.** $\frac{1}{x+1}$ **15.** $\frac{a}{1+2a}$ **17.** $6-x$ **19.** $\frac{xy}{x+y}$ **21.** $\frac{1}{x(x-2)}$

23. $\frac{x+3}{x+2}$ **25.** $\frac{x^2-4}{x^2-1}$ **27.** $\frac{x+2}{2x+1}$ **29.** $\frac{x-2}{2(x+1)}$ **31.** $\frac{x+7}{2(x+6)}$ **33.** $\frac{x+2}{x+6}$ **35.** $\frac{x+3}{x-4}$ **37.** 1 **39.** $\frac{1}{2x+3}$ **41.** $\frac{14}{5}$ **43.** $\frac{2}{2x-1}$

SECTION 7.6

1. $x=-3$ **3.** $x=3$ **5.** $x=-1$ **7.** $x=-1, x=2$ **9.** $x=13$ **11.** $x=-1, x=4$ **13.** $x=2$ **15.** No solution

17. $x=-3$ **19.** $x=2$ **21.** $x=-1$ **23.** $x=-2$ **25.** $x=-2, x=5$ **27.** $x=4$ **29.** $x=-\frac{1}{4}, x=4$

SECTION 7.7

1. 1.2 days **3.** 8.6 hrs **5.** 3.9 hrs **7.** 6.5 hrs **9.** 7.2 min **11.** 48 min **13.** $x=2$ **15.** $x=2$ and $x=3$

17. 15 mph **19.** 52 mph and 60 mph

CHAPTER 8

SECTION 8.1

1. -7 and 7 3. -3 and 3 5. -6 and 6 7. -2 and 2 9. -0.9 and 0.9 11. $-\frac{1}{5}$ and $\frac{1}{5}$ 13. rational

15. irrational 17. rational 19. not a real number 21. rational 23. irrational 25. 4 27. 11 29. 7 31. 9

33. -10 35. -0.9 37. $\frac{9}{10}$ 39. $-\frac{3}{5}$ 41. 0.8 43. -0.12 45. not possible 47. not possible 49. $-\frac{7}{11}$

51. not possible 53. -3 55. -3 57. $\frac{2}{3}$ 59. not possible 61. not possible 63. 2 65. 2 67. $\frac{9}{12}$ 69. $|x-4|$

71. $|x+3|$ 73. $|x-5|$ 75. $|x+1|$ 77. $b=5$ cm 79. 12 in 81. 15

SECTION 8.2

1. $2\sqrt{10}$ 3. $3\sqrt{3}$ 5. $4\sqrt{3}$ 7. $4\sqrt{5}$ 9. $5\sqrt{5}$ 11. $2\sqrt{15}$ 13. $-20\sqrt{2}$ 15. $16\sqrt{5}$ 17. x^4

19. $4y^2$ 21. $x^3\sqrt{x}$ 23. $3x^2\sqrt{7x}$ 25. $2x^3y^4\sqrt{2y}$ 27. $3x^8y^5\sqrt{10xy}$ 29. $50\,ab^4\sqrt{3bc}$

31. $40\,a^7b^3\sqrt{5bc}$ 33. $-8xy^3\sqrt{15xy}$ 35. $\frac{4x^2}{y^4}$ 37. $\frac{3x^5\sqrt{10}}{7}$ 39. $\frac{4a^2b^{10}\sqrt{2}}{13}$ 41. -1 43. $-5x\sqrt[3]{x}$

45. $2x^2y^5\sqrt[2]{6xy}$ 47. $\frac{3x^2\sqrt[3]{2}}{5}$

SECTION 8.3

1. $7\sqrt{3}$ 3. $14\sqrt{5}$ 5. $14\sqrt{x}$ 7. $-8\sqrt{6x}$ 9. $\sqrt{y+4}+\sqrt{x}$ 11. $9\sqrt{y}-4$ 13. $12\sqrt{2}$

15. $24\sqrt{7}$ 17. $11\sqrt{2}+10$ 19. $14\sqrt{5}$ 21. $6\sqrt{10}$ 23. 0 25. $-23\sqrt[3]{6}$ 27. $9\sqrt[3]{10}$
29. $4\sqrt{5}$ 31. $30\sqrt{15}+20\sqrt{7}$ 33. $3a^2b^2\sqrt{2a}$ 35. $-21xy\sqrt{2}$ 37. $14x^2y^2\sqrt{7x}$ 39. $4a^2b^2\sqrt{5ab}$

41. $-8x^2y^2\sqrt{2xy}$ 43. $a^5\sqrt[3]{4b}$ 45. $3xy\sqrt[3]{y}+4xy\sqrt[3]{x}-5xy$

SECTION 8.4

1. $2\sqrt{3}$ 3. $5\sqrt{2}$ 5. $3\sqrt{6}$ 7. $-40\sqrt{3}$ 9. 28 11. $4x^2y^2$ 13. $-20xy\sqrt{3xy}$ 15. $5x^2y^2\sqrt{2x}$

17. $3\sqrt{2}+6$ 19. $7+3\sqrt{7}$ 21. $5+8\sqrt[3]{5}$ 23. $x\sqrt{3}$ 25. $4x^3\sqrt{3}+2x^2$ 27. $2x^2y\sqrt{6}+5\sqrt{3xy}$

29. $4-2\sqrt{3}+2\sqrt{6}-3\sqrt{2}$ 31. $9+6\sqrt{6}$ 33. $2a^2-a\sqrt{15b}+2a\sqrt{3b}-3b\sqrt{5}$ 35. $15-10\sqrt{2}$

37. 2 39. -4 41. 71 43. $7a-b$ 45. $3a-4b^2$

SECTION 8.5

1. $\frac{3\sqrt{2}}{7x}$　**3.** $\frac{2\sqrt{5b}}{9b}$　**5.** $\frac{\sqrt{3}}{2b}$　**7.** $\frac{a\sqrt{15}}{3b}$　**9.** $\frac{4y\sqrt{x}}{7}$　**11.** $\frac{\sqrt{10}}{2}$　**13.** $\frac{\sqrt{3}}{2}$　**15.** $\frac{3\sqrt{2}}{2}$　**17.** $\frac{\sqrt{5}}{5}$

19. $\frac{\sqrt{6}}{4}$　**21.** $\frac{4\sqrt[3]{2x^2}}{x}$　**23.** $\frac{\sqrt{2}}{3}$　**25.** $\frac{a\sqrt{3b}}{3b}$　**27.** $\frac{a\sqrt{30b}}{10b}$　**29.** $3\sqrt{14}+3\sqrt{11}$　**31.** $2\sqrt{2}-2$

33. $\frac{4\sqrt{15}+6\sqrt{2}-6\sqrt{5}-3\sqrt{6}}{7}$　**35.** $\frac{2x+9+6\sqrt{2x}}{2x-9}$　**37.** $15-5\sqrt{6}$　**39.** $5+3\sqrt{3}$　**41.** $\frac{2x+2\sqrt{2x}+1}{2x-1}$　**43.** $\frac{\sqrt{2}+\sqrt{3}}{4}$

45. $-\sqrt{30}$　**47.** $\frac{7-2\sqrt{6}}{5}$　**49.** $\frac{37-20\sqrt{3}}{13}$　**51.** $\frac{a-2\sqrt{ab}+b}{a-b}$

SECTION 8.6

1. $x=16$　**3.** $x=121$　**5.** no solution　**7.** $x=5$　**9.** $x=\frac{4}{3}$　**11.** $x=12$　**13.** $x=9$　**15.** $x=20$　**17.** $x=14$　**19.** $x=2$

21. $x=2$　**23.** $x=\frac{5}{6}$　**25.** $x=-4, x=2$　**27.** $x=-\frac{1}{2}, x=3$　**29.** $x=8$　**31.** $x=1$　**33.** $x=1$　**35.** $x=10$　**37.** $x=2$

39. $x=3$　**41.** $x=4, x=9$　**43.** $x=5$　**45.** $x=20$　**47.** $x=8$　**49.** $x=3$　**51.** $x=5$　**53.** $x=3, x=\frac{19}{9}$

SECTION 8.7

1. $8i$　**3.** $9i$　**5.** $4i\sqrt{2}$　**7.** $2i\sqrt{5}$　**9.** $5i\sqrt{2}$　**11.** $4-5i$　**13.** $-6+2i\sqrt{6}$　**15.** $-8+30i\sqrt{2}$

17. $10+4i\sqrt{6}$　**19.** $2+3i$　**21.** $17+i$　**23.** $-1+i$　**25.** $10-2i$　**27.** $4+6i$　**29.** $6+i$

31. $-12+15i$　**33.** $3+3i$　**35.** 12　**37.** $-48i$　**39.** -9　**41.** $-6-14i$　**43.** $-66-18i$

45. $25-20i$　**47.** $16+11i$　**49.** $-2+42i$　**51.** $-5-56i$　**53.** $-60-32i$　**55.** $-12-5i$

57. $-10+10i$　**59.** 125　**61.** 43　**63.** 52　**65.** -8　**67.** -12　**69.** $-6-3\sqrt{6}$　**71.** $0-\frac{2}{7}i$

73. $-\frac{2}{3}+\frac{5}{3}i$　**75.** $0-\frac{5}{4}i$　**77.** $-\frac{15}{26}-\frac{10}{26}i$　**79.** $-\frac{8}{37}-\frac{48}{37}i$　**81.** $-\frac{1}{109}+\frac{33}{109}i$　**83.** $-\frac{63}{73}-\frac{22}{73}i$

85. $\frac{41}{58}+\frac{1}{58}i$　**87.** $-\frac{3}{2}+\frac{5}{2}i$　**89.** $\frac{1}{2}-\frac{3}{2}i$　**91.** -1　**93.** -1　**95.** $-i$

CHAPTER 9

SECTION 9.1

1. $\{-2,2\}$ 3. $\{-8,8\}$ 5. $\{-3\sqrt{2},3\sqrt{2}\}$ 7. $\{-5,5\}$ 9. $\left\{-\frac{3}{2},\frac{3}{2}\right\}$ 11. $\{-4\sqrt{2},4\sqrt{2}\}$ 13. $\left\{-\frac{\sqrt{10}}{2},\frac{\sqrt{10}}{2}\right\}$

15. $\{-1,5\}$ 17. $\{-7,1\}$ 19. $\{1+\sqrt{5},1-\sqrt{5}\}$ 21. $\{-13,-1\}$ 23. $\left\{-\frac{7}{2},\frac{13}{2}\right\}$ 25. $\left\{-\frac{11}{4},\frac{1}{4}\right\}$

27. $x=\frac{2\pm\sqrt{15}}{5}$ 29. $\{-2-\sqrt{6},-2+\sqrt{6}\}$ 31. $\{-2-\sqrt{2},-2+\sqrt{2}\}$ 33. $\{-1,0\}$ 35. $x=\frac{-2\pm\sqrt{7}}{3}$

37. $\left\{-\frac{1}{3},\frac{7}{3}\right\}$ 39. $\{-0.3,0.3\}$ 41. $\{-3i,3i\}$ 43. $\left\{\frac{1}{2},\frac{9}{2}\right\}$ 45. $\left\{-\frac{8}{3},0\right\}$ 47. $\left\{\frac{-7-2\sqrt{6}}{3},\frac{-7+2\sqrt{6}}{3}\right\}$

49. $\left\{-\frac{7}{11},\frac{5}{11}\right\}$ 51. $W=5\ cm,\ L=15\ cm$ 53. $\{3,18\}$ 55. $s=10\ in$ 57. $t=3\ sec$

SECTION 9.2

1. $\{-8,2\}$ 3. $\{-5,9\}$ 5. $\{-1,7\}$ 7. $\{-4,12\}$ 9. $\{2,10\}$ 11. $-1\pm\sqrt{6}$ 13. $x=-5\pm4\sqrt{2}$

15. $x=3\pm\sqrt{11}$ 17. $\{5\}$ 19. $\{-5,2\}$ 21. $\{-2,1\}$ 23. $x=\frac{5\pm\sqrt{13}}{2}$ 25. $\{1,10\}$ 27. $x=\frac{2\pm\sqrt{14}}{2}$

29. $\{-2,-1\}$ 31. $\left\{-\frac{3}{2},1\right\}$ 33. $\left\{-\frac{1}{2},\frac{3}{4}\right\}$ 35. $\left\{-\frac{2}{3},4\right\}$ 37. $x=\frac{2\pm\sqrt{15}}{5}$ 39. $x=\frac{-5\pm\sqrt{41}}{4}$

41. $x=\frac{-3\pm\sqrt{41}}{4}$ 43. $\{0,2\}$ 45. $\left\{0,\frac{7}{3}\right\}$ 47. $W=4\ in,\ L=8\ in$ 49. $14,4$ and $-4,-14$

51. $\{-21,-3\},\ \{3,21\}$ 53. $\{-6,-5\},\ \{5,6\}$ 55. $\{12,14\}$

SECTION 9.3

1. $4>0$, two distinct real sol. 3. $-39<0$, two complex sol. 5. 0, one real sol.

7. $112>0$, two distinct real sol. 9. $\{1,3\}$ 11. $\{-5,2\}$ 13. $\{-1,2\}$ 15. $\{5\}$ 17. $x=\pm\frac{\sqrt{10}}{2}$

19. $\left\{0,\frac{4}{3}\right\}$ 21. $\left\{-\frac{1}{3},\frac{3}{2}\right\}$ 23. $\left\{-3,\frac{1}{5}\right\}$ 25. $\left\{-5,\frac{4}{3}\right\}$ 27. $\left\{-1,\frac{5}{4}\right\}$ 29. $x=\frac{1\pm i\sqrt{3}}{2}$ 31. $x=\frac{-3\pm\sqrt{21}}{6}$

33. $\left\{-3,\frac{1}{2}\right\}$ 35. $\left\{-\frac{5}{6},1\right\}$ 37. $x=\frac{2\pm\sqrt{6}}{2}$ 39. $\{3,5\}$ 41. $-3\pm2\sqrt{3}$ 43. $\{-7\}$ 45. $\left\{-\frac{8}{5},1\right\}$

47. $W=5\ in,\ L=10\ in$ 49. $\{-11,-5\}$ 51. $t=4\ sec$ 53. $\{12,16\}$

SECTION 9.4

1. $\{4, 36\}$ **3.** $\{1, 16\}$ **5.** $\{25\}$ **7.** $\{8, -64\}$ **9.** $\left\{-27, \frac{1}{8}\right\}$ **11.** $\left\{\frac{1}{27}, 64\right\}$ **13.** $\{1, 32\}$

15. $\{32, 243\}$ **17.** $\{\pm 1, \pm 2\}$ **19.** $\{\pm 2, \pm 3\}$ **21.** $\{\pm 1, \pm 4\}$ **23.** $\left\{-\frac{2}{5}, 3\right\}$ **25.** $\left\{\frac{1}{3}, \frac{1}{6}\right\}$ **27.** $\left\{-\frac{1}{3}, \frac{1}{7}\right\}$

29. $\{\pm 2, \pm 2i\}$ **31.** $\{-4, -2, 0, 2\}$ **33.** $x = 9$ **35.** $x = 25$

SECTION 9.5

1. $a = 2 > 0$, upward   **3.** $a = -1 < 0$, downward   **5.** $a = 10 > 0$, upward   **7.** $a = -9 < 0$, downward   **9.** $a = -\frac{3}{4} < 0$, downward

11.

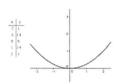

13.

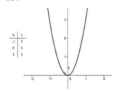

15.

17.

19.

21.

23.

25.

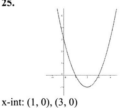

x-int: $(1, 0)$, $(3, 0)$
y-int: $(0, 3)$
vertex: $(2, -1)$

27.

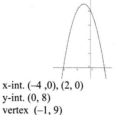

x-int. $(-4, 0)$, $(2, 0)$
y-int. $(0, 8)$
vertex $(-1, 9)$

29.

x-int. $(-5, 0)$, $(-1, 0)$
y-int. $(0, 5)$
vertex $(-3, -4)$

31.

x-int. $(-3, 0)$, $(1, 0)$
y-int. $(0, -3)$
vertex $(-1, -4)$

33.

x-int. $(-2, 0)$, $\left(\frac{1}{2}, 0\right)$
y-int. $(0, 2)$
vertex $\left(-\frac{3}{4}, \frac{25}{8}\right)$

35.

x-int. (–5, 0), (1, 0)
y-int. (0, –5)
vertex (–2, –9)

37.

x-int. $(-\frac{1}{2}, 0), (\frac{1}{2}, 0)$
y-int. (0, 1)
vertex (0, 1)

39.

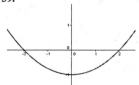

x-int. (–2,0), (2, 0)
y-int. (0, –1)
vertex (0, –1)

41.

x-int. (0, 0), (4, 0)
y-int. (0, 0)
vertex (2, –4)

43.

x-int. (0, 0), (2, 0)
y-int. (0, 0)
vertex (1, –3)

45.

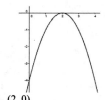

x-int. (2, 0)
y-int. (0, –4)
vertex (2, 0)

47.

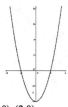

x-int: (–2, 0), (2,0)
y-int: (0, –4)
vertex: (0, –4)

49. a) t = 2 sec   b) 144 ft

51. a) 150 items   b) $4,200